# FORENSIC PSYCHOLOGY

## THIRD EDITION

### JOANNA POZZULO
Carleton University

### CRAIG BENNELL
Carleton University

### ADELLE FORTH
Carleton University

**Pearson Canada**
Toronto

**Library and Archives Canada Cataloguing in Publication**

Pozzulo, Joanna
 Forensic psychology / Joanna Pozzulo, Craig Bennell, Adelle Forth.—3rd ed.

Includes bibliographical references and index.
ISBN 978-0-13-706057-3

1. Forensic psychology—Textbooks.   I. Bennell, Craig   II. Forth, Adelle Elizabeth   III. Title.

RA1148.P69 2011      614'.15     C2010-906308-2

ISBN 978-0-13-706057-3

Vice-President, Editorial Director: Gary Bennett
Editor-in-Chief: Ky Pruesse
Acquisitions Editor: Matthew Christian
Sponsoring Editor: Carolin Sweig
Executive Marketing Manager: Judith Allen
Senior Developmental Editor: Patti Altridge
Project Manager: Marissa Lok
Production Editor: Deborah Cooper-Bullock
Copy Editor: Deborah Cooper-Bullock
Proofreader: Julia Hubble
Compositor: Aptara®, Inc.
Photo and Permissions Researcher: Mary Rose MacLachlan
Art Director: Julia Hall
Cover Designer: Miguel Acevedo
Cover Image: Getty Images/Superstock/Diana Ong

1 2 3 4 5      15 14 13 12 11

Printed and bound in the United States of America.

*This book is dedicated to our many students who challenge our thinking and inspire us.*

# Brief Contents

Chapter 1      An Introduction to Forensic Psychology    1

Chapter 2      Police Psychology    26

Chapter 3      The Psychology of Police Investigations    56

Chapter 4      Deception    89

Chapter 5      Eyewitness Testimony    118

Chapter 6      Child Victims and Witnesses    146

Chapter 7      Juries: Fact Finders    175

Chapter 8      The Role of Mental Illness in Court    201

Chapter 9      Sentencing and Parole in Canada: Practices and Public Opinions    230

Chapter 10     Risk Assessment    259

Chapter 11     Psychopaths    288

Chapter 12     Assessment and Treatment of Young Offenders    308

Chapter 13     Domestic Violence    331

Chapter 14     Sexual and Homicidal Offenders    354

# Contents

Preface   xii

## 1   An Introduction to Forensic Psychology   1

What Is Forensic Psychology?   2

*In the Media   The Reality of Reality TV*   3

**The Roles of a Forensic Psychologist   4**
The Forensic Psychologist as Clinician   4

**Box 1.1   Other Forensic Disciplines   6**

The Forensic Psychologist as Researcher   6
The Forensic Psychologist as Legal Scholar   7
**The Relationship between Psychology and Law   7**
Psychology and the Law   8
Psychology in the Law   8
Psychology of the Law   8
**The History of Forensic Psychology   9**
Early Research: Eyewitness Testimony
and Suggestibility   9
Early Court Cases in Europe   11
Advocates of Forensic Psychology
in North America   11
Forensic Psychology in Other Areas of the Criminal
Justice System   12

**Box 1.2   Biological, Sociological, and Psychological
Theories of Crime   13**

Landmark Court Cases in the United States   14
Signs of a Legitimate Field of Psychology   15

**Box 1.3   Influential Canadian Court Cases in the
History of Forensic Psychology   16**

**Modern-Day Debates: Psychological Experts
in Court   16**

**Box 1.4   Canadian Researcher Profile: Dr. James
Ogloff   17**

The Functions of the Expert Witness   18
The Challenges of Providing Expert Testimony   18
Criteria for Accepting Expert Testimony   20

*Case Study   You Be the Judge*   22

**Box 1.5   The Case of R. v. McIntosh
and McCarthy (1997): Potential Problems
with the Mohan Criteria   23**

## 2   Police Psychology   26

Police Selection   27

*In the Media   Using Social Media to Recruit
Police Officers*   28

A Brief History of Police Selection   28
The Police Selection Process   29

**Box 2.1   Validation and Police Selection   31**

The Validity of Police Selection Instruments   32
**Police Discretion   36**
Why Is Police Discretion Necessary?   37
Areas Where Police Discretion Is Used   38

**Box 2.2   Canadian Researcher Profile:
Dr. Dorothy Cotton   42**

*Case Study   You Be the Police Officer*   43

**Box 2.3   The Case of Ernst v.
Quinonez et al. (2003)   44**

Controlling Police Discretion   45

**Box 2.4   The National Use-of-Force
Model in Canada   47**

**Police Stress   48**
Sources of Police Stress   49
Consequences of Police Stress   51
Preventing and Managing Police Stress   52

**Box 2.5   The Buffalo Cardio-Metabolic Occupational
Police Stress (BCOPS) Study   53**

## 3   The Psychology of Police Investigations   56

Police Interrogations   57

**Box 3.1   The Mr. Big Technique   58**

The Reid Model of Interrogation   59
The Use of the Reid Model in Actual
Interrogations   60
Potential Problems with the Reid Model of
Interrogation   61
Interrogation Practices and the Courts   65

**Box 3.2   When the Police Go Too Far: The Case
of R. v. Hoilett (1999)   66**

An Alternative to the Reid Model   66
**False Confessions   67**
The Frequency of False Confessions   67
Different Types of False Confessions   68

**Box 3.3   False Confession in a Child-Abuse Case   70**

Studying False Confessions in the Lab   71
The Consequences of Falsely Confessing   73

*Case Study   You Be the Police Officer   74*

**Criminal Profiling   75**
What Is a Criminal Profile?   75

*In the Media   Hollywood Depictions of Criminal Profiling   76*

The Origins of Criminal Profiling   76

**Box 3.4   The RCMP's Violent Crime Linkage Analysis System (VICLAS)   78**

How Is a Criminal Profile Constructed?   78
Different Types of Profiling Methods   79
The Validity of Criminal Profiling   81
**Geographic Profiling   84**

**Box 3.5   Canadian Researcher Profile: Dr. Kim Rossmo   86**

**4   Deception   89**
**The Polygraph Technique   90**
Applications of the Polygraph Test   90
Types of Polygraph Tests   91
Validity of Polygraph Techniques   93

**Box 4.1   Seeing Through the Face of Deception   96**

Can the Guilty Learn to Beat the Polygraph?   96
Scientific Opinion: What Do the Experts Say?   96
Admissibility of Polygraph Evidence   97
**Brain-Based Deception Research   97**

**Box 4.2   Brain Fingerprinting: Evidence for a New Deception-Detection Technology?   99**

Verbal and Non-verbal Behaviour Cues to Lying   100
Verbal Cues to Lying   101

**Box 4.3   Quest for Love: Truth and Deception in Online Dating   103**

Are Some People Better at Detecting Deception?   103

*In the Media   TV and Lie Detection   104*

**Box 4.4   Detecting High-Stakes Lies   106**

**Box 4.5   Canadian Researcher Profile: Dr. Stephen Porter   107**

**Assessment of Malingering and Deception   108**
Disorders of Deception   108
Explanatory Models of Malingering   109
How to Study Malingering   110
Malingered Psychosis   111

**Box 4.6   Ethics of Deception Research   112**

**Box 4.7   Being Sane in Insane Places   113**

*Case Study   You Be the Forensic Psychology   115*

Assessment Methods to Detect Malingered Psychosis   115

**5   Eyewitness Testimony   118**
**Eyewitness Testimony: The Role of Memory   118**
**How Do We Study Eyewitness Issues?   120**
The Laboratory Simulation   120
**Recall Memory   121**
Interviewing Eyewitnesses   122
The Leading Question—The Misinformation Effect   122
**Procedures That Help Police Interview Eyewitnesses   124**
Hypnosis   124
The Cognitive Interview   125

*In the Media   Hypnotically Refreshed Memory Goes to Court, or Not   126*

**Recall of the Culprit   127**
Quantity and Accuracy of Descriptions   127
**Recognition Memory   128**
Lineup Identification   128

**Box 5.1   Canadian Researcher Profile: Dr. Rod Lindsay   132**

Voice Identification   134
Are Several Identifications Better Than One?   134
Are Confident Witnesses Accurate?   135
Estimator Variable Research in Recognition Memory   136
**Expert Testimony on Eyewitness Issues   139**

*Case Study   You Be the Judge   140*

**Public Policy Issues and Guidelines   141**

**Box 5.2   A Case of Wrongful Conviction   142**

## 6   Child Victims and Witnesses   146

History   147
Recall for Events   147

Box 6.1   The Martensville Babysitting Case   148

Free Recall versus Directed Questioning   148

*Case Study   You Be the Forensic Psychologist*   149

Box 6.2   Canadian Researcher Profile: Dr. Maggie Bruck   150

Why Are Children More Suggestible Than Adults?   150
Anatomically Detailed Dolls   151
Other Techniques for Interviewing Children   152
**Recall Memory Following a Long Delay   157**
Can Traumatic Memories Be Forgotten?   157

Box 6.3   Delayed Memory Goes to Court   158

Box 6.4   Delayed Prosecutions of Historic Child Sexual Abuse   159

Recall for People   160
Describing the Culprit   160
**Recognition   162**
Lineup Procedure and Identification Rates   162
**Testifying in Court   163**
Courtroom Accommodations   164
Child Maltreatment   165

Box 6.5   Corporal Punishment: Discipline or Physical Abuse?   166

Box 6.6   A Case of Neglect or Forgetfulness?   167

Box 6.7   One of the Worst Cases of Physical Abuse in Canada's History   168

Risk Factors Associated with Child Maltreatment   169
Short-Term and Long-Term Effects of Physical Abuse   170
Short-Term and Long-Term Effects of Sexual Abuse   171

Box 6.8   Luring Children over the Internet   172

*In the Media   To Catch a Predator*   172

## 7   Juries: Fact Finders   175

Jury Selection in Canada   176
The Cases Heard by Juries   176
Jury Selection   177

Characteristics and Responsibilities of Juries in Canada   178
Representativeness   178
Impartiality   178

Box 7.1   Balancing a Jury by Race   179

Box 7.2   Canada's Most Famous Partial Juror   179

Box 7.3   Cases Allowing a Challenge for Cause   181

**Jury Functions   182**

Box 7.4   Two Cases of Jury Nullification   183

**How Do We Study Juror and Jury Behaviour?   184**
Post-trial Interviews   184
Archives   184
Simulation   185
Field Studies   185
**Reaching a Verdict   186**
Listening to the Evidence   186
Disregarding Inadmissible Evidence   187

*In the Media   The CSI Effect*   188

Judge's Instructions   189
Jury Decision-Making Models   189
Deliberations   191
The Final Verdict   191
**Predicting Verdicts   192**
Demographic Variables   192
Personality Traits   192
Attitudes   193
Defendant Characteristics   194
Victim Characteristics   194

*Case Study   You Be the Juror*   195

Expert Testimony   196

Box 7.5   When Law Meets Religion   197

Box 7.6   Canadian Researcher Profile: Dr. Regina Schuller   198

## 8   The Role of Mental Illness in Court   201

Presumptions in Canada's Legal System   202
Fitness to Stand Trial   202
Raising the Issue of Fitness   203
How Many Defendants Are Referred for Fitness Evaluations?   203
Who Can Assess Fitness?   204
Fitness Instruments   204

Distinguishing between Fit and Unfit Defendants   205

Box 8.1   Fitness Instruments   207

*Case Study   You Be the Judge*   209

How Is Fitness Restored?   209
What Happens after a Finding of Unfitness?   209

Box 8.2   Mentally Ill but Competent to Make
Treatment Decisions?   210

**Mental State at Time of Offence   211**

Box 8.3   Sportscaster Shot Dead by Patient
with a Mental Illness   214

Raising the Issue of Insanity   215
Assessing Insanity   215
What Happens to a Defendant Found NCRMD?   216
**Automatism   217**

Box 8.4   A Gas Company, a Tire Company,
and a Case of Automatism   219

Box 8.5   Can Insults Lead to Automatism?   219

How Do NCRMD and Automatism Differ?   220
Intoxication as a Defence   220
**Defendants with Mental Disorders   221**

*In the Media   What to Do with Mentally Ill Offenders?*   222

Why Are There Such High Rates of Mental Illness
in Offender Populations?   222
Dealing with Offenders Who Are Mentally Ill   223
Bias against Mentally Ill Offenders   223
Are People with Mental Illnesses Violent?   224

Box 8.6   A Violent Crime Committed by a Mentally
Ill Man   225

Types of Offences Committed by People
with Mental Illnesses   225
Recidivism Rates and People with Mental Illnesses   225
Treatment of Offenders with Mental Disorders   226

Box 8.7   Canadian Researcher Profile: Dr. Marnie
Rice   227

**A New Court for the Mentally Ill: The Mental
Health Courts   228**
Are Mental Health Courts Effective?   228

**9   Sentencing and Parole in Canada:
Practices and Public Opinions   230**
**The Structure of the Canadian Court
System   231**

Aboriginal Courts   233

Box 9.1   The Gladue Court   235

**Sentencing in Canada   235**
The Purposes of Sentencing   236
The Principles of Sentencing   237
Sentencing Options in Canada   238

Box 9.2   Sentencing Options in Canada   238

Factors That Affect Sentencing Decisions   239

*Case Study   You Be the Judge*   240

Sentencing Disparity   240
Are the Goals of Sentencing Achieved?   244

Box 9.3   The Death Penalty in Canada: Were We
Right to Abolish It?   245

What Works in Offender Treatment?   246
**Parole in Canada   247**
Parole Decision Making   248

Box 9.4   Myths and Realities Concerning Parole
Decision Making   249

Types of Parole   250
Research on the Effectiveness of Parole   251

*In the Media   To Pardon . . . or Not to Pardon*   252

**Public Attitudes toward Sentencing
and Parole   253**

Box 9.5   Canadian Researcher Profile: Dr. Julian
V. Roberts   254

Factors That Influence Public Opinions   256

**10   Risk Assessment   259**
**What Is Risk Assessment?   260**
**Risk Assessments: When Are They
Conducted?   261**
Civil Setting   261
Criminal Settings   261
**A History of Risk Assessment   263**
**Types of Prediction Outcomes   264**
The Base Rate Problem   265
**Methodological Issues   265**
**Judgment Error and Biases   266**
**Approaches to the Assessment
of Risk   267**

Box 10.1   Dr. Death: A Legendary (Notorious)
Forensic Psychiatrist   268

Box 10.2    Canadian Researcher Profile:
Dr. Christopher Webster   269

Types of Predictors   270
**Important Risk Factors   270**
Dispositional Factors   271
Historical Factors   272
Clinical Factors   273
Contextual Factors   274

*In the Media   Sex Offender Registry Missed
Notorious Child Molester   275*

**Risk-Assessment Instruments   276**

Box 10.3    Risk-Assessment Instruments   277

**Current Issues   279**
Where Is the Theory?   279
What about Female Offenders?   279

Box 10.4    Coping-Relapse Model of Criminal
Recidivism   280

What about Protective Factors?   282

*Case Study   You Be the Forensic Psychologist   282*

Risk Assessment: Risky Business?   283
Are Decision Makers Using the Scientific
Research?   284
Why Do Some Individuals Stop Committing
Crimes?   285

Box 10.5    **Why Do High-Risk Violent Offenders
Stop Offending?   285**

**11   Psychopaths   288**
Assessment of Psychopathy   289

Box 11.1    Canadian Researcher Profile:
Dr. Robert Hare   291

Box 11.2    Subclinical Psychopaths: University
Samples   292

**Psychopathy and Antisocial Personality
Disorder   292
Forensic Use of Psychopathy   293
Psychopathy and Violence   294**

Box 11.3    Clifford Olson: A Predatory
Psychopath   295

Box 11.4    Psychopathy in Animals?   296

**Psychopaths in the Community   296
Psychopathy and Sexual Violence   297**

*In the Media   Mean on the Screen: Media's Portrayal
of Psychopaths   298*

**Psychopathy and Treatment   299
Psychopathy in Youth   300**

Box 11.5    **Psychopathy Label: The Potential
for Stigma   301**

**Psychopathy: Nature versus Nurture?   302**
Does Family Matter?   303
**Psychopathy and Law Enforcement   304
What Makes Them Tick? Cognitive
and Affective Models of Psychopathy   305**

*Case Study   You Be the Researcher   306*

**12   Assessment and Treatment
of Young Offenders   308**
**Historical Overview   309**
Naming Youth   311

Box 12.1    Sex, Text, and Murder   312

**Youth Crime Rates   313**

*In the Media   Canada's Youth Crime Legislation   313*

**Assessment of Young Offenders   314**
Assessing Those under Age 12   314

*Case Study   You Be the Police Officer   315*

Assessing the Adolescent   316
Rates of Behaviour Disorders in Youth   317
Trajectories of Youthful Offenders   317

Box 12.2    Risk-Assessment Tools Used with Young
Offenders in Canada   318

**Theories to Explain Antisocial Behaviour   319**
Biological Theories   319
Cognitive Theories   319
Social Theories   320
**Risk Factors   320**
Individual Risk Factors   320
Familial Risk Factors   321
School and Social Risk Factors   321

Box 12.3    **Running Around with the Wrong
Crowd: A Look at Gangs   322**

**Protective Factors   323**
Individual Protective Factors   323
Familial Protective Factors   323
Social/External Protective Factors   324

Prevention, Intervention, and Treatment
of Young Offending  324
Primary Intervention Strategies  324
Secondary Intervention Strategies  326

Box 12.4  Canadian Researcher Profile:
Dr. Alan Leschied  328

Tertiary Intervention Strategies  329

Box 12.5  Let the Music Play: An Alternative
to Offending  329


13  Domestic Violence  331
Types of Violence and Measurement  332

Box 13.1  Myths and Realities Concerning
Domestic Violence  333

Intimate Partners: A Risky Relationship  334

Box 13.2  Husband Battering Does Exist  335

Theories of Intimate Violence  337
Why Do Battered Women Stay?  338

Box 13.3  Canadian Researcher Profile: Dr. Donald
Dutton  339

Box 13.4  Woman's Best Friend: Pet Abuse
and Intimate Violence  341

A Heterogeneous Population: Typologies
of Male Batterers  342
Criminal Justice Response  342

Case Study  You Be the Researcher  343

Does Treatment of Male Batterers Work?  345

Box 13.5  The Correctional Service of Canada's Family
Violence Prevention Programs  347

Stalking  348

In the Media  Dangerous Fixations: Celebrity
Stalkers  351


14  Sexual and Homicidal Offenders  354
Sexual Offenders  355
Nature and Extent of Sexual Violence  355
Definition of Sexual Assault  356

Consequences for Victims  356

Box 14.1  Sexual Assault: Discounting Rape
Myths  357

Classification of Sexual Offenders  358

Box 14.2  Is Resisting a Sexual Attack
a Good Idea?  360

Adolescent Sexual Offenders  361
Female Sexual Offenders  361
Theories of Sexual Aggression  363
Assessment and Treatment of Sexual Offenders  364

Case Study  You Be the Forensic Psychologist  365

Effectiveness of Treatment for Sexual Offenders  367

Box 14.3  Relapse Prevention with Sexual
Offenders  367

Homicidal Offenders  369

In the Media  The Double Life of Col. Russell
Williams  370

Nature and Extent of Homicidal Violence  370
Bimodal Classification of Homicide  372
Filicide: When Parents Kill  372

Box 14.4  From Devotion to Depression: Mothers
Who Kill  374

Youth Who Kill  375
Spousal Killers  376
Serial Murderers: The Ultimate Predator  376
Mass Murderers  379
Theories of Homicidal Aggression  380

Box 14.5  Canada's Deadliest Mass Murder  381

Box 14.6  Canadian Researcher Profile:
Dr. Martin Daly  382

Treatment of Homicidal Offenders  384

Glossary  387
References  394
Credits  442
Case and Legislation Index  445
Name Index  447
Subject Index  454

# Preface

We remember the day that the three of us gathered in Adelle's office to lament our teaching assignment: an introductory course in forensic psychology. Not that we weren't interested in teaching the course, but we worried about not having an undergraduate Canadian textbook on the subject. Given the need to discuss the law when studying forensic psychology, a text based on U.S. or British law would not do. We decided to write a Canadian forensic psychology textbook that was directed at Canadian undergraduates, a comprehensive book with as much Canadian content as possible.

We have taken a broad-based perspective that incorporates both experimental and clinical topics. The text covers topics that might otherwise be discussed in traditional social and cognitive psychology courses—including eyewitness testimony, jury decision making, and police procedures—as well as topics that are clinical in nature and might otherwise be discussed in traditional personality or abnormal psychology courses—such as the meaning of being unfit to stand trial, mentally disordered offenders, and psychopathy. Our goal is to present the important ideas, issues, and research in a way that students will understand and enjoy, and in some cases find useful in their professional careers. We hope that the academic community will find this textbook a valuable teaching tool that provides a comprehensive and current coverage of forensic psychology.

## NEW TO THE THIRD EDITION

- **Case Studies** take an active role—"You be the . . ." Judge, Forensic Psychologist, and so on boxes provide students with an opportunity to apply the material in the chapter to a related scenario
- **In the Media** boxes highlight current issues being portrayed in the media which relate to the chapter topics
- **Increased coverage** on psychopathy (Ch. 11), young offenders (Ch. 12), domestic violence (Ch. 13), and homicidal offenders (Ch. 14), and new profiles of prominent Canadian researchers
- **Reorganization** of chapters to allow for easier delivery of course material
- **Updated**—All chapters have been updated to reflect the expanding field of forensic psychology, including recent changes to Canadian legislation
- **New profiles** of prominent Canadian researchers

    Dr. Dorothy Cotton, Correctional Service of Canada

    Dr. Stephen Porter, University of British Columbia-Okanagan

    Dr. Maggie Bruck, Johns Hopkins University

    Dr. Marnie Rice, Mental Health Centre Penetanguishene

    Dr. Alan Leschied, University of Western Ontario

    Dr. Donald Dutton, University of British Columbia

    Dr. Martin Daly, McMaster University

- **New** online **MyPsychKit** offering additional course material, including a Study Guide, practice tests, and more!
- The updated testbank for this edition will be provided in **MyTest**, Pearson's powerful and convenient online assessment generation program, as well as in Word. Go to **www.pearsonmytest.com**.

## RETAINED FEATURES

The pedagogical aids are designed to promote student learning and assist instructors in presenting key material. Important features include the following:

- **Learning Objectives** and **End-of-Chapter Summaries.** Each chapter starts with a list of learning objectives to guide students' learning of the material and closes with a summary linked to the learning objectives.
- **Vignettes.** Chapter-opening vignettes provide students with a context for the key concepts they will encounter in each chapter. These engaging vignettes present real-world scenarios in which students, or people they know, could potentially find themselves.
- **Boxes.** Boxed features within the chapters provide interesting asides to the main text. Some detail current Canadian cases and legal rulings, while others highlight "hot" topics in the news that have not yet been the subject of much psychological research. These boxes will develop students' consciousness of current issues and spark some research ideas.
- **Profiles of Canadian Researchers.** To expose students to the varied and excellent research in forensic psychology being conducted by Canadians, each chapter includes a profile of a key Canadian researcher whose work is relevant to the chapter topic. These profiles highlight educational background, current position, and research interests, along with a little about the researcher's personal life, so students realize the researchers featured are people too.
- **Research Methodology.** Research methodology specific to forensic topics is described in the relevant chapters, with the goal of helping students understand how studies in forensic psychology are conducted.
- **Research Studies.** Data reported in original studies is cited throughout the textbook, often in graph or table form for easy interpretation. Diagrams of psychological models and flow charts demonstrate key processes that occur through the criminal justice system.
- **Theoretical Perspectives.** Theories that provide accounts for specific topic areas are discussed in each chapter. The discussion of the various theories emphasizes a multidisciplinary approach, showing the interplay among cognitive, biological, and social factors in understanding the different forensic psychology areas.
- **Law.** *Forensic Psychology* provides the student with information on current Canadian law relevant to the psychological issues discussed. At times, Canadian law is contrasted with U.S. and/or British law; however, it is important to remember that the emphasis is on Canadian case law, statutes, regulations, and so on. We do not provide full coverage of law that is not Canadian, so students who are interested in the laws of other countries should refer to other resources.

- **Discussion Questions.** Several discussion questions are offered at the end of each chapter. Instructors can assign these questions for group discussion, or students can use the questions to examine their comprehension and retention of the chapter material. We hope these questions will inspire critical thought in students.

- **Key Terms and Glossary.** Throughout the chapters, keywords with which students in forensic psychology should be familiar appear in bold type and are defined in marginal notes. These key terms and their definitions are also provided in a glossary at the end of the book for easy reference.

## SUPPLEMENTS FOR INSTRUCTORS

The following supplements specific to *Forensic Psychology*, Third Edition, can be downloaded by instructors from a password-protected location on Pearson Education Canada's online catalogue (**vig.pearsoned.ca**). Contact your local sales representative for further information.

- **Instructor's Manual.** The Instructor's Manual is a comprehensive resource that provides chapter outlines, class activities, and summaries of select cases cited. We hope our colleagues will use the textbook and Instructor's Manual as a foundation that they can build on in the classroom lecture.

- **Test Item File.** This test bank, offered in Microsoft Word format, contains multiple-choice and short-answer questions. Each question is classified according to difficulty level and is keyed to the appropriate page number in the textbook.

- **MyTest.** The new edition test bank comes with MyTest, a powerful assessment-generation program that helps instructors easily create and print quizzes, tests, and exams, as well as homework or practice handouts. Questions and tests can all be authored online, allowing instructors ultimate flexibility and the ability to efficiently manage assessments at anytime, from anywhere.

- **PowerPoint Presentations.** PowerPoint slides highlight the key concepts in each chapter of the text.

**CourseSmart** goes beyond traditional expectations–providing instant, online access to the textbooks and course materials you need at a lower cost for students. And even as students save money, you can save time and hassle with a digital eTextbook that allows you to search for the most relevant content at the very moment you need it. Whether it's evaluating textbooks or creating lecture notes to help students with difficult concepts, CourseSmart can make life a little easier. See how when you visit **www.coursesmart.com/instructors**.

## SUPPLEMENTS FOR STUDENTS

**NEW to the third edition: MyPsychKit** is an online supplement that offers book-specific learning objectives, chapter summaries, and practice tests as well as a Study Guide and activities to aid student learning and comprehension. Also included in MyPsychKit are weblinks and further reading, both of which provide assistance with and access to powerful and reliable research material. *Student Access Code Cards for MyPsychKit are available with every new copy of the text.

**CourseSmart** goes beyond traditional expectations—providing instant, online access to the textbooks and course materials you need at an average savings of 60%. With instant access from any computer and the ability to search your text, you'll find the content you need quickly, no matter where you are. And with online tools such as highlighting and note-taking, you can save time and study efficiently. See all the benefits at **www.coursesmart.com/students**.

## ACKNOWLEDGMENTS

This book would never have come to fruition had we not been mentored by outstanding forensic researchers. Joanna Pozzulo is indebted to Rod Lindsay at Queen's University for his unfailing support, his rich insights, and his commitment to academic excellence that she aspires to achieve. Craig Bennell is grateful to David Canter at the University of Liverpool for providing a stimulating intellectual environment in which to study and for teaching him how to think critically. Adelle Forth wishes to express her admiration, respect, and gratitude to Robert Hare at the University of British Columbia, who nurtured her interest in the area of psychopathy and who has provided consistent support and guidance. These researchers continue to be a source of inspiration to us.

We would like to acknowledge that the forensic program at Carleton University, of which we are part, would not exist without our colleagues Shelley Brown, Kevin Nunes, Ralph Serin, and Evelyn Maeder.

We are thankful to the exceptional researchers we profiled in this textbook for giving us their time and insight into their lives. Specifically, Jim Ogloff, Dorothy Cotton, Kim Rossmo, Julian Roberts, Martin Daly, Bob Hare, Regina Schuller, Rod Lindsay, Maggie Bruck, Marnie Rice, Alan Leschied, Don Dutton, Chris Webster, Steve Porter.

All have made significant contributions to the field of forensic psychology.

We would like to thank the reviewers who provided us with exceptional feedback that allowed us to make the textbook stronger. Reviewers include the following:

Angela Book, Brock University

Deborah A. Connolly, Simon Fraser University

Jack J. Hirschberg, Concordia University

Peter N.S. Hoaken, University of Western Ontario

Connie Korpan, Grande Prairie Regional College

Carla MacLean, University of Victoria

Marc Paltry, Saint Mary's University

Kristine A. Peace, Grant MacEwan University

Edouard St. Pierre, Lakehead University

Alan Scoboria, University of Windsor

Brent Snook, Memorial University of Newfoundland

Michael Woodworth, UBC Okanagan

Abe Worenklein, Concordia University

We have tried to incorporate as many of the suggestions as possible, but of course we were restricted in terms of page length. In the end, we feel this third edition provides excellent breadth and good depth.

We thank our many undergraduate and graduate students who over the years have challenged our thinking and who have influenced the ideas expressed in this book.

We would like to thank the great staff at Pearson Education Canada. Ky Pruesse (editor-in-chief), Carolin Sweig (sponsoring editor), and Patti Altridge (developmental editor) deserve special mention—this book would not exist without their enthusiasm, expertise, and dedication. Marissa Lok (project manager), Deborah Cooper-Bullock (production and copy editor), and Mary Rose MacLachlan (photo researcher) also played important roles in making *Forensic Psychology*, Third Edition, become a reality.

Finally on a personal note, Joanna Pozzulo would like to thank her nieces, Jessica and Emma for making her feel like the coolest aunt ever. She also would like to thank Craig and Adelle for being great collaborators and dear friends. Craig Bennell would like to thank his wife Cindy for her love, patience, and support during the long hours of writing, and his sons Noah and Elijah for making him always remember what is most important. Adelle Forth would like to thank her partner, colleague, and friend, John Logan, for his insights, suggestions, and feedback that improved the book, as well as his understanding and support while preparing the book. She would also like to acknowledge the contribution of her numerous four-legged furry friends for keeping her sane.

# Chapter 1
## An Introduction to Forensic Psychology

## Learning Objectives

- Provide a narrow and a broad definition of forensic psychology.

- Describe the differences between clinical and experimental forensic psychology.

- List the three ways in which psychology and the law can interact.

- Identify some of the major milestones in the history of forensic psychology.

- List the criteria used in Canada to decide when expert testimony is admissible.

Jennifer Chen is an undergraduate university student who wants to become a forensic psychologist. She has just finished watching her favourite movie, *The Silence of the Lambs*. In fact, Jennifer always seems to be watching movies like this. If she's not watching movies, Jennifer is watching television shows such as *CSI* and *Criminal Minds,* or reading the latest true-crime book. Fortunately, Jennifer's neighbour works as a probation officer and she has regular contact with forensic psychologists. This neighbour has repeatedly told Jennifer that forensic psychology isn't necessarily what you see in the movies. Jennifer finally decides to find out for herself what forensic psychology is all about and enrols in a course, much like the one you are currently taking.

Although you may not appreciate it yet, **forensic psychology** is all around you. Every time you turn on the television or pick up the newspaper, there are stories that relate directly to the field of forensic psychology. Hollywood has also gotten in on the act. More and more often, blockbuster movies focus on issues that are related directly to the field of forensic psychology—whether it is profiling serial killers, selecting jury members, or determining someone's sanity. Unfortunately, the way in which the media portray forensic psychology is usually inaccurate. Although forensic psychologists often carry out the sorts of tasks you see depicted in the movies, the way in which they carry them out is typically very different from (and certainly less glamorous than) the typical Hollywood image. One of our primary goals throughout this book is to provide you with a more accurate picture of what forensic psychology is and to encourage you to think more critically about the things you see and hear in the media. See the In the Media box for further discussion about this issue.

**Forensic psychology:** A field of psychology that deals with all aspects of human behaviour as it relates to the law or legal system

Gene Hackman's role as a jury consultant in John Grisham's *Runaway Jury* relates to a task that some forensic psychologists are involved in. Much of what is seen in this Hollywood movie is an exaggeration of what actually occurs in jury selection.

## WHAT IS FORENSIC PSYCHOLOGY?

So, if Hollywood hasn't gotten it right, what exactly is forensic psychology? On the surface, this seems like a relatively simple question to answer, and it is undoubtedly an important question to ask. When being introduced to a new field of psychology, as you are now, one of the first questions you probably ask yourself is, "What am I going to be studying?" Although providing a clear and comprehensive definition of the discipline is obviously a logical way to begin a textbook on forensic psychology, this task is far more difficult than it seems because there is no generally accepted definition of the field (Brigham, 1999). Indeed, experts in this area don't even agree on what the field should be called, let alone how it should be defined (Ogloff, 2002). For example, you will often see forensic psychology being referred to as legal psychology or criminological psychology.

Much of the ongoing debate about how forensic psychology should be defined centres on whether the definition should be narrow or broad (Brigham, 1999). A narrow definition of forensic psychology would focus on certain aspects of the field while ignoring other, potentially important, aspects. For example, a narrow definition of forensic psychology might focus on clinical aspects of the field while ignoring the experimental research that many psychologists (who refer to themselves as forensic psychologists) conduct. Many leading psychologists, and the professional associations to which they belong, prefer to define the discipline in this way. For example, reflecting on the petition made to the American Psychological Association in 2001 to recognize forensic psychology as a specialization, Otto and Heilbrun (2002) state that "it was ultimately decided that the petition . . . should define forensic psychology narrowly, to include the primarily clinical aspects of forensic assessment, treatment, and consultation" (p. 8).

# The Reality of Reality TV

Crime has always been a popular topic for television shows, and researchers are interested in understanding the role that television plays in shaping the perceptions and attitudes of viewers toward crime-related matters. Recently, this line of research has taken on a new twist due largely to the introduction of crime-based reality TV (Doyle, 2003). And no crime-based reality show has been more popular than *Cops*, originally introduced by Fox network in 1989.

If shows such as *Cops* are influencing the perceptions and attitudes of viewers (e.g., toward the police and their response to crime), one obvious question to ask is whether this is problematic. Of course, asking this question leads to a range of other questions, such as whether these shows present an accurate portrayal of crime and our legal system's response to it. A colleague of ours at Carleton University, Aaron Doyle, has recently explored these types of issues in his 2003 book *Arresting Images: Crime and Policing in Front of the Television Camera*.

Some of what he finds when analyzing shows such as *Cops* might surprise you. For example, despite the fact that its producers refer to the show as "unfiltered television," Doyle's analysis of *Cops* indicates quite the opposite. In contrast to how the show is pitched to viewers, Doyle argues that *Cops* "offers a very particular and select vision of policing" (p. 34). Indeed, rather than referring to *Cops* as reality TV, Doyle suggests it is probably best seen as reality fiction, a "constructed version of reality with its own biases, rather than a neutral record" (p. 35). Once one understands how shows such as *Cops* are actually produced, Doyle's argument probably becomes more convincing. Consider the following examples.

Although the producers of *Cops* state that the show allows viewers to share a cop's point of view in "real time," this is not actually true. As Doyle (2003) shows, while each of the seven to eight minute vignettes that make up a *Cops* episode do tend to unfold in a linear fashion, the sequence of events is not typically presented in real time. Instead, the various parts of the vignette that are ultimately aired have often taken place over many hours, only to be edited together later. In fact, each hour of *Cops* airtime is typically edited down from between 50 to 60 hours of actual footage (Doyle, 2003).

Clever techniques for giving the illusion of real time flow are also regularly used by the editors of *Cops*. For example, as Doyle (2003) reveals, although it appears as if the visual and sound elements of *Cops* were both captured simultaneously, this is often not the case. Rather, "sound is edited to overlap cuts in the visuals . . . [with the continuing sound suggesting] continuity in time, as if the viewer has simply looked in a different direction during continuous action . . . although in fact an hour's worth of action and dialogue could have been omitted between the cuts" (p. 36). *Cops* is also made more realistic by ensuring that the camera crew is never seen, even during those segments of the episode when police officers are driving the camera crew to and from incidents (Doyle, 2003). According to Doyle, this involves considerable editing (e.g., of civilians reacting to the cameras). It also ensures that viewers are never left with the impression that the presence of television cameras could have had an impact on what they are watching. Unsurprisingly, the stories selected for ultimate airing on a *Cops* episode are also delivered in a way that ensures certain audience reactions. As highlighted by Doyle (2003), *Cops* uses a range of storytelling techniques to encourage viewers to identify with the police but not with suspects. For example, most *Cops* vignettes are hosted by a particular officer who we get to know throughout the vignette (e.g., at the beginning of the vignette we are given the officer's name and rank, and are told details about him or her). Suspects in all vignettes remain nameless; they are criminals who have given their consent to be shown but who otherwise remain anonymous and detached from the viewer.

So, as you proceed through this course, take some time to think about the shows that you watch. Think also about how these shows may have an impact on your perceptions and attitudes toward the topics we cover and whether this is a good thing. Of course, reality fiction can make for great television, but perhaps it should not shape our perceptions and attitudes about crime-related matters as much as it sometimes does.

Thus, according to this definition, the only individuals who should call themselves forensic psychologists are those individuals engaged in clinical practice (i.e., assessing, treating, or consulting) within the legal system. Psychologists who spend all their time conducting forensic-related research—for example, studying the memory of eyewitnesses, examining the decision-making processes of jurors, or evaluating the effectiveness of offender treatment programs—would not technically be considered forensic psychologists according to this narrow definition of forensic psychology. For reasons such as these, many psychologists have problems with using narrow definitions to define the field of forensic psychology (e.g., Bartol & Bartol, 2006).

By their very nature, broad definitions of forensic psychology are less restrictive than narrow definitions. One of the most commonly cited examples of a broad definition of forensic psychology is the one proposed by Bartol and Bartol (2006). They define the discipline as "(a) the research endeavour that examines aspects of human behaviour directly related to the legal process ... and (b) the professional practice of psychology within, or in consultation with, a legal system that embraces both civil and criminal law" (p. 3). Thus, unlike the narrow definition of forensic psychology provided above, which focuses solely on the *application* of psychology, this definition does not restrict forensic psychology to applied issues. It also focuses on the *research* that is required to inform applied practice in the field of forensic psychology.

Throughout this textbook, we adopt a broad definition of forensic psychology. Although we will often focus on the application of psychological knowledge to various aspects of the Canadian legal system, our primary goal is to demonstrate that this application of knowledge must always be based on a solid grounding of psychological research. In line with a broad definition of forensic psychology, this research frequently originates in areas of psychology that are often not obviously connected with the forensic area, such as social, cognitive, personality, and developmental psychology. The fact that forensic psychology is such an eclectic field is just one of the reasons why it is such an exciting area of study.

## THE ROLES OF A FORENSIC PSYCHOLOGIST

What is consistent across the various definitions of forensic psychology that currently exist is that individuals who call themselves forensic psychologists are always interested in issues that arise at the intersection between psychology and the law. What typically differs across the definitions is the particular focus the forensic psychologist takes. For example, by looking at the definitions provided above, it is clear that forensic psychologists can take on the role of clinician or researcher. In reality, however, these roles are not mutually exclusive, and one individual can take on more than one role. Indeed, some of the best-known forensic psychologists, many of whom will be profiled in this book, are both clinicians *and* researchers, while others are clinicians, researchers, *and* legal scholars. Since we will continually touch on these various roles throughout the upcoming chapters, we will briefly clarify what each role entails.

### The Forensic Psychologist as Clinician

**Clinical forensic psychologists:**
Psychologists who are broadly concerned with the assessment and treatment of mental health issues as they pertain to the law or legal system

**Clinical forensic psychologists** are broadly concerned with mental health issues as they pertain to the legal system (Otto & Heilbrun, 2002). This can include both research and practice in a wide variety of settings, such as schools, prisons, and hospitals. For example, clinical forensic psychologists are often concerned with the assessment and treatment of persons with mental disorders within the context of the law. On the research side, a frequent task for the clinical forensic psychologist might involve the validation of an assessment tool that has been developed to predict the risk of an offender being violent (e.g., Kropp & Hart, 2000). On the practical side, a frequent task might involve the assessment of an offender to assist the parole board in making an accurate determination of whether that offender is likely to pose a risk to the community if released. Other issues that clinical forensic psychologists are interested in may include, but are certainly not limited to, the following:

- Divorce and child custody mediation
- Determinations of criminal responsibility (insanity) and fitness to stand trial
- Providing expert testimony on questions of a psychological nature
- Personnel selection (e.g., for law enforcement agencies)
- Conducting critical incident stress debriefings with police officers
- Designing and conducting treatment programs for offenders

As in the United States, a clinical forensic psychologist in Canada must be a licensed clinical psychologist who has specialized in the forensic area. The educational requirements to obtain a licence vary across provinces and territories, but some form of graduate-level training is always required (Canadian Psychological Association, 2010). In Alberta, Saskatchewan, Newfoundland and Labrador, Nova Scotia, Prince Edward Island, and New Brunswick, the requirement is a master's degree in psychology (although New Brunswick will move to a Ph.D. degree standard in 2011). In British Columbia, Manitoba, Ontario, and Quebec, a Ph.D. degree in psychology is required. The forensic specialization typically takes the form of an intense period of supervised practice, before and/or after the completion of the required degree, in an applied forensic setting under the watchful eye of an experienced clinical supervisor. The last step of the licensing process is a comprehensive exam, which often involves an oral component.

One of the most common questions that undergraduate students ask is, "What is the difference between forensic psychology and **forensic psychiatry**?" In fact, many people, including those in the media, often confuse these two fields. To some extent in Canada, clinical forensic psychology and forensic psychiatry are more similar than they are different and, as a result, it is often difficult to separate them clearly. For example, both clinical forensic psychologists and forensic psychiatrists are trained to assess and treat individuals experiencing mental health problems who come into contact with the law, and you will see psychologists and psychiatrists involved in nearly every component of the criminal justice system. In addition, clinical forensic psychologists and forensic psychiatrists often engage in similar sorts of research (e.g., developing causal models of violent behaviour).

However, there are also important differences between the two fields. Probably the most obvious difference is that psychiatrists, including forensic psychiatrists, are medical doctors who can prescribe medication. Therefore, forensic psychiatrists undergo training that is quite different from the training clinical forensic psychologists receive, and this leads to several other distinctions between the fields. For example, in contrast to a psychiatrist's general (but not sole) reliance on a medical model of mental illness, psychologists tend to view mental illness more as a product of an individual's physiology, personality, and environment. See Box 1.1, which looks at some other important forensic-related disciplines that are often confused with the field of forensic psychology.

**Forensic psychiatry:** A field of medicine that deals with all aspects of human behaviour as it relates to the law or legal system

# Other Forensic Disciplines

Nowadays, people are being bombarded by media portrayals of various forensic disciplines, beyond just forensic psychology and forensic psychiatry. Although this does much to promote the respective specialties, it can also be the source of a lot of confusion. Listed below are brief descriptions of just a few forensic specialty areas. Each of these disciplines is sometimes confused with forensic psychology.

■ *Forensic anthropology*. Forensic anthropologists examine the remains of deceased victims to determine key facts about them, such as their gender, age, and appearance.

■ *Forensic linguistics*. Forensic linguists examine the spoken and written word in an attempt to assist criminal investigators. For example, they can assess the language in suicide notes to determine whether the notes are fake or genuine.

■ *Forensic chemistry*. Forensic chemists study the chemical aspects of crime scenes, which can include an analysis of paint particles, dyes, fibres, and other materials.

■ *Forensic ondontology*. Forensic ondontologists study the dental aspects of criminal activity, which can include identifying deceased victims through dental records and determining whether bite marks were made by an adult or a child.

■ *Forensic pathology*. Forensic pathologists examine the remains of dead bodies in an attempt to determine the time and cause of death through physical autopsy.

■ *Forensic entomology*. Forensic entomologists are concerned with how insects can assist with criminal investigations. For example, they can help to determine when someone died based on an analysis of insect presence (e.g., different types of insects will be present on a corpse at different points in time) and/or insect development (e.g., certain insects who are attracted to corpses soon after death develop in predictable, set cycles).

Source: Decaire, 1999.

## The Forensic Psychologist as Researcher

A second role for the forensic psychologist is that of experimenter, or researcher. As we have indicated above, although this role does not necessarily have to be separate from the clinical role, it often is. As with clinical forensic psychologists, **experimental forensic psychologists** are concerned with mental health issues as they pertain to the legal system, and they can be found in a variety of criminal justice settings. However, researchers in the forensic area are usually concerned with much more than just mental health issues. Indeed, they can be interested in any research issue that relates to the law or legal system. The list of research issues that are of interest to this type of forensic psychologist is far too long to present here, but they include the following:

■ Examining the effectiveness of risk-assessment strategies

■ Determining what factors influence jury decision making

■ Developing and testing better ways to conduct eyewitness lineups

■ Evaluating offender and victim treatment programs

■ Studying the impact of questioning style on eyewitness memory recall

■ Examining the effect of stress management interventions on police officers

Not only do clinical forensic psychologists differ from experimental forensic psychologists in terms of what they do, but they also differ in terms of their training. The forensic psychologist who is interested primarily in research will have undergone Ph.D.-level

**Experimental forensic psychologists:** Psychologists who are broadly concerned with the study of human behaviour as it relates to the law or legal system

graduate training in one of many different types of experimental graduate programs (and no internship is typically required). Only some of these graduate programs will be devoted solely to the study of forensic psychology. Others will be programs in social, cognitive, personality, or developmental psychology, although the program will have a faculty member associated with it who is conducting research in a forensic area. Regardless of the type of graduate program chosen, the individual's graduate research will be focused primarily on a topic related to forensic psychology (e.g., the malleability of child eyewitness memory). As can be seen in the short list of topics provided above, research in forensic psychology is eclectic and requires expertise in areas such as memory processing, decision making, and organizational issues. This is one of the reasons why training for experimental forensic psychology is more varied than the training for clinical forensic psychology.

## The Forensic Psychologist as Legal Scholar

A third role for the forensic psychologist, which is far less common than the previous two but no less important, is that of legal scholar. Because this role is less common, we will not deal with it as much throughout this textbook, but it is important to discuss this role briefly, especially because of the attention it has received in Canada. Two initiatives at Simon Fraser University (SFU) in Burnaby, B.C., are particularly important to mention. The first of these initiatives was SFU's Psychology and Law Program, originally established in 1991. More recently, this program has partnered with the University of British Columbia to allow students to obtain both their Ph.D. in psychology as well as their L.L.B. in law. This program produces forensic psychologists who are much more informed about the legal process and the legal system than was the case previously. The second initiative was the formation, also in 1991, of the Mental Health, Law, and Policy Institute (MHLPI) at SFU. The purpose of the MHLPI is to "promote interdisciplinary collaboration in research and training in areas related to mental health law and policy" (MHLPI, 2010). According to Brigham (1999), forensic psychologists in their role as legal scholars "would most likely engage in scholarly analyses of mental health law and psychologically oriented legal movements," whereas their applied work "would most likely center around policy analysis and legislative consultation" (p. 281).

## THE RELATIONSHIP BETWEEN PSYCHOLOGY AND LAW

Not only is forensic psychology a challenging field to be in because of the diversity of roles that a forensic psychologist can play, but it is also challenging because forensic psychology can be approached from many different angles. One way of thinking about these various angles has been proposed by Craig Haney, a professor of psychology at the University of California, Santa Cruz. Haney (1980) suggests that there are three primary ways in which psychology and the law can relate to each other. He calls these relationships **psychology *and* the law**, **psychology *in* the law**, and **psychology *of* the law**. Throughout this textbook, we will focus on the first two relationships, psychology and the law and psychology in the law. Clinical and experimental forensic psychologists are typically involved in these areas much more often than in the third. Psychology of the law is largely the domain of the legal scholar role and, therefore, we will touch on it only briefly.

**Psychology *and* the law:** The use of psychology to examine the operation of the legal system

**Psychology *in* the law:** The use of psychology in the legal system as that system operates

**Psychology *of* the law:** The use of psychology to examine the law itself

## Psychology and the Law

In this relationship, "psychology is viewed as a separate discipline [to the law], examining and analysing various components of the law [and the legal system] from a psychological perspective" (Bartol & Bartol, 1994, p. 2). Frequently, research that falls under the category of psychology *and* the law examines assumptions made by the law or our legal system, asking questions such as "Are eyewitnesses accurate?" "Do certain interrogation techniques cause people to falsely confess?" "Are judges fair in the way they hand down sentences?" and "Is it possible to accurately predict whether an offender will be violent when released from prison?" When working within the area of psychology *and* the law, forensic psychologists attempt to answer these sorts of questions so that the answers can be communicated to the legal community. Much of forensic psychology deals with this particular relationship. Therefore, research issues that fall under the general heading of "psychology and the law" will be thoroughly discussed throughout this textbook.

## Psychology in the Law

Once a body of psychological knowledge exists in any of the aforementioned areas of study, that knowledge can be used in the legal system by psychologists, lawyers, judges, and others. As the label indicates, psychology *in* the law involves the use of psychological knowledge in the legal system (Haney, 1980). As with psychology and the law, psychology in the law can take many different forms. It might consist of a psychologist in court providing expert testimony concerning some issue of relevance to a particular case. For example, the psychologist might testify that, based on his or her understanding of the psychological research, the eyewitness on the stand may have incorrectly identified the defendant from a police lineup. Alternatively, psychology in the law might consist of a police officer using his or her knowledge of psychology in an investigation. For example, the officer may base his questioning strategy during an interrogation on his knowledge of various psychological principles that are known to be useful for extracting confessions. Many of the research applications that we focus on in this textbook fit nicely with the label "psychology in the law."

## Psychology of the Law

Psychology *of* the law involves the use of psychology to study the law itself (Haney, 1980), and it addresses questions such as "What role should the police play in domestic disputes?" "Does the law reduce the amount of crime in our society?" and "Why is it important to allow for discretionary decision making in the Canadian criminal justice system?" Although often not considered a core topic in forensic psychology, there does appear to be a growing interest in the area of psychology of the law. The challenge in this case is that, to address the sorts of questions posed above, a set of skills from multiple disciplines (e.g., criminology, sociology, law) is often important and sometimes crucial. The new focus in North America and elsewhere on the role of forensic psychologist as legal scholar will no doubt do much to assist in this endeavour, and we are confident that in the future more research in the area of forensic psychology will focus on issues surrounding psychology of the law.

# THE HISTORY OF FORENSIC PSYCHOLOGY

Now that we have defined the field of forensic psychology and discussed the various roles that forensic psychologists can play, we will turn to a discussion of where the field came from and where it is currently headed. Compared with other areas of psychology, forensic psychology, when it is broadly defined, has a relatively short history, dating back roughly to the late nineteenth century. In the early days, this type of psychology was actually not referred to as forensic psychology and most of the psychologists conducting research in the area did not formally identify themselves as forensic psychologists. However, their research formed the building blocks of an emerging field of psychology that continues to be strong today. See Figure 1.1 for a timeline of some significant dates in the history of forensic psychology.

## Early Research: Eyewitness Testimony and Suggestibility

In the late nineteenth century, research in the area of forensic psychology was taking place in both North America and Europe, though as indicated above, it wasn't being referred to as forensic psychology at the time. Some of the first experiments were those of James McKeen Cattell (who is perhaps better known for his research in the area of intelligence testing) at Columbia University in New York. Cattell, a previous student of Wilhelm Wundt, who developed the first psychology laboratory in Leipzig, Germany, was one of the major powerhouses of psychology in North America. After developing an expertise in the study of human cognitive processes while in Leipzig, Cattell conducted some of the first North American experiments looking at what would later be called the *psychology of eyewitness testimony* (e.g., Cattell, 1895). Cattell would ask people to recall things they had witnessed in their everyday lives (e.g., "In which direction do apple seeds point?"), and he found that their answers were often inaccurate.

At around the same time, a number of other psychologists began studying eyewitness testimony and suggestibility (see Ceci & Bruck, 1993, for a review). For example, the famous French psychologist Alfred Binet conducted numerous studies in which he showed that the testimony provided by children was highly susceptible to suggestive questioning techniques. In a study discussed by Ceci and Bruck (1993), Binet (1900) presented children with a series of objects for a short period of time (e.g., a button glued to poster board). After viewing an object, some of the children were told to write down everything that they saw while others were asked questions. Some of these questions were direct (e.g., "How was the button attached to the board?"), others were mildly leading (e.g., "Wasn't the button attached by a thread?"), and still others were highly misleading (e.g., "What was the colour of the thread that attached the button to the board?"). As found in numerous studies since this experiment, Binet demonstrated that asking children to report everything they saw (i.e., free recall) resulted in the most accurate answers and that highly misleading questions resulted in the least accurate answers.

Shortly after Binet's study, a German psychologist named William Stern also began conducting studies examining the suggestibility of witnesses (Ceci & Bruck, 1993). The "reality experiment" that is now commonly used by eyewitness researchers to study eyewitness recall and recognition can in fact be attributed to Stern. Using this research paradigm, participants are exposed to staged events and are then asked to recall information about the

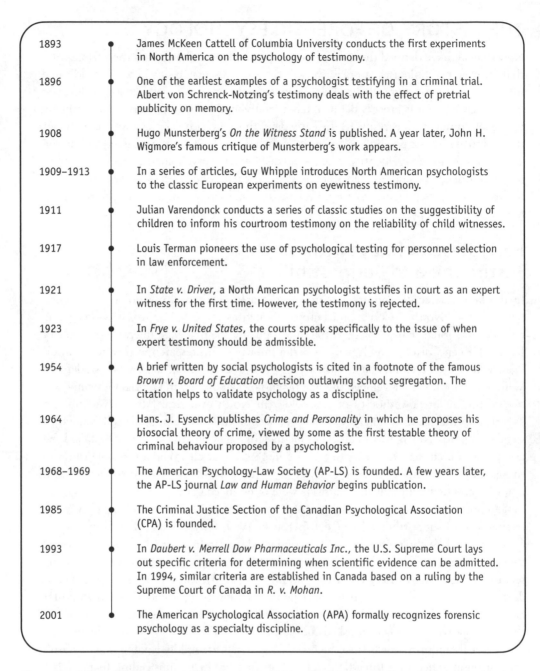

| 1893 | James McKeen Cattell of Columbia University conducts the first experiments in North America on the psychology of testimony. |
| 1896 | One of the earliest examples of a psychologist testifying in a criminal trial. Albert von Schrenck-Notzing's testimony deals with the effect of pretrial publicity on memory. |
| 1908 | Hugo Munsterberg's *On the Witness Stand* is published. A year later, John H. Wigmore's famous critique of Munsterberg's work appears. |
| 1909–1913 | In a series of articles, Guy Whipple introduces North American psychologists to the classic European experiments on eyewitness testimony. |
| 1911 | Julian Varendonck conducts a series of classic studies on the suggestibility of children to inform his courtroom testimony on the reliability of child witnesses. |
| 1917 | Louis Terman pioneers the use of psychological testing for personnel selection in law enforcement. |
| 1921 | In *State v. Driver*, a North American psychologist testifies in court as an expert witness for the first time. However, the testimony is rejected. |
| 1923 | In *Frye v. United States*, the courts speak specifically to the issue of when expert testimony should be admissible. |
| 1954 | A brief written by social psychologists is cited in a footnote of the famous *Brown v. Board of Education* decision outlawing school segregation. The citation helps to validate psychology as a discipline. |
| 1964 | Hans. J. Eysenck publishes *Crime and Personality* in which he proposes his biosocial theory of crime, viewed by some as the first testable theory of criminal behaviour proposed by a psychologist. |
| 1968–1969 | The American Psychology-Law Society (AP-LS) is founded. A few years later, the AP-LS journal *Law and Human Behavior* begins publication. |
| 1985 | The Criminal Justice Section of the Canadian Psychological Association (CPA) is founded. |
| 1993 | In *Daubert v. Merrell Dow Pharmaceuticals Inc.*, the U.S. Supreme Court lays out specific criteria for determining when scientific evidence can be admitted. In 1994, similar criteria are established in Canada based on a ruling by the Supreme Court of Canada in *R. v. Mohan*. |
| 2001 | The American Psychological Association (APA) formally recognizes forensic psychology as a specialty discipline. |

**Figure 1.1** Some Important European and North American Developments in the History of Forensic Psychology

Sources: Bartol & Bartol, 2004; Brigham, 1999.

event. In one of Stern's experiments, participants were exposed to a scenario that involved two students arguing in a classroom setting until one of the students drew a revolver (Stern, 1910). As was the case with Binet, Stern found that eyewitness testimony can often be incorrect, and he was perhaps the first researcher to demonstrate that a person's level of emotional arousal can have an impact on the accuracy of that person's testimony.

## Early Court Cases in Europe

Around the time that this research was being conducted, psychologists in Europe also started to appear as expert witnesses in court. Unsurprisingly, given the research being conducted at the time, much of the testimony that they were providing dealt with issues surrounding the accuracy of eyewitness testimony. For example, in 1896, Albert von Schrenck-Notzing was probably the first expert witness to provide testimony in court on the effect of pretrial publicity on memory. The case took place in Munich, Germany, and involved a series of three sexual murders. The court case attracted a great deal of attention from the press of the time, and Schrenck-Notzing testified that this extensive pretrial press coverage could influence the testimony of witnesses by causing what he called *retroactive memory falsification* (Bartol & Bartol, 2006). This term referred to a process whereby witnesses confuse actual memories of events with the events described by the media. Schrenck-Notzing supported his expert testimony with laboratory research, and this research is very much in line with what we know about the effects of pretrial publicity from more recent studies (e.g., Ogloff & Vidmar, 1994).

Following this case, Julian Varendonck, a Belgian psychologist, was called on to be an expert witness in a 1911 case involving the murder of a young girl, Cecile. Ceci and Bruck (1993) describe the case:

> Two of Cecile's friends who had played with her on the day of her murder were awakened that night by Cecile's mother to ask of her whereabouts. One of the children replied that she did not know. Later that night, she led the police to the spot where the children had played, not far from where Cecile's body was found. In the next month, the two children were repeatedly interviewed by authorities who asked many suggestive questions. The children quickly changed their original testimony of not knowing about Cecile's actions on the day of her murder. They provided details of the appearance of the murderer as well as his name. Because of an anonymous letter, the police arrested the father of one of the playmates for the murder of Cecile. On the basis of the details of the case, Varendonck was convinced of the defendant's innocence. He quickly conducted a series of studies with the specific intent of demonstrating the unreliability of children's testimony. (p. 406)

According to Ceci and Bruck (1993), in one of his studies, Varendonck (1911) asked a group of children to describe a person who had supposedly approached him in front of the children earlier that morning. Although this person did not exist, Varendonck was able to demonstrate, in line with more recent studies, that many of the children were easily led by suggestive questioning. Based on these findings, Varendonck concluded to the court that the testimony provided by the children in this case was likely to be inaccurate and that, as a group, children are very prone to suggestion.

## Advocates of Forensic Psychology in North America

Although it was not until years later that psychologists began testifying on similar issues in North America, psychology in North America was making great strides in other areas of the criminal justice system. Perhaps one of the most important landmarks was the publication in 1908 of Hugo Munsterberg's *On the Witness Stand* (Munsterberg, 1908).

The father of forensic psychology, Hugo Munsterberg, is best known for his controversial book *On the Witness Stand,* which many people believe pushed North American psychologists into the legal arena.

Another student of Wilhelm Wundt, Munsterberg is considered by many to be the father of forensic psychology. Coming from Germany to Harvard University in 1892, he quickly established a name for himself (Brigham, 1999). In his book, Munsterberg argued that psychology had much to offer the legal system. Through a collection of his essays, he discussed how psychology could assist with issues involving eyewitness testimony, crime detection, false confessions, suggestibility, hypnotism, and even crime prevention.

Unfortunately, he presented his ideas in a way that led to heavy criticism from the legal profession. This censure is unsurprising given the way in which he wrote. Consider the following quotation from the introduction to his book:

> The lawyer and the judge and the juryman are sure that they do not need the experimental psychologist. They do not wish to see that in this field pre-eminently applied experimental psychology has made strong strides. . . . They go on thinking that their legal instinct and their common sense supplies them with all that is needed and somewhat more . . . if the time is ever to come when even the jurist is to show some concession to the spirit of modern psychology, public opinion will have to exert some pressure. (Munsterberg, 1908, pp. 10–11)

Munsterberg's biggest critic was John Henry Wigmore, a well-respected law professor at Northwestern University in Chicago. Wigmore is known for many things, most notably his *Treatise on Evidence*, which is a critical examination of the laws of evidence. In the field of forensic psychology, however, what Wigmore is most commonly known for is his ruthless critique of Munsterberg's book. Through a series of fabricated "transcripts," Wigmore (1909) put Munsterberg on "trial," where he was sued, and found guilty of "claiming more than he could offer" (Brigham, 1999, p. 276). Wigmore criticized Munsterberg for the lack of relevant research publications to back up his claims and, more generally, for the lack of applied research in the field of forensic psychology as a whole. Perhaps because of Wigmore's comprehensive attack on Munsterberg's work, North American psychologists working in areas that we would now define as forensic psychology were largely ignored by the legal profession for a long period of time. However, according to some, Munsterberg was still instrumental in pushing North American psychologists into the legal arena (Bartol & Bartol, 2006).

## Forensic Psychology in Other Areas of the Criminal Justice System

After the publication of Munsterberg's controversial book, forensic psychology in North America gradually caught up to what was happening in Europe. Not only were theories of crime being proposed at a rapid rate (see Box 1.2), these theories were informing research conducted by North American psychologists. This research was also being practically applied in a wide range of criminal justice settings. For example, as Bartol and Bartol (2004) highlight, forensic psychologists were instrumental in establishing the first clinic for juvenile delinquents in 1909, psychologists began using psychological testing for law enforcement selection purposes in 1917, and 1919 saw the first forensic assessment laboratory (to conduct pretrial assessments) set up in a U.S. police agency. After these events, psychologists in the United States began to be more heavily involved in the judicial system as well, starting with the case of *State v. Driver* in 1921.

Box 1.2

# Biological, Sociological, and Psychological Theories of Crime

While an in-depth discussion of crime theories is beyond the scope of this book, efforts to develop such theories are clearly an important part of the history of forensic psychology. Over the last century, a variety of biological, sociological, and psychological theories of crime have been proposed and tested. Below are brief descriptions of some of the best-known theories.

## Biological Theories of Crime

■ *Sheldon's (1949) constitutional theory*. Sheldon proposed that crime is largely a product of an individual's body build, or somatotype, which is assumed to be linked to an individual's temperament. According to Sheldon, endomorphs (obese) are jolly, ectomorphs (thin) are introverted, and mesomorphs (muscular) are bold. Sheldon's studies indicated that, because of their aggressive nature, mesomorphs were more likely to become involved with crime.

■ *Jacobs, Brunton, Melville, Brittan, and McClemont's (1965) chromosomal theory*. Jacobs and her colleagues proposed that chromosomal irregularity is linked to criminal behaviour. A normal female has two X chromosomes, whereas a normal male has one X and one Y chromosome. However, it was discovered that there were men with two Y chromosomes, which, it was proposed, made them more masculine and, therefore, more aggressive. According to Jacobs and her colleagues, this enhanced aggressiveness would result in an increased chance that these men would commit violent crimes.

■ *Mark and Ervin's (1970) dyscontrol theory*. Mark and Ervin proposed that lesions in the temporal lobe and limbic system result in electrical disorganization within the brain, which can lead to a dyscontrol syndrome. According to Mark and Ervin, symptoms of this dyscontrol syndrome can include outbursts of sudden physical violence, impulsive sexual behaviour, and serious traffic violations.

## Sociological Theories of Crime

■ *Merton's (1938) strain theory*. Merton proposed that crime is largely a product of the strain felt by certain individuals in society (typically from the lower class) who have restricted access to legitimate means, such as education, of achieving valued goals of success. Merton argued that, while some of these individuals will be happy with the lesser goals that are achievable, others will turn to illegitimate means, such as crime, in an attempt to achieve the valued goals.

■ *Sutherland's (1939) differential association theory*. Sutherland proposed that criminal behaviour is learned through social interactions in which people are exposed to values that can be either favourable or unfavourable to violations of the law. More specifically, Sutherland maintained that people are likely to become involved in criminal activity when they learn more values (i.e., attitudes) that are favourable to violations of the law than values that are unfavourable to it.

■ *Becker's (1963) labelling theory*. Unlike most other theories of crime, Becker proposed that deviance (e.g., antisocial behaviour) is not inherent to an act but a label attached to an act by society. Thus, a "criminal" results primarily from a process of society labelling an individual as a criminal. This labelling process is thought to promote the individual's deviant behaviour through a self-fulfilling prophecy, defined by Becker as a prediction, which is originally false but which is made true by the person's actions.

## Psychological Theories of Crime

■ *Bowlby's (1944) theory of maternal deprivation*. Bowlby argued that the early separation of children from their mothers prevents effective social development from taking place. Without effective social development, Bowlby hypothesized that children will experience long-term problems in developing positive social relationships and will instead develop antisocial behaviour patterns.

■ *Eysenck's (1964) biosocial theory of crime*. Eysenck believed that some individuals (e.g., extraverts and neurotics) are born with cortical and autonomic nervous systems that influence their ability to learn from the consequences of their behaviour, especially the negative consequences experienced in childhood as part of the socialization and conscience-building process. Because of their poor conditionability, it is assumed that individuals who exhibit high levels of extraversion and neuroticism will have strong antisocial inclinations.

■ *Gottfredson and Hirschi's (1990) general theory of crime*. Gottfredson and Hirschi argue that low self-control, internalized early in life, in the presence of criminal opportunities explains an individual's propensity to commit crimes.

# Landmark Court Cases in the United States

Although psychologists in Europe had provided expert testimony in courts as early as the late nineteenth century, the first time this happened in the United States was 1921 (*State v. Driver*, 1921). However, according to Bartol and Bartol (2006), the *Driver* case was only a partial victory for forensic psychology. This West Virginia case involved the attempted rape of a young girl and the court accepted expert evidence from a psychologist in the area of juvenile delinquency. However, the court rejected the psychologist's testimony that the young girl was a "moron" and, therefore, could not be believed. In its ruling the court stated, "It is yet to be determined that psychological and medical tests are practical, and will detect the lie on the witness stand" (quoted in Bartol & Bartol, 2006, pp. 11–12).

A number of more recent U.S. court cases are also enormously important in the history of forensic psychology. Perhaps the best-known case is that of *Brown v. Board of Education* (1954). This case challenged the constitutionality of segregated public schools (Benjamin & Crouse, 2002). Opponents of school segregation argued that separating children based on their race creates feelings of inferiority, especially among African-American children. On May 17, 1954, the U.S. Supreme Court agreed. In the Court's ruling, Chief Justice Earl Warren stated,

> Segregation of White and colored children in public school has a detrimental effect upon the colored children. The impact is greater when it has the sanction of the law, for the policy of separating the races is usually interpreted as denoting the inferiority of the Negro group. A sense of inferiority affects the motivation of the child to learn. Segregation with the sanction of law, therefore, has a tendency to retard the educational and mental development of Negro children and to deprive them of some of the benefits they would receive in a racially integrated school system. Whatever may have been the extent of psychological knowledge [in previous court cases] this finding is amply supported by modern authority. (Benjamin & Crouse, 2002, p. 39)

Beyond the obvious social importance of this ruling, it is important in the field of forensic psychology because of a footnote that was attached to the last sentence of the ruling, the famous footnote 11. The "modern authority" that the U.S. Supreme Court was referring to in this ruling was research in the social sciences demonstrating the detrimental effect of segregation. At the top of the list of seven references included in footnote 11 was the work of Kenneth Clark, an African-American psychologist who taught psychology at City College in New York City and studied how prejudice and discrimination affected personality development. This was the first time that psychological research was cited in a U.S. Supreme Court decision, and some have argued that this validated psychology as a science (e.g., Benjamin & Crouse, 2002).

The last court case that we will discuss here is *Jenkins v. United States* (1962). The trial involved charges of breaking and entering, assault, and intent to rape, with the defendant, Jenkins, pleading not guilty by reason of insanity. Three clinical psychologists were presented by the defendant, each of them supporting an insanity defence on the basis that the defendant was suffering from schizophrenia at the time of the crimes. At the conclusion of the trial, the judge instructed the jury to disregard the testimony from the psychologists because "psychologists were not qualified to give expert testimony on the issue of mental disease" (American Psychological Association, 2007). The case was appealed. As part of the appeal, the American Psychological Association provided a report to the court stating their view that clinical psychologists are competent to provide opinions concerning the existence of mental illness. On appeal, the court reversed the conviction and ordered a new trial, stating that "some psychologists are qualified to render expert testimony on mental disorders . . . the determination of a psychologist's competence to render an expert opinion . . . must depend upon the nature and extent of his knowledge and not simply on the claim to the title 'psychologist'" (American Psychological Association, 2007). This decision helped to increase the extent to which psychologists could contribute directly to the legal system as expert witnesses.

Although the landmark U.S. court cases we have discussed so far have been fundamental in shaping forensic psychology, there are also numerous Canadian court cases that have been influential. A brief discussion of some of these cases is provided in Box 1.3. We will provide a more detailed discussion of some of the cases in the relevant chapters (where we focus on research relating to these rulings).

Despite the fact that he wasn't a forensic psychologist, Kenneth Clark made an extremely important contribution to this field. The citation of his work by the U.S. Supreme court in *Brown v. Board of Education* showed that psychological research could play a role in the courtroom.

## Signs of a Legitimate Field of Psychology

Although the field of forensic psychology has perhaps not come as far as many forensic psychologists would have hoped in its relatively short history, it has now become a recognized and legitimate field of study within psychology. Indeed, forensic psychology now appears to have many of the markings of an established discipline. As highlighted by Schuller and Ogloff (2001), this is reflected in numerous ways. First, a growing number of high-quality textbooks in the area provide the opportunity to teach students about forensic psychology. The availability of textbooks is particularly evident in the United States. Second, a large number of academic journals are now dedicated to various aspects of the field, and more mainstream psychology journals are beginning to publish research from the forensic domain at a regular rate. Third, a number of professional associations have now been developed to represent the interests of forensic psychologists and to promote research and practice in the area. The largest of these associations is the American Psychology-Law Society (AP-LS), founded in 1968–1969, in which Canadian forensic psychologists have played a crucial role (one of these individuals, Dr. James Ogloff, is profiled in Box 1.4). Other countries have developed similar professional associations. In Canada, for example, forensic psychologists can belong to the Criminal Justice Section of the Canadian Psychological Association (CPA), which was founded in 1985. Fourth, new training opportunities in forensic psychology, at both the undergraduate and graduate level, are being established in North America (some in Canada), and existing training opportunities are being improved. Finally, and perhaps most importantly, in 2001 the American Psychological Association (APA) formally recognized forensic psychology as a specialty discipline.

# Influential Canadian Court Cases in the History of Forensic Psychology

Some influential Canadian cases of particular interest to forensic psychologists include the following:

■ *R. v. Hubbert* (1975). The Ontario Court of Appeal states that jurors are presumed to be impartial (i.e., unbiased) and that numerous safeguards are in place within the Canadian judicial system to ensure this (e.g., limitations can be imposed on the press in terms of what they can report before the start of a trial).

■ *R. v. Sophonow* (1986). The Manitoba Court of Appeal overturns the murder conviction of Thomas Sophonow because of errors in law, many of which related to problems with the eyewitness evidence collected by the police as part of their investigation.

■ *R. v. Lavallee* (1990). The Supreme Court of Canada (SCC) sets guidelines for when, and how, expert testimony should be used in cases involving battered women syndrome. Since this ruling, expert testimony in cases of battered women who kill has increased.

■ *Wenden v. Trikha* (1991). The Alberta Court of Queen's Bench rules that mental health professionals have a duty to warn a third party if they have reasonable grounds to believe that their client intends to seriously harm that individual.

■ *R. v. Swain* (1991). The SCC makes a ruling that results in changes to the insanity defence standard in Canada, including the name of the defence, when the defence can be raised, and for how long insanity acquittees can be detained.

■ *R. v. Levogiannis* (1993). The SCC rules that children are allowed to testify in court behind screens that prevent them from seeing the accused.

■ *R. v. Mohan* (1994). The SCC establishes formal criteria for determining when expert testimony should be admitted into court.

■ *R. v. Williams* (1998). The SCC formally acknowledges that jurors can be biased by numerous sources, ranging from community sentiment on a particular issue to direct involvement with a case (e.g., being related to the accused).

■ *R. v. Gladue* (1999). The SCC rules that prison sentences are being relied on too often by judges as a way of dealing with criminal behaviour, especially for Aboriginal offenders, and that other sentencing options should be considered.

■ *R. v. Oickle* (2000). The SCC rules that police interrogation techniques, which consist of various forms of psychological coercion, are acceptable and that confessions extracted through their use can be admissible in court.

■ *R. v. L.T.H.* (2008). The SCC makes a ruling that, when determining the admissibility of a statement made by a young person to the police, the prosecution does not have to prove that the young person understood his or her legal rights as explained by police, but they do have to prove that these rights were explained to the young person by using language appropriate to his or her age and understanding.

## MODERN-DAY DEBATES: PSYCHOLOGICAL EXPERTS IN COURT

Since the field of forensic psychology has become more widely accepted, forensic psychologists have increasingly been asked to provide expert testimony in court. The variety of topics that forensic psychologists testify about is very broad indeed, including competency to stand trial, custody issues, malingering and deception, the accuracy of eyewitness identification, the effects of crime on victims, and the assessment of dangerousness. In order for forensic psychologists to increase the extent to which they can contribute to the judicial system in this way, it is important for them to become more knowledgeable about the

Box 1.4

## Canadian Researcher Profile: Dr. James Ogloff

James Ogloff entered the University of Calgary intending to major in commerce and to go on to complete a law degree. His career plan was to become a corporate lawyer. While majoring in commerce, during his second year he was required to complete an undergraduate course in social sciences. Viewing this as a largely useless requirement, he opted to complete Introduction to Psychology in an inter-session course in the summer to "get it over with." Much to his surprise, he ended up being captivated with psychology, so much so that the following fall semester, he ended up dropping out of his commerce courses and transferring to psychology. At that time, his interests were in the area of child psychology. Soon, though, his long-standing interests in law re-emerged and he completed his undergraduate research on the topic of eyewitness memory and hypnosis. Dr. Ogloff entered graduate school in clinical psychology, obtaining his M.A. at the University of Saskatchewan. While there, he spent a great deal of time at the Regional Psychiatric Centre, a secure prison hospital, where he trained, conducted research, and did clinical work. Although he was working in the forensic psychology area, he still felt the need to learn more about the law.

With a desire to learn more about the law and how it relates to psychology, Dr. Ogloff went on to attend the law/psychology program at the University of Nebraska at Lincoln. The University of Nebraska had established the first program that offered a combined law degree and Ph.D. in psychology. He completed his Juris Doctor in Law,

with distinction, and had a short stint of legal practice while still a student. He completed his Ph.D. in psychology, doing his doctoral research in the area of jury understanding of the insanity defence. His interest in this area was spawned by John Hinckley Jr.'s attempted assassination of President Ronald Reagan. Hinckley Jr. was found "not guilty by reason of insanity" and the verdict initiated a great deal of controversy regarding the use of the insanity defence in the United States. Numerous reforms were initiated—including changing the wording of the defence in many states with the intention to limit the number of people found "not guilty by reason of insanity." Curiously, though, no one had conducted research to determine whether varying the insanity defence standards produced changes in jury verdicts. Dr. Ogloff's research showed that even fairly dramatic changes to the insanity defence standards did not produce differences in verdicts by simulated jurors.

Following graduate school, Dr. Ogloff began his academic career at Simon Fraser University, where he eventually became the university endowed professor of law and forensic psychology. He helped to develop, and served as director of, the Program in Law and Forensic Psychology at Simon Fraser University. He also held an appointment as adjunct professor of law at the University of British Columbia, where he taught classes in mental health law and the psychology of litigation.

Dr. Ogloff has continued his research in the area of the comprehension of legal instructions, though his more recent work has focused more generally on jurors' comprehension of judges' legal instructions. In addition to his continued interest in jury research and judicial instructions, most of his research and scholarly writing has been in the areas of offenders with mental illnesses, training in law and psychology, the assessment of risk for violence, and professional ethics.

In 2001, Dr. Ogloff left Simon Fraser University to assume the position of foundation professor of clinical forensic psychology at Monash University in Melbourne, Australia. He is also director of psychological services for the Victorian Institute of Forensic Mental Health. As well, he has established and directs the Centre for Forensic Behavioural Science, a research, training, and consultation

*(continued)*

law and the legal system (Ogloff & Cronshaw, 2001). They need to become more aware of the role of an expert witness, the various ways in which psychology and the law differ from each other, and the criteria that courts consider when determining whether psychological testimony should be admitted.

## The Functions of the Expert Witness

**Expert witness:** A witness who provides the court with information (often an opinion on a particular matter) that assists the court in understanding an issue of relevance to a case

According to Ogloff and Cronshaw (2001), an **expert witness** generally serves one of two functions. One is to provide the court with information that assists them in understanding a particular issue, and the other is to provide the court with an opinion. Understanding these functions is important because they are what separate the expert witness from other witnesses who regularly appear in court (e.g., eyewitnesses). To be clear on this issue, in contrast to other witnesses in court, who can testify only about what they have directly observed, expert witnesses can provide the court with their personal opinion on matters relevant to the case and they are often allowed to draw inferences based on their observations (Ogloff & Cronshaw, 2001). These opinions and inferences must always fall within the limits of expert witnesses' areas of expertise, which they typically get through specialized training and experience, and the testimony must be deemed reliable and helpful to the court. In addition, it is important to point out that, when providing testimony to the courts, the expert witness is supposed to be there as an educator to the judge and jury, not as an advocate for the defence or the prosecution.

## The Challenges of Providing Expert Testimony

Providing expert testimony to the courts in an effective way is not a simple task, which probably explains why numerous manuals have been published to assist expert witnesses with the task of preparing for court (e.g., Brodsky, 1991, 1999). Even judges have provided suggestions on how forensic psychologists can increase their chances of being effective witnesses in court (e.g., Saunders, J.W.S., 2001). In large part, these difficulties arise because of the inherent differences (often conflicts) that exist between the fields of psychology and law. Numerous individuals have discussed these differences, but we will focus on one particular attempt to describe them.

According to Hess (1987, 1999), psychology and law differ along at least seven different dimensions:

1. *Knowledge*. Knowledge gain in psychology is accomplished through cumulative research. In the law, knowledge comes through legal precedent, logical thinking, and case law.

2. *Methodology*. Methodological approaches in psychology are predominantly nomothetic. In other words, the goal is to uncover broad patterns and general trends through the use of controlled experiments and statistical methods. In contrast, the law is idiographic in that it operates on a case-by-case basis.

3. *Epistemology*. Psychologists assume that it is possible to uncover hidden truths if the appropriate experiments are conducted. Truth in the law is defined subjectively and is based on who can provide the most convincing story of what really happened.

4. *Criteria*. In terms of a willingness to accept something as true, psychologists are cautious. To accept a hypothesis, results must be replicated, and conservative statistical criteria are used. The law decides what is true based on a single case and criteria that are often more lenient.

5. *Nature of law*. The goal in psychology is to describe how people behave. Law, however, is prescriptive. It tells people how they should behave.

6. *Principles*. Good psychologists always consider alternative explanations for their findings. Good lawyers always convince the judge and jury that their explanation of the findings is the only correct explanation.

7. *Latitude*. The behaviour of the psychologist when acting as an expert witness is severely limited by the court. The law imposes fewer restrictions on the behaviour of lawyers (though they are also restricted in numerous ways).

Understanding these differences is important because they help us appreciate why the courts are often so reluctant to admit testimony provided by psychological experts. For example, after considering how psychology and the law differ with respect to their methodological approach, it may not be surprising that judges often have difficulty seeing how psychologists can assist in court proceedings. Indeed, numerous legal scholars have questioned whether the general patterns and trends that result from a nomothetic psychological approach should ever be used in court. As Sheldon and Macleod (1991) state:

> The findings derived from empirical research are used by psychologists to formulate norms of human behaviour. From observations and experiments, psychologists may conclude that in circumstance X there is a likelihood that an individual . . . will behave in manner Y. . . . [N]ormative data of this sort are of little use to the courts. The courts are concerned to determine the past behaviour of accused *individuals*, and in carrying out that function, information about the past behaviour of *other individuals* is wholly irrelevant. (emphasis added, p. 815)

Currently, little attempt has been made to understand these differences between psychology and law, or their implications for the field of forensic psychology. Once we gain such an understanding, perhaps forensic psychologists will be in a better position to assist the courts with the decisions they are required to make. We believe that research conducted by forensic psychologists, particularly in their role as legal scholars, will greatly assist in this endeavour. This research will also increase our understanding of the criteria the courts use for determining the conditions under which they will accept expert testimony from psychologists.

## Criteria for Accepting Expert Testimony

In order for forensic psychologists to provide expert testimony in court, they must meet certain criteria. In the United States, criteria of one sort or another have been in place since the early twentieth century. In fact, until quite recently, the admissibility of expert testimony in the United States was based on a decision handed down by the courts in *Frye v. United States* (1923). Frye was being tried for murder and the court rejected his request to admit the results from a polygraph exam he had passed. On appeal, the court also rejected requests to allow the polygraph expert to present evidence on Frye's behalf (Bartol & Bartol, 1994). In the ruling, the court spoke specifically to the issue of when expert testimony should be admitted into court. The court indicated that, for novel scientific evidence to be admissible in court, it must be established that the procedure(s) used to arrive at the testimony is generally accepted in the scientific community. More specifically, the court stated, "while courts will go a long way in admitting expert testimony deduced from a well-recognized scientific principle or discovery, the thing from which the deduction is made must be sufficiently established to have gained general acceptance in the particular field in which it belongs" (*Frye v. United States*, 1923, p. 1).

This criterion came to be called the **general acceptance test**, and although it formed the basis of admissibility decisions in the United States for a long time, it is heavily criticized. The major criticism centres on the vagueness of the terms *general acceptance* and *the particular field in which it belongs*, and whether trial judges are able to make appropriate determinations of what these terms mean. As just one example of where problems might emerge, consider a defence lawyer who would like to have a criminal profiler provide expert testimony in court (as you will see in Chapter 3, a profiler is someone who attempts to predict the personality and demographic characteristics of unknown offenders based on how that offender's crimes were committed). How should the trial judge decide whether the profiler used generally accepted profiling techniques? If the courts turned to the profiling community (typically consisting of specially trained law enforcement personnel) to make this determination, the answer would most likely be far more favourable than if they had asked forensic psychologists who conduct research in the area of criminal profiling (e.g., Alison, Bennell, Mokros, & Ormerod, 2002). So, whom should the judge turn to and believe? In what "particular field" does criminal profiling belong?

This issue of vagueness was addressed more recently in the U.S. Supreme Court decision handed down in *Daubert v. Merrell Dow Pharmaceuticals, Inc.*(1993), when more specific admissibility criteria were set. Daubert sued Merrell Dow because he believed a morning sickness drug his mother ingested while pregnant, which was produced by the company, led to his birth defects. At trial, Merrell Dow presented experts who provided evidence that the use of the drug Bendectin does not result in birth defects. In turn, Daubert provided evidence from experts who claimed that Bendectin could lead to birth defects. The state court and the appeal court both rejected the testimony provided by Daubert's experts on the basis that the methods they used to arrive at their results were not generally accepted by the scientific community. On appeal before the U.S. Supreme Court, Daubert's lawyers challenged the state and appeal courts' interpretation of "general acceptance."

In addressing this issue, the U.S. Supreme Court stated that, for scientific evidence to be admitted into court, it must (1) be provided by a qualified expert, (2) be relevant, and (3) be reliable (meaning scientifically valid). To assist judges in making the decision as to whether evidence is in fact valid, the U.S. Supreme Court laid out four specific criteria, now commonly referred to as the **Daubert criteria**. Scientific evidence is considered valid if the following criteria are met:

1. The research has been peer reviewed.
2. The research is testable (i.e., falsifiable through experimentation).
3. The research has a recognized rate of error.
4. The research adheres to professional standards.

More recently, in the case of *Kumho Tire Company v. Carmichael* (1999), the U.S. Supreme Court ruled that the *Daubert* criteria apply to all expert testimony, not just scientific testimony.

Similar criteria are currently being used in Canada. The rules for admissibility in Canada were laid out in *R. v. Mohan* (1994). Mohan was a pediatrician charged with sexually assaulting several of his teenage female patients. At trial, Mohan wanted to provide expert testimony from a psychiatrist who was prepared to testify that the typical offender in such a case would be a pedophile and, in his opinion, Mohan was not a pedophile. The trial judge ruled that the testimony was inadmissible and, on appeal before the Supreme Court of Canada, the court agreed and established the standard for admitting expert testimony in Canada.

The standard is now referred to as the **Mohan criteria**. In addition to requiring that the testimony being offered by the expert is reliable (i.e., valid), the *Mohan* criteria includes four admissibility criteria, some of which are similar to the *Daubert* criteria:

1. The evidence must be relevant, in that it makes a fact at issue in the case more or less likely. Returning to our criminal profiling example, consider a serial rape case involving a white defendant and black victims. If an expert in the area of profiling concludes, as a result of reliable research, that 95% of all rapes are intraracial, it is possible that this testimony may be deemed relevant by the court since it makes it less likely that the defendant is guilty (Ormerod, 1999).

2. The evidence must be necessary for assisting the trier of fact. In other words, the testimony must be about something that goes beyond the common understanding of the court. For example, testimony from a profiler might suggest that the offender who committed a series of rapes is likely to have been unemployed or a shift worker at the time of the crimes. If that testimony were based on the fact that many of the rapes were committed during the day, it is doubtful that the testimony would be deemed admissible by the court because jurors applying their common sense will likely come to the same conclusion (Ormerod, 1999).

3. The evidence must not violate any other rules of exclusion (i.e., rules that would otherwise exclude the admissibility of the evidence). For example, even in cases where testimony was deemed relevant, it may still be ruled inadmissible if its potential prejudicial effect (on jurors) outweighs its probative value. Consider a trial where the defendant allegedly raped very young girls. In this case, it would be relevant that the defendant has previously been convicted of similar crimes in the past, and therefore

**Daubert criteria:** A standard for accepting expert testimony, which states that scientific evidence is valid if the research on which it is based has been peer reviewed, is testable, has a recognized rate of error, and adheres to professional standards

**Mohan criteria:** A standard for accepting expert testimony, which states that expert testimony will be admissible in court if the testimony is relevant, is necessary for assisting the trier of fact, does not violate any exclusionary rules, and is provided by a qualified expert

testimony about this fact has probative value. However, the prejudicial effect associated with this testimony is so great that it may lead jurors to convict the defendant, not because they are convinced of his guilt, but because, "he did it before so he deserves to be punished anyways" (Ormerod, 1999, p. 218).

4. The testimony must be provided by a qualified expert. Expertise in a court of law is typically determined by considering the type and amount of training and experience a witness possesses. Thus, if the testimony being considered relates to a criminal profile of the offender who committed a series of rapes, the witness must possess expertise in this specific domain for the testimony to be admissible. While determining this issue is usually straightforward, difficulties sometimes arise in determining what type of training and/or experience is valid, especially in cases where the testimony is based not in science but on "art" (as is arguably the case with profiling; Ormerod, 1999).

Using this information, read the scenario described in the Case Study box and see what challenges you might encounter as a judge when trying to apply the *Mohan* criteria.

Although these criteria probably make the judge's job of deciding when to admit expert testimony easier, they do not eliminate all possible problems. In large part, these problems occur because the criteria are still highly subjective and rely heavily on the discretion of the judge. An example of one potential problem is illustrated by the case of

## CASE STUDY  YOU BE THE JUDGE

You are a provincial court judge. The case before you involves a defendant who allegedly committed five sexual assaults against young women. The prosecutor on the case is trying to introduce testimony from an "expert" who will present evidence (referred to as similar fact evidence) that the defendant is responsible for all the crimes in question. Specifically, the witness plans to testify that the crimes in question were so similar that the same individual must have committed them: Not only did all the crimes occur in the same general geographic area, but the way the crimes were committed was also broadly similar (e.g., in terms of how the offender approached the victim, the type of weapon used, the sexual acts committed, and the level of violence exhibited).

### Your Turn . . .

Your task as the judge in this case is to determine whether this witness should be allowed to present her testimony in court.

What are the major issues that you would consider when making this decision? How would you go about determining whether the evidence that the witness plans to introduce is relevant and necessary for assisting the court in understanding the case? How would you go about determining whether the evidence is valid and whether the witness should in fact be considered an expert? What challenges might you face in answering these questions and what might assist you with your task?

R. v. McIntosh and McCarthy (1997), discussed in Box 1.5, in which a judge decided that testimony relating to the accuracy of eyewitness testimony was common knowledge and, as a result, inadmissible (Yarmey, 2001). Most of the research in the area of eyewitness accuracy indicates that the judge was most likely wrong in this case. This case highlights the need not only to conduct high-quality research in the area of forensic psychology, but also to get that research into the hands of the legal community. As you will see as you read through this textbook, much of the high-quality research already exists, but on the whole, forensic psychologists have not done a great job at transferring this research to the legal community.

## SUMMARY

1. Forensic psychology can be defined in a narrow or broad fashion. Narrow definitions focus only on the clinical *or* experimental aspects of the field, whereas broad definitions are less restrictive and encompass both aspects.

2. Forensic psychologists can play different roles. Clinical forensic psychologists are primarily interested in mental health issues as they pertain to law. Experimental forensic psychologists are interested in studying any aspect of human behaviour that relates to the law (e.g., eyewitness memory, jury decision making, risk assessment).

3. Psychology can relate to the field of law in three ways. Psychology and the law refers to the use of psychology to study the operation of the legal system. Psychology in the law refers to the use of psychology within the legal system as it operates. Psychology of the law refers to the use of psychology to study the legal system itself.

4. The history of forensic psychology is marked by many important milestones, in both the research laboratory and the courtroom. Early research consisted of studies of eyewitness testimony and suggestibility, and many of the early court cases in Europe where psychologists appeared as experts dealt with similar issues. Hugo Munsterberg played a significant role in establishing the field of forensic psychology in North America, and by the early 1900s, forensic psychologist were active in many different parts of the North American criminal justice system. Currently, forensic psychology is viewed as a distinct and specialized discipline, with its own textbooks, journals, and professional associations.

5. Expert witnesses differ from regular witnesses in that expert witnesses can testify about their opinions, whereas other witnesses can testify only as to what they know to be fact. In Canada, the criteria for determining whether an expert's testimony will be admitted into court relate to whether the testimony (1) is relevant, (2) goes beyond the common understanding of the court, (3) does not violate any exclusionary rules, and (4) comes from a qualified expert.

## Discussion Questions

1. You are sitting on a panel of experts that has been charged with the task of redefining the field of forensic psychology. In your role as a panel member, you have to consider whether forensic psychology should be defined in a narrow or broad fashion. What are some of the advantages and disadvantages of adopting a narrow definition? What are some of the advantages and disadvantages of adopting a broad definition? Decide what type of definition you prefer and explain why.

2. The majority of forensic psychologists have no formal training in law. Do you think this is appropriate given the extent to which many of these psychologists are involved in the judicial system?

3. You have just been hired as a summer intern at a law office. One of your tasks is to assist in preparing for a high-profile murder case that has attracted a great deal of media attention. One of the lawyers has found out that you've taken this course, and she wants to know whether the extensive pretrial press coverage the crime has received will make it difficult to find impartial jurors. Design a study to determine whether this is likely to be the case.

4. It took much longer for forensic psychology to become an established field of study in North America than in Europe. Why do you think this was the case?

5. Put yourself in the shoes of an expert witness. You are supposed to act as an educator to the judge and the jury, not as an advocate for the defence or the prosecution. To what extent do you think you could do this? Why?

# Chapter 2
## Police Psychology

## Learning Objectives

- Outline the major steps in developing a valid police selection procedure.

- Describe the various instruments that are used to select police officers.

- Define what is meant by the term *police discretion*.

- List some key decisions in policing that require the use of discretion.

- Outline some of the major sources and consequences of stress in policing.

- Describe various strategies for dealing with police stress.

It's Wednesday night, just after 2:00 a.m., and Constable Vincent Kwan is performing a routine patrol in a rough area of town. It's an area known for prostitution, drug dealing, and a large homeless population. Just when he was about to head back to the station, he receives a call from dispatch that gunshots have been heard coming from a nearby apartment. Being closest to the scene, Constable Kwan responds to the call. He pulls his cruiser in front of the apartment building and makes his way up the stairs. Outside the apartment door, he can hear a man yelling. The door is slightly ajar so he can see inside. It doesn't look like there's anyone else in the apartment so he knocks on the door. The man inside continues to yell as Constable Kwan enters the apartment. The man is only partially dressed and is yelling out his window. Constable Kwan can't understand what he is saying, but as the man turns around, Constable Kwan sees that he's holding a large knife in his hands and is bleeding from the arm. He tells the man to put down the knife, but the man runs to his balcony, backs up to the railing, and threatens to jump. He keeps swinging the knife in front of him and says he has a gun in his pocket. By his speech and demeanor, Constable Kwan can tell that something is seriously wrong with the man, but he doesn't know what. Constable Kwan now has to decide how to protect this man, while also protecting himself.

The scenario described above raises many questions about police officers and the nature of the work they do. For example, we might ask whether Constable Kwan is well suited to deal with this sort of situation. Is he the type of person who can think clearly under pressure? If not, why was he able to successfully graduate from the police academy? Alternatively, we might be curious about what Constable Kwan should do in this case. What options are available to him? How much force, if any, should he use to subdue the individual? Finally, we might be interested in how Constable Kwan is reacting to the events that are unfolding. Is he experiencing serious stress reactions? If so, what are they and how might they have an impact on his decisions? Will Constable Kwan suffer any long-term negative effects from being exposed to such a stressful incident? This chapter will provide some of the answers to these questions by examining a number of issues in the area of police psychology, including police selection, police discretion, and police stress.

## POLICE SELECTION

As part of ongoing recruitment efforts, the Vancouver Police Department (see the In the Media box) posts information about the policing profession on its recruitment web page:

> As an officer, on any given day, you will respond to burglar alarms, console victims of traumatic events and assist people in getting their lives back on track. You'll collect and log evidence at crime scenes, apprehend dangerous criminals and testify in court. You're as comfortable in front of a computer as you would be behind the wheel of a police car. . . . You will be skilled in investigation and interviewing techniques. Your strong communication and interpersonal skills will enable you to deal courteously, tactfully and firmly with the public in a variety of situations. . . . In some cases, you will need to exercise discretion and tact in persuading people to comply with directions so that an arrest is not necessary. . . . At crime scenes, you'll pay close attention to detail and make observations on suspects and the crime scene itself. You will gather relevant physical evidence and ensure that its storage is safe and uncontaminated. . . . Given the physical demand of police work, you must recognize the importance of maintaining a high level of fitness. . . . In addition to knowing arrest and control tactics, you will be trained to handle and care for a variety of firearms and to operate police vehicles in emergency situations. . . . Although high-stress and risky situations are the exception rather than the rule, you will need to be prepared for the unexpected. Long periods of routine tasks can be suddenly interrupted by an urgent call requiring immediate intervention. . . . At times you will deal with people who are intoxicated, high on drugs or mentally unstable and, on occasion, people who are hostile will direct their hostility at you. (City of Vancouver Police Department, 2010)

As this excerpt clearly indicates, police work is a complex, demanding, stressful, and potentially dangerous occupation. It requires intelligent, creative, patient, ethical, caring, and hard-working individuals. The job may not be for everyone and, therefore, it is important for all those involved to ensure that the individuals who are accepted for the job have the highest potential for success. The purpose of police selection is to ensure this happens (Ash, Slora, & Britton, 1990; Sanders, 2008). This requires the use of valid **police selection procedures** that allow police agencies to effectively screen out applicants who possess undesirable characteristics or select applicants who possess desirable characteristics (Fabricatore, 1979; Sanders, 2008). These characteristics may relate to a variety of personal features, including (but not limited to) an applicant's physical fitness, cognitive abilities, personality, and performance on various job-related tasks.

**Police selection procedures:** A set of procedures used by the police to either screen out undesirable candidates or select in desirable candidates

## Using Social Media to Recruit Police Officers

In the near future, police agencies across Canada will likely experience a substantial shortage of police officers (Hay Group, 2007). To fill the gap, young people will need to apply for policing jobs more frequently than is currently the case (Police Sector Council, 2006). This shortage is problematic because recent research has indicated that young people are not particularly interested in pursuing a policing career (Police Sector Council, 2005).

In an attempt to address this issue, some Canadian police agencies are using innovative advertising strategies. Specifically, they are capitalizing on young peoples' use of electronic social media to provide them with information about opportunities in policing. Rather than waiting for young people to come to them, police forces are taking their message to the computer screens of Canada's young people.

Perhaps more than any other police agency in Canada, the Vancouver Police Department (VPD) is taking the lead on this new initiative. For example, the VPD now has an excellent Internet recruitment site that has attracted much attention. It has also launched a Facebook page, which now has over 2000 fans, and a YouTube Channel, which has over 200,000 video views to date. Finally, in December 2008, the VPD launched a blog called Behind the Blue Line.

This blog is maintained by Constable Sandra Glendinning, a member of the VPD since 1995. According to Constable Glendinning, the blog is designed to "share with others what it's like to be a police officer in Vancouver" (2010). However, given many of the postings on the site, it may do more than that. For example, the blog clearly provides invaluable information for potential applicants to the VPD.

In terms of its impact on police recruitment, the social media strategy of the VPD has not been formally evaluated, but people involved in recruitment for the VPD say that it has had an impact on the number of applications they have received. Other forces appear to be taking notice and are adopting their own social media strategies, which they hope will assist in dealing with the impending staffing crisis.

## A Brief History of Police Selection

The task of selecting appropriate police officers is not a new one for police agencies, nor is it a new phenomenon in the world of psychology. Indeed, psychologists have been involved in police selection since the early twentieth century. In what is considered one of the earliest examples, Lewis Terman, in 1917, used the Stanford-Binet Intelligence Test to assist with police selection in California (Terman, 1917). Terman tested the intelligence of 30 police and firefighter applicants, which led him to recommend a minimum IQ score of 80 for future applicants. Following this, attempts were made to use personality tests to predict police performance in the mid-twentieth century (e.g., Humm & Humm, 1950). By the mid-1950s, psychological and psychiatric screening procedures of police applicants became a standard part of the selection procedure in several major police forces (Reiser, 1982).

In the 1960s and 1970s, major changes to police selection procedures took place in the United States, primarily as a result of two major events. In 1967, the U.S. president's Commission on Law Enforcement and Administration of Justice recommended that police forces adopt a higher educational requirement for police officers, obviously implying that intelligence is a core characteristic of successful officers. In 1973, the National Advisory Commission on Criminal Justice Standards and Goals in the United States recommended that police agencies establish formal selection processes, which would include the use of tests to measure the cognitive abilities and personality features of applicants

(Ho, 1999). Since that time, police selection has indeed become more formalized, with police forces using a wide range of selection procedures, as indicated in Table 2.1 (Cochrane, Tett, & Vandecreek, 2003).

Although police selection research is not as common in Canada as it is in the United States, many of the same selection procedures are used in both countries. For example, all Canadian police agencies currently conduct background checks of their applicants and require medical exams (Forcese, 1999). In addition, most Canadian police agencies use a range of cognitive ability and personality tests in their selection process, such as the RCMP's Police Aptitude Test and the Six Factor Personality Questionnaire, which measures conscientiousness (RCMP, 2010a). In general, the same selection procedures are used by police agencies across Canada, although there are some slight differences across provincial and territorial boundaries. For example, while some police agencies, such as the Edmonton Police Service, use polygraph tests for selection purposes, other police forces (e.g., Hamilton Police Service) do not.

A police recruit undergoing physical training

## The Police Selection Process

Regardless of whether a police agency decides to adopt a screening-out approach or a selecting-in approach, the general stages a force must go through to develop a valid selection process are the same (Gowan & Gatewood, 1995). In general terms, there are two separate stages to this process. Stage one is referred to as the job analysis stage. Here, the agency must define the knowledge, skills, and abilities (KSAs) of a "good" police officer. Stage two is referred to as the construction and validation stage. In this stage, the agency

**Table 2.1** U.S. Police Agency Selection Procedures

| Selection Procedure | Percentage of Police Agencies* |
| --- | --- |
| Background checks | 99.4 |
| Medical exams | 98.7 |
| Selection interviews | 98.1 |
| Personality tests | 91.6 |
| Drug testing | 88.4 |
| Physical agility tests | 80.0 |
| Polygraph tests | 65.8 |
| Recommendation letters | 46.5 |
| Cognitive ability tests | 46.5 |

*These data represent responses from 155 U.S. police agencies that responded to a survey sent out by Cochrane et al., 2003.

Source: Adapted from Cochrane et al., 2003.

must develop an instrument for measuring the extent to which police applicants possess these KSAs. A crucial part of this stage also requires that the agency determine the instrument's validity, or the extent to which the scores on the instrument actually relate to measures of actual, on-the-job police performance.

**Conducting a Job Analysis** As indicated above, a **job analysis** involves a procedure to identify and define the KSAs that make a good police officer. An organizational psychologist, working in conjunction with a police agency, frequently conducts the job analysis. These psychologists can use a range of techniques for identifying relevant KSAs, including survey methods and observational techniques. At other times, a job analysis can be conducted more informally, simply by asking members of a police agency to list the range of qualities they feel is essential for their job. Each of these approaches has certain advantages and disadvantages. However, for the moment, we will focus on some common problems that emerge when conducting any sort of job analysis in the policing context.

One of the major problems that can be encountered is that the KSAs of a good police officer may not be stable over time, making it difficult to determine what the selection procedures should actually be testing for. For example, Pugh (1985a, 1985b) found that, at two years of service, police officers who were enthusiastic and fit in well were rated as the best officers, while at four years of service officers who were stable and responsible were given the highest performance ratings. A potential explanation for this problem, and a problem in its own right, is the fact that different types of police officers, or different policing jobs, will be characterized by different KSAs. For example, Ainsworth (1993) draws attention to the fact that the KSAs that describe the ideal police constable will not be the same KSAs that describe the ideal police manager. Thus, as police officers move up through the ranks into supervisory positions, it should not be surprising to see relevant KSAs changing along the way.

Another problem with conducting a job analysis is that individuals may disagree over which KSAs are important. For example, if you were to ask a group of police constables and a group of senior police managers to define the characteristics of a good police officer, the answers could be quite different (though some similarities might also be expected). To illustrate this point, consider a survey in which Ainsworth (1993) asked police constables to list the qualities they thought were essential for effective policing. Topping their list was a sense of humour. In contrast, this personal quality is rarely, if ever, found to be important when senior police managers are asked to list the essential qualities for effective policing. When this is done, the most important KSAs typically relate to cognitive skills (Sanders, 2003).

Despite these problems, there does appear to be some agreement, even across police officers of varying ranks, on what type of person is "right for the job" (Sanders, 2003). For example, regardless of how the job analysis is conducted, the following KSAs are typically viewed as essential: honesty, reliability, sensitivity to others, good communication skills, high motivation, problem-solving skills, and being a team player.

**Constructing and Validating Selection Instruments** Recall that the goals in stage two of the police selection process are (1) to develop a selection instrument for measuring the extent to which police applicants possess relevant KSAs (construction) and (2) to ensure that this instrument relates to measures of police performance (validation). The measure of validation that we are most interested in is referred to as predictive validity, which is our ability to use a selection instrument to predict how applicants will perform in the future. Box 2.1 presents a more thorough discussion of predictive validity.

Researchers have identified a number of major problems with validation research in the area of police selection. Arguably, the most serious problem relates to how we measure the performance of police officers (Hargrave & Hiatt, 1987). This issue is crucial, since it will have a direct impact on the validity of any selection instrument. Unfortunately, no answer currently exists (Sanders, 2008). This is not to say that a variety of performance measures do not exist. Indeed, researchers have used several measures

## Box 2.1

# Validation and Police Selection

There are many different types of validation measures, and each measure refers to something slightly different. The most common validation measure used in police selection focuses on predictive validity in which the goal is to determine if there is a relationship between scores obtained from a selection instrument and measures of actual job performance (Gowan & Gatewood, 1995). In the policing context, predictive validity involves collecting data from police applicants by using a selection instrument, such as scores on a test of decision making under stress. Then, the results on this test are compared with a measure of job performance, such as performance scores provided by supervisors. If the selection data accurately predict job performance, then the selection instrument is said to have predictive validity.

A selection instrument's predictive validity can be determined by calculating validity coefficients, which range from +1.00 to −1.00. These coefficients indicate the strength and direction of the relationship between the scores from a selection instrument and the ratings of job performance. If a selection instrument is shown to have a validity coefficient near +1.00, then a very strong positive relationship exists, indicating that, as performance on the selection instrument increases, ratings of job performance also increase (see Figure 2.1). Conversely, if a selection instrument is shown to have a validity coefficient near −1.00, a very strong negative relationship exists: As performance on the selection instrument increases, ratings of job performance decrease (see Figure 2.2). Any value between these two extreme values represents an intermediate level of predictive validity.

**Figure 2.1** A Positive Relationship between Scores on a Selection Instrument and Job Performance Ratings

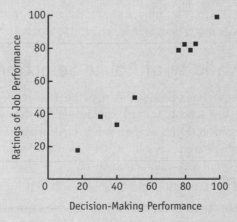

(continued)

(*continued*)

**Figure 2.2** A Negative Relationship between Scores on a Selection Instrument and Job Performance Ratings

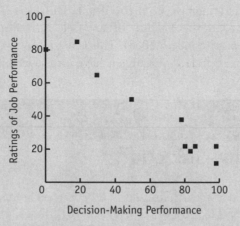

Note that validity coefficients of $+1.00$ and $-1.00$ both represent high levels of predictive validity, even if the values are not what we would expect. For example, it seems unlikely that a measure of decision-making performance under stress would relate negatively to the job performance of police officers, but if it did, we could still use those measures to predict job performance. We would simply predict that people who make poor decisions under stress make great police officers!

as indicators of job performance, including the number of times an officer is tardy, the number of complaints against an officer, the number of commendations received by an officer, graduation from training academy, academy exam scores, performance ratings by supervisors, performance ratings by peers, and so forth. The problem is that there is no evidence to suggest that one of these measures is any better than another, and even police agencies do not agree on how to define good performance (Falkenberg, Gaines, & Cordner, 1991). Furthermore, research suggests that a different picture of performance can emerge depending on what measure is used. For example, measures of performance during training often do not generalize to on-the-job performance (Kleinman & Gordon, 1986) and ratings by different individuals (e.g., peers versus supervisors) are often contradictory (Gardner, Scogin, Vipperman, & Varela, 1998).

## The Validity of Police Selection Instruments

Now that we have discussed some of the problems with constructing and validating police selection instruments, we will describe some of the instruments that are currently in use and present some research on their validity. Although some of these instruments might be new to you, there are many others, such as the selection interview, that you will be familiar with. We will focus our attention on three specific selection instruments; the selection interview, psychological tests, and the assessment centre.

**Selection interview:** In recruiting police officers, an interview used by the police to determine the extent to which an applicant possesses the knowledge, skills, and abilities deemed important for the job

**The Selection Interview** The **selection interview** is one of the most common selection instruments used by the police. Typically, selection interviews take the form of a semi-structured interview. In a semi-structured interview, the interviewer has a preset list of questions that are asked of each applicant, thus ensuring a more objective basis for comparing applicants (Gowan & Gatewood, 1995). One of the main goals of the selection interview is to determine the extent to which the applicant possesses the KSAs that have been deemed important in a job analysis. These qualities may differ from agency to agency and, as indicated above, they may depend on the job being applied for. As an example of the sort of criteria that may be considered, the criteria evaluated by the Hamilton Police Service's Essential Competency Interview include analytical thinking, self-confidence, communication, flexibility, self-control, relationship building, achievement orientation, physical skills/abilities, and dealing with diversity (Hamilton Police Service, 2010).

Surprisingly, given its frequent use as a selection instrument, there is relatively little research examining the predictive validity of the selection interview in the policing context (Aamodt, 2004). Based on the research that does exist, the results are somewhat mixed—that is, some research indicates that selection interviews can be used in a relatively accurate fashion to predict job performance (e.g., Hargrave & Hiatt, 1987), whereas other research suggests that basing police selection decisions on interviews can be potentially problematic (e.g., Doerner, 1997). These findings accord well with the general research literature from the field of organizational psychology, where mixed results regarding the predictive validity of the selection interview are also reported (McDaniel, Whetzel, Schmidt, & Maurer, 1994).

Despite the fact that some research suggests that interviews might provide information that is predictive of job performance, many police researchers remain cautious about their use. To understand why, consider Doerner's (1997) study, where he examined the degree to which different interviewers agree on their ratings of various attributes when interviewing the same applicant (where agreement could vary from +1.00, indicating total agreement between interviewers, to −1.00, indicating total disagreement). As illustrated in Table 2.2, Doerner found that the majority of inter-rater reliability measures were relatively low. This result was the case across a number of different interviewer pairs,

**Table 2.2** Measures of Inter-rater Reliability

| Attribute of Interviewee | Interviewers | | | | | |
|---|---|---|---|---|---|---|
| | 1 and 2 | 1 and 3 | 1 and 4 | 1 and 5 | 1 and 6 | 1 and 7 |
| Appearance | 0.55* | 0.14 | 0.58* | −0.25 | 0.50* | 0.18 |
| Self-confidence | 0.06 | 0.30 | 0.43* | 0.55 | 0.45* | 0.63 |
| Self-expression | 0.27 | 0.42 | 0.27 | 0.26 | 0.15 | 0.69* |
| Understanding | 0.85* | 0.03 | 0.67* | 0.46 | 0.35* | 0.47 |
| Comprehension | 0.47 | 0.56 | 0.24 | 0.14 | 0.42* | 0.59 |
| Background | 0.38 | 0.72* | 0.38* | −0.28 | 0.26 | 0.70* |
| Overall impression | 0.45 | 0.38 | 0.37* | 0.00 | 0.30 | 0.52 |
| N (number of interviews) | 15 | 10 | 22 | 10 | 28 | 10 |

*Denotes a significant finding.

Source: Adapted from Doerner, 1997.

who were assessing a range of personal attributes. Indeed, of the 42 comparisons Doerner made, only 14 were found to be statistically significant, and most of these came from only one pair of interviewers.

Given such findings, the validity of the interview technique as a method for selecting police officers must be considered, and interviewing should continue to be used with caution. It must also be remembered, however, that changing the way in which an interview is constructed and conducted can have a big impact on its validity (e.g., Campion, Palmer, & Campion, 1997). For example, the more structured an interview is, the more likely that it will predict future job performance with some degree of success (Cortina, Goldstein, Payne, Davison, & Gilliland, 2000). Therefore, police psychologists should continue to examine how selection interviews in the policing context can be improved and the predictive accuracy of new interview procedures should be established.

**Psychological Tests** In addition to the selection interview, psychological tests are also commonly used by police agencies to select suitable officers (Cochrane et al., 2003). Some of these tests have been developed to measure cognitive abilities, whereas others have been designed to assess an applicant's personality. In addition, some of these tests have been developed with police selection in mind, whereas others have been developed in other contexts, such as the mental health field. As with other selection instruments, there are still many unanswered questions when it comes to the use of psychological tests. However, there seems to be general agreement among police researchers that psychological tests are useful in deciding whether a person possesses certain attributes, and it is believed that this knowledge can be helpful, to some extent at least, in selecting applicants to become police officers.

**Cognitive ability tests:**
Procedure for measuring verbal, mathematical, memory, and reasoning abilities

**Cognitive Ability Tests** A wide variety of **cognitive ability tests** are available for police use. Although each test may emphasize something slightly different, they are typically used to measure verbal, mathematical, memory, and reasoning abilities. Such tests are used regularly when selecting police officers in Canada. Indeed, if you were to apply to the RCMP today, part of the selection procedure would require you to take the RCMP Police Aptitude Test (RPAT). The RPAT consists of 114 multiple-choice questions designed to evaluate an applicant's potential aptitude for police work. More specifically, the test measures seven core skills that are considered essential in performing the duties of a police officer: written composition, comprehension, memory, judgment, observation, logic, and computation (RCMP, 2010b).

In general, the reliance on cognitive ability tests for police selection purposes is supported by empirical research. However, these tests tend to be better at predicting performance during police academy training compared with future on-the-job performance (Gowan & Gatewood, 1995). For example, Hirsh, Northrop, and Schmidt (1986) conducted a meta-analysis of 40 validation studies involving cognitive ability tests. They found average validity coefficients of 0.36 and 0.13 for predicting training success and on-the-job performance, respectively. A more recent meta-analytic study reports similar results. Aamodt (2004) found validity coefficients of 0.41 and 0.16 when examining the use of cognitive ability tests for predicting academy performance and on-the-job performance, respectively, where on-the-job performance was assessed via supervisor ratings.

There are a variety of potential explanations for why higher scores are found when cognitive ability tests are used to predict academy performance versus on-the-job performance, but one interesting possibility is that personality variables play a role in determining job success, above and beyond one's cognitive abilities (e.g., Forero, Gallardo-Pujol, Maydeu-Olivares, Andres-Pueyo, 2009). Thus, it is worthwhile describing some of the personality tests used for police selection and the degree of validity associated with each.

**Personality Tests** A number of different personality tests are used for police selection, but only two of the most commonly used tests will be discussed here. Perhaps the most common test is an assessment instrument known as the **Minnesota Multiphasic Personality Inventory** (MMPI), now in its second version. According to Cochrane et al. (2003), of the 155 U.S. police agencies that responded to their survey, 71.9% of the agencies indicated that the MMPI-2 was the personality test they used most often for selection purposes. Interestingly, the MMPI, originally designed in the 1940s, was not developed for selecting police officers. Neither was the MMPI-2. Rather, this assessment instrument was developed as a general inventory for identifying people with psychopathological problems. Currently, the MMPI-2 consists of 567 true-false questions that attempt to identify psychopathological problems, including depression, paranoia, and schizophrenia.

**Minnesota Multiphasic Personality Inventory:** An assessment instrument for identifying people with psychopathological problems

Although Aamodt's (2004) meta-analysis of the MMPI revealed that it possesses little power in predicting academy performance or on-the-job behaviour, some research does suggest that the MMPI and the MMPI-2 can be associated with significant but relatively low validity coefficients. This may be especially true when the tests are used to predict problematic police behaviours (e.g., disciplinary suspensions; Chibnall & Detrick, 2003; Sanders, 2003). In part, the relatively low levels of predictive validity associated with the MMPI tests may be due to the fact that they were never developed as selection instruments. If this is true, then it may be that personality tests developed for police selection purposes will be associated with higher levels of predictive validity. In fact, this does appear to be the case, as indicated by studies examining the **Inwald Personality Inventory** (IPI).

**Inwald Personality Inventory:** An assessment instrument used to identify police applicants who are suitable for police work by measuring their personality attributes and behaviour patterns

Unlike the MMPI tests, the IPI was developed specifically for the law enforcement community. According to Inwald (1992), the creator of the IPI, the purpose of this selection instrument is to identify police applicants who are most suitable for police work by measuring their personality attributes and behaviour patterns. The instrument consists of 310 true-false questions that measure factors such as stress reactions, interpersonal difficulties, and alcohol and other drug use.

According to several researchers, the IPI appears to be more predictive of police officer performance than the MMPI (e.g., Inwald & Shusman, 1984; Scogin, Schumacher, Gardner, & Chaplin, 1995). For example, in one study, Scogin et al. (1995) compared the MMPI, the IPI, and the Shipley Institute of Living Scale (SILS), a brief intellectual screening device, on their ability to predict seven different job performance indicators: supervisor ratings, verbal reprimands, written reprimands, vehicular reprimands, citizen complaints, an overall composite of negative indicators, and an overall composite of positive recognitions.

The participants in the study were 82 trainees at the University of Alabama Law Enforcement Academy. Each participant completed the three selection instruments during the first week of academy training. One year following their graduation from the academy, each participant's police agency was contacted to obtain job performance indicators. The results found that the IPI was a slightly better predictor of on-the-job performance in the one-year follow-up period than both the MMPI and SILS. More specifically, the MMPI and the SILS could accurately predict only one of the seven performance indicators (supervisor ratings). The IPI, on the other hand, was able to predict three of the seven indicators (supervisor ratings, citizen complaints, and the overall composite of negative indicators). In addition, combining the MMPI and IPI scores did not appreciably improve predictive power over that observed with the IPI alone. As the authors of this study indicate, the one-year follow-up used in this study might not have been long enough for sufficient positive and negative on-the-job behaviour to occur. However, the results of this study do provide some preliminary evidence that the IPI performs slightly better than the MMPI under certain conditions, something that is confirmed in more recent meta-analytic studies (e.g., Aamodt, 2004).

**Assessment Centres** The last selection procedure we will discuss is the **assessment centre**, a procedure that is growing in popularity in Europe and North America (Lowry, 1996). An assessment centre is a facility at which the behaviour of police applicants can be observed in a number of different ways by multiple observers (Pynes & Bernardin, 1992). The primary selection instrument used within an assessment centre is the **situational test**, which involves simulations of real-world policing tasks. Trained observers evaluate how applicants perform during these tasks, and the performance appraisals are used for the purpose of selection.

The situational tests used in assessment centres attempt to tap into the KSAs identified as part of a job analysis. For example, the assessment centre evaluated by Pynes and Bernardin (1992) was based on a job analysis that identified eight core skill sets deemed crucial for effective policing: directing others, interpersonal skills, perception, decision making, decisiveness, adaptability, oral communication, and written communication. Based on these skill sets, four assessment exercises were developed, which allowed the applicants to be evaluated across the range of relevant KSAs. For example, one of the scenarios was a simulated domestic disturbance. Each applicant was given 15 minutes of the 35-minute exercise to meet with two people involved in a dispute. The applicant was expected to intervene in the dispute as a police officer and resolve it. At the end of the 15 minutes, the applicant is given 20 minutes to complete an incident report. This exercise requires excellent interpersonal skills in order to excel, in addition to good decision-making skills and written communication skills.

Although there is not a great deal of research examining the validity of assessment centres for police selection, some research does suggest that situational tests have moderate levels of predictive validity. For example, Pynes and Bernardin (1992) examined the scores given to each applicant across the four simulation exercises. These scores were then compared with training academy performance and future on-the-job performance. Overall assessment centre performance correlation coefficients were 0.14 and 0.20 for training academy performance and future on-the-job performance, respectively. Each of these validity coefficients was statistically significant. Similar results were presented by Aamodt (2004) in his meta-analysis of six studies where the predictive validity of assessment centres was examined.

## POLICE DISCRETION

As indicated by job analyses, many of the qualities deemed necessary for success as a police officer have to do with the applicant being adaptable, having common sense, possessing effective decision-making skills, and being a good problem solver (Sanders, 2003). In large part, these qualities are necessary because police officers are required to use discretion in

**Assessment centre:** A facility in which the behaviour of police applicants can be observed in a number of situations by multiple observers

**Situational test:** A simulation of a real-world policing task

much of their daily work (Walma & West, 2002). **Police discretion** can be defined in numerous ways, but McKenna (2002) has perhaps stated it best:

> Police discretion is the term that represents the critical faculty that individual officers must possess that will allow them to differentiate and discriminate between those circumstances that require absolute adherence to the letter of the law and those occasions when a degree of latitude is justified, based on the officer's knowledge, experience, or instinct. (p. 118)

To appreciate the extent to which the police use discretion, consider the following decisions that need to be made routinely by police officers:

- What street should I patrol tonight?
- Should I stop that vehicle for a traffic violation?
- What level of force is required to achieve my objective?
- Should I run after that suspect or wait for backup?
- Should I call an end to this investigation?
- Should I take this person to a psychiatric hospital or the police station?

The list of scenarios requiring some degree of police discretion is endless and, therefore, police discretion is a topic of major concern to researchers. More specifically, researchers are interested in whether police discretion is really necessary, the sorts of situations in which discretion is used, the factors that influence police decision making in these situations, and ways of controlling the inappropriate use of police discretion. Each of these issues will be examined in this section.

## Why Is Police Discretion Necessary?

Although some individuals and interest groups believe that police officers should always enforce the law, police officers clearly do not (and perhaps cannot) do this all the time. Indeed, police officers have great latitude in how they apply the law (McKenna, 2002). But is this discretion necessary? What good are laws if they are applied only under certain conditions? The typical answers that researchers offer for such questions are based on the fact that it is impossible to establish laws that adequately encompass all the possible situations an officer can encounter and, therefore, a degree of discretion is inevitable. For example, Walma and West (2002) argue the following:

> No manual or rule book can take into consideration every possible situation a police officer may face in doing his or her daily duties. No supervisor can follow a police officer around to monitor every decision he or she makes. As a result, police officers are entrusted with the discretion to apply their training and fulfill their duties in the manner they think is best. (p. 165)

In addition to this explanation, there are many other arguments for why police discretion is a necessary part of modern-day policing. For example, Sheehan and Cordner (1989) have provided the following important reasons for police discretion:

- A police officer who attempts to enforce all the laws all the time would be in the police station and in court all the time and, thus, of little use when serious problems arise in the community.

**Police discretion:** A policing task that involves discriminating between circumstances that require absolute adherence to the law and circumstances where a degree of latitude is justified

- Legislatures pass some laws that they clearly do not intend to have strictly enforced all the time.

- Legislatures pass some laws that are vague, making it necessary for the police to interpret them and decide when to apply them.

- Most law violations are minor in nature, such as driving slightly over the posted speed limit, and do not require full enforcement of the law.

- Full enforcement of all the laws all the time would alienate the public and undermine support for the police.

- Full enforcement of all the laws all the time would overwhelm the criminal justice system, including the prisons.

- The police have many duties to perform with limited resources. Good judgment must, therefore, be used in establishing enforcement priorities.

It should be stressed that by accepting police discretion as an inevitable part of policing, we as a society must be prepared to deal with the consequences. Although the arguments put forward by researchers such as Sheehan and Cordner (1989) highlight some obvious advantages of police discretion, there are also potential disadvantages. For police discretion to be advantageous, officers must exercise discretion in a nondiscriminatory manner (Walma & West, 2002), and unfortunately this does not always happen. Despite the fact that all members of Canadian society have their rights protected under the Charter of Rights and Freedoms, the police do, on occasion, use their discretion inappropriately.

## Areas Where Police Discretion Is Used

Having now established that there are a variety of rationales for police discretion, it is important that we consider some of the situations in which it is used. As indicated above, there are relatively few decisions that a police officer has to make that do not require at least some degree of discretion. However, several domains are worthy of a more in-depth discussion, including encounters with youths, offenders with mental illnesses, domestic violence, and use-of-force situations.

**Youth Crime** According to Siegal and Senna (1994), as the "initial gatekeepers" to the juvenile justice system, police officers have a great deal of discretion when dealing with young offenders. Common police responses to youth crime include formal arrests, police cautions, community referrals, and family conferences. Indeed, one study in the United States suggests that approximately 30% to 40% of youth crime is handled informally by police officers or through referrals to community services (Office of Juvenile Studies and Delinquency Prevention, 1992).

In Canada, police officers are actively encouraged to use discretion when dealing with youth crime (Department of Justice Canada, 2010a) and recent research suggests that most police services do consider informal action when interacting with young offenders (e.g., the use of informal or formal warnings, involving parents and/or social workers, arresting but releasing the young person, referring youths to community-based intervention programs; Carrington & Schulenberg, 2003). For example, in a recently interviewed sample of 200 police officers from across Canada, over 78% of the officers indicated that their police service would usually or always consider the use of informal action with young offenders. Only

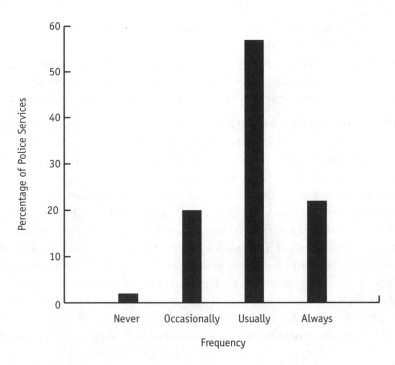

**Figure 2.3** Percentage of Police Services that Consider Using Informal Action with Young People

Source: Carrington and Schulenberg, 2003, Figure II.8 (p. 30).

22% of the officers indicated that their police services would never, or only occasionally, consider the use of informal action (see Figure 2.3; Carrington & Schulenberg, 2003).

The encouragement and use of informal action on the part of the police appears to be the result of a growing belief that formal criminal justice processing (e.g., sentences) is probably not the most effective response for dealing with many young offenders. Indeed, one common view is that custodial sentences make matters worse by putting young offenders into a situation in which they are forced to interact and associate with other, often more serious, offenders. Instead, community-based intervention strategies that involve family members, teachers, social workers, and the police are thought to be more useful (Department of Justice Canada, 2010a). In addition, to instil values of responsibility and accountability in young offenders, greater attention is now being paid to restorative justice options in which the youth is made to repay the victim.

A movement toward informal processing of youths is evident in some recent programs established in Canada. For example, the Sparwood Youth Assistance Program (SYAP), which began in 1995, provides young offenders in Sparwood, B.C., with an opportunity to be dealt with outside the formal court system. This intervention program is based in the community and involves the young person's family and the community as a whole. An integral part of the program is the **resolution conference**, in which the offender and his or her family are brought together with the victim and the police in an attempt to come up with a plan to (1) compensate the victim, (2) penalize the youth, (3) provide support to the youth's family, and (4) establish a monitoring scheme to ensure the youth complies with the program (SYAP, 2007).

**Resolution conference:** Involves an offender and his or her family coming together with the victim and the police in an attempt to solve a problem

For our purposes here, one of the most important aspects of the program is that it relies almost entirely on the discretion of the police. Not only is it up to the police to decide whether the program is suitable for the offender, it is also up to them to determine whether the program is working. If, in their view, the program is not having the intended effect, they can use their discretion to pursue a more serious course of action.

**Offenders with Mental Illnesses** As is the case with young offenders, police officers in Canada frequently come into contact with offenders with mental illnesses. According to Cotton and Coleman (2008), several factors have increased the likelihood of these encounters, but primary among these is the recent movement toward de-institutionalizing individuals who have mental illnesses. In an attempt to ensure these encounters are dealt with effectively, formal policies are often put in place that specify how police officers should deal with offenders who have mental illnesses. These policies typically instruct police officers to apprehend the individual whenever he or she poses a danger to self or others or is causing some other kind of serious disturbance (Teplin, 2000). However, although these policies provide the police with the legal power to intervene, police officers must still rely on their discretion to choose the most appropriate action.

When police officers encounter an individual with a mental illness who is creating a disturbance, there are generally three options available to them: (1) they can transport that person to a psychiatric institution of some kind, (2) they can arrest the person and take him or her to jail, or (3) they can resolve the matter informally (Teplin, 2000). Although this decision may not seem difficult, in practice it is. For example, as Teplin (2000, p. 9) states, "emergency hospitalization often is fraught with bureaucratic obstacles and the legal difficulties of obtaining commitment for treatment . . . many psychiatric programs will not accept everyone, particularly those considered dangerous, those who also have substance abuse disorders, or those with numerous previous hospitalizations." As a result, police officers may be forced to take actions that are not in the best interest of the offender, such as taking the individual to jail. Unfortunately, research indicates that this is often what happens (e.g., Bittner, 1967; Teplin, 1986).

The limited options that are often available to the police when they are dealing with mentally ill offenders can mean that these offenders become criminalized (e.g., Crocker, Hartford, & Heslop, 2009; Teplin, 1984, 2000). In other words, individuals who would have typically been treated within the mental health system are now dealt with by the criminal justice system. This criminalization process appears to be at work in the study conducted by Hoch, Hartford, Heslop, and Stitt (2009).

The aim of Hoch et al.'s (2009) study was to determine the rate at which individuals who suffered from a mental illness in the city of London, Ontario, came into contact with the police (and were charged and arrested) compared with individuals not identified as mentally ill. The data were restricted to a single year (January to December, 2001). In total, 817 people with a mental illness were identified from the London Police Service database who had at least one interaction with the police, and 111 095 people were identified who did not have a mental illness. As you can see in Figure 2.4, the results from this study indicate that people who definitely had a mental illness (PMI-Definite) had significantly more interactions with the police than people with no mental illness (NPMI). Similarly, people with a mental illness were more frequently charged and arrested compared with people without a mental illness. Specifically, Hoch et al. (2009) found that "people with mental illness were arrested, charged, or both 10% more often than those without mental illness" (p. 55).

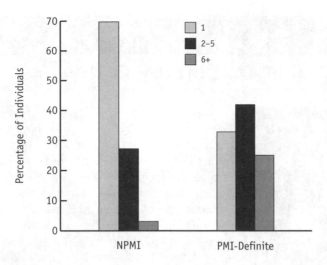

**Figure 2.4** Percentage of Police Interactions in 2001 by Mental Illness Group

Source: Hoch et al., 2009, Figure 1B (p. 54).

These figures raise many difficult questions. For example, does the charged and arrested figure mentioned in the previous paragraph reflect the discriminatory use of discretion on the part of the police or does it reflect the fact that mentally ill offenders commit more serious crimes? Alternatively, could it be that this figure simply reflects the fact that the hands of the police are often tied, with arrests being one of the few options available to ensure that individuals with mental illnesses remain free from harm? To know what these figures actually mean, more systematic research clearly needs to be conducted. We are thankful that Canadian researchers are beginning to conduct such research. One of these researchers is Dr. Dorothy Cotton, who is profiled in Box 2.2.

**Domestic Violence** Another area in which police officers have a great deal of discretion is in their response to domestic disputes. Historically, domestic violence by a husband against his wife was often ignored by the police. However, in the 1960s and 1970s, people became more aware of victim needs in domestic violence situations, and numerous individuals and interest groups began pushing for a more aggressive policy of arrest (Melton, 1999).

According to Melton (1999), a number of factors helped this push along. First, several lawsuits were successfully brought against U.S. police departments that had failed to arrest offenders of domestic violence. Second, domestic violence research began being conducted, with some of this research suggesting that arrests had a deterrent effect on offenders of domestic violence. Eventually, pro-arrest policies were put in place in many police agencies, in both Canada and the United States, and new government legislation was enacted. An example of such legislation in Canada is B.C.'s Violence Against Women in Relationships Policy (British Columbia Ministry of Attorney General, 2004), which attempts to ensure a strong criminal justice response to domestic violence.

Even with new policies and legislation in place, police officers still have a range of responses available to them when faced with domestic disputes. As a result, the police must still use their discretion to decide on the best course of action. For example, Melton

Box 2.2

# Canadian Researcher Profile: Dr. Dorothy Cotton

Dorothy Cotton came to Canada from Boston to study medicine at McGill University. She had no intention of studying psychology and certainly no intention of staying in Canada, but a second-year course in abnormal psychology piqued her interest and 30-something years after her arrival, she is still in Canada, having obtained her Ph.D. in social psychology from Queen's University.

In the early days of her career, Dr. Cotton worked in a frontline psychology position at a provincial psychiatric hospital, going on to become chief psychologist there as well as director of forensic services. While she has done a variety of work in clinical and forensic psychology, her work with police services has been her professional passion. Dr. Cotton says her interest in policing issues happened quite by accident. As psychiatric services downsized over the years, she discovered that the police were spending more time with her patients than she was. Curious as to why, she set out to explore.

As an associate member of the Canadian Association of Chiefs of Police (CACP), Dr. Cotton has been integral to the development of programs linking police services and mental health services, in the interest of meeting the needs of people with mental illnesses. Her research and publications in this area have examined the attitudes and knowledge of police in regard to mental illness, the nature and extent of police training and education about mental illness, as well as best practices for police services in dealing with mentally ill offenders. She is co-author of the CACP's *Contemporary Policing Guidelines for Working with the Mental Health System.*

Currently, Dr. Cotton is a clinical neuropsychologist with the Correctional Service of Canada, where she works with offenders with a variety of cognitive and neuropsychological problems. She appears to have an affinity for unique and underserviced areas of psychology, as she is one of only a handful of clinical correctional neuropsychologists in Canada. She is also the first—and only—person in Canada to hold diplomate status in police psychology (the highest recognition that is currently available in this field).

Dr. Cotton is a past president of the College of Psychologists of Ontario, and is a fellow of the Canadian Psychological Association. She is currently a member of the Mental Health and the Law Advisory Committee of the Mental Health Commission of Canada, which represents Canada's most significant attempt to address issues related to mental health and mental illness in Canada by developing a national mental health strategy—which will include issues related to the interface between people with mental illnesses and the criminal justice system, including the police.

Known to cops across the country as the author of a "psychology for cops" column that appears in the national police magazine, *Blueline*, Dr. Cotton is one of a very rare species of people in the world who are bassoon-playing psychologists. In fact, she has been known to suggest that she practices psychology only to support her bassoon-playing habit.

You are a police officer who has just received a call over your radio about a domestic disturbance. You arrive at the scene to find a woman and a man arguing. The woman has a bloody nose and a black eye, and it is clear that the man is the person who hit her. The woman pleads with you not to arrest the man. She states that she has a serious drinking problem, that she started the argument with her husband, and that it was totally her fault that she ended up getting hit. While crying, she also says that she can't take care of her fours kids by herself because she doesn't work and depends on the husband to take care of the house and pay the bills.

### Your Turn . . .

If you arrest the husband, then he may go to prison. What would you do and why?

(1999) indicates that arrest rates range from 12% to 40% of all cases of domestic violence seen by the police, with other responses being used in the remainder of cases. These other options regularly include mediation (e.g., talking to the victim), community referrals (e.g., recommending the couple seek professional help), and separation (e.g., asking one of the participants to leave). Indeed, some studies indicate that separation is used as an intervention strategy as often as arrests are used, if not more often. In addition, Melton (1999) argues that, in many domestic violence cases, the police still decide to do nothing at all.

If you were a police officer, how would you make decisions in cases of domestic disputes? To experience some of the challenges you might face when making an arrest decision, see the Case Study box.

**Use-of-Force Situations** Police officers are granted the right to use force—in fact, they are required to use force—to protect the general public and themselves (Walma & West, 2002). However, police officers have a great deal of discretion when deciding when (and how) to use force. They can use force when it is necessary to suppress a situation, but only to the extent that is necessary to accomplish this goal. When a police officer uses force for any other purpose, or in excess of what is needed, that officer has made inappropriate use of his or her discretionary power. When this happens, the result can be deadly. It can also be very costly for the police, who may have to deal with potential lawsuits.

In Canada, the authority to use force is laid out in our Criminal Code (Walma & West, 2002). For example, Section 25 of the Criminal Code states that "Everyone who is required by law to do anything in the administration of enforcement of the law . . . is, if he acts on reasonable grounds, justified in doing what he is required or authorized to do and in using as much force as is necessary for that purpose." However, problems arise in use-of-force situations because of the ambiguity of terms such as *reasonable grounds* and *as is necessary*. Indeed, there are many examples in which people disagree on these terms. When this happens, we must turn to our judicial system to resolve the problem. In some cases, the court will decide that the force used by the police was inappropriate (as in the

Box 2.3

# The Case of *Ernst v. Quinonez et al.* (2003)

In *Ernst v. Quinonez et al.* (2003), the court examined the methods used by the defendants to arrest the plaintiff, Edward Ernst. The plaintiff and his friend, Jason Steves, drove up to Niagara Falls, Ontario, from their home in Buffalo, New York. After leaving a nightclub, the pair decided to drive Steves' vehicle up and down a street that was known to be a popular tourist area. While stopped at a red light, Steves proceeded to squeal his tires. A nearby police officer observed the incident, approached the vehicle, and asked Steves for his licence and his registration. Steves retrieved some papers from his vehicle but could not locate the requested documentation. Noticing that the appropriate documentation was in Steves's hand, the police officer reached into the vehicle to take it. At this time, Steves put his car into gear and began to drive away with the police officer still halfway in his car. The officer yelled for Steves to stop the vehicle, as did the plaintiff. The plaintiff also attempted to reach the brake pedal of the car but was unable to do so. Eventually, the vehicle stopped and the police officer pulled Steves out of his car.

At this time, an unidentified uniformed officer approached the plaintiff, ordered him out of the vehicle, handcuffed him, and informed him he was under arrest. While the plaintiff was handcuffed, the unidentified officer knelt on the plaintiff's shoulder and neck to prevent him from moving. At this time, several other officers arrived at the scene. One of these officers pulled the plaintiff from the ground and wrapped his arm around the plaintiff's neck to drag him to the hood of the vehicle. While the plaintiff was being dragged, another of the defendants punched him in the stomach numerous times. According to videotape of the incident captured by an onlooker, the plaintiff did not show any sign of resisting the police officers.

Among the plaintiff's allegations was that the defendants assaulted him. All the defendants were required to describe and justify the actions they took in dealing with the situation. Throughout the hearing, the defendants explained it was their belief they acted reasonably in response to the situation. For example, in responding to why he put his arm around the plaintiff's neck, the defendant who was responsible claimed that, when he lifted the plaintiff off the ground, the plaintiff stiffened his back and was thus being uncooperative. In order to get control of Ernst, the defendant testified that he "grabbed Ernst by the front of the shirt . . . he had to reach over Ernst's shoulder in order to do this as [he] was standing slightly behind Ernst" (*Ernst v. Quinonez et al.*, 2003, para. 26). Likewise, another defendant claimed the plaintiff attempted to kick and spit at him and, as a result, he "punched Ernst with a closed fist in the upper chest area once" (para. 31).

Largely by analyzing the videotape of the incident, the judge found that the amount of force used by the defendants on the plaintiff was far more than was necessary. The defendants were convicted for assault and false arrest and imprisonment. The plaintiff was awarded a total of $38 300 in damages.

case described in Box 2.3). This ruling could occur because the use of force was viewed as unnecessary, was in excess of what was needed, or was based on factors that should not have been taken into account, such as the race of the suspect. In other cases, the courts find police use of force appropriate and justifiable.

Fortunately, police use of force is a relatively rare phenomenon. As MacDonald, Manz, Alpert, and Dunham (2003) state, "Whether measured by use-of-force reports, citizen complaints, victim surveys, or observational methods, the data consistently indicate that only a small percentage of police–public interactions involve use of force" (p. 120). Recently, for example, the Police Public Contact Survey developed by the U.S. Bureau of Justice Statistics found that only 1.5% of people who come into contact with police in the United States either experience force first-hand or are threatened by the use of force (U.S. Bureau of Justice Statistics, 2005). Furthermore, when police in the United States do decide to use force, it is often the minimal amount of force necessary (Adams, 1999), and it is typically in response to a resistant suspect (Alpert & Dunham, 1999).

Similar findings have recently emerged from a study in Canada where Butler and Hall (2008) examined data from the Calgary Police Service over a two-year period (January 1, 2006 to December 31, 2007). In line with studies conducted in the United States, Butler and Hall reporting the following:

- Use of force by the police was very rare, accounting for 0.07% of police–public encounters.

- Male subjects accounted for the vast majority (93.6%) of individuals where force was used.

- Approximately 88% of subjects requiring force were under the influence of drugs and/ or alcohol at the time or experiencing some degree of emotional distress.

- The use of neck restraints, tasers, and batons on subjects rarely resulted in the need for medical attention, although batons were the most injurious force intervention technique examined in the study (29% of subjects where a baton was used required medical treatment).

## Controlling Police Discretion

In an attempt to ensure that police officers exercise their discretion appropriately, a number of organizations have established guidelines that allow police discretion to be controlled. As indicated by Walma and West (2002), the Charter of Rights and Freedoms can, in a sense, be seen as a guideline to control police discretion because it makes clear that all people should be treated fairly and equally. In addition, specific codes of conduct for police officers have been developed that also help to control the use of discretion (Walma & West, 2002). For example, in Canada, one section of the Police Services Act states that police officers commit misconduct if they fail to treat or protect a person without discrimination. Another method for controlling police discretion is the enactment of government legislation to deal with a particular problem. As indicated previously, B.C.'s Violence Against Women in Relationships Policy is an example of such legislation.

In this section, we will deal specifically with methods for controlling inappropriate police discretion in use-of-force situations. One reason for focusing on such situations is the public's widespread interest in this area. The other reason is that numerous attempts have been made, in Canada particularly, to develop innovative approaches for controlling the abuse of force by the police. One approach is the development of administrative policies within police agencies, which are specifically meant to control the use of force by police officers. A related approach is the development of models (the most common being the **use-of-force continuum**) that help to guide a police officer's decision-making process in use-of-force situations.

**Use-of-force continuum:** A model that is supposed to guide police officer decision making in use-of-force situations by indicating what level of force is appropriate given the suspect's behaviour and other environmental conditions

**Departmental Policies** Departmental policies for restricting use of force by police officers are not new. Research on the effectiveness of these policies is also not new. For example, Fyfe (1979) examined the impact of use-of-force policies put in place by the New York Police Department (NYPD) in 1972. These policies were meant to decrease the use of lethal force by NYPD officers and Fyfe's study indicated just that. Not only did the frequency of police shooting decrease in New York from 1971 to 1975, but the numbers of officers injured and killed during the same period also decreased. Similar findings have been reported in several other U.S. cities, indicating that departmental policies can effectively restrict the use of inappropriate force (e.g., Geller & Scott, 1992). However, White (2001) draws attention to the fact that restrictive use-of-force policies do not always have the desired impact, and that other factors can minimize their effect. For instance, he has argued that the philosophies of senior police officers can often outweigh departmental polices. As White put it, if the police leadership has a "bust their heads" philosophy, departmental policies will likely not have their intended effect (p. 135).

In Canada, similar policies to those discussed above are sometimes put in place for the purpose of restricting various use-of-force options available to the police. For example, following the case of Robert Dziekanski in 2007, who died shortly after he was tasered by RCMP officers in the Vancouver International Airport, the RCMP introduced a new policy for taser use, which is intended to restrict when officers can use the weapon (in addition to providing new requirements for training on the taser). Following recommendations from the Braidwood Inquiry, which looked into the circumstances surrounding Dziekanski's death, the RCMP now plans to restrict the use of tasers to situations where individuals exhibit "active resistance"—that is, "situations where a subject is causing bodily harm or the [police officer] believes on reasonable grounds that the subject will imminently cause bodily harm" (Commission for Public Complaints Against the RCMP, 2010). This policy is quite different from the one that was in place at the time of Dziekanski's death, which essentially allowed the weapon to be used when people were simply not cooperating with police officers.

**The Use-of-Force Continuum** Although use-of-force continuums may not directly restrict the use of force by police officers in the same way that departmental policies do, they may indirectly control force by ensuring that officers carefully assess and evaluate

A photo of Robert Dziekanski moments before he was tasered by RCMP officers in the Vancouver International Airport (left) and just after he was restrained (right).

potential use-of-force situations when deciding what course of action to take. In the words of Walma and West (2002, p. 67),

> The theory behind the continuum is that, in order to subdue a suspect, the officer must be prepared to use a level of force that is one step higher than that used by the suspect in resisting the officer. There is no need for the officer to move up the continuum of force step by step since it is certainly unlikely that the suspect will do so. Once the suspect displays his or her level of resistance, the officer must react with subduing force. If, however, the officer moves to a level of force that is disproportionate to the force offered by the suspect, the officer is open to the accusation of using excessive force.

Thus, use-of-force continuums control police officer actions in the sense that they encourage them to use only what force is necessary to deal adequately with a situation.

In Canada, a lot of time and energy has been put into developing a national use-of-force model (Butler, 2009). For example, the Canadian Association of Chiefs of Police (CACP) has approved such a model, which is described more fully in Box 2.4 (CACP, 2007). It is hoped that this model will have its intended effect of assisting Canadian police officers with their decision making in use-of-force situations and in educating others on the subject.

## Box 2.4

# The National Use-of-Force Model in Canada

To provide guidelines to police officers with regard to what level of force is reasonable under various circumstances, Canadian police agencies have developed a National Use-of-Force Model (see Figure 2.5). The model represents the process by which a police officer assesses, plans, and responds to use-of-force situations (CACP, 2007, p. 11):

> The assessment process begins in the centre of the graphic [in Figure 2.5] with the situation confronting the officer. From there, the assessment process moves outward and addresses the subject's behaviour and the officer's perception and tactical considerations. Based on the officer's assessment of the conditions represented by these inner circles, the officer selects from the use of force options contained within the model's outer circle. After the officer chooses a response option, the officer must continue to assess, plan and act to determine if his or her actions are appropriate and/or effective or if a new strategy should be selected. The whole process should be seen as dynamic and constantly evolving until the situation is brought under control.

Even with this model, the decisions a police officer has to make when deciding whether to use force are not easy. For example, according to the CACP (2007), a police officer will have to consider, among many other factors, whether the incident is occurring in a public place, whether there is enough light to assess the situation properly, whether the location poses a risk to him or her or the subject, whether the subject is alone, and whether the subject is intoxicated. This deliberation must occur at the same time the officer is considering the subject's behaviour and the officer's own ability to deal with the situation. Based on this assessment, the police officer must then develop a plan that involves selecting what he or she feels to be an appropriate response. As indicated in the outermost ring of the diagram, there are five basic options. Officer presence is the least forceful option, followed by verbal and non-verbal communication, physical control, intermediate weapons, and, finally, use of lethal force. As the CACP (2007) notes, there is an approximate correspondence between the graphic's depiction of a subject's behaviour and the options available to the officer. For example, if a suspect is exhibiting potentially lethal behaviour, then it may be necessary for the police officer to use lethal force.

*(continued)*

(continued)

**Figure 2.5** The National Use-of-Force Model

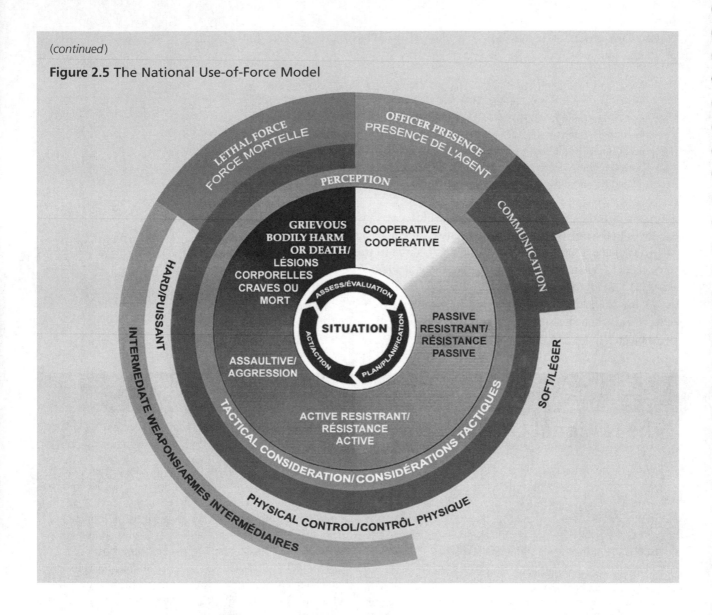

## POLICE STRESS

Many police psychologists, as well as police officers and their families, consider policing to be one of the most stressful occupations (Anshel, 2000). After our discussion of some of the dangerous situations police officers encounter, you will likely come to a similar conclusion yourself. Even if the extent of the stressfulness of policing is debatable, we can all probably agree that police officers are exposed to many stressful events. Not only has research demonstrated that this is the case, but it has also indicated that these stressful events can have a negative impact on police officers and their families, as well as the organizations they work for (Brown & Campbell, 1994). In this section, we will discuss some of the sources of police stress and examine the potential consequences. In addition, we will briefly focus on what can be done to prevent and manage police stress.

# Sources of Police Stress

As Finn and Tomz (1996) make clear, "different officers are likely to perceive different events as stressful, depending on their individual background, personalities, expectations, law enforcement experience, years on the job, type of law enforcement work they perform, and access to coping resources" (p. 6). However, research suggests that there are a number of common sources of police stress (Abdollahi, 2002). Although the labelling of these categories may differ depending on what article or book you read, the major sources of police stress tend to include organizational stressors, occupational stressors, criminal justice stressors, and public stressors. Finn and Tomz (1996) have provided a reasonably comprehensive list of specific stressors that fall into each of these categories, a partial listing of which is presented in Table 2.3.

Although the majority of people assume that **occupational stressors** are the most stressful for police officers, officers indicate that they experience a degree of stress for each of the stressors described in Table 2.3. In fact, many police researchers believe they have evidence to show that **organizational stressors** more strongly affect officers than occupational stressors (Finn & Tomz, 1996). Such claims are backed up by anecdotal evidence. For example, as reported by Finn and Tomz (1996), a wife of an officer who ended up resigning because of stress commented, "My husband came home more screwed up with department problems than with anything he ever encountered on the streets" (p. 7).

**Occupational stressors:** In policing, stressors relating to the job itself

**Organizational stressors:** In policing, stressors relating to organizational issues

---

**Table 2.3** Sources of Police Stress

1. **Organizational Stressors**
   - *Lack of career development.* In most police agencies, there is little room for advancement, regardless of the performance of the officer.
   - *Excessive paperwork.* The need for duplicate forms of every police transaction is often questioned.

2. **Occupational Stressors**
   - *Irregular work schedule.* Shift work is disruptive to the personal lives of most police officers.
   - *Human suffering.* Officers are constantly exposed to the inequities and brutalities of life.

3. **Criminal Justice Stressors**
   - *Ineffectiveness of the corrections system.* Officers are alarmed by the recidivism rate of criminals who seem to be perpetually "on the street" rather than incarcerated.
   - *Unfavourable court decisions.* Many court decisions are viewed by officers as unfairly increasing the difficulty of police work.

4. **Public Stressors**
   - *Distorted press accounts.* Reports of incidents are often inaccurate and perceived as derogatory by officers, whether or not the inaccuracy is intentional.
   - *Ineffectiveness of referral agencies.* The ineffectiveness of social service agencies frustrates officers who view these agencies as their only source of assistance.

Source: Adapted from Teplin, 2000.

Although occupational stressors, such as police shootings, can cause a great deal of stress for many police officers, organizational stressors, such as perceptions of inadequate departmental support, can also result in harmful levels of stress.

The stress associated with organizational stressors is also revealed in surveys of police officers. For example, Taylor and Bennell (2006) asked 154 full-time officers employed by a police agency in Ontario to fill out the Operational Police Stress Questionnaire and the Organizational Police Stress Questionnaire, both of which were developed by McCreary and Thompson (2006). More specifically, police officers were asked to rank each of the 40 stressors included on these surveys from 1 to 7, with a score of 1 indicating that the event caused them no stress at all in the previous six months and a score of 7 indicating that the event caused them a lot of stress in the previous six months. For illustrative purposes, the ten highest-ranked stressors across the two surveys are provided in Table 2.4. As you can

**Table 2.4** The Ten Highest-Ranked Police Stressors Among Ontario Police Officers

The feeling that different rules apply to different people (4.78)*

Fatigue (4.47)

Feeling like you always have to prove yourself to the organization (4.41)

Inconsistent leadership style (4.36)

Dealing with the court system (4.17)

Bureaucratic red tape (4.14)

Not enough time available to spend with friends and family (4.09)

Shift work (4.04)

Finding time to stay in good physical condition (3.98)

Perceived pressure to volunteer free time (3.91)

*Numbers in brackets are means out of 7.

Source: Adapted from Taylor & Bennell, 2006.

**Table 2.5** Possible Consequences of Police Stress

| Physical Health Problems | Psychological and Personal Problems | Job Performance Problems |
|---|---|---|
| High blood pressure | Depression and anxiety | Low morale |
| Cardiovascular disease | Aggression | Tardiness |
| High cholesterol | Post-traumatic stress disorder | Absenteeism |
| Stomach ulcers | Drug and alcohol abuse | Early retirement |
| Respiratory problems | Suicide | Reduced productivity |
| Skin problems | Domestic violence | Reduced efficiency |
| Weight gain | Separation and divorce | Citizen complaints |
| Diabetes | Extramarital affairs | Turnover |
| Death | Burnout | Hostile interactions |

Source: Adapted from Brown & Campbell, 1994.

see from the results, many of the highest-ranked events are actually organizational stressors (e.g., the feeling that different rules apply to different people), although a number of occupational stressors (e.g., fatigue) also rank very high.

## Consequences of Police Stress

When a police officer experiences a potentially life-threatening situation, the acute stress reactions that the officer experiences can have serious repercussions that last long after the actual event. Likewise, constant exposure to other police stressors, particularly organizational stressors, can affect police officers on a more chronic basis (McCraty, Tomasino, Atkinson, & Sundram, 1999). Without an effective prevention or management strategy (at both the individual and the organizational level) to deal with police stressors, police officers, their families, and the organizations they work for will suffer in numerous ways. Brown and Campbell (1994) have categorized the general consequences of police stress into physical health problems, psychological and personal problems, and job performance problems, and large-scale research projects such as the study discussed in Box 2.5 are starting to systematically examine these effects. See Table 2.5 for a summary of possible consequences of police stress that fall into each of these categories.

**Physical Health Problems** One of the major consequences of police stress is the impact it can have on an officer's physical health. As McCraty et al. (1999) explain, constant exposure to acutely stressful events can result in the chronic activation of the body's stress response systems to a point where physiological breakdown occurs. The result of such a breakdown can take many different forms. For example, research by Franke, Collins, and Hinz (1998) has suggested that police officers are more than twice as likely as people in other occupations to develop cardiovascular disease. In addition, Kroes, Margolis, and Hurrell (1974) reported that more than 32% of the police officers they examined experienced digestive disorders, which is significantly higher than the prevalence rate in the civilian population. Finally, in a large-scale study of 2376 police officers,

Violanti, Vena, and Marshall (1986) found that rates of death due to cancer were significantly higher among police officers than among the general population. However, the limited amount of research in the area makes it difficult to determine how many of these health problems are due to the stressful events police officers are exposed to and how many of them are due to the lifestyle habits adopted by police officers (Abdollahi, 2002).

**Psychological and Personal Problems** Psychological and personal problems, including depression, post-traumatic stress disorder, drug and alcohol abuse, marital problems, and suicide, can also emerge when police officers are exposed to stressful situations. However, it should be noted that, as in the case of physical health problems, the research in this area can often be contradictory and, therefore, caution must be used when interpreting the results of any single study. For example, although numerous studies have suggested that alcohol use may be particularly problematic among police officers (e.g., Violanti, Marshall, & Howe, 1985), Alexander, Innes, Irving, Sinclair, and Walker (1991) found that alcohol consumption by police officers was not statistically greater than consumption rates found for firefighters, prison officers, or nurses. Similarly, although some researchers have found indications of burnout among police officers (e.g., Anson & Bloom, 1988), other researchers have failed to find significant levels of burnout, especially among Canadian police managers (Loo, 1994).

Police-related suicide rates and divorce rates have also recently been examined, and here as well there are many contradictory findings. For example, in contrast to popular belief, studies of suicide in North American police agencies demonstrate that the rates are not significantly different from the suicide rates found in comparable male populations (Aamodt & Stalnaker, 2006). Likewise, despite the view voiced by some that the divorce rate is high in the police population (Territo & Sewell, 2007), recent research suggests that the divorce rate for law enforcement personnel in the United States is actually lower than that of the general population, even when controlling for demographic and various job-related variables (McCoy & Aamodt, 2010).

**Job Performance Problems** Job performance problems are the third major category of stress consequences. Often as a direct result of the physical and psychological problems discussed above, the way a police officer performs on the job can suffer greatly. As with other stress reactions, impaired job performance can take many forms, including a decrease in work efficiency and productivity, increased absenteeism and tardiness, and early retirement. Although these consequences may not seem as serious as the physical and psychological problems caused by police stress, from an organizational perspective they certainly are significant. For example, consider the problem of absenteeism because of illness. According to one newspaper article from the late 1980s, it was estimated that each year in England and Wales the police service lost approximately 1.6 million working days through sickness, some of which can undoubtedly be attributed to stress (*The Guardian*, October 28, 1988). Similar statistics are unavailable in Canada for police agencies specifically, but if more general Canadian research is anything to go by, the issue certainly requires serious attention (e.g., Duxbury & Higgins, 2003; Duxbury, Higgins, & Coghill, 2003).

## Preventing and Managing Police Stress

Most police officers and police agencies have now recognized the need to prevent and manage negative reactions to stressful events. Indeed, over the last 20 years, formal stress

# The Buffalo Cardio-Metabolic Occupational Police Stress (BCOPS) Study

Over the past several years, the largest, most comprehensive study of police stress ever conducted has been taking place in Buffalo, under the lead of Dr. John Violanti, a long-serving (now retired) member of the New York State Police and a leader in the field of police stress research at the University of Buffalo.

The primary purpose of the research is to study the effects of police stress on adverse metabolic and cardiovascular outcomes with the goal being to prevent stress-related disorders. To date, hundreds of police officers have participated in the study, which involves the collection of a huge amount of data, including the following:

- The completion of questionnaires, which measure demographic, lifestyle, and psychological factors (e.g., depression)
- Measurements of bone density and body composition
- Ultrasounds of arteries
- 18 salivary cortisol samples throughout the day, and in response to a series of challenges
- Blood samples
- The quantity and quality of sleep that the officers are getting, as measured by a watchlike device called an *actigraph*
- Work history records

The plan is to sample the *entire* Buffalo Police Department, which would make this the first ever population-based study of police stress that examines both psychological and physiological measures of stress. Already the data that has emerged from this study is revealing important information. For example, it appears that female officers may suffer more from certain post-traumatic stress symptoms and depressive symptoms than male officers. In addition, officers with more post-traumatic stress symptoms appear to experience more adverse physiological effects.

For years to come, this study will provide valuable information about the consequences of police stress that will benefit police officers and the people they serve.

Source: Hartley, Burchfiel, & Violanti, 2010.

programs have been set up in most agencies to combat the effects of police stress. A variety of strategies are included in these programs, including informal support networks, physical fitness programs, professional counselling services, family assistance programs, and special assessments following exposure to critical events such as shootings or accidents (Brown & Campbell, 1994). A thorough discussion of each of these strategies is beyond the scope of this chapter, but such a discussion can be found in Brown and Campbell (1994). Here, we will simply focus on one particular strategy: training police officers to use effective coping strategies.

Police stress is not only a result of being exposed to stressful events, but also a result of the poor coping skills that some police officers use when faced with these events (Anshel, 2000). Many coping strategies are maladaptive and can lead to further, more serious problems for the police officer. For example, in a study of Canadian police officers, Burke (1993) found that officers who coped with stress by using alcohol, other drugs, anger, or withdrawal were more likely to suffer from health problems and further stress than were officers who used more adaptive coping strategies. Thus, one potential method for preventing and managing stress at the level of the individual police officer is to teach officers how to use adaptive coping strategies. Many of these strategies are fairly basic, such as teaching police officers how to communicate with others more effectively (given that ineffective communication is a primary cause of stress). Other strategies are more specific stress-relieving techniques, such as the use of Freeze-Frame®, which forms part of the Heart-Math Stress Management Program (McCraty et al., 1999). Using this technique, officers are taught to "consciously disengage from negative mental and emotional reactions as they occur by shifting their attention to the area of the heart, then self-generating a positive or neutral feeling" (McCraty et al., 1999, p. 6).

As Anshel (2000) points out, training police officers how to use adaptive coping strategies may be a particularly useful approach because "although police officers often cannot control the sources of job-related stress, their effective use of coping strategies following unpleasant events is controllable" (p. 377). Furthermore, this intervention has been shown to have a significant and positive impact, not only on the health and general well-being of police officers, but also on how they deal with stressful policing events in the future (McCraty et al., 1999).

## SUMMARY

1.  The development of a useful police selection process requires two major steps: (1) an analysis of the knowledge, skills, and abilities that are required for the job, and (2) the construction and validation of selection instruments that measure these qualities and compare them with job performance.

2.  Some of the most common police selection procedures are semi-structured interviews, psychological tests, and the use of assessment centres.

3.  Police discretion refers to the power that police officers have to decide which laws apply to a given situation and whether to apply them. Many view police discretion as an inevitable part of police work and, so long as it is used in an unbiased manner, police discretion can be very useful.

4.  Nearly every decision that a police officer makes requires some degree of discretion. However, four of the most commonly studied areas of police discretion deal with youth crime, offenders with mental illnesses, domestic violence, and use-of-force situations. A major effort has been made in Canada to develop policies to guide police decision making in each of these areas. One example is the National Use-of-Force Model, which provides guidelines to police officers with regard to what level of force is reasonable under various circumstances.

5.  Policing is considered by many to be one of the most stressful occupations. Sources of stress include organizational stressors, occupational stressors, criminal justice stressors, and public stressors. These stressors can lead to serious physical health problems, psychological and personal problems, and job performance problems if they are not dealt with appropriately.

6.  To combat the negative effects of stress, police forces are developing and using a variety of prevention and management strategies. One strategy that looks particularly promising involves teaching police officers how to use adaptive coping skills when faced with stressful events.

## Discussion Questions

1.  You are a member of a community group that has been put together to provide your local police agency with recommendations regarding police selection criteria. What do you, as a community citizen, feel are the most important characteristics of a good police officer? Do you think these characteristics should be considered when police forces select police officers? Why or why not?

2.  Members of police forces have rated sense of humour an important characteristic of an effective police officer. As a researcher in the area of police psychology, what problems might you encounter when developing a situational test to determine whether police applicants have a good sense of humour?

3.  Imagine you are a police officer who encounters a well-dressed woman walking down the street who is obviously intoxicated. What would you do? Would you arrest her and take her to jail, or would you drive her home? What factors would you consider when making your decision? Would your decision have been different if you encountered an older man who was dressed in dirty and ripped clothes? Why or why not?

4.  Your friend has been a police officer for five years. He constantly talks to you about the stress he feels but rarely does he raise any issues about occupational stressors. Instead, he seems most upset with his organization. Why do you think organizational stressors have such a big impact on police officers?

5.  What sorts of things could you do as a police psychologist to help the police officer in question 4 deal with his stress? What do you think his police force could do, as an organization, to prevent and manage his stress?

# Chapter 3
## The Psychology of Police Investigations

## Learning Objectives

- Describe the Reid model of interrogation and summarize the rationale for its use.

- Outline three potential problems with the Reid model of interrogation.

- Differentiate among false, retracted, and disputed confessions.

- Define the three major types of false confessions.

- Explain why the police use criminal profiling and outline three potential problems with its use.

- Explain what geographic profiling is and how it can be used in police investigations.

Mark Jackson was arrested for shooting a man inside a convenience store. After his arrest, he was taken to the police station for questioning. Over the course of a 24-hour period, Mark was interrogated five times. The last interrogation took place at 2:00 a.m. Although Mark stated he was exhausted, he was told the interrogation would not take long and that it was best to "get it over with." In reality, the interrogation lasted for more than three hours.

Initially, Mark maintained that, although he was at the store on the day of the shooting, he had nothing to do with the crime. However, throughout the interrogations, the police challenged him, stating they had hard evidence proving he was the killer. This evidence not only included a security video, but also several eyewitnesses. None of this evidence actually existed. In addition, the police minimized the seriousness of the crime, stating that the victim was a known drug dealer who "had it coming" and that Mark "did everyone a favour."

Over the course of his interrogations, the police continually pressured Mark to stop denying his involvement in the crime and said that if he told the truth "all of this would end." Finally, during his last interrogation, Mark admitted to the shooting. The case went to court, and Mark was convicted, largely on the basis of his confession. Months later, it was discovered that he had not committed the crime. Mark had confessed to a crime he had nothing to do with.

As seen in Chapter 2, forensic psychology plays an important role in many aspects of police work. One element we have yet to discuss, however, is psychology's role in criminal investigations, such as the Mark Jackson investigation described above. Many people are aware that psychology is used in criminal investigations, and recent movies and television shows have done much to promote this fact. However, as you will see throughout this chapter, psychology played an important role in the investigative process long before Hollywood became interested in the topic, and it continues to do so today.

Psychologists have identified a number of key investigative tasks where psychology is particularly relevant. One of these tasks relates to the collection and evaluation of investigative information—information that is often obtained from suspects. Another task relates to investigative decision making, especially decisions that require an in-depth understanding of criminal behaviour. This chapter will focus on how psychology contributes to these tasks by looking first at how the police interrogate suspects, and some possible consequences of their interrogation practices, and then by examining the practice of profiling the characteristics of criminals based on the way they commit their crimes.

## POLICE INTERROGATIONS

Confession evidence is often viewed as "a prosecutor's most potent weapon" (Kassin, 1997, p. 221), and police officers will often go to great lengths to secure such evidence (see Box 3.1 for an example of how far Canadian police agencies will sometimes go). In some countries, people may be convicted solely on the basis of their confession, although in North America, a confession usually has to be backed up by some other form of evidence (Gudjonsson, 2003). Regardless of whether corroborative evidence is required, it is likely that people who confess to a crime are more likely to be prosecuted and convicted than those who do not. Indeed, some legal scholars have gone so far as to claim that a confession makes other aspects of a trial unnecessary, because "the real trial, for all practical purposes, occurs when the confession is obtained" (McCormick, 1972, p. 316). Given the importance of confession evidence, it should come as no surprise that, although one of the goals of a **police interrogation** is to gain information from the suspect that furthers the investigation, such as the location of important evidence, another key goal is to obtain a confession (Kassin, 1997).

**Police interrogation:** A process whereby the police interview a suspect for the purpose of gathering evidence and obtaining a confession

Being interrogated by the police for the purpose of extracting a confession is often considered to be inherently coercive. Imagine yourself being interrogated for the very first time. You would probably be in an environment that is foreign to you, faced with one, possibly two, police officers whom you have never met. You would know little of what the police officers are going to do to you and would have no one to turn to for support. Even if you were innocent of the crime in question, the situation would no doubt be an extremely intimidating one. In large part, this is due to the fact that the police interrogators are part of a system that gives them certain powers over you, the suspect (Gudjonsson, 2003).

There is no question that police interrogations were coercive in the past. Consider police tactics in the mid-twentieth century, for example, when whipping was occasionally used to obtain confessions (e.g., *Brown v. Mississippi*, 1936). Or consider a more recent episode occurring in the 1980s, where New York City police officers jolted a suspect with a stun gun to extract a confession (Huff, Rattner, & Sagarin, 1996). Although these overt acts of physical coercion have become much less frequent with time, they have been replaced with more subtle, psychologically based interrogation techniques, such as lying about evidence, promising lenient treatment, and implying threats to loved ones (Leo, 1992).

## Box 3.1

# The Mr. Big Technique

Recently it has become clear that some Canadian police forces will go to great lengths to secure a confession. In addition to the Reid model of interrogation, which is discussed in this chapter, another procedure that is commonly used is referred to as the Mr. Big technique (Smith, Stinson, & Patry, 2009). Unlike the Reid model, the Mr. Big technique is a noncustodial procedure in that it happens outside of the interrogation room.

According to Smith et al. (2009), the procedure generally involves undercover police officers who pose as members of a criminal organization and attempt to lure the suspect into the gang (e.g., by showing the suspect how lucrative it can be). Often the suspect is made to commit some minor crimes (for which he may be rewarded) and once committed to the organization, the suspect is "interviewed" for a higher level job. However, before the suspect can seal the deal with the boss, Mr. Big, he must confess to a serious crime (the one under investigation).

According to the researchers, one of several reasons is usually given to the suspect for why he needs to confess: "as a form of 'insurance' for the criminal gang, so they have something 'on' the suspect if he ever turns against them; so that Mr. Big can draw on his purported influence and connections to make the evidence or 'problem' disappear; or both" (Smith et al., 2009, p. 170). Once the confession is elicited, it is used against the suspect in his trial.

Although not used as frequently as other interrogation techniques such as the Reid model, the Mr. Big technique is used often. For example, Smith et al. (2009) present evidence that prior to 2004, the technique had been used at least 350 times in Canada. The technique also seems to be very effective, resulting in a 75% success rate and a 95% conviction rate.

One of the cases where this technique was used will be familiar to most of you: the Mayerthorpe RCMP murders in 2005, when James Roszko shot and killed four police officers (Smith et al., 2009). Although Rosko had acted alone at his ranch, a Mr. Big undercover operation was set up to show how two of Roszko's acquaintances—Dennis Cheeseman and Shawn Hennessey—were involved in the killing. The operation involved over 50 undercover officers and ultimately led to confessions from Cheeseman and Hennessey, who "admitted to giving Roszko a shotgun and giving him a ride back to his property when they knew that Roszko was planning to kill the RCMP officers" (Smith, Stinson, & Patry, 2009, p. 171).

Obviously, the use of this technique raises some interesting ethical and legal questions. For example, does this technique boil down to entrapment, where a person is induced to commit an illegal act they otherwise would not commit? According to Smith et al.'s (2009) review of the case law (e.g., *R. v. Mack*, 1988) the answer is no: "[b]ecause the Mr. Big operation is designed to elicit . . . a confession regarding an event that occurred before the operation started and not for criminal activity during the undercover operation, this type of sting operation falls outside of the Canadian definition of entrapment" (p. 179).

From a legal perspective, does the technique raise other questions, beyond the issue of entrapment? Again, the answer appears to be no according to the Canadian courts (e.g., *R. v. Mentuck*, 2000). Indeed, as highlighted by Smith et al. (2009), the technique has been approved by the Canadian courts, which seem to view the "the Mr. Big technique [as] a reasonable use of police trickery that would not bring the administration of justice into disrepute" (pp. 179–180).

Despite these positions taken by the courts, psychological research that has examined coercive interrogation tactics has raised concerns, some of which will be discussed later in the chapter (e.g., the chance that the tactics may lead people to falsely confess). Although this research doesn't relate directly to the Mr. Big technique, Smith et al. (2009) convincingly argue that the results may generalize to this procedure and therefore caution should always be used when planning to introduce suspects to "Mr. Big."

Although not all interrogators use these strategies, police officers sometimes view these techniques as a necessary evil to obtain confessions from guilty persons. Indeed, leading authorities in the field of interrogation training openly state that, because offenders are typically reluctant to confess, they must often be tricked into doing so (Inbau, Reid, Buckley, & Jayne, 2004).

# The Reid Model of Interrogation

Police officers around the world often receive specialized training in exactly how to extract confessions from suspects. Depending on where this training is provided, different approaches are taught. For example, as discussed later in this chapter, police officers in England and Wales are trained to use interrogation techniques that are far less coercive than those used in North America (Kassin & Gudjonsson, 2004; Sear & Williamson, 1999; Snook, Eastwood, Stinson, Tedeschini, & House, 2010). These different techniques are used primarily because courts in England have begun to recognize some of the potential problems associated with coercive interrogation practices, such as false confessions (Meissner & Russano, 2003). Before moving on to discuss these potential problems, let us look closely at the type of interrogation training provided to police officers in North America.

A police officer interrogating a suspect

The most common interrogation training program offered to North American police officers is based on a book written by Inbau et al. (2004) called *Criminal Interrogation and Confessions*. Within this manual, the authors describe the now-famous **Reid model** of interrogation, a technique originally developed by John E. Reid, a polygrapher from Chicago (Meissner & Russano, 2003).

**Reid model:** A nine-step model of interrogation used frequently in North America to extract confessions from suspects

At a general level, the Reid model consists of a three-part process. The first stage is to gather evidence related to the crime and to interview witnesses and victims. The second stage is to conduct a nonaccusatorial interview of the suspect to assess any evidence of deception (i.e., to determine whether the suspect is lying when he or she claims to be innocent). The third stage is to conduct an accusatorial interrogation of the suspect (if he or she is perceived to be guilty) in which a nine-step procedure is implemented, with the primary objective being to secure a confession (Inbau et al., 2004).

This nine-step procedure in stage three consists of the following steps:

1. The suspect is immediately confronted with his or her guilt. If the police do not have any evidence against the suspect at this time, then the interrogator can hide this fact and, if necessary, pretend that such evidence exists.

2. Psychological themes are then developed that allow the suspect to justify, rationalize, or excuse the crime. For example, a suspected rapist may be told that the victim must have been asking for it.

3. The interrogator interrupts any statements of denial by the suspect to ensure the suspect does not get the upper hand in the interrogation.

4. The interrogator overcomes the suspect's objections to the charges to a point at which the suspect becomes quiet and withdrawn.

5. Once the suspect has become withdrawn, the interrogator ensures that the suspect does not tune out of the interrogation by reducing the psychological distance between the interrogator and the suspect, such as by physically moving closer to the suspect.

6. The interrogator then exhibits sympathy and understanding, and the suspect is urged to come clean. For example, the interrogator might try to appeal to the suspect's sense of decency.

7.   The suspect is offered face-saving explanations for the crime, which makes self-incrimination easier to achieve.

8.   Once the suspect accepts responsibility for the crime (typically by agreeing with one of the face-saving explanations), the interrogator develops this admission into a full confession.

9.   Finally, the interrogator gets the suspect to write and sign a full confession.

In addition to the techniques included in these nine steps, Inbau et al. (2004) provide many other suggestions for how to effectively interrogate suspects. These suggestions include things such as using a plainly decorated interrogation room to avoid distractions, having the evidence folder in your hand when beginning the interrogation, and making sure that the suspect is alone in the interrogation suite prior to the interrogator entering the room.

The Reid model of interrogation is based on the idea that suspects do not confess to crimes they have committed because they fear the potential consequences that await them if they do (Inbau et al., 2004). In addition, their fear of the potential consequences is not sufficiently outweighed by their internal feelings of anxiety associated with remaining deceptive (i.e., by maintaining they did not commit the crime in question). The goal of the Reid model, therefore, is to reverse this state of affairs, by making the consequences of confessing more desirable than the anxiety related to the deception (Gudjonsson, 2003). It is assumed that this can be done by using psychologically based techniques, such as the minimization and maximization techniques described below (Jayne, 1986). For example, many believe that providing the suspect with a way to rationalize his or her behaviour can reduce the perceived consequences of confessing. Conversely, appealing to one's sense of morality can sometimes increase the anxiety associated with deception.

Techniques used in the Reid model of interrogation can be broken down into two general categories. These categories are often referred to by different names, including *friendly and unfriendly techniques*, *Mutt and Jeff techniques*, and *minimization and maximization techniques*. You will probably know them as good cop–bad cop techniques. Throughout this chapter, the labels *minimization* and *maximization* will be used to refer to the categories, since these terms are the most commonly accepted.

**Minimization techniques:**
Soft sell tactics used by police interrogators that are designed to lull the suspect into a false sense of security

**Maximization techniques:** Scare tactics used by police interrogators that are designed to intimidate a suspect believed to be guilty

**Minimization techniques** refer to "soft sell" tactics used by police interrogators that are designed to "lull the suspect into a false sense of security" (Kassin, 1997, p. 223). These tactics include the use of sympathy, excuses, and justifications. For example, when the interrogator in the opening scenario suggested to Mark Jackson that the victim "had it coming" because he was a drug dealer, and that Mark "did everyone a favour" by shooting the victim, that interrogator was using minimization techniques. In contrast to minimization techniques, **maximization techniques** refer to "scare tactics" that interrogators often use "to intimidate a suspect believed to be guilty" (Kassin, 1997, p. 223). This intimidation is typically achieved by exaggerating the seriousness of the offence and by making false claims about evidence the police supposedly have. References to the nonexistent security videotape and the eyewitnesses in the opening scenario are examples of such a scare tactic.

## The Use of the Reid Model in Actual Interrogations

Simply because the Reid model of interrogation is the most widely taught interrogation procedure in North America does not necessarily mean that police officers rely on the model in practice. Currently, it is not possible to say with any degree of confidence how often police officers in North America use Reid interrogation techniques, but studies are beginning to shed some light on this issue.

For example, Kassin et al. (2007) recently conducted a survey of 631 police investigators about their interrogation practices. They had the officers rate, on a 5-point scale ranging from never to always, how often they used different types of interrogation techniques. The results of the survey indicated that many of the techniques included in the Reid model of interrogation are used in actual police interrogations, although the frequency of use varied across techniques. For instance, interrogators almost always used techniques such as isolating suspects from friends and family and trying to establish rapport with suspects to gain their trust. Other common but less frequently used techniques included confronting suspects with their guilt and appealing to their self-interest. Less common still, but sometimes used, were techniques such as providing justifications for the crime and implying or pretending to have evidence. Very rare were instances of threatening the suspect with consequences for not cooperating and physically intimidating the suspect.

Given that Kassin et al.'s (2007) results are based on interrogators' self-reported behaviour, there is, of course, the chance that their responses are biased. Building on research by Leo (1996), King and Snook (2009) recently conducted a more objective analysis. They obtained 44 videotaped interrogations conducted by Canadian police officers and coded the various techniques the interrogators used. Their results, which are partially illustrated in Table 3.1, provide the first glimpse into what goes on in Canadian interrogation rooms.

Like Kassin et al.'s (2007) survey, the results indicate that Canadian interrogators do not strictly adhere to the core components of the Reid model of interrogation, many of which are outlined above, although some of the guidelines suggested by Inbau et al. (2004) were regularly observed. In addition, very few coercive strategies were observed in the interrogations, although a reasonable number of suspects were not read their rights to silence and legal counsel (although this could have occurred before the videotaping of the interrogation). Interestingly, the number of Reid techniques used by the interrogators in this study did relate to interrogation outcomes, with more confessions being given when interrogations contained a greater proportion of Reid techniques. However, as King and Snook (2009) state, this result does not necessarily prove the effectiveness of the Reid model, since there are many possible explanations for this finding (e.g., an interrogator could expend more effort when there is clearer evidence of a suspect's guilt and the number of interrogation techniques they use could reflect this effort).

## Potential Problems with the Reid Model of Interrogation

Because many police officers are trained to use the Reid model of interrogation, especially in North America, it has been the subject of much research. This research indicates that the technique has a number of potential problems. Three problems in particular deserve our attention. The first two relate to the ability of investigators to detect deception (Memon, Vrij, & Bull, 2003) and to the biases that may result when an interrogator believes, perhaps incorrectly, that a suspect is guilty (Kassin, Goldstein, & Savitsky, 2003). The third problem has to do with the coercive nature of certain interrogation practices,

**Table 3.1** The Percentage of Interrogation Tactics Used in Canadian Interrogations (*N* = 44)

| Coding Category | Percentage |
|---|---|
| **Reid Themes** | |
| Appeal to suspect's pride with flattery | 57 |
| Play one suspect against the other | 43 |
| Minimize the seriousness of the offence | 36 |
| Sympathize with the suspect by condemning others | 25 |
| Suggest noncriminal intent for the offence | 9 |
| Exaggerate the seriousness of the offence | 0 |
| **Reid Suggestions** | |
| Suspect not handcuffed during the interrogation | 100 |
| No telephone in the interrogation room | 86 |
| No handshake prior to the interrogation | 80 |
| Suspect alone prior to the interrogation | 61 |
| Interrogator seated across from the suspect | 46 |
| Polygraph offer made to the suspect | 9 |
| **Influence Tactics** | |
| Confront suspect with evidence of his or her guilt | 82 |
| Identify contradictions in the suspect's account | 46 |
| Appeal to interrogator's authority | 27 |
| Touch suspect in a friendly manner | 14 |
| Use good cop–bad cop routine | 2 |
| Exaggerate the facts of the offence | 0 |
| **Coercive Strategies** | |
| Suspect not read rights to silence and legal counsel | 21 |
| Suspect threatened with psychological pain | 5 |
| Promises of leniency in exchange for admission of guilt | 2 |
| Suspect not permitted to invoke his or her rights | 0 |
| Deprivation of essential necessities | 0 |
| Interrogation lasted longer than six hours | 0 |

Note that the percentages in this table are based on each technique being observed at least once during the interrogation (the total number of times that each technique was observed was not coded).

Source: King and Snook, 2009, Tables 2–5.

and the possibility that these practices will result in false confessions (Ofshe & Leo, 1997). We will briefly discuss the first two problems here and reserve our discussion of false confessions for the next section of this chapter.

**Deception detection:** Detecting when someone is being deceptive

**Detecting Deception** A more thorough discussion of **deception detection** will be provided in Chapter 4, so our discussion here will be limited to how deception detection relates to police interrogations. The issue of whether investigators are effective deception detectors is an important one, especially when using the Reid model of interrogation, because the actual interrogation of a suspect begins only after an initial interview has allowed the interrogator to determine whether the suspect is guilty (Inbau et al., 2004). The decision to commence a full-blown police interrogation, therefore, relies on an accurate assessment of whether the suspect is being deceptive when he or she claims to be innocent.

As you will see in Chapter 4, there is currently very little research available to suggest that police officers, or anyone else for that matter, can detect deception with any degree of accuracy (e.g., Memon et al., 2003). This finding often appears to be true even after people receive specialized training (Köhnken, 1987), although there are some recent exceptions to this in Canada, where certain training programs have been shown to increase lie detection accuracy (Porter, Juodis, ten Brinke, Klein, & Wilson, 2010; Porter, Woodworth, & Birt, 2000). As a result, it seems likely that the decision to interrogate a suspect when using the Reid model of interrogation will often be based on an incorrect determination that the suspect is guilty (Kassin et al., 2003).

Of course, procedural safeguards are in place to protect an individual during the transition to the interrogation phase of the Reid model (Kassin & Gudjonsson, 2004). Most notably in the United States are an individual's *Miranda* rights (*Miranda v. Arizona*, 1966). In Canada, the rights of suspects are included in The Charter of Rights and Freedoms, and include the rights to silence and legal counsel (King & Snook, 2009). In both countries, it is only when suspects knowingly and voluntarily waive these rights that their statements can be used as evidence against them (Kassin & Gudjonsson, 2004; King & Snook, 2009). Research, however, has demonstrated that *Miranda*-type rights may not provide the protection that they are assumed to provide.

One significant problem is that many individuals do not understand their rights when they are presented to them. Particularly vulnerable populations in this regard appear to include young people and those with impaired intellectual capacity (Fulero & Everington, 2004; Oberlander & Goldstein, 2001), but healthy adults and even police officers also exhibit problems with comprehension (Eastwood & Snook, 2010; Grisso, 1981; Gudjonsson, Clare, & Cross, 1992; Moore & Gagnier, 2008).

Consider a recent Canadian study by Eastwood and Snook (2010). They sampled 56 undergraduate students, nearly half whom were enrolled in a police recruitment program. Each participant was presented with the two legal cautions that are supposed to be presented to suspects in Canada—the right to silence and the right to legal counsel—first in verbal format and then in written format, one element at a time (e.g., the right to silence includes multiple elements, such as (1) you need not say anything, (2) you have nothing to hope from any promise or favour, and (3) you have nothing to fear from any threat). After each type of presentation, participants recorded their understanding of the caution and rated how confident they were with their answer. The researchers coded these responses for degree of accuracy, with points being provided for each element of the caution that the participants correctly understood.

The results of this study were consistent with previous research (e.g., Moore & Gagnier, 2008). In general, participants had difficulty understanding each of the cautions, particularly certain elements, but presenting the cautions in written format, one element at a time, allowed for a greater degree of comprehension. This increased comprehension is demonstrated in Table 3.2 for the right to silence caution. Importantly, self-reported confidence was not a good predictor of a participant's degree of comprehension and demographic variables, such as group status (student versus police recruit), were not related to comprehension. Based on these results, Eastwood and Snook (2010) concluded that "Canadians facing an investigative interview situation will not fully

**Table 3.2** Percentage of Participants Comprehending the Components of the Right to Silence

| | | Number of Components Comprehended (out of 4) | | | |
|---|---|---|---|---|---|
| **Format type** | 4 | 3 | 2 | 1 | 0 |
| Verbal | 3.6 | 8.9 | 57.1 | 21.4 | 8.9 |
| Written | 48.2 | 14.3 | 35.7 | 1.8 | 0.0 |

Source: Eastman and Snook, 2009 (p. 372; Table 1).

comprehend their rights, and therefore are unable to make a fully informed decision regarding whether or not they should waive their rights" (p. 375). Not only does this mean that the rights and freedoms of Canadian suspects are not always being protected, it also means that evidence collected by the police in their interviews could be deemed inadmissible in court.

**Investigator Bias** The second problem with the Reid model of interrogation occurs during the actual interrogation and results from the fact that when the police begin their interrogation they already believe the suspect to be guilty. The problem here is that when people form a belief about something before they enter a situation, they often unknowingly seek out and interpret information in that situation in a way that verifies their initial belief. A study by Kassin et al. (2003) demonstrates some of the potential dangers that can result from this particular form of **investigator bias**.

In a mock interrogation study, the researchers had students act as interrogators or suspects. Some of the interrogators were led to believe that the suspect was guilty of a mock crime (finding a hidden key and stealing $100 from a locked cabinet), while others were led to believe that the suspect was innocent. In reality, some of the suspects were guilty of the mock crime whereas others were innocent. Interrogators were instructed to devise an interrogation strategy to use on the suspects, and the suspects were told to deny any involvement in the crime and to convince the interrogator of their innocence. The interrogation was taped, and a group of neutral observers then listened to the recording and were asked questions about the interrogator and the suspect.

A number of important results emerged from this study:

1. Interrogators with guilty expectations asked more questions that indicated their belief in the suspect's guilt. For example, they would ask, "How did you find the key that was hidden behind the DVD player?" instead of "Do you know anything about the key that was hidden behind the DVD player?"

2. Interrogators with guilty expectations used a higher frequency of interrogation techniques compared with interrogators with innocent expectations, especially at the outset of the interrogation.

3. Interrogators with guilty expectations judged more suspects to be guilty, regardless of whether the suspect was actually guilty.

4. Interrogators indicated that they exerted more pressure on suspects to confess when, unbeknownst to them, the suspect was innocent.

**Investigator bias:** Bias that can result when police officers enter an interrogation setting already believing that the suspect is guilty

5. Suspects had fairly accurate perceptions of interrogator behaviour (i.e., innocent suspects believed their interrogators were exerting more pressure).

6. Neutral observers viewed interrogators with guilty expectations as more coercive, especially against innocent suspects, and they viewed suspects in the guilty expectation condition as more defensive.

In sum, these findings indicate that investigative biases led to coercive interrogations that caused suspects to appear more guilty (to both the interrogator and neutral observers), even when the suspect had committed no crime.

## Interrogation Practices and the Courts

The decision to admit confession evidence into court rests on the shoulders of the trial judge. Within North America, the key issues a judge must consider when faced with a questionable confession are whether the confession was made voluntarily and whether the defendant was competent when he or she provided the confession (Wakefield & Underwager, 1998). The reason for using these criteria is that involuntary confessions and confessions provided when a person's mind is unstable are more likely to be unreliable.

What is meant by "voluntary" and "competent" is not always clear, which is why debate continues over the issue. What does seem clear, however, is that confessions resulting from overt forms of coercion will not be admitted in court. As Kassin (1997) states, "A confession is typically excluded if it was elicited by brute force; prolonged isolation; deprivation of food or sleep; threats of harm or punishment; promises of immunity or leniency; or, barring exceptional circumstances, without notifying the suspect of his or her constitutional rights" (p. 221).

Conversely, confessions that result from more subtle forms of psychological coercion are regularly admitted into court, in both Canada and the United States. For example, in the Canadian case of *R. v. Oickle* (2000), Richard Oickle confessed to seven counts of arson occurring in and around Waterville, Nova Scotia, between 1994 and 1995. The confession was obtained after a police interrogation in which several questionable interrogation techniques were used. These tactics included exaggerating the infallibility of a polygraph exam, implying that psychiatric help would be provided if the defendant confessed, minimizing the seriousness of the crimes, and suggesting that a confession would spare Oickle's girlfriend from having to undergo a stressful interrogation. After considering whether Oickle's confession was voluntarily given, the trial judge deemed the confession admissible and convicted him on all counts. The Court of Appeal subsequently deemed the confession evidence inadmissible and entered an acquittal. On appeal before the Supreme Court of Canada, a ruling was handed down, which stated that Oickle's confession was properly admitted by the trial judge, and therefore his conviction should stand, despite the interrogation techniques employed by the police. So, if these sorts of interrogation practices are condoned by the court, what sorts of practices are not? Box 3.2 provides a brief account of another recent Canadian case, *R. v. Hoilett* (1999), in which the Ontario Court of Appeal did rule that the defendant's confession was involuntary and therefore should not have been admitted at his trial. This ruling gives some indication as to how far Canadian police officers can go with their coercive interrogation tactics before the courts consider that the police have gone too far.

Box 3.2

# When the Police Go Too Far: The Case of *R. v. Hoilett* (1999)

Hoilett was arrested for sexual assault in Toronto at 11:25 p.m. on November 28, 1997. At the time of his arrest, Hoilett was under the influence of alcohol and crack cocaine. He was taken to the police station and placed in a cell. At 1:24 a.m. on November 29, police officers came to Hoilett's cell to remove his clothing in order for them to be forensically examined. All his clothing was taken, including his underwear, shoes, and socks, and he was left naked in his cell with just a metal bed to sit on for one-and-a-half hours.

At 3:06 a.m., Hoilett was awakened and given some light clothes, but no underwear, and shoes that did not fit. When he asked for a tissue to wipe his nose, the police officers did not provide him with one. Hoilett was then taken from his cell to be interrogated. The interviewing officer was aware that Hoilett had consumed alcohol and crack cocaine that evening but believed the suspect was not impaired during the interrogation, only tired, which was why he kept nodding off. Although Hoilett was detained and under arrest, the interviewing officer testified that "the reason he proceeded with the interview at that hour . . . was because he was not sure he would have another opportunity to do so" (*R. v. Hoilett*, 1999, para. 5).

Hoilett made an incriminating statement to the police at this time, and the trial judge ruled that the statement was made voluntarily and knowingly and, therefore, it was admissible. In his ruling, the trial judge recognized and openly disapproved of the inhumane conduct demonstrated by the police in this case. However, the judge concluded that this treatment did not affect the free will of the defendant, and Hoilett was convicted on one count of sexual assault.

On appeal before the Ontario Court of Appeal, the court pointed out that, in reaching his conclusion that Hoilett's confession was voluntary, "the trial judge made no reference to . . . the accused's testimony where he said that his decision to speak was influenced by how cold he was and that he needed a tissue, and that the officers suggested these things could be made available to him after the interrogation" (para. 23). The Court of Appeal went on to state that "virtually everyone would have their . . . will to say no to the police significantly influenced by . . . receiving inhumane treatment . . ." (para. 25).

Referring to whether Hoilett was competent at the time he made his statement, the Court of Appeal added that there was substantial evidence that he was not (e.g., Hoilett was awakened and interviewed at 3:06 a.m., he stated he was tired, and on several occasions the interrogators had to ask him whether he was awake).

As a result of their findings, the Ontario Court of Appeal reversed the decision of the trial judge, ruled that the statement of the accused was involuntary, and ordered that a new trial be held.

## An Alternative to the Reid Model

Because of the potential problems that can result from using coercive interrogation tactics, police agencies in several countries have recently introduced changes to their procedures. Perhaps more than anywhere else, these changes have been most obvious in England and Wales, where courts have restricted the use of many techniques found in the Reid model of interrogation (Gudjonsson, 2003).

Over the last 20 years, police agencies in England and Wales have gone through several phases of change in an attempt to reduce oppressive interrogation practices. Currently, these agencies use the so-called PEACE model to guide their interrogations. PEACE is an acronym for *planning* and *preparation*, *engage* and *explain*, *account, closure*, and *evaluation*. According to Meissner and Russano (2003), this model provides an inquisitorial framework within which to conduct police interrogations (compared with the accusatorial framework used in the Reid model) and is based on an interview method known as conversation management, which encourages information gathering more than securing a confession.

In fact, police agencies in England and Wales have all but abandoned the term *interrogation* in favour of *investigative interviewing* to get away from the negative connotations associated with North American–style interrogation practices. Although little research has been conducted to examine the impact of the PEACE model, some research indicates that a decrease in the use of coercive interrogation tactics does not necessarily result in a substantial reduction in the number of confessions that can be obtained (Meissner & Russano, 2003). For example, one analysis shows that approximately 50% of all suspects confessed to crimes before and after the PEACE model was introduced (Milne & Bull, 1999).

Recently, a call has been made by Canadian researchers to replace the Reid model of interrogation that is typically taught in Canada with the PEACE model (Snook et al., 2010). While one police force (the Royal Newfoundland Constabulary) has committed to reforming its interrogation practices, it is still too early to know if the PEACE model will be incorporated into Canadian policing as it has been in England and Wales.

## FALSE CONFESSIONS

Perhaps the biggest problem that people have with the use of coercive interrogation tactics is that these techniques can contribute to the likelihood of suspects making **false confessions** (Kassin & Gudjonsson, 2004; Kassin, 2008). False confessions can be defined in a number of ways. However, Ofshe (1989) provides a definition that appears to be well accepted. He suggests that a confession should be considered false "if it is elicited in response to a demand for a confession and is either intentionally fabricated or is not based on actual knowledge of the facts that form its content" (p. 13). When false confessions do occur, they should be taken seriously, especially considering the weight that juries put on confessions when determining the guilt or innocence of a defendant (Kassin & Sukel, 1997). Research indicates that when people have been wrongfully convicted of a crime, a false confession is often to blame. For example, Scheck, Neufeld, and Dwyer (2000) discovered that, in the 70 cases of wrongful convictions they examined, 21% included confession evidence that was later found to be false.

Before examining the extent of this problem, it is important to define two additional terms that are often confused with false confessions: **retracted confessions** and **disputed confessions**. Retracted confession consists of an individual declaring that the confession he or she made is false (regardless of whether it actually is) (Gudjonsson, 2003). Disputed confessions, however, are confessions that are disputed at trial, which does not necessarily mean the confession is false or that it was retracted. Instead, disputed confessions may arise because of legal technicalities, or because the suspect disputes the confession was ever made (Gudjonsson, 2003).

**False confession:** A confession that is either intentionally fabricated or is not based on actual knowledge of the facts that form its content

**Retracted confession:** A confession that the confessor later declares to be false

**Disputed confession:** A confession that is later disputed at trial

## The Frequency of False Confessions

Most researchers readily admit that no one knows how frequently false confessions are made. The major problem is that in most cases it is almost impossible to determine whether a confession is actually false. The fact that a confession is coerced does not mean the confession is false, just as a conviction based on confession evidence does not mean the confession is true (Kassin, 1997). As a result of this problem, researchers come up with drastically different estimates of how frequently false confessions occur. For example, the incidence of self-reported false confessions among prison inmates has been found to vary from 0.6% (Cassell, 1998) to 12% (Gudjonsson & Sigurdsson, 1994). Regardless of the exact number, most researchers believe there are enough cases to treat the issue very seriously.

## Different Types of False Confessions

One thing researchers do agree on is that there are different types of false confessions. While several different typologies exist for classifying false confessions (e.g., Gudjonsson, 2003; McCann, 1998), the most common typology still appears to be the one proposed by Kassin and Wrightsman (1985), which states that false confessions consist of voluntary false confessions, coerced-compliant false confessions, and coerced-internalized false confessions.

**Voluntary false confession:** A false confession that is provided without any elicitation from the police

**Voluntary False Confessions** Voluntary false confessions occur when someone voluntarily confesses to a crime he or she did not commit without any elicitation from the police. Research has indicated that people voluntarily false confess for a variety of reasons. For example, Gudjonsson (1992) suggests that such confessions may arise out of (1) a morbid desire for notoriety, (2) the person being unable to distinguish fact from fantasy, (3) the need to make up for pathological feelings of guilt by receiving punishment, or (4) a desire to protect somebody else from harm (which may be particularly prevalent among juveniles).

Although it may seem surprising, highly publicized cases do occasionally result in voluntary false confessions. Perhaps the most famous case was the kidnapping and murder of Charles Lindbergh's baby son. Charles Lindbergh was famous for being the first pilot to fly solo across the Atlantic Ocean in 1927. On March 1, 1932, Charles Lindbergh Jr., at the age of 20 months, was kidnapped. Two-and-a-half months later, the decomposed body of the baby was found with a fractured skull. It is estimated that some 200 people falsely confessed to the kidnapping and the murder (Note, 1953). In the end, only one man was convicted for the crime, a German immigrant named Bruno Richard Hauptman, who was executed for the crime in 1936, despite his repeated claims of being innocent. To this day, questions are still raised about Hauptman's guilt (e.g., Jones, 1997).

Another, more recent case involved the high profile voluntary false confession made by John Mark Karr to the unsolved 1996 murder of JonBenet Ramsey, the 6-year-old American beauty pageant queen. Karr was living in Thailand when he confessed to being with JonBenet when she died but claimed that her death was an accident (Aglionby, 2006). He was released to the U.S. authorities and returned to Boulder, Colorado, where the murder had taken place. Shortly after his arrival, prosecutors announced that they would not pursue charges against Karr because his version of events did not match details of the case and because his DNA did not match samples found at the scene (CNN, 2006). However, Karr was quickly extradited to California on several other child pornography charges.

**Coerced-compliant false confession:** A confession that results from a desire to escape a coercive interrogation environment or gain a benefit promised by the police

**Coerced-Compliant False Confessions** Coerced-compliant false confessions are those in which the suspect confesses to a crime, even though the suspect is fully aware that he or she did not commit it. This type of false confession is perhaps the most common (Gudjonsson & MacKeith, 1988). Unlike voluntary false confessions, these confessions are caused by the use of coercive interrogation tactics on the part of the police, such as the maximization techniques described earlier. Specifically, coerced-compliant confes-

A plea for help in the famous Lindbergh baby kidnapping case. It is estimated that 200 people falsely confessed to the kidnapping and murder of 20-month-old Charles Lindbergh, Jr.

# WANTED

## INFORMATION AS TO THE WHEREABOUTS OF

## CHAS. A. LINDBERGH, Jr.
### OF HOPEWELL, N. J.

## SON OF COL. CHAS. A. LINDBERGH
### World-Famous Aviator

**This child was kidnaped from his home in Hopewell, N. J., between 8 and 10 p. m. on Tuesday, March 1, 1932.**

### DESCRIPTION:

| | |
|---|---|
| Age, 20 months | Hair, blond, curly |
| Weight, 27 to 30 lbs. | Eyes, dark blue |
| Height, 29 inches | Complexion, light |

**Deep dimple in center of chin**
**Dressed in one-piece coverall night suit**

ADDRESS ALL COMMUNICATIONS TO
COL. H. N. SCHWARZKOPF, TRENTON, N. J., or
COL. CHAS. A. LINDBERGH, HOPEWELL, N. J.

ALL COMMUNICATIONS WILL BE TREATED IN CONFIDENCE

COL. H. NORMAN SCHWARZKOPF
Supt. New Jersey State Police, Trenton, N. J.

March 11, 1932

sions may be given so the suspect can (1) escape further interrogation, (2) gain a promised benefit, or (3) avoid a threatened punishment (Gudjonsson, 1992).

As with voluntary false confessions, there are a number of reported cases of coerced-compliant false confessions. For example, the 1993 movie *In the Name of the Father* starring Daniel Day-Lewis is based on such a case. Gerry Conlon, along with three other Irishmen, falsely confessed to bombing two pubs in Surrey, England, as a result of coercive police interrogations. The coercive tactics included making up false evidence and threatening to harm members of Conlon's family unless he confessed. Conlon and his acquaintances were subsequently convicted and sent to prison but were later released (Gudjonsson, 2003). Box 3.3 provides an example of a recent coerced-compliant false confession that occurred in Canada.

### Coerced-Internalized False Confessions
The third, and perhaps the most bizarre, type of false confession proposed by Kassin and Wrightsman (1985) is the **coerced-internalized false confession**. Here, individuals recall and confess to a crime they

**Coerced-internalized false confession:** A confession that results from suggestive interrogation techniques, whereby the confessor actually comes to believe he or she committed the crime

Box 3.3

# False Confession in a Child-Abuse Case

In the case *R. v. M.J.S.* (2000), M.J.S. was accused of aggravated assault on his baby son (J.S.) and, after supplying the police with a written confession, was charged with the crime. But was M.J.S. responsible for the crime, or was this a case of a coerced-compliant false confession?

J.S. was one to three months old at the time the abuse was supposed to have happened. The boy had been admitted to the hospital for a suspected chest infection and vomiting problems. While in the hospital, X-rays were taken, and it was later discovered that the baby had several rib fractures. The injuries were unusual for a baby so young, leading the baby's pediatrician to notify child welfare. The testimony of an expert suggested that the most likely cause of the fractures was that the baby was shaken.

A police investigation was begun. Both M.J.S and his wife cooperated with the police throughout the investigation. On four occasions, the police interrogated the accused. During these interrogations, the police used techniques similar to those used in the Reid model of interrogation, which eventually led the accused to confess. Fortunately, all the interrogations were videotaped, which provided the courts with a means to determine whether the confession was coerced.

Much of the interrogation consisted of developing various psychological themes to justify the crime. For example, one of the interrogating officers stated, "No doubt it was probably accidental on your part. . . . I don't believe it was intentional. . . . Children's bones are so fragile. . . . You made a mistake" (*R. v. M.J.S.*, para. 16). In addition, every time the accused denied his involvement in the crime, the officers interrupted with statements such as "We are beyond that point—we know you did it" (para. 19).

The officers also lied to the accused, stating they had talked to everyone else who might have been involved with the incident and cleared them all. This had not happened. Furthermore, the interviewing officers appealed to the accused's sense of honour and decency, and stressed how much better he would feel if he confessed. For example, one officer stated, "You'll be able to say to yourself . . . I'm going to sleep tonight, knowing that I told the truth" (para. 20). Still denying his involvement in any wrongdoing, the accused was presented with threatening statements. One interrogator stated, "If you run from this mistake, your family disintegrates, your family falls apart. . . . If you want your kids to be raised in a foster home, or adopted somewhere, that is a decision that you have to make" (para. 25).

In ruling on the confession evidence, the judge stated that the alleged confession in this case was extracted by threats and implied promises. The judge decided that the techniques employed by the investigators were coercive and that the accused confessed to the crime to escape the oppressive atmosphere created by the interrogations. The judge concluded by stating, "This case is a classic illustration of how slavish adherence to a technique can produce a coerced-compliant false 'apology' [confession] even from an accused who has denied 34 times that he did anything wrong when caring for his child" (para. 45). As a result of these findings, the confession evidence was deemed inadmissible.

did not commit, usually after they are exposed to highly suggestible questions, such as the minimization techniques described earlier in the chapter (Gudjonsson, 2003). In contrast to the coerced-compliant false confessor, however, these individuals actually end up believing they are responsible for the crime. According to Gudjonsson (1992), several vulnerability factors are associated with this type of false confession, including (1) a history of substance abuse or some other interference with brain function, (2) the inability of people to detect discrepancies between what they observed and what has been erroneously suggested to them, and (3) factors associated with mental state, such as severe anxiety, confusion, or feelings of guilt.

Perhaps the most frequently cited case of a false confession falls under the heading of a coerced-internalized false confession (Ofshe & Watters, 1994). The case involves Paul

Ingram, who, in 1988, was accused by his two adult daughters of committing crimes against them, crimes that included sexual assault, rape, and satanic ritual abuse that involved slaughtering newborn babies. As if some of these allegations were not strange enough, Ingram confessed to the crimes after initially being adamant he had never committed them. In addition, he was eventually able to recall the crimes in vivid detail despite originally claiming he could not remember ever abusing his daughters. Ingram ended up pleading guilty to six counts of rape and was sentenced to 20 years in prison. In prison, Ingram came to believe he was not guilty of the crimes he confessed to. After having initial appeals rejected, Ingram was released from prison on April 8, 2003.

Many people feel that Ingram falsely confessed to the crimes he was sentenced for. Supporters of this position typically draw on two related pieces of evidence (see Olio & Cornell, 1998, for evidence to the contrary). First, it is known that Ingram was exposed to highly suggestive interrogation techniques that have been shown to adversely influence people's memory of events. For example, over the course of five months, Ingram took part in 23 interrogations in which he was instructed (on some of these occasions) to visualize scenes of satanic cult activity that he could not remember (Wrightsman, 2001). Second, a psychologist hired to evaluate the case, Dr. Richard Ofshe from the University of California, concluded that Ingram had been brainwashed into believing he was responsible for the crimes (Ofshe & Watters, 1994). To demonstrate this belief, Ofshe conducted an experiment in which he presented Ingram with a fabricated scenario: that Ingram had forced his son and daughter to have sex together while he watched (Olio & Cornell, 1998). According to Olio and Cornell (1998), phase 1 of the experiment consisted of Ofshe asking Ingram if he could remember the incident (Ingram indicated that he could not). Ofshe then instructed Ingram to use the same visualization techniques he had used during his previous interview sessions. The next day, Ingram informed Ofshe he could now remember the incident and he produced a written confession providing details of his involvement. In phase 2 of the experiment, Ofshe pressured Ingram to retract his confession, but Ingram was not willing to do so.

## Studying False Confessions in the Lab

It is obviously difficult to study if, and how, false confessions occur. Even in the research laboratory it is not an easy task because of obvious ethical constraints (Kassin & Kiechel, 1996). Nowadays, no university ethics committee would allow research participants to be led to believe they had committed crimes of the sort that Paul Ingram was accused of. As a result, researchers have attempted to develop innovative laboratory paradigms that allow them to study the processes that may cause false confessions to occur without putting their participants at risk. One such paradigm was proposed by Dr. Saul Kassin and his student.

In their classic study, Kassin and Kiechel (1996) tested whether individuals would confess to a crime they did not commit. They had participants take part in what they thought was a reaction time study. A co-conspirator read a list of letters out loud to a participant who had to type these letters into a computer. However, before each session began, the participant was warned that if he or she hit the ALT key on the keyboard while typing in the letters, all the data would be lost. Sixty seconds after beginning the task, the computer automatically crashed, which brought the head researcher into the lab with accusations that the participant had hit the key.

Kassin and Kiechel were specifically interested in how two factors would affect participant reactions to the allegations. Participant vulnerability (defined as the participant's

**Table 3.3** Compliance, Internalization, and Confabulation in Kassin and Kiechel's Study

| | No False Evidence (No Witness) | | False Evidence (Witness) | |
| --- | --- | --- | --- | --- |
| | *Not Vulnerable (Slow Pace)* | *Vulnerable (Fast Pace)* | *Not Vulnerable (Slow Pace)* | *Vulnerable (Fast Pace)* |
| Compliance | 35% | 65% | 89% | 100% |
| Internalization | 0% | 12% | 44% | 65% |
| Confabulation | 0% | 0% | 6% | 35% |

Source: Adapted from Kassin and Kiechel, 1996.

certainty concerning his or her own innocence) was manipulated by varying the speed that participants had to type. In the "not vulnerable" condition, letters were read at a rate of 43 letters per minute; in the "vulnerable" condition, letters were read at a rate of 67 letters per minute. The researchers also varied whether false evidence was presented. In the "no false evidence" condition, the co-conspirator stated she did not see what happened; in the "false evidence" condition, she stated she saw the participant hit the ALT key. The results from the study are presented in Table 3.3.

**Compliance:** A tendency to go along with demands made by people perceived to be in authority, even though the person may not agree with them

To measure the degree to which participants exhibited **compliance** with the allegations, the researchers presented each participant with a written confession and recorded how many participants signed it. As indicated in Table 3.3, many participants accepted responsibility for the crime despite the fact that they were innocent, particularly the vulnerable participants presented with false evidence. To measure the degree to which participants internalized their confession, the researchers recorded comments made by participants to another co-conspirator outside the lab who asked them what had happened. If the participant accepted blame for the crime, he or she was recorded as exhibiting **internalization**. Based on the results from this study, many participants also internalized their confession. Again, this was especially true for vulnerable participants presented with false evidence. Finally, to measure the degree to which participants made up details to fit with their confession, known as **confabulation**, the researchers brought the participant back into the lab, read the list of letters again, and asked the participant to try to reconstruct where things had gone wrong. Vulnerable participants presented with false evidence were once again found to be particularly susceptible to confabulation.

**Internalization:** The acceptance of guilt for an act, even if the person did not actually commit the act

**Confabulation:** The reporting of events that never actually occurred

Thus, Kassin and Kiechel's (1996) findings suggest that it is possible to demonstrate, under laboratory conditions, that people can admit to acts they are not responsible for and come to believe in their guilt to such a point that they can reconstruct details of an act that never occurred (Kassin & Kiechel, 1996). However, whether these findings can be generalized to actual police interrogations is unclear because the Kassin and Kiechel paradigm fails to capture a number of elements found in real-world interrogations: (1) while the participants in Kassin and Kiechel's study had nothing to lose if they couldn't convince others of their innocence, real suspects have much to lose if they are found guilty, (2) while all participants in the Kassin and Kiechel's study were actually innocent of the crime, all suspects in real interrogations aren't, and (3) while the participants in Kassin and Kiechel's study could have easily been confused about their guilt (they may have accidentally hit the key), real suspects typically aren't confused about their involvement in a crime (Russano, Meissner, Narchet, & Kassin, 2005).

Fortunately, more recent research is helping to clarify these issues (e.g., Horselenberg, Merckelbach, & Josephs, 2003; Russano et al., 2005). For example, Russano et al. (2005) dealt with these problems by devising a novel paradigm where only some of the participants were guilty of a crime (a crime which involved specific intent) and where a confession resulted in known consequences. Specifically, they paired participants with a confederate and were asked to solve a logic problem, either individually or jointly. In the guilty condition, "the confederate asked for help on a problem that was supposed to be solved individually. . . . Participants who provided an answer were guilty of cheating. In the innocent condition, the confederate did not make this request, and so participants did not violate the experimental rule" (p. 482).

To examine the impact of various interrogation strategies on confessions, participants in both the innocent and guilty conditions were either presented with minimization tactics (e.g., offered face-saving excuses for committing the crime) or no minimizing tactics. The offer of a deal was also manipulated across conditions. In the deal condition, participants were told that if they confessed, the consequences would be less severe than if they didn't. In the no-deal condition, the consequences were consistent regardless of whether the participant confessed.

The results were as expected. Guilty participants were much more likely to confess (71.6%) than innocent participants (20.3%). In addition, participants who were offered a deal were more likely to confess than participants who were not offered a deal. This was the case for both guilty participants (who exhibited a 26% increase in true confessions when a deal was offered) and innocent suspects (who exhibited an 8% increase in false confessions). Furthermore, participants were more likely to confess when minimization tactics were used than when they were not used. Again, this was the case for both guilty participants (who exhibited a 35% increase in true confessions when minimization tactics were used) and innocent suspects (who exhibited a 12% increase in false confessions). Finally, the largest increase in confession rates occurred when both tactics (i.e., minimization and deals) were used together. For example, compared to when no tactics were used, the use of both tactics led to a 41% increase in true confessions from guilty participants and a 37% increase in false confessions from innocent suspects.

## The Consequences of Falsely Confessing

False confessions cause problems for both the person making the false confession and the police agencies tasked with investigating the crime. The obvious problem that the person making the false confession faces is that, if the confession is admitted in court, the jury could convict the suspect for a crime he or she did not commit (Leo & Ofshe, 1998). Recent studies have shown that jurors might be likely to convict a suspect based on confession evidence even when the jurors are aware that the suspect's confession resulted from a coercive interrogation.

For example, in one study, Kassin and Sukel (1997) presented participants with transcripts of a mock murder trial. One group of participants received a transcript in which the defendant immediately confessed to the police during questioning (the low-pressure condition). A second group of participants received a transcript in which the defendant was coerced into confessing by having his hands handcuffed behind his back and by being threatened by the interrogator (the high-pressure condition). A third group of participants received a transcript in which the defendant never confessed to the murder (the control condition). The results of the study indicate that those participants presented with a confession obtained in the high-pressure condition recognized the confession was involuntary and said it would not affect their decisions. However, when actual verdicts were examined across the three groups, the presence of a confession was found to significantly increase the conviction rate, even for those participants in the high-pressure condition. Thus, not only can people be convicted of crimes they did not commit based on their false confession, but this can also happen even when the confession appears to have been obtained through coercive interrogation tactics.

A second, and less commonly recognized, consequence of false confessions involves the consequences for the police and, therefore, the public. When somebody makes a false confession, the police are diverted down a false trail that may waste valuable time, time that they could have used to identify and apprehend the real offender. Such was the case in both the Lindbergh kidnapping case and the Ramsey murder case, which were described above. Howitt (2002) also provides an example of this happening in the Yorkshire Ripper serial murder investigation that took place in England during the 1970s. At one point in the investigation, the police were sent several tape recordings supposedly from the Ripper himself. Howitt states that senior police officers on the case, believing the tapes to be genuine, used up valuable resources investigating the tapes. However, the tapes were not genuine, and these actions probably delayed the eventual arrest of Peter Sutcliffe and allowed further murders to take place.

Obviously the police have to be very concerned about false confessions and need to minimize the chance of them occurring. Read the scenario in the Case Study box and

## CASE STUDY YOU BE THE POLICE OFFICER

Edward Chen is a 42-year-old Chinese immigrant who has just been picked up by the police on suspicion of murdering Emily Jones, a 30-year-old nurse who was killed when coming home from a late shift at the hospital where she worked. Edward fits the suspect descriptions that were given by several eyewitnesses and he has no alibi for the night when the murder took place. He also has a criminal record, which consists of several drug charges. He denies knowing the victim and says he had nothing to do with the murder. When he is brought into the police station for questioning, he appears very anxious, shows potential signs of being slightly learning disabled, and does not speak fluent English.

### Your Turn . . .

As a police officer working on this case, what approach would you suggest be taken when interrogating Edward? What should be the primary goals of the interrogation? What would you be concerned with when developing the interrogation strategy? Would you be worried about Edward possibly confessing to the crime even if he didn't commit it? Why or why not? If you think a false confession is a possibility, what could you do to prevent this from happening?

determine what you could do to reduce the likelihood of the suspect falsely confessing to the crime he is being questioned for.

# CRIMINAL PROFILING

To conduct interrogations, police need to have a viable suspect in custody. In some instances, the identification of probable suspects is relatively straightforward, because in many crimes the victim and the offender know each other and there is often a clear motivation for the crime, such as passion, greed, or revenge. But what about those crimes in which it is more difficult to identify a suspect, crimes in which the victim and offender are strangers and there is no clear motive? In these cases, the police often rely on unconventional investigative techniques, such as criminal profiling.

## What Is a Criminal Profile?

Perhaps more than any other investigative technique, criminal profiling has caught the attention of the public, and Hollywood depictions of criminal profiling are common (as illustrated in the In the Media box). But what is criminal profiling in reality? There is no single definition of *criminal profiling* (Alison, Bennell, Mokros, & Ormerod, 2002). Indeed, there is even little agreement as to what the technique should be called (Wilson, Lincoln, & Kocsis, 1997). However, the definition proposed by John Douglas and his former colleagues from the Federal Bureau of Investigation (FBI) fairly accurately describes the procedure: **criminal profiling** is "a technique for identifying the major personality and behavioural characteristics of an individual based upon an analysis of the crimes he or she has committed" (Douglas, Ressler, Burgess, & Hartman, 1986, p. 405).

**Criminal profiling:** An investigative technique for identifying the major personality and behavioural characteristics of an individual based upon an analysis of the crimes he or she has committed

Although criminal profiling is now used in a range of contexts, it is most commonly used in cases of serial homicide and rape (Holmes & Holmes, 2002). In particular, profiling is thought to be most applicable in cases in which extreme forms of psychopathology are exhibited by the offender, including sadistic torture and ritualistic behaviour (Geberth, 1990). Criminal profiling was originally intended to help the police identify the criminal in these sorts of cases, either by narrowing down a list of suspects or by providing new lines of inquiry. However, criminal profiling is now used for a number of purposes, including the following (Homant & Kennedy, 1998):

- To help set traps to flush out an offender
- To determine whether a threatening note should be taken seriously
- To give advice on how best to interrogate a suspect
- To tell prosecutors how to break down defendants in cross-examination

Although every criminal profile will undoubtedly be different in terms of the information it contains, some of the most common personality and behavioural characteristics that profilers try to predict include the offender's age, sex, race, level of intelligence, educational history, hobbies, family background, residential location, criminal history, employment status, psychosexual development, and post-offence behaviour (Holmes & Holmes, 2002). Often these predictions are made by forensic psychologists and psychiatrists who have either clinical or research experience with offenders (Wilson et al., 1997). In North America, however, the majority of profilers are experienced and specially trained law enforcement officers (Rossmo, 2000).

# Hollywood Depictions of Criminal Profiling

Countless television shows and films have profiling built into their plots, and there seems to be no end in sight to Hollywood portrayals of this topic. We are often asked by students about these media depictions: "Do profilers like this actually exist?" "Can they actually do in real life what they are seen to do on the screen?" And most often, "what do I need to do to get that kind of job?"

We are sometimes tempted to tell these students that these shows are all fake—after all, the chance of gaining full-time employment as a profiler is very small. However, the truth is that these shows are not entirely fake, even though many aspects of them are. Indeed, audiences have become too smart, and too demanding, for Hollywood to pull the wool over their eyes entirely. Audiences require a degree of realism in these shows to stay interested, although we also need to have directors spice things up a bit.

In fact, audiences have gotten so demanding that it is now common practice to have researchers attached to these shows and to even hire technical consultants (real-life profilers) who help make the shows appear more realistic. These individuals provide information about what terms to use, what places to go to, and what names to drop so that there is a ring of truth to what the actors are saying and doing. It is then up to Hollywood to make this all sound (and look) sexy so that the audience keeps coming back for more.

Consider the following examples:

### The Silence of the Lambs

Adapted from Thomas Harris's book, *The Silence of the Lambs,* much of this movie is set in Quantico, VA, where the FBI's Investigative Support Unit (ISU) actually resides. In addition, parts of this film were largely based on the work of John Douglas, previous chief of the ISU. Indeed, Scott Glenn's character (Jack Crawford) was largely modelled after Douglas and Douglas served as a technical consultant on the film (Douglas, 2010). The serial killer depicted in the movie, Buffalo Bill, was also based loosely on a real-life killer. In particular, many of the things that Buffalo Bill did, such as the skinning of bodies, resemble the crimes of Ed Gein, a Wisconsin man who was a frequent grave robber. Interestingly, on some DVD versions of this film, Douglas provides a commentary informing the audience as to what parts of the movie are real and what parts are fake.

### Numb3rs

The first episode of *Numb3rs* was broadcast on January 23, 2005. In that show, an FBI agent recruits his brother Charlie, who happens to be a mathematical genius, to help solve challenging crimes. One of the problems encountered in the first episode is to identify the residential location of an offender based on where he committed his crimes. Stumped, Charlie goes back to his university office and derives a formula for determining a "hot zone" where the offender is likely to live. The formula he writes on his blackboard was actually the work of Dr. Kim Rossmo, who is profiled in Box 3.5. Rossmo, a former detective, helped to develop the field of geographic profiling while a Ph.D. student at Simon Fraser University (Devlin & Lorden, 2007).

## The Origins of Criminal Profiling

Criminal profiling is usually thought to have been developed by agents from the FBI in the 1970s. However, there are numerous examples of profiling techniques being used long before that time (Canter, 2000; Holmes & Holmes, 2002; Turvey, 2002; Woodworth & Porter, 2001). The investigation that you may be most familiar with is the famous case of Jack the Ripper (Harrison, 1993).

**Early Attempts at Criminal Profiling** In 1888, a series of murders were committed in the east end of London, around an area known as Whitechapel. The victims were all women, and all were mutilated by the offender. At one point, the unknown offender sent a letter to the newspapers, and at the end of it he signed his name, Jack the Ripper (Holmes & Holmes, 2002). A police surgeon involved with the investigation of the murders engaged in a form of criminal profiling. As Woodworth and Porter (2001, p. 244) reveal,

> Dr. George Phillips attempted to create a reconstruction of various crime scenes and describe the wounds of the victims for the purpose of gaining a greater insight into the offender's psychological make-up. In particular, Phillips believed that a circumspect examination of the wound patterns of murder victims could provide clues about both the behaviour and personality of the offender who committed the crimes.

This instance is probably one of the first times that criminal profiling was used in a criminal investigation. Unfortunately, it assisted little, evidenced by the fact that we still have no idea who Jack the Ripper actually was.

Another well-known case, often cited as an example of how accurate some profilers can be, is the case of New York City's Mad Bomber. Starting in 1940, an unknown offender began detonating bombs in public places around New York (Wrightsman, 2001). Stumped, the New York City Police Department turned to a local forensic psychiatrist, Dr. James Brussel, for help with the case. By examining the actions of the bomber, Brussel began to develop a profile of the unknown offender. Dr. Brussel's profile included characteristics such as the following: the offender would be a middle-aged male, he would suffer from paranoia, he would be pathologically self-centred, he would be reasonably educated, he would be unmarried and possibly a virgin, he would be Roman Catholic, and he would wear buttoned-up double-breasted suits (Turvey, 2002). In 1957, almost 17 years after the bombings started, the police finally arrested George Metesky. Metesky fit most of the characteristics that Dr. Brussel had profiled, even down to the double-breasted suit he wore to the police station (Holmes & Holmes, 2002). Metesky was subsequently sent to a mental institution for the criminally insane. He was released in 1973 and died in 1994.

**The FBI and Beyond** The next big milestone in the history of criminal profiling was the development of a criminal profiling program at the FBI in the 1970s (Turvey, 2002). Not only was this the first time that profiles were produced in a systematic way by a law enforcement agency, but it was also the first time that training was provided in how to construct criminal profiles. Subsequent to the development of the FBI's Behavioral Sciences Unit in 1972, the National Center for the Analysis of Violent Crime was opened for the purpose of conducting research in the area of criminal profiling and providing formal guidance to police agencies around the United States that were investigating serial crimes, serial murder in particular. Similar units have now sprung up in police agencies around the world, including Canada, Germany, and England. These outfits typically provide operational support to police agencies in cases in which profiling may be useful, and many conduct their own research into criminal profiling. See Box 3.4 for an example of how the RCMP has been moving the criminal profiling field forward.

**Investigative Psychology** Since the early 1990s, some of the most important advances in the area of criminal profiling have been made by David Canter, the founder of a relatively new field of psychology that he has named *investigative psychology*. The origins of this field can be traced back to Canter's involvement in the John Duffy (a.k.a., Railway Rapist) rape/murder case. Canter was called in by Scotland Yard to provide a profile of the unknown offender, and in doing so, he drew on his knowledge of human behaviour that he had gained as an academic psychologist (especially in the area of environmental

Box 3.4

## The RCMP's Violent Crime Linkage Analysis System (VICLAS)

In recent years, the RCMP has played a pivotal role in developing the field of criminal profiling. In large part, it has been able to do this by drawing on the best of modern computer technology. One of the RCMP's most significant advances has been the development in the mid-1990s of an automated system for linking serial crimes, the Violent Crime Linkage Analysis System, or **VICLAS** (Martineau & Corey, 2008). One of the biggest problems the police encounter when they are faced with a possible crime series is **linkage blindness**, which refers to an inability on the part of the police to link geographically dispersed serial crimes committed by the same offender because of a lack of communication among police agencies (Egger, 2002). VICLAS was developed, in part, to prevent such linkage blindness.

The backbone of VICLAS is a booklet that police officers fill out. The questions in this booklet are supposed to capture crucial behavioural information on crimes of a serious nature. These crimes include motiveless homicides, sexual assaults, missing persons, and nonparental abductions (Collins, Johnson, Choy, Davidson, & Mackay, 1998). The booklet contains more than a hundred questions about the offender's behaviour, the victim, and any available forensic information. This information is then entered into a computer and downloaded into a centralized database where it is carefully compared with other crimes. Specially trained VICLAS analysts determine if there are any possible crime linkages. If any potential links are identified, then the crimes are highlighted as a series and the relevant police agencies are notified and encouraged to share information (Collins et al., 1998).

According to Woodworth and Porter (2001), as of 2000, "there were more than 30 000 cases in the system, and although there are no official statistics on its success rate, there were 3200 known linkages" (p. 253). These results, in addition to anecdotal evidence that suggests the system holds promise, have earned VICLAS a reputation as one of the best crime linkage analysis systems in existence (Collins et al., 1998). Police from around the world, including agencies in England, Australia, and Germany, are currently using VICLAS to help to identify serial crimes.

**VICLAS:** The Violent Crime Linkage Analysis System, which was developed by the RCMP to collect and analyze information on serious crimes from across Canada

**Linkage blindness:** An inability on the part of the police to link geographically dispersed serial crimes committed by the same offender because of a lack of information sharing among police agencies

psychology) (Canter, 1994). Since that early successful contribution, Canter and his colleagues have spent the last 20 years developing the field of profiling into a scientific practice. These individuals have also made countless contributions to other areas of investigative psychology (Canter & Youngs, 2009).

## How Is a Criminal Profile Constructed?

Profiles are constructed differently by different profilers. In fact, different "schools" of profiling now exist that guide the profile construction process (Hicks & Sales, 2006). However, regardless of what approach is taken to generate a profile, relatively little is known about the profiling process. While some individuals have attempted to change this (e.g., Canter, 2000), such attempts are not common. Indeed, the descriptions of the profiling process provided by many researchers and profilers are incredibly vague.

For example, in a now-classic study of criminal profiling, Pinizzotto and Finkel (1990) describe the process of profiling as an equation in the form: WHAT + WHY = WHO. The WHAT of the crime refers to the material that profilers collect at the start of an investigation, such as crime-scene photos, autopsy reports, and descriptions of victims. The WHY of the crime refers to the motivation for the crime and each crime scene behaviour. The WHO of the crime refers to the actual profile that is eventually constructed once the WHAT and the WHY components have been determined. Although this conceptual model may make sense at a general level, it is clearly too vague to be useful.

As Pinizzotto and Finkel (1990) themselves point out, the model "does not tell us precisely how . . . the profiler gets from the WHAT to the WHY, or from the WHY to the WHO" (p. 217).

Other conceptual models have also been produced, particularly by profilers at the FBI (e.g., Douglas & Burgess, 1986), but these models also lack the specificity required to truly understand the profiling process. Part of the problem with providing such detail is that profiling is still viewed primarily as an art, not a science. Although some are making an effort to change this (see Hicks & Sales, 2006, for a review), profiling is currently based to a large extent on the profiler's experience and intuition (Douglas & Olshaker, 1995). As a result, asking profilers to provide specific details of how they construct profiles may be similar to asking Picasso to explain how he painted.

## Different Types of Profiling Methods

Although it is not clear how criminal profilers construct their profiles, it is evident that they can draw on different types of profiling methods (Hicks & Sales, 2006). Specifically, profilers can use two approaches: the deductive profiling method and the inductive profiling method. **Deductive criminal profiling** involves the prediction of an offender's background characteristics generated from a thorough analysis of the evidence left at the crime scenes by that particular offender (Holmes & Holmes, 2002). This method largely relies on logical reasoning, as indicated in an example provided by Canter (2000) in which the victim of an unidentified assailant noticed that the offender had short fingernails on his right hand and long fingernails on his left hand. According to Canter, "Somebody with specialist knowledge suggested that this was a characteristic of people who are serious guitar players. It was therefore a reasonable deduction that the assailant was somebody who played the guitar" (p. 24). The primary disadvantage of this profiling method is that the underlying logic of the argument can sometimes be faulty. Take the prediction we just described. Although the argument appears to be logical, it is in fact wrong. The offender in this case did not play the guitar at all. Instead, the reason he had short fingernails on his right hand was that he had a job repairing old tires.

In contrast to deductive profiling, **inductive criminal profiling** involves the prediction of an offender's background characteristics generated from a comparison of that particular offender's crimes with similar crimes committed by other, known offenders. This method is based on the premise that "if certain crimes committed by different people are similar, then the offenders must also share some common personality traits" (Holmes & Holmes, 2002, p. 5). The inductive method of profiling relies largely on a determination of how likely it is an offender will possess certain background characteristics given the prevalence of these characteristics among known offenders who have committed similar crimes. An example of the inductive profiling method is provided by Aitken et al. (1996), who developed a statistical profile of a murderer of children. Based on their analysis of similar crimes committed by known offenders, they predicted that there was a probability of 0.96 that the offender would know the victim, a probability of 0.92 that the offender would have a previous criminal conviction, a probability of 0.91 that the offender would be single, a probability of 0.79 that the offender would live within 8 kilometres of the crime scene, and a probability of 0.65 that the offender would be under the age of 20. In this case, the profile turned out to be very accurate.

**Deductive criminal profiling:** Profiling the background characteristics of an unknown offender based on evidence left at the crime scenes by that particular offender

**Inductive criminal profiling:** Profiling the background characteristics of an unknown offender based on what we know about other solved cases

The Psychology of Police Investigations  **79**

**Table 3.4** Organized and Disorganized Crime Scene Behaviours

| Organized Behaviours | Disorganized Behaviours |
|---|---|
| Planned offence | Spontaneous offence |
| Use of restraints on the victim | No restraints used on the victim |
| Ante-mortem sexual acts committed | Post-mortem sexual acts committed |
| Use of a vehicle in the crime | No use of a vehicle in the crime |
| No post-mortem mutilation | Post-mortem mutilation |
| Corpse not taken | Corpse (or body parts) taken |
| Little evidence left at the scene | Evidence left at the scene |

Source: Adapted from Ressler et al., 1986.

In contrast to deductive profiling, the major problem with the inductive method of profiling is with sampling issues (Turvey, 2002). The key problem is that it will never be possible to have a representative sample of serial offenders from which to draw profiling conclusions. That is, if we encounter a serial crime with behaviours A, B, and C, but no crimes in our database have behaviours A, B, and C, how do we construct an accurate profile?

**The Organized-Disorganized Model** Many profilers today use an inductive profiling approach developed by the FBI in the 1980s. This model was developed largely through interviews with incarcerated offenders and has come to be called the **organized-disorganized model** (Hazelwood & Douglas, 1980). The model suggests that an offender's crime scene can be classified as either organized or disorganized (see Table 3.4). Organized crime scene behaviours reflect a well-planned and controlled crime, while disorganized behaviours reflect an impulsive crime, which is chaotic in nature. Similarly, an offender's background can be classified as either organized or disorganized (see Table 3.5). Organized background characteristics reflect a methodical individual, while disorganized characteristics reflect a disturbed individual, who is usually suffering from some form of

**Organized-disorganized model:** A profiling model used by the FBI that assumes the crime scenes and backgrounds of serial offenders can be categorized as *organized* or *disorganized*

**Table 3.5** Organized and Disorganized Background Characteristics

| Organized Behaviours | Disorganized Behaviours |
|---|---|
| High intelligence | Low intelligence |
| Skilled occupation | Unskilled occupation |
| Sexually adequate | Sexually inadequate |
| Lives with a partner | Lives alone |
| Geographically mobile | Geographically stable |
| Lives and works far away from crimes | Lives and works close to crimes |
| Follows crimes in media | Little interest in media |
| Maintains residence and vehicle | Does not maintain residence and vehicle |

Source: Adapted from Ressler et al., 1986.

psychopathology. The basic idea is that, when encountering a disorganized crime scene, the investigator should profile the background characteristics of a disorganized offender, and likewise for organized crime scenes and organized background characteristics. Although little research has examined whether the organized-disorganized model actually works, the research that does exist raises serious doubts (e.g., Canter, Alison, Alison, & Wentink, 2004). Indeed, even the FBI has refined this model to account for the many offenders who display mixtures of organized and disorganized features (Douglas, Burgess, Burgess, & Ressler, 1992).

## The Validity of Criminal Profiling

Because profiling is used by the police, it is important to consider whether the technique is actually reliable and valid. Profilers certainly claim that they have experienced much success with their profiles (Woodworth & Porter, 2001), and it appears that police officers hold generally positive (although somewhat cautious) views of profiling (e.g., Copson, 1995; Jackson, van Koppen, & Herbrink, 1993; Snook, Haines, Taylor, & Bennell, 2007; Trager & Brewster, 2001). For example, Snook et al. (2007) found that the majority of Canadian police officers they surveyed felt that profiling is a valuable investigative tool that can help to solve cases and further an investigator's understanding of a case. However, these officers also recognized the limitations of profiling, indicating that it shouldn't be used as evidence in court, that it shouldn't be used for all types of crimes, and that it does have the potential to seriously mislead an investigation. There is also some, albeit very limited, empirical evidence for the basic assumptions underlying criminal profiling. For example, in a recent review of the profiling field, Alison, Goodwill, Almond, van den Heuvel, and Winter (2010) show that, under limited conditions, it is possible to use certain crime scene behaviours to predict certain background characteristics of serial offenders.

Despite these findings indicating that criminal profiling may be useful, the practice is still often criticized. Three criticisms in particular have received attention from researchers:

1. Many forms of profiling are based on a theoretical model of personality that lacks strong empirical support.

2. Many profiles contain information that is so vague and ambiguous they can potentially fit many suspects.

3. Professional profilers may be no better than untrained individuals at constructing accurate criminal profiles.

Let's now look at each of these criticisms in turn.

**Does Profiling Have a Strong Theoretical Base?** There seems to be general agreement that most forms of profiling, including the FBI's organized-disorganized approach, rely on a **classic trait model** of personality that was popular in psychology before the 1970s (Alison et al., 2002). In this model, the primary determinants of behaviour are stable, internal traits (Mischel, 1968). These traits are assumed to result in the expression of consistent patterns of behaviour over time and across situations. In the criminal context, this consistency is thought to persist across an offender's crimes and into the offender's noncriminal lifestyle, thus allowing him or her to be accurately profiled (Homant & Kennedy, 1998). Thus, an offender characterized by a trait of "organization"

**Classic trait model:** A model of personality that assumes the primary determinants of behaviour are stable, internal traits

is expected to exhibit organized behaviours across his or her crimes (e.g., the offender will consistently plan the crimes, use restraints, and use weapons), as well as in his or her non-criminal life (e.g., the offender will be highly intelligent, sexually adequate, and geographically mobile) (Alison et al., 2002).

Although some researchers believe this classic trait model provides a solid basis for criminal profiling (e.g., Homant & Kennedy, 1998), other researchers disagree (e.g., Alison et al., 2002). Those who disagree draw on research from the field of personality psychology, which demonstrates that traits are not the only (or even primary) determinant of behaviour (Cervone & Shoda, 1999). Rather, situational influences are also known to be very important in shaping our behaviour, and some researchers argue that there is no reason to suspect that serial offenders will be any different (Bennell & Canter, 2002; Bennell & Jones, 2005). From a profiling perspective, the impact of various situational factors (e.g., an extremely resistant victim, an interruption during a crime, or a bad day at work) may create behavioural inconsistencies across an offender's crimes, and between different aspects of his or her life, making it very difficult to create an accurate profile.

Those who believe the classic trait model forms a strong basis for criminal profiling also acknowledge the "checkered past" that this model has experienced (e.g., Homant & Kennedy, 1998). However, these individuals refer to instances in which behavioural consistency has been found in the noncriminal context and highlight the fact that higher levels of behavioural consistency typically emerge when we examine pathological populations (Pinizzotto & Finkel, 1990). Assuming that most serial offenders do in fact fall into this pathological population, these supporters argue that the level of behavioural consistency that they express may be adequate to develop accurate criminal profiles. Clearly, more empirical research dealing with this issue is required before any firm conclusions can be made. Until then, the debate over the validity of criminal profiling will continue.

**What Is the Impact of Ambiguous Profiles?** Another common criticism of criminal profiling is that many profiles are so ambiguous that they can fit many suspects. If one of the goals of profiling is to help to prioritize potential suspects, this concern clearly needs to be addressed. To examine this issue, Alison, Smith, Eastman, and Rainbow (2003) examined the content of 21 profiling reports and found that almost a quarter (24%) of all the profiling opinions provided in these reports could be considered ambiguous (i.e., the opinion could be interpreted differently by different people). Of more direct relevance to the ambiguity criticism, however, is an interesting follow-up study conducted by Alison, Smith, and Morgan (2003), in which they examined whether ambiguous profiles could in fact be interpreted to fit more than one suspect.

Alison et al. (2003) provided details of a genuine crime to two groups of forensic professionals, including senior detectives. The crime involved the murder of a young woman. Each group of participants was then provided with a criminal profile constructed for this case by the FBI. They were asked to read the profile and compare it with the description of a suspect. Unbeknownst to the participants, each group was provided with a different suspect description. One group was provided with the description of the genuine offender, while the other group was provided with a suspect constructed by the researchers, who was different from the genuine offender on a number of key points. After comparing the profile with their suspect, each participant was asked to rate the accuracy of the profile and to state if (and why) he or she thought the profile would be operationally useful. Despite the fact that each group received different suspect descriptions, both groups of participants rated the profile as fairly accurate, with no significant difference between the groups. In addition, both groups viewed the profile as generally useful and indicated they thought it would allow the police to narrow down the list of potential suspects and develop new lines of inquiry. This study, therefore, provides preliminary support for the criticism that ambiguous profiles can in fact be interpreted to fit more than one suspect, even when those suspects are quite different from each other.

Although such a finding could have serious implications, we must be careful when interpreting these results. For example, it would be important to know how closely the profile used in this study matches the typical criminal profile provided in the field. In addition, it should be emphasized that this study is far from realistic in that the crime scene details and suspect descriptions provided to the participants in this study contained much less information than would be the case in an actual police investigation. Also of note is a more recent study, which showed that a more up-to-date sample of profiles did not contain the same degree of ambiguity (13% instead of 24%; Almond, Alison, & Porter, 2007). This result suggests that in certain jurisdictions at least this potential problem may be waning.

**How Accurate Are Professional Profilers?** The last criticism that we will deal with here is the possibility that professional profilers may be no more accurate in their profiling predictions than individuals who have received no specialized training. In early writings on criminal profiling, claims were even made that profilers may be no better than bartenders at predicting the characteristics of unknown offenders (Campbell, 1976). If this is in fact the case, the police must consider how much weight they will put on statements made by professional profilers. Unlike the previous two criticisms, this issue has been examined on numerous occasions and the results have been mixed (Kocsis, 2003; Pinizzotto & Finkel, 1990). In other words, profilers are sometimes found to be more accurate than other groups when asked to construct profiles under laboratory conditions, but at other times they are found to be no more accurate.

In a fairly representative study, Kocsis, Irwin, Hayes, and Nunn (2000) compared profile accuracy across five groups of individuals: profilers, psychologists, police officers, students, and psychics. All participants were provided with the details of a genuine crime, which they were asked to review. The participants were then given a series of questionnaires that dealt with various aspects of the offender's background, including his or her physical characteristics, cognitions related to the offence, pre- and post-offence behaviours, social history, and personality characteristics. The participants' task with these questionnaires was to select the alternatives that best described the unknown offender. Accuracy was determined for each group by comparing the responses from the participants with the correct answers. The results from this study are presented in Table 3.6, which indicates the mean number of questions that each group got correct for each subset of characteristics.

As you can see from this table, professional profilers were the most accurate when it came to profiling cognitive processes (e.g., degree of planning) and social history (e.g., marital status). Therefore, they have received the highest total accuracy score, which is an aggregate score for all subsets of characteristics, excluding personality predictions. On

**Table 3.6** Comparing Profilers, Psychologists, Police Officers, Students, and Psychics[*]

| Measure | Profilers | Psychologists | Police | Students | Psychics |
|---|---|---|---|---|---|
| Cognitions | 3.20 | 2.27 | 2.49 | 2.03 | 2.60 |
| Physical | 3.60 | 3.63 | 3.43 | 3.42 | 2.80 |
| Offence | 4.00 | 4.03 | 3.09 | 3.64 | 3.65 |
| Social | 3.00 | 2.63 | 2.60 | 2.94 | 2.25 |
| Total | 13.80 | 12.57 | 11.60 | 12.03 | 11.30 |
| Personality | 24.60 | 34.03 | 22.03 | 26.84 | 27.70 |

[*]Numbers refer to the mean number of correct questions. The number of correct questions that participants could have predicted was 7 for cognitions, 6 for physical characteristics, 7 for offence behaviours, and 10 for social history (total accuracy is, therefore, out of 30). Kocsis and colleagues did not provide information relating to the total number of correct predictions for personality characteristics.

Source: Adapted from Kocsis et al., 2000.

the other hand, psychologists were the most accurate when it came to profiling physical characteristics (e.g., offender age), offence behaviours (e.g., degree of control), and personality features (e.g., temperament). When the results of the four nonprofiler groups were combined, Kocsis et al. found that the combined score of the nonprofiler groups was lower than the profilers, leading them to conclude that "the collective skills of profilers are superior to the individual skills represented by each of the comparison groups" (p. 325). This result has recently been endorsed by other researchers who have reanalyzed the data by using sophisticated statistical techniques (Snook, Eastwood, Gendreau, Goggin, & Cullen, 2007). However, given the preliminary nature of these sorts of studies, the marginal accuracy differences between groups, and the artificial conditions under which these studies are conducted, it seems likely that the debate over whether professional profilers can provide more accurate profiles than untrained individuals will continue (Bennell, Jones, Taylor, & Snook, 2006).

# GEOGRAPHIC PROFILING

**Geographic profiling:** An investigative technique that uses crime scene locations to predict the most likely area where an offender resides

In addition to criminal profiling, another form of profiling is commonly used by the police: **geographic profiling**. In simple terms, geographic profiling uses crime scene locations to predict the most likely area where the offender resides (Rossmo, 2000). As is the case with criminal profiling, geographic profiling is used most often in cases of serial homicide and rape, though it has also been used in cases of serial robbery, arson, and burglary. Geographic profiling is used primarily for prioritizing potential suspects. This prioritization is accomplished by rank ordering the suspects based on how close they live to the predicted home location, so the suspect who lives closest to the predicted home location would be focused on first (Rossmo, 2000). This task is important, considering the number of suspects who can enter a serial crime investigation. For example, in the Green River serial murder case in Washington State, which was solved in 2001, the police collected more than 18 000 suspect names (Rossmo, 1995).

The basic assumption behind geographic profiling is that most serial offenders do not travel far from home to commit their crimes and, therefore, it should be possible to make a reasonably accurate prediction about where an offender lives. Fortunately for the geographic profiler, research supports this assumption. Perhaps surprisingly, it turns out that serial offenders tend to be consistent in their crime site selection choices, often committing their crimes very close to where they reside (Rossmo, 2000). Indeed, even many of the most bizarre serial killers commit their crimes close to home (Canter, Coffey, Huntley, & Missen, 2000). For travelling offenders, particularly those who travel in a particular direction to commit their crimes, geographic profiling is typically not a useful investigative strategy. However, for the majority of serial offenders who do commit their crimes locally, a number of profiling strategies can be used (Snook, Zito, Bennell, & Taylor, 2005).

One of the first cases in which geographic profiling techniques were used was the case of the Yorkshire Ripper in England. After five years of unsolved murders, an advisory team was set up to review the investigation. Although some of the investigators felt the offender lived in a different part of the country from where the crimes were happening, the advisory team believed the offender was a local man. To provide support for this claim, the team constructed a type of geographic profile (Kind, 1987). They plotted the 17 murders onto a map and calculated the centre of gravity for the points. That is, by adding up the x-y coordinates for each crime and dividing by the 17 crimes, they could calculate the x-y coordinate for the centre of gravity. In this case, the centre of gravity was near Bradford, a city close to where the majority of the murders had taken place. When Peter Sutcliffe was eventually arrested for the crimes, he was found to reside in a district of Bradford.

Since the time of the Yorkshire Ripper murders, a number of individuals have built computerized **geographic profiling systems** that can assist with the profiling task (Canter et al., 2000; Levine, 2007; Rossmo, 2000). One of these individuals was Dr. Kim Rossmo, who is profiled in Box 3.5. The locations of linked crime sites are input into these systems and are represented as points on a map. The systems then perform calculations by using mathematical models of offender spatial behaviour, which reflect the probability that the offender lives at particular points in the area where the offences have taken place. Every single location on the map is assigned an overall probability and these probabilities are designated a colour. For example, the top 10% of probabilities might be assigned the colour red, and so on. The eventual output is a coloured map, in which each colour band corresponds to the probability that the offender lives in the area (see Figure 3.1). The police use this map to prioritize their investigative activities. Geographic profilers also consider other factors that may affect an offender's spatial behaviour, such as the density of suitable victims in an area, but this probability map forms the basis of their prediction.

Whether these computerized geographic profiling systems are necessary for constructing accurate profiles, or whether less sophisticated and potentially more cost effective alternatives are possible, is a question that has recently begun to be explored (see Bennell, Taylor, & Snook, 2007). For example, Snook, Taylor, and Bennell (2004) examined whether individuals trained to use simple **heuristics** (e.g., predicting that serial offenders will live close to the locations of the majority of their crimes) would make profiling predictions that are as accurate as computerized systems. In that study, they found that, even

**Geographic profiling systems:** Computer systems that use mathematical models of offender spatial behaviour to make predictions about where unknown serial offenders are likely to reside

**Heuristics:** Simple general rules that can be used to make decisions and solve problems. In some instances, a reliance on heuristics can result in biased decisions. In other cases, heuristics can result in reasonably accurate decisions

Box 3.5

## Canadian Researcher Profile: Dr. Kim Rossmo

Dr. Kim Rossmo had been a police officer with the Vancouver Police Department for 16 years when he became the first Canadian police officer to get his Ph.D. in criminology. At Simon Fraser University in Burnaby, B.C., Rossmo began his doctoral studies with Paul Brantingham, a well-known environmental criminologist. Drawing on his background in mathematics and his experience as a street-wise police officer, Rossmo decided to take what was known about offender spatial behaviour from fields such as environmental criminology and put them to practical use by developing an investigative tool for predicting where unknown serial offenders are likely to live.

After years of research, Rossmo developed an approach he called *geographic profiling* and designed a computer system named *Rigel*, which is now one of the most sought-after investigative tools by police agencies around the world. Dr. Rossmo is regularly called in to assist with serial crime investigations by the RCMP, the FBI, and Scotland Yard. Based on his most recent estimation, he has consulted on over 200 cases, ranging from murders, to bombings, to robberies. One of his most recent cases was the high-profile Washington sniper case, which proved to be a particularly interesting and difficult case for geographic profiling because of the transient nature of the suspects.

After working as a detective inspector in charge of the Geographic Profiling Section of the Vancouver Police Department for a number of years, Dr. Rossmo moved on to serve a two-year term as the director of research for the prestigious Police Foundation in Washington, D.C. Dr. Rossmo now calls Texas State University home, where he directs the Center for Geospatial Intelligence and Investigation in the Department of Criminal Justice.

In addition to his ongoing consultancy work, Dr. Rossmo continues to conduct research on geographic profiling and is expanding his focus to deal with other issues of importance. He is currently engaged in research projects exploring the spatial patterns of illegal border crossing, insurgency attacks, and terrorist planning. Recently, he completed a collaborative study by using Rigel to study the foraging patterns of great white shark attacks off the coast of South Africa. In 2009, he published a book on criminal investigative failures and their causes. When asked where he sees the field going in the future, he replied that environmental criminology research has the potential to provide immediate solutions to problems in public safety and homeland security.

Dr. Rossmo has been the recipient of many awards for his achievements as a police officer and an academic, and he made an appearance as a character in the crime novel *Burnt Bones* by Michael Slade. He is the author of numerous articles and *Geographic Profiling*, the first book on the subject. This text provides an excellent example of how academic research can successfully be applied to real-world policing problems.

before any training, approximately 50% of participants made predictions that were as accurate as a computerized system. After training, there was no difference between the average accuracy of the participants and the system, when accuracy was measured by calculating the distance between the actual and predicted home location. Such findings have resulted in a debate over the relative merits of various profiling approaches (e.g., Canter, 2005; Rossmo, 2005; Snook, Taylor, & Bennell, 2005), and research is currently being conducted in an attempt to resolve this debate.

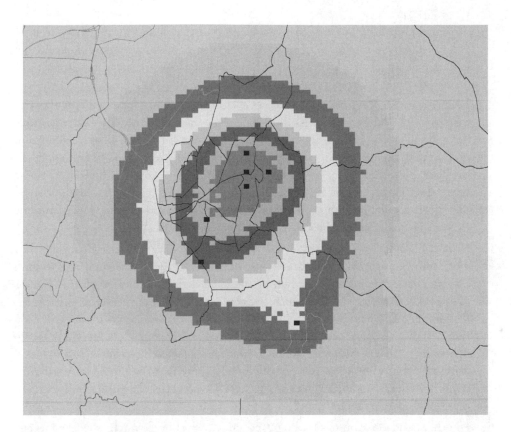

**Figure 3.1** A Computerized Geographic Profile

The black dots represent the crime locations and the different coloured bands (represented here by different shades of grey) correspond to the probability that the offender resides in that particular geographic area. The high-priority search area in this case centres on the four crimes in the upper half of the map. This profile was constructed by using Dragnet, a computerized geographic profiling system developed by David Canter.

## SUMMARY

1.  The police attempt to achieve two goals when conducting interrogations: (1) to gain information that furthers the investigation and (2) to obtain a confession from the suspect. Police officers in North America sometimes use the Reid model of interrogation to interrogate suspects. This model advocates the use of psychologically based interrogation tactics to break down a suspect's resistance to telling the truth. The tactics used in the Reid model of interrogation can be broken down into minimization and maximization techniques.

2.  The three potential problems with the Reid model of interrogation are (1) the inability of police officers to accurately detect deception, (2) biases that result from presuming a suspect is guilty, and (3) an increased likelihood that suspects will make false confessions.

3.  False confessions must be differentiated from retracted confessions and disputed confessions. A false confession is one that is either intentionally fabricated or is not based

on actual knowledge of the facts in a case. A retracted confession is simply an individual's statement that his or her confession is false. A disputed confession is one that is disputed at trial, often because of a legal technicality or because the suspect disputes the confession was ever made.

4. There are three types of false confessions, each having its own set of vulnerability factors. Voluntary false confessions occur when someone voluntarily confesses to a crime he or she did not commit without any elicitation from the police. Coerced-compliant false confessions are those in which the suspect confesses to a crime, even though the suspect is fully aware that he or she did not commit it. Coerced-internalized false confessions consist of individuals confessing to a crime they did not commit—and subsequently coming to the belief they committed the crime—usually after they are exposed to highly suggestible questions.

5. Criminal profiling is sometimes used by the police in serial crime investigations. They use it for prioritizing suspects, developing new lines of inquiry, setting traps to flush out offenders, determining whether an offender's actions should be taken seriously, giving advice on how to interrogate suspects, and developing courtroom strategies. Despite its use, criminal profiling is often criticized. One major criticism centres on the lack of a strong theoretical base underlying the approach. A second criticism relates to the fact that many profiles contain ambiguous information and this may cause problems when police officers are asked to interpret the profile. A third criticism is that professionally trained profilers may be no better than other individuals at constructing accurate profiles.

6. Another common form of profiling is geographic profiling, which is defined as any technique that uses crime scene locations to predict the most likely area where the offender resides. This form is often used to prioritize suspects, by rank ordering them based on the proximity of their residence to the predicted home location.

## Discussion Questions

1. Many police agencies now video-record their interrogations, thus presenting potential advantages for the police, suspects, and the courts. Do you see any potential problems with using this procedure? What are some other possible ways to minimize the problems that result from modern-day interrogation practices?

2. Because the Reid model of interrogation can increase the degree to which people falsely confess to crimes, people seem to agree that it should not be used with particular individuals (e.g., those who have a severe learning disability). However, few police agencies have policies in place to indicate when it is not appropriate to use the Reid model. Put yourself in the role of a police psychologist and develop a set of recommendations for when the technique should and shouldn't be used.

3. You are a criminal profiler who uses the inductive approach to profiling. You encounter a series of crimes in which the offender consistently attacks elderly women in their apartments at night. How would you go about constructing a profile in this case? What sorts of problems would a deductive profiler have with your profile? How could you attempt to counter some of the arguments?

4. Geographic profiling works in large part because offenders commit most of their crimes close to home. Why do you think offenders do this?

# Chapter 4
## Deception

## Learning Objectives

- Describe the two types of polygraph tests.

- Describe the most common types of errors made by the Comparison Question Test (CQT) and the Concealed Information Test (CIT).

- Describe physiologically based alternatives to the polygraph, including event-related brain potentials and functional brain-imaging techniques.

- Outline the verbal and non-verbal characteristics of deception.

- Define malingering, and list the three explanatory models of malingering.

- Differentiate between the types of studies used to examine malingering.

Dimitri Adonis is in trouble. He is a suspect in a vicious attack that occurred outside a popular nightclub. He was seen driving away from the scene of the attack. He has been asked by the police to take a polygraph exam. On the date of the first scheduled test, he tells the polygraph examiner that he has a bad cold. The police examiner asks him to come back the following week to take the exam. At the next exam, his numerical score is −10. The police examiner informs him of his deceptive scoring and attempts to obtain a confession from him about his role in the attack. Dimitri maintains that he is innocent and the polygraph must be wrong.

How do we know whether someone is telling the truth or lying? A person may lie to the police about his or her involvement in a crime, lie to a psychologist about psychological symptoms, lie to a probation officer by claiming to be following conditional release requirements, or lie in a job interview. Several techniques have been developed to try to answer this question. As seen in Chapter 3, police attempt to detect whether someone is telling them the truth during an interrogation. Psychologists have participated in the development and testing of a variety of techniques to detect deception. In this chapter, we focus on several issues associated with deception, including the use of the polygraph and alternatives to the polygraph, the relationship between verbal and non-verbal cues to deception, and methods for detecting the malingering of mental disorders.

# THE POLYGRAPH TECHNIQUE

Physiological measures have long been used in an attempt to detect deception. For example, at one time the Chinese forced suspects to chew on dry rice powder and then to spit it out. If the powder was dry, the suspect was judged to be lying (Kleinmuntz & Szucko, 1984). The rationale for this technique was that anxiety causes a person's mouth to be dry. A person telling the truth would not be anxious and, therefore, would not have a dry mouth. In contrast, a person lying would be anxious and would have a dry mouth. Polygraphy relies on the same underlying principle: deception is associated with physiological change. The origins of modern polygraphy date from 1917 when William Marston, a Harvard psychologist also trained as a lawyer, developed a systolic blood pressure test (Iacono & Patrick, 1999) and attempted to use this physiological response as evidence for a person's innocence (see Lykken, 1998). Marston's testimony was rejected by the courts in *Frye v. United States* (1923) because they felt the test had not gained acceptance by the scientific community, foreshadowing the debate associated with physiological measures that continues to the present day.

**Polygraph:** A device for recording an individual's autonomic nervous system responses

A **polygraph** (the word is a combination of two Greek words, *poly* = "many" and *grapho* = "write") is a device for recording an individual's autonomic nervous system responses. Measurement devices are attached to the upper chest and abdomen to measure breathing. The amount of sweat on the skin is measured by attaching electrodes to the fingertips. Sweat changes the conductance of the skin, which is known as the galvanic skin response. Finally, heart rate is measured by a partially inflated blood pressure cuff attached to an arm. Each of these measures is amplified and can be printed out on paper or stored in a computer to be analyzed. In a forensic context, a polygraph is used to measure a person's physiological responses to questions asked by an examiner.

In Canada, polygraph training is provided by the Canadian Police College. In the United States, the American Polygraph Association accredits independent polygraph schools. The polygraph course at the Canadian Police College is restricted to police officers. The college offers a 12-week intensive course that covers the various techniques, interviewing practices, and scoring.

## Applications of the Polygraph Test

Polygraph tests are used for a range of purposes. In Canada, the police often use them to help in their criminal investigations. The police may ask a suspect to take a polygraph test as a means to resolve the case. If the suspect fails the polygraph test, that person may be pressured to confess, thereby giving the police incriminating evidence. Although not common, police may ask alleged victims of crimes to take a polygraph

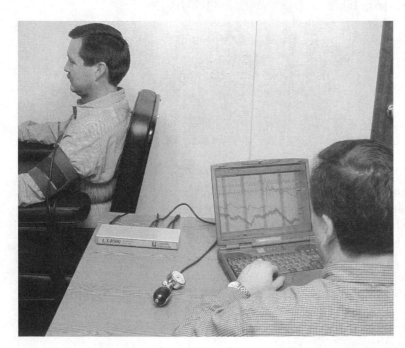

A suspect being given a polygraph test

test to help to verify whether a crime has occurred. Insurance companies may request a polygraph test to verify the claims of the insured. More recently, the polygraph has been used in the United States to assess and monitor sexual offenders on probation. **Polygraph disclosure tests** are used to uncover information about an offender's past behaviour. In addition, polygraph tests are used to determine whether the offender is violating the conditions of probation or are used to test for evidence of risky behaviour, such as sexual fantasies about children.

**Polygraph disclosure tests:** Polygraph tests that are used to uncover information about an offender's past behaviour

The most widespread applications of polygraph testing in the United States were for the periodic testing of employees to identify those engaged in theft or using drugs at work and for the screening of prospective employees, to weed out those with criminal tendencies or substance-abuse problems. However, the Employee Polygraph Protection Act of 1988 restricted private companies from using the polygraph for these purposes and limited the use of the polygraph to specific investigations of job-related wrongdoing. Nonetheless, governmental agencies in the United States and Canada still use the polygraph as a general screening tool. For example, some police departments require applicants to take a polygraph test, and the Canadian Security Intelligence Service (CSIS) also requires that its potential employees take a polygraph test to assess "the candidate's reliability and loyalty."

## Types of Polygraph Tests

The polygraph does not detect lies per se, since the physiological states associated with lying share much in common with many other states, including anxiety, anger, embarrassment, and fear. Instead, polygraph tests rely on measuring physiological responses to different types of questions. Some questions are designed to elicit a larger physiological response in guilty individuals than in those who are innocent. The two main types of polygraph tests are reviewed below.

**The Comparison Question Test** The **Comparison Question Test** (CQT; also known as the Control Question Test) is the most commonly used test to investigate criminal acts. The typical CQT includes a pretest interview, followed by a series of questions administered while the suspect's physiological responses are measured (usually three separate question sequences are asked). The polygraph examiner then scores the charts and ends the CQT with a post-test interview in which the test results are discussed.

**Comparison Question Test:** Type of polygraph test that includes irrelevant questions that are unrelated to the crime, relevant questions concerning the crime being investigated, and comparison questions concerning the person's honesty and past history prior to the event being investigated

A critical component of this technique is the pretest interview. During the pretest interview, the polygraph examiner develops the control questions, learns about the background of the suspect, and attempts to convince the suspect of the accuracy of the polygraph test. The examiner will do this by quoting very high accuracy rates and conducting a stimulation test. For example, the suspect will pick a card with a number on it from a deck of cards, and the examiner will determine the number by examining the polygraph chart. The deck of cards is rigged so the examiner knows which card the suspect picked.

The examiner then asks ten questions to be answered with either "yes" or "no." Table 4.1 provides an example of a typical question series used in a CQT. Three types of questions are asked. Irrelevant questions, referring to the respondent's identity or personal background (e.g., "Is your first name *Beatrice?*") are included as a baseline but are not scored. Relevant and control questions establish guilt or innocence. Relevant questions deal with the crime being investigated (e.g., "On June 12, did you stab your ex-wife?"). Probable-lie comparison questions (a.k.a. control questions) are designed to be emotionally arousing for all respondents and typically focus on the person's honesty and past history

**Table 4.1** Typical Question Series Used in a Comparison Question Test

| Type of Question | Questions |
| --- | --- |
| Irrelevant | Do you understand that I will be asking only questions we have discussed before? |
| Irrelevant | Do you live in Canada? |
| Comparison | Between the ages of 18 and 28, did you ever deliberatively plan to physically hurt someone? |
| Relevant | Did you stab Petunia Bottoms on the night of March 10? |
| Irrelevant | Is your first name *Craig*? |
| Comparison | Prior to 2003, did you ever verbally threaten to hurt anyone? |
| Relevant | Did you use a knife to stab Petunia Bottoms? |
| Irrelevant | Were you born in November? |
| Comparison | During the first 20 years of your life, did you ever do anything illegal? |
| Relevant | On March 10, did you participate, in any way, in the stabbing of Petunia Bottoms? |

prior to the event being investigated (e.g., "Before the age of 45, did you ever try to seriously hurt someone?"). Polygraph examiners assume they can detect deception by comparing reactions to the relevant and comparison questions. Guilty suspects are assumed to react more to relevant questions than comparison questions. In contrast, innocent suspects are assumed to react more to comparison questions than relevant questions. The reasoning behind these assumptions is that innocent people know they are telling the truth about the relevant question so they will react more strongly to general questions about their honesty and past history.

Examiners in the past used global scoring, incorporating all available information—including physiological responses, the suspect's demeanour during the examination, and information in the case file—to make a decision about the guilt or the innocence of the suspect. Most examiners now numerically score the charts to ensure that decisions are based solely on the physiological responses. There are three possible outcomes of a polygraph test: truthful, deceptive, and inconclusive. During the post-test interview, the examiner tells the suspect the outcome, and if the outcome is deceptive the examiner attempts to elicit a confession.

Several psychologists have questioned the underlying rationale of the CQT (Cross & Saxe, 2001; Furedy, 1996; Iacono & Patrick, 2006). Imagine yourself being falsely accused of a serious crime and taking a polygraph exam. Being innocent, you might react more strongly to questions about a crime that you could get punished for (i.e., relevant questions) than about vague questions concerning your past behaviour (i.e., comparison questions). In contrast, guilty suspects might actually respond more to comparison questions because they are novel or because they believe they have other crimes to hide. In addition, the guilty suspect may no longer react to the crime-relevant questions because he or she may have been asked repeatedly about the crime. The validity of the CQT is discussed later in the chapter.

**The Concealed Information Test** This test was developed by Lykken (1960) and was originally called the *Guilty Knowledge Test* but is currently known as the **Concealed Information Test** (CIT). The CIT does not assess deception but instead seeks to determine whether the suspect knows details about a crime that only the person who committed the crime would know. The general form of the CIT is a series of questions in multiple-choice format. Each question has one correct option (often called the *critical option*) and four options that are foils—alternatives that could fit the crime but that are incorrect. A CIT question in the context of a homicide might take the following form: "Did you kill the person with (a) a knife, (b) an axe, (c) a handgun, (d) a crowbar, or (e) a rifle?" The guilty suspect is assumed to display a larger physiological response to the correct option than to the incorrect options. An innocent person, conversely, who does not know the details of the crime, will show the same physiological response to all options.

**Concealed Information Test:**
Type of polygraph test designed
to determine if the person knows
details about a crime

Underlying the CIT is the principle that people will react more strongly to information they recognize as distinctive or important than to unimportant information. Suspects who consistently respond to critical items are assumed to have knowledge of the crime. The likelihood that an innocent person with no knowledge of the crime would react most strongly to the critical alternative is one in five for each question. If ten questions are asked, the odds that an innocent person will consistently react to the critical alternative are exceedingly small (less than 1 in 10 000 000). Critiques of the CIT have warned that this test will work only if the suspect remembers the details of the crime (Honts & Schweinle, 2009).

The most common physiological response measured when administering the CIT is palmar sweating (i.e., skin conductance response measured in the palm of the hand). In recent years, three other responses have been studied in the lab. Preliminary research suggests that response times to questions can accurately identify participants with guilty knowledge (Seymour, Seifert, Shafto, & Mosmann, 2000). Some researchers have also investigated using eyeblinks as an index of guilty knowledge (Fukuda, 2001; Thonney, Kanachi, Sasaki, & Hatayama, 2005). More recently, pupil diameter has been effective in detecting deception (Webb, Honts, Kircher, Bernhardt, & Cooke, 2009).

Although law enforcement in Canada and the United States does not routinely use the CIT, it is used regularly in a limited number of other jurisdictions, such as Israel and Japan (Ben-Shakhar & Furedy, 1990). Iacono and Patrick (1999) suggest two reasons for the lack of widespread acceptance of the CIT. First, since polygraph examiners believe in the accuracy of the CQT, they are not motivated to use the more difficult-to-construct CIT. Second, for law enforcement to use the CIT, salient features of the crime must be known only to the perpetrator. If details of a crime appear in the media, the crime-related details given cannot be used to construct a CIT.

## Validity of Polygraph Techniques

**Types of Studies** How is the accuracy of polygraph tests assessed? Accuracy is determined under ideal circumstances by presenting information known to be true and false to individuals and measuring their corresponding physiological responses. In practice, studies assessing the validity of polygraph techniques vary in how closely they are able to achieve this ideal. Studies of the validity of polygraph techniques can be classified into two types: laboratory and field studies.

In laboratory studies, volunteers (often university students) simulate criminal behaviour by committing a mock crime. Volunteers come to a laboratory and are randomly assigned to one of two conditions: committing a mock crime or not committing a mock crime. The main advantage of these studies is that the experimenter knows **ground truth** (i.e., who is truly guilty or innocent). In addition, laboratory studies can also compare the relative merits of different types of polygraph tests and control for variables such as the time between the crime and the polygraph exam. However, because of the large motivational and emotional differences between volunteers in laboratory studies and actual suspects in real-life situations, the results of laboratory studies may have limited application to real life. In laboratory studies, guilty participants cannot ethically be given strong incentives to "beat" the polygraph, and both guilty and innocent participants have little to fear if they "fail" the polygraph exam.

Field studies involve real-life situations and actual criminal suspects, together with actual polygraph examinations. Field studies often compare the accuracy of "original" examiners to "blind" evaluators. Original examiners conduct the actual evaluation of the suspect. Blind evaluators are provided with only the original examiner's charts and are given no information about the suspect or the case. Original examiners are exposed to extra polygraph cues—information about the case in addition to that obtained via the polygraph, such as the case facts and the behaviour of the suspect during the examination. Although polygraph examiners are taught to ignore these cues, Patrick and Iacono (1991) found that examiners are nonetheless significantly influenced by them.

The largest problem with field studies is establishing ground truth. Indicators of guilt, such as physical evidence, eyewitness testimony, or DNA evidence, are often not available. In such situations, truth is more difficult to establish. To deal with this problem, two additional ways of establishing ground truth have been developed: judicial outcomes and confessions. Judicial outcomes are problematic because some people are falsely convicted and some guilty people are not convicted. Confessions are also problematic. Although rare, some people may falsely confess. More significant, however, is the problem that confessions are often not independent from the polygraph examiner's decisions. Confessions are often elicited because a person fails a polygraph exam. Moreover, cases in which a guilty suspect beats the polygraph are not included in research studies. Thus, reliance on confessions to establish ground truth likely inflates polygraph accuracy rates (Iacono & Patrick, 2006). Most field studies have used confessions to establish ground truth.

**Polygraph Tests: Accurate or Not?** The accuracy of the polygraph for detecting lies is controversial. Numerous laboratory studies have assessed the accuracy of the CQT and the CIT (see Iacono & Patrick, 1999, for a review). However, as pointed out above, there are problems when relying on typical mock crime scenarios to estimate real-life accuracy. As a consequence, only field studies of the CQT will be described here. The situation concerning the CIT is different. Since the CIT is almost never used in Canada or the United States, no relevant North American data are available. Thus, we will describe assessments of the CIT based on laboratory and field studies done in Israel.

Although the CQT has been investigated for more than 30 years, its ability to accurately measure deception remains controversial (Furedy, 1996; National Research Council, 2003). Most of the studies have used confessions to classify suspects as guilty or innocent, and as noted above, there are problems with using this as the criterion. Most guilty suspects (84% to 92%) are correctly classified as guilty (Patrick & Iacono, 1991;

**Table 4.2** Field Studies of the Comparison Question Test*

| Study | Guilty Condition | | | Innocent Condition | | |
|---|---|---|---|---|---|---|
| | Guilty | Innocent | Inconclusive | Guilty | Innocent | Inconclusive |
| Honts and Raskin (1988) | 92% (92%) | 8% (8%) | 0% (0%) | 0% (15%) | 91% (62%) | 9% (23%) |
| Patrick and Iacono (1991) | 98% (92%) | 0% (2%) | 2% (6%) | 8% (24%) | 73% (30%) | 19% (46%) |

*Blind examiners' results appear in parentheses.

Raskin, Honts, & Kircher, 1997). However, the picture for innocent suspects is less optimistic, with accuracy rates ranging from 55% to 78% (Honts & Raskin, 1988; Patrick & Iacono, 1991). Many of the innocent suspects were classified as inconclusive. Between 9% and 24% of innocent suspects were falsely identified as guilty. Such a high false-positive rate indicates that innocent people respond more to relevant than control questions, suggesting that the premise underlying the CQT does not apply to all suspects.

Table 4.2 presents data from several field studies comparing the accuracy of the original examiner with the blind evaluators. The accuracy rates of the original examiner are higher than the accuracy of the blind evaluator, especially for innocent suspects. For example, Patrick and Iacono (1991) examined the accuracy of original examiner opinions to blind scoring for 37 innocent verified cases. The hit rate (in this context, cases classified as innocent when actually innocent, excluding inconclusives) for original examiners was 90%, compared with 55% for blind scorers. The main reason original examiners are more accurate than blind examiners is that the original examiners appear to be using extra polygraph cues (such as the attitude of the suspect, other evidence about the case, and verbal cues), whereas blind chart evaluators have access only to polygraph information. Additional research is needed to confirm the source of these extra polygraphic cues used by examiners.

Mock-crime laboratory studies evaluating the CIT indicate that it is very effective at identifying innocent participants (hit rates of up to 95%) and slightly less effective at identifying guilty participants (hit rates between 76% and 85%) (Gamer, Rill, Vossel, & Gödert, 2005; Iacono & Patrick, 1988; Jokinen, Santilla, Ravaja, & Puttonen, 2006; Lykken, 1998). A meta-analysis of 80 CIT studies examined what factors are associated with higher accuracies (Ben-Shakhar & Elaad, 2003). Correct outcomes were better in studies that included motives to succeed, verbal response to alternatives, five or more questions, and in laboratory mock-crime studies. Two published field studies, both done in Israel, have assessed the accuracy of the CIT. Elaad (1990) found that 98% of innocent suspects were correctly classified, but only 42% of guilty suspects were correctly classified. Elaad, Ginton, and Jungman (1992) measured both respiration and skin conductance and found that 94% of innocent and 76% of guilty suspects were correctly classified.

Based on the research described above, the CIT appears to be vulnerable to false-negative errors (falsely classifying guilty suspects as innocent), whereas the CQT is vulnerable to false-positive errors (falsely classifying innocent suspects as guilty). See Box 4.1 for a new way of measuring deception.

Box 4.1

## Seeing Through the Face of Deception

If you travel by air, you will be subjected to intense scrutiny. Airport security officers have become increasingly vigilant in their attempts to detect passengers intent on harm. Technologies that can provide a rapid, accurate assessment of deceit are becoming more and more important.

Pavlidis, Eberhardt, and Levine (2002) examined whether high-definition thermal imaging of the face could be used to detect deceit. Thermal imaging measures the amount of facial warming, which is linked to regional blood flow. Imaging can be done quickly without the individual even knowing his or her facial temperature is being measured. Pavlidis and colleagues wanted to know whether facial warming was associated with deception. Individuals were randomly assigned to commit a mock crime (stab a mannequin and rob it of $20) or to a control condition in which they had no knowledge of the crime. Use of thermal imaging (in particular around the eyes) correctly classified 6 of the 8 guilty participants and 11 of the 12 innocent participants. This accuracy rate was similar to a polygraph exam administered to participants that correctly classified 6 of 8 guilty and 8 of 12 innocent participants. In the future, when security or customs officers ask you questions, they may be paying more attention to your facial temperature than to your answers.

## Can the Guilty Learn to Beat the Polygraph?

**Countermeasures:** As applied to polygraph research, techniques used to try to conceal guilt

Is it possible to use **countermeasures** to beat the polygraph? There are websites that describe the best ways to beat the polygraph. Honts, Raskin, and Kircher (1994) showed that 30 minutes of instruction on the rationale underlying the CQT was sufficient for community volunteers to learn how to escape detection in a mock-crime study. Participants were told to use either physical countermeasures (e.g., biting their tongue or pressing their toes on the floor) or mental countermeasures (e.g., counting backward by 7 from a number greater than 200) when asked a control question during the polygraph exam. Both countermeasures worked, with 50% of the guilty suspects beating the polygraph test. In addition, the polygraph examiners were not able to accurately detect which participants had used the countermeasures.

Iacono, Cerri, Patrick, and Fleming (1992) investigated whether anti-anxiety drugs would allow guilty subjects to appear innocent on the CIT. Undergraduate students were divided into one innocent group (who watched a noncrime videotape) and four guilty groups. Participants in the guilty groups watched a videotaped crime and then were given one of three drugs (Diazepam, meprobamate, or propranolol) or a placebo prior to being administered a CIT. None of the drugs had an effect on the accuracy of the CIT. In addition, the polygraph examiner was able to identify 90% of the participants receiving drugs.

## Scientific Opinion: What Do the Experts Say?

Most knowledgeable scientists are skeptical about the rationale underlying the CQT and its accuracy. The United States National Research Council (NRC) established a panel of 14 scientists and four staff to review the validity of the polygraph (NRC, 2003). In a comprehensive report, the committee concluded the following:

■ "The theoretical rationale for the polygraph is quite weak, especially in terms of differential fear, arousal, or other emotional states that are triggered in response to relevant and comparison questions" (NRC, 2003, p. 213).

- "The existing validation studies have serious limitations. Laboratory test findings on polygraph validity are not a good guide to accuracy in field settings. They are likely to overestimate accuracy in field practice, but by an unknown amount" (p. 210).

- "In summary, we were unable to find any field experiments, field quasi-experiments, or prospective research-oriented data collection specifically designed to assess polygraph validity and satisfying minimal standards of research quality" (p. 115).

- "What is remarkable, given the large body of relevant research, is that claims about the accuracy of the polygraph made today parallel those made throughout the history of the polygraph: practitioners have always claimed extremely high levels of accuracy, and these claims have rarely been reflected in empirical research" (p. 107).

Despite scientists' negative view of it, the CQT is still used by law enforcement as an investigative tool. To understand why, we have to know only that whatever its actual validity, the polygraph will cause many suspects to confess, thereby providing resolution of the criminal investigation.

## Admissibility of Polygraph Evidence

Polygraph results were first submitted as evidence in court in the United States in *Frye v. United States* (1923). James Frye was denied the opportunity to have the results of a polygraph test conducted by William Marston admitted as evidence. This ruling led to the requirement that a technique must obtain "general acceptance" by the relevant scientific community before it can be admitted as evidence. This precedent was replaced by a new admissibility standard that required courts to render scientific decisions (*Daubert v. Merrell Dow Pharmaceuticals*,1993) and was later extended to nonscientific experts who could provide unique specialized information to the court (*Kumho Tire Co. Ltd. v. Carmichael*,1999). Some states permit the admission of polygraph evidence if there is a prior agreement between prosecuting and defence lawyers. The United States Supreme Court (*U.S. v. Scheffer*,1998) rejected the admissibility of the polygraph because of the belief that polygraph evidence will usurp the role of the jury as determinant of the credibility of a witness. Justice Thomas ruled, "Jurisdictions, in promulgating rules of evidence, may legitimately be concerned about the risk that juries will give excessive weight to the opinions of the polygrapher, clothed as they are in scientific expertise and at times offering, as in respondent's case, a conclusion about the ultimate issue in the trial" (p. 422).

Polygraph evidence is not admissible in Canadian criminal courts of law. The same concerns that U.S. courts have raised have been a focus of concern in Canadian courts. In *R. v. Beland*(1987), the Supreme Court of Canada ruled that polygraph evidence should not be admitted to help to determine whether a person is telling the truth. The court referred to the polygraph as being falsely imbued with the "mystique of science," thus causing jurors to weight polygraph evidence more than it deserves when determining the verdict.

## BRAIN-BASED DECEPTION RESEARCH

In the past decade, researchers have attempted to use brain-based responses to detect deception. **Event-related brain potentials** (ERPs) are a type of brain-based response that has been investigated for detecting deception. ERPs are measured by placing electrodes on the scalp and by noting changes in electrical patterns related to presentation of a

**Event-related brain potentials:** Brain activity measured by placing electrodes on the scalp and by recording electrical patterns related to presentation of a stimulus

stimulus. ERPs reflect underlying electrical activity in the cerebral cortex. One type of ERP that has shown promise is known as the P300. This ERP occurs in response to significant stimuli that occur infrequently. When using CIT procedures, guilty suspects should respond to such crime-relevant events with a large P300 response, compared with noncrime-relevant events. No difference in P300 responses to crime-relevant and irrelevant events should be observed in innocent suspects. One of the advantages of ERPs is that they have been proposed as a measure resistant to manipulation. (However, Rosenfeld, Soskins, Bosh, and Ryan, [2004], have obtained results suggesting that participants who are knowledgeable about ERPs can evade detection.)

Several studies have been conducted to assess the validity of the P300 as a guilt detector (e.g., Abootalebi, Moradi, & Khalilzadeh, 2006; Allen & Iacono, 1997; Farwell & Donchin, 1991; Rosenfeld, Angell, Johnson, & Qian, 1991; Rosenfeld, Nasman, Whalen, Cantwell, & Mazzeri, 1987). Farwell and Donchin (1991) conducted one of the first studies on the use of the P300 to detect the presence of guilty knowledge. The study consisted of two experiments. In the first experiment, participants role-played one of two espionage scenarios, which involved the exchange of information with a foreign agent, during which they were exposed to six critical details (e.g., the colour of the agent's hat). In the second experiment, participants were asked about details of minor offences they had committed in their day-to-day lives. In the first experiment, using P300 as the measure, 18 of 20 participants were correctly classified in the guilty condition, and 17 of 20 were correctly classified in the innocent condition. In the second experiment, all four of the guilty participants were correctly classified, and three of the four innocent participants were correctly classified. Although the results look impressive, there are several limitations to this study. First, guilty participants reviewed the crime-relevant details just prior to taking the CIT. In addition, there were no aversive consequences linked to performance in this study. Finally, the sample size, especially in the second experiment, was very small. Abootalebi and colleagues (2006) recently reported lower detection rates than previously reported (e.g., Rosenfeld et al., 1991) when employing the P300-CIT paradigm, with correct identification ranging from 74% to 80%, depending on the approach. In summary, although the P300 has shown potential for detecting deception, its application remains limited to laboratory settings.

More recently, investigators have also begun to use functional magnetic resonance imaging (fMRI) to determine which areas of the brain are associated with deception (Ganis, Kosslyn, Stose, Thompson, & Yurgelun-Todd, 2003; Langleben et al., 2002). For example, Ganis and colleagues (2003) examined which brain areas were activated when someone told a spontaneous or rehearsed lie. Lies that were part of a story and that had been rehearsed repeatedly produced a higher level of activation in the right anterior frontal cortex than did spontaneous isolated lies. In contrast, spontaneous isolated lies produced a higher level of activation in the anterior cingulate and posterior visual cortices. These findings and others indicate that brain-imaging techniques can differentiate which parts

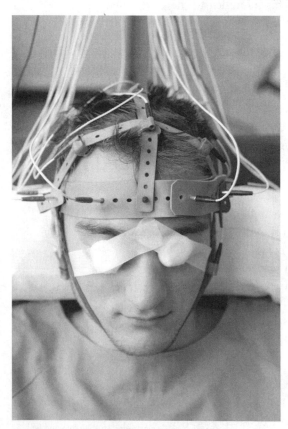

Measuring brain activity during a deception task

of the brain are involved in lying and can even indicate which areas are associated with different types of lying. A limitation of this research, however, is that it is typically based on averaging fMRI data across multiple participants, which constrains its use for detecting deception in individuals. More recent research has employed fMRI to detect deception at the individual level (Kozel et al., 2005; Langleben et al., 2005) and found increased prefrontal and parietal activity when someone is lying. Kozel and colleagues (2005) note that, to better treat and diagnose patients, this methodology is important for examining the neurological factors of disorders for which deception plays a prominent role (e.g., malingering or psychopathy).

Box 4.2 describes the case of Terry Harrington, a man convicted of murder who attempted to use the results of brain-based deception testing to prove his innocence.

---

## Box 4.2

# Brain Fingerprinting: Evidence for a New Deception-Detection Technology?

The case that put brain fingerprinting in the news was *State v. Harrington* (2003). On July 22, 1977, retired police officer John Schweer was shot and killed while working as a security guard for a car dealership in Iowa. Seventeen-year-old Terry Harrington and Curtis McGhee were arrested for the murder. At his trial, Terry Harrington claimed he was not at the crime scene and several witnesses testified that Harrington had been at a concert on the night of the murder. The prosecution's key witness was another teenager, Kevin Hughes, who testified that he was with Harrington and McGhee on the night of the murder. According to Hughes, the three teenagers decided to steal a car. They went to the car dealership. Hughes testified that he waited in the car while Harrington, who first removed a shotgun from the trunk, and McGhee went around a building at the car dealership. Hughes claims he heard a gunshot and Harrington and McGhee came running back to the car. Hughes testified that Harrington had stated he had just shot a cop. Both Terry Harrington and Curtis McGhee were convicted of first-degree murder and sentenced to life in prison without the possibility of parole.

Throughout his 25 years of imprisonment, Terry Harrington maintained his innocence, but all his attempts to appeal his conviction were unsuccessful. From his prison cell, Harrington heard about a new technology that might help his case. He contacted Lawrence Farwell, a cognitive psychophysiologist and head of Brain Fingerprinting Laboratories. On April 18 and 25, 2000, Farwell came to the Iowa State Penitentiary to test Harrington to determine if he had knowledge of the crime scene and of details about his alibi (the

concert he claims he attended). Farwell measured the amplitude of Harrington's P300 brain potential to irrelevant and relevant crime scene and concert details. According to Farwell, Harrington's lack of P300 response to crime-relevant details indicated that Harrington had not participated in the murder. In contrast, Harrington showed a prominent P300 to alibi-relevant information.

Harrington's case received national attention in December 2001 when the CBS show *60 Minutes* featured Farwell's research and his testing of Harrington. In March 2002, Harrington's lawyer submitted a report describing the results of Farwell's testing to the Supreme Court of Iowa.

Although the results of the brain fingerprinting were entered as evidence, the judges relied on other evidence to overturn the murder conviction. During the hearing, three of the prosecution witnesses recanted their testimony. Kevin Hughes stated that he had made up the story about what happened the night of the murder. Hughes claimed that he lied to obtain the $5000 reward being offered about the murder and to avoid being charged with the crime. In addition, the police failed to turn over all the police reports to Harrington's defence lawyer. These reports documented the police investigation of an alternative suspect. On February 26, 2003, the Supreme Court of Iowa overturned the murder conviction of Terry Harrington and the case was remanded for a new trial. On October 24, 2003, the Pottawattamie County Attorney announced that he was dropping the murder charges against Terry Harrington.

# Verbal and Non-verbal Behaviour Cues to Lying

On average, North Americans tell one to two lies per day (Serota, Levine, & Boster, 2010). However, a small number of people are prolific liars. The most common method of deception detection is through the analysis of verbal characteristics and non-verbal behaviours. The underlying assumption is the same as that for polygraphy: The act of deception produces a physiological change compared with telling the truth. The argument here is that it is more difficult for people to control aspects of their non-verbal behaviour than their verbal behaviour (DePaulo & Kirkendol, 1989). The typical experiment involves one group of participants (called the *message source*) who are told to provide either true or deceptive messages. For example, DePaulo, Lassiter, and Stone (1982) asked participants to honestly describe people they liked and disliked. They also asked participants to describe the same people dishonestly (i.e., to pretend to like the person they disliked, and vice versa). Another group of participants was asked to detect when the message source participants were truthful or deceptive. Participants who were instructed to focus their attention on the message source participants' tone of voice were more successful at detecting deception than those participants given no special instructions.

Researchers have also assessed facial cues and other non-verbal cues to deception. For example, Ekman and Friesen (1974) showed student nurses a film of an ocean scene and videotaped them describing what they were seeing and how they felt while watching the film. They also watched a gruesome medical training film (e.g., the amputation of a hand or a severe industrial burn) and were videotaped while pretending that the film they were watching was pleasant. To motivate the nurses watching the gruesome film, the researchers told them that to be successful in nursing, they would have to be able to mask feelings when dealing with unpleasant events. Ekman and Friesen found that the nurses focused on controlling their facial expressions when attempting to deceive. Observers who watched videotapes of the nurses attempting to deceive were more likely to detect deception when they were shown a videotape of the nurses' bodies (with the faces blacked out) than when shown a videotape of their faces. Subsequent research on whether non-verbal cues can be used as an indicator of deception is mixed (Vrij, 2008). Non-verbal behaviours such as gaze aversion, smiling, and self-manipulation (e.g., rubbing one's hands) are not reliable indicators of deception.

If a liar is not feeling excited, scared, or guilty, or when the lie is easy to fabricate, behavioural cues to deception will likely not be present. In a study of everyday lying, DePaulo, Kashy, Kirkendol, Wyer, and Epstein (1996) found that both college students and community members practised deception daily. Most of the deception was not considered serious, and the participants reported they were not concerned or worried about being caught. Participants lied about their opinions, feelings, achievements, reasons for doing things, and possessions. Most of the lies were told for psychological reasons, such as protecting the liar from embarrassment. For example, "I told her Ted and I still liked each other when really I don't know if he likes me at all." The reason this person lied was "because I'm ashamed of the fact that he doesn't like me anymore."

Ekman (1992) has hypothesized that when people are attempting to conceal an emotion, the true emotion may be manifest as a micro facial expression. These microexpressions are brief facial expressions reflecting the true emotions the person is experiencing. In response to terrorists concerns, the United States has been training security officers at airports to use this technique (reading concealed emotions in people) to identify potential threats. There has been relatively little empirical research measuring microexpressions and deception. Recently, Porter and ten Brinke (2008) examined the frequency of microexpressions while students viewed a variety of pleasant, unpleasant, and neutral photos, and either responded with a genuine or deceptive facial expression. The researchers found that participants did display inconsistent expressions of emotions during deception. However, most of these expressions lasted longer than a brief period (thus, they would not be considered microexpressions). In addition, when students were trying to be deceptive, they manifested only partial, rather than whole-face, microexpressions (i.e., the expressions occurred only in the upper and lower face). Additional research is needed to evaluate whether microexpressions are a reliable indicator of deception.

Strömwall, Hartwig, and Granhag (2006) explored the role of stress by creating a realistic deception scenario by using experienced police officers, employing long interrogations, and generating suspects who were motive-driven and had adequate time to prepare their deception. Participants were offered $30 to tell a biographical story to a police officer and were randomly instructed to be honest or deceitful. To create motivation and higher risk, participants were offered an additional $20 if they were able to convince the officer that they were being truthful. Liars felt more anxious and stressed during the task when compared to truth-tellers. No differences in non-verbal behaviours were observed. For verbal strategies, the majority of truth-tellers claimed to "keep it real" (50%), whereas liars would "keep it simple" (46.7%). (For more on verbal cues to lying, see the next section).

Do students and offenders display similar cues to deception? Much of the deception research uses students as the participants, but in the real-world, students tend not to be crime suspects. Porter and his colleagues (2008) examined verbal and non-verbal behaviours while students and offenders told true and false stories about emotional events in their past history. Both groups provided fewer details when they were lying than when honest. Offenders also engaged in more self-manipulations and smiled less when lying about emotional events.

Table 4.3 describes the types of verbal and non-verbal indicators used to detect deception. The verbal indicator that has been most strongly associated with deception is voice pitch. Liars tend to speak in a higher-pitched voice than those telling the truth. Most studies have found increased use of speech disturbances ("ah," "umm") and a slower rate of speech during deception (DePaulo et al., 1982; Fiedler & Walka, 1993; Sporer & Schwandt, 2006). However, if you ask participants only to conceal information or instruct them on what they should lie about, deception is associated with fewer speech disturbances and a faster speech rate (Vrij, 1995). In summary, it appears that cognitively more difficult lies (lies in which you have to fabricate an answer) may be associated with one pattern of speech disturbances, whereas cognitively simpler lies (lies in which you must conceal something) may be associated with a different pattern of speech disturbances.

## Verbal Cues to Lying

In a comprehensive meta-analysis, DePaulo and colleagues (2003) coded 158 cues to deception from 120 samples of adults. Most of the verbal and non-verbal behaviours coded did not discriminate between liars and truth-tellers. One of the most reliable

> **Table 4.3** Verbal and Non-verbal Characteristics of Deception
>
> **Verbal Characteristics**
>
> - Speech fillers (frequency of saying "ah" or "umm")
> - Speech errors (word or sentence repetition, sentence change, sentence incompletion, or slips of the tongue)
> - Pitch of voice (changes in pitch)
> - Rate of speech (number of words spoken in a specific time period)
> - Speech pauses (length of silence between question asked and answer given; number of noticeable pauses in speech)
>
> **Non-verbal Characteristics**
>
> - Gaze aversion (avoiding looking at the face of conversation partner or interviewer)
> - Smiling (frequency of smiles or laughs)
> - Blinking (frequency of eyeblinks)
> - Fidgeting (scratching head, playing with jewellery)
> - Illustrators (gestures to modify or supplement what is being said)
> - Hand or finger movements
> - Leg or foot movements
> - Body movements
> - Shrugs (frequency of shoulders raised in an "I-don't-know"–type gesture)
> - Head movements (nods or shakes head)
> - Shifting positions
>
> Source: Adapted from Vrij, 1998.

indicators was that liars provide fewer details than do truth-tellers. Liars also told less compelling accounts as compared with truth-tellers. For example, liars' stories were less likely to make sense (less plausible, lack logical structure, have discrepancies), were less engaging, and were less fluent than were truth-tellers' stories. Liars were also rated as less cooperative and more nervous and tense than truth-tellers. Finally, truth-tellers were more likely to spontaneously correct their stories and more likely to admit to a lack of memory than liars were. Deception cues were easier to detect when liars were motivated to lie or when they were attempting to cover up personal failings or transgressions.

Sporer and Schwandt completed two recent meta-analyses, which examined verbal cues (2006) and non-verbal cues (2007) to deception. Verbal indices that were positively associated with deception were pitch, response latency, and errors in speech, with length of description negatively associated with deception. For non-verbal behaviour, only 3 of 11 behaviours were negatively (i.e., these behaviours decreased in frequency while lying) associated with deception: nodding, foot and leg movements, and hand movements.

What about online deception? Computer-mediated communication is extremely common and researchers have began to study when, where, and how people lie online. See Box 4.3 for an example of such research.

# Quest for Love: Truth and Deception in Online Dating

Approximately 16 million Americans have used online dating services. Recently Canada was described as a "hotbed of online dating" (Globe and Mail, 2010). Canadians are heavy users of online dating sites and *Plenty of Fish*, one of the more popular online dating sites, was developed and is run by a now very wealthy Canadian.

### How Accurate Are Internet-dating Profiles?

Most users of online dating sites believe that others misrepresent themselves (Gibbs, Ellison, & Heino, 2006), and some potential users avoid using these sites because of fear of deception. People who post profiles may embellish their profiles to attract potential mates. In contrast, users may want to ensure they present themselves accurately, quirks and shortcomings, since they are seeking a potential mate who will be compatible with their personality and interests. Do men and women engage in different types of impression management online? For example, are men more likely to enhance their occupations and earnings, and women their youthfulness and physical attractiveness?

Toma, Hancock, and Ellison (2008) invited online daters to participate in a study on self-presentation in online dating profiles. Participants needed to be a subscriber to popular dating sites in which the users create their own profile (this requirement excluded sites such as *eHarmony* in which subscribers are matched based on their responses to questionnaires). Forty men and forty women were invited

to the lab, and the accuracies of their dating profiles were examined.

### Self-Reported Accuracy

Participants self-reported they were most accurate about their relationship information (e.g., married, divorced, single) and whether they had children. However, when photos were included in profiles, the participants rated them as less accurate than other information, such as their occupation, education, habits (e.g., smoking and drinking), and political and religious beliefs.

### Observed Accuracy

In the study, the participant's height and weight were measured and their age was obtained from their driver's licences. The majority (81%) of the participants provided inaccurate information about height, weight, or age. Participants were more likely to lie about their weight than their age or height. Men were more likely overestimate their height, and women were more likely to underestimate their weight. Most of these deceptions were small in magnitude. However, in some cases they were larger in magnitude, such as a 7.5 centimetre difference in height, a 16 kilogram difference in weight, and an 11 year difference in age.

The authors conclude that "online daters in the present study used deception strategically as a resource in the construction of their online self-presentation and in the engineering of their romantic lives" (p. 1035).

# Are Some People Better at Detecting Deception?

If you believe what you see on the television, there are lie detection wizards out there. See the In the Media box for a description of popular recent television series. Across studies, the ability to distinguish lies from truth tends to be only slightly better than chance. For example, a meta-analysis by Aamondt and Custer (2008) found that on average the accuracy rate for detecting deception for "professional lie catchers," such as police officers, judges, and psychologists, was 55.5%: a rate that is not more accurate than students and other citizens (who had 54.2% accuracy). This poor performance in deception detection has been explained in two ways. First, people tend to rely on behaviours that lack predictive validity (Fiedler & Walka, 1993). Laypeople have a number of beliefs about lying. In a study that measured stereotypic beliefs about lying in 75 different countries, the Global Deception Research Team (2006) found that the most common stereotype about liars is

# TV and Lie Detection

Television shows about detecting deception are popular. In this box, we describe three shows whose underlying premise is using physiological, linguistic, or behavioural cues to detect deception.

### Lie to Me

*Lie to Me*'s main character is Dr. Cal Lightman, a lie detection expert who has an uncanny ability to detect lies. He watches your face for micro-expressions, reads your body language, listens to your voice, and monitors what you say. His only challenge is the stress caused by being able to detect all the lies told by those around him, even those told by his family and his friends. This TV drama, launched in 2009, was an instant success. Although the accuracy of Dr. Lightman's abilities are unrealistic, a true expert on lie detection comments on each episode.

### Lie Detector

You may also have heard of the reality TV show *Lie Detector*. The most recent version of this show was aired in 2005. Its premise was to provide people who had been accused of lying with the opportunity to vindicate themselves. Dr. Ed Gelb, a forensic psychophysiologist and a trained polygraph examiner, would conduct a polygraph examination on the show. Guests on the show ranged from a woman claiming to have contact with extraterrestrials, to Paula Jones, who claimed Bill Clinton sexually harassed her. Although some reality shows maintain their popularity, *Lie Detector* was cut after only one season.

### The Moment of Truth

In this game show, contestants were asked increasingly embarrassing personal questions that they had to answer honestly to win money. To determine whether the person was telling the truth a polygraph test was administered prior to the show. The polygraph results were used to determine when the contestants were telling the truth or a lie The show premiered in January 2008 and ended in August 2009.

---

**Truth-bias:** The tendency of people to judge more messages as truthful than deceptive

that they avoid eye contact. Police officers share belief in these stereotypes: They believe that two cues indicative of deceit are eye gaze and fidgeting. Unfortunately these two cues have not been found to be related to deception (Vrij, 2008). Second, most people have a **truth-bias**. Truth-bias refers to the tendency of people to judge more messages as truthful than deceptive (Bond & DePaulo, 2006).

Several studies by Ekman and colleagues have investigated the abilities of diverse professional groups to detect deception. In the 1991 study by Ekman and O'Sullivan, forensic psychiatrists, customs agents, FBI agents, and judges all performed around chance levels in detecting deception. The only group that performed better than chance (64% correct) were U.S. Secret Service agents. About a third of Secret Service agents were 80% accurate or better. The most accurate participants were those who relied on multiple cues to assess credibility rather than on any one cue.

More recently, Ekman, O'Sullivan, and Frank (1999) showed professional groups videotaped speakers describing a true or false opinion. Both federal law-enforcement officers and clinical psychologists were able to detect deceit at above chance levels (around 70% correct). In a Canadian study, Porter, Woodworth, and Birt (2000) found that parole officers performed below chance levels (40% correct) at distinguishing videotaped speakers describing a truthful or fictitious stressful personal experience, such as an animal attack or a serious car accident. However, after attending a deception-detection workshop, they were significantly more accurate (77% correct). Thus, although detecting deception is difficult, it is possible to improve judgment accuracy through training.

**Table 4.4** Accuracy Rates of Professional Lie Catchers

| Study | Accuracy Rates | | |
|---|---|---|---|
| | Truth | Lie | Total |
| DePaulo & Pfeifer, 1996 (Experienced police)* | 64% | 42% | 52% |
| DePaulo & Pfeifer, 1996 (New police recruits)* | 64% | 42% | 53% |
| Ekman & O'Sullivan, 1991 (Federal polygraphers) | | | 56% |
| Ekman & O'Sullivan, 1991 (Police officers) | | | 56% |
| Ekman & O'Sullivan, 1991 (Secret Service) | | | 64% |
| Köehnken, 1987 (Police officers) | 58% | 31% | 45% |
| Vrij, 1994 (Police detectives) | 51% | 46% | 49% |
| Ekman et al., 1999 (Federal law-enforcement officers) | 66% | 89% | 73% |
| Ekman et al., 1999 (Sheriffs) | 56% | 78% | 67% |
| Porter et al., 2000 (Parole officers) | 41% | 47% | 52% |
| Mann et al., 2004 (Police officers) | 64% | 66% | 65% |

*Accuracy rates for experienced police and new recruits were collapsed together.

In a review of 40 studies, Vrij (2000) found a 67% accuracy rate for detecting truths and a 44% accuracy rate for detecting lies. Table 4.4 presents the accuracy rates of professional lie catchers. In most of the studies, the professional lie catchers were not very accurate at detecting deception. The results also showed that in most studies, truthful messages were identified with more accuracy than deceptive ones. Thus, even professional lie catchers have a truthfulness bias. One reason even professionals are not good at detecting lies is that they rely on the wrong cues. For example, Vrij and Semin (1996) found that 75% of police and customs officers believe that gaze aversion is a reliable indicator of deception, but empirical research has not found it to be a reliable indicator of deception (Vrij, 1998). Mann, Vrij, and Bull (2004) examined police officers' ability to detect lies and truths told by suspects during police interrogations. These police officers were able to reach accuracy rates similar to more specialized law-enforcement groups, such as U.S. Secret Service agents (Ekman et al., 1999). There are two potential explanations for the higher-than-usual accuracy. First, the suspects were highly motivated to lie and research has shown that high-stakes lies are easier to detect than low-stakes ones. Second, the police are more familiar with the setting and type of individual they were judging, namely suspects. Box 4.4 looks at police detection of high-stakes lies.

Two factors one might think would be related to deception-detection ability are level of job experience and confidence in judgment. DePaulo and Pfeifer (1996) compared the proficiency of deception detection of university students, new police recruits, and experienced police officers. None of the groups were better than others at detecting deception; however, the experienced police officers reported being more confident in their decisions. This finding is consistent with more recent research (Ekman & O'Sullivan, 1991; Leach, Talwar, Lee, Bala, & Lindsay, 2004; Porter et al., 2000) indicating that neither level of experience nor confidence in deception-detection ability are associated with accuracy rates. For example, in a meta-analysis examining the relation between judges' accuracy at

Box 4.4

## Detecting High-Stakes Lies

You are watching the news, and a mother is being interviewed outside her home, begging for the return of her two sons. She says that while stopped at a stop light, a black man approached her car with a gun and demanded she get out of the car. Her two young sons were in the backseat. Frightened for her life, she got out of the car and the carjacker jumped into the car and drove off with the children in the back. Over the next nine days, she is often on the news pleading with the carjacker to return her sons. Your initial reaction is concern for the mother and hope that the children will be found unharmed. On the ninth day, the mother confesses to police that there was no carjacker and that she had driven her car to a local lake, left the car on the boat ramp in neutral, got out, and watched as the car slowly rolled into the lake and sank. The two children's bodies were found in the car, still in their car seats.

This story is the true case of 23-year-old Susan Smith. Smith was convicted of first-degree murder of 3-year-old Michael and 14-month-old Alex. During the penalty phase of the trial, the assistant prosecutor, Keith Giese, stated, "We're going to go back over the nine days of lies, the nine days of deceit, the nine days of trickery, the nine days of begging this country to help her find her children, while the whole time they lay dead at the bottom of that lake" (Reuter, 1995).

Would you have been able to detect if Susan Smith was lying by what she said or by her behaviour during her numerous press conferences? Vrij and Mann (2001) asked a similar question. They asked 52 police officers to view videotaped press conferences of people who were asking the public's help in locating their missing relatives or the murderers of their relatives. Vrij and Mann asked the officers to determine who was lying and who was telling the truth. What they didn't tell the officers was that every video showed people who had actually been found guilty of killing their own relatives. The officers were not very accurate at detecting the deception. Moreover, accuracy was not related to age, years of police work, level of experience interviewing suspects, or confidence.

detecting deception and confidence in their judgments, DePaulo, Charlton, Cooper, Lindsay, and Muhlenbruck (1997) found that the average correlation was 0.04. The reason that confidence is unrelated to accuracy may be that people rely on cues they believe are related to deception and when they see these cues, their confidence increases. However, since the cues people believe are related to deception are often not valid, their accuracy tends to be poor.

Research by Bond and DePaulo (2008) has found that there are no specific traits related to detecting deception in others. They conclude that "deception judgments depend more on the liar than the judge" (p. 489).

Porter, Campbell, Stapleton, and Birt (2002) investigated several factors related to the ability to detect deceit, including characteristics of the judge (e.g., handedness, type of cues used, personality), characteristics of the target (e.g., attractiveness, gender), and modality of reports (e.g., audiovisual or audio only). The findings were intriguing. In university students, detection accuracy was highest when the judge was left-handed, the target was unattractive, the target and judge were of opposite genders, and if facial cues were relied on. Porter and colleagues interpreted the left-handed advantage as being due to left-handers relying more on right-hemisphere processes, which in turn may be associated with greater emphasis on processing facial cues rather than relying on other, less informative, cues. Attractive liars are assumed to be more readily believed because of the activation of the stereotype that attractive people are more likely to tell the truth. Gender differences may also arise via the activation of stereotypes. See Box 4.5 to read about Dr. Porter and his research.

Box 4.5

# Canadian Researcher Profile: Dr. Stephen Porter

Dr. Stephen Porter completed his undergraduate degree at Acadia University and then moved west to complete his master's and doctorate at the University of British Columbia (UBC), working with Dr. John Yuille. His doctoral thesis focused on whether it was possible to implant memories of stressful childhood events (such as a serious medical procedure, a vicious dog attack, or a car accident). Over three suggestive interviews, more than half of the participants came to recall the false events either partially or in complete detail. Dr. Porter was surprised at the extent to which emotional memory can be so powerfully manipulated. This study was one of the factors contributing to the demise of the repressed memory movement.

Dr. Porter's first job was working in a medium security federal prison, and although he found it a fascinating experience, he decided he did not want to spend the rest of his life in prison and began his academic career at Dalhousie University. Currently Dr. Porter is a professor of psychology at the UBC—Okanagan and the director of the newly developed forensic psychology honours program.

Dr. Porter has diverse research interests that include credibility assessment, memory for crime (including eyewitness memory, false memory, and traumatic memory), violent behaviour, and psychopathy. His interest in each of these areas was sparked by the research of the three forensic faculty members at UBC: Drs. Yuille, Hare, and Dutton. Dr. Porter reports that his fascination with human behaviour is what maintains his continued interest in these areas. Both Dr. Porter and his productive group of graduate students use multiple research methods, including lab-based studies, longitudinal and prospective studies, field studies, and archival studies.

He has two favourite studies. He is very fond of a 2002 *Journal of Abnormal Psychology* paper co-authored with Mike Woodworth called "In Cold Blood." It was the first investigation of the types of homicides committed by psychopathic and nonpsychopathic offenders. They found that psychopathic murderers, with very few exceptions, carefully planned out their murders for instrumental gain, unlike other offenders. This finding challenged the traditional view that psychopaths are impulsive, or unable to inhibit their behaviour. Another of Dr. Porter's favourite studies is a 2008 *Psychological Science* paper that he wrote with his graduate student Leanne ten Brinke called "Reading Between the Lies." This study was the first to document exactly what happens on the human face when people try to deceive others about their emotional states.

Dr. Porter has been a consultant for both Crown and defence lawyers, as well as law enforcement officers. He remembers one particularly horrific double homicide case where he helped police investigators develop interrogation strategies for two potential suspects. He reports that he would enjoy being consulted on some current Canadian cases in which people plead for the return of their missing relatives.

There are two changes to the criminal justice system he would like to see. First, Dr. Porter wishes that the system would eliminate the automatic statutory release after two-thirds of a federal sentence. He believes that early release should be earned rather than automatic. Second, he thinks that the jury system should be eliminated because of the numerous flaws in jurors' decision making.

Dr. Porter believes that students in forensic psychology should be passionate about their research and learn the necessary skills to excel at research. He enjoys teaching abnormal, personality, and forensic psychology. When not at work, Dr. Porter enjoys riding a motorcycle, listening to punk music, and eating rich food.

# ASSESSMENT OF MALINGERING AND DECEPTION
## Disorders of Deception

Deception is a central component of some psychological disorders. The disorders described below vary on two dimensions: (1) whether the person intentionally or consciously produces the symptoms, and (2) whether the motivation is internal or external.

The *Diagnostic and Statistical Manual of Mental Disorders*, Fourth Edition (*DSM-IV*) (American Psychiatric Association [APA], 1994) diagnostic criteria for a **factitious disorder** include (1) physical or psychological symptoms that are intentionally produced, (2) internal motivation to assume the sick role, and (3) an absence of external incentives. Eisendrath (1996) has suggested that patients with factitious disorders might be aware they are intentionally producing the symptoms, but they may lack insight into the underlying psychological motivation.

**Factitious disorder:** A disorder in which the person's physical and psychological symptoms are intentionally produced and are adopted to assume the role of a sick person

There are many different subtypes of factitious disorders, with most being rare. An example of a physical factitious disorder is **Munchausen syndrome**. In this syndrome, the patient intentionally produces a physical complaint, such as abdominal pain, and constantly seeks physician consultations, hospitalizations, and even surgery to treat the nonexistent illness. In some cases, patients will ingest poison or purposely infect wounds to maintain a patient role. This disorder often emerges by age 20, is difficult to treat, and is chronic in nature (APA, 1994). Meadow (1977) coined the term *Munchausen syndrome by proxy* (MBP) to describe cases in which parents or caregivers falsified symptoms in their children. A study by Rosenberg (1987) evaluated 117 reported cases of MBP and found 98% of the individuals were the biological mother of the child; in almost 9% of the cases, the child died. In a more recent review of this syndrome, Sheridan (2003) analyzed the characteristics of 451 MBP cases. Although the most common perpetrator was the child's biological mother (77%), other perpetrators were also identified (the father in 7% of cases). Most the victims were young (age 4 or younger), with 6% of the victims dying and 7% suffering long-term physical injuries. Nearly a third (29%) of the perpetrators had some symptoms of Munchausen syndrome.

**Munchausen syndrome:** A rare factitious disorder in which a person intentionally produces a physical complaint and constantly seeks physician consultations, hospitalizations, and even surgery to treat the nonexistent illness

The two key components of **somatoform disorders** include (1) physical symptoms that cannot be explained by an underlying organic impairment, and (2) the symptoms are not intentionally produced. In this disorder, patients truly believe they have a physical problem and often consult with their physicians for treatment of their physical problems. Somatoform disorders are rare and often co-occur with other disorders, such as depression or anxiety (Gureje, Simon, Ustun, & Goldberg, 1997).

**Somatoform disorders:** A disorder in which physical symptoms suggest a physical illness but have no known underlying physiological cause and the symptoms are not intentionally produced

The two key components to **malingering** are that (1) the psychological or physical symptoms are clearly under voluntary control and (2) there are external motivations for the production of symptoms. People typically malinger mental illness for one of the following external motivations:

**Malingering:** Intentionally faking psychological or physical symptoms for some type of external gain

- A criminal may attempt to avoid punishment by pretending to be unfit to stand trial, to have a mental illness at the time of a criminal act, or to have an acute mental illness to avoid being executed.

- Prisoners or patients may seek drugs, or prisoners may want to be transferred to a psychiatric facility to do easier time or escape.

- Malingerers may seek to avoid conscription to the military or to avoid certain military duties.

- Malingerers may seek financial gain from disability claims, workers' compensation, or damages from alleged injury.

- Malingerers may seek admission to a hospital to obtain free room and board.

Any psychiatric or physical disorder may be malingered. As new syndromes are developed, such as post-traumatic stress disorder, they provide new opportunities for people to attempt to malinger them. Malingering varies in terms of severity from benign (e.g., "Not tonight, honey; I have a headache.") to serious (e.g., "I heard a voice telling me to kill my neighbour, so I obeyed it.").

Individuals with factitious and somatoform disorders often encourage and even insist on having physical tests and invasive procedures, whereas malingerers will often refuse to cooperate with invasive procedures to determine the veracity of their symptoms. The incidence of malingering in the general population is unknown. Patients who malinger rarely admit it. Thus, individuals who successfully malinger are never included in the statistics. Moreover, mental health professionals are often reluctant to label a patient as a malingerer.

The prevalence rate of malingering is relatively high in forensic contexts. For example, Frederick, Crosby, and Wynkoop (2000) reported that 45% of patients evaluated for competency or mental state at the time of offence produced invalid psychological test profiles. Rogers, Ustad, and Salekin (1998) reported that 20% of emergency jail referrals feigned psychological symptoms. Rogers (1986) reported that 4.5% of defendants evaluated for mental state at the time of offence were definite malingerers and another 20% were suspected. Given these large numbers, it is clear that malingering should be considered in all forensic evaluations. Estimates of malingering psychological symptoms following personal injury range widely. For example, Lees-Haley (1997) reported that about 25% of personal injury claimants were feigning post-traumatic symptoms in an attempt to receive financial compensation.

The opposite of malingering is called **defensiveness**. Defensiveness refers to the conscious denial or extreme minimization of physical or psychological symptoms. Patients or offenders of this sort seek to present themselves in a favourable light. Minimization of physical and psychological symptoms varies both in degree and motivation. Some people might want to appear to be functioning well to meet an external need, such as being a fit parent, or an internal need, such as unwillingness to acknowledge they are a "patient." Degree of defensiveness can range from mild, such as downplaying a minor symptom, to outright denial of a more serious psychological impairment, such as denying hearing command hallucinations.

**Defensiveness:** Conscious denial or extreme minimization of physical or psychological symptoms

## Explanatory Models of Malingering

Based on motivations, Rogers (1990) described three explanatory models of malingering: pathogenic, criminological, and adaptational. The pathogenic model assumes that people are motivated to malinger because of an underlying mental disorder. According to this model, the patient attempts to gain control over his or her pathology by creating bogus symptoms. Over time, these patients experience more severe mental disorders and the true symptoms emerge. Little empirical support exists for this model.

The criminological model focuses on "badness": "a bad person (Antisocial Personality Disorder), in bad circumstances (legal difficulties), who is performing badly (uncooperative)" (Rogers, 1997, p. 7). This definition is similar to the malingering definition described in the *DSM-IV* (APA, 1994). According to this definition, malingering should be strongly suspected if two or more of the following factors are evident: (1) presence of antisocial personality disorder, (2) forensic assessment, (3) lack of cooperation, and (4) marked discrepancy between subjective complaints and objective findings. Like the pathogenic model, little empirical support exists for this model. No research indicates that persons with antisocial personality disorder are any more likely to malinger than are other offenders (Rogers, 1990). In addition, many different types of patients are uncooperative with evaluations, including those with eating disorders or substance-use problems. In contrast, some malingerers appear to be highly cooperative. Rogers (1990) found that *DSM-IV* indicators of malingering tended to overdiagnose malingering in a forensic sample.

According to the adaptational model, malingering is likely to occur when (1) there is a perceived adversarial context, (2) personal stakes are very high, and (3) no other viable alternatives are perceived. Research findings support this model in that there are higher rates of malingering in adversarial settings or when the personal stakes are high. This model provides the broadest and least pejorative explanation of malingering. Rogers, Sewell, and Goldstein (1994) asked 320 forensic psychologists to rate 32 items subdivided into pathogenic, criminological, and adaptational models on how important the item was to malingering. The adaptational model was rated the most important and the pathogenic model as the least important.

## How to Study Malingering

Research comprises three basic designs: case study, simulation, and known groups. Each of these designs has its associated strengths and weaknesses. Although case studies are not used as often as they once were, they are useful for generating a wide variety of hypotheses that can be tested by using designs with more experimental rigour. In addition, a case study is the only way to examine rare syndromes such as MBP syndrome.

**Simulation design:** As applied to malingering research, people are told to pretend they have specific symptoms or a disorder

Most research on malingering has used a **simulation design** (similar to polygraph laboratory studies). Participants are told to malinger a specific disorder and are typically compared with two groups: (1) a control group randomly selected from the same population as the malingerers and (2) a clinical comparison group representing the disorders or symptoms that are being feigned. These studies address whether measures can detect malingering in nonclinical samples. However, individuals with mental disorders may also malinger. Studies have begun to ask patients with mental disorders to feign a different mental disorder or to exaggerate the severity of their symptoms. These studies address how effectively participants with mental disorders can malinger. In an early study using a clinical sample, Rogers (1988) reported that nearly half of the psychiatric in-patients either did not remember or did not follow the instructions to malinger. To examine the relative efficacy of detection methods for disordered and nondisordered samples, the optimal simulation design would use four groups: nonclinical experimental, nonclinical-control, clinical-experimental, and clinical-control.

The primary strength of the simulation design is its experimental rigour. The main disadvantage is its limited generalizability to the real world. Simulation studies are often limited in their clinical usefulness because of the minimal levels of preparation and level of motivation by participants. Early studies used brief and nonspecific instructions, such as, "Appear mentally ill." Instructions are now more specific, with some studies giving participants a scenario to follow: For example, "Imagine you have been in a car accident and you hit your head. You have decided to exaggerate the amount of memory problems you are having to obtain a larger monetary settlement from the car insurance company." In addition, participants may be given time to prepare.

Some studies have coached participants by providing information about genuine mental disorders or by telling them about detection strategies. Research suggests that telling participants about disorders does not help them, whereas information about detection strategies does help them avoid detection (Baer, Wetter, & Berry, 1995; Storm & Graham, 2000). In contrast, Bagby et al. (2002) found that providing students with information about validity scales designed to detect deception did not enhance their ability to feign successfully.

Ethical concerns have been raised about whether participants should be taught how to become skilled malingerers. Ben-Porath (1994) has argued that such research does not "appear to have sufficient scientific justification to make up for the potential harm that might be caused by publishing such a study" (p. 150). A survey of lawyers and law students indicates that about 50% would provide information about psychological testing, including whether the test had any validity scales to detect deception (Wetter & Corrigan, 1995). See Box 4.6 for a discussion of the conflict between ethics and research design when doing this type of research.

When individuals engage in malingering in applied settings, the stakes are often high. For example, they may obtain funding for a disability or avoid a harsher sentence. Both the type and magnitude of incentives are typically limited in simulation studies. Studies that use incentives often offer monetary rewards to malingerers for being successful. The magnitude of the incentive ranges from very modest (e.g., $5) to more substantial (e.g., having their names placed in a lottery for the chance to win $100). Simulation studies have rarely used negative incentives. For example, the researcher could offer money for participating in a malingering study but take some of the money away if the participant is detected as unsuccessfully using deception.

Studies investigating malingering in applied settings would ideally use the known-groups design. The **known-groups design** involves two stages: (1) the establishment of the criterion groups (e.g., genuine patients and malingerers), and (2) an analysis of the similarities and differences between these criterion groups. The main strength of the known-groups design is its generalizability to real-world settings. Its chief limitation is the establishment of the criterion groups. Samples of the genuine patients likely include errors, and some of the classified malingerers may be genuine patients. Because of the difficulty with the reliable and accurate classification of criterion groups, this design is rarely used in malingering research.

**Known-groups design:** As applied to malingering research, it involves comparing genuine patients and malingerers attempting to fake the disorder the patients have

## Malingered Psychosis

How often people attempt to feign psychosis is unknown. Pope, Jonas, and Jones (1982) found nine patients with factitious psychosis in a sample of 219 consecutive admissions to a forensic psychiatric hospital. They followed these patients for seven years, and none went on to develop a psychotic disorder, although all were diagnosed with either borderline personality disorder (a personality disorder defined by instability in mood, self-image, and interpersonal relationships) or histrionic personality disorder (a personality disorder

Box 4.6

# Ethics of Deception Research

Simulation laboratory studies are often used to study the accuracy of detection measures. To make these experiments more similar to real-world situations, rewards are given for successful deception, but punishment can be meted out for unsuccessful deception. In the studies described below, both positive and negative incentives were used to approximate real-life criminal investigation settings.

## Psychopathy, Threat, and Polygraph Test Accuracy

The participants in a laboratory polygraph study by Patrick and Iacono (1989) were incarcerated Canadian male offenders. The experimenters wanted to "create a realistic threat context for the polygraph tests. . . . A failure to live up to group expectations can provoke responses much stronger than mere disapproval: Peer labelling in the prison environment frequently leads to ostracism, persecution, and physical brutality" (p. 348). Offenders were offered $10 for participating in the experiment and the potential of a $20 bonus. Offenders were told that if more than ten offenders were judged by the polygraph examiner as deceptive, no one would receive the $20 bonus. To increase the offenders' motivation, they were told that a list of the names of participants who failed would be made public.

Offenders were randomly assigned to commit or not commit a mock crime. The mock crime consisted of sneaking into the doctor's office and removing $20 from the pocket of the doctor's jacket. Each participant was given a polygraph test. It was clear that some of the participants were concerned about their test outcomes. For example, one offender stated, "I hope they [the other inmates] don't beat my head if I fail" (Patrick & Iacono, 1989, p. 353).

At the end of the study, all participants were given the $20 bonus and participants' polygraph test outcomes were not made public.

## Detecting Deceit and Different Types of High-Stakes Lies

In a study of observers' ability to detect deception, Frank and Ekman (1997) used both positive and negative incentives to motivate their participants. Participants engaged in a mock crime, which involved stealing $50 from a briefcase. They were told they could keep this money if they were able to convince an interviewer they had not taken the money (positive incentive). However, they were also warned that if the interviewer judged them as lying, they would have to give back the $50 and would not get the $10 for participating in the study (negative incentive). Some participants were also told that if they were unsuccessful liars, they would have to sit on a metal chair in a cold, small, darkened room and listen to repeated blasts of 110 decibel white noise for an hour (even more negative incentive). At the end of the experiment, all participants received their $10 and were told they did not need to face the additional punishment.

Researchers often have to balance ethical concerns with attempts to increase the validity of their research. In the two studies described here, deception was used to motivate the participants. Some researchers might consider that the level of deception borders on unethical, whereas others would argue that this level of deception is necessary to make the research meaningful. Researchers submit their research protocols to ethical committees for review to ensure the rights of participants are protected. Thus, although you may have some concerns about the level of deception, both of these studies were approved by ethical review.

defined by excessive emotionality and attention-seeking behaviours). The presence of malingering does not negate the possibility that other psychiatric illnesses or psychological disorders are present. In fact, the term *instrumental psychosis* was developed to identify patients (many with psychiatric histories) attempting to feign symptoms to secure special accommodations (Waite & Geddes, 2006). Cornell and Hawk (1989) reported that 8% of 314 consecutive psychiatric admissions were diagnosed as malingering psychotic symptoms by experienced forensic psychologists. Box 4.7 describes one of the first studies of malingered psychosis.

# Being Sane in Insane Places

In 1973, David Rosenhan published a paper in the journal *Science* titled "Being Sane in Insane Places." Rosenhan's goal was to investigate the accuracy of psychiatric diagnoses and the consequences of diagnostic labels. In the first part of his study, eight individuals with no history of a mental disorder tried to gain admission to several mental hospitals. Imagine you are one of the pseudo-patients taking part in Rosenhan's study. You go to your local hospital complaining that you have been hearing voices. When asked what the voices are saying, you reply that it is sometimes unclear but you think they are saying "empty," "hollow," and "thud." You state that you do not recognize the voice. Other than falsifying your name and occupation, everything else about your personal history is true. Like the actual eight pseudo-patients in the study, you also have no history of any serious pathology. To your surprise, you are immediately admitted to the psychiatric in-patient ward with a diagnosis of schizophrenia. Once you are admitted, you tell the staff that your auditory hallucinations have disappeared. Like the real pseudo-patients, you are feeling somewhat apprehensive about what might happen to you. You are cooperative and friendly toward staff and patients. When the staff member asks you how you are feeling, you answer, "I am fine." You follow the rules in the hospital and pretend to take the medication given to you. You have been told that you have to get out of the hospital on your own. So you try to convince the staff you are "sane." To deal with the boredom, you pace up and down the hall, engage staff and patients in conversation, and write extensive notes about your daily activities. The staff members do not question you about this behaviour, although the other patients on the ward comment on your note-taking and accuse you of being "a journalist or a professor."

In the actual experiment, pseudo-patients were hospitalized from 7 to 52 days. Staff failed to recognize the lack of symptoms in the pseudo-patients. Not one of the pseudo-patients was identified as "normal" by staff. As noted by Rosenhan (1973), "once a person is designated abnormal, all of his other behaviors are colored by that label" (p. 253). For example, the nurses interpret your pacing behaviour as a manifestation of anxiety and your note-taking as a behavioural manifestation of your pathology. Pseudo-patients' attempts to initiate conversations with staff were not very successful, since the staff would "give a brief response while they were on the move and with head averted, or no response at all" (Rosenhan, 1973, p. 255). An example of one conversation was,

> **[Pseudo-patient]:** "Pardon me, Dr. X. Could you tell me when I am eligible for grounds privileges?"
>
> **[Physician]:** "Good morning, Dave. How are you today?" (Moves off without waiting for a reply.) (p. 255)

This study raises concerns about the use of labels and how such labels can influence the meaning of behaviours. What are the consequences of psychiatric diagnoses? As stated by Rosenhan (1973), "A diagnosis of cancer that has been found to be in error is cause for celebration. But psychiatric diagnoses are rarely found to be in error. The label sticks, a mark of inadequacy forever" (p. 257).

**What Are the Indicators of Malingered Psychosis?** Table 4.5 provides a list of the potential indicators of malingered psychosis. Resnick (1997) provides a comprehensive description of these indicators. Malingerers often tend to overact, believing the more bizarre they are, the more psychotic they will appear. Early observers have also reported this. For example, Jones and Llewellyn (1917) stated the malingerer "sees less than the blind, he hears less than the deaf, and is more lame than the paralysed. . . . He . . . piles symptom upon symptom and so outstrips madness itself" (p. 17). Malingerers are often willing to discuss their symptoms when asked, whereas actual patients with schizophrenia are often reluctant to discuss their symptoms. Some malingerers may attempt to control the assessment by behaving in an intimidating manner or by accusing the clinician of not believing them. In an interview, a malingerer may be evasive when asked to provide

### Table 4.5 Cues to Malingered Psychosis in Criminal Defendants

- Understandable motive for committing crime
- Presence of a partner in the crime
- Current crime fits pattern of previous criminal history
- Suspicious hallucinations
  - Continuous rather than intermittent
  - Vague or inaudible hallucinations
  - Hallucinations with no delusions
  - Inability to describe strategies to diminish voices
  - Claiming all command hallucinations are obeyed
  - Visual hallucinations in black and white
- Suspicious delusions
  - Abrupt onset or termination
  - Eagerness to discuss delusions
  - Conduct markedly inconsistent with delusions
  - Elaborate delusions that lack paranoid, grandiose, or religious themes
- Marked discrepancies in interview versus noninterview behaviour
- Sudden emergence of psychotic symptoms to explain criminal act
- Absence of any subtle signs of psychosis

Source: Adapted from Resnick, 1997.

details, take a long time to answer, or answer, "I don't know." Malingerers often report rare or atypical symptoms, blatant symptoms, or absurd symptoms that are usually not endorsed by genuine patients. For example, a person attempting to malinger psychosis may claim to have seen "a large 60-foot Christ who told me to kill my mother."

Malingerers are more likely to report positive symptoms of schizophrenia, such as delusions (a false belief that is persistently held) or hallucinations (a perceptual experience in absence of external stimulation), as compared with negative or subtle symptoms of schizophrenia, such as blunted affect, concreteness, or peculiar thinking. Both auditory and visual hallucinations are common in psychotic patients. When a person is suspected of malingering auditory hallucinations, he or she should be asked the vocal characteristics (e.g., clarity, loudness, duration), source (inside or outside of the head), characteristics (e.g., gender, familiar or unfamiliar voice, command), and response (insight into unreality, coping strategies, obeying them). Comparing genuine and feigned auditory hallucinations is one way to detect a malingerer. For example, actual patients often report coping strategies to make the "voices go away," such as watching television, seeking out interpersonal contact, or taking medications (Kanas & Barr, 1984). The malingerer may report there is nothing that will make the voices go away. In other cases, malingerers may report atypical auditory command hallucinations (hallucinations telling people to act in a certain way), such as "Go commit a sex offence" or "Rob, rob, rob."

Jason King is a 30-year-old, single, white man charged with aggravated sexual assault. He is being assessed for fitness to stand trial at a pretrial jail. The police report indicated he acted alone and had stalked the victim prior to the sexual assault. The arresting police officers and correctional officers at the jail observed no signs of abnormal behaviour in Jason. During the psychological evaluation, Jason rocked back and forth and sang songs. He constantly interrupted the psychologist and claimed he had ESP powers and was being held as a political prisoner. He answered all the questions, although he refused to elaborate on some of his symptoms and would often say "I don't know." He claimed his lawyer was a communist and was out to convert him. He also stated the courtroom was actually a circus, with the judge being the ringmaster and the jury the audience.

### Your Turn . . .

What are the clues that Jason might be malingering a mental disorder? If you were the forensic psychologist doing the assessment, which malingering tests would you use? Who else might you want to interview to help your assessment?

Genuine visual hallucinations are usually of normal-sized people seen in colour, and remain the same if eyes are open or closed. Atypical visual hallucinations, such as seeing "a green devil in the corner laughing," "a dog that would change in size when giving messages," or hallucinations only in black and white, are indicative of malingering.

## Assessment Methods to Detect Malingered Psychosis

**Interview-Based Methods** The Structured Interview of Reported Symptoms (SIRS) (Rogers, Bagby, & Dickens, 1992) was initially developed in 1985, and in its most recent version, it consists of 172 items that are scored from a structured interview. The items are organized into the following eight scales that represent different strategies that a person may employ when malingering:

1. Rare symptoms: symptoms that true patients endorse very infrequently
2. Symptom combinations: uncommon pairings of symptoms
3. Improbable or absurd symptoms: symptoms unlikely to be true, since true patients rarely endorsed them
4. Blatant symptoms: items that are obvious signs of mental disorder
5. Subtle symptoms: items that contain what most people consider everyday problems
6. Selectivity of symptoms: ratio of symptoms endorsed versus those not endorsed
7. Severity of symptoms: number of severe symptoms reported
8. Reported versus observed symptoms: discrepancy between self-report and observable symptoms

The SIRS has been extensively validated by using both simulation and known-groups designs, and research has consistently demonstrated differences in SIRS scores between honest and simulating samples, and between clinical samples and suspected malingerers (Rogers, 2008). The SIRS also correlates strongly with validity indices from the Minnesota Multiphasic Personality Inventory (MMPI-2; Boccaccini, Murrie, & Duncan, 2006; Edens, Poythress, & Watkins-Clay, 2007) and is used widely by clinical forensic psychologists (Archer, Buffington-Vollum, Stredny, & Handel, 2006).

Another interview-based method is the Miller-Forensic Assessment of Symptoms Test(M-FAST; Miller, 2001), which was developed on 330 forensic patients and 216 undergraduate students and was intended as a brief, structured interview (25 items, 10-minute administration) to provide clinicians with a valid and reliable measure for detecting feigned mental illness. The M-FAST contains nine content items that resemble SIRS scales, including unusual hallucinations, reported versus observed symptoms, contradictory symptoms, extreme symptoms, trigger questions, rare combinations, negative image, unusual symptom onset, and suggestibility. A number of recent studies suggest that the M-FAST is a useful, reliable tool for detecting malingering (Guy, Kwartner, & Miller, 2006; Guy & Miller, 2004; Jackson, Rogers, & Sewell, 2005; Miller, 2001, 2005). The M-FAST is intended as a screening tool and is not recommended for use in isolation.

**Self-Report Questionnaire** The most widely used personality inventory to assess nonoffenders and offenders is the MMPI-2 (Butcher, Dahlstrom, Graham, Tellegen, & Kaemmer, 1989). The MMPI-2 includes several clinical scales to assess psychopathology but also includes several scales specifically designed to test "faking-bad" or malingering. For example, the items on the Infrequency ($F$) scale and the Back F ($F_B$) scale were developed to detect unusual or atypical symptoms and consist of items endorsed by less than 10% of a normative sample.

A comprehensive meta-analysis of the MMPI-2 and malingering found that the $F$ and $F_B$ scales were the most useful at detecting malingerers (Rogers, Sewell, Martin, & Vitacco, 2003). However, the optimal cut-off score to use varies across the samples studied. A study by Storm and Graham (2000) examined whether the MMPI-2 validity scales would be able to correctly classify college students who have been coached on malingering strategies, students told to malinger but given no coaching, and psychiatric in-patients. Some validity indicators were more susceptible to coaching, whereas others, such as the Infrequency Scale, could still discriminate coached malingerers from psychiatric in-patients. Recent research with criminal defendants, classified as malingerers or not based on the SIRS, has also supported the use of the Infrequency ($F$) scale to identify malingerers in forensic populations (Toomey, Kucharski, & Duncan, 2009).

## SUMMARY

1. The Comparison Question Test (CQT) is the most commonly used polygraph exam in North America. It consists of three types of questions: irrelevant, comparison (questions relating to past behaviours that are supposed to generate emotion), and relevant (questions relating to the crime being investigated). The Concealed Information Test (CIT) probes for whether the suspect has knowledge about the details of a crime that only the guilty person would have.

2. The CQT is quite accurate at detecting guilt but is not very good at determining a suspect's innocence (i.e., it has a high false-positive rate). The CIT is quite accurate in detecting innocence but is not very good at determining a suspect's guilt (i.e., it has a high false-negative rate).

3. Event-related brain potentials (ERPs) and brain-imaging techniques can be used to detect deception in laboratory settings. However, these techniques have not yet been used extensively in forensic settings.

4. Another method of attempting to detect whether someone is lying is through the analysis of verbal characteristics and non-verbal behaviours. The non-verbal indicator most strongly associated with deception is voice pitch. A verbal characteristic associated with deception is that liars provide fewer details when lying compared with those telling the truth.

5. The two key components to malingering are that the psychological or physical symptoms are clearly under voluntary control and that there are external motivations for the production of symptoms. Malingering should be considered in any forensic evaluation. Three explanatory models of malingering have been proposed: pathogenic, criminological, and adaptational. Only the adaptational model has received empirical support.

6. Malingering research utilizes three basic designs: case study, simulation, and known groups. The most common is the simulation design.

## Discussion Questions

1. You are a forensic psychologist hired to determine if a defendant is truly psychotic. What sorts of information would you base your assessment on? What clinical indicators would you look for?

2. Many of the studies designed to detect deception involve deceiving research participants. What ethical concerns have been raised? What types of studies should be allowed?

3. The Comparison Question Test is the polygraph test commonly used by police in North America. Do you think this test has sufficient validity for use by the police? Should it be admissible in court?

4. You recently got hired as a customs agent. Knowing what you do about non-verbal and verbal cues to deception, what cues would you watch out for to catch someone smuggling?

# Chapter 5
## Eyewitness Testimony

## Learning Objectives

- Describe two categories of independent variables and three general dependent variables found in eyewitness research.

- Describe and explain the misinformation effect.

- Outline the components of the cognitive interview.

- Describe lineup procedures and how they may be biased.

- Summarize the debate surrounding expert testimony on eyewitness issues.

- Outline the recommendations for collecting eyewitness identification evidence.

Lucy Peluso went to the bank on her lunch hour. As she approached the teller, a man pushed her out of the way so that he could quickly exit the bank. Seconds later, Lucy found out that the man had robbed the teller. Lucy was an eyewitness. The police interviewed her along with the others in the bank. The witnesses were able to hear one another describe what they saw. Six months after the robbery, Lucy was asked to go to the police station to view a series of photographs. When she was asked whether the man who robbed the bank was pictured, Lucy very quickly pointed and said, "That's him, I'm certain."

Eyewitness evidence is one of the earliest and most widely studied topics in forensic psychology. As you read in Chapter 1, the German psychologist Albert von Schrenck-Notzing testified during a serial killer trial about the influence of pretrial media exposure on witnesses' memory. Today, both the police and the courts rely on eyewitness evidence. Eyewitness testimony is one of the most compelling types of evidence presented in criminal trials. Thus, information about the likelihood and types of mistakes made by eyewitnesses is vitally important in terms of justice. In this chapter, we will focus on how memory works when it comes to remembering in an eyewitness context. As well, we will examine the various factors and police procedures that can influence how accurate eyewitnesses can be.

## EYEWITNESS TESTIMONY: THE ROLE OF MEMORY

A large part of eyewitness testimony rests on memory. The concept of memory can be viewed as a process involving several stages. The encoding stage occurs first, when you perceive and pay attention to details in your environment. For example, you are perceiving and paying attention when you look at a stranger's face and notice his big, bushy eyebrows. To some extent, the stranger's face and eyebrows have been encoded. The encoded information then passes into your short-term holding facility, known as your short-term memory. Your short-term memory has a limited capacity. Consequently, to make room for other, new information, information in your short-term memory passes into your longer-term holding facility, known as your long-term memory. Information from long-term memory can be accessed or retrieved as needed. For example, if you are asked to describe the stranger you saw, you will retrieve the information you stored in your long-term memory and report that the stranger had bushy eyebrows. It is important to remember that not every piece of information will go through all the memory stages and factors can affect each stage. For example, not all details from an event will be encoded; nor will all information in short-term memory move to long-term memory. Using our example of Lucy Peluso witnessing a bank robbery, consider the factors that are occurring to affect memory and retrieval.

Look at this scene for five seconds

Lucy is filling out a deposit slip so she will be ready for the bank teller. She is not paying attention to her environment (factor: inattention). Unexpectedly, there is a brief interaction between her and an unfamiliar male (factors: unexpectedness; amount of time to view environmental details). Lucy is now a witness, and she is interviewed with several other people in the bank by police (factor: hearing others describe the same environmental details she saw). The police officer asks Lucy a few, brief questions (factor: the wording of the questions). Lucy is called six months after the crime to examine a lineup (factors: the amount of time elapsed between having witnessed the event and having to retrieve the information; type of lineup procedure used). Lucy is confident when she identifies the culprit (factor: relation between confidence and accuracy). Figure 5.1 delineates the stages of memory.

As you may have figured out by now, memory is not like a video recording in which an identical representation of the event is stored and then can be played on request (Loftus, 1979b). Our memory can change each time we retrieve the event; some parts of the event may be embellished or guessed at because we cannot remember all the details. Often in our everyday life, our memory fallibilities are insignificant. For example, remembering that you bought a coffee at a Second Cup when actually it came from a Tim Hortons is harmless, most likely. In contrast, remembering whether the culprit was right- or left-handed may be critical if police are going to arrest the guilty suspect.

Eyewitness memory retrieval can be broadly partitioned into either recall or recognition memory. **Recall memory** refers to reporting details of a previously witnessed event or person. For example, describing what the culprit did and what the culprit looked like are both recall tasks. In contrast, **recognition memory** refers to determining whether a previously seen item or person is the same as what is currently being viewed. For example, hearing a set of voices and identifying the culprit's voice or identifying clothing worn by the culprit during the crime are both recognition tasks.

**Recall memory:** Reporting details of a previously witnessed event or person

**Recognition memory:** Determining whether a previously seen item or person is the same as what is currently being viewed

**Figure 5.1** Stages of Memory

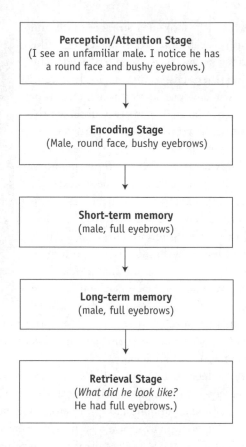

**Perception/Attention Stage**
(I see an unfamiliar male. I notice he has
a round face and bushy eyebrows.)

↓

**Encoding Stage**
(Male, round face, bushy eyebrows)

↓

**Short-term memory**
(male, full eyebrows)

↓

**Long-term memory**
(male, full eyebrows)

↓

**Retrieval Stage**
(*What did he look like?*
He had full eyebrows.)

## HOW DO WE STUDY EYEWITNESS ISSUES?

Researchers interested in studying eyewitness issues can examine data from actual crimes. For example, they can use archival data such as police reports, or they can examine witnesses in naturalistic environments by accompanying police to crime scenes and interviewing witnesses after the police have done their job. Alternatively, they can conduct laboratory simulations. The laboratory simulation study is the most common paradigm used to study eyewitness issues.

### The Laboratory Simulation

To study eyewitness memory by using a laboratory simulation, an unknowing participant views a critical event, such as a crime, through a slide sequence, a video recording, or live. The participant is unaware that he or she will be questioned about the event until after the event is witnessed. Now a witness, the participant is asked to describe what happened and the target/culprit involved. Following the descriptions of what was witnessed, the witness may be asked to examine a lineup. Many independent variables can be manipulated or examined; however, there are only three general dependent variables in eyewitness studies.

**Independent Variables** Numerous independent variables can be manipulated or examined within the laboratory simulation. Wells (1978) has coined the terms estimator variable and system variable to help classify them. **Estimator variables** are those variables or factors that are present at the time of the crime and that cannot be changed. These can

**Estimator variables:** Variables that are present at the time of the crime and that cannot be changed include the age of the witness, the amount of lighting, the presence of a weapon, and whether the witness was intoxicated. The criminal justice system cannot exert control over these variables. Thus, their effect on eyewitness accuracy can be estimated only after the crime. **System variables** are those variables or factors that can be manipulated to increase (or decrease) eyewitness accuracy, such as the type of procedure used by police to interview the witness or the type of lineup procedure used to present the suspect to the witness. These variables are under the control of the justice system. Both estimator and system variables can be manipulated in eyewitness laboratory studies.

**System variables:** Variables that can be manipulated to increase (or decrease) eyewitness accuracy

**Dependent Variables** The three general dependent variables in eyewitness studies are (1) recall of the event/crime, (2) recall of the culprit, and (3) recognition of the culprit.

Recall of the crime or the culprit can take two formats. With **open-ended recall**, also known as a **free narrative**, witnesses are asked to either write or orally state all they remember about the event without the officer (or experimenter) asking questions. With this type of recall, the witness also may be asked to describe the culprit. With **direct question recall**, witnesses are asked a series of specific questions about the crime or the culprit. For example, the witness may be asked the colour of the getaway car or the length of the culprit's hair.

**Open-ended recall:** Witnesses are asked to either write or orally state all they remember about the event without the officer (or experimenter) asking questions. Also known as a *free narrative*

**Free narrative:** Witnesses are asked to either write or orally state all they remember about the event without the officer (or experimenter) asking questions. Also known as *open-ended recall*

**Direct question recall:** Witnesses are asked a series of specific questions about the crime or the culprit

A witness's recall of the crime or the culprit can be examined for the following:

■ *The amount of information reported.* How many descriptors of the crime do witnesses report? How many descriptors of the culprit do witnesses report?

■ *The type of information reported.* What is the proportion of peripheral details versus central details? What is the proportion of culprit details versus environment details?

■ *The accuracy of information reported.* What is the proportion of correct descriptors reported? What is the proportion of omission errors (information the witness failed to report)? What is the proportion of commission errors (details falsely reported to be present)?

As for the recognition of the culprit, the typical recognition task is a lineup. A culprit **lineup** is a set of people presented to the witness, who in turn must identify the culprit if he or she is present. Another type of lineup takes the form of a set of voices, and the witness is asked to identify the culprit's voice. Clothing lineups, in which the witness examines clothing that may have been worn by the culprit, sometimes are also used.

**Lineup:** A set of people presented to the witness, who in turn must state whether the culprit is present and, if so, which one

A witness's recognition response can be examined for the following:

■ *Accuracy of decision.* What is the rate of correctly identifying the culprit in the lineup? What is the rate of correctly stating that the culprit is not present in the lineup?

■ *Types of errors made.* What is the rate of identifying an innocent person? What is the rate of stating that the culprit is not present when he or she is actually in the lineup?

# RECALL MEMORY

The primary goal for an officer interviewing an eyewitness is to extract from the witness a complete and accurate report of what happened (Fisher, Geiselman, & Raymond, 1987; Jackson, Sijlbing, & Thiecke, 1996). Insufficient information may provide the officer with few leads to pursue, resulting in a case that will not be solved. In this situation, the culprit will remain free to commit further crimes. If inaccurate information is supplied, then an officer may pursue innocent suspects, thus reducing the likelihood that the guilty person will be caught.

Now test your own recall. Without looking back at the crime scene photo on page 119, how many details can you remember?

## Interviewing Eyewitnesses

Fisher et al. (1987) were curious about the techniques police were using to interview eyewitnesses. They analyzed 11 tape-recorded interviews from a police department in Florida. Eight different detectives, who averaged 10.5 years of experience each, conducted these interviews. The researchers found that the interviews were conducted with a lot of variation. In general, however, the researchers found that the officers would introduce themselves, ask the eyewitnesses to report what they remembered by using an open-ended format, and then ask the witnesses a series of direct questions to determine specific information, such as the age or height of the culprit. The officers usually ended the interview by asking the eyewitnesses if there was any additional information that they could remember.

Fisher et al. (1987) found that the police officers' approach limited their ability to collect complete and accurate information in a number of ways. First, the researchers found that police often interrupted eyewitnesses when they were providing an open-ended recall report. The police may limit the amount of information eyewitnesses have in their conscious memory by preventing them from speaking or distracting them with questions.

Second, police questioned eyewitnesses with very short, specific questions. This type of question format uses a more superficial level of concentration than open-ended questions and tends to result in very short answers. The other problem with short, specific questions is that a police officer may not ask a relevant question that would provide critical information. For example, the culprit may have a tattoo, but if the officer does not ask about tattoos, the eyewitness may not report this feature. Thus, the police officer may miss a descriptor that could help in narrowing the suspect pool and arresting the culprit.

Third, police officers tended to ask questions in a predetermined or random order that was inconsistent with the information that witnesses were providing at the time. For example, a police officer may have asked a question about the culprit's voice while the witness was describing the culprit's clothing. Mixing visual and auditory questions has been found to decrease recall by approximately 19% (Fisher & Price-Roush, as cited in Fisher et al., 1987). Lastly, officers tended to ask questions that are "leading" or suggestive, which can be very dangerous when trying to collect accurate information.

## The Leading Question—The Misinformation Effect

Elizabeth Loftus, one of the most prominent researchers in the area of leading questions, has conducted many experiments demonstrating that a witness's recall report can be altered by the phrasing of a question. In one study, Loftus and Palmer (1974) had university students watch a videotape of a car accident. After viewing the accident, the participants were asked the identical question with a variation in one critical word, *hit*: "About how fast were the cars going when they hit each other?" *Hit* was replaced with either *smashed*, *collided*, *bumped*, or *contacted*. Even though all participants saw the same videotape, the speed reported by the participants varied depending on which critical word was used. Participants reported the highest rate of speed when the word *smashed* was used and the lowest rates of speed when the words *bumped* and *contacted* were used.

The experiment did not end there. The researchers called participants back a week later and asked whether they had seen any broken glass. Participants who were questioned with the word *smashed* were more likely to recall seeing broken glass than were the other participants. However, there was no broken glass in the videotape. This study illustrates how the wording of a question can influence memory for the incident.

Loftus went on to demonstrate that simply introducing an inaccurate detail to witnesses could lead them to report that inaccurate detail when questioned later (Loftus, Altman, & Geballe, 1975). The **misinformation effect**, also called the **post-event information effect**, is a phenomenon in which a witness who is presented with inaccurate information after an event will incorporate that misinformation in a subsequent recall task (Loftus, 1975).

In one classic study, Loftus conducted four experiments demonstrating that how a question is worded can influence an eyewitness's recall at a later date. We'll discuss one of these experiments below.

Past misinformation studies have used a common method or paradigm. Participants were exposed to an event via slides, video, or live action. They were then given a series of questions about the event, some of which contained misinformation. Later, the participants were asked a series of questions about the event, probing their response to the misinformation introduced. They were asked to respond from a forced-choice/multiple-choice set. That is, they were given a set of responses to choose from, with one response being correct, one response containing the misinformation, and one or two incorrect responses.

**Experiment** Forty university students watched a three-minute film clip of a class being interrupted by eight demonstrators. Following the clip, participants were given 20 questions. Half of the participants were asked, "Was the leader of the 4 demonstrators who entered the classroom a male? The remaining participants were asked, "Was the leader of the 12 demonstrators who entered the classroom a male?" All other questions were the same for the two groups. After a one-week delay, the participants were asked 20 new questions about the film. The critical question in this new set was, "How many demonstrators did you see entering the classroom?" The participants that were asked a question about 12 demonstrators reported seeing an average of almost 9 demonstrators (8.85). Those who were asked about 4 demonstrators reported seeing an average of 6.40 demonstrators. Thus, incorporating the number of demonstrators into the question posed to witnesses affected the number of demonstrators witnesses recalled seeing later.

The misinformation effect occurs when a variety of different types of questions and methodology are used. But why does it occur?

**Explaining the Misinformation Effect** Many studies have demonstrated that a witness's report can include misinformation that was previously supplied (Cole & Loftus, 1979; Loftus, 1979a), and these have fuelled debates on how and why this phenomenon occurs (Loftus, Miller, & Burns, 1978; McCloskey & Zaragoza, 1985). Were witnesses' memories changed? Were the participants just going along with the experimenter (or guessing) and providing the answer they thought was wanted? Or maybe the witness had two memories, a correct one and an incorrect one, and could not remember where each

**Misinformation effect:**
Phenomenon where a witness who is presented with inaccurate information after an event will incorporate that misinformation in a subsequent recall task. Also known as the *post-event information effect*

**Post-event information effect:**
Phenomenon where a witness who is presented with inaccurate information after an event will incorporate that misinformation in a subsequent recall task. Also known as the *misinformation effect*

memory came from. Researchers have tried to advance or argue against these three general positions; each position has different implications for memory:

1. With changes in the methodology, some studies have found support for guessing or experimenter pleasing. Some witnesses will guess at the answer they think the experimenter wants, resulting in the misinformation effect. This explanation is known as the **misinformation acceptance hypothesis** (McCloskey & Zaragoza, 1985).

2. Some studies have found that witnesses can recall both memories—the original, accurate one and the inaccurate one. However, witnesses cannot remember where each memory came from. When asked to recall what was seen, the witness chooses the incorrect memory. This explanation is called the **source misattribution hypothesis** (Lindsay, 1994).

3. Loftus is perhaps the biggest proponent of the **memory impairment hypothesis**. This hypothesis refers to the original memory being replaced or altered with the new, incorrect memory (Loftus, 1979b). The original memory is no longer accessible.

The debate on which explanation is responsible for the misinformation effect is far from over. Researchers continue to come up with different methodologies that point to alternative explanations. One issue that has been put to rest, though, is whether the misinformation effect happens. The misinformation effect is a real phenomenon.

How can the misinformation effect happen in real life? A witness can be exposed to inaccurate information in a number of ways:

1. An officer may make assumptions about what occurred or what was witnessed and then inadvertently phrase a question consistent with his or her assumption. For example, the officer may ask the witness, "Did you see *the* gun?" rather than asking the more neutral question, "Did you see *a* gun?"

2. There may be more than one witness, and the witnesses overhear one another's statements. If there are discrepancies between the witnesses, then a witness may change his or her report to make it consistent.

3. A police officer may incorporate an erroneous detail from a previous witness's interview. For example, the officer may ask the witness, "What was the culprit with the scar wearing?" The witness may subsequently report that the culprit had a scar when in fact there was none.

## PROCEDURES THAT HELP POLICE INTERVIEW EYEWITNESSES

Psychologists have been instrumental in developing procedures that can be beneficial at eliciting accurate information from witnesses.

### Hypnosis

In some cases, eyewitnesses may be unable to recall very much that was witnessed, possibly because they were traumatized. With the help of hypnosis, they may be able to recall a greater amount of information. In a survey of ten forensic hypnosis experts, all felt that hypnosis could help witnesses remember crime details (Vingoe, 1995). It is assumed that a person

**Misinformation acceptance hypothesis:** Explanation for the misinformation effect where the incorrect information is provided because the witness guesses what the officer or experimenter wants the response to be

**Source misattribution hypothesis:** Explanation for the misinformation effect where the witness has two memories, the original and the misinformation; however, the witness cannot remember where each memory originated or the source of each

**Memory impairment hypothesis:** Explanation for the misinformation effect where the original memory is replaced with the new, incorrect, information

under hypnosis is able to retrieve memories that are otherwise inaccessible. A hypnotized witness may be able to produce a greater number of details than a nonhypnotized witness; this phenomenon is termed *hypnotically refreshed memory* (Steblay & Bothwell, 1994).

According to Kebbell and Wagstaff (1998), two techniques that are often used in hypnosis are age regression and the television technique. With age regression, the witness goes back in time and re-experiences the original event. With the television technique, the witness imagines that he or she is watching an imaginary television screen with the events being played as they were witnessed. Further instructions stating that the eyewitness's memory will improve over time and in future sessions are provided once the witness has recalled the event. The witness is then awoken from the hypnosis.

Several reviews have examined the effectiveness of hypnosis in enhancing memory recall (e.g., Brown, Scheflin, & Hammond, 1998; Reiser, 1989; Steblay & Bothwell, 1994). These reviews find that individuals under hypnosis will provide more details, but those details are just as likely to be inaccurate as accurate (see also Fisher, 1995). Some researchers have suggested that one aspect of hypnosis that might help to increase recall of details is when individuals close their eyes. Both visual and auditory information is recalled to a greater degree when individuals close their eyes than when they keep their eyes open when trying to remember (Perfect, Wagstaff, Moore, Andrews, Cleveland, Newcombe et al., 2008). The hypnotized individual seems to be more suggestible to subtle cues by the interviewer than under normal conditions. The difficulty with using hypnosis is not being able to differentiate between the accurate and inaccurate details. In addition, witnesses recall both accurate and inaccurate details with the same degree of confidence (Sheehan & Tilden, 1984), and as we will see later, this confidence may be misleading.

Police are not interested in using hypnosis simply to collect more information; they are interested in collecting accurate information. For hypnosis to be useful in a forensic context, police need to know about the accuracy of the information recalled while under hypnosis. The Canadian courts are aware of the difficulties with hypnotically induced recall and typically do not permit information gained that way to be used as evidence. Hypnotically induced memories have recently been in the Canadian media. See the In the Media box to learn more about hypnotically refreshed memory.

## The Cognitive Interview

Given the limitations of hypnosis, researchers have developed an interview procedure based on principles of memory storage and retrieval called the **cognitive interview** (Geiselman et al., 1984). The cognitive interview can be used with eyewitnesses, but it is not a procedure recommended for use with unwilling participants, such as suspects (see Chapter 3). The cognitive interview is based on four memory-retrieval techniques to increase recall: (1) reinstating the context, (2) reporting everything, (3) reversing order, and (4) changing perspective.

In an initial study, Geiselman, Fisher, MacKinnon, and Holland (1985) compared the "standard" police interview, hypnosis, and the cognitive interview to determine differences in the amount and accuracy of information recalled by witnesses. Participants watched a police training film of a crime. Forty-six hours after viewing the film, each participant was interviewed with one of the procedures by experienced law enforcement professionals. Compared with the "standard" police interview and hypnosis, the cognitive interview produced the greatest amount of accurate information without an increase in inaccurate details.

**Cognitive interview:** Interview procedure for use with eyewitnesses based on principles of memory storage and retrieval

## Hypnotically Refreshed Memory Goes to Court, or Not

On June 19, 1990, Elizabeth Bain was a 22-year-old student at the University of Toronto, Scarborough campus studying psychology. She disappeared on her way to the university to check the tennis schedule. Two days later, Elizabeth's car was found with a bloodstain on the floor of the back seat. Her boyfriend, Robert Baltovich, was put under surveillance. Although a number of massive searches were undertaken, Elizabeth's body was not found. Investigators decided to hypnotize four witnesses who had seen Bain and Baltovich before Bain's disappearance to try and have the witnesses remember as much as possible. Baltovich was charged with first-degree murder five months later, and in 1992, he was convicted of the second-degree murder of his girlfriend. Baltovich's lawyers appealed the case and cited hypnotically refreshed memory as one of the reasons the conviction should be set aside. Baltovich spent almost nine years in prison until the Ontario Court of Appeal overturned his conviction in 2004 and ordered a new trial.

In 2007, the Supreme Court of Canada ruled that testimony elicited under hypnosis was inadmissible because individuals under hypnosis may be more suggestible and may have a difficult time distinguishing between accurate and fabricated memories. Moreover, there is no way of determining when the memories are accurate. So, in 2008, at the time of Baltovich's retrial, hypnotically refreshed memory was inadmissible in court.

Following several legal arguments in the Baltovich retrial, the Crown decided it would not call any evidence and Baltovich was acquitted of murder in April 2008. Some believe that Paul Bernardo was responsible for Elizabeth Bain's murder.

Sources: Karl, S. (2009, December 21). On memory: Hypnotically refreshed memory. *National Post.* Retrieved from www.nationalpost.com/story. html?id=2368653; Robert Baltovitch: Not guilty. (2008, April 22). *CBC News.* Retrieved from www.cbc.ca/news/background/baltovich_robert/

Bekerian and Dennett (1993) reviewed 27 studies that tested the cognitive interview. Across the studies, the cognitive interview produced more accurate information than the alternatives, such as the "standard" police interview. Approximately, a 30% increase in accurate information was obtained with the cognitive interview over other procedures, and there was an insignificant decrease in errors for the cognitive interview compared with other methods.

Over the years, Fisher and Geiselman (1992) expanded the cognitive interview into the **enhanced cognitive interview**, including various principles of social dynamics in addition to the memory retrieval principles used in the original cognitive interview. The additional components include the following:

**Enhanced cognitive interview:** Interview procedure that includes various principles of social dynamics in addition to the memory retrieval principles used in the original cognitive interview

1. *Rapport building.* An officer should spend time building rapport with the witness and make him or her feel comfortable and supported.

2. *Supportive interviewer behaviour.* A witness's free recall should not be interrupted; pauses should be waited out by the officer, who should express attention to what the witness is saying.

3. *Transfer of control.* The witness, not the officer, should control the flow of the interview; the witness is the expert—that is, the witness, not the officer, was the person who saw the crime.

4. *Focused retrieval.* Questions should be open-ended and not leading or suggestive; after free recall, the officer should use focused memory techniques to facilitate retrieval.

5. *Witness-compatible questioning.* An officer's questions should match the witness's thinking; if the witness is talking about clothing, the officer should be asking about clothing.

The enhanced cognitive interview, the original cognitive interview, and the standard police interview have been compared (Memon & Bull, 1991). Both cognitive interviews produced more accurate information, without an increase in inaccurate information, than standard interviews. Significant differences between the two cognitive interviews have not been found (Köehnken, 1995). The question remains as to which components are responsible for the increase in accurate information (Kebbell & Wagstaff, 1998).

The cognitive interview has been tested in the United Kingdom with different-aged participants, including younger adults (age 17 to 31), older adults (age 60 to 74), and older-older adults (age 75 to 95) (Wright & Holliday, 2007). Compared with a "standard" police interview conducted in the United Kingdom, the cognitive interview increased the amount of accurate "person," "action," "object," and "surrounding" details for each age group without increasing the amount of inaccurate information recalled.

Although some officers in Canada (and in other countries such as the United States and the United Kingdom) have been trained to conduct cognitive interviews, some are reluctant to use it, stating that it requires too much time to conduct and that the appropriate environment is not always available. However, trained officers report that they use some of the cognitive interview components on a regular basis when interviewing witnesses (see also Dando, Wilcock, & Milne, 2009).

## RECALL OF THE CULPRIT

Along with a description of what happened, the witness will be asked to describe the culprit's appearance. Perusal of newspapers and news broadcasts finds that descriptions are vague and apply to many people. For example, a culprit may be described as white, male, between 1.75 metres and 1.83 metres tall, with short, brown hair. Think of how many people you know who fit this description.

## Quantity and Accuracy of Descriptions

Research examining culprit descriptions provided by witnesses finds that descriptions are limited in detail and accuracy (Sporer, 1996). Lindsay, Martin, and Webber (1994) examined descriptions provided by adults in real and staged crimes. Witnesses to staged crimes reported an average of 7.35 descriptors. In contrast, witnesses to real crimes reported significantly fewer descriptors—3.94 on average. Hair and clothing items were commonly reported descriptors.

In a study examining real-life descriptions, Van Koppen and Lochun (1997) conducted an archival review of official court records examining descriptions of culprits from 400 robberies. Data were coded from 1300 witnesses and 1650 descriptions of culprits were analyzed. Consistent with anecdotal evidence, witnesses provided few descriptors. On average, witnesses reported eight descriptors. The researchers found that sex and height were the items most often reported. Witnesses were correct 100% of the time when identifying the sex of the culprit. Unfortunately, sex is not a great discriminator. Only 52% of witnesses were accurate when identifying the height of the culprit.

Wagstafff, MacVeigh, Boston, Scott, Brunas-Wagstaff, and Cole (2003) found that hair colour and hairstyle were reported most accurately. Yarmey, Jacob, and Porter (2002) found that witnesses had difficulty correctly reporting weight (27% accuracy), eye colour, (24% accuracy), and type of footwear (13% accuracy).

As you can see, culprit descriptions are limited in quantity and accuracy, which, in turn, limits their usefulness to the police in their investigation. Given the strides psychologists have made in other areas of police procedure, such as interviewing techniques, it would be worthwhile for psychologists to develop a technique or procedure that could be used to increase the amount and accuracy of witnesses' descriptions of culprits.

In one such attempt to increase the amount of descriptive information about an unfamiliar other, Kask, Bull, and Davies (2006) examined the effectiveness of having a "standard" for witnesses to use when answering questions about the target person. Participants saw an unfamiliar person interact with one of three experimenters. For half of the participants, the experimenter posed questions about the target stranger in reference to himself or herself (i.e., the experimenter functioned as a "standard" by which to be used as a reference). For example, when the experimenter was used as a standard, he or she would ask the participant, "My hair is this long; how long was his hair?" For the participants in the no-standard condition, the experimenter would ask the participant, "How long was his hair?" Unfortunately, the researchers found that the use of a standard did not help witnesses to recall accurate person information; however, it did aid somewhat when it came to recalling descriptors that are not typically remembered well (e.g., appearance of eyes, nose, or mouth).

## RECOGNITION MEMORY

As defined at the beginning of the chapter, recognition memory involves determining whether a previously seen item or person is the one that is currently being viewed. A witness's recognition memory can be tested in a number of ways:

- Live lineups or photo arrays
- Video surveillance records
- Voice identification

## Lineup Identification

"It's number 5; I'll never forget that face!" The typical method used to gain proof about the identity of the culprit is to conduct a lineup identification, in which a witness views a group of possible suspects and determines whether one is the culprit.

### Why Conduct a Lineup? A critical distinction needs to be made between the terms *suspect* and *culprit*. A **suspect** is a person the police "suspect" committed the crime. However, a suspect may be guilty or innocent of the crime in question. In contrast, a **culprit** is the guilty person who committed the crime.

A lineup identification reduces the uncertainty of whether a suspect is the culprit beyond the verbal description provided (Wells, 1993). A witness identifying the suspect increases the likelihood that the suspect is the culprit. In contrast, not identifying the suspect decreases the likelihood that the suspect is the culprit.

An alternative view of a lineup identification is that it provides police with information about the physical similarity between the lineup member chosen and the culprit (Navon, 1990). Police will have some notion of what the culprit looks like based on the person selected from the lineup.

**Suspect:** A person the police "suspect" committed the crime, who may be guilty or innocent for the crime in question

**Culprit:** The guilty person who committed the crime

**Lineup Distractors** In addition to placing a suspect in a lineup, other lineup members may be included. These members are called **foils** or **distractors**, and they are known to be innocent of the crime in question. Police can use two types of strategies to decide on the physical appearance of the lineup distractors. A similarity-to-suspect strategy matches lineup members to the suspect's appearance. For example, if the suspect had brown hair, blue eyes, and a moustache, then each lineup member would have these characteristics. A difficulty with this strategy, however, is that there are many physical features that could be matched, such as width of eyebrows, length of nose, and thickness of lips. If taken to the extreme, this strategy would produce a lineup of clones—everyone would look exactly like the suspect, making it virtually impossible to identify the culprit. In contrast, a match-to-description strategy sets limits on the number of features that need to be matched. With this strategy, distractors are matched only on the items that the witness provided in his or her description. For example, if a witness stated that the criminal had brown hair, blue eyes, a round face, and no facial hair, then those would be the features on which each lineup member is matched.

Lindsay et al. (1994) noted that some general characteristics that might not be mentioned would need to be included to produce a "fair" lineup. A **fair lineup** is one in which the suspect does not stand out from the other lineup members. For example, if skin colour was not mentioned, then a lineup could be constructed with one white face (the suspect) and five black faces. Thus, the lineup would be unfair or biased. Some characteristics, such as sex and race, are known as default values and should be matched even if not mentioned in the witness's description.

Also, to avoid a biased lineup, Luus and Wells (1991; Wells, Rydell, & Seelau, 1993) suggest that if a feature is provided in the witness's description but does not match the suspect's appearance, then the distractors should match the suspect's appearance on that feature. For example, if the culprit is described as having brown hair but the suspect has blond hair, then the distractors should have blond hair.

**Estimating Identification Accuracy** When we are interested in finding out how often witnesses will make an accurate (or inaccurate) identification decision, we need to create the condition when police have arrested the right person, the guilty suspect. We also need to create the condition when police have arrested the wrong person, an innocent suspect. Thus, we create two lineups in our research. One lineup—the **target-present lineup**—contains a picture of the culprit. In the other lineup—the **target-absent lineup**—we substitute the culprit's picture with another photo. Identification decisions are different with each type of lineup. See Table 5.1 for the types of identification decisions possible as a function of type of lineup.

Three types of identification decisions can occur with a target-present lineup. The witness can identify the guilty suspect, which is a correct identification. If the witness identifies a foil, that is a foil identification. In addition, the witness may state that the culprit is not present, which is a false rejection.

Three types of identification decisions can occur with a target-absent lineup. The witness can state that the culprit is not present, which is a correct rejection. The witness can identify a foil, which is a foil identification. The witness can also identify an innocent suspect, in which case the witness makes a false identification. Sometimes, researchers will not make a distinction between false identifications and foil identifications from a target-absent lineup and will refer to these two errors simply as false positives.

**Foils:** Lineup members who are known to be innocent for the crime in question. Also known as *distractors*

**Distractors:** Lineup members who are known to be innocent for the crime in question. Also known as *foils*

**Fair lineup:** A lineup where the suspect does not stand out from the other lineup members

**Target-present lineup:** A lineup that contains the culprit

**Target-absent lineup:** A lineup that does not contain the culprit but rather an innocent suspect

**Table 5.1** Possible Identification Decisions as a Function of Lineup Type

| Type of Lineup | Identification Decision | | | | |
|---|---|---|---|---|---|
| | Correct Indentification | False Rejection | Foil Indentification | Correct Rejection | False Indentification |
| Target-present | X | X | X | Not possible | Not possible |
| Target-absent | Not possible | Not possible | X | X | X |

Source: Wells, 1993.

**Identification Decision Implications** The only correct decision with a target-present lineup is to make a correct identification. The only correct decision with a target-absent lineup is to make a correct rejection. The other decisions with each type of lineup are errors and have different implications for the witness and the justice system (Wells & Turtle, 1986):

■ A foil identification (with either a target-present lineup or a target-absent lineup) is a known error to the police, so the person identified will not be prosecuted. The witness, however, may be perceived as having a faulty memory. Moreover, the other details provided by this witness may be viewed with some skepticism because a known recognition error was made.

■ A false rejection is an unknown error and may result in the guilty suspect going free and possibly committing further crimes.

■ A false identification also is an unknown error in real life and may result in the innocent suspect being prosecuted and convicted for a crime he or she did not commit. Moreover, with a false identification, the real criminal remains free to commit further crimes. False identifications may be the most serious type of identification error a witness can make.

**Live Lineups or Photo Arrays?** Most often, police will use a set of photographs rather than live persons to assemble a lineup (Turtle, Lindsay, & Wells, 2003). *Photo array* is the term used for photographic lineups. Photo arrays are more common than lineups for a number of reasons:

■ They are less time-consuming to construct. The police can choose foils from their mug shot (pictures of people who have been charged with crimes in the past) files rather than find live persons.

■ They are portable. The police are able to bring the photo array to the witness rather than have the witness go to the police department.

■ The suspect does not have the right to counsel being present when a witness looks at a photo array. This right is present with live lineups.

■ Because photos are static, the police need not worry that the suspect's behaviour may draw attention to himself or herself, thus invalidating the photo array.

■ A witness may be less anxious examining a photo array than a live lineup.

An alternative to photographs or live lineups is to use video-recorded lineups. Advantages to video lineups include the ability to enlarge faces or focus on particular features. Lineup members can be shown walking, turning, and talking. In a study by Cutler, Fisher, and Chicvara (1989), they found that correct identification and correct rejection rates did not differ across live and video-recorded lineups. So far there has been some movement in the United Kingdom to use video-recorded lineups. Further research is needed to examine identification differences, if any, between video-recorded lineups and photo lineups.

**Lineup Presentation Procedures** Lineups can be presented in different formats or with different procedures to the witness. Perhaps most common is the procedure known as the **simultaneous lineup** (Wells, 1993). The simultaneous procedure presents all lineup members at one time to the witness. Wells (1993) suggested that this procedure encourages the witness to make a **relative judgment**, whereby lineup members are compared with one another and the person who looks most like the culprit is identified.

An alternative lineup procedure is the **sequential lineup**. This lineup procedure involves presenting the lineup members serially to the witness. The witness must make a decision as to whether the lineup member is the culprit before seeing the next lineup member (Lindsay & Wells, 1985). Also, with the sequential procedure, a witness cannot ask to see previously seen photos and the witness is unaware of the number of photos to be shown. Wells (1993) suggested that the sequential procedure reduces the likelihood that the witness can make a relative judgment. Instead, witnesses may be more likely to make an **absolute judgment**, whereby each lineup member is compared with the witness's memory of the culprit and the witness decides whether it is the culprit.

Lindsay and Wells (1985) compared the identification accuracy rate achieved with the simultaneous and sequential lineup procedures. University students witnessed a videotaped theft and were asked to identify the culprit from six photographs. Half the students saw a target-present lineup and the other half of students saw a target-absent lineup. Across target-present and target-absent conditions, the lineups were either presented using a simultaneous procedure or a sequential procedure.

Correct identification (target-present lineups) rates did not differ across lineup procedures. However, correct rejection rates were significantly different across lineup procedures. Only 42% of the participants made a correct rejection with a simultaneous lineup, whereas 65% of the participants made a correct rejection with a sequential lineup. In other words, if the culprit was not included in the lineup, witnesses were more likely to correctly indicate that he or she was not present if they were shown a sequential lineup rather than a simultaneous lineup. The higher correct rejection rate with the sequential procedure compared with the simultaneous procedure has been replicated numerous times (Steblay, Dysart, Fulero, & Lindsay, 2001). Across several studies however, correct identifications have been shown to decrease with the sequential lineup compared with the simultaneous lineup (Lindsay, Mansour, Beaudry, Leach, & Bertrand, 2009). The sequential lineup is the procedure used in some Canadian jurisdictions, such as Ontario, and some U.S. states, such as New Jersey. Recent research, however, has called into question the "sequential superiority effect" (McQuinston-Surrett, Malpass, & Tredoux, 2006). The researchers suggest that when certain methodological factors are considered, the simultaneous procedure produces correct rejection rates similar to those of the sequential procedure without a drop in correct identifications. Thus, the debate continues (see also Malpass, Tredoux, & McQuiston-Surrett, 2009).

**Simultaneous lineup:** A common lineup procedure that presents all lineup members at one time to the witness

**Relative judgment:** Witness compares lineup members to one another and the person that looks most like the culprit is identified

**Sequential lineup:** Alternative lineup procedure where the lineup members are presented serially to the witness, and the witness must make a decision as to whether the lineup member is the culprit before seeing another member. Also, a witness cannot ask to see previously seen photos and is unaware of the number of photos to be shown.

**Absolute judgment:** Witness compares each lineup member to his or her memory of the culprit to decide whether the lineup member is the culprit

Dr. Rod Lindsay has been a key researcher in the area of lineup identification. See Box 5.1 to read about him and his research.

**Showup:** Identification procedure that shows one person to the witness: the suspect

An alternative identification procedure to the lineup is a **showup**. This procedure shows one person to the witness: the suspect. The witness is asked whether the person is the culprit. Although an absolute judgment is likely with a showup, it has a number of other difficulties, making it a less-than-ideal procedure. Both courts and researchers have

## Box 5.1

# Canadian Researcher Profile: Dr. Rod Lindsay

Dr. Rod Lindsay recalls the fortuitous meeting that started his more than 30-year career researching eyewitness issues. While he was working in his office one day, during his time as a graduate student at the University of Alberta, a new faculty member walked in and introduced himself as Gary Wells. It was January 1978 and Dr. Wells was looking for graduate students who would be interested in working on a research project he was planning. The project was examining jurors' perceptions of eyewitness identification. In 1979, this project was published in the *Journal of Applied Psychology*, and it would be one of the first in a long list of articles that would follow for Dr. Lindsay.

In the early 1980s, Dr. Lindsay joined the faculty at Queen's University, where he continued conducting eyewitness research. Dr. Lindsay describes his favourite research questions as those that can lead to real-world applications. He prefers to use experimental methodology to investigate the research questions that intrigue him. Although he respects surveys, case studies, and many other forms of methodology, he likes how a good experiment can answer a very specific and narrowly defined question, such as "Which of two lineup procedures will generate more accurate identifications?"

Dr. Lindsay's extensive eyewitness expertise has led him to the courts as an expert witness in a number of cases. Perhaps one of the most emotionally difficult cases for him

was a Rwandan war-crime trial. The defendants were charged with 20 000 counts of murder in a single afternoon.

Recently, Dr. Lindsay consulted on two Canadian cases that he found both professionally interesting and very frustrating. In one of the cases, a First Nations suspect was placed in a 12-person lineup in which no other lineup member was First Nations. In the other case, a Filipino suspect also was placed in a 12-person lineup; this time, all the other lineup members were First Nations! In each case, the court decided there was nothing wrong with the lineup—decisions that Dr. Lindsay did not agree with.

To deal with eyewitness issues on a practical level, Dr. Lindsay would like to see the Canadian government create something like the United Kingdom's Home Office. Such an organization could take responsibility for researching police procedures, and then decide on the best practices, and write and distribute this information through directives for law enforcement. Moreover, the courts would have the clout to back up a Home Office–type department by throwing out any evidence that resulted from procedures that did not meet the standards outlined.

In addition to informing the justice system on how to improve eyewitness evidence, Dr. Lindsay is committed to teaching and training future eyewitness researchers. He enjoys getting students excited about the eyewitness world: "If you love it, they will."

Eyewitness research is not the only thing Dr. Lindsay is passionate about. Often, he will escape the lab on a Friday afternoon only to re-emerge on Monday morning, having spent the time in between playing duplicate bridge and more duplicate bridge.

Dr. Lindsay has received numerous distinctions for his work. Most recently, in 2002, Dr. Lindsay's contribution to the eyewitness field was recognized by the Canadian Psychological Association, with the Career Award for Distinguished Contributions to the Application of Psychology.

argued (*Stovall v. Denno*, 1967; Wells, Leippe, & Ostrom, 1979) that because there are no other lineup members shown, the witness is aware of whom the police suspect, and this knowledge may increase a witness's likelihood of making an identification that may be false.

Not everyone agrees with this view, however. In the early 1990s, a series of studies were conducted by Gonzalez, Ellsworth, and Pembroke (1993). They did not find false identifications to be higher with a showup than with a lineup. In fact, they found that witnesses were more likely to reject a showup than all members of a lineup. Gonzalez et al. concluded that witnesses are more cautious with their decision making when presented with a showup rather than a lineup, and as a result, they will err on making a rejection rather than an identification. Yarmey, Yarmey, and Yarmey (1996), however, reached a different conclusion. They found that lineups produced lower false-identification rates than showups. In a recent meta-analysis comparing showups and lineups, Steblay, Dysart, Fulero, and Lindsay (2003) found that false identifications were higher with showups than with lineups. Also, in an analysis of 271 actual police cases, the suspect was more likely to be identified in a field showup (76%) than in a photographic lineup (48%) (Behrman & Davey, 2001). These results are consistent with the notion that showups are suggestive. Further research is needed to understand the discrepancy in identification rates for showups across studies.

For now, there are only two acceptable uses of a showup. It may be used for deathbed identifications, when there is a fear that the witness will not be alive by the time a lineup is assembled (Wells, Malpass, Lindsay, Turtle, & Fulero, 2000). Also, police may use a showup if a suspect is apprehended immediately at or near the crime scene.

One other identification procedure that may precede a lineup identification is known as a **walk-by**. This identification occurs in a naturalistic environment. The police take the witness to a public location where the suspect is likely to be. Once the suspect is in view, the witness is asked whether he or she sees the culprit.

**Walk-by:** Identification procedure that occurs in a naturalistic environment. The police take the witness to a public location where the suspect is likely to be. Once the suspect is in view, the witness is asked whether he or she sees the culprit

**Biased lineup:** A lineup that "suggests" who the police suspect and thereby who the witness should identify

**Lineup Biases** Constructing a fair lineup is a challenging task. **Biased lineups** suggest who the police suspect and thereby who the witness should identify. In some way, the suspect stands out from the other lineup members in a biased lineup. The following biases have been investigated and found to increase false positives:

1. *Foil bias*. The suspect is the only lineup member who matches the description of the culprit. For example, the suspect has a beard and moustache while the other lineup members are clean-shaven (Lindsay, Lea, & Fulford, 1991).

2. *Clothing bias*. The suspect is the only lineup member wearing similar clothing to that worn by the culprit. For example, the culprit was described as wearing a blue baseball cap. The suspect is wearing a blue baseball cap while the foils are not (Dysart, Lindsay, & Dupuis, 2006; Lindsay et al., 1991; Lindsay, Wallbridge, & Drennan, 1987).

What is wrong with this lineup?

3.  *Instruction bias*. The police fail to mention to the witness that the culprit may not be present; rather, the police imply that the culprit is present and that the witness should pick him or her out (Malpass & Devine, 1981; Steblay, 1997: Clark, 2005).

## Voice Identification

Perhaps one of the first and most prominent cases involving voice identification (or "ear-witness" identification) occurred in the United States in 1937. The infant son of Charles Lindbergh, a well-known doctor and aviator, was kidnapped and murdered (see Chapter 3). Lindberg identified Bruno Hauptmann's voice as the one he heard three years earlier when he paid the ransom. The kidnapper had said, "Hey, doctor, over here, over here." Hauptmann was convicted of kidnapping and murder. At the time, no studies on voice identification existed. Unfortunately, little has changed over the past 65 years, as very few studies have been conducted in this area.

In one study examining many key voice variables, Orchard and Yarmey (1995) had 156 university students listen to a taped voice of a mock kidnapper that varied in length—either 30 seconds or 8 minutes. The voice was varied such that the kidnapper either had a distinctive or nondistinctive voice. The researchers also varied whether the speaker spoke in a whisper or a normal tone. Voice-identification accuracy was tested using six-person voice lineups two days after the participants heard the taped voice. Here are some of the results:

- Identification accuracy was higher with longer voice samples.
- Whispering significantly decreased identification accuracy.
- Distinctiveness interacted with whispering, influencing identification accuracy.

### Factors That Decrease the Likelihood of Correct Voice Identification

Other studies have found that the likelihood of a correct identification is decreased if a voice is changed by whispering or muffling, or through emotion (Bull & Clifford, 1984; Saslove & Yarmey, 1980). Orchard and Yarmey (1995) have stated that "when voices are disguised as whispers, or changed in tone between first hearing the perpetrator and the conduction of the voice lineup, identification evidence should be accepted with critical caution" (p. 259).

Kerstholt, Jansen, Van Amelsvoort, and Broeders (2006) examined the question of whether the perpetrator and witness having different accents would affect voice identification. There was a trend for participants to be more accurate when the speaker had a familiar versus a different accent: 41% correct identifications versus 34% correct identifications, respectively, and 56% correct rejections versus 35% correct rejections, respectively.

In terms of target-voice position in a lineup, if the target voice occurs later in the lineup, correct identification decreases compared with an earlier presentation (Doehring & Ross, 1972). Cook and Wilding (1997) reported that when the target's face was visible when participants originally heard the voice at encoding, correct identification decreased greatly. Also, as the number of foils increased from four to eight voices, correct identification decreased (Clifford, 1980).

## Are Several Identifications Better Than One?

If identification decisions for different pieces of evidence were combined, would the decision regarding the suspect's guilt be more accurate? Pryke, Lindsay, Dysart, and Dupuis (2004) conducted two experiments examining the usefulness of multiple independent

lineups to identify a culprit: for example, having the participants identify the clothing worn by the culprit in one lineup and identify the culprit's face in another lineup. If both of these identification decisions are of the suspect, then the likelihood that the suspect is the culprit should be greater than if just one identification decision implicates the suspect. In the first experiment, following exposure to a live target, participants were shown a face lineup, then a voice lineup, and lastly a body lineup (Pryke et al., 2004). In the second experiment, a clothing lineup was added to the other three lineups. The researchers found that exposing witnesses to more than one lineup, each consisting of a different aspect of the suspect, increased the ability to determine the reliability of an eyewitness's identification of the suspect. Thus, the likelihood of the suspect's guilt increased as the number of independent identifications of the suspect increased by any one witness. This research presents an interesting avenue for future research, with many questions still unanswered. For example, are certain types of lineups more diagnostic of a suspect's guilt than others?

## Are Confident Witnesses Accurate?

In a landmark U.S. Supreme Court Case in 1972 (*Neil v. Biggers*), the Court stated that the confidence of a witness should be taken as an indicator of accuracy. This assertion implies that witnesses who are certain in their identification of the culprit are likely to be accurate. Many studies, however, have investigated this relationship and found a different result (Cutler & Penrod, 1989a, 1989b; Penrod & Cutler, 1995; Sporer, Penrod, Read, & Cutler, 1995). Overall, there appears to be a small positive correlation between accuracy and confidence. There also are a number of moderator variables that can increase or decrease this relation.

Wells and his colleagues have investigated post-lineup identification feedback and its effect on the confidence–accuracy relationship (Bradfield, Wells, & Olson, 2002; Luus & Wells, 1994; Wells & Bradfield, 1998). In one study (Wells & Bradfield, 1998), after the witness made a lineup identification decision, the experimenter provided one of the following:

1. Confirming feedback: "Good, you identified the actual suspect."
2. Disconfirming feedback: "Actually, the suspect is number __."
3. No feedback.

Participants were asked to make a number of judgments following the feedback or lack thereof. Of key interest were the ratings the participants made regarding how confident they were that they identified the correct person on a 1-to-7-point scale in which 1 means not at all certain and 7 means totally certain. See Figure 5.2 for the confidence ratings as a function of feedback condition.

Participants who were informed that they had identified the culprit reported significantly higher confidence ratings than did participants who received disconfirming feedback or no feedback. Thus, confidence can be manipulated and inflated, thereby affecting the confidence–accuracy relation. A recent meta-analysis of post-identification feedback has shown it to be a reliable and robust effect, having an impact on a number of factors, including how certain a witness feels and how much attention they think they paid to the culprit (Douglass & Steblay, 2006).

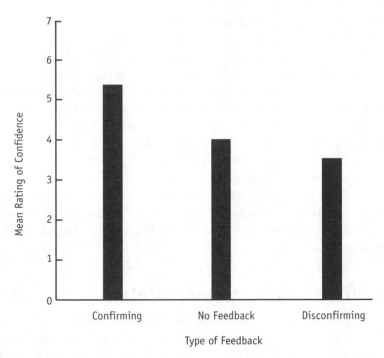

**Figure 5.2** Mean Confidence Ratings as a Function of Feedback

Source: Wells & Bradfield, 1998.

Research also indicates that the more often you express a decision, the greater your confidence in subsequent reports (Shaw, 1996; Shaw & McClure, 1996). You can imagine that by the time a witness testifies in court, he or she has been interviewed many times. Consequently, the confidence the witness expresses in the courtroom may be inflated. Inflated confidence may be problematic given that it is an indicator used by fact-finders (i.e., judges and juries) to assess accuracy. Moreover, mock jurors do not appear sensitive to "inflated confidence" (Bradfield & McQuiston, 2004). Wells, Small, Penrod, Malpass, Fulero, and Brimacombe (1998) have recommended that police ask witnesses for their confidence rating immediately following their identification decision prior to any feedback and that this rating be used in court. This rating may be more informative with regard to accuracy. Also, it is recommended that the person administering the lineup not know who the suspect to limit post-identification feedback.

## Estimator Variable Research in Recognition Memory

Three estimator variables have received much attention in eyewitness research: age, race, and weapon focus.

**Age** Differences in the ability to make correct identifications have not been found between younger and older adults. Although older adults (over age 60) are just as likely as younger adults to correctly identify the culprit from a target-present lineup, older adults are more likely to make an incorrect decision from a target-absent lineup than are younger adults (Wells & Olson, 2003). In other words, older adults make similar correct identifications but fewer correct rejections than do younger adults. This pattern of responding

can also be found between children and young adults (Pozzulo & Lindsay, 1998; see Chapter 6 for more on this topic).

Memon and Gabbert (2003) tested younger (age 18 to 30) and older (age 60 to 80) witnesses' identification abilities. A crime video was shown, and target-present and target-absent lineups were presented by using either a simultaneous or sequential lineup. Younger and older witnesses did not differ in their correct identification rate with the simultaneous lineup or the sequential lineup. Greater correct identifications were obtained with the simultaneous lineup than with the sequential lineup for both groups. Older witnesses made fewer correct rejections with the simultaneous and the sequential lineup than did younger witnesses. Thus, older witnesses were more likely to make a false positive than were younger witnesses when shown a target-absent lineup, regardless of the procedure used. However, older witnesses made more correct rejections with a sequential lineup than with the simultaneous lineup (as did younger adults). Overall, though, older adult witnesses may have more difficulty than younger adult witnesses in making correct rejection decisions.

**Race** The **cross-race effect**, also known as the **other-race effect** and the **own-race bias**, is the phenomenon of witnesses remembering faces of people of their own race with greater accuracy than they remember faces of people of other races. In a meta-analysis, Meissner and Brigham (2001) examined 30 years of research, including almost 5000 participants, on the topic of cross-race identification. They found that own-race faces produced higher correct identifications and lower false positives than other-race faces. In a Canadian study, the cross-race effect was examined by using Caucasian and First Nation samples (Jackiw, Arbuthnott, Pfeifer, Marcon, & Meissner, 2008). Similar to other studies, both Caucasian and First Nations participants were more accurate at recognizing faces from their own race compared with the "other" race. Intriguingly, both Caucasians and First Nations participants were more likely to choose a face when trying to identify a First Nations face. The authors suggest that the potential for mistaken identification of First Nations people is high regardless of the race of the eyewitness. Moreover, it is important to note that many different bands fit within the First Nations designation. Thus, individuals from different bands may be experiencing the cross-race effect.

A number of explanations for this phenomenon have been suggested. Below are three of the more common explanations.

**Attitudes** One hypothesis to explain the other-race effect is based on attitudes. More specifically, people with less prejudicial attitudes may be more inclined to distinguish among members of other races. However, research to date does not support this explanation (Platz & Hosch, 1988; Slone, Brigham, & Meissner, 2000). Having said that, Meissner and Brigham (2001) do note that prejudicial attitudes may be related to the amount of contact a person has with other-race members, which, in turn, may help to explain the other-race effect (see below).

**Physiognomic Homogeneity** An alternative hypothesis to explain the other-race effect suggests that some races have less variability in their faces—that is, "they all look alike." This hypothesis has not received much empirical support either. Goldstein (1979) for example, examined Japanese, black, and white faces and did not find that one group was more similar across members than the others were. Although physical similarity may not explain the other-race effect, some physical features may be more appropriate for discriminating among faces of certain races, such as hair colour (Deregowski, Ellis, &

**Cross-race effect:** The phenomenon of witnesses remembering own-race faces with greater accuracy than faces from other races. Also known as the *other-race effect* and the *own-race bias*

**Other-race effect:** Phenomenon of witnesses remembering own-race faces with greater accuracy than faces from other races. Also known as the *cross-race effect* and *the own-race bias*

**Own-race bias:** Phenomenon of witnesses remembering own-race faces with greater accuracy than faces from other races. Also known as the *cross-race effect* and *the other-race effect*

Shepherd, 1975; Shepherd, 1981; Shepherd & Deregowski, 1981). Thus, persons from other races may not pay attention or encode relevant features that distinguish between members of a particular race. For example, paying attention to hair colour for Asian faces may be less discriminating than hair colour for Caucasian faces. This explanation, however, does not seem adequate at explaining the cross-race phenomenon.

**Interracial Contact** Perhaps the hypothesis receiving the most attention examines the amount or type of contact people have had with other races. This hypothesis states that the more contact you have with other races, the better you will be able to identify them. In the 1970s, some researchers examined children and adolescents living in integrated neighbourhoods versus those living in segregated neighbourhoods. It was predicted that participants from integrated neighbourhoods would be better at recognizing other-race faces than would those living in segregated neighbourhoods. Some support for this prediction was found (Cross, Cross, & Daly, 1971; Feinman & Entwisle, 1976).

In another test of this hypothesis, Li, Dunning, and Malpass (as cited in Meissner & Brigham, 2001) examined the ability of white basketball "experts" (dedicated fans) and white basketball novices to recognize black faces. Given that the majority of U.S. professional basketball players are black, it was thought that the experts would have more experience distinguishing black faces because of their experience watching basketball. Indeed, the experts were better at identifying black faces than were the novices.

It is important to note that not all studies that have investigated interracial contact have found the predicted effect. For example, Ng and Lindsay (1994) examined university students from Canada and Singapore and the other-race effect was not completely supported.

A definitive conclusion on the contact hypothesis and how it factors into the other-race effect remains unclear. Further work in this area is needed.

**Weapon Focus** **Weapon focus** is the term used to describe the phenomenon of a witness's attention being focused on the culprit's weapon rather than on the culprit (Steblay, 1992). The witness will remember less about the crime and culprit when a weapon is present than when no weapon is present. It is clear that this phenomenon occurs, but why it occurs is less clear. There have been two primary explanations for the weapon focus effect: arousal and unusualness.

**Arousal** The **cue-utilization hypothesis** was proposed by Easterbrook (1959) to explain why a witness may focus on the weapon rather than other details. The hypothesis suggests that when emotional arousal increases, attentional capacity decreases. With limited attentional capacity, central details, such as the weapon, are more likely to be encoded than are peripheral details, such as the colour of the culprit's hair. There is limited support for this hypothesis.

**Unusualness** An alternative explanation for the weapon focus phenomenon has to do with unusualness, in that weapons are unusual and thus attract a witness's attention. Because a witness is not paying attention to and encoding other details, these other details are not remembered (Mitchell, Livosky, & Mather, 1998; Pickel, 1998). To follow this line of thinking, you would predict that not only weapons, but also other objects might produce a "weapon focus" effect, if they were unusual for the situation.

Pickel (1999) conducted two experiments to investigate the unusualness explanation. In one of the experiments, university students watched one of four videotapes in which a

**Weapon focus:** Term used to describe the phenomenon of a witness's attention being focused on the culprit's weapon rather than on the culprit

**Cue-utilization hypothesis:** Proposed by Easterbrook (1959) to explain why a witness may focus on the weapon rather than other details. The hypothesis suggests that when emotional arousal increases, attentional capacity decreases

woman was approached by a man with a handgun. The scenarios differed in their location and the degree of threat posed to the witness. In one video, the interaction occurred at a baseball game in the stadium parking lot. In the other video, the interaction occurred at a shooting range. In the low-threat condition, the man kept the gun pointed to the ground. In the high-threat condition, the man pointed the gun at the woman. Participants provided less accurate descriptions of the man if he was carrying a gun in the parking lot rather than at the shooting range. The degree of threat did not influence the descriptions of the man. These data suggest that unusualness can produce the weapon focus phenomenon. However, it should be noted that identification of the target was not affected.

Thus, there is support for the unusualness explanation for the weapon focus effect. More research, however, is needed to definitively conclude why the weapon focus effect occurs. It may be encouraging to know that Pickel, Ross, and Truelove (2006) found that participants could be trained not to focus on a weapon, thus reducing the weapon focus effect.

## EXPERT TESTIMONY ON EYEWITNESS ISSUES

Eyewitness testimony is an area for which experts may be able to provide the courts with data that can help the fact-finders with their decision making. However, not all eyewitness experts agree as to whether there is sufficient reliability across eyewitness studies and whether it is appropriate to apply the results of laboratory simulations to the real world. An additional criticism lodged against the testimony of eyewitness experts is that the information provided is common sense and, therefore, not necessary for the fact-finder.

Kassin, Tubb, Hosch, and Memon (2001; Kassin, Ellsworth, & Smith, 1989) surveyed researchers to determine which eyewitness issues they felt were reliable enough to provide expert testimony in court. Issues that were deemed sufficiently reliable included lineup procedures, interview procedures, and the confidence–accuracy relationship.

There are, however, some dissenters (e.g., Egeth, 1993; McCloskey & Egeth, 1983). In one critique, Ebbesen and Konecni (1997) argue that eyewitness experts are overconfident in their conclusions and have thus misled the courts about the validity, consistency, and generalizability of the data. The researchers take issue with the lack of theory in the eyewitness area and argue that the studies are too far removed from real-world eyewitness situations to be useful in predicting how "actual" witnesses would behave. They outline a number of weaknesses in eyewitness research that should limit its usefulness to real-world application and experts testifying:

1. Studies examining the same issue produce different results.
2. Most of the studies use university students; real-life witnesses vary in age and other demographic variables.
3. Most studies allow a witness to view the culprit for approximately six seconds; in reality, witnesses may view the culprit for five or more minutes.

In defence of eyewitness research, Leippe (1995) noted that eyewitness research uses a number of methodologies and types of participants (see also Loftus, 1983). In addition, a number of studies are highly reliable. In support of the laboratory simulation using staged crimes, Wells (1993) asks, "If subjects believe that they are witnessing real crime, for instance, in what important way are they different from people who witness a real crime?" (p. 555). Perhaps the eyewitness field will always have critics on each side.

Overall, several studies have suggested that the lay public may not be sufficiently knowledgeable about eyewitness issues to evaluate this evidence in court (e.g., Benton, Ross, Bradshaw, Thomas, & Bradshaw, 2006; Brewer, Potter, Fisher, Bond, & Luszcz, 1999). Furthermore, Yarmey (2001) has concluded that many results found with eyewitness studies are counterintuitive and contradict the common-sense beliefs of those in the community. In a recent Canadian survey by Read and Desmarais (2009) however, they found that participants demonstrated a greater accuracy with regard to eyewitness issues than has been found in the past with the lay public. Moreover, these responses were similar to those provided by eyewitness experts.

Currently, the Canadian justice system tends to limit, and might not allow, the testimony of eyewitness experts on these issues in court. For example, the Ontario Court of Appeal in *R. v. McIntosh and McCarthy* (1997) ruled not to permit expert testimony on eyewitness-identification issues. However, in a recent murder case, *R. v. Henderson* (2009), a Manitoba judge allowed a jury to hear expert testimony on the limitations of eyewitness identification. The case involved several eyewitnesses that allegedly saw a barroom fight between Henderson and the victim several hours before the murder. It is unclear how the Canadian courts will respond to eyewitness experts providing testimony on the topic in the future. See the Case Study box to see how you would evaluate eyewitness testimony.

## CASE STUDY YOU BE THE JUDGE

One Saturday evening in Vancouver during the holiday season, Kenji Hattori (a Japanese tourist) stopped at a bank machine on his way back to his hotel after having several drinks at a nearby bar. He withdrew $200 and left the bank. As he walked back to his car in a nearby parking lot, he was approached by a Caucasian man with a knife who robbed him of his wallet, watch, and cellphone. Unfortunately, the incident occurred outside the view of the bank's security cameras, and passersby didn't seem to notice.

At the police station, the police asked Kenji about the incident. Kenji stated that he was quite shaken by the incident, but he tried to provide as much information as he could about the appearance of the robber.

The police were certain they had the right man and asked Kenji to identify the robber from a simultaneous lineup. To ensure Kenji didn't make a mistake, they took a photo of the robber standing outside the bank where Kenji was held up. Kenji identified the suspect as the man who had robbed him. He was certain he had selected the correct person. The police congratulated Kenji for picking out the robber.

### Your Turn . . .
Based on Kenji's identification, the police arrested and charged the suspect.

What factors do you think influenced Kenji's identification? Should his identification be admissible in court? Why or why not? What recommendations would you make to police for future identifications?

# PUBLIC POLICY ISSUES AND GUIDELINES

In the mid-1990s, then-U.S. attorney general Janet Reno commissioned a set of guidelines for the collection and preservation of eyewitness evidence. She was prompted by the large body of empirical literature on eyewitness issues. In addition, the more sensational factor that caught her attention involved a review of DNA exoneration cases (Wells et al., 2000). According to Turtle et al. (2003; also www.innocenceproject.org), in more than 75% of DNA exoneration cases, the primary evidence used to convict was eyewitness identification. See Table 5.2 for some of the cases that involved mistaken identification in the United States. In 1997, Osgoode Hall Law School at York University set up an Innocence Project for Canadians. This group often works with the Association for the Defence of the Wrongfully Convicted; a group of pro bono lawyers who worked to free Donald Marshall, David Milgaard, and Guy Paul Morin; all of who were wrongfully convicted.

Eyewitness researchers, along with police officers and lawyers, constituted the Technical Working Group for Eyewitness Evidence (1999) that was commissioned in the United States to respond to Janet Reno's request. They developed a national set of guidelines known as *Eyewitness Evidence: A Guide for Law Enforcement*. In terms of lineup identification, Wells et al. (1998) proposed that the guidelines be limited to four recommendations:

1. The person who conducts the lineup or photo array should not know which person is the suspect.

2. Eyewitnesses should be told explicitly that the criminal may not be present in the lineup and, therefore, witnesses should not feel that they must make an identification.

3. The suspect should not stand out in the lineup as being different from the foils based on the eyewitness' previous description of the criminal or based on other factors that would draw extra attention to the suspect.

**Table 5.2** DNA Exoneration Cases (United States)

| Name | State | Crime | Years in Prison | Contributing Cause(s) |
|------|-------|-------|-----------------|------------------------|
| Steven Barnes | NY | Rape | 19.5 years | Witness ID*, IFS** |
| Ronnie Bullock | IL | Sexual Assault | 10.5 years | Witness ID |
| Willie Davidson | VA | Rape | 12 years | Witness ID, IFS |
| Frederick Daye | CA | Rape | 10 years | Witness ID, IFS |
| Anthony Gray | MD | Murder | 7 years | False Confession |
| Clarence Harrison | GA | Rape | 17.5 years | Witness ID, IFS |
| Ray Krone | AZ | Murder | 10 years | IFS |
| Clark McMillan | TN | Rape | 22 years | Witness ID |
| Vincent Moto | PA | Rape | 8.5 years | Witness ID |
| Miguel Roman | CT | Murder | 18.5 years | Snitches |

*ID = identification
**IFS = improper forensic science
Source: www.innocenceproject.org.

4. A clear statement should be taken from the eyewitness at the time of the identification and prior to any feedback as to his or her confidence that the identified person is the actual criminal.

Kassin (1998) added one more rule for lineup identification. He stated that the entire lineup procedure should be recorded on video to ensure accuracy in the process. In particular, the lineup and the interaction between the officer and the witness should be on video so that lawyers, the judge, and the jurors can later assess for themselves whether the reports of the procedure made by police are accurate.

Parallel guidelines have also been developed in Canada. In the early 1980s, law professor Neil Brooks (1983) prepared Canadian guidelines titled *Police Guidelines: Pretrial Eyewitness Identification Procedures*. In addition, psychologists (eyewitness researchers) were asked to consult in the preparation of these guidelines. Thirty-eight recommendations were made with the goal of increasing the reliability of eyewitness identification. These recommendations, however, have not always been followed.

One Canadian case involving poor police techniques in collecting eyewitness identification was that of Thomas Sophonow (*R. v. Sophonow*, 1986). Sophonow was convicted of murdering Barbara Stoppel in Winnipeg, Manitoba. Sophonow spent four years in prison for a murder that he did not commit. DNA evidence exonerated him 15 years later. Supreme Court Justice Peter Cory requested a public inquiry into the case. Forty-three recommendations were made, including the following:

- The photo lineup procedure with the witness should be videotaped or audiotaped from the point the officer greets the witness to the completion of the interview.

- Officers should inform witnesses that it is just as important to clear innocent suspects as it is to identify guilty suspects.

- The photo lineup should be presented sequentially.

- Officers should not discuss a witness's identification decision with him or her.

See Box 5.2 to read more about the Sophonow case. It will be interesting to examine future cases to determine whether the recommendations from the inquiry are met.

## Box 5.2

# A Case of Wrongful Conviction

On the evening of December 23, 1981, Barbara Stoppel was working as a waitress at the Ideal Donut Shop in Winnipeg, Manitoba. At about 8:45 p.m., several patrons found her in the women's washroom of the shop, where she had been strangled and was close to death. Stoppel later died in hospital.

A number of eyewitnesses were available in this case. For example, Mrs. Janower worked at a drugstore in the same plaza as the doughnut shop. She went to the doughnut shop at about 8:20 p.m. She saw a man standing inside who had locked the door and headed toward the washroom. Mr. Doerksen was selling Christmas trees near the doughnut shop. He chased a man who walked out of the doughnut shop when Stoppel's body was found. Mr. McDonald sat in his parked truck as he waited for his wife to finish her shopping in the plaza. He could see into the doughnut shop and noticed a man talking to the waitress. He saw the man walk with the waitress to the back of the shop. He then came out to lock the front door of the doughnut shop. In addition to eyewitness accounts, police accumulated much physical evidence.

Police discovered that Thomas Sophonow was in Winnipeg visiting his daughter on the night Stoppel was murdered. Sophonow was forthcoming with hair samples and so on. The police interview notes suggested that Sophonow might have been at the doughnut shop between 8:00 and 9:00 p.m. A few days later, Sophonow was interrogated for more than four hours. He was arrested in Vancouver and charged with Stoppel's murder on March 12, 1982.

Sophonow's first trial was a mistrial, but he was convicted in the second trial. The verdict was appealed, and the court of appeal overturned the guilty verdict from the second trial and ordered a new trial. After the third trial, the court of appeal overturned the guilty verdict and acquitted Sophonow. For the 15 years that followed, he sought his exoneration for the crime.

In 1998, the Winnipeg Police Service reopened the investigation into Stoppel's murder. On June 8, 2000, it was announced that Sophonow was not responsible for the murder and that another suspect had been identified. The Manitoba government issued a news release stating that the attorney general had made an apology to Sophonow, as he had endured three trials and two appeals, and spent 45 months in jail for an offence he did not commit. An inquiry was ordered into the police investigation and court proceedings to determine if mistakes were made and whether compensation should be provided.

The following are some of the issues that may have contributed to Sophonow's wrongful conviction:

- Detective notes when interviewing Sophonow were not verbatim, and a misquote was recorded. For example, Sophonow stated, "I could not have been in Ideal Donut Shop," but the statement recorded was "I could have been in Ideal Donut Shop."

- Winnipeg police did not inform Sophonow that he could call a lawyer at any time or inform him that the statements he made could be used against him. Sophonow stated that he asked for a lawyer on several occasions during interrogation, but the officers did not allow him to call one.

- Sophonow was strip-searched and a search of his anal cavity was done to determine if he was carrying any drugs, even though there was no reason to believe this was the case. Sophonow felt that there was nothing he could say that the police would believe and felt it best to keep quiet.

- Mr. Doerksen was hypnotized and asked to describe the assailant. Mr. Doerksen called the police when he thought he saw the culprit at a hotel. This man was quickly exonerated. Mr. Doerksen also identified a reporter as the culprit, who was also quickly exonerated. Mr. Doerksen failed to identify Sophonow from a lineup that the police assembled. The sergeant conducting the lineup told Mr. Doerksen to consider number 7—Sophonow was number 7.

- Sophonow had an alibi that was not considered seriously. He had stopped at a Canadian Tire the night of the murder, spoke to a woman and her daughter waiting for their car repairs, went to a Safeway store, bought some red stockings, and went to hospitals to deliver the stockings for Christmas. These events occurred around 8:00 p.m. and, given the timeline of the killing, ruled Sophonow out as the murderer.

- Terry Arnold lived near the doughnut shop and reportedly had a crush on Stoppel. He fit the description and did not have an alibi. He was not fully investigated.

Dr. Elizabeth Loftus testified in the inquiry and noted a number of problems with the eyewitness evidence:

- When there is more than one witness, they can inadvertently influence one another.

- People under hypnosis are suggestible and often assume that what they retrieve under hypnosis is accurate, even though it may not be.

- The photo arrays shown to Mrs. Janower had Sophonow's picture stand out: His picture had a yellow background and his hat was off to the side, as was the suspect's hat in the composite drawing initially issued to the public. There also was a live lineup in which Sophonow stood out in terms of his height.

Source: *R. v. Sophonow*, 1986.

# SUMMARY

1. Independent variables in the eyewitness area can be categorized as estimator or system variables. The effect of estimator variables on eyewitness accuracy can be estimated only after the crime. In contrast, system variables can be manipulated by the criminal justice system to increase (or decrease) eyewitness accuracy. The three dependent variables in the eyewitness area are recall of the event, recall of the culprit, and recognition of the culprit.

2. The misinformation effect is a phenomenon in which a witness who is presented with inaccurate information after an event will incorporate that misinformation into a subsequent recall task. This effect could occur as a result of a witness guessing what the officer wants the response to be. Alternatively, this effect could occur because a witness has two memories—one for the correct information and one for the incorrect information—but cannot accurately remember how he or she acquired each piece of information. The misinformation effect could also occur because the inaccurate information replaces the accurate information in memory.

3. The cognitive interview is based on four memory-retrieval techniques to increase recall: reinstating the context, reporting everything that comes to mind, recalling the event in different orders, and changing the perspective from which the information is recalled. In addition to these techniques, the enhanced cognitive interview includes five more techniques: building rapport, exhibiting supportive interviewer behaviour, transferring the control of the interview to the witness, asking for focused recall with open-ended questions, and asking the witness questions that match what the witness is recalling.

4. The simultaneous lineup, sequential lineup, showup, and walk-by are lineup procedures used by police to determine whether the suspect is the culprit. Biased lineups suggest who the police suspect and thereby who the witness should identify. In a biased lineups, the suspect stands out from the other lineup members in some way. Foil bias, instruction bias, and clothing bias have been investigated and shown to increase false-positive responding.

5. Not all eyewitness experts agree on the reliability of research findings and whether we can apply the results of laboratory simulations to the real world. An additional criticism lodged against the eyewitness expert testifying is whether the information provided is common sense and therefore not necessary for the fact-finder.

6. Four rules were outlined to reduce the likelihood of false identification. First, the person who conducts the lineup should not know which member of the lineup is the suspect. Second, eyewitnesses should be told explicitly that the criminal may not be present in the lineup and, therefore, witnesses should not feel that they must make an identification. Third, the suspect should not stand out in the lineup as being different from the foils based on the eyewitness's previous description of the criminal or based on other factors that would draw extra attention to the suspect. Fourth, a clear statement should be taken from the eyewitness at the time of the identification (and prior to any feedback) as to his or her confidence that the identified person is the actual criminal.

## Discussion Questions

1. Imagine you are a judge and are allowing an eyewitness psychological expert to testify. What factors would you consider appropriate for the expert to testify about? What factors would you disallow testimony about?

2. One of your friends is training to be a police officer. His training is almost complete, but he is worried that he has not received sufficient training on how to interview eyewitnesses. He asks whether you can describe some of the techniques you learned in your forensic class. Explain interview strategies to elicit complete and accurate recall, as well as a technique that may hinder the process.

3. There has been a considerable amount of research on the misinformation effect. Design an experiment to test whether the misinformation effect also occurs if participants witness a violent crime.

4. Police use different types of lineup procedures. Describe these different types of procedures, and distinguish among the types of identification decisions that can occur in both target-present and target-absent lineups.

# Chapter 6
## Child Victims and Witnesses

## Learning Objectives

- Differentiate between techniques that decrease versus increase the likelihood of accurate recall in child witnesses.

- Summarize children's ability to recall/describe people's appearances.

- Describe a lineup technique designed for children's identification.

- Outline the courtroom accommodations available for child witnesses.

- Explain child maltreatment categories and related consequences.

Suzie James lay asleep in the bed across from her older sister's when she heard something; someone was at the bedroom window. Suzie was 8 years old and Samantha (Sam) was 13 years old. They shared a bedroom with a large pullout window. In the summer, it could get very warm in the city so they kept their window open most nights. As Suzie opened her eyes, she saw a tall, thin, white man cover her sister's mouth and say, "Don't scream and I won't hurt you." Suzie pretended she was still asleep but tried to peek at the man so she could describe him later. In a few seconds, Sam was gone with this man who had come through the window. Suzie started yelling for help immediately. Her parents rushed in and asked what had happened and where was Sam. They called 911 and within minutes police arrived to interview Suzie.

Suzie sat on her mother's lap as she recounted what had happened moments earlier. Unfortunately, Suzie did not provide a lot of detail. Many questions remained regarding the identity of the man. The police officer started to ask Suzie direct questions, such as "Did you ever see this man before? Did he have a weapon? How old was he? How tall was he? Did he have any facial hair?" When the abduction occurred, the only light in the room came from a dim nightlight between the beds. Suzie could not see much in that light, but she provided answers to all the questions the officer asked.

A former gardener was arrested about three months after the crime, and his picture was placed in a lineup shown to Suzie. Suzie stared at his picture but could not make an identification. Almost a year after the abduction, Sam was spotted at a Quickie Mart with a man fitting the description her sister had provided. The store clerk quickly called police and tried to detain the two. Police arrived to arrest the abductor, who was the gardener, and bring Sam back home to her family. The abductor was charged with numerous offences.

How do we interview children? Should the justice system rely on children's memory? We will explore these questions and others in this chapter. We will focus on the historical legal context around children testifying in court, children's memory abilities, how best to tap into children's memory, and, lastly, the various forms of child abuse and their consequences.

## HISTORY

The way in which child victims and witnesses have been viewed by the justice system has changed dramatically over the years. Some early views can be traced back to the Salem witch trials in 1692, when children told falsehoods and claimed to have witnessed the defendants perform supernatural feats (Ceci & Bruck, 1993). Several years following the execution of the defendants for witchcraft, some of the children recanted their testimonies. For the most part, the prevailing legal attitude toward child witnesses for the following 300 years was that of skepticism.

Research testing the validity of these negative attitudes toward child witnesses started in Europe in the early twentieth century. Reviews from this time seemed to conclude that young children were highly suggestible and had difficulty separating fact from fantasy, and thus were capable of providing inaccurate testimony, even if the testimony was of personal significance (Whipple, 1909, 1910, 1911, 1912). Unfortunately, little is known about the details of the research on which these conclusions were based. Also, the criminal justice system was not very interested in these reviews. As a result, few studies were conducted on children's competencies during the early and mid-twentieth century.

A flurry of research on children's witness abilities started in the 1970s and continues to this day. Ceci and Bruck (1993) outlined four factors that led to the renewed interest in child witnesses:

1. Expert psychological testimony was becoming more acceptable in the courtroom.

2. Social scientists were interested in research that could be applied to real-world problems.

3. Studies on adult eyewitness testimony were increasing.

4. The legal community became interested in behavioural science research regarding child witnesses.

This last point was in response to the increasing number of reported sexual and physical abuse cases where a child was a victim or witness. These cases, arising in both the United States and Canada, often involved numerous children and numerous defendants. Box 6.1 describes a Canadian case in which children were the primary victims and witnesses.

## RECALL FOR EVENTS

Are children able to recall events accurately? How does their performance compare with the recall of adults? The Martensville case and others similar to it may suggest that children do not make very reliable witnesses, even about events they supposedly experienced. However, studies have found that children are capable of accurately recalling forensically

# The Martensville Babysitting Case

In the fall of 1991 in Martensville, Saskatchewan, Ms. L. noticed a rash on her 2.5-year-old daughter's bottom. Ms. L. suspected that child abuse had occurred at the babysitting service run by Linda Sterling. Following a medical examination of the child, a doctor concluded that the rash was not indicative of abuse.

The investigation continued, however, and several claims were made against Linda Sterling, her husband, Ronald, and her son Travis. The child in question was interviewed intensely and eventually stated that a man had touched her. Many more children were subsequently interviewed, some claiming that they had been confined in cages, penetrated with axe handles, forced to drink blood, whipped, and thrown naked into freezers. The children also claimed to have witnessed a ritual murder, a child's nipple being bitten off, a body dumped into an acid bath, and a dog stabbed to death.

Linda, Ronald, and Travis Sterling, along with one other woman and five other men, were arrested and charged. More than 40 charges, including sexual assault, sexual assault with a weapon, unlawful confinement, and intercourse with a minor, were laid against the Sterlings.

Dr. John Yuille from the University of British Columbia was an expert witness in the case. He noted that the interviews with the children were fraught with leading questions and that rewards were offered to children for giving the "right answer." Moreover, there was a lack of physical evidence consistent with the claims being made.

The investigation and trial spanned more than two and a half years. Linda and Ronald Sterling were acquitted, while Travis was convicted on several of the charges. Eventually, six of eight convictions were overturned because of the inappropriate interview techniques that were used with the children.

Source: *R. v. Sterling*, 1995.

---

relevant details of events (e.g., Ceci & Bruck, 1993). Moreover, children are capable of recalling much that is accurate. The challenge, of course, is determining when children are recalling accurately and when they are **fabricating** (i.e., making false claims). Research suggests that the accuracy of children's reporting is highly dependent on how they are asked to report. Examine the Case Study box. How would you interview children about an event that occurred?

**Fabricating:** Making false claims

## Free Recall versus Directed Questioning

When children are asked to report all they can remember, using a free narrative approach, their accuracy in reporting is comparable with that of adults (Ceci & Bruck, 1993). Unfortunately, children tend to report very little information using a free narrative. Direct questions or probes, such as "What else do you remember?" or "Tell me more about what you remember" are often necessary to elicit the required information. The dilemma arises when we consider the accuracy of direct questioning.

As we have seen with adult eyewitnesses in Chapter 5, when children are asked leading, direct questions, they are more likely to produce an erroneous response than when they are asked nonleading, direct questions (Roebers, Bjorklund, Schneider, & Cassel, 2002). Generally, older children are more resistant to leading questions than are younger children, and adults are even more resistant to leading questions (Ceci & Bruck, 1993). Dr. Maggie Bruck has been a key researcher in the area of children's

## CASE STUDY YOU BE THE FORENSIC PSYCHOLOGIST

Five-year-old Caitlin attends Sunshine Daycare in the town of Mindon, Ontario, which has a population of 7500. One day when Caitlin's mother picked Caitlin up from daycare, Caitlin seemed upset. This mood was unusual for Caitlin, typically Caitlin would run into her mother's arms, overjoyed to see her mom. When Caitlin's mom asked what was wrong, the girl didn't reply.

That night when Caitlin was going into the tub for a bath, her mother noticed Caitlin had some red welts on her bottom. When Caitlin's mom asked, "Why is your bottom red?" Caitlin started crying. After calming Caitlin down, her mother asked, "Did something happen at daycare today?" Caitlin nodded "yes." After her mother asked her what happened, Caitlin said that Miss Mimi got angry with the kids and hit them with a wooden spoon. When her mother asked if all the children got hit, Caitlin nodded "yes."

After Caitlin went to bed, Caitlin's mom called some of the other mothers to find out whether their kids had red marks as well and whether their children's demeanour was unusual. The other mothers inspected their children and started asking them very specific questions. Some children had bruises, and some children had other marks. The next morning, the mothers kept their children home and called the police and the Children's Aid Society to report the physical abuse.

Children were interviewed by police officers and then again by social workers. Miss Mimi was ordered to close her daycare and was charged with the physical abuse of children.

### Your Turn . . .

What would you do if you were Caitlin's mother or father? How should children be interviewed to increase the likelihood of reporting reliable information?

---

eyewitness memory and suggestibility. See Box 6.2 to learn more about Dr. Bruck and her research.

Direct questions that require yes or no responses or use a forced-choice format are particularly problematic for preschoolers (Peterson & Biggs, 1997). For example, Waterman, Blades, and Spencer (2004) interviewed children between the ages of 5 and 9. First, a woman went into children's classrooms and engaged them in a discussion about familiar topics for approximately ten minutes. The woman showed children four photographs: two of pets and two of food items. After the woman had left, researchers then interviewed the children using questions that required yes or no answers—that is, *yes/no questions*—(e.g., "Did the lady show you a picture of a banana?") and *wh-* questions (e.g., "What was the lady's name?"). Half of both types of questions were unknown to the children (e.g., "How did the lady get to school this morning?"). In these cases, the correct response should be "I don't know." Children performed similarly across both types of questions when they were answerable. However, when questions were unanswerable, children were more likely to say "I don't know" to *wh-* questions than yes/no questions. We see that yes/no questions are particularly problematic for children. Melnyk, Crossman, and Scullin (2006) suggest that

## Canadian Researcher Profile: Dr. Maggie Bruck

Dr. Maggie Bruck is a leading researcher in the area of developmental forensic psychology. Dr. Bruck started on this path with a B.A. from Wheaton College in Norton, Massachusetts. She then completed her Ph.D. at McGill University, researching social class differences in children's language acquisition. She stayed in Montreal after graduating and became a research associate at the McGill-Montreal Children's Hospital Learning Centre. So how did Dr. Bruck transition from examining language acquisition to understanding children's suggestibility? Dr. Bruck was intrigued and horrified by the McMartin case: a child abuse case in the United States that involved many preschoolers and daycare workers who were charged with numerous counts of committing horrific child abuse during the late 1980s. Dr. Bruck states, "I had so many questions about the whole workings of the legal system and why children would say these things and why adults would believe them." These types of daycare cases continued to surface through the 1990s and formed the basis of much of

Dr. Bruck's research and writing (with Dr. Steve Ceci), and they still do. At the time though, Dr. Bruck felt that the theoretical issues that were being proposed to understand or account for children's memory distortions were inadequate, and they left her "cold." Dr. Bruck notes, "They do not come near to explaining much of what actually goes on."

After almost 20 years of research, Dr. Bruck is impressed by the surge of empirical studies that continue to provide data for some very complicated issues related to child testimony. Dr. Bruck describes her favourite study as one that she co-authored with Patrick Cavanagh (a vision scientist and her high school classmate) and Steve Ceci, which examined the ability to recognize high school classmates at a twenty-fifth high school reunion (Drs. Bruck and Cavanagh attended that high school and organized the reunion). Dr. Bruck states, "The study was so much fun to put together. The results were very interesting and the participants were my classmates. The paper has since been featured in many textbooks."

Dr. Bruck stayed at McGill until the mid-2000s, at which point she moved to Johns Hopkins University as a professor of psychiatry and behavioral sciences. Dr. Bruck has consulted on many cases that involve children providing testimony. Dr. Bruck's one recommendation to the criminal justice system is to legislate mandated electronic recording of interviews. Dr. Bruck is currently conducting two large-scale projects. These involve children's understanding of touching as well as interviewing techniques that contribute to accurate reports. She and her colleague Stephen Ceci are also writing a new book on the role of developmental forensic psychology in the courtroom.

Dr. Bruck balances her work life with her cat by her side while gardening, cooking, and playing tennis.

this may be the case because these questions rely on recognition rather than recall, thus increasing the likelihood of error. Using recall (e.g, "Tell me everything you remember") may elicit brief responses, but those responses are more likely to be accurate. We will discuss recall and recognition in greater detail later in the chapter.

## Why Are Children More Suggestible Than Adults?

Generally, two directions have been taken to understand children's greater propensity toward suggestibility (Bruck & Ceci, 1999). One focus has investigated the "social characteristics" of the interview. It has been argued that children respond to interviewers in the manner they feel the interviewer desires, a tendency known as *social compliance*. The alternative area researchers have concentrated on to understand children's responses has been the investigation of developmental changes in their cognitive or memory system.

**Social Compliance or Social Pressure** It has been argued that children may respond to suggestive influences because they trust and want to cooperate with adult interviewers, even if the children do not understand or have the knowledge to answer the question. Children may infer the desired response in keeping with the "gist" or general idea of the question (Brainerd & Reyna, 1996). In a study by Hughes and Greive (1980), young children between the ages of 5 and 7 were asked nonsensical questions, such as "Is milk bigger than water?" and "Is red heavier than yellow?" Even though these questions are illogical and do not have correct responses, many children provided a yes or no answer rather than saying, "I don't know." It should be noted, however, that although children may respond according to a suggestion provided, their memory for the actual event may remain intact, and, if later questioned, they may report the accurate response (if asked about it in a nonsuggestive manner).

**Changes to the Cognitive System** Some research has found developmental differences in the ways children and adults encode, store, and retrieve memories (Brainerd & Reyna, 2004). Moreover, differences between children and adults also have been found in terms of forgetting and retention. Also related to memory is the notion that children "misattribute" where information came from (Parker, 1995). For example, children may report on an event that they heard about (e.g., through suggestive questioning from an interviewer) as if it were something they had experienced. For example, children may not remember that Ms. Z suggested that an event had occurred, and, when later asked about it, children report the "suggestion," believing that the event actually occurred.

Currently, researchers believe that an interaction of social and cognitive factors is likely responsible for children's suggestibility and their reporting of false information. The content and format of questions posed to child witnesses should be considered carefully. Interviewers need to balance asking direct questions with the risk of obtaining false information. Many researchers would recommend relying on free recall as much as possible to obtain accurate information.

A number of techniques, protocols, and procedures to aid child witnesses with recalling information have been investigated. Below, we describe some of these options for use with child witnesses and their efficacy for recalling accurate information.

## Anatomically Detailed Dolls

If children have difficulty providing a verbal account of what they witnessed or experienced, props may be useful. When interviewing children suspected of being sexually abused, some mental health professionals may introduce **anatomically detailed dolls**. Just as the name implies, anatomically detailed dolls, sometimes like a rag doll, are consistent with the male or female anatomy. Dolls may be of an adult male or female or a young male or female. The assumption underlying the use of these dolls is that children may have difficulty verbalizing what occurred, and in their play with the dolls they will demonstrate the events they experienced (Vizard & Trantor, 1988). Is this assumption correct, though? The research provides some contradictory results (Aldridge, 1998).

**Anatomically detailed dolls:** A doll, sometimes like a rag doll, that is consistent with the male or female anatomy

Anatomically detailed dolls being used in a therapy session

In a field study, Thierry, Lamb, Orbach, and Pipe (2005) examined the impact of anatomically detailed dolls on reports provided by 3- to 12-year-old alleged sexual abuse victims. The children were separated into two groups: younger (age 3 to 6) and older (age 7 to 12). The number of details provided were comparable in response to open-ended questions, whether or not dolls were used. When direct questions were posed, children 3 to 6 years old were more likely to use the dolls to re-enact what occurred than to report verbally. In contrast, 7 to 12 year olds reported more details verbally than with the dolls. Younger children were more likely to play with the dolls in a suggestive manner and to contradict details that were reported verbally. Overall, both younger and older children reported proportionally more "fantastic" details with the dolls than without. Similar results were found by DeLoache and Marzolf (1995).

Contrary to the above results, Goodman, Quas, Batterman-Faunce, Riddlesberger, and Kuhn (1997) found that 3- to 10-year-olds who had been touched during an examination were more likely to report such touching with dolls than when questioned orally. In another study, Saywitz, Goodman, Nicholas, and Moan (1991) interviewed 5- and 7-year-old girls who had received a physical examination. For half the girls, a genital examination was included. In this study, many of the children failed to report genital touching when they were asked for a verbal report of their examination, or they failed to show on the dolls what had actually happened. However, when asked a direct question—such as "Did the doctor touch you here?"—many of the children correctly agreed. Children who had not received the genital examination never made false reports of genital touching in either the oral free recall or the doll-enactment conditions. For this group, very few errors were made when the experimenter pointed to the genital area of the doll and asked, "Did the doctor touch you here?"

**Should Anatomically Detailed Dolls Be Used?** A number of difficulties have been identified for using these dolls to determine if sexual abuse occurred (Koocher, Goodman, White, Friedrich, Sivan, & Reynolds, 1995). For example, no specifications or guidelines are available for manufacturers of these dolls. Consequently, wide variation exists and some mental health professionals even make their own dolls. Not only is there no standardization for what the dolls should look like, but also there are no standard procedures for scoring the behaviours that children exhibit when interacting with the dolls. Research is not available to answer how nonabused versus abused children play with the dolls, and whether the groups of children play with the dolls differently. Thus, the use of anatomically detailed dolls for diagnosing sexual abuse can be inaccurate and dangerous (Dickinson, Poole, & Bruck, 2005).

## Other Techniques for Interviewing Children

**Criterion-Based Content Analysis** Criterion-based content analysis (CBCA) was developed in Germany in the 1950s by Udo Undeutsch (1989) to facilitate distinguishing truthful from false statements made by children. It has gone through some revision over the years by Stellar and Kohnken (1989) and Raskin and Esplin (1991) (Stellar, 1989). CBCA is part of a more comprehensive protocol called **statement validity analysis** (SVA) for credibility assessment for sexual abuse allegations. SVA consists of three parts: (1) a structured interview with the victim; (2) a systematic analysis of the verbal content

**Criterion-based content analysis:** Analysis that uses criteria to distinguish truthful from false statements made by children

**Statement validity analysis:** A comprehensive protocol to distinguish truthful or false statements made by children containing three parts: (1) a structured interview of the child witness, (2) a systematic analysis of the verbal content of the child's statements (criterion-based content analysis), and (3) the application of the statement validity checklist

of the victim's statements by using CBCA, and (3) the application of a statement validity checklist. Although some suggest the need to use the entire SVA system when assessing allegations, the CBCA is considered the most important part and is often used as a stand-alone protocol.

The underlying assumption of the CBCA is that descriptions of real events differ in quality and content from memories that are fabricated. Eighteen criteria were developed to discriminate between true and fabricated events of sexual abuse. See Table 6.1 for a list of CBCA criteria. It is assumed that true events are more likely to contain the CBCA criteria than fabricated events.

---

**Table 6.1** Criterion-Based Content Analysis Criteria

**General Characteristics**

1. *Logical structure.* Is the statement coherent? Do the statements fit together?
2. *Unstructured production.* Is the account consistently organized?
3. *Quality of details.* Are there specific descriptions of place, time, person, etc.?

**Specific Contents**

4. *Contextual embedding.* Is the action connected to other daily routine events?
5. *Interactions.* Are there reports of conversation between the victim and the perpetrator?
6. *Reproduction of speech.* Is conversation in its original form?
7. *Unexpected complications.* Was there an unplanned interruption in the sexual activity?
8. *Unusual details.* Are there details that are unusual but meaningful?
9. *Superfluous details.* Are peripheral details described in connection to the sexual event?
10. *Accurately reported details misunderstood.* Did the child describe a detail accurately but interpret it incorrectly?
11. *Related external associations.* Is there reference to a sexually toned event that is not related to the alleged offence?
12. *Subjective experience.* Did the child describe feelings or thoughts experienced at the time of the incident?
13. *Attribution of the accused's mental state.* Is there reference to the perpetrator's feelings or thoughts during the incident?

**Motivation-Related Contents**

14. *Spontaneous corrections or additions.* Were corrections offered or information added?
15. *Admitting lack of memory or knowledge.* Did the child indicate lack of memory or knowledge of an aspect of the incident?
16. *Raising doubts about one's own testimony.* Did the child express concern that some part of the statement seems incorrect?
17. *Self-depreciation.* Did the child describe some aspect of their behaviour related to the alleged offence as inappropriate?
18. *Pardoning the accused.* Did the child make excuses for or fail to blame the alleged perpetrator?

Source: Raskin, D.C., & Esplin, P.W. (1991). Statement validity assessment: Interview procedures and content analysis of children's statements of sexual abuse. *Behavioral Assessment, 12*, p. 279.

CBCA is not without its critics, however. For example, Ruby and Brigham (1997) note a number of difficulties with CBCA, such as inconsistencies with the number of criteria that need to be present to conclude truthfulness and the different decision rules for reaching a conclusion. Research has shown that age of the interviewee is positively correlated with scores on the CBCA (e.g., Buck, Warren, Betman, & Brigham, 2002; Vrij, Akenhurst, Soukara, & Bull, 2002). Younger children do not possess the cognitive abilities and command of the language to provide as detailed statements as older children. As a result, truthful statements by younger interviewees may be judged as doubtful because the statements are missing certain CBCA criteria (Vrij, 2005). Also, Pezdek et al. (2004) raise concerns about the forensic suitability of the CBCA for discriminating between children's accounts of real and fabricated events. They note that CBCA scores are influenced by both how familiar the event is to the child and how old the child is.

Overall, CBCA scores are calculated by using a truth–lie classification that requires the assessor to classify the statement as truthful or untruthful, based on his or her own interpretation of the statement. As a result, this method is highly subjective and does not ensure inter-rater reliability. Despite the criticisms, CBCA and SVA are being used in parts of Europe to distinguish between children's truthful and false reports. Recently, SVA has also been applied to adult statements to distinguish between truthful and false reports, and studies report great success (Parker & Brown, 2000).

**Step-Wise Interview** An alternative procedure for interviewing children that aims to keep false claims at a minimum is the **step-wise interview** developed by Yuille and his colleagues (e.g., Yuille, Hunter, Joffe, & Zaparniuk, 1993). This interview protocol consists of a series of "steps" designed to start the interview with the least leading and directive type of questioning, and then proceed to more specific forms of questioning as necessary (see Table 6.2). The objective with this protocol is to provide the child with lots of opportunity to report by using a free narrative before other types of questioning are used.

Lindberg, Chapman, Samsock, Thomas, and Lindberg (2003) have tested the step-wise procedure, along with a procedure they developed, the modified structured interview, and a procedure developed by Action for Child Protection in West Virginia that uses doll play. The three procedures are similar in terms of rapport building and the general question phases. The major difference is in terms of specific questioning. With the step-wise procedure, specific questioning occurs through progressively more focused questions and probes information obtained from the more general questions. With the modified structured interview, specific questioning occurs through the use of *wh-* questions. With the Action for Child Protection procedure, specific questioning occurs through doll play.

To test these three procedures, children in Grades 1 and 2 watched a video of a mother hitting her son. The children were then randomly assigned to be interviewed by using one of the three procedures. The interviewers were blind to what the children witnessed on the video. Interviews were transcribed and then coded for correct and incorrect statements. The results indicated that the procedure developed by the Action for Child Protection group was less effective than the other two, and the step-wise and modified interviews produced a comparable amount of information during the free-narrative portions. The modified procedure was superior to the step-wise or the Action for Child Protection procedure for *where* questions.

**Step-wise interview:** Interview protocol with a series of "steps" designed to start the interview with the least leading and directive type of questioning, and then proceed to more specific forms of questioning, as necessary

**Table 6.2** The Step-Wise Interview

| Step | Goal | How |
|------|------|-----|
| 1 | Rapport building | Talk to the child about neutral topics, trying to make him or her feel comfortable. |
| 2 | Recall of two nonabuse events | Have the child describe two experienced events, such as a birthday party and going to the zoo. |
| 3 | Explanation of truth | Explain truth in general and have the child agree to tell the truth. |
| 4 | Introduction of critical topic | Start with open-ended questions, such as "Do you know why you are talking with me today?" Proceed to more specific questions if disclosure does not occur, such as "Who are the people you like/don't like to be with?" |
| 5 | Free-narrative | Ask the child to describe what happened by using a free-narrative approach. |
| 6 | General questions | Ask questions based on what the child said, in a manner the child understands. |
| 7 | Specific questions (if necessary) | Follow up and clarify inconsistencies with more specific questions. |
| 8 | Interview aids (if necessary) | Have the child draw if he or she is not responding. Dolls may be introduced only after disclosure has occurred. |
| 9 | Conclude | Thank the child for helping and explain what will happen next. |

Source: Yuille et al., 1993.

Overall, the step-wise procedure is consistent with what we know about children's recall abilities and how to elicit accurate information. The step-wise interview is the procedure commonly used in Canada.

**Narrative Elaboration** In the United States, Saywitz and Snyder (1996) developed an interview procedure called **narrative elaboration**. With this procedure, children learn to organize stories into relevant categories:

- Participants
- Settings
- Actions
- Conversation/affective states
- Consequences

**Narrative elaboration:** An interview procedure whereby children learn to organize their story into relevant categories: participants, settings, actions, conversation/affective states, and consequences

A card containing a line drawing is available for each category (see Figure 6.1 for four of them). These visual cues help children remember to state all that they can. Children practise telling stories with each card before being questioned about the critical event. Then, they are asked for a free narrative about the critical event—for example, "What

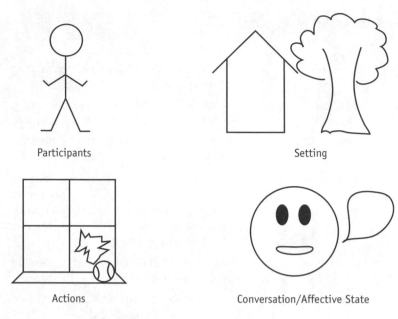

Participants

Setting

Actions

Conversation/Affective State

**Figure 6.1** Line Drawings Appearing on Card Categories

Source: Saywitz & Snyder, 1996, p. 1348.

happened?" Lastly, children are presented with each card and asked, "Does this card remind you to tell something else?"

To test the narrative elaboration procedure, children in Grades 1 and 2 and children in Grades 4, 5, and 6 witnessed a staged event (Saywitz & Snyder, 1996). The children were then interviewed with either the narrative-elaboration procedure (involving training in the use of reminder cue cards), exposure to the cue cards without training, or a "standard" interview without training or cue cards. Children interviewed with the narrative elaboration procedure reported more accurate information but not more inaccurate information for the staged event compared with when just the cue cards were presented without training or the standard interview. Also, children did not fabricate more information with the narrative-elaboration procedure.

Given the positive effects of the narrative-elaboration procedure, Brown and Pipe (2003) considered whether they could further improve the procedure if it was coupled with mental reinstatement. The recall of 6- to 9-year-olds was compared when they received narrative-elaboration training, the narrative-elaboration training with mental reinstatement, or the control condition without training for narrative elaboration. Children trained with the narrative elaboration reported almost twice as much information and were more accurate compared with the control group. Mental reinstatement did not increase accuracy. Moreover, research has found that simply asking children to report what they saw and heard, or to talk about information across categories was sufficient to produce increases in the amount of information recalled (Quas, Schaaf, Alexander, & Goodman, 2000).

**National Institute of Child Health and Human Development (NICHD) Interview Protocol** After having examined a number of interviewing protocols for use with children, Dr. Michael Lamb and his colleagues at the National Institute of Child Health and Human Development (NICHD) have developed an interviewing procedure that relies on open-ended questioning with two types of prompts available to interviewers (Sternberg, Lamb, Esplin, Orbach, & Hershkowitz, 2002). Interviewers can use time prompts to have the child fill in details and a timeline. For example, the interviewer may ask, "What happened next?" Also, interviewers can use cue question prompts where details that the child has reported are used in the question and children are asked to elaborate. For example, the interviewer may say, "You said the teacher took off his belt. Tell me more about that." This protocol also provides direction on how to start the interview and how to introduce the topic of abuse. For example, children are initially engaged to describe neutral events (e.g., the child's guitar lessons) in a nonleading manner. The topic of abuse may be introduced by asking the child why he or she has come to talk to you. A number of studies have been conducted investigating the NICHD protocol with positive results (Lamb, Hershkowitz, Orbach, & Esplin, 2008). In related research, Dr. Kim Roberts at Wilfrid Laurier University has collaborated with Dr. Lamb on a variety of research studies examining children's reporting abilities (e.g., Roberts & Lamb, 1999) and factors that may influence children's reports, such as report-building style (Roberts, Lamb, & Sternberg, 2004).

**Cognitive Interview** You may recall the cognitive interview from Chapter 5; this interview can be adapted and used with children (Geiselman & Padilla, 1988). A meta-analysis found that children interviewed with the cognitive interview reported more accurate information than children interviewed in control conditions (Kohnken, Milne, Memon, & Bull, 1999; also Holliday & Albon, 2004).

As you can see, there are a number of protocols available to those who interview children. These protocols limit the use of direct questions and attempt to have the child provide as much information as possible by using a free-recall format (Larsson & Lamb, 2009). The interview protocols being used by police vary by jurisdiction.

# RECALL MEMORY FOLLOWING A LONG DELAY

Is it possible to forget a traumatic event, such as abuse, only to recall it many years later? This question is at the centre of a heated debate about memory repression. Some argue that childhood sexual abuse memories are so traumatic for some individuals that they repress them in their unconscious. It is only as adults, with the help of therapy, that they come to recall the abuse, through what are known as recovered memories. Others argue that it is only through therapy and the use of suggestive techniques that clients come to believe that they were sexually abused as children when in fact they were not; such recollections are known as false memories. Loftus (whose research is described in Chapter 5) is among the proponents of this second group. **False memory syndrome** was a term coined to describe a client's false belief that he or she was sexually abused as a child. Clients may have no memories of this abuse until they enter therapy to deal with some other psychological problem, such as depression or substance abuse (Read, 1999). See Box 6.3 for a case involving "delayed" memory.

**False memory syndrome:** Term to describe clients' false beliefs that they were sexually abused as children, having no memories of this abuse until they enter therapy to deal with some other psychological problem, such as depression or substance abuse

## Can Traumatic Memories Be Forgotten?

Perhaps the greatest point of contention regarding false memory syndrome is whether traumatic memories can be completely forgotten only to be remembered many years later.

Box 6.3

# Delayed Memory Goes to Court

On October 2, 1992, a 48-year-old teacher, Michael Kliman, from Richmond, B.C., was arrested and charged with the sexual abuse of two female students. The complainants (A and B) were in their late 20s when they made the allegations, but the abuse allegedly occurred in 1975, when the complainants were in Grade 6.

The complaints alleged that Kliman would take each of them out of class three or four times a week for up to 20 minutes at a time. It was alleged that Kliman would bring them to a small room in the school where he would sexually fondle them or they would fondle him. In addition, one of the complainants claimed that when she was on a class camping trip in Grade 7, Kliman took her to his tent and raped her. Both complainants alleged that they suffered from dissociative amnesia—that is, memory loss of an event because of the trauma of the event.

Both A and B testified that they had no memory of the abuse until many years later. A stated that she recovered the repressed memory after she was admitted to a hospital psychiatric ward for an eating disorder when she was 19. B stated that she recalled the past events after she was questioned by police following A's claim.

In A's hospital record for anorexia, Kliman's name was not mentioned. A testified that while she worked at an insurance company a superior sexually abused and harassed her. She also testified that she was repeatedly abused and stalked by a man between October 1990 and December 1991. She consulted a therapist as a result of this abuse in February 1991. The therapist specialized in adult survivorship of childhood sexual abuse, post-trauma reactions, dissociation, and memory. At the time A sought therapy, she had no memory of abuse at her elementary school. It was during the course of this therapy that A first identified Kliman as an abuser.

B was sexually abused by a foster brother and neighbour when she was 11 years old. She has a continuous memory of this abuse. B had no memory of abuse by Kliman until interviewed by the police officer following up A's allegation of abuse.

Dr. John Yuille and Dr. Elizabeth Loftus were called in to discuss memory and dissociative amnesia. The experts reached somewhat differing conclusions. Dr. Loftus noted that at present no scientific evidence supports the notion that several incidents of traumatic sexual abuse could cause memory of the events to be lost. She also testified that the use of leading questions and suggestive interviewing techniques could contaminate memory. Dr. Yuille testified that some literature, including some of his work, supports the notion of dissociative amnesia.

Kliman was tried three times. In the first trial, the jury convicted him. The decision was appealed and the court of appeal set aside the conviction because of inadequate disclosure. In the second trial, the jury was unable to reach a unanimous verdict. In the third trial, Kliman was acquitted on all counts. The trial judge noted that there were many improbabilities about the details of the complainants' testimony that made it difficult to believe, aside from the memory issues. For example, it is hard to imagine how Kliman could excuse himself from class several times a week.

Source: *R. v. Kliman*, 1998.

In a study by Porter and Birt (2001), university students were asked to describe their most traumatic experience and their most positive experience. A number of different experiences were reported in each condition. Approximately 5% of their sample of 306 participants reported sexual assault or abuse as their most traumatic experience. The majority of these participants stated that they had consciously forced the memory out of their minds rather than never having a memory of it. Proponents of the false memory argument contend that not having any memory of abuse is different from preferring not to think about it. When there is absolutely no memory of abuse, and it is only through the use of suggestive techniques that the abuse is remembered, many argue that these memories should be interpreted cautiously.

Lindsay and Read (1995) suggest five criteria to consider when determining the veracity of a recovered memory:

1. *Age of complainant at the time of the alleged abuse.* It is unlikely that anyone would have a memory (of abuse or otherwise) prior to age 2.

2. *Techniques used to recover memory.* Techniques such as hypnosis and guided imagery heighten suggestibility and encourage fantasy.

3. *Similarity of reports across interview sessions.* Do the reports become increasingly more fantastic, or are they similar?

4. *Motivation for recall.* Is the client experiencing other psychological distress and wanting an answer to explain such feelings?

5. *Time elapsed since the alleged abuse.* It may be more difficult to recall abuse that occurred 25 years ago than 2 years ago.

Although some may "recover" memories of abuse and others never truly forget this traumatic experience, the courts are seeing a number of cases where there has been a delay in reporting the abuse. See Box 6.4 for a discussion regarding the phenomenon of historic child sexual abuse.

**Historic child sexual abuse (HCSA):** Allegations of child abuse having occurred several years, often decades, prior to when they are being prosecuted

## Box 6.4

# Delayed Prosecutions of Historic Child Sexual Abuse

Courts are having to deal with a relatively new phenomenon known as **historic child sexual abuse** (HCSA)—that is, allegations of child abuse having occurred several years, often decades, prior to the time at which they are being prosecuted (Connolly & Read, 2006). It should be noted that the vast majority of these cases involve memories of abuse that have been continuous. The alleged victim does not claim to have ever "forgotten" the abuse. From the results of a national survey in the United States, Smith, Letourneau, Saunders, Kilpatrick, Resnick, and Best (2000) found that 47% of adults who reported having been abused as children delayed reporting the abuse for over five years. Even more intriguing is that approximately 27% of this sample noted that they reported the abuse for the first time on the survey. Being male seems to be a reliable predictor of delayed reporting (Finkelhor, Hotaling, Lewis, & Smith, 1990).

In Canada (as well as in the United Kingdom, Australia, and New Zealand), there is no time limit during which a victim must report sexual abuse. Connolly and Read (2006) examined 2064 criminal complaints of HCSA in Canada with the objective of describing these criminal prosecutions. "Historic abuse" was defined as abuse in which the last offence occurred two or more years prior to the time of trial. Connolly and Read (2006) stated that the "typical" HCSA case had the following characteristics:

> The complainant is probably female. On average, she was 9 years old when the abuse began, 12 years old when it ended, and 26 years old at trial. She is unlikely to be reported to have been in therapy, and she is very likely to report continuous memory for the offence. Her abuser is more likely than not to be a male relative and he is on average 23 years older than her. On average, he was 33 years old when the abuse began, 36 years old when it ended and 51 years old at trial. In the majority of cases, the complainant reports repeated abuse that was sustained over an average period of almost 4 years. A threat is probably not reported to have accompanied the abuse, but if one is reported, it is likely to be against the complainant's or her family's physical safety. (p. 424)

Read, Connolly, and Welsh (2006) examined the factors that predicted the verdicts in actual HCSA cases between 1980 and 2002 in Canada. Four hundred and sixty-six cases were heard before a jury (434 cases resulted in a guilty verdict). Six hundred and forty-four cases were heard by a judge alone (442 cases resulted in a guilty

*(continued)*

verdict). In each case, the complainant was 19 years old or younger when the alleged offence began, and two or more years had elapsed from the end of the alleged offence to the trial date. Eleven independent variables were examined: (1) length of delay, (2) age of complainant at the time the alleged abuse began, (3) repressed memory testimony, (4) involvement in therapy, (5) expert testimony, (6) frequency of alleged abuse, (7) intrusiveness of alleged abuse, (8) duration of alleged abuse, (9) presence of threat, (10) complainant's gender, and (11) relationship of accused to complainant. The following section discusses the researchers' results, for both jury trials and judge-alone trials.

### Results for Jury Trials

In 93% of the HCSAs prosecuted before a jury, a guilty verdict was reached. Guilty verdicts were lower with older-aged complainants (Mean [M] = 12.67 years) than with younger-aged complainants (M = 9.52 years). Fewer guilty verdicts were obtained when experts provided an opinion for one side or the other, but not when there was an expert on each side. Surprisingly, when an expert testified on behalf of the Crown, fewer guilty verdicts were obtained than when there was no expert testifying. An expert testifying for the defence also resulted in somewhat fewer convictions than when there was no expert. When the abuse was accompanied by threats (i.e., physical and/or emotional), guilty verdicts were more likely than when there were no threats. Also, guilty verdicts were higher for defendants who had a familial relationship with the complainant rather than a community connection to the complainant. Other independent variables did not differ significantly in their influence on the verdict.

### Results for Judge-Alone Trials

In approximately 69% of the HCSAs prosecuted before a judge alone, a guilty verdict was reached. The increase in likelihood of acquittal corresponded with the increase in length of delay. The average delay period was 14.98 years for acquittals as compared with an average delay of 12.36 years for guilty verdicts. Guilty verdicts were more likely when a claim of repression was made than when no repression claim was made by the complainant. Guilty verdicts were more likely with more intrusive sexual abuse than with less intrusive sexual abuse, such as sexual exposure or sexual touching. Judges were more likely to reach a guilty verdict when the defendant was a family member rather than someone in the community. When the defence had an unchallenged expert testify, guilty verdicts were less likely than if no expert testified.

## RECALL FOR PEOPLE

Not only must children report the events that happened, it is likely they will have to describe the culprit, especially if he or she is a stranger. Culprit descriptions—also known as recall for people—by child witnesses have been examined in only a few studies relative to the number of studies that have examined recall for an event.

## Describing the Culprit

In one study, Davies, Tarrant, and Flin (1989) asked for descriptions of a stranger from younger (age 6 to 7) and older (age 10 to 11) children. The younger children recalled fewer items (M = 1 descriptor) than the older children (M = 2.21 descriptors). The researchers also found that older children recalled more interior facial features, such as freckles and nose, than younger children. Hair was the most frequently mentioned feature by both younger and older children.

The exterior feature of hair seems to be a dominant descriptor focused on by both children and adults (Ellis, Shepherd, & Davies, 1980; Sporer, 1996). Pozzulo and Warren (2003) found that exterior facial descriptors such as hair colour and style were predominant and accurately reported by 10- to 14-year-olds and adults. Moreover, interior facial features were problematic for both youth and adults.

Height, weight, and age are descriptors commonly reported, and if they are not reported, police may ask about them directly. Unfortunately, children and youth may have considerable difficulty with their estimates of such characteristics. Davies, Stevenson-Robb, and Flin (1988) found that children/youth (age 7 to 12 years) were inaccurate when asked to report the height, weight, and age of an unfamiliar visitor. Pozzulo and Warren (2003) found that accuracy for body descriptors such as height and weight were consistently problematic for youth. One possible explanation for this result is that children and youth may not understand the relation between height and weight—that is, taller people are heavier than shorter people of similar girth. Alternatively, children and youth simply may lack experience with height and weight. It is only in later adolescence that people become body conscious and more familiar with weight (and height proportions).

Leichtman and Ceci (1995) examined the effect of stereotypes and suggestions on preschoolers' reports. Children between the ages of 3 and 6 were assigned to one of four groups:

- Control—no interviews contained suggestive questions.
- Stereotype—children were given expectations about a stranger who visited the class.
- Suggestion—children were given misinformation about acts committed by the stranger.
- Stereotype plus suggestion—children were given expectations plus misinformation about the stranger.

Children witnessed a stranger by the name of Sam Stone visit their classroom. Sam was present for a story that was read by the teacher. All children were interviewed repeatedly after the event in one of the four conditions described above. For example, in the stereotype condition, children were told that Sam was kind and well meaning but very clumsy and bumbling. In the suggestion condition, children were misled that Sam ripped a book and soiled a teddy bear during his classroom visit. So, which group had the most accurate interview answers?

Using open-ended interviews, children were most accurate in the control condition and least accurate in the stereotype plus suggestion condition. Children in the stereotype condition produced a fair number of false reports. Children in the stereotype plus suggestion condition produced a great number of false reports. Overall, the older children were more accurate than the younger children.

In a follow-up study, Memon, Holliday, and Hill (2006) provided youngsters ages 5 to 6 with picture books of a man called Jim Step, who either paints his house, bakes a cake, or goes to the zoo. There were three versions of each story:

- Jim was portrayed as a clumsy person
- Jim was portrayed as a careful person
- Jim was portrayed neutrally

All children received post-storybook information that was consistent with the stereotype (e.g., Jim was described as clumsy in the book and then given stereotypical information about a clumsy person) and inconsistent with the stereotype (e.g., Jim was described as a careful person in the book and then given stereotypical information that is inconsistent with being a careful person) of Jim's character in the storybook.

The data revealed that children were more likely to accept positive, inaccurate information than negative, inaccurate information. Thus, negative information was more likely to be rejected and positive information was more likely to be accepted.

As these studies illustrate, it is important for interviewers not to introduce their own biases or inaccurate information when interviewing children. Once again, the argument can be made that children should be asked to describe the culprit in terms of what he or she did and looked like by using a free narrative. Given the few descriptors children provide, it may be important to probe this information for detail. Some of the techniques described above for event recall may be helpful with person recall. More research is needed on how to elicit person descriptions from children (as well as adults).

## RECOGNITION

One other task a child victim or witness may be asked to perform is an identification of the culprit from a lineup. In a meta-analysis comparing children's identification abilities to adults', Pozzulo and Lindsay (1998) found that children over age 5 produced comparable correct identification rates to adults, provided the culprit was present in the lineup (target-present lineup). However, when the culprit was not in the lineup (target-absent lineup), children as old as age 14 produced greater false positives than adults. That is, children were more likely to select an innocent person from a lineup than were adults (see Chapter 5 for a review of general lineup identification issues).

## Lineup Procedure and Identification Rates

Pozzulo and Lindsay (1998) examined whether identification rates differed between children and adults as a function of the lineup procedure used. As you may recall from Chapter 5, the sequential lineup has been demonstrated to decrease false-positive responding compared with simultaneous presentation for adults (Lindsay & Wells, 1985), although recently there has been some debate on the sequential superiority effect (McQuiston-Surrett, Malpass, & Tredoux, 2006). Nonetheless, we can examine whether the use of the sequential lineup with children decreases their false-positive responding. Pozzulo and Lindsay (1998) found that with sequential lineup presentation, the gap for false-positive responding between children and adults increased. Thus, the sequential lineup increased false-positive responding with child witnesses, whereas for adults the sequential lineup decreased false-positive responding.

**An Identification Procedure for Children** In an attempt to develop an identification procedure that decreases children's false-positive responding, Pozzulo and Lindsay (1999) proposed a two-judgment theory of identification accuracy. The researchers postulated that to reach an accurate identification decision, witnesses conduct two judgments: relative and absolute. First, witnesses compare across lineup members and choose the most similar-looking lineup member to the culprit, a relative judgment. Second, witnesses compare the most-similar lineup member to their memory of the culprit and decide if it is in fact the culprit, an absolute judgment. Pozzulo and Lindsay (1999) speculated that children often fail to make an absolute judgment and thereby produce greater false positives than adults.

The researchers explain how a failure of making an absolute judgment would result in greater false positives. They argue that with target-present lineups, a relative judgment is sufficient to lead to a correct identification because it is likely that the culprit looks most like himself or herself compared with the other lineup members. Thus, the culprit is selected. In contrast, with target-absent lineups, solely relying on a relative judgment may lead to an identification of an innocent person because the most similar-looking lineup member is not the culprit—recall that with a target-absent lineup the culprit is not there. An absolute judgment is necessary with target-absent lineups. If children fail to conduct an absolute judgment, a greater false-positive rate may result.

Based on these notions, Pozzulo and Lindsay (1999) developed an identification procedure for children, known as the **elimination lineup**, that is consistent with the two-judgment theory of identification accuracy. The elimination lineup procedure requests two judgments from the child:

1. All lineup photos are presented to the child, and the child is asked to select the lineup member who looks most like the culprit (relative judgment). Once this decision is made, the remaining photos are removed.

2. The child is asked to compare his or her memory of the culprit with the most-similar photo selected in the first stage and to decide if the photo is of the culprit (absolute judgment).

Pozzulo and Lindsay (1999) tested variations of this procedure and the "standard" simultaneous procedure with children and adults. The elimination procedure was found to significantly decrease children's false-positive responding with target-absent lineups compared with the simultaneous procedure. In other words, children's correct rejection rate increased by using the elimination procedure compared with the simultaneous procedure. Moreover, children's false-positive rate (or correct-rejection rate) with the elimination procedure was similar to that of adults when the simultaneous procedure was used.

The elimination procedure continues to be tested with different-aged children and adults while varying the conditions under which an identification needs to be made to determine its robustness and viability for use in "real life" (e.g., Dempsey & Pozzulo, 2008; Pozzulo & Balfour, 2006; Pozzulo, Dempsey, Corey, Girardi, Lawandi, & Aston, 2008; Pozzulo, Dempsey, & Crescini, 2009). For example, in a study by Pozzulo and Balfour (2006), children between the ages of 8 and 13 were tested along with adults when a culprit underwent a change in appearance following the commission of a theft. Simultaneous and elimination lineup procedures were examined under conditions when the culprit was or was not present in the lineup. The researchers found that correct identification rates decreased following a change in appearance regardless of the witness's age and lineup procedure used. In terms of correct-rejection rates, children had an overall lower correct-rejection rate compared with adults. Compared with the simultaneous procedure, the elimination procedure was more effective at increasing correct rejections when there was no change in the culprit's appearance from the time the crime was committed to the time a lineup was viewed. When a change occurred, however, correct-rejection rates were similar across the two identification procedures for both children and adults.

## TESTIFYING IN COURT

Prior to 2006, in Canada (as well as in the United States and some European countries), children under age 14 had to pass a **competency inquiry** before testifying. The notion behind the competency inquiry was that children must demonstrate that they can communicate

**Elimination lineup:** Lineup procedure for children that first asks them to pick out the person who looks most like the culprit from the photos displayed. Next, children are asked whether the most similar person selected is in fact the culprit

**Competency inquiry:** Questions posed to child witnesses under age 14 to determine whether they are able to communicate the evidence and understand the difference between the truth and a lie, and, in the circumstances of testifying, to see if they feel compelled to tell the truth what they witnessed or experienced. Also, it was felt that it was critical for children to understand the difference between saying the truth and lying, and to feel compelled to tell the truth. It could be argued that the competency inquiry was historically entrenched in the negative views of child witnesses discussed earlier in this chapter.

Bill C-2 came into effect in Canada in the winter of 2006, amending the Canada Evidence Act and the Criminal Code of Canada.

Under the old legislation of the Canada Evidence Act, section 16 stated that witnesses under age 14 must (1) be able to communicate the evidence and (2) understand the difference between the truth and a lie, and, in the circumstances of testifying, feel compelled to tell the truth.

In the first part of the inquiry, children need only demonstrate a general ability to perceive, recall, and communicate rather than demonstrate specific abilities for describing the event/crime in question. Common questions may include the following:

- What grade are you in?
- What is your teacher's name?
- How many siblings do you have?

Children as young as age 2 or 3 may be able to demonstrate a general ability to communicate.

For the second part of the exam, children are questioned regarding their ability to distinguish between the truth and a lie, and must demonstrate an understanding of the meaning of *oath*. Common themes for questioning in this section include the following:

- Defining terms
- Religion and church
- Consequences of lying

The second part of the inquiry may be particularly difficult for young children (even for some adults).

Under the new Canada Evidence Act, section 16.1, there is a presumption that children have a capacity to testify. Children (defined as persons under the age of 14) are asked simple questions about past events to determine their ability to understand and respond to questions. Children are requested to promise to tell the truth and testify under such a promise. No questions are asked about their understanding of the notion of an *oath* or *truth*.

## Courtroom Accommodations

Child witnesses may experience extreme stress and trauma because of having to testify in court while facing the defendant (Goodman et al., 1992). The Canadian justice system has responded to child victims and witnesses by providing a set of alternatives to testifying in court in the presence of the defendant. For example, in 1988, legislation was enacted that allowed children to testify from behind a screen or from another room by way of closed-circuit television (Bala, 1999a). These provisions applied to children under the age of 18 who were the complainants in sexual offence cases. Further amendments in 1997 extended these provisions to any child witness for any sexual offence or assault. Bill C-2 further extends these provisions to any offence for which a child (i.e., someone who is under the age of 18) testifies.

Professor Nicholas Bala has conducted extensive work in the area of child witness testimony. Bala (1999a) identifies a number of alternatives to in-court testimony that have been used in the Canadian system and are now available to any witness under the age of 18 and to vulnerable witnesses upon application.

A screen used when a child testifies

1. A shield/screen to separate the child and defendant so that the child does not see the defendant's face. However, the child is visible to the defendant and the rest of the courtroom and may be able to see the defendant's feet.

2. The child is allowed to provide testimony via a closed-circuit television monitor. The child and lawyers are in a separate room from the courtroom and the child's testimony is televised to the courtroom where the defendant, judge, and jury are present. The defendant can be in touch with his or her lawyer by telephone.

3. The child may have a support person with him or her while providing testimony. The child can decide whom he or she wants, although a person who is a witness in the same case cannot be a support person unless he or she has already provided testimony.

4. A child may be video-recorded while being interviewed about the details of the crime. The video may be admitted into evidence, so that the child does not have to repeat the details in court.

5. Generally, previous statements made by a witness are considered hearsay and not admissible. However, in sexual abuse cases, judges can apply the rules liberally, and statements made by the child during the initial disclosure of the abuse may be allowed as evidence. For example, a mother may testify about what her child said when disclosing the abuse.

6. The judge may close the courtroom to the public and/or media to protect the privacy of the child. A publication ban prohibiting any information that would identify the complainant or any witness also may be granted to protect the child's identity.

These alternatives also are available in the United States.

In addition, with Bill C-2, children under the age of 18 can no longer be cross-examined personally by the accused (s. 486.2).

## CHILD MALTREATMENT

So far, we have highlighted sexual abuse against children; however, there are other forms of maltreatment that a child may experience. Other forms of maltreatment require the same considerations as sexual abuse. The Child Maltreatment Section (CMS) of Health Canada distinguishes four categories of child maltreatment:

1. **Physical abuse** is defined as the deliberate application of force to any part of a child's body that results or may result in a nonaccidental injury. Examples include shaking, choking, biting, kicking, burning, and poisoning. See Box 6.5 for a debate on whether corporal punishment is physical abuse.

**Physical abuse:** The deliberate application of force to any part of a child's body that results in or may result in a nonaccidental injury

# Corporal Punishment: Discipline or Physical Abuse?

Seventy-eight-year-old Lucille Poulin was a religious leader in a commune on Prince Edward Island. Poulin was given the responsibility of looking after the children in the commune while their parents worked. She believed children needed discipline to prevent them from engaging in evil acts. Poulin used a wooden paddle when disciplining the children, resulting in assault charges in 2002.

At Poulin's trial, several children testified that she often beat them, at times causing them to pass out. Poulin was found guilty of assaulting five children. The court ruled that Poulin went beyond discipline. She was sentenced to eight months in jail and ordered not to live with or care for children younger than age 14 for three years following her release.

Corporal punishment has been put to the Supreme Court of Canada in a challenge by the Canadian Foundation for Children, Youth, and the Law (*Canadian Foundation for Children, Youth, and the Law v. The Attorney General in Right of Canada*, 2004). The legislation under scrutiny was section 43 of the Canadian Criminal Code, which states, "Every schoolteacher, parent, or person standing in the place of a parent is justified in using force by way of correction toward a pupil or child, as the case may be, who is under his or her care, if the force does not exceed what is reasonable under the circumstances."

The Canadian Foundation for Children, Youth, and the Law argued that section 43 of the Criminal Code violates sections 7 (security of the person), 12 (cruel and unusual punishment), and 15 (equality) of the Canadian Charter of Rights and Freedoms and that it conflicts with Canada's obligations under the United Nations' Convention of the Rights of the Child.

In July 2000, the Ontario Superior Court of Justice upheld the constitutionality of section 43. In January 2002, the decision went to the Ontario Court of Appeal, which upheld the lower court's decision and dismissed the appeal. The appeal then went to the Supreme Court of Canada. In January 2004, the Supreme Court held that section 43 was constitutional. The Supreme Court also ruled the following:

- Corporal punishment is prohibited in schools. Teachers in Canada will still be able to use physical force to remove a student or prevent immediate threats of harm to person or property, but a student can no longer be physically punished.

- Parents are not permitted to spank, slap, or otherwise use any corporal punishment on children younger than age 2 or older than age 12.

- Parents may use physical force on children between the ages of 3 and 12 but may not use an object to hit them.

- Parents are not permitted to strike children between the ages of 3 and 12 on the head or the face, under any circumstances.

Source: *R. v. Poulin*, 2002.

**Sexual abuse:** When an adult or youth uses a child for sexual purposes

**Neglect/failure to provide:** When a child's caregivers do not provide the requisite attention to the child's emotional, psychological, or physical development

**Emotional maltreatment:** Acts or omissions by caregivers that cause or could cause serious behavioural, cognitive, emotional, or mental disorders

2. **Sexual abuse** occurs when an adult or youth uses a child for sexual purposes. Examples include fondling, intercourse, incest, sodomy, exhibitionism, and exploitation through prostitution or the production of pornographic materials.

3. **Neglect/failure to provide** occurs when a child's caregivers do not provide the requisite attention to the child's emotional, psychological, or physical development. Examples include failure to supervise or protect leading to physical harm (such as drunk driving with a child), failure to provide adequate nutrition or clothing, failure to provide medical treatment, and exposing the child to unhygienic or dangerous living conditions. See Box 6.6 for a case in which a father forgot his child in a hot car, and read about whether the court found this to be a case of neglect.

4. **Emotional maltreatment** is defined as acts or omissions by caregivers that cause or could cause serious behavioural, cognitive, emotional, or mental disorders. Examples

Box 6.6

## A Case of Neglect or Forgetfulness?

For Dominic Martin and Sylvie Dubé of Montreal, a weekday's typical morning routine involved dropping off their daughter, Audrey, at daycare. Then Martin would drop his wife off at work and head to work himself. Martin would park his car in the subway parking lot and take the subway to work. On Thursday, July 17, 2003, Martin was running late so he dropped his wife off first. He then headed to the subway parking lot, as he did so many times before, while Audrey lay asleep in the backseat of the car. Martin got on the subway and went to work, forgetting to drop off his 23-month-old daughter.

After approximately eight hours, Martin returned to his car and found Audrey unconscious. It was estimated that the temperature in the car was hotter than 60°C. Audrey later died in the hospital, and Martin was charged with manslaughter.

Martin argued that with the change in his morning routine, he had forgotten to drop off his daughter. Audrey was asleep so he did not hear her in the back seat. The initial charges against Martin of manslaughter were dropped (Hanes, 2004).

General Motors commissioned a study in 2001 to determine the number of children who had died of hyperthermia—that is, severe heatstroke or heat exhaustion (as cited in Picard, 2003). One hundred and twenty children were reported to have died from being left in hot, parked cars since 1996. Of course, not all cases are a result of forgetfulness.

Source: Picard, 2003.

include verbal threats, socially isolating a child, intimidation, exploitation, terrorizing, or routinely making unreasonable demands on a child.

It is likely that children experience multiple forms of maltreatment simultaneously. For example, it is hard to imagine that a child who is neglected is not also emotionally abused.

Government agencies have the authority and responsibility to remove children from their caregivers when they are maltreated or at risk for maltreatment. Also, a child may be removed if a caregiver is unwilling or unable to prevent abuse by a third party. For example, children may be removed from their caregivers' custody because of neglect, physical and sexual abuse, alcohol or other drug use, and mental illness. It is important to recognize that for children to be apprehended, these factors must have negative effects on parenting to the extent that the caregiver cannot adequately parent. The term **in need of protection** is used to describe a child's need to be separated from his or her caregiver because of maltreatment.

**In need of protection:** A term used to describe a child's need to be separated from his or her caregiver because of maltreatment

With the exception of Yukon, Canadian jurisdictions require the reporting of children suspected to be in need of protection. Legislation across Canada varies the age below which an individual is considered a child. Generally, an individual is no longer considered a child between the ages of 16 and 19. In Ontario, for example, the Child and Family Services Act (i.e., legislation pertaining to children) denotes children as people under 18 years of age. See Box 6.7 for a case of physical abuse in which the child was in need of protection but did not receive it.

Beck and Ogloff (1995) surveyed Canadian psychologists and found that more than 98% of the respondents were aware of mandatory reporting laws in their jurisdiction. Although psychologists may be aware of reporting laws, they do not necessarily comply. According to the survey results, psychologists may not report child

Box 6.7

# One of the Worst Cases of Physical Abuse in Canada's History

Until Randal Dooley was 6 years old, he lived in Jamaica with his older brother, Teego, and a number of relatives. Randal's biological father, Tony Dooley, left when Randal was 1 year old, moving to Canada with his new wife, Marcia. The couple sent for the boys in the fall of 1997.

Shortly after Randal started school in Toronto, Randal's Grade 1 teacher wondered if Randal was maltreated. The first incident that caused her concern was when Randal lost a mitten. He was frantic about finding it. Randal mentioned that he would get a "licking from his mother." By the end of the same month, Randal had a badly broken elbow. The second incident that led his teacher to notify officials occurred when she noticed Randal had welts on his arm. She took Randal to the vice-principal's office, where they looked at his back and saw more than 25 welts. They called the Toronto police. No charges were laid at the time, however.

In April 1998, the Dooley family moved to the east end of Toronto. Mr. Dooley registered Teego at a new school but not Randal. There was no mention of another school-aged child.

Randal was found dead on the lower bunk bed that he shared with Teego on September 25, 1998. Mr. Dooley called 911 to report that his son had committed suicide. Randal's autopsy, however, raised doubts about a suicidal cause. The autopsy described Randal as a gaunt boy, his entire body almost completely covered with welts, bruises, scratches, and U-shaped marks. The report also said that Randal's body had extreme internal damage, usually seen when someone has been hit by a car. Randal had four separate brain injuries, 14 fractured ribs, and a lacerated liver.

His elbow had been broken in three places and his own tooth was in his stomach.

Mr. Dooley explained that in late August he had "flogged" Randal with a belt and was concerned that the Children's Aid Society would be called. It also was reported that Marcia Dooley made Randal eat his vomit and would not let him use the bathroom. She was reported to have punched him in the head, kicked him, broken his arm by putting her foot in his back and twisting it, and to have thrown Randal against a door where his eye was struck by the doorknob, which caused it to swell shut for three days. Moreover, it was reported that Mr. Dooley beat Randal on various occasions.

Tony and Marcia Dooley were charged with second-degree murder in Randal's death. At the trial, medical experts suggested that Randal's vomiting and incontinence were likely a result of a brain injury. Moreover, a pediatric neurosurgeon who testified at the trial noted that in his opinion Randal's death came from a fatal brain injury that caused a seizure.

After three days of deliberation, on April 18, 2002, Tony and Marcia Dooley were convicted of second-degree murder. Superior Court Justice Eugene Ewaschuk who presided over the case stated that Randal "may very well be the worst victim of child abuse in Canadian penal history." Marcia received a life sentence without eligibility for parole for 18 years. Tony also received a life sentence without eligibility for parole for 13 years.

Source: Blatchford, 2002.

maltreatment because of insufficient evidence or a belief that child protection agencies cannot help.

When trying to understand how often maltreatment occurs, it is important to clarify the distinction between incidence and prevalence. The CMS defines **incidence** as the "number of new cases in a specific population occurring in a given time period, usually a year." In contrast, the **prevalence** of maltreatment is defined as "the proportion of a population at a specific point in time that was maltreated during childhood."

The second Canadian Incidence Study of Reported Child Abuse and Neglect provides a national estimate of the number of instances of child maltreatment reported to and investigated by child welfare services in 2003. According to the report by Trocme et al. (2005), approximately 217 319 child investigations were conducted across Canada (excluding

**Incidence:** Number of new child-maltreatment cases in a specific population occurring in a given time period, usually a year

**Prevalence:** In the study of child abuse, the proportion of a population at a specific point in time that was maltreated during childhood

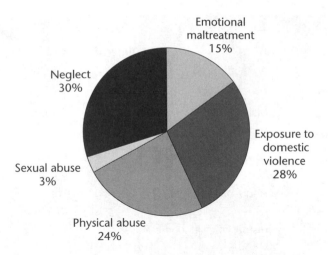

**Figure 6.2** Primary Categories of Substantiated Child Maltreatment in Canada (Excluding Quebec)*

*Based on a sample of 5660 substantiated child-maltreatment investigations.

Source: Trocme et al., 2005.

Quebec because of differences in data collection methodologies in that province)—a rate of 45.68 investigations per 1000 children in Canada. Of these investigations, 47% were substantiated, involving an estimated 103 298 child investigations—an incidence rate of 21.71 substantiated investigations per 1000 children. The rate of substantiated maltreatment in Canada, excluding Quebec, has increased 125%, from 9.64 substantiated cases per 1000 children in 1998 to 21.71 in 2003. This increase in documented maltreatment may be explained by improved and expanded reporting and investigation procedures such as the following:

1. Changes in case-substantiation practices
2. More systematic identification of victimized siblings
3. Greater awareness of emotional maltreatment and exposure to domestic violence

Neglect (30%), exposure to domestic violence (28%), and physical abuse (24%) were the three primary categories of substantiated maltreatment. Emotional maltreatment accounted for another 15% of cases while sexual-abuse cases represented 3% of all substantiated investigations. See Figure 6.2 for the distribution of child-maltreatment categories.

## Risk Factors Associated with Child Maltreatment

A number of **risk factors**—factors that increase the likelihood for emotional and/or behavioural problems—have been identified for physical and sexual abuse. These can be categorized as child factors, parental factors, and social factors (see Table 6.3).

The risk factors for physical and sexual abuse differ. Physical abuse risk factors are varied and include a parent's past childhood physical abuse as well as the parent's attitude toward pregnancy. In contrast, sexual abuse risk factors tend to revolve around family composition.

**Risk factor:** A factor that increases the likelihood for emotional and/or behavioural problems

**Table 6.3** Risk Factors for Abuse

| | Type of Abuse | |
|---|---|---|
| | *Physical Abuse* | *Sexual Abuse* |
| **Child Factors** | | |
| | Male | Female |
| **Parental Factors** | | |
| | Young maternal age | Living in a family without a biological parent |
| | Single-parent status | Poor relationship between parents |
| | History of childhood physical abuse | Presence of a stepfather |
| | Spousal assault | Poor child–parent relations |
| | Unplanned pregnancy or negative attitude toward pregnancy | |
| | History of substance abuse | |
| | Social isolation or lack of social support | |
| **Social Factors** | | |
| | Low socioeconomic status | |
| | Large family size | |

Source: MacMillan, 2000, p. 704.

# Short-Term and Long-Term Effects of Physical Abuse

A number of short-term effects of physical abuse have been determined. These include greater perceptual-motor deficits, lower measured intellectual functioning, lower academic achievement, externalizing behaviour such as aggression, and internalizing mental health difficulties such as hopelessness and depression (Ammerman, Cassisi, Hersen, & Van Hasselt, 1986; Conaway & Hansen, 1989; Lamphear, 1985).

In a review of studies examining the long-term effects of physical abuse, Malinosky-Rummell and Hansen (1993) report strong relations between physical abuse and nonfamilial and familial violence. Physically abused persons, especially males, engage in more nonfamilial violence than nonabused persons. In terms of familial violence, about 30% of physically abused or neglected persons abuse their own children (Kaufman & Zigler, 1987; Widom, 1989a). Moreover, being abused as a child predicted inflicting and receiving dating violence in a sample of university students. Also, spouses who were abusive reported higher rates of physical abuse than nonabusive spouses. Thus, experiencing physical abuse appears to increase the likelihood of perpetrating physical abuse.

# Short-Term and Long-Term Effects of Sexual Abuse

Kendall-Tackett, Williams, and Finkelhor (1993) examined 45 studies that considered the short-term effects of childhood sexual abuse. Common effects across the studies were behaviour problems, lowered self-esteem, inappropriate sexuality, and symptoms consistent with post-traumatic stress disorder. Research has found that within two years of being abused, children report a number of physical difficulties such as sleep disturbance, eating disorders, stomach problems, and headaches (Adams-Tucker, 1982).

Putnam (2003) identified three categories of outcomes in adults with a history of childhood sexual abuse: (1) psychiatric disorders, (2) dysfunctional behaviours, and (3) neurobiological dysregulation.

Under psychiatric disorders, major depression in adulthood has been found to be strongly related to sexual abuse in childhood (Paolucci, Genuis, & Violato, 2001). Sexualized behaviour is one of the most closely related dysfunctional behaviours with those who have a history of childhood sexual abuse (Widom & Ames, 1994). In terms of neurobiological dysregulation, magnetic resonance imaging (MRI) studies have found reduced hippocampal volume in adults who experienced sexual abuse as children, similar to that found in war veterans experiencing post-traumatic stress disorder (Stein et al., 1997). Messman-Moore and Long (2003) reported that adults who were sexually abused as children have an increased risk of being sexually abused as adults. Other long-term risks for sexually abused children include depression, self-injurious behaviours, anxiety, and interpersonal distrust (Browne & Finkelhor, 1986).

In a retrospective study conducted from 1995 to 1997, over 17 000 community members in California were surveyed (Dube et al., 2005). Participants were asked about abuse and dysfunction during childhood and other health-related issues. Childhood sexual abuse was reported by 16% of the male and 25% of the female respondents. If a person suffered childhood sexual abuse, it was found that there would be an increase in the risk of various outcomes. For example, suicide attempts were twice as likely among both men and women who had reported experiencing childhood sexual abuse compared with those who had not reported experiencing it. Also, there was an increased risk of alcohol problems, illicit drug use, and family problems when respondents had experienced childhood sexual abuse.

A recent survey in the United States found that roughly one in five young people is solicited for sex over the Internet each year (Mitchell, Finkelhor, & Wolak, 2001; see also Box 6.8). Canadian law is catching up to computer technology with the enactment of Bill C-15A in 2002. Now, it is a criminal offence to use the Internet to communicate with a child for the purpose of committing a sexual act (s. 172.1 of the Criminal Code of Canada). This offence carries a maximum five-year prison sentence. This legislation in part satisfies Canada's commitment to a United Nations protocol on the rights of the child that was signed by 105 countries in 2002. An advantage of this protocol is that it sets out consistent law to deal with child issues across countries. Given that the Internet does not have borders, this type of consistency is critical. See the In the Media box to learn more about the media's involvement in the battle against Internet luring.

**A Caveat to the Outcomes of Child Maltreatment** Although child maltreatment is always horrific, it is important to note that not all children who experience maltreatment will suffer negative outcomes. Although some children who have undergone

Box 6.8

## Luring Children over the Internet

Advances in computer technology provide a host of benefits to its users. Unfortunately, this technology can also be abused. With the Internet, sexual predators have access to countless children, and they can remain anonymous until they decide to meet a child. Some sexual predators conceal their true ages, and a child may assume that he or she is meeting another child, however, sometimes predators do not conceal their ages, as was the case with Kenneth Symes.

Symes was a 36-year-old former church pastor from Ajax, Ontario. Between April 18 and August 10, 2005, Symes began a series of Internet chats with two girls that

he thought were 12 to 13 years of age. In fact, the girls were undercover investigators. The chat exchange between Symes and the "girls" was sexually explicit and left no doubt that he wanted to have sexual relations with both girls. Symes arranged to meet one of the girls, and when he attended the meeting, police arrested him. Symes pled guilty to two counts of Internet luring and was sentenced to 12 months in prison, which was reduced to 2 months after double credit was given for time served.

Source: *R. v. Symes*, 2005.

## *To Catch a Predator*

You may have heard of the show *To Catch a Predator*. *Dateline NBC*, a television show based in the United States, got into the business of crime-busting with its series *To Catch a Predator*. It is estimated that one in four children are invited to meet for a sexual encounter. On this reality show, tables get turned on men who attempt to lure a child for a sexual encounter. Adult men chat online with youngsters, or so they believe, and eventually, these men arrange to meet the child for a sexual encounter. The child however is an operative: an adult trained to pretend to be a child while chatting online. When the male arrives at a prearranged location, he is met with a camera crew and is confronted by the host of the show. These men are shown on-air, and the police may be contacted. The men's names and faces are shown to the viewing audience.

A similar version was conducted in Canada by W-FIVE. A house rented in Toronto for five weeks was the place where the men would be told to go to meet the decoy. Although the police were invited to participate, they declined. However, with the aid of the New Hampshire police department, six "child personas" were developed; for example, 12-year-old Katie, 13-year-old Jenny, and 12-year-old Alex. The operatives had to be clear about their ages and could never initiate the subject of sex or a meeting for sex.

Because of these restrictions on the operatives, the predator had to use sexually explicit chat and be clear about his intent to meet for a sexual encounter with the underage child. Within the first few nights that the operatives were

online in chat groups directed at teens, there were sexually explicit chat and invitations. For example, "Yamaha man" made a date to meet "Katie" for a sexual encounter at the staged house. When "Yamaha man" showed up, he did not meet "Katie"; instead, he met a W-FIVE reporter and was asked why he was there.

What happens when the predator is part of the criminal justice system? In 2006, Louis Conradt, a 56-year-old Texas prosecutor, reportedly shot himself when police officers tried to arrest him for allegedly attempting to solicit a minor online. The cast and crew of *Dateline*'s *To Catch a Predator* were waiting outside his house to film his arrest. Allegedly Conradt attempted to set up a sexual encounter with a 13-year-old boy but failed to show up at the decoy house. A lawsuit against NBC was brought by Conradt's sister alleging that Conradt's civil rights were violated and the show intentionally inflicted emotional distress. Was NBC irresponsible? Should the company be allowed to film these interactions? Should these men's faces be shown? Conradt's sister sued for $100 million compensatory and punitive damages. The case was settled out of court. *Dateline NBC* has since decided to stop producing *To Catch a Predator*.

Sources: NBC resolves lawsuit over 'To Catch a Predator' suicide. (2008, June 24) *Los Angeles Times*. Retrieved from http://latimesblogs.latimes.com/showtracker/2008/06/nbc-resolves-la.html; Finlay, P. (2007, March 24). An easy catch. *CTV News*. Retrieved from http://www.ctv.ca/servlet/ArticleNews/story/CTVNews/20070323/wfive_aneasycatch_070324/20070324?hub=WFive

maltreatment will experience negative short-term and/or long-term effects, others will not. Moreover, some children who have *not* experienced maltreatment will experience negative effects (and, of course, some children who have not undergone maltreatment will not experience negative effects). A number of factors may increase or protect against negative outcomes (see Chapter 12 for a greater discussion on risk and protective factors for children and youth). Thus, it is important to keep in mind that no one factor in childhood can predict outcomes in adulthood with absolute accuracy.

## SUMMARY

1.  The accuracy of children's reporting is highly dependent on how they are asked to report. When children are asked to recall memories using the free-narrative method, the children's recall is as accurate as adults. A number of procedures and protocols to increase children's accurate responding have been investigated, including statement validity analysis, the step-wise interview, and narrative elaboration. Leading questions and the use of anatomically correct dolls are problematic for accurate reporting.

2.  Children report few person descriptors when asked to describe a stranger or culprit. Interior facial items such as freckles and nose shape are more likely to be reported by older children than younger children. However, accurately reporting these features is difficult. The exterior feature of hair is frequently mentioned by both children and adults. Height, weight, and age are unlikely to be reported accurately by children and youth.

3.  Children produce comparable correct identification rates with adults' when presented with a target-present lineup. However, children are more likely than are adults to select an innocent person with a target-absent lineup. The elimination lineup procedure decreases children's false-positive responding compared with a simultaneous lineup procedure.

4.  Historically in Canada (and other countries), children under the age of 14 had to pass a competency inquiry before being allowed to testify. Under the new Bill C-2, children are asked simple questions to demonstrate their ability to communicate. Children testify under a promise to tell the truth. Also as a result of Bill C-2, a number of alternatives to in-court testimony (e.g., screens, a pre-recorded interview, and the presence of a support person) are available for persons under the age of 18.

5.  Maltreatment can be categorized into sexual abuse, physical abuse, neglect/failure to provide, and emotional abuse. A number of short-term and long-term effects can result from physical abuse; for example, perceptual-motor deficits, lower measured intellectual functioning, lower academic achievement, externalizing behaviour, internalizing mental health difficulties, and nonfamilial and familial violence. A number of short-term and long-term effects can result from sexual abuse; for example, behaviour problems, lowered self-esteem, inappropriate sexuality, physical symptoms consistent with post-traumatic stress disorder, and continued abuse when an adult.

## Discussion Questions

1. In your local community newspaper, you read of a 7-year-old boy who has been physically abused and then abandoned. You wonder what difficulties this boy may experience in the next couple of years and when he becomes an adult. Describe the possible short-term and long-term effects of maltreatment.

2. Why is the use of anatomically correct dolls controversial when assessing child sexual abuse?

3. After completing an undergraduate course in forensic psychology, you are interested in telling your colleagues in the police department the best interview techniques to use with child witnesses. You decide to develop a mini-workshop on good and bad interview techniques. Put together a curriculum for your workshop.

4. An 8-year-old girl has witnessed the abduction of her best friend by an adult male. What factors will likely influence this child's ability to describe the kidnapper? What procedures should the police use when conducting a lineup with this child witness?

# Chapter 7

## Juries: Fact Finders

## Learning Objectives

- Describe how jurors are selected in Canada.

- Distinguish between representativeness and impartiality.

- Describe the effects of pretrial publicity and the available options for dealing with it.

- Outline the stages to reaching a jury verdict.

- Describe the categories of variables that have been examined to predict a verdict.

Kathy Kramer is juror 10. Along with 11 other jurors, she is seated in the jury box, listening to evidence about how the defendant, Melissa Vincent, brutally murdered her roommate in a fit of rage when she found out that her boyfriend and roommate were having an affair. Melissa isn't your "typical" defendant; she is 21 years old and was on an exchange program in Australia, completing her undergraduate degree in psychology, when the crime occurred. She comes from a wealthy family: Both her parents are surgeons. The Crown argues that Melissa left the school library early one night and, as she was nearing her apartment complex, she saw her boyfriend, Mark Carson, leaving the building. Melissa is alleged to have confronted her room-mate, Marcy Metcalfe, and when she learned that Mark and Marcy were having a sexual relationship, she became enraged, grabbed a kitchen knife, and stabbed her roommate, leaving Marcy dead. A phone record shows that Melissa called Mark around the time the victim died. Melissa claimed she was just leaving the library when she made this call to ask Mark to meet her at her apartment. According to Melissa, she arrived after Mark was at the apartment and it was Mark who called the police to report the murder. Mark admits to having a relationship with Marcy. He also claims Melissa was extremely jealous of the friendship he had with Marcy. Melissa argued that the apartment complex was located in a "rough" part of town where drug dealers and prostitutes hung around. It was not uncommon to hear that apartments were broken into for money or drugs. The murder weapon was never recovered. No one could verify what time Melissa left the library. Mark did not have an alibi, either. Kathy needs to decide on a verdict for this case. What factors should influence her verdict?

In this chapter, we will focus on the jury-selection process, how jury research is conducted, and issues related to understanding the rules of law and how well we can predict verdicts. The information we provide in this chapter will focus on criminal trials exclusively unless otherwise stated.

In Canada, the courts deal with both civil and criminal cases. Criminal cases are those in which an act was allegedly committed as found in the Criminal Code of Canada. In contrast, civil cases are those that involve a breach of contract or other claims of "harm" (known as torts). Civil cases can be heard by jury or judge alone, as can criminal cases. However, the process, jury selection, and decision rules for civil cases are quite different from criminal cases. For example, jury trials for civil cases can have fewer jurors than criminal trials. Six- or eight-member jury trials often occur in civil cases, whereas twelve-member juries are typical in criminal cases. Also, verdicts do not necessarily have to be unanimous in civil trials. This chapter will focus on issues as they relate to criminal cases.

## JURY SELECTION IN CANADA

Before a jury trial can begin, a jury needs to be selected or "seated." The process of jury selection differs by province and territory (and country), although there are a number of commonalities across jurisdictions. Before we discuss jury selection, it is important to consider the types of cases juries will hear.

### The Cases Heard by Juries

Television has bombarded us with crime shows such as *Law and Order* and *CSI*. Talk shows, such as *Larry King Live*, also highlight the latest developments in various high-profile cases. All this media coverage may distort perceptions of the frequency of trials heard by juries. Only some types of offences can proceed with jury trials. Moreover, in some instances defendants are given an option of a jury trial, but they may opt to be tried by judge alone. Thus, in Canada, relative to the total number of trials that take place, only a few are tried by jury. The remainder of trials are heard and ruled on by judges alone.

There are three types of offences in Canada: (1) summary offences, (2) indictable offences, and (3) hybrid offences.

Summary offences involve a sentence of less than six months in prison and a fine of less than $2000 (section 787[1] of the Criminal Code). However, for some offences the maximum sentence is 18 months (R.S.C. 1985, C-46, s. 787[1]). These offences are tried by judge alone. Moreover, the defendant charged with a summary offence does not have a right to a trial by jury.

There are three categories of indictable offences:

1. Less serious indictable offences are heard by a judge sitting alone. These are found in section 553 of the Criminal Code and include theft (other than theft of cattle), obtaining money or property by false pretences, and failure to comply with a probation order.

2. Highly serious indictable offences must be tried by judge and jury. These offences include treason, murder, and piracy. However, an exception under section 473 of the Criminal Code indicates that if the attorney general and the accused agree, the trial can proceed without a jury and the judge alone tries the case.

3. For some indictable offences, the accused can choose whether the trial proceeds by judge and jury or judge alone. These are the indictable offences not listed in either section 553 or 469 of the Criminal Code, such as robbery (R.S.C. 1985, C-46, s. 343; 1995, C-34, s. 302), arson (R.S.C. 1985, C-46, s. 433; 1990, C-15, s. 1), and sexual assault with a weapon (R.S.C. 1985, C-46, s. 272; 1995, C-39, s. 145). The defendant has the option to choose (1) to be tried by a provincial or territorial court judge without a jury and without having had a preliminary inquiry, (2) to have a preliminary inquiry and to be tried by a judge without a jury, or (3) to have a preliminary inquiry and to be tried by a judge and a jury. If a defendant does not make a selection, he or she will have a preliminary inquiry and be tried by a judge and jury.

Hybrid offences are a cross between indictable offences and summary offences. These are offences for which the maximum sentence is five or more years in prison if they proceed by indictment. If the Crown proceeds summarily, the maximum penalty is 6 months, or 18 months in some cases, such as sexual assault. It is up to the Crown attorney to decide whether to proceed with the case as an indictable offence or a summary offence. If the Crown opts for a summary offence, the case is tried by judge alone and the defendant does not have the right to a jury trial.

As you can see, these criteria greatly reduce the number of cases that are tried by jury. Also, it is important to keep in mind that jury trial options vary somewhat across provinces and territories.

## Jury Selection

The **Juries Act** is provincial and territorial legislation that outlines the eligibility criteria for jury service and how prospective jurors must be selected. Although legislation varies across jurisdictions, there are a number of commonalities. Differences in eligibility criteria across jurisdictions may include the minimum age to be a juror (e.g., 18 years in Ontario and 19 years in British Columbia) and the professions (e.g., lawyer, police officer) that keep individuals exempt from jury duty.

**Juries Act:** Provincial and territorial legislation that outlines the eligibility criteria for jury service and how prospective jurors must be selected

Prospective jurors (i.e., random community members) receive a **jury summons**—that is, a court order that states a time and place for jury duty. Receiving a jury summons does not guarantee that you will be a juror, though. It simply means that you are expected to show up, typically at the courthouse, prepared to be a juror. If you ignore a summons and do not show up, you may incur a severe legal penalty, such as a fine or jail time.

**Jury summons:** A court order that states a time and place to go for jury duty

In Canada, criminal trials have 12-person juries. If you are selected from the juror pool, you will be a juror unless one of the lawyers presents a challenge. Generally, there are two types of challenges lawyers can use to reject a potential juror: (1) peremptory challenge and (2) challenge for cause.

Both the Crown and defence are allowed a limited number of peremptory challenges. In murder trials, each side has 20 peremptory challenges, whereas for most other crimes each side has 12 peremptory challenges. The Crown or defence can use a peremptory challenge to reject jurors who they believe are unlikely to reach a verdict in their favour. When using a peremptory challenge, the lawyer does not need to provide a reason for rejecting the prospective juror.

In contrast, when using a challenge for cause, the lawyer must give a reason for rejecting the prospective juror. We will discuss challenge for cause later in this chapter. Keep in mind that Canadian lawyers have very limited information about prospective jurors. This information includes name, address, occupation, and physical demeanour. Also, in many Canadian cases the lawyers are not allowed to ask prospective jurors questions to gain more information about them. Consequently, lawyers have very little information on which to decide whether a juror will reach a verdict in their favour. Although a prospective juror may be challenged and not able to sit for one trial, he or she may be selected for another trial.

## Characteristics and Responsibilities of Juries in Canada

The Supreme Court of Canada indicated two fundamental characteristics of juries (*R. v. Sherratt*, 1991):

1.  A composition that represents the community in which the crime occurred. This is known as **representativeness**.
2.  A lack of bias on the part of jurors, known as **impartiality**.

## Representativeness

For a jury to be considered "representative," it must allow any possible eligible person from the community the opportunity to be part of the jury. Representativeness is achieved through randomness. For example, a community's telephone directory or voter registration is used as a pool from which to randomly draw 100 or so names for potential jury duty. Of course, one could argue that neither of these "pools" is truly representative of the community because there may be people who can serve on a jury but whose names do not appear on these lists. For example, a homeless person may not have a phone but may be eligible to serve on a jury. Also, the Juries Act lists "exemptions" for those who cannot serve on a jury, thus limiting the true representativeness of the jury pool.

In some cases, the Crown or the defence may challenge the composition of the jury, arguing that it does not represent the community on some characteristic. For example, in *R. v. Nepoose* (1991), the defendant was an Aboriginal woman. The jury composition for her trial was successfully challenged for having too few women. See Box 7.1 for a jury-composition challenge of representativeness on the basis of race.

## Impartiality

The juror characteristic of impartiality centres on three issues:

1.  For a juror to be impartial, he or she must set aside any pre-existing biases, prejudices, or attitudes and judge the case based solely on the admissible evidence. For example, a juror must ignore that the defendant belongs to an ethnic group against which he or she holds a bias. An impartial juror will not let his or her prejudice cloud the evaluation of the evidence.
2.  To be impartial also means that the juror must ignore any information that is not part of the admissible evidence. For example, prior to the start of a trial, a case may have

## Balancing a Jury by Race

In 2001, two Caucasian men, Jeffrey Brown and Jeffrey Kindrat, were charged with sexually assaulting a 12-year-old Aboriginal girl. Of approximately 100 potential jurors who showed up for jury duty in Melfort, Saskatchewan, only one was visibly Aboriginal. Not surprisingly, once the jury was composed, all those sitting on the jury were Caucasian.

During the trial, the defendants admitted to picking the girl up, giving her five beers to drink, and then engaging in sexual activity with her outside a truck belonging to a third man, Dean Edmondson. The jury heard the evidence and then deliberated to reach verdicts of not guilty for both Brown and Kindrat.

Were these verdicts a product of a racist jury? The case raised concern about the jury-selection process. The Saskatchewan Justice Department stated that it would contact officials across Canada to determine whether changes to the selection process could be made to make juries more racially balanced. The effect of this case on jury selection has yet to be determined.

Interestingly, in the trial of Edmondson, he was found guilty, also with an all-Caucasian jury. One main difference between the cases was the testimony of the victim. The victim testified more fully against Edmondson; however, she was reluctant to testify against Brown and Kindrat, providing far less information.

An appeal from the Crown was allowed in 2005 by the Saskatchewan Court of Appeal. The acquittals were set aside, and a new trial was ordered for Brown and Kindrat. The appeal was not based on the racial composition of the jury, however, but rather on the judge's instruction to the jury.

Sources: Warick, 2003; *R. v. Brown*, 2005.

received media attention highlighting facts about the defendant that are biased, irrelevant, or inadmissible.

3. It also is important that the juror have no connection to the defendant so that the juror does not view the evidence subjectively or unduly influence the other jurors. See Box 7.2 for a Canadian case dealing with juror partiality.

## Canada's Most Famous Partial Juror

Peter Gill and five others were tried in Vancouver for two gang-style murders in 1995. Gillian Guess was one of the 12 jurors hearing Peter Gill's case. During the trial, Guess and Gill ran into each other outside the courtroom; thereafter, they began to flirt in the courtroom. This flirtation led to a meeting outside the courtroom and escalated into a sexual relationship. Their relationship was ongoing as Guess continued to serve on the jury hearing Gill's case.

The jury, including Guess, found Peter Gill and the other defendants not guilty. When the court became aware of the relationship, both Guess and Gill were charged with obstruction of justice. Guess was found guilty and sentenced to 18 months in jail. She was the first juror in North America to be convicted of attempting to obstruct justice and ended up serving three months in prison. Peter Gill had been convicted of obstruction of justice in the past and was sentenced to five years and ten months in prison. Justice Barry Davies of the Supreme Court of British Columbia noted, "Mr. Gill pursued a deliberate and persistent attack upon one of society's most fundamental democratic institutions" (*R. v. Gill*, 2002, para. 29) by getting involved with Guess.

A new murder trial was ordered for Peter Gill and two other men. The appeal court noted that Guess's impartiality had been compromised and that it was hard to imagine a more remarkable violation of a juror's duty.

Sources: *R. v. Budai, Gill, and Kim*, 2001; *R. v. Gill*, 2002; *R. v. Guess*, 1998.

**Threats to Impartiality** A number of threats to impartiality exist. For example, is it possible to forget the emotionally charged headlines that we read before going to jury duty? Typically, the media attention is negative for the defendant, and that could mean that the defendant does not receive a fair trial. Thus, the concern is that verdicts will be based on emotion and biased media coverage rather than on admissible evidence. Steblay, Besirevic, Fulero, and Jimenez-Lorente (1999) conducted a meta-analysis of 44 studies examining the effects of pretrial publicity. They found a modest, positive relationship between exposure to negative pretrial publicity and judgments of guilt. This relation means that as exposure to negative pretrial publicity increases, so do the number of guilty verdicts.

Postive pretrial publicity also seems to have an impact on verdict. In one study examining negative and positive pretrial publicity, Ruva and McEvoy (2008) had mock jurors read news clips with negative, positive, or unrelated pretrial publicity. Mock jurors watched a murder trial and rendered a verdict along with a number of other ratings. Pretrial publicity, whether positive or negative, influenced verdict, perceptions of the defendant, and attorneys. Positive information biased jurors positively toward the defendant (e.g., less guilty verdicts), and negative information biased jurors negatively against the defendant (e.g., more guilty verdicts).

**Keeping Potential Jurors Impartial** Before a case goes to trial, a preliminary hearing occurs in which the Crown presents the evidence against the defendant. The judge then determines whether there is sufficient evidence for the case to proceed to trial. In Canada, at the preliminary hearing, the judge typically places a ban on the media's reporting of the evidence before the end of the trial process. If the details of the case can be kept from the public, then the likelihood of potential jurors being exposed to information that may compromise their ability to remain impartial is decreased. Moreover, the likelihood of jurors using only the evidence presented during the trial to reach their verdict is increased.

Unfortunately, details do get leaked, especially in high-profile cases involving child victims or violent offences. For example, details about numerous missing women from Vancouver found buried on Robert Pickton's farm in Port Coquitlam made headlines across Canada before Pickton's case was heard (e.g., Saunders & Thompson, 2002). What are the legal options when the defence or Crown fears a partial or biased jury pool?

Some methods for increasing the likelihood of an impartial jury are as follows:

1. The Crown or defence may argue that the trial should be moved to another community because it would be very difficult to obtain an impartial jury from the local community. This option is called a **change of venue** and is found in section 599(1) of the Criminal Code (R.S.C., 1985, C-46, s. 599). The party raising the issue must demonstrate that there is a reasonable likelihood that the local community is biased or prejudiced against the defendant. Factors that may lead to a biased community include extensive pretrial publicity, a heinous crime, and a small community in which many people know the victim and/or the defendant (Granger, 1996).

   A change of venue is not granted very often, but when it is, the trial typically stays within the province or territory in which the crime occurred. An example was the trial of Kelly Ellard, a teen charged with the murder of 14-year-old Reena Virk in a suburb of Victoria, B.C. Adrian Brooks, the defence lawyer, successfully argued to move the trial from Victoria to Vancouver. Brooks claimed that the media attention the case received would prohibit Ellard from getting a fair trial in Victoria (Meissner, 2000).

**Change of venue:** Moving a trial to a community other than the one in which the crime occurred

2. An alternative to moving a trial to a new community is to allow sufficient time to pass so that the biasing effect of any pretrial prejudicial information has dissipated by the time the trial takes place. Thus, the judge may call for an **adjournment**, delaying the trial until sometime in the future. A major limitation to adjourning cases is that not only can prospective jurors' memories fade, so might those of the witnesses. Witnesses may forget critical details that they are to testify about. Also, witnesses may move or die. Consequently, courts infrequently call for an adjournment.

**Adjournment:** Delaying the trial until sometime in the future

3. Another option that may be granted in cases for which bias is suspected among the prospective jury pool is known as a **challenge for cause**. The Crown or defence may argue that, although the prospective jury pool may be partial, if questioned, these prospective jurors could be identified and rejected from serving on the jury. As with the change of venue, the side desiring the judge to allow a challenge for cause must demonstrate that there is reasonable partiality in the community from which the jury pool will be drawn. If the judge grants a challenge for cause, prospective jurors can be probed with a set of predetermined questions approved by the judge. The questions are relatively few (perhaps five or so) and only the prospective jurors' state of mind or thinking can be examined. Lawyers are not allowed to ask prospective jurors about their backgrounds or personalities. See Box 7.3 for two cases where a challenge for cause was granted.

**Challenge for cause:** An option to reject biased jurors

---

## Box 7.3

# Cases Allowing a Challenge for Cause

### Questions Focused on Racial Bias Ruled Appropriate

In *R. v. McLeod* (2005), two black men of Jamaican origin, Germaine McLeod and Christopher Chung, were charged with murdering a man of Asian descent. The Crown's theory was that all three men were involved in drug trafficking or other illegal activities and that the deceased was killed because he was believed to be a police informant.

The following questions were allowed to be posed to the prospective jurors:

1. Do you believe that black Jamaican men, as a group, are more likely to be violent than other persons generally?

2. Would your ability to judge the evidence in this case without bias, prejudice, or partiality be affected by the fact that the accused persons are black Jamaican men, and the deceased was Asian?

As is the practice in the province of Alberta, where this trial occurred, the trial judge, Judge Slatter, was responsible for posing the questions to the prospective jurors.

Source: *R. v. McLeod*, 2005.

### Seating a Jury for the Pig Farmer Trial: A Challenge for Cause Granted in Part Because of Intense Pretrial Publicity

Robert Pickton, a pig farmer from Port Coquitlam, B.C., was charged with the first-degree murder of 26 women. The charges were divided into two trials to facilitate the hearing of testimony and evidence. Pickton's first trial focused on six counts of murder. A challenge for cause was declared.

The jury selection occurred in December 2006, with Judge Williams questioning potential jurors. Jury selection started with 600 prospective jurors to find 12 jurors and 2 alternates. Once a trial begins, alternate jurors cannot replace jurors and the alternates are dismissed. In December 2007, the jury found Picton guilty of 6 counts of second-degree murder. He was sentenced to life in prison with no chance of parole for 25 years. The Crown has decided not to pursue prosecution of the remaining murders.

Sources: Hunter & Baron, 2006; *CBC News*, 2007, August 28; Skelton, C. (2010, August 5). Crown drops 20 murder charges against Picton. *Times Colonist*. Retrieved from http://www.timescolonist.com/news/Crown+drops+murder+charges+against+Picton/3362068/story.html

A challenge for cause changes how the jury is selected. This process is unique to Canada (Granger, 1996). First, two individuals are selected from the jury pool and are sworn to act as triers. A third person is selected as a prospective juror. The lawyers or judge question the prospective juror, while the two triers listen to the answers provided. The triers then discuss the answers with each other to reach a unanimous decision as to whether the prospective juror is impartial. If the triers decide that the prospective juror is not impartial, another person is selected and the process begins again. If the triers decide that the prospective juror is impartial, then that person becomes the first member of the jury (unless the Crown or defence uses a peremptory challenge) and replaces one of the triers. This first juror acts as a trier for a second juror. Thus, jurors 1 and 2 will act as triers for juror 3, jurors 2 and 3 will act as triers for juror 4, and so on, until 12 jurors are selected.

When trying to evaluate whether a challenge for cause is useful for identifying biased individuals, a number of issues need to be considered:

1. The process may be conducted in open court, where the jury pool can hear the questions the lawyers ask and the responses provided. Moreover, they can hear the answers that lead to a positive or negative decision from the triers. Thus, it is possible for prospective jurors to alter their answers according to whether they want to serve on the jury.

2. Prospective jurors may find it difficult to be honest when answering questions about bias that may put them in an unflattering light, especially if the questioning is conducted in open court.

3. Prospective jurors must be aware of their biases and how their biases may influence their behaviour. Some classic work by Nisbett and Wilson (1977) suggests that individuals are unaware of their biases and how their biases affect their behaviour.

## JURY FUNCTIONS

The main legal function of a jury is to apply the law, as provided by the judge, to the admissible evidence in the case and to render a verdict of guilt or innocence. As we will discuss, there are cases in which the jury will ignore the law and apply some other criteria to reach a verdict. In addition to the main legal function of juries, four other jury functions have been identified:

1. To use the wisdom of 12 (rather than the wisdom of 1) to reach a verdict
2. To act as the conscience of the community
3. To protect against out-of-date laws
4. To increase knowledge about the justice system

**Ignoring the Law** The jury has a responsibility to apply the law as defined by the judge to the admissible evidence and to render a verdict. Ignoring that law and the evidence, and rendering a verdict based on some other criteria is known as **jury nullification**. Juries may choose to ignore the law for a number of reasons. For example, they may believe the law is unfair given the circumstances of the case or the punishment accompanying a conviction is too harsh for the crime. In both these instances, jury nullification may result.

Jury nullification typically can occur when the case involves controversial issues, such as abortion and euthanasia (see Box 7.4).

**Jury nullification:** Occurs when a jury ignores the law and the evidence, rendering a verdict based on some other criteria

Box 7.4

# Two Cases of Jury Nullification

## Dr. Henry Morgentaler: Baby Killer or Champion of Women's Rights?

Dr. Henry Morgentaler conducted his first abortion, secretly, in 1968. He began performing illegal abortions openly in Montreal in 1969, and in 1970 he was arrested for conducting an abortion. Intriguingly, the arrest occurred three years before the U.S. Supreme Court landmark case of *Roe v. Wade* (1973), which made abortion a constitutional right for American women.

A Quebec jury of 11 men and 1 woman found Dr. Morgentaler not guilty. The verdict was appealed and overturned in 1974. Dr. Morgentaler was sentenced to prison. When he was released, he continued conducting illegal abortions. In two more trials, juries returned not guilty verdicts. In 1975, a significant change to Quebec law occurred in which a jury verdict could no longer be overturned on appeal, known as the Morgentaler Amendment. Furthermore, in 1976, the Quebec government announced it would no longer prosecute abortion cases.

In 1983, while conducting abortions in Ontario, Dr. Morgentaler and two colleagues were charged with conducting illegal miscarriages. The jury found them not guilty. The Ontario Court of Appeal then reversed this verdict.

Clearly, the voice of the community, via the jury, was incongruent with the law. Change in legislation occurred in 1988 when the Supreme Court of Canada ruled that Canadian women have the right to a safe abortion. More than 100 000 abortions are conducted in Canada each year.

## Robert Latimer: A Loving Father?

Tracy Latimer lived with her family in Wilkie, Saskatchewan. She had severe cerebral palsy, was quadriplegic, and could communicate only by means of facial expression, laughter, and crying. It was estimated that she had the mental capacity of a 4-month-old baby. Tracy had five to six seizures a day and it was believed that she was in constant pain. She also underwent several surgeries. Another surgery was scheduled for Tracy when she was 12 years old.

Robert Latimer, Tracy's father, felt that this surgery would be a mutilation and could no longer live with seeing his daughter suffer. He decided that he would end his daughter's life. In 1993, he connected a hose to his pickup truck's exhaust pipe, put the hose into the truck's cab, and seated Tracy in the running truck. Tracy died from carbon monoxide inhalation. At first, Latimer claimed that Tracy had passed away in her sleep, but he later confessed to taking Tracy's life. The jury found Robert Latimer guilty of second-degree murder.

Second-degree murder carries a life sentence without eligibility for parole for a minimum of 10 years and up to 25 years. Juries are allowed to make sentencing recommendations in this situation. The jury sent the judge a note asking if they could recommend less than ten years. The judge explained the mandatory minimum recommendation as outlined in the Criminal Code; however, they could make any recommendation they liked. The jury recommended one year before parole eligibility.

The judge granted a constitutional exemption from the mandatory minimum and sentenced Robert Latimer to one year in prison and one year of probation. In keeping with the law, however, the Court of Appeal upheld the conviction but changed the sentence to life imprisonment with eligibility for parole in ten years. Once again, the law was inconsistent with the community's sentiment, which was expressed by the jury.

Sources: *R. v. Morgentaler*, 1988; *O'Malley & Wood*, 2003; *R. v. Latimer*, 2001.

If juries are allowed to ignore the law and vote with their conscience, won't we end up with a biased or random system? Meissner, Brigham, and Pfeifer (2003) examined the influence of a jury nullification instruction in a euthanasia case. Mock jurors were more likely to find the defendant not guilty with a nullification instruction when the jurors had a positive attitude toward euthanasia. Intriguingly, when jurors were given a standard jury instruction, they reported referring to the legal aspects of the case to make their decisions. However, when they were given a nullification instruction they reported that they relied on their attitudes of euthanasia and their perceptions of the defendant's behaviour. Overall, nullification instructions may influence jury decision making, "producing both socially favourably (e.g., sympathetic) and socially unfavourably (e.g., prejudical) verdicts" (Meissner, Brigham, & Pfeifer, 2003, p. 253).

## HOW DO WE STUDY JUROR AND JURY BEHAVIOUR?

Now that we know how juries are selected, and what their characteristics and responsibilities are, we can start understanding and predicting their behaviour. Many researchers in the forensic area have focused their careers on trying to predict verdicts and the variables that affect verdicts. We will now discuss four methodologies that have been used to gain understanding of juror and jury behaviour.

### Post-trial Interviews

In trying to understand why juries reached particular verdicts, perhaps it seems most logical and simple to ask the jurors themselves why they reached the verdicts they did. In Canada, however, actual jurors are not allowed to discuss what occurred in deliberations. All discourse that occurs during the deliberations is confidential. Breaking this confidentiality is a violation of section 649 of the Criminal Code (R.S.C., 1985, C-46, s. 649). A juror who discusses any part of the deliberation process would be committing a summary offence that carries a fine of up to $2000 and/or imprisonment for up to six months. Although researchers cannot talk to Canadian jurors regarding their deliberations, they can turn to the United States or other countries that do not have this rule.

The main strength of post-trial interviews is high external validity; that is, results come from using real cases and the actual jurors that deliberated. Consequently, results may be more likely to generalize to the real world. This methodology, however, also has a number of weaknesses. For one, jurors' accounts may not be reliable. For example, jurors may recall details inaccurately, they may forget critical aspects of the deliberation, they may embellish or downplay elements to present themselves more favourably, or they may be unaware of the reasons for their decisions and behaviour. Thus, conclusions may be based on data that are unreliable. Moreover, a cause-and-effect relationship cannot be established with this type of methodology. At best, researchers can talk about variables that occur together. Alternative hypotheses cannot be ruled out with this methodology.

### Archives

Records of trials, such as transcripts and police interviews of witnesses, can be reviewed to uncover relationships between variables. The strength of this methodology is similar to post-trial interviews in that external validity is high. A similar weakness, however, is the inability to establish cause-and-effect relationships. Also, the researcher is restricted to the data available in that the types of questions that can be posed are limited by the information that can be accessed. The researcher is unable to go back and collect more information. Furthermore, the researcher is unaware of how the information was collected and the reliability of that information. For example, police interviews may have been conducted by using biased procedures.

## Simulation

One of the most common methodologies used to investigate jury issues is the simulation. Researchers simulate a trial, or aspects of it, by using a written, audio, or video format. Participants are presented with the trial information, and the researcher can vary and manipulate this trial information. Examples of possible independent variables of interest include the age of the witness or the race of the defendant. Following the presentation of the trial, participants are asked to respond individually (juror research) or in groups (jury research). Typically, jurors and juries will be asked to render a verdict or make other judgments. Verdicts and other participants' responses can be compared to determine whether the independent variable(s) had an effect.

Participants deliberate a mock trial

One of the major strengths of this methodology is its high internal validity; that is, researchers can reveal cause-and-effect relationships because they systematically manipulated the independent variables. However, the control the researchers have over the independent variables limits the external validity of this methodology. For example, in simulations, cases are not real and there are no consequences to the verdicts or decisions the jurors render. Furthermore, the participants typically are university students, who may not be representative of real jury pools. These factors limit the generalizability of the results obtained with simulations.

## Field Studies

This methodology involves using actual jurors while they are serving on jury duty, so cooperation from the courts and the jurors is required. Researchers are able to observe variables of interest as they are occurring. For example, they may be interested in how prospective jurors respond to questions posed during the voir dire (i.e., preliminary examination of the jurors before they are assigned to the case). Alternatively, researchers may be able to introduce variables that they want to examine. The court may agree to let jurors take notes while the evidence is being presented, for example. Trials in which jurors were allowed to take notes can be compared with trials in which jurors were not allowed to take notes. A comparison of the verdicts can be undertaken across these cases.

The strength of field studies is high external validity. A number of limitations, however, are also present. For example, receiving approval from the courts for conducting the research may be difficult. Even when approval is granted, it is likely that only a small sample of participants will be available, and appropriate comparison groups may be too difficult to identify. Additionally, there are a host of confounding variables that the researcher may not be able to control, such as the gender of lawyers and witnesses.

As you can see, the researcher interested in juror/jury issues has a variety of methodologies to choose from. Each methodology has some strengths and weaknesses. By using all these methodologies, we may be able to gain a more accurate understanding of juror and jury behaviour.

# REACHING A VERDICT

Once a jury has been selected, their work begins. Jurors must listen to the admissible evidence and disregard any evidence that the judge does not allow. Once the lawyers deliver their closing arguments, the judge provides the jury with the law that they must apply to the evidence to reach a verdict. The jury then makes its **deliberation**—that is, they discuss the evidence privately among themselves to reach a verdict, which is then provided to the court. We will discuss each stage involved in reaching a jury verdict and the factors that may affect each stage.

## Listening to the Evidence

Two innovations have been proposed as aids for jurors while they listen to the evidence: note-taking and asking questions. Advantages and disadvantages have been identified for each aid. We will discuss each aid in turn and the Canadian justice system's position on each.

**Note-Taking** Trials can be lengthy and complex, resulting in missed or forgotten evidence by the time the jury is asked to deliberate. Some have suggested that allowing jurors to take notes may facilitate memory and understanding of the evidence (e.g., Heuer & Penrod, 1994). Moreover, note-takers may be more attentive during the trial than those who do not take notes. Not everyone is in agreement, however, that allowing jurors to take notes is advantageous or even preferable. For example, in the Canadian case of *R. v. Andrade* (1985), a number of disadvantages to juror note-taking were identified:

- Jurors who take notes may exert influence while in deliberation over those who do not.
- If disagreements occur about the evidence, jurors will rely on those who took notes to clarify the issue.

A review of the research examining juror note-taking was conducted by Penrod and Heuer (1997). They reached the following conclusions regarding juror note-taking:

- Jurors' notes serve as a memory aid.
- Jurors do not overemphasize the evidence that they have noted at the expense of evidence they have not recorded.
- Notes do not produce a distorted view of the case.
- Note-takers can keep up with the evidence as it is being presented.
- Note-takers do not distract jurors who do not take notes.
- Note-takers do not have an undue influence over those who do not take notes.
- Jurors' notes are an accurate record of the trial.
- Juror note-taking does not favour either the prosecution/Crown or the defence.

As you can see, allowing jurors to take notes does not appear to pose major difficulties. Hartley (2002) also concluded that note-taking does not have a significant impact on a juror's memory of the evidence. At present in Canada, the trial judge in each case decides whether jurors will be allowed to take notes (Granger, 1996).

**Asking Questions** When watching trials on television, or if you have ever had the opportunity to listen to a trial in court, you may have found yourself wondering about a detail that was mentioned. Would it not help if you could stop the trial and ask a question? The courts have considered the issue of jurors being allowed to ask questions. Heurer and Penrod (1994) reported that typically juries have few questions (usually not more than three), and the questions tend to be concerned with the meaning of key legal terms, such as *reasonable doubt*. In a review of the research examining juror questions, Penrod and Heuer (1997) reached the following conclusions:

- Jury questioning promotes juror understanding of the facts and the issues.
- Juror questions do not clearly help to get to the truth.
- Juror questions do not increase the jurors', judges', or lawyers' satisfaction with the trial and verdict.
- Jurors ask legally appropriate questions.
- If counsel objects, and the objection is sustained, the jury does not draw inappropriate inferences from unanswered questions.
- Jurors do not become advocates.

Thus, the research on allowing jurors to ask questions does not appear to indicate that jurors' questions are particularly harmful or helpful. At present in Canada, jurors may submit their questions in writing to the judge after the lawyers have completed their questioning of the witness. The judge then determines whether the question is permissible. Questions that are permissible then are posed by the judge. Ultimately, allowing jurors to ask questions is up to the judge presiding over the trial.

Does the relatively recent influx of forensic science television programming increase jurors' quest for scientific evidence? Shows such as *CSI: Crime Scene Investigation* and its two spinoffs, *CSI: Miami* and *CSI: NY* "educate" potential jurors on the latest scientific evidence. Do the shows raise the bar too high? Do they influence the jury pool? See the In the Media box for a discussion of the "*CSI* effect."

## Disregarding Inadmissible Evidence

Are jurors able to "forget" what they heard? This question is not only relevant when we consider pretrial publicity, but also when judges request that jurors disregard inadmissible evidence. Often, juries will hear inadmissible evidence when lawyers or witnesses make statements that are not allowed according to legal procedure. Following an inadmissible statement or inadmissible evidence, the judge will instruct the jury to disregard it. The critical component to a fair trial and a just verdict is that the jury uses only admissible statements and evidence. But are jurors able to disregard evidence they have heard?

Kassin and Sommers (1997) argued that whether jurors will follow a judge's instruction to disregard inadmissible evidence is related to the reason for the instruction rather than to the instruction itself. In their study, mock jurors were presented with a murder trial, and a piece of evidence was manipulated. Jurors in the control condition received only circumstantial and ambiguous evidence. In the experimental conditions, an audiotaped telephone conversation in which the defendant confessed to the murder was included. When this audiotape was admitted into evidence, the defence lawyer objected. The judge either overruled the objection, allowing it into evidence, or sustained the objection and asked jurors to disregard it because it was either illegally obtained or difficult to

# The *CSI* Effect

Do you watch any of the *CSI* shows? If you do, you are not alone. Approximately 60 million people each week watch these programs. The *CSI* shows typically start with a crime, some evidence is collected, high-tech analysis is undertaken, and the crime is solved all in about 60 minutes. If only real-life happened like this. Unfortunately, the more we watch these shows, the more we believe that they demonstrate how our justice system should work, and we may even begin to think that our justice system has failed if it does not mimic what we see on television.

The "*CSI* effect" can be described as the education of jurors whereby they are more likely to convict a suspect if the procedures and techniques from television are used in real life. Their mode of thinking may go something like this, for example: "Why wasn't DNA collected? Is it a match? You can't beat DNA." The *CSI* effect is viewed as the infallibility of forensic science as a function of seeing it on television. This phenomenon has been around for about ten years, shortly after the first *CSI* installment aired on television.

Are you a product of the *CSI* effect? You need not be a juror to be influenced by these television shows. Universities in the United States report a dramatic increase in forensic science–type undergraduate and graduate programs. A similar pattern can be seen in Canadian universities. For example, the Criminology and Criminal Justice program at Carleton University is one of the largest undergraduate programs at the school. The number of Canadian schools offering forensic psychology courses has also spiked; you may be reading this as part of one of these very courses.

Jurors who have watched these programs may rely on what they have seen on television to evaluate the evidence presented in real-life court. Jeffrey Heinrick (2006) reports on a number of cases where real-life investigation did not live up to the *CSI* shows.

For example, a man from Illinois accused of trying to kill his ex-girlfriend was found not guilty by the jury, reportedly because the police did not test the blood-stained sheets for DNA. After the man was released from jail, he stabbed his ex-girlfriend to death. A jury also found a man from Phoenix not guilty because his bloodstained coat was not tested for DNA. Thanks to the *CSI* effect, jurors now require expensive and sometimes unnecessary DNA tests, gun residue tests, and handwriting analyses, for example. Jurors also may not understand that some lab tests may take months and even years to complete.

Some argue that the *CSI* effect has a negative impact on the justice system, while others argue that it makes jurors more informed about what it takes to find someone guilty. Prosecutors argue that it raises the bar unfairly, making the case easier for the defence. What do you think?

A group of Canadian researchers from St. Mary's University, Drs. Smith, Patry, and Stinson (2008) found evidence that crime dramas do indeed influence the perceptions of forensic science and, in turn, of what lawyers do in the courtroom. Kim, Barak, and Shelton (2009) found that watching *CSI* shows did not influence jurors' verdicts independently. The *CSI* effect was found to have an indirect influence on conviction in circumstantial cases where it raised expectations about scientific evidence. Presently, we must conclude that the verdict is still out on whether and how crime shows influence the justice system. With no shortage of crime drama on television, further research is needed in this area.

Sources: Heinrick, J. (Fall, 2006). Everyone's an expert: The CSI effect's negative impact on juries. The Triple Helix. Arizona State University; Smith, S.M., Patry, M., & Stinson, V. (2008). Is the CSI effect real? If it is, what is it? In G. Bourgon, R.K. Hanson, J.D. Pozzulo, K.E. Morton Bourgon, & C.L. Tanasichuk (Eds.), *Proceedings of the 2007 North American Correctional & Criminal Justice Psychology Conference (User Report)*. Ottawa, ON: Public Safety Canada.

comprehend. When jurors were asked to disregard the evidence because it was illegally collected, their verdicts were similar to the jurors who received the ruling that the tape was admissible. In contrast, when jurors were instructed to disregard the tape because of comprehension difficulty, they rendered verdicts similar to the control jurors who had not heard about the inadmissible evidence. Thus, Kassin and Sommers concluded that jurors will disregard evidence when they are provided with a logical and legitimate reason for the judge's decision to disregard it.

One other interesting result has been found with the instruction to disregard. Some researchers have found that a judge's instruction to disregard evidence simply makes the evidence more memorable than if no instruction were given, which is known as the back-fire effect (Paglia & Schuller, 1998). Thus, jurors are more likely to pay attention to inadmissible evidence following a disregard instruction than if no instruction was provided. Similarly, Pickel, Karam, & Warner (2009) found that if the inadmissible evidence was memorable, it was harder for the jury to ignore.

Overall, the influence of the disregard instruction is not straightforward. Other factors come into play and interact with the effect of the instruction.

## Judge's Instructions

A number of studies have examined jurors' abilities to understand the legally dense instructions that the judge charges the jury with prior to its deliberation. The results of these studies generally are not positive. Lieberman and Sales (1997) have concluded that jurors do not remember, understand, or accurately apply judges' instructions. Reifman, Gusick, and Ellsworth (1992) surveyed 224 citizens from Michigan who were called for jury duty. The goal was to assess jurors' comprehension of judges' instructions. These prospective jurors understood less than 50% of the instructions they received.

Four reforms for judges' instructions have been proposed: (1) rewriting instructions, (2) providing a written copy of the instructions to jurors, (3) providing jurors with pre- and post-evidence instructions, and (4) having lawyers clarify legal instruction during their presentation to the jury. However, these reforms do not necessarily significantly increase comprehension. These four proposed reforms have not been implemented with any consistency within the Canadian justice system.

## Jury Decision-Making Models

How do jurors combine the trial evidence to reach a verdict? Moreover, what is the process by which verdicts are reached? Although a number of models of juror/jury decision making have been proposed, they may be categorized as using either a mathematical or explanation-based approach.

**Mathematical Models** The common theme with mathematical models is that they view jurors as conducting a set of mental calculations regarding the importance and strength of each piece of evidence (Hastie, 1993). A guilty or not guilty verdict is determined by the outcome of the calculations for all the relevant evidence. For example, an eyewitness who identified the defendant may be perceived as strong evidence and be weighed heavily toward a guilty verdict; however, learning that the DNA found at the crime scene does not match the defendant's decreases the likelihood of a guilty verdict. The verdict is a function of the calculation of all the relevant evidence.

Ellsworth and Mauro (1998) examined the congruency of mental calculations and how jurors perceive their process of reaching a verdict. They found that a mathematical approach was inconsistent with how jurors report that they reach verdicts. Jurors do not appear to provide a value for each piece of evidence presented. Moreover, it may be difficult to partition evidence into discrete pieces of evidence that can then be assigned a value. Perhaps an explanation-based approach is more consistent with how jurors process the trial evidence.

A jury listens to evidence

**Explanation Models** In contrast to mathematical models, explanation models suggest that evidence is organized into a coherent whole. Pennington and Hastie's (1986) explanation approach is called the *story model*. They proposed that jurors are active at understanding and processing the evidence. Jurors interpret and elaborate on the evidence and make causal connections, and in doing so, they create a story structure. These "stories" are then compared with each verdict option presented by the judge. The verdict option most consistent with the story is the verdict reached.

Of course, jurors listening to the same evidence may construct different stories that are consistent with alternative verdicts. That is to say, individual differences can influence the story-construction process. Jurors bring in their personal experiences, knowledge, beliefs, and attitudes when constructing their story. Thus, jurors may reach different decisions after hearing the same evidence.

To test the story model, Pennington and Hastie (1986) had 26 participants watch a simulated murder trial and then make individual verdicts at the end of the trial. Following their verdicts, participants were interviewed to determine how they thought about the evidence. The researchers found that participants put the evidence into a story format and different stories were related to different verdicts.

In a follow-up study, Pennington and Hastie (1988) varied how easily a particular story could be constructed by altering the order in which the evidence was presented. They found that when the evidence was presented in a chronological order, it was more likely that the verdict reached was consistent with that story order. This information could be useful to lawyers who may choose to present evidence in a story format that is consistent with the verdict they want. The story model seems to be consistent with how jurors process trial evidence and reach a verdict. The story model continues to be used to understand jury decision making.

# Deliberations

As you may recall, a 12-person jury is necessary for criminal cases in Canada. However, cases can continue as long as no more than two members are excused, possibly for illness or other reasons, during the trial (Granger, 1996). For example, in the 2003 murder trial of Matti Baranovski in Toronto, an 11-person jury convicted Lee Cochrane and Meir Mariani of manslaughter.

Once all the evidence has been heard and the judge has delivered instructions to the jurors, the jury retires to a secluded room to deliberate. In Canada, the jury is sequestered until the final verdict is reached—then, the jury is dismissed by the judge (Granger, 1996). This means that the jury is not allowed to talk to anyone outside their 12-person panel, with the exception of the court-appointed officer in the event that they have a request or question.

The expectation from the justice system is that the jury reviews the evidence and determines the most consistent match between the verdict options that were provided by the judge and the admissible evidence. A number of factors can influence a juror's position on the case. A phenomenon known as **polarization** occurs when individuals tend to become more extreme in their initial position following a group discussion (Baron & Bryne, 1991). In contrast, a **leniency bias** also has been found whereby jurors move toward greater leniency following deliberations (MacCoun & Kerr, 1988).

**Polarization:** When individuals tend to become more extreme in their initial position following a group discussion

**Leniency bias:** When jurors move toward greater leniency during deliberations

## The Final Verdict

A Canadian jury must reach a unanimous verdict. If it cannot, the jury is said to be a **hung jury** or deadlocked, and a mistrial is declared. Following a hung-jury outcome, the Crown must decide whether it will retry the case.

**Hung jury:** A jury that cannot reach a unanimous verdict

In contrast to required unanimous verdicts in Canada, the United States has permitted majority votes of eleven to one, ten to two, and nine to three. Similarly, the United Kingdom has allowed juries to render eleven-to-one or ten-to-two majority votes provided that the jury has deliberated for a minimum of two hours. In a meta-analysis examining the effects of jury size, Saks and Marti (1997) found that six-person juries are less representative of the community, they remember less of the evidence, they return quicker verdicts, and they are more likely to reach a unanimous verdict than 12-person juries. Hastie, Penrod, and Pennington (1983) found that when a jury could retire with a majority vote, they tended to reach a decision faster and did not fully discuss both the evidence and the law, compared with when the jury was required to reach a unanimous verdict.

In general, when a first verdict poll is taken, the final verdict tends to be consistent with the first poll in about 90% of cases (Kalvern & Zeisel, 1966; Sandys & Dillehay, 1995). MacCoun and Kerr (1988) conducted a meta-analysis of 12 studies examining juror preferences at the beginning of deliberation as well as final verdicts. They found that a pro-defence faction was more persuasive than a pro-prosecution faction. More specifically, if seven or fewer jurors vote guilty at the beginning of deliberation, the jury will tend to render a not guilty verdict. If ten or more jurors initially vote guilty, the final verdict will likely be guilty. If eight or nine jurors initially vote guilty, the final verdict is unpredictable.

Hastie, Penrod, and Pennington (1983) identified two broad styles that juries tend to adopt when trying to reach a verdict: verdict driven and evidence driven. Verdict-driven juries tend to start the deliberation process by taking an initial verdict poll. In contrast, evidence-driven juries tend to start the deliberation process by discussing the evidence. A verdict poll is not taken until much later during the deliberation. These two styles can influence the outcome of the initial verdict poll (Sandys & Dillehay, 1995).

## PREDICTING VERDICTS

A great deal of research on juror characteristics has been conducted to determine whether verdicts can be predicted based on these characteristics. We will examine the following six types of variables that have been studied and their relation to the verdict: (1) demographic variables, (2) personality traits, (3) attitudes, (4) defendant characteristics, (5) victim characteristics, and (6) expert testimony.

## Demographic Variables

**Racial bias:** The disparate treatment of racial out-groups

Variables such as the gender, race, socioeconomic status, and education of jurors are demographic variables that have been examined, in part because they are readily available to lawyers but also because they can be used to challenge witnesses. For example, are female jurors more lenient? Are Caucasians more likely to render guilty verdicts?

**Racial bias** as it relates to jury decision making can be defined as disparate treatment of racial out-groups. In a recent meta-analysis examining racial bias on verdict and sentencing decisions, Mitchell, Haw, Pfeifer, and Meissner (2005) found a small significant effect of racial bias on jury decisions. Participants were more likely to render guilty verdicts for "other-race" defendants than for defendants of their own race. Also, participants rendered longer sentences for other-race defendants. Is it possible to reduce this effect? Cohn, Bucolo, Pride, and Sommers (2009) found that when a defendant's race was made salient, white juror racial bias toward a black defendant was reduced. Moreover, jurors' prejudicial beliefs were related to verdict only when the defendant's race was not made salient.

Other factors also may interact with defendant race. For example, Perez, Hosch, Ponder, and Trejo (1993) found that strength of the evidence may come into play along with race. When the evidence was weak or ambiguous (not clearly favouring one side), race similarity between defendant and jury led to leniency. When evidence was strong, race similarity between defendant and jury led to punitiveness. This is known as the **black sheep effect** (Chadee, 1996).

**Black sheep effect:** When evidence is strong, similarity between defendant and jury leads to punitiveness

Eberhardt, Davies, Purdie-Vaughns, and Johnson (2006) examined racial stereotypes in a death sentence case. The researchers used photos of black defendants and had ethnically diverse university students rate how stereotypically black they looked. They found that in cases where there was a white victim, black defendants who looked more stereotypical were more likely to be sentenced to death than those who looked less stereotypical.

Unfortunately, when using juror demographic variables to predict verdicts, results are less than reliable. Overall, only a small and inconsistent relation exists between juror demographic variables and jury verdicts (e.g., Bonazzoli, 1998).

## Personality Traits

The two personality traits that have been commonly measured in connection to jurors are authoritarianism and dogmatism. Individuals high in authoritarianism tend to have right-wing political views and are conservative and rigid thinkers who acquiesce to authority.

Similarly, individuals high in dogmatism also tend to be rigid and closed-minded but without the political overtones found with the authoritarianism construct. Are personality traits better for predicting verdicts than demographic variables?

Given the underlying traits associated with dogmatism and authoritarianism, anyone would predict that jurors who score high on these constructs would be more likely to align themselves with the prosecution and, thus, render more guilty verdicts than jurors who score low on these constructs. In a meta-analysis that examined authoritarianism and juror verdicts across 20 studies, Narby, Cutler, and Moran (1993) found a moderate, positive relationship between authoritarianism and verdict such that those who score high on these traits tend to be more inclined to render guilty verdicts. That is, they have a pro-prosecution bias.

One also needs to consider that jurors are required to reach a unanimous decision, possibly by persuading other jurors. What type of person or what personality traits tend to be the most persuasive? In a study by Rotenberg, Hewlett, and Siegwart (1998), mock jurors who were extroverted and had higher moral reasoning were found to be more persuasive than other mock jurors. In another study, Marcus, Lyons, and Guyton (2000) examined the "big five" personality dimensions for persuasiveness:

- Extroversion: outgoing, sociable, and animated
- Agreeableness: altruistic, interpersonally pleasant, and positive
- Conscientiousness: self-disciplined, determined, and dutiful
- Emotional stability: calm, even-tempered, and able to handle stressful situations
- Openness to experience: imaginative, sensitive, intellectually curious, and unconventional

The researchers found that participants who showed a high level on conscientiousness were most likely to report being persuaded by other participants. In contrast, participants who scored high on openness were least likely to be persuaded by other participants. Those exhibiting high levels of extroversion were most persuasive, and being male wielded more influence than being female. Intriguingly, extroverted, tall males were even more persuasive than extroverted, shorter males. Jurors' personality traits seem to be more reliable for predicting verdicts than demographic variables.

## Attitudes

Researchers have examined a variety of attitudes linked to specific topics or issues that may be present in cases, such as drunk driving, rape, child sexual abuse, and capital punishment. For example, Spanos, DuBreuil, and Gwynn (1991–1992) examined rape myths (e.g., a woman who wears provocative clothing is interested in having sex) in connection to a date-rape case. University students heard a version of a date-rape case involving expert testimony about rape myths and cross-examination of such, and then deliberated in small groups to reach a verdict. A gender split was observed in which females did not believe the defendant and voted him guilty more often than male mock jurors. However, regardless of the gender of the mock jurors, those with feminist attitudes were more likely not to believe the defendant's testimony.

Devine et al. (2001) reported that no group of attitudes or values has received sufficient investigation to reach a definitive conclusion at this point. The one notable exception is attitudes toward capital punishment. For example, Horowitz and Seguin (1986) reported that juries comprising death-qualified jurors (i.e., jurors who are willing to impose the death sentence) had a 19% higher conviction rate than non-death-qualified jurors. In general, death-qualified jurors are more likely than non-death-qualified jurors to vote for conviction at the end of a trial (Ellsworth & Mauro, 1998).

Overall, attitudes that are case-specific seem to have more predictive power over verdict than more general attitudes do.

## Defendant Characteristics

A number of studies have examined defendant characteristics and their influence on verdicts. For example, if jurors hear about a defendant's prior criminal record that contains one or more convictions, they are more likely to find the defendant guilty than if the jurors did not have this knowledge (Hans & Doob, 1976).

There also seems to be a small relationship between the attractiveness of the defendant and jury verdict. Izzett and Leginski (1974) provided mock jurors with either a picture of an unattractive defendant or an attractive defendant, and found verdict preferences to be more lenient for the attractive defendant and more severe for the unattractive defendant. Patry (2008) examined whether defendant attractiveness and the act of deliberation would have an effect on guilt decision. Indeed, "plain-looking" defendants were more often found to be guilty when mock jurors did not deliberate. However, when mock jurors did deliberate, the attractive defendant was more likely to be found guilty.

Defendant characteristics often are examined in relation to other characteristics, such as victim characteristics. Pozzulo, Dempsey, Maeder, and Allen (2010) examined defendant gender, defendant age (age 15 versus age 40), and victim gender in a sexual assault case of a 12-year-old student by her teacher. Male defendants received higher guilt ratings than female defendants. Female jurors found the victim more accurate, truthful, and believable than male jurors did. In contrast, male jurors found the defendant more reliable, credible, truthful, and believable than female jurors did. Moreover, female jurors held the defendant more responsible for the crime than male jurors did. Overall, mock jurors perceived that the younger defendant desired the event more than the older defendant, but only when the victim was a female. As you can see, a number of variables other than perceptions of the defendant and victim can interact and influence verdict.

## Victim Characteristics

Characteristics of the victim may become particularly relevant in cases of sexual assault in which a guilty verdict may hinge on the testimony of the alleged victim. In Canada, before the mid-1980s, a woman's prior sexual history was admissible and could be used to infer her credibility and the likelihood that she consented to sexual relations with the defendant. In 1985, rape-shield provisions were legislated, which prevented lawyers from introducing a woman's prior sexual history (R.S.C. 1985, C-46, s. 276).

In the early 1990s, however, some people began to challenge these provisions on the grounds that they prevented defendants from receiving a fair trial (*R. v. Seaboyer*, 1991; *R. v. Gayme*, 1991). Defence lawyers argued that it was necessary to admit the accuser's prior sexual history because it would support defendants' claims of an honest but mistaken belief in consent. The rape shield provisions were amended in 1992, allowing inquiry into a woman's sexual history at the judge's discretion (R.S.C. 1985, C-46, s. 276; 1992, c. 38, s. 2). Only if a woman's sexual history was deemed relevant would the judge allow it to be heard by the jury. Further, the Supreme Court of Canada (*R. v. Seaboyer*, 1991) recommended that the trial judge provide the jury with cautionary instructions on how this evidence should be used. More specifically, the jurors must be cautioned that a woman's sexual history should be used only in determining a defendant's claim of an "honest but mistaken belief in consent." A woman's sexual history must not be used to demonstrate that the woman is less trustworthy or that she is likely to consent to sexual intercourse. Some have argued that such a distinction is too fine to be made by jurors. How would you interpret a woman's sexual history in a "date-rape" case? (See the Case Study box.)

Schuller and Hastings (2002) conducted a study in which the victim's sexual history was varied to include either sexual intercourse, kissing and touching, or no history

## CASE STUDY  YOU BE THE JUROR

Jenny Jones was in her second year at university. She had met Matt Grayson in her introductory psychology class. They didn't know each other very well but had a few classes together and knew some of the same people. Jenny thought Matt was cute and told her friends that she'd go out with him if he asked.

Matt had been dating a female from his high school for almost three years. Matt had gone off to university and his girlfriend stayed in town and went to a local community college. Matt's girlfriend decided she no longer wanted a long-distance relationship. She broke up with Matt just before reading break. Matt was upset but decided there were lots of women at university that he could go out with instead. He figured it would be his ex-girlfriend's loss. That weekend, a friend of Jenny's and Matt's had a house party to mark the end of reading week. Both Jenny and Matt went to the party.

At the party, Jenny and Matt started chatting and were having a good time together. Both Jenny and Matt had a couple of drinks but neither considered themselves drunk. As the party was breaking up, around 2:00 a.m., Matt asked if Jenny wanted to go back to his room in residence to "hang out." Jenny said, "Sure." While in Matt's room, Matt and Jenny started to get intimate. After a few minutes though, Jenny said she should go home. Matt asked her to stay and continued to kiss Jenny. Jenny repeated that she should go. Jenny and Matt had intercourse and the next morning, Jenny claimed that Matt sexually assaulted her. Matt agrees that they had sex but insists that it was consensual. Matt claimed that Jenny could have left at any time.

The case went to trial and the judge allowed the defence to question Jenny on her sexual history. Jenny stated that she had, in the past, had intercourse with five other boyfriends; however, she stated that she did not want to have intercourse with Matt that night.

### Your Turn . . .

Do you think Matt sexually assaulted Jenny? Would you change your verdict if you did not know about Jenny's sexual history? Do you think an alleged victim's sexual history is relevant? Should the history be admissible in court?

information in a sexual assault trial. In addition, a judge's instructions limiting the use of the sexual history information was examined. Compared with the participants who heard no sexual history information, those who heard that the victim and defendant had sexual intercourse in the past were less likely to find the alleged victim credible, more likely to find her blameworthy, and more likely to believe she consented to sexual intercourse. Thus, they were more likely to find the defendant not guilty. The sexual history information did not influence participants' judgments about the defendant's belief in consent, which is contrary to the goal of judges' instructions as intended by the Supreme Court of Canada. It would appear that a judge's instruction to limit the use of the sexual history information is not effective. If a woman's sexual history is admitted into evidence, it is used to assess her credibility.

Cases have continued to challenge the 1992 rape shield provisions. In *R. v. Darrach* (2000), the defendant, Andrew Darrach, was found guilty of sexually assaulting his former girlfriend. Darrach appealed his conviction, arguing that he did not receive a fair trial because he was unable to present information about his prior sexual history with the accuser. Darrach stated that, given his past relationship with the accused, he thought that the sexual encounter was consensual. During the trial, the judge heard the defence's arguments and ruled that the evidence was inadmissible when Darrach refused to testify or be cross-examined on the claims he was making. In Darrach's appeal, he claimed that the law unfairly required him to testify and denied him access to a full defence. In October 2000, the Supreme Court of Canada upheld Darrach's conviction and upheld the country's rape-shield provisions. The Supreme Court noted that the onus is on the defendant to demonstrate that the accuser's sexual history is relevant before it will be allowed (*R. v. Darrach*, 2000).

Should religious beliefs matter in sexual assault cases? For example, should a female victim be asked to remove her religious veil when providing testimony in a sexual assault case? In a recent case in Ontario, the judge determined that the woman would have to remove her niqab (i.e., a full face and body covering that leaves just the eyes exposed) to provide testimony. Currently, there is no legal precedent in Canada regarding this type of covering when providing testimony. Should the onus be on the victim/witness to demonstrate the need to wear such coverings when providing testimony? As a juror, would you be influenced by whether you could see the victim's face? See Box 7.5 to learn more about this possible precedent-setting case.

## Expert Testimony

How well do jurors understand the evidence presented? Sometimes, jurors don't have the background knowledge to understand certain types of evidence, such as DNA. Lawyers may ask that an expert be allowed to testify to explain the evidence. What influence does expert evidence have on jurors' decisions?

A number of findings about expert testimony are available, but no simple conclusion has emerged. For example, Schuller, Terry, and McKimmie (2005) examined whether the expert's gender is used as a cue to evaluate the testimony provided. Along with the gender of the expert, the complexity of the testimony was varied such that the testimony was either more or less complex (e.g., by using technical jargon). In a civil case that involved an alleged price-fixing arrangement between a crushed-rock supplier and a road construction company, the plaintiff was suing the two companies for damages of $490 000 because of the price-fixing agreement. When the expert testimony was more complex, the jury

Box 7.5

# When Law Meets Religion

Should Muslim women be allowed to testify wearing a veil that covers their entire face and body except for their eyes? This question is currently before Canadian courts. At this time, no Canadian case law addresses this issue. But as there are approximately 580 000 Muslims living in Canada, the ruling may have implications for Muslim women in future criminal cases.

Currently, a Muslim woman who wears a niqab is the alleged victim in a sexual assault case before a court in Toronto.

The woman did not want to remove her veil to testify at her trial. The woman stated that, for religious reasons, she did not want to show her face to "men you are able to marry." The defence argued that showing her face was necessary to assess demeanour so that the defence could tailor its questioning. It also indicated that a visible face is necessary to assess credibility.

In October 2008, Ontario Court Justice Norris Weisman ruled that the Muslim woman would have to show her face when providing testimony in court. In his ruling, Justice Weisman determined that this woman's religious beliefs were "not that strong" and the wearing of the niqab was a "matter of comfort" for her. Justice Weisman also noted that this woman's driver's licence photo shows her face without the veil (i.e., as a result, a variety of men, such as police officers and border guards, could ask to see this driver's licence and see the woman's unveiled face).

Alia Hogben, the executive director of the Canadian Council of Muslim Women weighed in on the issue. She accepted the judge's decision, saying that in court "the laws of the country should be acceptable." She also pointed out, however, that when enacting this requirement, "sensitivity [should] be shown" (as quoted in Powell, 2009).

The Muslim woman in question appealed Justice Weisman's ruling. In May 2009, Superior Court Justice Frank Marrocco heard arguments in the case and decided to turn the issue back to Justice Weisman. Justice Marrocco instructed Justice Weisman to undertake another inquiry into why the woman wears the niqab. After Justice Weisman explores the woman's beliefs, he can decide whether the woman can wear a niqab when testifying.

Sources: Powell, B. (2009, February 2). Order to take off niqab pits law against religion. *TheStar.com*. Retrieved from http://www.thestar.com/printarticle/580790; Partial court victory for Muslim woman over niqab (2009, May 1). *Ctvtoronto.ca*. Retrieved from http://montreal.ctv.ca/servlet/an/local/CTVNews/20090501/niqab_ruling_090501?hub=MontrealHome

awarded higher damages to the plaintiff when the expert was male, rather than female. When the expert testimony was less complex, although not significantly so, the jury awarded higher damages when the expert was female, rather than male. Jurors may be affected by gender differently, depending on their ability to process expert testimony.

Expert testimony need not produce a positive effect, however, and jurors may disregard it completely. For example, Sundby (1997) examined the transcripts of 152 jurors who participated in 36 first-degree murder cases in California. Jurors were asked about their perceptions and reactions to three types of witnesses: professional experts, lay experts, and families or friends of the defendant. Of the three types of witnesses, jurors were most likely to view professional experts negatively, believing they had little credibility and hurt the side they were testifying for. Overall, jurors may carefully consider expert testimony.

## A Special Case of Expert Testimony on Battered Women's Syndrome

Dr. Regina Schuller and her colleagues have conducted a number of studies examining battered women who kill their abusers and the influence of expert testimony in their trials (Schuller, 1992, 1995; Schuller & Hastings, 1996; Schuller & Rzepa, 2002; Schuller, Smith, & Olson, 1994). See Box 7.6 to learn more about Dr. Schuller and her research.

Box 7.6

# Canadian Researcher Profile: Dr. Regina Schuller

Dr. Regina Schuller mentions how she was bitten by the jury bug as a graduate student at the University of Western Ontario. Her supervisor, Neil Vidmar, was just finishing up his now classic book *Judging the Jury* (co-authored with Valerie Hans) and asked her to read a preliminary copy. Dr. Schuller has never looked back. She immersed herself in the psychology-law area, completing her Ph.D. at Western and also spending two years at Northwestern University in the United States, where she was part of an interdisciplinary program focused on the law and social science.

While in the United States, she also spent a significant amount of time working with Tom Tyler at the American Bar Foundation in Chicago. Dr. Schuller joined the faculty in the department of psychology at York University in Toronto in 1990. She has been there ever since, and has received numerous awards and distinctions for her work. At York, she has also held a number of important administrative positions in the department, such as undergraduate program director (1997–2000) and, more recently, graduate program director (2004–2007).

Dr. Schuller's program of research centres on issues of gender in the legal system. For example, she has investigated violence against women in the form of expert testimony pertaining to battered women in the trials of women who killed their abusers. She also has an interest in investigating the impact of legislative changes that allow for greater information about a claimant's (typically a woman's) sexual history into the court. And more recently, she has turned her attention to the issue of racial bias in the courtroom.

Dr. Schuller notes that one of her favourite pieces of research was a study conducted with Patricia Hastings examining alternative ways to introduce expert testimony on battered women and its influence on juror verdicts and evaluations of the defendant (i.e., the woman who killed her abuser). She states that it was important to consider empirically whether there might be some negative effects associated with battered woman syndrome testimony. For instance, might it pathologize battered women, as some critics were suggesting? This research study was published in the journal *Law and Human Behavior*.

Dr. Schuller primarily uses laboratory simulations to conduct her research. She says that the reason for this methodology is twofold. First, in Canada, researchers are restricted from talking to actual jurors, so fieldwork is virtually impossible. Second, simulation provides a strong methodology when researchers are trying to isolate the impact of numerous variables on the decision process.

When asked what keeps her going in the field of jury research, she emphatically says, "It's fun." She believes the entire process is fun, from creating mock trials to collecting the data and writing it up for others to read. She also states how jury research is an application of the broader area of social psychology, and she finds it fascinating to see how social psychological phenomena occur in the microcosm of the jury, such as how group processes can affect jury verdicts.

Her philosophy for training future leaders in the field includes a strong suggestion for psychologists to immerse themselves in reading case law. Dr. Schuller stresses that we need to keep in mind that if we want lawyers, judges, and the justice system to listen to what we have to say, we need to understand the context in which the research will be applied.

Dr. Schuller uses an apprenticeship model with the students she trains. She works closely with them, from conceptualizing research ideas, to designing studies and manuscript writing. It is clear that Dr. Schuller is a great role model and mentor for future researchers in the psychology-law area.

Regina Schuller lives with her partner, Richard, two children, René and Andrée, and their dog, Ootsie, in the Toronto area. In her spare time, she enjoys running marathons and tries to maintain a long-distance running schedule.

In one study, Schuller, Smith, and Olson (1994) examined the impact of four variables, including jurors' pre-existing beliefs about wife abuse, jurors' beliefs in a "just world" (i.e., believing that you receive what you deserve), the presence or absence of expert testimony on battered women's syndrome, and sex of the juror (male versus female). Mock jurors listened to a homicide trial involving a woman who killed her abusive husband. They then made various judgments about the case. The mock jurors who heard the expert testimony were more likely to believe the woman's account of what happened than were those who did not hear the expert testimony. Those who had a weak belief in a just world were more lenient in their judgments and felt that the expert testimony was more relevant to the battered woman than did those who had a strong belief in a just world. Female mock jurors who had a weak belief in a just world were more likely to find the defendant not guilty.

## SUMMARY

1. In Canada, prospective jurors are selected from a set of random names from the community. These prospective jurors receive a jury summons stating the time and place to go for jury duty. If you are randomly selected from this juror pool, you will be a juror unless one of the lawyers presents a challenge.

2. For a jury to be considered representative, it must allow any possible eligible juror from the community the opportunity to be part of the jury. Juror impartiality centres on three issues: (1) being able to set aside any pre-existing biases, prejudices, or attitudes to judge the case solely on admissible evidence; (2) ignoring any information that is not part of the admissible evidence; and (3) not being connected to the defendant in any way.

3. Pretrial publicity threatens juror impartiality. The concern is that verdicts will be based on emotion and biased media coverage rather than on admissible evidence. To reduce or limit the negative effects of pretrial publicity, the judge can order a publication ban until the end of the trial. Other options for dealing with pretrial publicity include a change of venue, an adjournment, or a challenge for cause.

4. Once a jury has been selected, its work begins by listening to the admissible evidence and disregarding any evidence that the judge does not allow. Once the lawyers deliver their closing arguments, the judge provides the jury with the law that they must apply to the evidence to reach a verdict. The jury then deliberates to reach a verdict.

5. Categories that have been examined in terms of predicting verdicts include demographic variables, personality variables, attitudes, defendant characteristics, victim characteristics, and expert testimony.

### Discussion Questions

1. Design a study to evaluate the advantages and disadvantages of jury aids (e.g., note-taking, asking questions).

2. A battered woman who shot and killed her sleeping abusive husband is standing trial for murder. The defence has retained a prominent forensic psychologist to give expert testimony. What impact do you think this expert will have on the jury? Discuss factors that can interact with expert testimony.

3. Should juries be permitted to ignore the law? Discuss the issues surrounding jury nullification.

4. To study juror decision making, researchers have used four different methodologies. Describe the advantages and disadvantages of each method.

# Chapter 8
## The Role of Mental Illness in Court

## Learning Objectives

■ Outline the fitness standard and the changes made to legislation.

■ Contrast unfit and fit offenders.

■ Explain Canada's insanity standard.

■ Describe automatism and examples of cases in which it was used as a defence.

■ State the explanations for high rates of mental illness in offender populations.

■ Explain the various treatment goals and options for offenders with mental disorders.

Johnny Duchane was adopted by Mr. and Mrs. DeLaroche when he was 2 years old. He had become a ward of the state because his birth mother was a cocaine addict and his father was a drug dealer serving a life sentence for killing one of his drug runners. Mr. and Mrs. DeLaroche were from a small town outside of Vancouver.

Johnny started showing some odd behaviour when he was a teenager. He was often found talking to himself, and he seemed to think everyone was against him. He thought that the only way to protect himself was to become a police officer. Johnny managed to be hired on as an officer but it quickly became clear that he was not well, and Johnny was diagnosed with paranoid schizophrenia. When he was taking his medication, he could function in most of his daily activities; however, Johnny did not like how the medication made him feel so he would stop taking his medication without warning.

Mr. and Mrs. DeLaroche had not heard from their son in a month and could not find him. He wasn't in his apartment, and he had been dismissed from the police force. While watching the news, Mr. and Mrs. DeLaroche heard that a local police officer had been murdered outside the police station where Johnny had once been employed. Mr. and Mrs. DeLaroche feared that the voices Johnny sometimes heard in his head had told Johnny to kill. The following day, a news report announced that former police officer Johnny Duchane had murdered the officer and was in custody, awaiting a psychological assessment.

Although a number of people convicted of crimes may suffer from mental illness, this chapter will consider mental illness as it relates to the ability to stand trial and to the commission of a crime. In this chapter, we will explore what is meant by the term *fitness to stand trial* within the Canadian criminal justice system. We also will examine the term *mental state at the time of offence* as it pertains to Canadian criminal law and forensic psychology.

## PRESUMPTIONS IN CANADA'S LEGAL SYSTEM

The cornerstone of English-Canadian law identifies two elements that must be present for criminal guilt to be established: (1) a wrongful deed, also known as **actus reus**, and (2) criminal intent, also known as **mens rea**. Both of these elements (and the elements of the specific case) must be found beyond a reasonable doubt for a guilty verdict to be reached. Issues of fitness, insanity, automatism, and mental disorders all call into question these two basic elements of criminal law.

## FITNESS TO STAND TRIAL

It is reasonable to expect that in order for individuals who are charged with the commission of a crime to be tried fairly, they should have some understanding of the charges and proceedings and be able to help in preparing their defence. A defendant who is deficient in these domains, possibly because of a mental disorder, may be considered unfit to stand

trial. Thus, **unfit to stand trial** refers to a defendant's inability to conduct a defence at any stage of the proceedings on account of a mental disorder. For example, a defendant may be found unfit to stand trial if he or she is experiencing an episode of schizophrenia and lacks the ability to understand the situation and tell the lawyer the facts of the case. Also, in a recent Canadian case, *R. v. Balliram* (2003), it was concluded that an unfit person could not be sentenced. The degree of impairment necessary for an unfit determination has been difficult to pinpoint, however.

Historically, little direction was provided by means of legislation for a finding of unfitness; rather, case law was used to determine the criteria that should be met. Specifically, the case of *R. v. Prichard* (1836) has been considered the key case for the fitness standard (Lindsay, 1977). Three criteria were delineated in the Prichard case:

- Whether the defendant is mute of malice (i.e., intentionality)
- Whether the defendant can plead to the indictment
- Whether the defendant has sufficient cognitive capacity to understand the trial proceedings

Prior to the enactment of Bill C-30 (1992) and by the mid-1980s, the federal Department of Justice acknowledged a number of problems with the mental disorder provisions of the Criminal Code of Canada (e.g., inconsistencies, omissions, lack of clarity and guidance). Also, there were issues regarding the incompatibility of these provisions with the Canadian Charter of Rights and Freedoms. For example, someone who was declared unfit to stand trial could be confined indefinitely. A number of changes were instituted with the enactment of Bill C-30.

With the enactment of Bill C-30 in 1992, the Criminal Code stated a fitness standard. The fitness standard can be found in section 2 of the Code: A defendant is unfit to stand trial if he or she is

unable on account of mental disorder to conduct a defence at any stage of the proceedings before a verdict is rendered or to instruct counsel to do so, and, in particular, unable on account of mental disorder to a) understand the nature or object of the proceedings, b) understand the possible consequences of the proceedings, or c) communicate with counsel. (R.S.C., 1985, C-46, s. 2; 1992, c. 20, s. 216, c. 51, s. 32)

This last point about communicating with counsel has been further specified in case law in R. v. Taylor (1992). In this case, the Ontario Court of Appeal stated that the test to be applied in terms of "communication with counsel" is with regard to limited cognitive capacity. The court ruled that a defendant need only be able to state the facts relating to the offence that would allow an appropriate defence. Moreover, the defendant need not be able to communicate facts that are in his or her best interests. The court decided that applying the "best interest rule" was too strict a criterion.

One other issue that was altered with Bill C-30 was the length of time a defendant could be held in custody for a fitness evaluation. A five-day limit on court-ordered assessments was legislated, with provisions for extensions, if necessary, to complete the evaluation. The extension, however, is not to exceed 30 days, and the entire length of detention should not exceed 60 days (R.S.C., 1985, C-46, s. 672.15). The evaluation can occur while the defendant is in a detention, outpatient, or in-patient facility. Roesch, Ogloff, Hart, Dempster, Zapf, and Whittemore (1997) found that the average length of time for evaluation was approximately three weeks and that 88% occurred in in-patient facilities (also Zapf & Roesch, 1998). It should be noted that mental health law (i.e., commitment and treatment in psychiatric facilities) is under provincial/territorial jurisdiction.

## Raising the Issue of Fitness

The issue of a defendant's fitness may be raised at various points from the time of arrest to the defendant's sentence determination. Examples of instances in which the issue of fitness may be raised include when a plea is entered, when a defendant chooses not to be represented by counsel, and during sentencing (Ogloff, Wallace, & Otto, 1991). The Criminal Code of Canada states that a defendant is assumed to be fit to stand trial unless the court is satisfied on the balance of probabilities that he or she is unfit (R.S.C., 1985, C-46, s. 672.22). The defence or Crown may raise the issue of a defendant's fitness. Also noted in the Code is that the burden of proving unfitness is on the party who raises the issue (R.S.C., 1985, C-46, s. 672.23[2]).

## How Many Defendants Are Referred for Fitness Evaluations?

Webster, Menzies, Butler, and Turner (1982) estimated that approximately 5000 fitness evaluations were conducted annually in Canada. In a more recent investigation, Roesch et al. (1997) found that 61% of a sample from a remand facility in B.C. underwent fitness evaluations. Moreover, 24% were held for assessments of both fitness and criminal responsibility (we will discuss criminal responsibility in more detail later in the chapter). In the United States, Bonnie and Grisso (2000) estimated that somewhere between 2% and 8% of all felony defendants are referred for fitness evaluations—that is, about 25 000 to 38 000 defendants (Hoge, Poythress, Bonnie, Monahan, Eisenberg, & Feucht-Haviar, 1997). See Table 8.1 for a distribution of the number of accused ruled unfit in seven Canadian jurisdictions during the period 1992–2004. (See also Table 8.3 on page 215

**Table 8.1** Number of Accused Given the Legal Status of Unfit, by Jurisdiction (1992–2004)

| Jurisdiction | Number of Accused Ruled Unfit |
|---|---|
| Prince Edward Island | 4 |
| Quebec | 399 |
| Ontario | 1151 |
| Alberta | 94 |
| British Columbia | 216 |
| Nunavut | 2 |
| Yukon | 10 |

Source: Latimer & Lawrence, 2006.

for the total percentage of cases in which the accused is ruled as unfit or not criminally responsible on account of mental disorder across seven jurisdictions in Canada for the period 1992–2004.)

## Who Can Assess Fitness?

Traditionally, only medical practitioners have been allowed to conduct court-ordered assessments of such aspects as fitness to stand trial and criminal responsibility (Viljoen, Roesch, Ogloff, & Zapf, 2003). Unlike in the United States and Australia, the Canadian Criminal Justice system continues to take this position. In fact, the Canadian Criminal Code excludes psychologists from conducting court-ordered assessments. The Code specifies that these assessments must be carried out by medical practitioners (R.S.C., 1985, C-46, s. 672.1). It is important to note that the medical practitioners need not have any background in psychiatry or experience with forensic populations. In contrast, Farkas, DeLeon, and Newman (1997) reported that 47 U.S. states allow psychologists to conduct fitness and criminal responsibility evaluations.

Canadian psychologists can, however, be involved in court-ordered assessments in a variety of ways. For example, psychologists may be asked to conduct psychological testing and to assist with the assessment of defendants who are referred for evaluation. Psychologists submit their results to psychiatrists or other medical practitioners, who then incorporate the results into a report for the court.

## Fitness Instruments

A number of screening instruments have been developed to help evaluators quickly screen out defendants who are competent to stand trial. Comprehensive fitness assessments can then be reserved for those defendants who are "screened in." Zapf and Roesch (1998) compared the fitness decisions that were made by using a screening instrument with decisions that were made following a defendant's stay in a psychiatric facility. The researchers found that the two sets of decisions were consistent with each other. They concluded that long stays in mental facilities were unnecessary for most of the fitness decisions. Rather, many fitness decisions could be made quickly by using a screening instrument, which would result in a more cost-effective system.

One screening instrument that has particular relevance for Canadians is the Fitness Interview Test Revised (FIT-R) (Roesch, Zapf, Eaves, & Webster, 1998), which was developed to meet the fitness criteria outlined in the Canadian Criminal Code. The FIT-R is in the form of a semi-structured interview and assesses the three psychological abilities stated in the Code's fitness standard. Each section contains several items that the evaluator probes with the defendant. For example,

■ Understand the nature or object of the proceedings
  – Factual knowledge of criminal procedure
    i defendant's understanding of the arrest process
    ii the nature and severity of the current charges
    iii the role of key participants
■ Understand the possible consequences of the proceedings
  – Appreciation of personal involvement in and importance of the proceedings
    i appreciation of range and nature of possible penalties and defences
■ Communicate with counsel
  – Ability to participate in defence
    i defendant's ability to communicate facts
    ii defendant's ability to relate to his or her attorney
    iii defendant's ability to plan legal strategy

Each response is rated on a 3-point scale, ranging from 0 (indicates no to little impairment) to 2 (indicates severe impairment). Once the interview is complete, the evaluator must make a decision regarding overall fitness. The final decision involves three stages: (1) determining the existence of a mental disorder, (2) determining the defendant's capacity regarding each of the three psychological abilities stated above, and (3) examining the previous information. Although performance on the items contained in each section is considered in determining the section rating, decisions are not made based on a specific cut-off score. Instead, these section ratings constitute a separate judgment based on the severity of impairment and its perceived importance. See Box 8.1 for a look at some other fitness instruments.

## Distinguishing between Fit and Unfit Defendants

Viljoen and Zapf (2002) examined the characteristics of 80 defendants who were referred for fitness evaluations and 80 defendants who were not referred. As shown in Table 8.2, a number of characteristics differed significantly between the referred and nonreferred defendants.

Using the Fit-R, referred defendants were significantly more likely to show impairment on one or more sections. For example, referred defendants were less likely to understand the nature and object of the proceedings, and possible consequences of the proceedings. No significant difference between the referred and nonreferred defendants was found in terms of being able to communicate with counsel.

**Table 8.2** Demographic, Criminological, and Mental Health Characteristics for Defendants Referred versus Nonreferred for Fitness Evaluations

| Characteristic | Referred Defendants | Nonreferred Defendants |
|---|---|---|
| | (n = 80) | (n = 80) |
| Never married | 56.3% (45) | 46.3% (37)** |
| White | 81.3% (65) | 72.5% (58) |
| Didn't complete high school | 56.3% (45) | 68.8% (55) |
| Living alone | 32.5% (26) | 13.8% (11)** |
| Unemployed | 55.0% (44) | 48.8% (39) |
| Current violent offence | 71.3% (57) | 26.3% (21)** |
| Previous arrests | 76.3% (61) | 92.5% (74)* |
| Current primary diagnosis | | |
| Psychotic | 41.3% (33) | 3.8% (3)** |
| Affective disorder | 20.0% (16) | 12.5% (10) |
| Substance abuse | 10.0% (8) | 41.3% (33)** |
| No diagnosis | 28.8% (23) | 42.5% (34) |
| Lifetime diagnosis | | |
| Psychotic | 41.3% (33) | 5.0% (4)** |
| Affective disorder | 53.7% (43) | 28.8% (23)** |
| Substance abuse | 71.3% (57) | 85.0% (68)* |
| No diagnosis | 7.5% (6) | 12.5% (10) |
| Antisocial personality disorder | 32.5% (26) | 47.5% (38)* |
| Previous mental health services | 85.0% (68) | 56.3% (45)** |
| Previous hospitalizations | 66.3% (53) | 11.3% (9)** |

\* $p < 0.05$

\*\* $p < 0.01$

Source: Viljoen & Zapf, 2002.

Zapf and Roesch (1998) examined the demographic, mental health, and criminal characteristics that differentiate fit from unfit defendants by using a sample of 180 males undergoing evaluation in a facility in B.C. Using the fit/unfit decision offered to the court by the psychiatrist, the data were divided into these two categories and then compared across criteria.

In examining the demographic variables, only marital status was significant. Fit defendants were significantly more likely to have been married (married, divorced, separated, common law) than were unfit defendants. Previous studies have found defendants who are referred for fitness evaluations to be primarily single, unemployed, and living alone (Roesch et al., 1981; Webster et al., 1982). In a meta-analysis of 30 studies conducted in both Canada and the United States, Nicholson and Kugler (1991) found that fit and unfit defendants differed on age, gender, race, and marital resources. Unfit defendants

Box 8.1

# Fitness Instruments

## Competency Screening Test (CST)

The CST (Lipsitt, Lelos, & McGarry, 1971) has 22 uncompleted sentences that the respondent must finish. For example,

- The lawyer told Bill that . . .
- When I go to court the lawyer will . . .
- Jack felt that the judge . . .

The items measure three constructs: the potential for a constructive relationship between the defendant and his lawyer, the defendant's understanding of the court process, and the ability of the defendant to emotionally cope with the criminal process. Responses are scored by using a 3-point scale (0, 1, 2), depending on the relation between the defendant's response and example responses provided in the scoring manual. A score of 0 would be assigned if the response demonstrated a low level of legal understanding. For example, "The lawyer told Bill that he is guilty" would receive 0 points (Ackerman, 1999). A score of 2 would be assigned if the response demonstrated a high level of legal understanding. For example, "The lawyer told Bill that he should plead guilty" would receive 2 points (Ackerman, 1999). Scores for each of the items are summed to produce a total CST score. The CST score, in addition to a brief psychiatric interview, is aimed at distinguishing between competent defendants who could proceed to trial and those defendants who should undergo a more complete competency assessment. A score of 20 or below suggests that the defendant should undergo a more comprehensive evaluation.

## Competency to Stand Trial Assessment Instrument (CAI)

The CAI (Laboratory of Community Psychiatry, Harvard Medical School, 1973) was designed to accompany the CST in that the CAI is a semi-structured interview and constitutes a comprehensive competency evaluation. The CAI assesses 13 functions corresponding to a defendant's ability to participate in the criminal process on behalf of his or her best interests. Each function is represented in a statement with two or three sample questions that the evaluator may pose to the defendant. For example (Ackerman, 1999),

Function:  Appraisal of available legal defences

Statement:  The defendant's awareness of possible legal defences and how consistent they are with the reality of his or her particular circumstances

Question:  How do you think you can be defended against these charges?

Following a response, the evaluator can ask follow-up questions to further probe the defendant's response if it is unclear or ambiguous. For each function, responses are rated on a scale from 1 (reflecting a total lack of capacity for function) to 5 (reflecting no impairment—i.e., defendant can function adequately). A score of 6 can be given when there is insufficient information to rate the function. The evaluator examines the scores for each function and then makes an overall determination.

## Interdisciplinary Fitness Interview (IFI)

The IFI (Golding, Roesch, & Schreiber, 1984) was developed following an analysis of the CAI. As with the CAI, the IFI is a semi-structured interview measuring three areas of competency: functional memory, appropriate relationship with lawyer, and understanding of the justice system. There are four main sections to the IFI:

Section A: Legal items

Section B: Psychopathological items

Section C: Overall evaluation

Section D: Consensual judgment

Each section has a number of subsections and areas within each subsection that can be assessed. The revision of the IFI (IFI-R) (Golding, 1993) retains the semi-structured interview protocol; however, there are only two sections: Current Clinical Condition and Psycho-Legal Abilities. Each section has a number of subsections. For example, under the heading Current Clinical Condition are the following categories:

- Attention/consciousness
- Delusions
- Hallucinations
- Impaired reasoning and judgment
- Impaired memory
- Mood and affect

*(continued)*

*(continued)*

The evaluator assesses these major areas of clinical dysfunction. Responses are rated with a scale ranging from 0 (absent or does not bear on defendant's fitness) to 2 (symptom is likely to significantly impair the defendant's fitness).

Under the Psycho-Legal Abilities heading, there are four subsections:

■ Capacity to appreciate charges and to disclose pertinent facts, events, and motives

■ Courtroom demeanour and capacity to understand the adversarial nature of proceedings

■ Quality of relationship with attorney

■ Appreciation of and reasoned choice with respect to legal option and consequences

Responses are rated on a scale ranging from 0 (no or minimal capacity) to 2 (substantial capacity). It also has been recommended that when conducting a competency assessment, the defendant's lawyer, previous mental health contacts, and jail personnel are interviewed. In addition, mental health reports, police reports, and prior arrest history should be reviewed (Golding, as cited in Ackerman, 1999).

## MacArthur Competence Assessment Tool— Criminal Adjudication (MacCAT-CA)

The MacCAT-CA (Hoge, Bonnie, Poythress, & Monahan, 1992) is a structured interview containing 22 items that assess competencies in three areas:

■ Factual understanding of the legal system and the adjudication process

■ Reasoning ability

■ Understanding of own legal situation and circumstances

These areas are assessed via hypothetical scenarios. Following the presentation of the scenario, the defendant is asked a series of specific questions. The evaluator assigns a score of 0, 1, or 2, based on the scoring criteria. For each area, score ranges are provided for three levels of impairment: none to minimal, mild, or clinically significant.

were more likely to be older females belonging to a minority group and to have fewer marital resources. Hubbard, Zapf, and Ronan (2003) examined the *competency* (the term used in the United States for *fitness*) reports of 468 defendants. Differences between competent and incompetent defendants were found on employment status, psychiatric diagnosis, ethnicity, and criminal charges. Incompetent defendants were less likely to maintain employment and had more serious mental illness than competent defendants. Also, more African-American defendants were found incompetent compared with Caucasian defendants. Hubbard et al. (2003) also found that incompetent defendants were more likely to be charged with property and miscellaneous crimes rather than violent crimes compared with competent defendants.

Zapf and Roesch (1998) also found that defendants who were unfit were four times more likely to have met criteria for a psychotic disorder, whereas defendants who were fit were about as likely to have been diagnosed with a psychotic disorder as not. It is important to note that not all psychotic defendants are unfit, and the presence of psychosis is not sufficient or equivalent to unfitness (Golding et al., 1984). Substance abuse disorders were significantly less likely to be found in unfit defendants than in the fit defendants.

In examining criminological variables, Zapf and Roesch (1998) found that there were no significant differences between fit and unfit defendants. The two groups were similar in the frequency with which they had committed violent, property, and miscellaneous crimes. Moreover, both groups had a similar criminal history and were just as likely to have previously been in prison.

How would you rule on the defendant in the Case Study box? Is he fit or unfit?

Jack Chow was a graduate student in psychology working on his Ph.D. He would often spend his days in the lab conducting file reviews of offenders for his dissertation research. Jack shared the lab with two other students who were also completing their graduate studies. One day, Jack accused his lab mates of tapping into his data set and changing the data. His lab mates didn't know what he was talking about. These accusations escalated when Jack accused them of going into his email account and sending computer viruses to his friends who were contacts in his email list. Jack's lab mates were getting tired of these accusations.

One Friday afternoon, Jack opened his data file and was convinced it had been tampered with. In a rage, Jack threw his chair at one of his lab mates and started punching him. A student walking by quickly called campus security and the police. Jack was charged with assault. On the way to the police station, Jack started yelling that his lab mates had orchestrated his arrest so that they could steal his data and publish his groundbreaking research. Jack was given a court-appointed lawyer. In a preliminary hearing, Jack's lawyer stated Jack had no understanding of what he was being charged with and could not answer any of his questions. Jack kept repeating that he had to get back to his data and didn't have time for these games because he had a Nobel Prize to win. Jack's lawyer claimed Jack was unfit to stand trial and requested an assessment.

### Your Turn . . .

Would you grant Jack this assessment? Do you think Jack is showing signs of unfitness? What are some of your concerns regarding Jack's behaviour?

## How Is Fitness Restored?

When a defendant is found unfit to stand trial, the goal of the criminal justice system is to get the defendant fit. The most common form of treatment for fitness is medication. A question facing the justice system concerning this form of treatment is whether a defendant has the right to refuse medication. The courts will take into account the individual's capacity to comprehend and appreciate the consequences of his or her actions and public safety. Defendants sometimes may argue for not taking medication because of the serious side effects. A treatment order may be imposed by the court (R.S.C., 1985, C-46, s. 672.58); however, the courts also must grapple with having a heavily medicated defendant and whether this serves justice. See Box 8.2 for a look at a case involving a defendant with a mental illness, who fought against taking medication.

## What Happens after a Finding of Unfitness?

The proceedings against a defendant who is found unfit to stand trial are halted until competency is restored. In the United States, almost all jurisdictions limit the time a defendant may be "held" as unfit. In the landmark case of *Jackson v. Indiana* (1972), the United States Supreme Court stated that a defendant should not be held for more than a

Box 8.2

# Mentally Ill but Competent to Make Treatment Decisions?

Scott Starson (a.k.a. Scott Jeffery Schutzman) has a special skill in physics. Without having formal training, he works with the top physics researchers in the world. In 1991, he co-authored an article with a physics professor from Stanford University. In addition to his physics ability, Starson also has a long history of battling a mental disorder. He has been diagnosed as having bipolar affective disorder. Starson has been admitted to several mental health facilities over the years.

In 1998, Starson was charged with uttering two death threats to tenants in his apartment complex. He was found not criminally responsible on account of mental disorder. In January 1999, the Ontario Review Board ordered that he be detained at the Centre for Addiction and Mental Health (CAMH) in Toronto. Dr. Ian Swayze and Dr. Paul Posner, both psychiatrists at CAMH, proposed to treat Starson with mood stabilizers, antipsychotic, anti-anxiety, and anti-Parkinsonian medication. Starson refused pharmaceutical intervention and appealed the Ontario Review Board's decision in provincial court. He argued that "he would not be able to do his work while on the proposed medication, not because of the side effects, but because of the very effects that the drugs are intended to achieve. . . . Starson said that after periods of treatment with such medications, it would always take him some time to 'work his way up the academic ladder'" (*Starson v. Swayze*, 1999, para 55).

In November 1999, the Ontario Superior Court of Justice overturned the Ontario Review Board's decision, stating that it was unreasonable. Justice Anne Molloy stated that the Board's conclusion that Starson was in denial of his mental illness was an error and that it was wrong for the Board to accept unsubstantiated claims that Starson suffered delusions that others were out to harm him. Starson's doctors appealed the decision to the Ontario Court of Appeal. The appeal court ruled that Starson was capable of making treatment decisions and could appreciate the possible consequences of refusing treatment. The doctors appealed to the Supreme Court of Canada. In June 2003, the Supreme Court upheld the lower court's decision that Starson had the capacity to refuse medical treatment.

Sources: *Starson v. Swayze*, 1999; *Starson v. Swayze*, 2003.

reasonable period of time to determine whether there is a likelihood of the person gaining competency (fitness). Of course, what constitutes a reasonable period of time is open to interpretation.

For unfit defendants in Canada, the judge may order that the defendant be detained in a hospital or that the defendant be conditionally discharged. The defendant is reassessed for fitness within 45 days. In the event that the defendant becomes fit, he or she returns to court and the proceedings resume (R.S.C., 1985, C-46, s. 672.28). If the defendant remains unfit after 90 days, he or she is referred to a review board for assessment and disposition (R.S.C., 1985, C-46, s. 672.47). Cases of defendants who continue to be unfit are reviewed on an annual basis by the review board. In these cases, the Crown must prove that there is sufficient evidence to bring the case to trial (referred to as making a **prima facie case**) every two years and at any time the defendant requests the proceeding. For youth found unfit, the court must review the case every year instead of every two years, according to section 141(10) of the Youth Criminal Justice Act. If the court determines that sufficient evidence is no longer available to prosecute the case, the case is dropped and the defendant is found not guilty (R.S.C., 1985, C-46, s. 672.33).

Even though a defendant may be restored to fitness, it is possible that he or she will become unfit once again during the trial proceedings. If unfitness occurs again, the proceedings stop until the defendant becomes fit. If a defendant becomes fit while in custody (e.g., detained in a mental facility) and there is reason to believe that he or she may

**Prima facie case:** Case in which the Crown prosecutor must prove there is sufficient evidence to bring the case to trial

become unfit if released, the defendant will be required to remain in the mental facility until the trial is complete (R.S.C., 1985, C-46, s. 672.29). Also, it is possible for a defendant to become unfit while waiting to be sentenced (Manson, 2006).

What if a defendant is unlikely to become fit (e.g., possibly because of permanent brain damage)? Until recently, an absolute discharge could not be issued to defendants unlikely to become fit. However, in *R. v. Demers* (2004), the Supreme Court of Canada ruled that the inability of the courts or review boards to issue an absolute discharge to defendants who are unlikely to become fit and who pose no significant threat to society was in violation of the liberties guaranteed under section 7 of the Charter of Rights and Freedoms. This infringement was addressed by an amendment to the Criminal Code with the passing of Bill C-10, occurring in January 2006. A court now has the authority to stay the proceedings for a defendant who is unlikely to become fit if any the following are true:

- The accused is unlikely ever to become fit.
- The accused does not pose a significant threat to the safety of the public.
- A stay of proceedings is in the interests of the proper administration of justice.

Bill C-10 still does not provide review boards with the ability to absolutely discharge an accused who is found unfit; only the courts have this power. A review board, however, can recommend to a court that an inquiry be undertaken to determine if a stay of proceedings is in the interests of the proper administration of justice. If a stay is not ordered, the accused remains under the disposition determined by the review board.

See Figure 8.1 for key processes in cases involving fitness.

## MENTAL STATE AT TIME OF OFFENCE

**Insanity** has been defined as not being of sound mind, and being mentally deranged and irrational (Sykes, 1982). In a legal context, insanity removes the responsibility for performing a particular act because of uncontrollable impulses or delusions, such as hearing voices. There have been two primary British cases that have shaped the current standard of insanity in Canada (as cited in Moran, 1985). The first was that of James Hadfield who in 1800 attempted to assassinate King George III. Hadfield had suffered a brain injury while fighting against the French. His lawyer successfully argued that he was out of touch with reality and therefore met the insanity standard of the time. Following this case, the Criminal Lunatics Act (1800) was established, and it stated the insanity standard of the day.

**Insanity:** Impairment of mental or emotional functioning that affects perceptions, beliefs, and motivations at the time of the offence

The second case influencing Canada's current insanity standard was that of Daniel McNaughton in 1843 (*R. v. McNaughton*, 1843). Daniel McNaughton was born and raised in Glasgow, Scotland. Eventually he found his way to London in July 1842. While in London, he purchased two pistols that he carried in his waistcoat. On Friday, January 20, 1843, he walked behind Edward Drummond, one of Prime Minister Robert Peel's secretaries, who was coming back from Drummonds Bank. McNaughton approached Drummond from behind, took a pistol out of his pocket, and shot Drummond in the back. Drummond then turned to see who shot him and saw McNaughton and pointed to him. McNaughton reached for his other pistol and at that point was tackled by James Silver, a constable. McNaughton was handcuffed and his weapons were removed. Drummond died five days later.

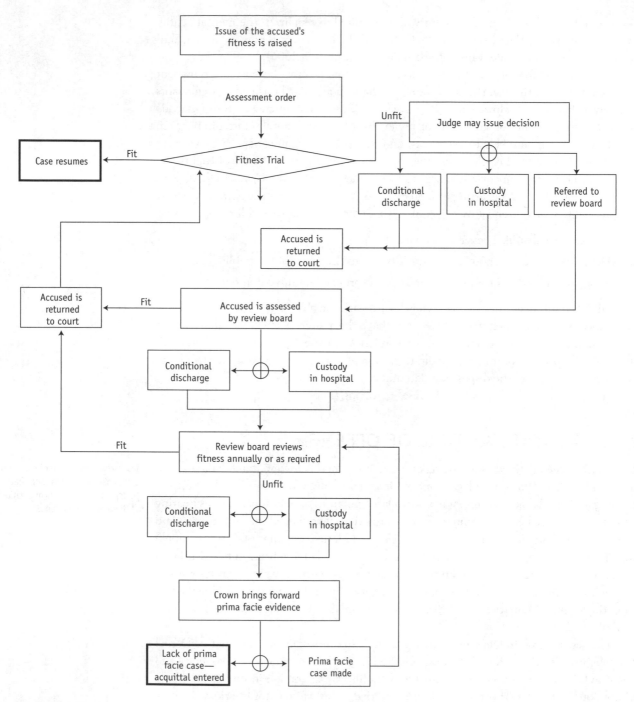

**Figure 8.1** Key Processes in Cases Involving Fitness

*Although both the court and review board have the authority to detain a person found not criminally responsible on account of mental disorder in hospital, the accused may refuse treatment while detained.

**In accordance with the decision of the Supreme Court of Canada in *R. v. Swain* in 1991, the Crown may not "raise the issue of the defendant's mental capacity before the Crown proved that the crime had been committed or until the accused had put their mental capacity into issue."

There is some debate as to McNaughton's reason for shooting and whether Drummond or Peel was the intended target.

McNaughton was charged with murder, and the judge interpreted his plea as "not guilty." McNaughton was found not guilty because of his mental status: insanity. He would serve out his life in a mental institute (see Dalby, 2006, for the full details of the story).

Five critical elements emerged from the McNaughton verdict, with three specific to the insanity defences of today:

1. A defendant must be found to be suffering from a defect of reason/disease of the mind.

2. A defendant must not know the nature and quality of the act he or she is performing.

3. A defendant must not know that what he or she is doing is wrong.

The elements in the McNaughton standard emerged in legislation in parts of the United States, England, and Canada. Little would change for the insanity standard in Canada for many years.

In the mid-1970s, a review of the policies for offenders with mental disorders was undertaken by the Law Reform Commission of Canada. Forty-four recommendations on law and policy were provided (Law Reform Commission of Canada, 1976). In response to this review, the Department of Justice commissioned the Mental Disorder Project in the early 1980s. This review found that the mental disorder legislation in the Criminal Code was in conflict with the Charter of Rights and Freedoms. The ruling from the Supreme Court of Canada in *R. v. Swain* (1991) was consistent with the review and foreshadowed the changes to the Criminal Code. For example, in *R. v. Swain* (1991), the Supreme Court determined that defendants who were found not guilty by reason of insanity could not be automatically detained until their level of dangerousness was decided or an appropriate disposition was determined. Finding a defendant guilty before either of these things was done would be in conflict with the Charter. Moreover, the Court also decided that the defendant could raise the issue of his or her mental capacity at any point in the trial, but the Crown could not do so until it had proved the crime against the defendant or until the defendant raised his or her mental capacity.

In 1992, Bill C-30 was enacted and the following changes were made to the justice system:

- The term *not guilty by reason of insanity* was changed to *not criminally responsible on account of mental disorder* (NCRMD).

- The wording of the standard was altered and stated in section 16 of the Criminal Code of Canada: "No person is criminally responsible for an act committed or an omission made while suffering from a mental disorder that rendered the person incapable of appreciating the nature and quality of the act or omission or of knowing that it was wrong."

- **Review boards** were created. These legal bodies were mandated to oversee the care and disposition of defendants found unfit and/or not criminally responsible on account of a mental disorder. Review boards were required to review each unfit and NCRMD case every year.

**Review boards**: Legal bodies mandated to oversee the care and disposition of defendants found unfit and/or not criminally responsible on account of a mental disorder

Another change occurred in 1999. In *Winko v. British Columbia*, the Supreme Court of Canada stated that a defendant who is NCRMD should be detained only if he or she poses a criminal threat to the public; otherwise, the defendant should receive an absolute discharge. Another review on justice and human rights was undertaken in 2002 concerning mental disorder provisions in the Criminal Code. A second review for 2007 has been recommended, and it will allow data to be collected on the issues that have emerged. See Box 8.3 for a description of a case in which the defendant was found NCRMD.

**Table 8.3** Number of Accused Given the Legal Status of NCRMD and Unfit, by Jurisdiction (1992–2004)

| Jurisdiction | Number of NCRMD | % of Total Cases That Are NCRMD and Unfit |
|---|---|---|
| Prince Edward Island | 8 | 0.1% |
| Quebec | 3378 | 43.5% |
| Ontario | 2059 | 37.0% |
| Alberta | 306 | 4.6% |
| British Columbia | 1036 | 14.4% |
| Nunavut | 6 | 0.1% |

Source: Latimer & Lawrence, 2006.

## Raising the Issue of Insanity

Studies find that few defendants use the insanity defence. For example, in the United States, one study found that less than 1% of all felony cases will argue an insanity defence (Steadman, McGreevy, Morrissey, Callahan, Robbins, & Cirincione, 1993). Moreover, the success rate of such a defence is variable. It has been reported that approximately 25% of defendants who argue an insanity defence succeed (Steadman et al., 1993). See Table 8.3 for a distribution of NCRMD and unfit cases in Canada.

Insanity defences typically occur when opposing sides (prosecution and defence) agree to such a verdict (Melton, Petrila, Poythress, & Slobogin, 1997). It is not common to have opposing experts testify on this issue in jury trials. Ogloff, Schweighofer, Turnbull, and Whittemore (1992) reported that defendants found NCRMD are likely to have major psychiatric disorders, such as schizophrenia, and many past mental health problems that resulted in hospitalization or prior rulings of unfitness.

Within the Canadian criminal justice system, a defendant is considered not to suffer from a mental disorder. Of course, the defendant may raise the issue of insanity for his or her defence. In Canada, there are only two situations in which the Crown may raise the issue of insanity:

1. Following a guilty verdict, the Crown could argue that the defendant was NCRMD. This situation may occur if the Crown believes that the defendant requires psychiatric treatment and a mental facility is best suited for the defendant's needs.

2. If the defence states that the defendant has a mental illness, the Crown can then argue it.

The party that raises the issue must prove it beyond a balance of the probabilities (R.S.C., 1985, C-46, s. 16).

## Assessing Insanity

Just as with fitness to stand trial, an insanity defence requires a psychiatric assessment. Richard Rogers developed the first standardized assessment scales for criminal responsibility: the Rogers Criminal Responsibility Assessment Scales (R-CRAS) (Rogers, 1984).

The R-CRAS is the only instrument of its kind. It has five scales:

1. Patient reliability
2. Organicity
3. Psychopathology
4. Cognitive control
5. Behavioural control

Each scale has 30 items, which are given a score from 0 to 6, with higher values representing greater severity (Rogers & Sewell, 1999). It is important to note that the R-CRAS was developed to standardize evaluations and ensure particular areas are evaluated, rather than produce a cut-off score to indicate criminal responsibility (Rogers & Ewing, 1992). The clinician is to take all the information into account and use it as the basis for a decision regarding the defendant's mental status and criminal responsibility.

## What Happens to a Defendant Found NCRMD?

Three dispositions can be made following a finding of NCRMD. If the defendant is not a threat to society or poses low risk for reoffending, the court or review board can order an **absolute discharge**. That is, the defendant is released into the community without restrictions on his or her behaviour. A second disposition option is to order a discharge with conditions, known as a **conditional discharge**. In this case, the defendant is released but must meet certain conditions, such as not possessing firearms. Failure to meet the conditions imposed with a conditional discharge may result in the defendant being incarcerated or sent to a psychiatric facility. Lastly, the court or review board may order that the defendant be sent to a psychiatric facility (R.S.C., 1985, C-46, s. 672.54).

It is important to note that a defendant who is sent to a psychiatric facility need not comply with treatment. It is only when the defendant's mental health has deteriorated to a point that he or she is no longer competent to make treatment decisions that steps may be taken to force treatment on the defendant (R.S.C., 1985, C-46, s. 672.54). In such instances, the provincial and territorial mental health policies would be followed.

In Canada, dispositions may be made by the court or referred to a provincial or territorial review board. Dispositions that are made by the court also are reviewed by a review board within 90 days and can be changed at any point. An exception to this rule occurs if the court makes an absolute discharge (R.S.C., 1985, C-46, s. 672.81). This decision does not go before a review board. In addition, review boards review the defendant's disposition every year. There is a great deal of information that review boards will take into account, including

- charge information
- trial transcript
- criminal history
- risk assessment
- clinical history, such as previous admissions to hospital
- psychological testing
- hospital's recommendation

**Absolute discharge:** The defendant is released into the community without restrictions to his or her behaviour

**Conditional discharge:** A defendant is released; however, release carries certain conditions (e.g., not to possess firearms) that the defendant must meet. Failure to meet the conditions imposed with a conditional discharge may result in the defendant being incarcerated or sent to a psychiatric facility

As you read earlier, historically, defendants who were found insane would spend the remainder of their lives in an insane asylum. More recently, it was not uncommon for "insane" defendants to be given indeterminate sentences, only to be released when they were deemed sane. Moreover, insane defendants often would serve more time in a mental institute than their prison sentence would have been following a standard guilty verdict. Bill C-30 introduced **capping**, which refers to the maximum period of time a person with a mental illness can be affected by his or her disposition. For example, the disposition period for a defendant with a mental illness who committed a violent offence is ten years, the same length of time as the prison term. Once the cap is reached, the defendant may be released without restrictions. However, if the defendant is still perceived to be dangerous, he or she could be involuntarily committed to a secure hospital. Moreover, if the defendant was declared a mentally disordered dangerous/violent offender, this designation could increase the cap.

**Capping**: Notion introduced through Bill C-30 where there is a maximum period of time a person with a mental illness could be affected by their disposition

When deciding on a disposition, the court and review board must choose the option that is least limiting to the defendant. Four main criteria are considered when deciding a disposition:

- Public safety
- Mental state of the defendant
- Reintegration of the defendant into society
- Other needs of the defendant

See Figure 8.2 for key processes in cases involving NCRMD defences.

# AUTOMATISM

If you don't have control over your behaviour, should you be held responsible for your actions? Consider the case of Kenneth Parks (*R. v. Parks*, 1992). He got up in the middle of the night, got dressed, got into his car, and drove to where his parents-in-law lived. He went into their home, got a kitchen knife, stabbed his mother-in-law to death and almost killed his father-in-law. He then drove to the police station and turned himself in. He was charged and tried for murder and attempted murder. Parks's defence was that he was sleepwalking, a form of automatism. **Automatism** refers to unconscious, involuntary behaviour; that is, the person committing the act is not aware of what he or she is doing. Parks was acquitted on both charges. See Box 8.4 for an example of automatism involving a Canadian socialite.

**Automatism:** Unconscious, involuntary behaviour such that the person committing the act is not aware of what he or she is doing

The Criminal Code of Canada does not specifically address automatism as a defence; rather, judges have had to rely on their own judgment and case law when such defences are raised. In *R. v. Stone* (1999) (see Box 8.5), the Supreme Court of Canada stated that there were two forms of automatism: noninsane and insane. Noninsane automatism refers to involuntary behaviour that occurs because of an external factor. The verdict in such cases is "not guilty." Insane automatism refers to an involuntary action that occurs because of a mental disorder. In these cases, a finding of NCRMD would be entered and the legislation for NCRMD would be applied.

In *R. v. Stone* (1999) the Supreme Court outlined a two-stage process for addressing defences of automatism. First, the trial judge must decide whether there is sufficient evidence

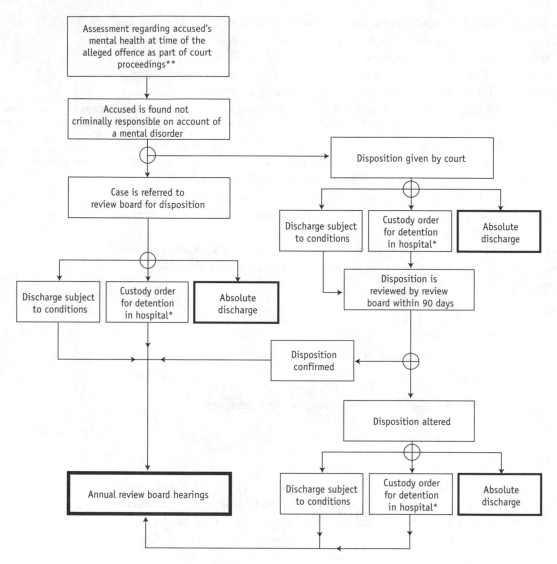

**Figure 8.2** Key Processes in Cases Involving NCRMD Defences

*Although both the court and review board have the authority to detain a person found NCRMD in hospital, the accused may refuse treatment while detained.

**In accordance with the decision of the Supreme Court of Canada in *R. v. Swain* in 1991, the Crown may not "raise the issue of the defendant's mental capacity before the Crown proved that the crime had been committed or until the accused had put their mental capacity into issue."

that a jury could find that the defendant's behaviour was involuntary. The following factors are considered:

- Psychiatric assessments
- Severity of triggering event
- History of automatic behaviour

Second, the trial judge determines if the condition is a mental disorder (insane) or non-mental-disorder (noninsane) automatism.

## A Gas Company, a Tire Company, and a Case of Automatism

Dorothy and Earl Joudrie were teen sweethearts. They married in 1957 and although they had only $25 at the time, they managed to amass quite a fortune. They had a 650-square-metre home, a vacation home in Hawaii, and were millionaires. Earl had become the chair of both Gulf Canada Resources Limited and the Canadian Tire Corporation, to name just two of his many accomplishments. In 1989, the couple separated. In 1994, Earl petitioned for a divorce but Dorothy contested the petition.

It was January 21, 1995, when Dorothy Joudrie took a handgun and shot Earl Joudrie six times. The motivation for the shooting was unclear. Abuse early in the marriage? Loss of marital status? Or some other reason? Dorothy had no memory of the shooting. Three psychiatrists told the court that Dorothy was in a dissociative state at the time of the shooting. One psychiatrist for the Crown, Dr. Arboleda-Florez, stated that Dorothy was in an automatistic state at the time of the shooting. There are two types of automatism: sane and insane. Dorothy's state was determined to be insane automatism (more about this distinction in the main text). The jury of 11 women and 1 man reached the same conclusion, returning a "not criminally responsible on account of mental disorder" decision. Dorothy Joudrie was ordered to undergo a psychiatric assessment. Dorothy spent five months in a psychiatric facility after the verdict and then was given an absolute discharge. The Joudries were divorced in 1995.

Source: Adapted from Nemeth, 1996.

If the judge decides that the condition is the result of an external factor, the defence can argue noninsane automatism. The judge and/or jury will need to decide whether the defendant acted involuntarily. If so, the defendant will be found not guilty. If the judge decides that the condition is the result of a mental disorder, the defence can argue insane automatism, and the case proceeds as an NCRMD case. The NCRMD standard as outlined in section 16 of the Canadian Criminal Code must be met. A successful defence in this situation would result in an NCRMD verdict.

Canadian courts have recognized defences of noninsane automatism in the following circumstances:

- A physical blow (e.g., a blow to the head)
- Physical ailments, such as stroke

## Can Insults Lead to Automatism?

There was no question that Bert Stone stabbed his wife 47 times (R. v. Stone, 1999). He was holding a hunting knife and his wife was dead in her seat. His defence was that his behaviour was not under his control. Stone argued that when he stabbed her, he was in an automatistic state that was triggered by his wife's insults. After Stone stabbed his wife, he got rid of the body, cleaned up, left a note for his stepdaughter, and then checked into a hotel. Later, he sold his car and flew to Mexico. It was here that he woke up one morning to a feeling of having his throat cut. While trying to remember this bad dream, he remembered stabbing his wife two times. After about six weeks, Stone returned to Canada and gave himself up to police. He was charged with murder. Stone was found guilty and sentenced to seven years in prison.

- Hypoglycemia (e.g., low blood sugar)
- Carbon monoxide poisoning
- Sleepwalking
- Involuntary intoxication
- Psychological blow from an extraordinary external event that might reasonably be expected to cause a dissociative state in an average, normal person

It is important to note that everyday life stresses that may lead to a dissociative state would not be sufficient for a defence of automatism. Dissociative states from psychological factors, such as grief and mourning or anxiety, are more consistent with diseases of the mind and may be applicable for the insanity defence.

## How Do NCRMD and Automatism Differ?

The main difference between defences of NCRMD and automatism lies in their verdict outcomes. An NCRMD verdict may result in the defendant being sent to a mental health facility. In contrast, a successful (noninsane) automatism verdict means that the defendant is not guilty and is then released without conditions. Insane automatism verdicts result in an NCRMD ruling. The defendants in these cases are subject to the same dispositions as those with a successful NCRMD defence.

## Intoxication as a Defence

One evening, Mr. Daviault brought a 40-ounce bottle of brandy over to Ms. X's home at her request (*R. v. Daviault*, 1994). X was 65 years old and partially paralyzed. She was confined to a wheelchair. X had a half glass of brandy and fell asleep in her wheelchair. During the middle of the night, she awoke to go to the bathroom, at which point Daviault sexually assaulted her and left the apartment. X noticed that the bottle of brandy was empty. Daviault had drunk the remainder of the bottle; he was an alcoholic. During the trial proceedings, Daviault stated that he had had seven or eight bottles of beer earlier that day. Although he remembered having a glass of brandy when he arrived at X's, he did not remember what happened afterward and that he awoke naked in X's bed. He denied sexually assaulting her.

A pharmacologist testified for the defence and stated that "an individual with this level of alcohol in his blood might suffer an episode of 'L'amnesie-automatisme,' also known as a blackout. In such a state the individual loses contact with reality and the brain is temporarily dissociated from normal functioning. The individual has no awareness of his actions when he is in such a state and will likely have no memory of them the next day" (*R. v. Daviault*, 1994, para. 73).

The judge found that the defendant committed the offence but, because of the level of intoxication, found that he did not have the intent to commit the act. Daviault was found not guilty. On appeal, the court reversed the judge's decision, entering a guilty verdict for Daviault. The appeal court stated that self-induced intoxication resulting in a state similar to automatism is not available as a defence for a general intent offence—that is, an offence that requires only an intention to commit the act. Moreover, in 1995 Bill C-72 was passed, which stated that intoxication was not recognized as a defence for violent crimes.

As you can see, automatism is not a straightforward defence. It is a challenge to prove and may result in variable verdicts. Until legislation can clarify this defence, there will remain ambiguity in the use and success of this defence.

## DEFENDANTS WITH MENTAL DISORDERS

If a defendant does not receive an unfit finding or an NCRMD verdict, this does not necessarily mean that he or she does not have mental health difficulties. In a Canadian study examining males from the Edmonton Remand Centre, Bland, Newman, Dyck, and Orn (1990) found that 92% of the sample had a lifetime prevalence of psychiatric disorders (see Table 8.4). To give you a comparison, in 2002, (in Canada) approximately 10% of the general population reported mental health problems (Statistics Canada, 2003). In 2006 to 2007, 10% of incarcerated offenders were found to have a mental disorder at the time of admission (Public Safety Canada Portfolio Corrections Statistics Committee, 2007). A substantial number of offenders in the United States also have mental health needs. For example, 25% of offenders incarcerated in Colorado suffer from mental illness (O'Keefe & Schnell, 2007). Also, it is important to note that mentally ill offenders are likely to have more than one mental health issue. It is estimated that approximately 75% of mentally ill offenders (in the United States) have dual diagnoses (Chandler, Peters, Field, & Duliano-Bult, 2004).

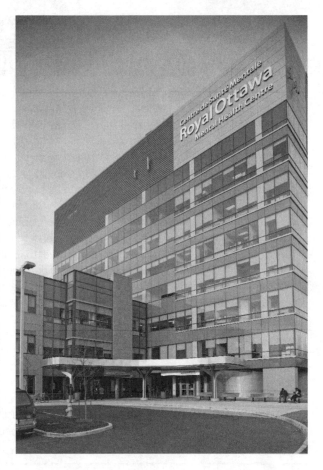

Royal Ottawa Mental Health Centre

Recently, the issue of what to do with mentally ill offenders has been in the Canadian media. See the In the Media box for a discussion of what to do with offenders who have mental illness but do not meet criteria for unfitness or NCRMD.

**Table 8.4** Prevalence Rates of Psychiatric Disorders in an Edmonton Sample of Defendants

| Type of Mental Disorder | Rate |
| --- | --- |
| Substance abuse | 87% |
| Antisocial personality disorder | 57% |
| Affective disorder | 23% |
| Anxiety/somatoform disorders | 16% |
| Schizophrenia | 2% |

Source: Bland et al., 1990.

## What to Do with Mentally Ill Offenders?

What happens to offenders who do not meet criteria to be considered unfit or NCRMD? Currently, inmates who are mentally ill are segregated from other offenders. Segregation is used if inmates are suicidal or at risk of seriously injuring themselves. Recently however, the Correctional Service of Canada has taken steps to change this. Howard Sapers, Canada's federal prison ombudsman, stated that, "The practice of confining mentally ill offenders to prolonged periods of isolation in austere conditions with limited meaningful social interaction must end." (as quoted in Quan, 2010). Sapers also noted that the Correctional Service of Canada has hired outside experts to examine the practice of segregating mentally ill offenders. Sapers would like to see alternatives to segregation for those who are mentally ill.

Offenders who experience acute mental illness are sent to one of five regional psychiatric hospitals in Canada. Unfortunately, there are virtually no options if an offender does not meet hospital admission criteria but suffers mental illness. Sapers has suggested the development of intermediate-care units that would be located within the prison to offer offenders a therapeutic setting.

Correctional Service of Canada is investigating this option. Moreover, they are looking into a computerized intake system that would allow offenders who need mental health services to be identified earlier and easier.

Intriguingly, Vic Toews, the Minister of Public Safety has stated that, "Although we've taken significant steps to improve services for the mentally ill in our corrections system, prisons should not be relied on to provide treatment for mental illness" (quoted in Quan, 2010).

Interest in these issues follows an investigation report in 2008 regarding the death of Ashley Smith who died from self-asphyxiation while in custody in a prison in Kitchener, Ontario. The report found that Smith, who was 19 years old at the time of her death, did not receive proper mental health services and was placed in solitary confinement for the entire time she was in custody (11.5 months). The report noted that the prison staff did not adequately respond to her needs, which often resulted in medical emergencies.

Source: Quan, D. (2010, March 25). Stop isolating mentally ill inmates: Ombudsman. *Canwest News Service*. Retrieved from http://www.globalmontreal.com/health/ Stop+isolaing+mentally+inmates+Ombudsman/2726481/ story.html?hub=WFive

## Why Are There Such High Rates of Mental Illness in Offender Populations?

A variety of explanations have been postulated to understand the high rates of mental illness in offender populations in Canada (Bland et al., 1990):

1. Individuals with a mental illness are likely to be arrested at a disproportionately high rate compared with those who do not have a mental illness.

2. Individuals with a mental illness are less adept at committing crime and therefore more likely to get caught.

3. Individuals with a mental illness are more likely to plead guilty, possibly because of an inability to access good representation or to understand the consequences of their plea.

In 2004, the Canadian Mental Health Association suggested that individuals with mental health issues are likely to be detected and arrested for nuisance offences such as trespassing and disorderly conduct, and are more likely to be remanded into custody for these minor offences.

It is possible that all these explanations are appropriate. Moreover, there may be alternative explanations to the high rates of mental illness in offender populations that have yet to be articulated. Further research is needed to explain this phenomenon.

# Dealing with Offenders Who Are Mentally Ill

Police have great latitude in how they deal with offenders who are mentally ill in the community. Provincial and territorial mental health legislation grants police two options for handling these offenders. If an individual has a mental disorder and poses a threat to him- or herself or to others, the police may bring the individual to a hospital or a mental health facility for assessment and possible treatment. As an alternative, the police may charge and arrest the individual. In this scenario, mental health services may be obtained through the criminal justice system. Thus, the mental health system and the criminal justice system are both available to police, providing two alternative routes for dealing with people with a mental illness. Some have argued that people with mental illnesses are more likely to be processed through the justice system because of the difficulty of obtaining services for them through the mental health system (Teplin, 1984).

# Bias against Mentally Ill Offenders

As part of a Canadian national study examining mental health problems in federally incarcerated offenders, Porporino and Motiuk (1995) compared 36 male offenders meeting criteria for a mental disorder (e.g., mania or schizophrenia) with 36 male offenders not meeting these criteria. The two groups were similar on a number of variables, including age, type of crime committed, and history of criminal activity. The researchers were interested in the conditional release patterns for both groups. Specifically, they wanted to know whether offenders with a mental illness were treated differently.

Offenders can receive a conditional release from a federal facility in Canada in two ways: parole or mandatory supervision. Parole is determined by a parole board and is dependent on eligibility criteria. Ultimately, the National Parole Board has discretionary power in whether parole is granted. In contrast, mandatory supervision occurs after serving two-thirds of a sentence.

Porporino and Mortiuk found that a similar proportion of offenders from both groups (67% of those with a mental disorder versus 75% of those without one) received conditional releases. However, the reason for granting a conditional release differed across the two groups. Offenders with mental disorders were more likely to be conditionally released as a result of mandatory supervision, whereas offenders who did not have a mental disorder were more likely to be conditionally released because of parole.

Moreover, the researchers found that the offenders with mental disorders were more likely to have their release suspended (e.g., for not abiding by their supervision order) compared with other offenders. The offenders without mental disorders were likely to be re-admitted for committing a new offence.

In one study, individuals with mental illness, according to police records, were twice as likely to be at risk for coming back into contact with the criminal justice system compared with other offenders (Hartford, Heslp, Stitt, & Hoch, 2005). Thus, offenders with mental disorders may be treated cautiously by the criminal justice system because of a presumption that they are a greater risk for committing more crime. Is this presumption correct?

In a six-year follow-up study, Teplin, Abram, and McClelland (1994) examined the relationship between post-release arrest rates for violent crime and mental disorders. Offenders with either schizophrenia or a major affective disorder had a 43% likelihood of re-arrest. Those with substance abuse had a similar re-arrest rate of 46%. Moreover, offenders with a prior history of violent crime were twice as likely to be re-arrested as those with no prior history. Offenders with a history of hallucinations and delusions (i.e., schizophrenia symptoms) were not more likely to be subsequently arrested. As you can see, a number of factors can be related to rates of re-arrest, not just mental illness.

## Are People with Mental Illnesses Violent?

A commonly held belief is that those who have a mental illness are violent predators. Does the research support this view? Two epidemiological surveys were conducted to examine the relationship between violence and mental disorders. In a Canadian study conducted in Edmonton, violence referred to physical acts, such as fist fighting and using weapons (Bland & Orn, 1986). Mental disorders included antisocial personality disorder, major depression, and alcohol/drug dependence. Approximately 55% of respondents who met criteria for a psychiatric diagnosis committed violent acts. In contrast, only about 16% of respondents who did not meet criteria for a psychiatric diagnosis engaged in violent behaviour. When respondents met criteria for two diagnoses—for example, alcoholism and antisocial personality disorder and/or depression—80% to 93% of these respondents committed violent acts. Similar results were found in a sample from the United States (Swanson, Holzer, Ganju, & Jono, 1990). Over 50% of the U.S. respondents who met criteria for a psychiatric disorder committed violent acts. In both studies, substance abuse increased the risk of engaging in violence.

Examining a European sample, Hodgins (1992, 1993) reviewed the criminal and mental health records of approximately fifteen thousand 30-year-olds born in Stockholm, Sweden, in 1953. Persons who had been admitted to mental health facilities were classified according to their most serious diagnosis. For example, participants were grouped according to whether they had a major mental disorder, such as schizophrenia or an alcohol and/or drug abuse or dependency, or another mental disorder. Hodgins found that individuals with a major mental disorder, especially those individuals with a substance abuse or dependency, were significantly more likely to have committed a crime than those without a mental disorder. However, most persons with a major mental disorder who committed offences committed them before the age of 18, before the symptoms of the major mental disorder would have been present. Thus, these results cast doubt on the notion that major mental illness precipitates violence.

Cirincione, Steadman, Clark-Robbins, and Monahan (1992) examined the degree to which a diagnosis of schizophrenia was predictive of violence, after controlling for arrest history. Two cohorts, one from 1968 and one from 1978, in a New York State psychiatric facility were reviewed. Results differed across cohorts. Prior arrest was a significant predictor of violence in both cohorts. A schizophrenia diagnosis was predictive of violence in the 1968 cohort but not in the 1978 cohort. For those without a history of prior arrest, a diagnosis of schizophrenia did not predict engaging in later violence. This research indicates that prior violence and substance abuse seem to have much greater effects on the likelihood of future violence than psychiatric diagnoses, such as schizophrenia.

A meta-analysis examining the recidivism of more than 15 000 mentally disordered offenders was conducted by Bonta, Law, and Hanson (1998). The disordered offenders were followed for an average of 4.8 years in the community after having been released from prisons and hospitals. Mentally disordered offenders were found less likely to recidivate

## A Violent Crime Committed by a Mentally Ill Man

On July 30, 2008, 22-year-old Tim McLean boarded a Greyhound bus in Edmonton on his way home to Winnipeg. McLean put his headphones on and fell asleep in one of the bus seats. A man named Vincent Li sat beside him. While McLean was asleep, Li started stabbing him with a hunting knife. He then beheaded and cannibalized McLean. Who could commit such a horrific, violent act? Li was a 40-year-old who had immigrated to Canada from China in 2001. He had worked at a number of jobs—for example, he had worked as a contractor, a newspaper deliverer, and a fast-food employee. Li had no previous criminal record. Li was charged with second-degree murder and his trial started on March 3, 2009, with Li pleading not criminally responsible on account of mental disorder.

According to a psychiatrist who testified, Li was a schizophrenic who heard a voice telling him to kill. Li was found to suffer hallucinations even though he was on medication. Li was found NCRMD and was sent to a high-security mental health facility for a year. After that time, he will be re-assessed.

McLean's mother has created the deDelley Foundation for Life to change criminal law. She wants people who voluntarily take someone else's life to lose their freedom for the rest of their lives, regardless of whether they are declared not criminally responsible.

Sources: McIntyre, M. (2009, March 5). Victim's family incensed as beheading killer avoids jail time. *National Post*. Retrieved from http://www.nationalpost.com/related/topics/story.html?id=1356797; Suspect in bus killing delivered newspapers, worked at McDonald's: employer (2008, August 1). *CBC News*. Retrieved from http://www.cbc.ca/canada/story/2008/08/01/stabbing-victim.html

violently than offenders who did not have major psychological or psychiatric disorders. The researchers suggest that some data finds a greater likelihood of violence when an individual is experiencing a psychotic phase with symptoms of a paranoid nature. Overall, the notion that people with mental illness are more violent may not be a completely accurate view. However, see Box 8.6 for an example of an extremely violent crime committed by a mentally ill individual.

## Types of Offences Committed by People with Mental Illnesses

Rice and Harris (1990) compared three groups of offenders: a group of males found NCRMD, a random group of convicted offenders who were sent for pretrial psychiatric evaluations, and a group of convicted offenders who were matched on the offence committed. The researchers found that NCRMD defendants were more likely to have committed murder or attempted murder than the other groups. Overall, however, offenders with mental disorders committed a variety of crimes, such as fraud, shoplifting, and murder. In other words, mentally disordered offenders were similar to other offenders and not distinguishable based solely on offence type (Rice & Harris, 1997b).

## Recidivism Rates and People with Mental Illnesses

To determine whether offenders with mental disorders are more likely to reoffend, Rice and Harris (1992) examined 96 NCRMD defendants who were diagnosed with schizophrenia and 96 nonschizophrenic offenders. The two groups were matched on age, offence, and criminal history. The schizophrenics were less likely, although not significantly so, to violently reoffend than were the nonschizophrenics. In another study using some of the same participants as in the Rice and Harris (1992) examination, 210 NCRMD defendants were compared on post-release recidivism to a matched convicted group (Rice & Harris, 1990). The NCRMD defendants had lower rates of both general and violent recidivism than the convicted offenders. It appears that, compared with other offenders, those with a major mental illness are not more likely to commit future crimes, especially violent crimes. Rice has conducted considerable research with mentally disordered offenders. See Box 8.7 to learn more about Rice and her work.

## Treatment of Offenders with Mental Disorders

The goals for treatment for offenders with mental disorders vary greatly and are somewhat dependent on whether the offender is dealt with through the mental health system or the criminal justice system. Some of the treatment goals identified for those with mental disorders include symptom reduction, decreased length of stay in the facility, and no need to be re-admitted to hospital (Test, 1992). Of course, reducing the risk of recidivism has garnered much attention as a treatment goal among those in the criminal justice system (Lipsey, 1992).

There are a number of types of facilities at which mentally disordered offenders can receive treatment: psychiatric institutions, general hospitals, and assisted housing units. There appears to be little agreement on which type of treatment is appropriate for offenders with mental disorders (Quinsey & Maguire, 1983). However, for those who experience active psychotic symptoms, such as delusions, hallucinations, suspicion, and noncompliance with medication, there are two key treatment options: antipsychotic drugs and behaviour therapy (Breslin, 1992). Medication can help to control psychotic symptoms, while behaviour therapy can help to ensure that patients take the medication consistently. The critical aspects of behaviour therapy appear to be in providing positive social and material reward for appropriate behaviour, while decreasing or eliminating attention for symptomatic behaviour (Beck, Menditto, Baldwin, Angelone, & Maddox, 1991; Paul & Lentz, 1977).

The availability of facilities and the treatment programs offered vary across the country. Moreover, the willingness of an offender to engage in a particular program will vary. Even if an offender is motivated to receive treatment, an appropriate program may not be available at a particular facility. Thus, there are difficulties in matching programs to offenders' needs and willingness to participate.

One overarching treatment goal of many offender programs is to reintegrate the offender into society. The mental health and criminal justice system has developed options with this goal in mind. For example, a **community treatment order** allows the offender who has a mental illness to live in the community, with the stipulation that he or she will agree to treatment or detention in the event that his or her condition deteriorates. Another option for the courts dealing with offenders with mental illnesses who are facing minor charges is **diversion**—that is,

**Community treatment order:** Sentence that allows the mentally ill offender to live in the community, with the stipulation that the person will agree to treatment or detention in the event that his or her condition deteriorates

**Diversion:** A decision not to prosecute a young offender, but rather have him or her undergo an educational or community-service program. Also an option for the courts dealing with offenders with mental illnesses who are facing minor charges. The court can divert the offender directly into a treatment program rather than have him or her go through the court process

Mental Health Centre Penetanguishene

diverting them directly into a treatment program rather than having them go through the court process. Generally, only defendants who are willing to participate in treatment will be diverted.

Treatment can be critical for offenders who have certain mental disorders, such as schizophrenia.

## Box 8.7

# Canadian Researcher Profile: Dr. Marnie Rice

Dr. Marnie Rice completed her undergraduate degree with a major in psychology from McMaster University. She completed an M.A. at the University of Toronto and then moved to York University to complete a Ph.D. Dr. Rice's doctoral research focused on vicarious reinforcement learning in preschool children. Dr. Rice states, "I was very interested in how it was that children learned so much by imitation. I found evidence that supported my hypothesis that humans are 'prepared' to learn vicariously. Research on 'preparedness' was a precursor of my later work on evolutionary psychology."

In 1975, Dr. Rice started working as a clinical psychologist at the Oak Ridge Division of the Mental Health Centre in Penetanguishene. Although she wasn't initially drawn to this position of working with adult male patients in a maximum security hospital, she was interested in using her knowledge in applied behavioural analysis. Some 35 years later, Dr. Rice is still there! In 2002, Dr. Rice took advantage of an early retirement opportunity, although she never really intended to retire. Dr. Rice has been working part-time as a researcher in the Research Department at Mental Health Centre Penetanguishene since 2002.

Dr. Rice's current areas of research are practically the same as they've always been: violence risk assessment for offenders, mentally disordered offenders, and sex offenders.

More recently, domestic assaulters have also become a population of interest for Dr. Rice. The study of psychopathy and evolutionary explanations of human violence are also long-term research interests of hers. Dr. Rice's interest in working with forensic populations came as soon as she started working at Mental Health Centre Penetanguishene. She notes that it seemed like a natural fit to do research that could eventually help to improve the assessment and treatment of the sorts of patients at the hospital. Along with Drs. Vern Quinsey and Grant Harris, she continues to work on these issues today. Dr. Rice's interest is maintained by continuing to discover findings that allow her to refine the problem and ask new and more sophisticated questions. "Sometimes our findings confirm what we thought, but other times they force us to rethink our hypotheses. It's still very exciting to me," states Dr. Rice.

Dr. Rice has two favourite studies: (1) an evaluation of a maximum security therapeutic community (Rice, Harris, & Cormier, 1992) "because the results surprised me"—for example, this study found that a treatment program actually made psychopathic offenders worse rather than better (to learn more about psychopathy see Chapter 11)—and (2) an evaluation of the effects of a staff training program to reduce the amount and seriousness of violence in the hospital (Rice, Helzel, Varney, & Quinsey, 1985) because it had a positive effect on violence at the hospital and (with some modification) is still in use today at a number of hospitals.

On a personal note, Dr. Rice has always tried to balance her professional life with her home life and leisure time. She enjoys spending time with her two children. She also takes time to participate in outdoor activities to clear her mind. Whenever possible, Dr. Rice loves to travel, especially to developing countries. She finds that travelling allows her to return to work renewed and refreshed. Overall, Dr. Rice notes how extremely grateful she is for the opportunities she has had.

# A NEW COURT FOR THE MENTALLY ILL: THE MENTAL HEALTH COURTS

A new court is in town, designed for those in need of fitness examinations and criminal responsibility assessments, guilty pleas, and sentencing hearings. These courts, known as mental health courts, have been emerging across Canada since the mid-1990s (Bloom & Schneider, 2007). These courts attempt to redirect those with mental health needs back into the mental health care system rather than the criminal justice system. Mental health courts have four main objectives (Schneider, Bloom, & Heerema, 2007):

1. To divert accused who have been charged with minor to moderately serious criminal offences and offer them an alternative
2. To facilitate evaluation of a defendant's fitness to stand trial
3. To ensure treatment for a defendant's mental disorders
4. To decrease the cycle that mentally disordered offenders experience by becoming repeat offenders

In general, mental health courts offer a rehabilitative reaction to behaviour that would otherwise have been dealt with through the criminal justice system. Alternatives to serving a sentence in prison for less serious offences, such as theft, shoplifting, property damage, and minor assaults, are available. One goal for these courts is to ensure that defendants and offenders receive the proper assessments and treatments. The courts make referrals to medical experts, as well as case workers who help to develop a "release plan" (e.g., provide clothes, find housing, and select treatment options) once the accused is in the community. Mental health courts can be found in a number of communities across Canada, including those in Saskatchewan, Ontario, and Newfoundland and Labrador.

## Are Mental Health Courts Effective?

At the outset, it must be noted that little research has been conducted to evaluate mental health courts. What we do know is that there is a lot of variability across different courts. For example, courts may differ on how defendants are referred, the criteria for a defendant's eligibility, and the quality and quantity of services available. It also appears to be the case that defendants going through mental health courts are more likely to be connected to services than those not going through such a court (Schneider, Bloom, & Heerema, 2007). Those having gone through the mental health system also report being more satisfied with the process and perceiving higher levels of fairness, lower levels of coercion, and increased confidence with the administration of justice. As for whether recidivism rates are lower for those going through these courts, the data are not yet in. We will have to wait to see what the research says.

## SUMMARY

1. A defendant is found to be unfit if he or she is unable, because of a mental disorder, to understand the nature of the proceedings, to understand the consequences of the proceedings, or to communicate with counsel. Bill C-30 in 1992 legislated the length of time a defendant could be held in custody for a fitness evaluation.

2. Compared with fit defendants, unfit defendants are more likely to be unemployed and living alone, and are less likely to have ever been married. They also tend to be older females belonging to a minority group who have fewer marital resources, and they are more likely to have met criteria for a psychotic disorder. Defendants who are found fit are about as likely to have been diagnosed with a psychotic disorder as not. Also, unfit defendants are less likely to have problems with substance abuse than fit defendants.

3. The term used for Canada's insanity standard is *not criminally responsible on account of mental disorder* (NCRMD). The defendant is not criminally responsible for an act that was committed (or omitted) while he or she was suffering from a mental disorder to the extent that he or she could not appreciate the nature or quality of the act or of knowing that it was wrong.

4. Automatism is defined as unconscious, involuntary behaviour. Canadian courts have recognized factors such as a physical blow, carbon monoxide poisoning, and sleep-walking as defences for automatism.

5. A number of explanations have been suggested for the high rates of mental illness in offender populations. For example, individuals with a mental illness may be less adept at committing crime and, therefore, more likely to get caught.

6. Treatment goals for offenders with mental disorders vary greatly. Some goals are symptom reduction, decreased length of stay in the facility, no need to be re-admitted to hospital, and reduced recidivism.

## Discussion Questions

1. As part of your summer internship program at the courthouse, the judge has asked you to review the cases heard over the past year and identify the ones in which noninsane automatism was used as a defence. Describe some factors that may lead to automatism which may come up in the cases you will review.

2. While having dinner with your parents, your father mentions an article that he read in the newspaper highlighting the dangerousness of offenders with mental disorders. He makes the inference that mental illness leads to violent offending. Describe the data that calls your father's conclusion into question.

3. When you show up for your social psychology class, you are informed that the professor has been arrested for voyeurism. When she was arrested, she was confused and incoherent. She is scheduled to undergo a fitness to stand trial evaluation. Your friends mention that they heard a rumour about the professor having some sort of mental illness. Describe the characteristics associated with unfit defendants and the process your professor will undergo following an unfit determination.

4. You have been hired by the police department to help police quickly identify those who may need psychiatric services—that is, those who should not be processed through the criminal justice system. Develop a brief checklist for police to use when they come in contact with disorderly individuals so that they can take the most appropriate action.

# Chapter 9

## Sentencing and Parole in Canada: Practices and Public Opinions

## Learning Objectives

- Describe the structure of the Canadian court system, including Aboriginal courts.

- List the primary purposes and principles of sentencing.

- Describe the various sentencing options available in Canada.

- Define the term *sentencing disparity* and explain how it can be studied.

- List the principles that form the basis for effective correctional interventions.

- Describe some of the myths associated with parole decision making.

In an Edmonton courtroom, Jamie Harrison was just found guilty of breaking and entering, and Judge Singh, who presided over the case, has made the difficult decision to incarcerate Jamie for his crime. In part, the decision was based on the seriousness of the crime—more than $10 000 worth of valuables was stolen from the property Jamie burglarized—but it didn't help that this was not Jamie's first crime.

In fact, starting from a very young age, Jamie has had a lot of encounters with the police and he has a long criminal record to show for it. Most of his crimes have involved property offences, but he has also been charged with a serious assault and drug possession. Jamie has also been incarcerated on several other occasions, and he has always managed to find trouble very quickly upon his release.

Given all these facts, Judge Singh feels he has few options for Jamie. He is not confident that prison will turn Jamie's life around, but given the seriousness of the crime and Jamie's constant reoffending, he thinks that prison is probably the best place for him. Judge Singh also hopes that a prison sentence will send a message to other criminals in the community that the sort of behaviour exhibited by Jamie will not be tolerated by the criminal justice system.

Throughout this chapter, we will discuss sentencing and parole of adult offenders in Canada by focusing on some of the issues raised in the opening vignette. We will first describe the structure of the Canadian court system and discuss the sentencing process, focusing specifically on the purposes and principles that guide sentencing decisions and the various sentencing options available to Canadian judges like Judge Singh. Our attention will then turn to one of the major problems that can result from this process and various solutions that have been proposed to solve this problem. Specifically, we will focus on the sentencing disparity that can often result from the high degree of discretion Canadian judges have when deciding on appropriate sentences. We will finish our discussion of sentencing by reviewing research that examines whether the goals of sentencing are actually achieved. We will then move on to describe in some detail the parole process as it is commonly practised by Canada's National Parole Board. We will focus our attention on how parole decisions are made and on research that looks at the effectiveness of these decisions. To conclude the chapter, we will present research findings that deal with Canadians' perceptions toward sentencing and parole and discuss where these perceptions might come from.

# THE STRUCTURE OF THE CANADIAN COURT SYSTEM

The Canadian court system is one component of the larger Canadian criminal justice system that includes policing agencies and correctional institutions. Some of the major roles of courts in Canada include hearing evidence presented at trial, determining guilt and innocence, and rendering sentencing decisions across a wide range of criminal and civil cases. In this chapter, we will focus on the sentencing aspect of the Canadian court system. However, before we do that, we will first briefly discuss the structure of our court system in Canada.

As illustrated in Figure 9.1, the court system in Canada is relatively complex in that it is made up of numerous types of courts that are separated by jurisdiction and levels of legal superiority (Horner, 2007). In terms of jurisdiction, courts in Canada can be split into provincial/territorial courts and federal courts. Canadian courts can be conceptualized as forming a four-tier hierarchy of legal superiority; the ones at higher levels of the

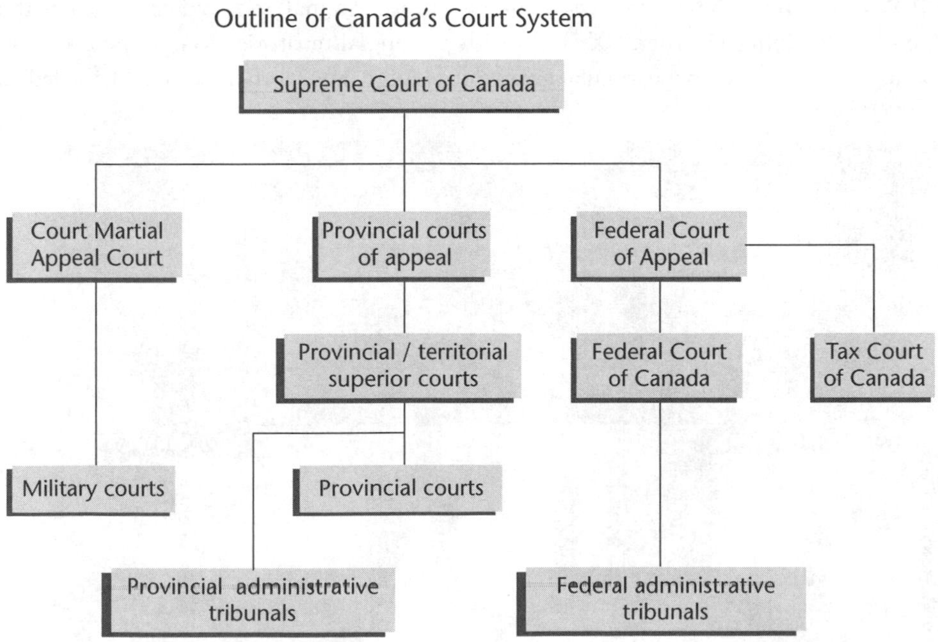

Outline of Canada's Court System

**Figure 9.1** The Canadian Court System

Source: Department of Justice Canada (DOJ), 2010.

hierarchy possess more legal authority than courts at lower levels. By this, we mean that Canadian courts are essentially bound by the rulings of courts positioned above them in the hierarchy (Horner, 2007).

The bottom layer of Figure 9.1 represents administrative tribunals. These tribunals resemble courts in a variety of ways, but they are not officially part of the Canadian court system (DOJ, 2010; Horner, 2007). These tribunals are responsible for resolving disputes over a wide range of administrative issues in both provincial/territorial and federal jurisdictions (e.g., disability benefits). One example of a provincial administrative tribunal is the Liquor Licensing Board. An example at the federal level is the National Parole Board, which will be discussed at the end of this chapter.

Thus, the lowest level of the *actual* court hierarchy in Canada consists of provincial/territorial courts, sometimes referred to as "inferior" courts, which can be found in all provinces and territories with the exception of Nunavut (Nunavut has its own Nunavut Court of Justice, which basically combines the power of the inferior and superior courts; DOJ, 2010). The range of cases heard in these courts is broad and can include criminal offences (e.g., traffic violations) and civil issues (e.g., small claims) (DOJ, 2010). In addition, a number of courts at this level of the hierarchy specialize in particular areas (e.g., drug treatment courts; Horner, 2007). Furthermore, provincial/territorial courts can hear appeals from administrative tribunals. Military courts, which will not be discussed in detail here, deal with offences committed by members of the Canadian Armed Forces (including civilians who work for the Canadian Armed Forces) under the National Defence Act.

The next level up in the court system hierarchy in provincial/territorial jurisdictions includes provincial/territorial "superior" courts. One of the primary roles of these courts is to act as the court of first appeal for courts at the lowest level of the hierarchy (DOJ, 2010). In addition, these courts try the most serious criminal and civil cases—cases that often involve juries (Horner, 2007). As with provincial/territorial courts, these superior courts often specialize in a particular area (e.g., family law) (Horner, 2007). At the federal

The Supreme Court of Canada in Ottawa

level, the court at this position in the hierarchy is referred to simply as the Federal Court of Canada. This court primarily serves to review administrative decisions made by federal administrative tribunals (e.g., related to matters such as immigration). A specialized court in the federal system, the Tax Court of Canada, deals with tax disputes between the federal government and Canadian taxpayers (DOJ, 2010).

Above these courts in the hierarchy can be found the provincial courts of appeal and the Federal Court of Appeal (the Court Martial Appeal Court hears appeals from military courts). The function of these courts is to review decisions rendered by the superior-level courts. Unlike superior-level courts, however, appellate courts do not normally conduct trials or hear evidence from witnesses (Horner, 2007).

Finally, at the top of the court hierarchy in Canada is the **Supreme Court of Canada** (SCC), which was created in 1875 (SCC, 2010). The SCC is the final court of appeal in Canada. However, before the SCC will hear an appeal, the case must typically have been appealed in the relevant courts lower in the hierarchy—and even then, people still have limited rights to appeal to the SCC (Horner, 2007). The SCC also provides guidance to the federal government on law-related matters (e.g., interpretation of the Canadian Constitution). The SCC consists of eight judges plus the chief justice (currently Beverley McLachlin). These judges are all appointed by the federal government.

**Supreme Court of Canada:** Created in 1875, the Supreme Court of Canada consists of eight judges plus the chief justice, who are all appointed by the federal government. The Supreme Court is the final court of appeal in Canada, and lower Canadian courts are bound by its rulings. The Supreme Court also provides guidance to the federal government on law-related matters, such as the interpretation of the Canadian Constitution

## Aboriginal Courts

Although Figure 9.1 captures the basic structure of Canada's court system, it is important to highlight a number of issues related to Aboriginal offenders in Canada and to examine how these issues have had an impact on our court system. Perhaps the most important issue that needs to be discussed is the disproportionate involvement of Aboriginals in the Canadian criminal justice system, or **Aboriginal overrepresentation** (LaPrairie, 1996; Rugge, 2006).

Despite attempts to reduce the problem, Aboriginal offenders are still greatly overrepresented in our criminal justice system. For example, according to 2006 census data, Aboriginal people make up about 3.1% of the general population in Canada (Perreault, 2009). However, in 2007/2008, "Aboriginal adults accounted for 17% of adults admitted to remand, 18% admitted to provincial and territorial custody, 16% admitted to probation, and 19% admitted to a conditional [community] sentence" (Perreault, 2009). As can be seen in Figure 9.2, Aboriginal overrepresentation is a problem across Canada, although it is more of a problem in certain regions (i.e., the Prairie provinces; Trevethan, Moore, & Rastin, 2002).

**Aboriginal overrepresentation:** The discrepancy between the relatively low proportion of Aboriginal people in the general Canadian population and the relatively high proportion of Aboriginal people involved in the criminal justice system

Much effort has gone into understanding the potential causes of Aboriginal overrepresentation, and several factors appear to contribute to the overrepresentation problem:

1. Existing data suggests that Aboriginal people may commit more crimes than non-Aboriginal people (Brzozowski, Taylor-Butts, & Johnson, 2006) and that the crimes they commit may be of a more serious nature (i.e., crimes that are more likely to result in sentences of incarceration; Quann & Trevethan, 2000).

2. Aboriginal people appear to be processed by the criminal justice system in a different way than non-Aboriginal people, potentially indicating the presence of systemic (and perhaps overt) racism (Rudin, 2006). For instance, access to adequate legal representation appears to be more problematic for Aboriginal people involved in the criminal justice system (Aboriginal Justice Inquiry of Manitoba, 2009).

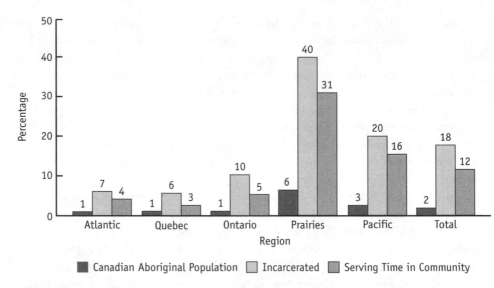

**Figure 9.2** Proportion of Aboriginal Offenders Serving Time in Federal Prisons and in the Community

Source: Trevethan, Moore, & Rastin, 2002.

3. On average, Aboriginal people in Canada are more economically disadvantaged than non-Aboriginal people (Weinrath, 2007). Because of this, criminal justice policies and practices, such as fining offenders, appear to have a differential impact on offenders. For example, it is known that Aboriginal people are more likely than non-Aboriginal people to be serving time in prison for fine defaults (Haslip, 2001).

For our purposes, rather than focusing on why Aboriginal offenders are overrepresented in the criminal justice system, we will focus on some of the things being done in Canada to reduce this problem; specifically things being done to the Canadian court system (see LaPraire, 1996, and Rudin, 2006, for a discussion of why Aboriginal overrepresentation might exist). Of particular importance is legislation that has been proposed and passed by the federal government to deal with the Aboriginal overrepresentation problem and court rulings that have provided guidance in how this legislation should be interpreted.

Perhaps no other piece of legislation is more important to discuss than Bill C-41, which was passed by Parliament in 1996. Bill C-41 discusses the principles and purposes of sentencing in Canada, and it introduced new sentencing options, such as the conditional (community) sentence. In section 718.2 of Bill C-41, which deals with the use of incarceration, the government included the qualification "all available sanctions other than imprisonment should be considered for all offenders, *with particular attention to the circumstances of Aboriginal offenders*" (italics added; R.S.C., 1985, s. 718.2[e]). As discussed by Roberts and Melchers (2003), that section of Bill C-41 has been interpreted by the Supreme Court of Canada in *R. v. Gladue* (1999) as an attempt to "ameliorate the serious problem of over-representation of Aboriginal people in prisons" (para. 93).

One significant result of this Supreme Court ruling has been the development of courts in Canada that focus on processing Aboriginal offenders. For reasons discussed in Box 9.1, some of these courts are known as Gladue Courts. In a Gladue court, special cultural considerations and adverse background conditions are taken into account when

## The Gladue Court

In the trial of *R v. Gladue*, Jamie Tanis Gladue pleaded guilty to the manslaughter of her common-law husband whom she suspected was cheating on her. Although Gladue was Cree, the trial judge did not consider her Aboriginal status as an important factor at sentencing. For her sentence, Gladue received three years in prison. The case proceeded through the British Columbia Court of Appeal and then to the Supreme Court of Canada.

On April 23, 1999, the Supreme Court of Canada released its decision in *R. v. Gladue*, stating that section 718.2 of the Criminal Code should change the way judges approach the sentencing process. The Court stressed that prison terms were being relied on too often in Canada as a way of dealing with criminal behaviour, especially when it came to Aboriginal offenders.

Following this ruling, Canadian judges expressed concern over how the Gladue decision should be applied. Judges had concerns about whether the courts had the time or expertise to deal with the special circumstances of Aboriginal offenders. In response to these concerns, it was proposed that a special court be developed, the Gladue Court, as a way of addressing the special circumstances of Aboriginal offenders.

The Gladue Court, located in Toronto, is now available to all Aboriginal people whose cases would normally have gone through the Old City Hall Courts in Toronto. Currently, the Gladue Court performs the same activities as the Old City Hall Court: It accepts guilty pleas, sentences offenders, and does bail hearings. The difference is that the people working in the Gladue Court have an in-depth understanding of the background of Aboriginal offenders, as well as the culturally appropriate programs and services available to these individuals.

Source: Aboriginal Legal Services of Toronto, 2001.

assessing the case of the Aboriginal person on trial, which may work to mitigate or reduce the culpability of the offender. These factors can include, but are not limited to, issues related to substance abuse, poverty, exposure to abuse, lack of employment, loss of identity, culture, or ancestral knowledge, and attendance at a residential school (Law Courts Education Society of B.C., 2009).

Consideration of Gladue factors will sometimes result in the application of a **restorative justice** approach to sentencing in order to heal those affected by the criminal act, instead of using prison as a deterrent (Law Courts Education Society of B.C., 2009). More consistent with Aboriginal culture, restorative justice "responds to a criminal act by putting the emphasis on the wrong done to a person as well as the wrong done to the community" (Serin et al., 2009, p. 115). As the graphic in Figure 9.3 makes clear, the goal is typically for the victim of a crime, the offender, and members of the community to voluntarily meet in an attempt to restore the imbalance that was caused by the crime. The primary objectives are to prevent further damage from occurring (community safety), to ensure that the offender is made responsible for the crime and "repays" the victim and/or the community (accountability), and to provide the offender with whatever he or she needs (e.g., with respect to skill development) to become a law-abiding citizen in the future (competency development).

**Restorative justice:** An approach for dealing with the crime problem that emphasizes repairing the harm caused by crime. Based on the philosophy that when victims, offenders, and community members meet voluntarily to decide how to achieve this, transformation can result

## SENTENCING IN CANADA

Probably the most visible and controversial component of the court system in Canada is the sentencing process, which is defined as "the judicial determination of a legal sanction upon a person convicted of an offence" (Canadian Centre for Justice Statistics, 1997).

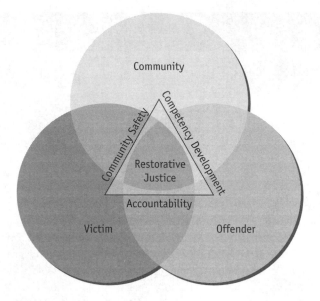

**Figure 9.3** The Concept of Restorative Justice

Source: Department of Juvenile Justice, 2010.

According to Roberts (1991), the sentencing process is highly visible because, unlike the majority of decisions made in the criminal justice system, sentencing decisions are made in the open and presented before the court. The sentencing process is highly controversial because of the great number of problems that can potentially result from the sentencing process, such as issues with sentencing effectiveness (Roberts, 1991). As a result, the sentencing process in Canada has been the subject of extensive research.

## The Purposes of Sentencing

To understand the sentencing process in Canada, we must begin by discussing the reasons that we sentence offenders. Perhaps the most obvious goal of sentencing is to change the behaviour of convicted offenders and the behaviour of potential offenders who reside in the community. More specifically, offenders are sentenced to reduce the probability that they, and the rest of the community, will violate the law (referred to as **specific deterrence** and **general deterrence**, respectively). One of the reasons that sentencing attracts so much attention from forensic psychologists is that psychologists are interested in understanding human behaviour and how that behaviour can be changed (Roberts, 1991). The area of sentencing provides fertile ground for psychologists to explore many issues.

    As made clear in the Criminal Code of Canada, judges also sentence offenders for many other reasons. For example, as stated in section 718 of the Criminal Code, the fundamental purpose of sentencing is to contribute to respect for the law and the maintenance of a just, peaceful, and safe society by imposing sanctions on individuals who commit crimes. Other objectives include the following:

- To denounce unlawful conduct
- To separate offenders from society

**Specific deterrence:** Sentencing to reduce the probability that an offender will reoffend in the future

**General deterrence:** Sentencing to reduce the probability that members of the general public will offend in the future

- To assist in rehabilitating offenders
- To provide **reparations** for harm done to victims or the community
- To promote a sense of responsibility in offenders

**Reparations:** A sentence where the offender has to make a monetary payment to the victim or the community. See *restitution* on page 238

At present, it is not clear if one of these sentencing goals is any more dominant than another. The following facts, however, are clear:

1. Judges often consider more than one goal when handing down a sentence. For example, an offender may be sentenced to prison to reduce the probability that he or she will commit another crime and to separate that offender from society.

2. These goals can, at times, be incompatible with one another. For example, handing down a long prison sentence will separate an offender from society. However, as will be discussed later in this chapter, long sentences may not be an effective way of rehabilitating an offender (i.e., reducing the probability that they will reoffend in the future).

3. Different judges across Canada likely hand down sentences for different reasons, even when dealing with offenders and offences that are similar. For example, under similar circumstances, one judge may hand down a sentence that he or she feels promotes a sense of responsibility in the offender, while another judge may hand down a sentence primarily intended to deter the general public from violating the law.

## The Principles of Sentencing

Just as there are numerous reasons for imposing sanctions on offenders, there are also numerous sentencing principles in Canada, which are meant to guide sentencing decisions. Again, these are laid out explicitly in the Criminal Code. The **fundamental principle of sentencing**, as defined in section 718.1 of the Criminal Code, is that a sentence must be proportionate to the gravity of the offence and the degree of responsibility of the offender. Thus, when handing down a sentence in Canada, judges should consider the seriousness of the specific offence in addition to any other factor that might relate to the offender's degree of responsibility, such as the offender's age at the time of the offence.

Beyond this fundamental principle, however, the Criminal Code also consists of other sentencing principles. For example, section 718.2 indicates that when handing down sentences judges should take into account the following principles:

- A sentence should be adjusted to account for any relevant aggravating or mitigating circumstances relating to the offence or the offender. For example, if the offender abused a position of authority when committing his or her offence, this should be considered.
- Sentences should be similar for similar offenders committing similar offences under similar circumstances.
- Where consecutive sentences are imposed, the combined sentence should not be unduly harsh.
- An offender should not be deprived of liberty (e.g., imprisoned) if less restrictive sanctions are appropriate under the circumstances.
- If reasonable, sanctions other than imprisonment should be considered for all offenders.

**Fundamental principle of sentencing:** The belief that sentences should be proportionate to the gravity of the offence and the degree of responsibility of the offender

# Sentencing Options in Canada

**Restitution:** A sentence where the offender has to make a monetary payment to the victim or the community

**Fine:** A sentence where the offender has to make a monetary payment to the courts

**Community service:** A sentence that involves the offender performing a duty in the community, often as a way of paying off a fine

**Conditional sentence:** A sentence served in the community

**Imprisonment:** A sentence served in prison

In addition to the purposes and principles of sentencing, Canada's Criminal Code also describes the various sentencing options available for particular offences and the maximum (and minimum) penalties that can be handed down. However, while the Criminal Code provides a general framework for making sentencing decisions, judges still have a great deal of discretion. For example, while it may be possible to sentence a petty criminal to prison, it is highly likely that some other sentencing option will be used instead, such as a fine. Indeed, Roberts and Birkenmayer (1997) found that judges in Canada rarely provide the maximum penalty that is prescribed in the Criminal Code for any offence. For example, the maximum penalty for breaking and entering in Canada is life in prison, but the median sentence length reported by Roberts and Birkenmayer for Canadian judges was just three months' imprisonment. Box 9.2 provides a detailed description of some of the sentencing options available to judges in Canada.

## Box 9.2

## Sentencing Options in Canada

Depending on the offence being considered, judges in Canada have many sentencing options available to them Some of these options include the following:

- *Absolute or conditional discharge.* Canadian judges have the option to impose an absolute discharge or conditional discharge. When making this decision, judges will consider whether a discharge would be in the best interest of the offender and the community. If an offender is given an absolute discharge, that person is released and is free to do as he or she wishes in the community. An offender who is given a conditional discharge will have to follow certain rules in the community for a specified period of time in order for the discharge to become absolute. If the offender breaks these rules, he or she can serve time in prison. The important point about a discharge, which makes it different from, say, a conditional sentence (see below) is that the accused is not convicted of an offence, despite being found guilty of the offence, and therefore he or she is spared the stigmatizing consequences of a criminal record.

- *Restitution.* **Restitution** is a payment made by an offender to the victim to cover expenses resulting from a crime, such as monetary loss resulting from property damage. When someone is injured, restitution can be used to cover medical bills and lost income.

- *Fines and community service.* The most common sentencing option in Canada is the **fine**. A court that fines an offender will set the amount of the fine, the way the fine is to be paid, and the time by which the fine must be paid. In many cases, the offender will be able to pay off the fine by performing **community service**. If an offender, without a reasonable excuse, does not pay the fine, then he or she can serve a term of imprisonment.

- *Conditional sentence.* A **conditional sentence** is a prison sentence served in the community. This sentencing option was introduced to Canada only in 1996 as part of Bill C-41. An offender serving a conditional sentence is released into the community and must follow a set of rules for a specific period of time. The prison sentence is suspended as long as the offender abides by these rules. If an offender breaks these rules, he or she may be required to serve the remainder of the sentence in prison.

- *Imprisonment.* **Imprisonment** is a last resort reserved for situations in which less restrictive sanctions are inappropriate. For summary (i.e., less serious) offences, the maximum term of incarceration is six months. For indictable (i.e., more serious) offences, the term of incarceration varies by offence and can include life imprisonment. Offenders sentenced to prison terms of less than two years serve their sentences in provincial or territorial prisons. Sentences of two or more years are served in federal penitentiaries.

Source: John Howard Society, 1999.

In addition to the options discussed in Box 9.2, Canadian judges have a number of additional options open to them when handing down sentences of imprisonment, especially for high-risk offenders. One of these options is to declare the offender a **dangerous offender**. The prosecution can submit a dangerous offender application to the court for any offender convicted of a serious personal injury offence who constitutes a danger to others (John Howard Society, 1999). According to the Criminal Code, the determination of dangerousness in these cases is based on evidence that one of the following conditions is met:

1. The offender exhibits a pattern of unrestrained behaviour that is likely to cause danger.
2. The offender exhibits a pattern of aggressive behaviour with indifference as to the consequences of this behaviour.
3. The offender exhibits behaviour that is of such a brutal nature that ordinary standards of restraint will not control it.
4. The offender shows a failure to control sexual impulses that are likely to harm others.

If someone receives the dangerous offender designation, that person can be imprisoned for an indefinite period of time.

Alternatively, prosecutors can submit an application to the court to have an offender designated as a **long-term offender**. Based on the description provided in section 753.1 of the Criminal Code, any offender who meets the following criteria can be designated a long-term offender:

1. It would be appropriate to impose a sentence of two years or more for the offence.
2. There is a substantial risk that the offender will reoffend.
3. There is a reasonable possibility of eventual control of risk in the community.

A long-term offender will be given a sentence of imprisonment of at least two years, followed by a period of supervision in the community (John Howard Society, 1999).

**Dangerous offender:** A label attached to offenders who are proven to constitute a significant danger to others

**Long-term offender:** A label attached to offenders who are proven to be a high risk for reoffending

## Factors That Affect Sentencing Decisions

As indicated above, the Criminal Code highlights various factors that should be taken into account when judges decide on sentences in Canada. These include the seriousness of the offence, the offender's degree of responsibility, various aggravating and mitigating factors, the harshness of the sentence, and so forth. According to Roberts (1991), some researchers suggest that these legally relevant factors can explain most of the variation that occurs in sentencing decisions across judges (e.g., Andrews, Robblee, & Saunders, 1984). This clearly is as it should be. However, other researchers argue that many judges appear to rely on extra-legal factors (i.e., factors that have little to do with the crime) when making their sentencing decisions, which is cause for concern.

For example, an important study by Hogarth (1971) found that "only about 9% of the variation in sentencing could be explained by objectively defined facts, while more than 50% of such variation could be accounted for simply by knowing certain pieces of information about the judge himself" (p. 382). Likewise, in a more recent study, Ulmer (1997) found that a variety of extra-legal factors influence sentencing even when relevant factors, such as crime seriousness and prior criminal history, are held constant. Some of these

Steve Patterson, a young man of 26, has pleaded guilty to robbery. Late one night, Steve entered a local grocery store. Pointing a plastic replica gun at the cashier, Steve demanded that he hand him all the money from the cash register. Steve ran out of the store with over $500 in cash, but the police picked him up later that night.

This is the first time Steve has ever been charged with a crime. For the last four years, he had been working as a forklift driver, but he was recently laid off from the company because it went bankrupt. Steve tells the court he robbed the store to buy food for his wife and newborn child. He pleads with the judge to spare him from prison and states that his wife and child depend on him.

### Your Turn . . .

If you were the judge presiding over this case, what sort of sentence do you feel Steve should receive? What factors would you consider when determining an appropriate sentence and why? What goals would you try to achieve by handing down your sentence and how confident would you be that those goals would actually be achieved?

factors included the gender and race of the defendant (e.g., in Pennsylvania, males and blacks were approximately 50% more likely than women and whites to be incarcerated for their crimes).

There are clearly many factors that judges need to consider when making sentencing decisions. Review the case of Steve Patterson in the Case Study box and determine what factors you would consider when handing down a sentence.

## Sentencing Disparity

**Sentencing disparity:** Variations in sentencing severity for similar crimes committed under similar circumstances

**Unwarranted sentencing disparity:** Variations in sentencing severity for similar crimes committed under similar circumstances that result from reliance by the judge on legally irrelevant factors

**Systematic disparity:** Consistent disagreement among judges about sentencing decisions because of factors such as how lenient judges think sentences should be

**Unsystematic disparity:** Inconsistencies in a judge's sentencing decisions over time when judging the same type of offender or crime because of factors such as the judge's mood

One of the reasons that it is important to appreciate the various factors that affect sentencing decisions is so that we can understand **sentencing disparity**. Sentencing disparity is defined as "any difference in severity between the sentence that an offender receives from one judge on a particular occasion and what an identical offender with the identical crime would receive from either the same judge on a different occasion or a different judge on the same or a different occasion" (McFatter, 1986, pp. 151–152). Because sentencing disparity can lead to serious injustices, it is commonly viewed as a major problem within our criminal justice system. Indeed, a number of leading Canadian researchers have proposed that sentencing disparity is one of the most important problems with sentencing (e.g., Roberts, 1991).

**Sources of Unwarranted Sentencing Disparity** The real problem occurs when disparities in sentencing happen because of a reliance on extra-legal factors. In this case, we can refer to the disparity as **unwarranted sentencing disparity** (Roberts, 1991). Unwarranted sentencing disparity can result from many factors, and researchers have attempted to classify these factors into groups. For example, McFatter (1986) discusses two major sources of unwarranted sentencing disparity: **systematic disparity** and **unsystematic disparity**. Systematic

A prison cell in one of Canada's maximum-security prisons

disparity represents *consistent* disagreement among judges about sentencing, such as how lenient they feel sentences should be. Sources of systematic disparity can include differences between judges in terms of their personality, philosophy, experience, and so on.

Unsystematic disparity, conversely, results from a given judge's *inconsistency* over occasions in judging the same type of offender or crime. This type of disparity can also arise from a number of sources, including fluctuations in mood, focusing on irrelevant stimuli, or the way in which the facts of the case are interpreted by the judge on any particular day (McFatter, 1986). Why is it important to understand these different sources of sentencing disparity? As McFatter (1986) suggests, only by understanding the various sources of sentencing disparity can we come up with effective strategies to combat its existence.

**Studying Sentencing Disparity** Researchers in this area typically use one of two procedures to study sentencing disparity—laboratory-based simulation studies (e.g., McFatter, 1986) or the examination of official sentencing statistics in an attempt to uncover variations in judicial sentencing decisions (e.g., Birkenmayer & Roberts, 1997). Of the two procedures, simulation studies are more common so we will focus our discussion on this procedure. In a simulation study, researchers present mock judges, or real judges, with the details of a trial, and the researcher manipulates particular variables of interest, such as the defendant's age, ethnicity, or gender. The goal is to manipulate these variables while attempting to control for as many other variables as possible, so that if evidence for sentencing disparity is found, the researcher can be fairly confident as to what caused it.

The experiment conducted by McFatter (1986) provides an excellent example of a simulation study. He provided six judges with 13 crime and offender descriptions, which included brief details of the crime and the offender's age, prior record, drug use, and

## Table 9.1 Sentencing Severity Scores

| Sentence | Severity Score |
|---|---|
| Fine or suspended sentence | 1 |
| Probation (months) | |
|     1–12 | 1 |
|     13–36 | 2 |
|     Over 36 | 3 |
| Split sentence (jail and probation) | 4 |
| Prison | |
|     1–6 months | 3 |
|     7–12 months | 5 |
|     13–24 months | 7 |
|     25–36 months | 9 |
|     (Add 2 points for every year up to 50 years) | |
|     50 years | 103 |
| Life imprisonment or death | 103 |

Source: Adapted from McFatter, 1986.

employment status. The descriptions were chosen to represent a wide range of typical crimes and offender descriptions. For example, the crimes ranged from a fight that broke out after a minor traffic accident to a rape and murder of an 11-year-old girl. In the first phase of the study, judges were asked to rate various aspects of the crime, such as its seriousness, and to recommend a sentence. Approximately two months later, the judges were given the same crime and offender descriptions and were asked to make ratings and recommend sentences once again. In both phases, the severity of sentences handed down by judges was transformed into numbers by using the scale developed by Diamond and Zeisel (1975), which is provided in Table 9.1.

The raw severity scores for the sentences handed down by the judges in each phase of McFatter's (1986) experiment are presented in Table 9.2. Three interesting things emerge from these data:

1. The results indicate that there is a good deal of agreement among judges about the severity of sentences appropriate for each crime. For example, all six judges consistently handed down very lenient sentences for crime 1 (the fight that resulted from a minor traffic accident), while five of the six judges consistently handed down very serious sentences for crime 13 (the rape and murder of the 11-year-old girl).

2. However, despite these similarities, there are also many instances of unwarranted sentencing disparity. For example, the sentences handed down for crime 9 (an armed robbery that took place on the street) varied drastically across judges, with severity scores ranging from 2 to 53.

3. Most of this disparity appears to come from unsystematic sources. In a large number of cases, the same judge handed down different sentences when presented with the

**Table 9.2** Sentencing Severity Scores for the Judges

| | Judge (Phase) | | | | | | | | | | | |
|---|---|---|---|---|---|---|---|---|---|---|---|---|
| **Crime** | **1(1)** | **1(2)** | **2(1)** | **2(2)** | **3(1)** | **3(2)** | **4(1)** | **4(2)** | **5(1)** | **5(2)** | **6(1)** | **6(2)** |
| 1 | 1 | 1 | 2 | 4 | 2 | 2 | 2 | 3 | 1 | 4 | 1 | 4 |
| 2 | 3 | 2 | 4 | 4 | 1 | 2 | 2 | 2 | 1 | 4 | 3 | 2 |
| 3 | 2 | 1 | 5 | 4 | 4 | 2 | 3 | 4 | 2 | 2 | 2 | 3 |
| 4 | 5 | 5 | 9 | 9 | 3 | 3 | 3 | 3 | 3 | 3 | 2 | 3 |
| 5 | 3 | 3 | 4 | 9 | 4 | 4 | 3 | 4 | 7 | 4 | 7 | 3 |
| 6 | 5 | 2 | 7 | 7 | 4 | 4 | 3 | 3 | 3 | 3 | 3 | 13 |
| 7 | 2 | 4 | 5 | 4 | 3 | 3 | 4 | 5 | 13 | 3 | 4 | 13 |
| 8 | 4 | 3 | 5 | 9 | 23 | 5 | 13 | 4 | 1 | 4 | 4 | 3 |
| 9 | 53 | 39 | 53 | 43 | 2 | 5 | 13 | 5 | 3 | 4 | 13 | 23 |
| 10 | 103 | 103 | 103 | 103 | 5 | 103 | 23 | 23 | 12 | 23 | 103 | 53 |
| 11 | 63 | 103 | 103 | 103 | 103 | 43 | 13 | 13 | 103 | 103 | 13 | 23 |
| 12 | 103 | 103 | 103 | 103 | 103 | 103 | 53 | 103 | 103 | 103 | 103 | 103 |
| 13 | 103 | 103 | 103 | 103 | 103 | 103 | 53 | 103 | 103 | 103 | 103 | 103 |

Source: McFatter, 1986.

same crime and offender after a two-month delay. Indeed, in some cases the degree of disparity was extremely high, as in the case of crime 12 and 13, where judge 4 handed down much more lenient sentences in phase 1 compared with phase 2.

Similar findings have also been reported in simulation studies conducted in Canada (e.g., Palys & Divorski, 1986).

**Reducing Sentencing Disparity** Regardless of how sentencing disparity is studied, the conclusion is often that a reasonably high degree of disparity exists across sentences handed down by different judges considering similar crimes and across sentences handed down by the same judge when considering similar crimes on different occasions. As discussed above, a number of sources can account for this disparity, but ultimately, sentencing disparity exists because the law in Canada allows judges a great deal of discretion when making sentencing decisions. Although sentencing guidelines exist in Canada's Criminal Code, these guidelines are often so broad that they do little to decrease sentencing disparity. For example, as Roberts (1991) points out, "There are over 70 offences contained in the Criminal Code that can be punished by dispositions ranging from a discharge to a sentence of imprisonment of 14 years or life" (p. 471).

Although certain forms of sentencing disparity are probably inevitable, there has been a move within Canada in recent years to try to reduce unwarranted disparity. Just as people debate the extent to which sentencing disparity exists, debates are also ongoing as to how this disparity can best be minimized. The most common approach for reducing sentencing disparity, especially in Canada, is to implement **sentencing guidelines**. These guidelines attempt to provide a more consistent, structured way of arriving at sentencing decisions. Unfortunately, there is little in the way of empirical research to suggest whether

**Sentencing guidelines:** Guidelines that are intended to reduce the degree of discretion that judges have when handing down sentences current sentencing guidelines in this country are effective. Research from other countries produces mixed results, with some studies showing increased sentencing uniformity when using guidelines (e.g., Roberts, 1991) and other studies showing less impressive results (e.g., Wallace, 1993).

## Are the Goals of Sentencing Achieved?

Recall from the beginning of this chapter that sentencing has many different goals. As a result, the question of whether the goals of sentencing are achieved is a difficult one to answer because, to a large extent, the answer depends on what goal we are most concerned with. For some goals, the answer to this question is often "yes." For example, if we sentence an offender to a term in prison, we can be reasonably confident that the offender will be separated from society for a certain period of time. However, with respect to some other goals, the answer is less clear-cut. In particular, there is an ongoing debate as to whether current sentencing practices in Canada achieve the goals of deterring people from committing crimes and whether they assist in the rehabilitation of offenders. Canadian forensic psychologists have played, and continue to play, a crucial role in this debate. See Motiuk and Serin (2001) for an excellent overview of the contributions made by these psychologists.

A great deal of recent research has focused specifically on the effectiveness of "get tough" strategies (Cullen & Gendreau, 2000), which include a range of punishment-based sentencing options, some consisting of incarceration. Other strategies fall under the heading of intermediate strategies, which are less severe than incarceration but more severe than probation (Gendreau, Goggin, Cullen, & Andrews, 2001). Examples would include house arrest, curfews, and electronic monitoring (Gendreau et al., 2001). It has long been assumed that experiencing one of these sanctions would change the antisocial behaviour

Recent research suggests that "get-tough" strategies for offenders, such as incarceration, may not reduce the chance of reoffending

Box 9.3

## The Death Penalty in Canada: Were We Right to Abolish It?

At 12:02 a.m. on December 11, 1962, in Toronto, Arthur Lucas and Robert Turpin were the last people to be executed in Canada. Although the death penalty in Canada was formally abolished in 1976 for offences under the Criminal Code, and in 1999 for military offences under the National Defence Act, there are three very good reasons that it is still important to discuss this issue. The first reason is that, since the time when the death penalty was abolished in Canada, there have been attempts to reinstate capital punishment. Indeed, as recently as 1987, Canadian Members of Parliament voted on the issue in the House of Commons, with a close vote (148 versus 127) in favour of not reinstating the death penalty. The second reason is that these attempts to reinstate the death penalty seem to reflect public opinion on the issue. Although public support for the death penalty has varied over time, recent Canadian polls indicate that the majority of Canadians are in favour of reinstating the death penalty (notably, the 1998 Gallup poll indicates that 61% of Canadians are in favour of the death penalty for murder) (Edwards & Mazzuca, 1998). The third reason, and one that we will explore here, is that most of the research examining the death penalty suggests that it should not be reinstated in Canada. Although many members of the public believe that the death penalty acts as an effective crime deterrent, research does not support this view.

Existing research suggests there are a number of problems with the crime deterrent argument. First, this argument assumes that offenders think about the punishment before acting, which simply does not appear to be the case for the majority of offenders (Benaquisto, 2000). In fact, a very large number of murders are committed in the heat of passion, or under the influence of alcohol or other drugs, with the offenders paying very little attention to the consequences of their crimes. Second, if the death penalty did act as a crime deterrent, we would expect to see an increase in the Canadian murder rate since abolition. However, the murder rate in Canada has generally declined since 1975. Third, the argument that the death penalty ensures that offenders will never murder again is based on the belief that a high proportion of those released will murder again. In fact, as you will see when we get to the section on parole later in this chapter, it is relatively rare for convicted murderers to commit another murder after their release from prison.

Source: John Howard Society, 2007.

of offenders and reduce the likelihood that they will reoffend. However, as is the case with the most serious of sanctions, the death penalty, recent research does not support this hypothesis (Gendreau et al., 2001). See Box 9.3 for a discussion of this issue as it relates to the death penalty.

In a review, Gendreau et al. (2001) examined the rehabilitative and deterrent effect of various community-based sanctions and prison sentences. These researchers used the technique of meta-analysis to summarize findings from research studies that examined the impact of specific sanctions. For our purposes here, the most important measures to focus on from the study are the rate of recidivism for offenders who experienced the sanction, the rate of recidivism for offenders who experienced regular probation (used as a control group), and the average effect size that resulted from a comparison of these two rates. The consideration of effect size is particularly important since this measure summarizes the impact that a particular sanction was found to have across a range of studies. In this case, effect sizes can range from $+1.00$ to $-1.00$, with positive effect sizes indicating that the sanction increased recidivism (i.e., compared with probation, those offenders who received the sanction reoffended at a higher rate) and negative effect sizes indicating that the sanction decreased recidivism (i.e., compared with probation, those offenders who received the sanction reoffended at a lower rate).

**Table 9.3** Effects of Community-Based Sanctions and Incarceration on Recidivism

| Type of Sanction | Sample Size | Average Effect Size |
|---|---|---|
| Supervision program | 19 403 | 0.00 |
| Arrest | 7 779 | 0.01 |
| Fine | 7 162 | −0.04 |
| Restitution | 8 715 | −0.02 |
| Boot camp | 6 831 | 0.00 |
| Scared straight | 1 891 | 0.07 |
| Drug testing | 419 | 0.05 |
| Electronic monitoring | 1 414 | 0.05 |
| More versus less prison | 68 248 | 0.03 |
| Prison versus community | 267 804 | 0.07 |

Source: Adapted from Gendreau et al., 2001.

Based on the results from this study, it must be concluded that there is very little evidence that community sanctions lead to substantial decreases in recidivism rates (compared with regular probation). Indeed, most of the average effect sizes listed in Table 9.3 are positive, indicating that, on average, the particular sanctions listed in this table resulted in moderate increases in recidivism. Only two sanctions (fines and restitution) resulted in average effect sizes that were negative, and in these cases, the observed decrease in recidivism rates was very small (−0.04 and −0.02, respectively). In addition, this study found that sanctions consisting of incarceration also had little impact on recidivism. In fact, longer periods of incarceration led to slightly higher rates of recidivism across the studies that were examined (+0.03). In addition, those offenders who were sent to prison for brief periods of time also exhibited higher rates of recidivism compared with offenders who received a community-based sanction (+0.07).

## What Works in Offender Treatment?

So, given these results, does this mean that nothing can be done to deter or rehabilitate offenders? Historically, some researchers have taken the view that nothing will work with offenders (most notably Martinson, 1974), but new research suggests that this is not the case. In fact, Canadian researchers have led the way in establishing principles of effective correctional intervention, and a growing body of research is beginning to show the value of these principles (Andrews & Bonta, 2006). Although quite a large number of principles are emerging as potentially important (Andrews, 2001), we will focus on three that appear to be particularly valuable in determining which correctional interventions will be effective.

The first of these principles is known as the **need principle**. It states that effective intervention will target known criminogenic needs (i.e., factors that are known to contribute to reoffending), including (1) antisocial attitudes, beliefs, and values, (2) antisocial associates, (3) antisocial personality factors (such as impulsivity, risk-taking, and low self-control), and (4) antisocial behaviours (Cullen & Gendreau, 2000).

**Need principle:** Principle that correctional interventions should target known criminogenic needs (i.e., factors that relate to reoffending)

The second principle is known as the **risk principle**. It states that effective interventions will focus on those offenders who are at high risk of reoffending (Cullen & Gendreau, 2000). Not only are low-risk offenders unlikely to reoffend, but also their chances of reoffending may actually increase if exposed to an intervention, because of the fact that they will be brought into contact with people who hold antisocial attitudes (Andrews, 2001).

**Risk principle:** Principle that correctional interventions should target offenders who are at high risk to reoffend

The third principle is known as the **responsivity principle**. It states that effective interventions will match the general learning styles, motivations, and abilities of the offender being targeted as well as more specific factors such as the offender's personality, gender, and ethnicity (Cullen & Gendreau, 2000).

**Responsivity principle:** Principle that correctional interventions should match the general learning style of offenders

The often-cited meta-analytic study conducted by Andrews, Zinger, Hoge, Bonta, Gendreau, and Cullen (1990) was one of the first attempts to determine whether interventions with a wide range of juvenile and adult offenders, which consist of these core principles, do in fact lead to reductions in recidivism. These researchers examined 80 program evaluation studies and coded the interventions in each study as appropriate, inappropriate, or unspecified. Interventions were defined as appropriate if they included the three principles of effective intervention described above (most of these programs involved the use of behavioural and social learning principles, which included techniques such as behavioural modelling, rehearsal, role-playing, and reinforcement). Interventions were coded as inappropriate if they were inconsistent with these principles (many of these programs were based on get-tough or psychodynamic strategies). Interventions were coded as unspecified if they could not be categorized as appropriate or inappropriate because of a lack of information. The hypothesis in this study was that offenders exposed to appropriate interventions would exhibit lower rates of recidivism compared with offenders exposed to inappropriate interventions. This is exactly what was found. Offenders taking part in appropriate programs exhibited a decrease in recidivism, whereas offenders taking part in inappropriate programs exhibited an increase in recidivism. Offenders taking part in unspecified programs exhibited a decrease in recidivism, though less of a decrease compared with offenders in appropriate programs. Since this study, this same general pattern of results has been found on numerous occasions, for various offending groups (e.g., Andrews, Dowden, & Gendreau, 1999; Antonowicz & Ross, 1994; Pearson, Lipton, & Cleland, 1996).

In conclusion, then, it does appear that something can be done to deter and rehabilitate offenders. By focusing on current research in the area of forensic psychology, interventions can be developed that significantly reduce the chance that offenders will go on to commit further crimes. Certainly, this does not suggest that all new sentencing options will be effective, since many of these new options will not be consistent with the principles of effective correctional programming. However, a number of options have been developed—many in Canada—that do correspond with these principles. Early indications suggest that they hold promise for achieving some of the goals of sentencing that we discussed at the beginning of this chapter (Motiuk & Serin, 2001).

## PAROLE IN CANADA

Ever since August 11, 1899, when Parliament enacted the Ticket of Leave Act, **parole** has played an important part in the history of criminal justice in Canada. Sir Wilfrid Laurier, the prime minister at the time, recognized the value of actively reintegrating certain

**Parole:** The release of offenders from prison into the community before their sentence term is complete

offenders into society as soon as possible to enhance their chances of rehabilitation (NPB, 2010a). Indeed, he even went so far as to describe the sort of offender that the Act was meant for:

> . . . a young man of good character, who may have committed a crime in a moment of passion, or perhaps, have fallen victim to bad example, or the influence of unworthy friends. There is a good report on him while in confinement and it is supposed that if he were given another chance, he would be a good citizen. (NPB, 2010a)

Since the time of Laurier, many things about parole have changed, but the essence of parole remains the same. Notably, parole still involves (1) the conditional release of offenders into a community so they can serve the remainder of their sentences outside an institution, (2) an attempt to rehabilitate offenders so they can become productive contributors to society, (3) a high degree of community supervision to ensure the parolee is abiding by certain rules, and (4) a clause that, if the conditions of parole are not complied with, an offender's parole can be revoked and he or she can be sent back to prison.

## Parole Decision Making

Although the essence of parole may be similar to what it was a century ago, parole decision making has changed drastically. Compared with how parole decisions were once made, the decision-making process is now far more complex and objective. The process that currently exists is more complex because of the range of information that is considered when making parole decisions and because of the way in which that information is evaluated. The process is more objective because, unlike parole decisions made in the past, where an elected member of government was responsible for the decision, parole decisions are now made by a group of individuals forming Canada's **National Parole Board** (NPB). The process that the NPB goes through when making its decisions is open to scrutiny by the public because members of the public are allowed to attend and observe parole hearings and to request copies of written parole board decisions (NPB, 2010b). See Box 9.4 for more information about the NPB.

So, how are parole decisions made? In Canada, an offender must usually serve the first third of their sentence or the first seven years, whichever is less, before being eligible for full parole. Most parole decisions are made after a formal hearing with the offender. When making their decisions, NPB members carefully review the risk that an offender might present to society if he or she is released. According to the NPB (2010d), this involves an initial risk assessment where the following issues should be considered:

- Information about the offender's current offence
- The offender's criminal history
- Social problems experienced by the offender, such as drug use and family violence
- The offender's mental status
- Performance on earlier releases
- Information about the offender's relationships and employment history

**National Parole Board:** The organization in Canada responsible for making parole decisions

Box 9.4

# Myths and Realities Concerning Parole Decision Making

The general public has many misconceptions when it comes to issues of parole, and the NPB continually strives to correct them. The following list provides some of the myths people adhere to, along with the correct information provided by the NPB.

**Myth 1: Parole reduces the sentence imposed by the courts.**

Parole does not reduce the sentence imposed by the courts; it affects only the way in which a sentence will be served. Parole allows offenders to serve their sentences in the community under strict conditions and the supervision of a parole officer. If offenders abide by these conditions, they will remain in the community until their sentence is completed in full, or for life in the case of offenders serving life or indeterminate sentences.

**Myth 2: Parole is automatically granted when an inmate becomes eligible for parole consideration.**

Parole is not automatically granted when inmates become eligible. In fact, the NPB denies full parole to approximately six out of ten offenders at their first parole review date.

**Myth 3: The NPB grants parole to offenders who express remorse for the offences they have committed.**

Whether offenders express remorse is only one of the factors the NPB considers. Of greater importance is whether

offenders understand the factors that contributed to their criminal behaviour, the progress they made while incarcerated, and the feasibility of their plans upon release.

**Myth 4: Most of the offenders released on parole are convicted of new crimes.**

Most offenders released on parole successfully complete their sentences without committing new offences or breaching the conditions of their parole.

**Myth 5: Victims do not have a role in the parole process, and their views are not taken into account.**

Victims and their families have a significant role in the parole process. They have the opportunity to present a statement directly to the NPB about any concerns they have for their safety or the safety of the community. In addition, victims may remain in contact with the NPB while the offender is under sentence. Moreover, the NPB allows victims, as well as other members of the public, to observe parole hearings and to request copies of written decisions.

Source: NPB, 2010c.

- Psychological or psychiatric reports
- Opinions from other professionals, such as police officers
- Information from victims
- Any other information indicating whether release would pose a risk to society

  After this initial assessment, the NPB examines specific risk factors, such as

- The offender's institutional behaviour
- Information that indicates evidence of change and insight into the offender's own behaviour
- Benefits derived from treatment that may reduce the risk posed by the offender
- The feasibility of the offender's release plans

The NPB members then decide whether to grant parole.

Importantly, despite the fact that NPB members are instructed to consider all these factors, recent research in Canada indicates that they may not actually consider them when making release decisions. Using hypothetical offender vignettes, Gobeil and Serin (2009) examined the release decisions made by 31 parole board members from Canada and New Zealand. The vignettes summarized the cases of different types of offenders (e.g., a male violent offender, a woman offender, a male Aboriginal offender), while keeping the length of the vignettes constant and incorporating very similar information in each vignette (e.g., risk assessments, correctional staff recommendations, and other information). After reading each vignette, the parole board member was asked to make a release decision or access additional information in one of six areas that is mandated for consideration by parole boards: risk-assessment information, mental health information, victim information, program information, release plan information, and criminal history information. Once parole board members decided not to access any additional information, or after all information had been accessed, they were forced to make a release decision.

The results of Gobeil and Serin's (2009) study indicate that release decisions varied as a function of offender type. For example, "the release rate was considerably higher for the woman offender and sex offender vignettes than for the other vignettes, [whereas] the release rate was notably lower for the Aboriginal offender and domestic violence offender vignettes" (p. 100). Interestingly, these differences were not related to potentially important participant characteristics (e.g., the age, gender, experience, or professional background of the parole board member). In addition, variability was also found to be present in the amount and type of information accessed by the parole board members. For example, information related to risk assessment and release plan was commonly accessed, but not mental health or victim information. This finding is potentially problematic because, as indicated above, parole board members are required to consider these sources of information when making release decisions.

## Types of Parole

In addition to making pardoning decisions (see the In the Media box), the NPB can grant various types of parole to offenders. These include temporary absence, day parole, full parole, and statutory release.

**Temporary Absence** A **temporary absence** is usually the first type of release an offender will be granted (NPB, 2010e). Offenders may be granted unescorted or escorted temporary absences (unescorted absences would typically follow successful escorted absences) so that they can take part in activities such as substance abuse programs, family violence counselling, and technical training courses.

**Day Parole** **Day parole** allows offenders to participate in community-based activities. Offenders on day parole must typically return to their institution or halfway house at the end of the day (NPB, 2010e). Performance on day parole is considered when the NPB reviews an offender's application for full parole.

**Full Parole** **Full parole** allows the offender to serve the remainder of the sentence under supervision in the community. Before an offender is granted full parole, a thorough assessment is done to predict the likelihood of reoffending (NPB, 2010e). Consideration is also

**Temporary absence:** A form of parole that allows the offender to enter the community on a temporary basis (e.g., for the purpose of attending correctional programs)

**Day parole:** A form of parole that allows the offender to enter the community for up to one day (e.g., for the purpose of holding down a job)

**Full parole:** A form of parole that allows the offender to serve the remainder of his or her sentence under supervision in the community

given to what conditions should be implemented to address the chance of risk. To be granted full parole, offenders must usually have been granted (and must have successfully completed) unescorted temporary absences and day parole.

**Statutory Release** By law, most federal inmates must be released with supervision after serving two-thirds of their sentence, which is known as **statutory release** (NPB, 2010e). (Offenders serving life, however, are not eligible for statutory release.) As with full parole, an assessment is done to predict the likelihood of reoffending and consideration is given as to what conditions should be implemented to address the chance of risk.

**Statutory release:** The release of offenders from prison after they have served two-thirds of their sentence

In each of the above cases, the Correctional Service of Canada is responsible for supervising offenders on parole, usually with the assistance of community agencies such as the John Howard Society. If an offender does not abide by the parole conditions, he or she may be returned to prison. The following is a partial list of general parole conditions provided by the NPB:

- Offenders must report to their residences immediately upon release.
- Offenders must report to their parole offices on dates set by their parole officers.
- Offenders must remain in Canada.
- Offenders must obey the law and keep the peace.
- Offenders must inform their parole officers if they come into contact with the police.
- Offenders must advise their parole officers of any changes in address or employment.
- Offenders must not own or possess any weapons.

Other parole conditions may be specific to the crime that the offender was convicted for (e.g., convicted child molesters may be required to avoid contact with children).

## Research on the Effectiveness of Parole

As we noted earlier with regard to sentencing, a great deal of research has examined the effectiveness of parole decision making. In fact, the NPB provides updates on the success of their parolees on an annual basis. Many of the statistics published by the NPB compare the success rates of offenders granted day and full parole to those offenders granted statutory release. Recall that, by law, most federal inmates must be released with supervision after serving two-thirds of their sentence. If the NPB is making effective decisions, we would expect to see higher rates of success for offenders on day and full parole, compared with those who have been granted statutory release. Statistics suggest exactly this.

For example, as indicated in the most recent *Performance Monitoring Report* published by the NPB (2009), offenders who are granted parole based on an assessment of their risk of reoffending, are more likely to complete their supervision period in the community compared with offenders released as a result of statute-based systems. Of course, this is not to say that offenders granted day or full parole never breach the conditions of their paroles or commit further crimes—just that this tends to be the exception rather than the rule.

# To Pardon . . . or Not to Pardon

Graham James is a convicted offender. He was pardoned in 2007.

In case anyone was unaware of the fact before 2010, media stories about Graham James have now made it widely known that in addition to making parole decisions, Canada's NPB is also responsible for making decisions about whether offenders should be pardoned. James, a former junior hockey coach who pled guilty to sexually molesting two of his players, received a pardon in 2007 after serving a 3.5-year prison sentence, but that information was made public only in 2010.

Nearly all offenders can apply to the NPB for a pardon. If granted, a pardon means that information about a person's criminal record is removed from Canada's criminal records database and information about that person's conviction(s) cannot be given out without the approval of Canada's Minister of Public Safety. The purpose of a pardon is to give people a second chance—according to the NPB, a pardon is a way of trying to ensure that a conviction no longer reflects negatively on a person's character. Imagine being an ex-convict who's trying to secure a job and how difficult that task might become if potential employers were able to find out that you have a criminal record (and also how much more likely it might be that you would commit further crimes if you were unable to secure employment). A pardon can help with this because the Canadian Human Rights Act forbids discrimination based on a pardoned conviction.

Of course, assisting with the rehabilitation of offenders is the bright side of pardons. The media has also painted a darker picture. Consider a recent *Maclean's* article written by Michael Friscolanti (April 22, 2010). In his article, Friscolanti discusses pardons given to convicted sex offenders. According to Friscolanti, "over the last two years, 1,554 sex offenders have applied for a pardon [and] only 41 were rejected." He also discusses the fact that, in Ontario, if a convicted sex offender is granted a pardon from the NPB, he or she must be deleted from the Ontario Sex Offender Registry, a computer database, which was initiated in 2001 and is regularly used by the police to identify potential suspects in criminal investigations. Friscolanti reports that, in 2007, 62 convicted sex offenders were removed from that database and that by the end of 2010 an estimated 700 convicted offenders will have been removed. Given these figures, and the negative implications they carry for police investigations, it is perhaps understandable that many people have a problem with the current pardoning process, especially those whose lives have been affected by sex offenders.

So what do you think about pardoning offenders? Should we or should we not grant pardons? Should different rules apply to different offenders?

Sources: CBC News, 2010a; Friscolanti, 2007; NPB, 2010f.

In support of these claims by the NPB, Figure 9.4 provides data relating to the rate of parole revocation for breach of conditions across different types of parole. This graph clearly indicates that, during the period 2004 to 2009, offenders who were granted statutory release were far more likely to have their parole revoked because of a breach of conditions than those on full or day parole were; however, even in the case of statutory release, a large majority of offenders do not breach their conditions.

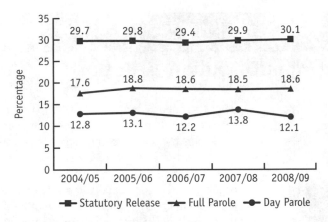

**Figure 9.4** Parole Revocation for Breach of Conditions

Source: NPB, 2009.

A similar picture emerges when we examine the rate of revocation because of non-violent or violent offences. As indicated in Figure 9.5, offenders granted statutory release are again the most likely to have their parole revoked because of the commission of a nonviolent or violent offence; however, even these offenders are unlikely to commit further crimes.

## PUBLIC ATTITUDES TOWARD SENTENCING AND PAROLE

Having examined in some detail the sentencing and parole process in Canada, let us now focus our attention on the attitudes that Canadians have about these processes. Studying these attitudes is important for several reasons. For example, Roberts (2007) highlights the fact that public confidence in the criminal justice system is important to its functioning, in that the system relies on victims reporting crimes to the police and in assisting with the prosecution of accused persons. The general public will carry out these duties only if they have confidence in the criminal justice system.

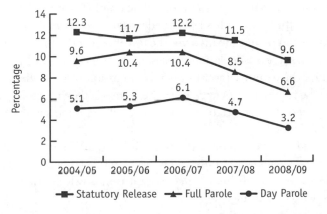

**Figure 9.5** Parole Revocation for Nonviolent and Violent Offences

Source: NPB, 2009.

Box 9.5

# Canadian Researcher Profile: Dr. Julian V. Roberts

Since being a graduate student at the University of Toronto, Dr. Julian Roberts has been interested in what the public thinks about sentencing and other criminal justice issues. In fact, this interest is what led him to the area of sentencing research in the first place. He realized this criminal justice topic was of greatest concern to members of the public. Over the past 30 years, Dr. Roberts has built up a research program around this general issue and has conducted research that is both academically important and practically important in terms of its impact on criminal justice policy.

For example, Dr. Roberts recalls a favourite study he conducted with one of his graduate students. The study examined peoples' attitudes toward community-based punishments, specifically conditional sentences. Respon-

dents to a national survey were asked to read a scenario and sentence the offender. When respondents were simply given the choice between a prison sentence and a community-based sentence, they favoured the prison sentence. However, when they were given specific details of what a conditional sentence entails, the large majority favoured that option, which clearly indicates that public opposition to the conditional sentence reflects a lack of knowledge. Since this study was published in the *Canadian Journal of Behavioural Science* in 2000, it has been cited in numerous legal judgments.

After working in various government agencies, such as the Department of Justice Canada and the Canadian Sentencing Commission, Dr. Roberts is now a professor of criminology at the University of Oxford. He is well known for his research in the area of public attitudes toward criminal justice, especially as those attitudes relate to sentencing. Much of this research is available in the books he has written or co-written, including *Understanding Public Attitudes to Criminal Justice; Public Opinion, Crime, and Criminal Justice; Making Sense of Sentencing;* and *Criminal Justice in Canada: A Reader.* In addition, Dr. Roberts was the editor of the *Canadian Journal of Criminology* for 14 years and is currently the editor of the *European Journal of Criminology.* In 2010, he became the only academic to be appointed to the Sentencing Council of England and Wales.

A fair amount of research has examined public opinion of the criminal justice system in Canada. Much of this research has been conducted by Dr. Julian Roberts, who is profiled in Box 9.5. This research typically involves the use of one of the following research methods: public opinion surveys, simulation studies, or focus groups (in which a small number of people are brought together for an in-depth discussion of their views on a particular topic). Mostly, the results that emerge from these three different approaches are similar, so we will focus our discussion on the results from public opinion surveys because they are the most commonly used.

As summarized by several researchers (e.g., Roberts, 2007; Stein, 2001; Tufts, 2000), a number of general trends can be observed from the results of public opinion surveys. We will provide details of four of the more consistent trends before briefly exploring where these attitudes may come from.

1. Although Canadians often express a lack of confidence in the criminal justice system, more people view it in a positive light than a negative light (Roberts, 2007). For

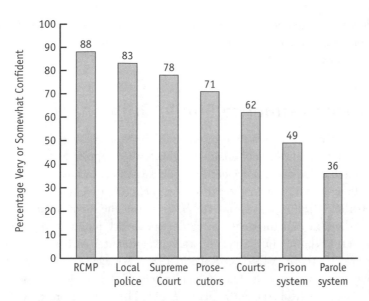

**Figure 9.6** Public Confidence in Different Branches of the Canadian Criminal Justice System

Source: Roberts, 2007.

example, as Roberts highlights, when asked about their confidence in the justice system generally, the majority of Canadians indicate that they have a relatively high degree of confidence. While these views vary somewhat across Canada (Tufts, 2000), Canada fairs reasonably well as a nation compared to other countries (Halman, 2001; cited by Roberts, 2007). For example, according to data provided by Roberts, compared with the attitudes of those in the United States (where 27% have a great deal or quite a lot of confidence in their justice system), we exhibit a greater degree of confidence (57% have a great deal or quite a lot of confidence).

2. This result must be qualified by the fact that Canadians possess different levels of confidence in different branches of the criminal justice system (Roberts, 2007). As indicated in Figure 9.6, respondents to a 2002 Ipsos-Reid survey indicated that Canadians have the most confidence in the police and the least confidence in the prison and parole system. According to Roberts (2007), this particular finding is stable across surveys conducted in Canada, and is also found in public opinion polls conducted in other countries.

3. In part, the findings listed above can be explained by the fact that Canadians think offenders are treated too leniently (Stein, 2001). For example, when respondents are asked about how particular criminal justice institutions deal with offenders, their view is that the courts and the federal government do not treat criminals harshly enough (although people also consistently underestimate how harshly criminals are treated in reality; Doob & Roberts, 1988; Hough & Roberts, 1998). Interestingly, Canadians do not necessarily hold the same view of police agencies, which may indicate, as Stein (2001) argues, that these views are specific to agencies involved in the sentencing process.

4. Canadians support alternatives to prison but only under certain conditions. For example, community-based sanctions are preferred over incarceration for first-time

offenders when offenders are convicted for relatively minor crimes (Tufts, 2000). Even for repeat offenders, Canadians support alternatives to prison, but only for young offenders (Tufts, 2000).

## Factors That Influence Public Opinions

Many researchers have claimed that public opinion on issues of sentencing and parole does not fairly reflect the state of affairs in Canada (e.g., Sprott & Doob, 1997). It has been suggested that this discrepancy between public opinion and reality occurs because of an inadequate understanding on the part of the public of crime and our criminal justice system (Roberts, 2007; Sprott & Doob, 1997). Certainly, the results of public opinion surveys support the idea that the public lacks the knowledge required to develop accurate perceptions of the criminal justice system, as do experimental studies that have looked at this issue more directly (e.g., Doob & Roberts, 1988). For example, a very common finding in public opinion surveys is that the public believe that violent crime in general is increasing in Canada (Roberts, 2007; Stein, 2001). This perception, however, does not correspond to actual crime trends in Canada, which indicate a steady decrease in violent crime (Wallace, 2003).

So, if public opinion is not based on fact, where does public opinion come from? As we have tried to demonstrate in the In the Media boxes you have encountered in each chapter of this textbook, one obvious source of public opinion is the media or, more specifically, the way in which the media portrays criminal justice issues in Canada (Sprott & Doob, 1997). Many studies have shown that the media provide a biased view of our criminal justice system (Doob, 1985), and many researchers hold the view that "members of the public do not adequately correct for the unrepresentative range of cases they hear about in the news media [and] . . . [a]s a result, the negative feelings and perceptions of leniency that the news media create are perpetuated" (Sprott & Doob, 1997, p. 276). The few experiments that have been done to examine media effects on public opinion in the area of sentencing and parole confirm these views (e.g., Doob & Roberts, 1988).

Another factor that may contribute to this discrepancy, particularly the discrepancy between public opinion of sentencing severity and actual sentencing severity, is the fear people have about being victimized. For example, Sprott and Doob (1997) hypothesized that the higher the fear of victimization, the more likely a person will be to view the criminal justice system in a negative light. Their reasoning is that fear of crime may motivate an individual to look to the judicial system for safety. Since the judicial system has been unable to adequately deal with the crime problem, those with the most fear might be more likely to view the courts as being too lenient. Because many Canadians are afraid of being victims of crime (Hung & Bowles, 1995), Sprott and Doob's reasoning leads to an expectation that a large portion of the Canadian public will view the criminal justice as lenient, which is exactly what public opinion surveys indicate. By using pre-existing data, Sprott and Doob (1997) were able to examine the relationship between fear of crime and attitudes toward the criminal justice system. Their results confirmed their hypotheses. Generally, they found that as "level of fear increased, so did perceptions of leniency in sentencing, dissatisfaction with the courts generally, and dissatisfaction with the police" (Sprott & Doob, 1997, pp. 285–286).

# SUMMARY

1. The Canadian court system is one component of the larger Canadian criminal justice system that includes policing agencies and correctional institutions. The court system in Canada is made up of numerous types of courts that are separated by jurisdiction and levels of legal superiority. Courts that are designed to deal specifically with Aboriginal offenders are also part of this system.

2. Sentences are supposed to serve a number of different purposes in Canada. Deterring people from committing crimes and offender rehabilitation are two of the primary purposes. Sentencing in Canada is also guided by numerous principles, such as the fundamental sentencing principle, which states that a sentence must be proportionate to the gravity of the offence and the degree of responsibility of the offender. Such principles are meant to provide judges with guidance when handing down sentences.

3. Judges have many sentencing options at their disposal. The most serious option is imprisonment. New sentencing options have also been recently proposed, such as the conditional sentence, in which an offender can serve his or her prison time in the community.

4. One of the major problems with sentencing in Canada is unwarranted sentencing disparity, which refers to differences in the severity of sentences handed down by different judges (or the same judge on different occasions) because of a reliance on extra-legal factors. These factors can include the judge's personality, philosophy, experience, and so on. One of the primary strategies for reducing sentencing disparity is to implement sentencing guidelines.

5. Research examining the impact of punishment-based sentences suggests they are not effective for reducing recidivism. In contrast, correctional interventions based on core correctional principles show more promise. These principles include the need principle (effective interventions target criminogenic needs), the risk principle (effective interventions target high-risk offenders), and the responsivity principle (effective interventions match the general learning style, and the particular characteristics, of the offender).

6. The NPB makes parole decisions in Canada. Contrary to popular belief, parole is not automatically granted to offenders as soon as they become eligible. Offender remorse plays only a very small part in parole decisions. Most offenders let out on parole do not go on to commit more crimes, and victims do have a significant say in the parole process.

## Discussion Questions

1. In your opinion, should offenders who are convicted of serious crimes, such as sexual assault, ever become eligible for parole? Why or why not?

2. You have just been hired as a research assistant by one of your professors. She is working on a government project looking at ways to deal with sentencing disparity. Together, you and your professor must propose strategies, beyond the sentencing guidelines that currently exist, that could be used to reduce unwarranted sentencing disparity in Canada. What types of strategies would you propose?

3. Your neighbour thinks Canada is getting soft on crime by providing community "rehabilitation" programs. He thinks the only way to really rehabilitate offenders is to lock them up in cells with nothing to do but ruminate on the crimes they've committed. Do you think your neighbour is right? Explain.

4. Recent results from public opinion polls suggest that, even when the public is told that the death penalty has little impact as a crime deterrent, the majority still support the death penalty. Why do you think this happens?

5. Beyond the factors we have discussed in this chapter, what might account for the inaccurate perceptions of the public when it comes to sentencing and parole practices in Canada? What can be done to decrease these inaccurate perceptions?

# Chapter 10
## Risk Assessment

## Learning Objectives

■ Define the components of risk assessment.

■ List what role risk assessments play in Canada.

■ Describe the types of correct and incorrect risk predictions.

■ Differentiate among static, stable, and acute dynamic risk factors.

■ Describe unstructured clinical judgment, actuarial prediction, and structured professional judgment.

■ List the four major types of risk factors.

Jason Marshall and his spouse, Susan, have a history of engaging in verbal and physical violence. When Jason and Susan were living together, their neighbours called the police on three occasions because of domestic violence. Six months ago, the Marshalls separated and are currently involved in a custody dispute regarding their two children. Susan wants to have sole custody, whereas Jason wants to have joint custody. Jason has been emailing and calling Susan constantly, demanding to see his children. For the past two weeks, he has been seen parked outside her new apartment for hours at a time. He left a threatening note on her car windshield, and Susan called the police, indicating she was frightened of what Jason might do to her or their children. The police need to consider what level of risk Jason poses and whether they should charge him with criminal harassment.

Every day, individuals make judgments about the likelihood of events. Predictions are made about being admitted into law school, recovering from an episode of depression, or committing a criminal act after release from prison. Our legal system frequently requires decisions about the likelihood of future criminal acts that can significantly influence the lives of individuals. With the possibility that offenders could spend years or even the remainder of their lives in confinement, decisions by psychologists can have a significant impact. Predicting future violence has been described as "one of the most complex and controversial issues in behavioral science and law" (Borum, 1996, p. 945).

Although it is clear that significant advances have taken place since the 1990s, risk assessment and prediction remains imperfect. Bonta (2002) concludes that "risk assessment is a double-edged sword. It can be used to justify the application of severe sanctions or to moderate extreme penalties. . . . However, the identification of the violent recidivist is not infallible. We are not at the point where we can achieve a level of prediction free of error" (p. 375). Nonetheless, the systematic assessment of risk provides judicial decision makers, such as judges and the National Parole Board (NPB), with much needed information to help them make challenging decisions.

The goal of this chapter is to explore the major issues associated with risk prediction in a forensic context. In particular, the focus will be on understanding the task of assessing risk and predicting violence.

## WHAT IS RISK ASSESSMENT?

In the past two decades, we have seen a change in the way risk is viewed. Prior to the 1990s, risk was seen as a dichotomy—the individual was either dangerous or not dangerous. Nowadays, risk is regarded as a range—the individual can vary in the degree to which he or she is considered dangerous (Steadman, 2000). In other words, the shift has added a dimension of probability to the assessment of whether a person will commit violence. The focus on probability reflects two considerations. First, it highlights the idea that probabilities may change across time. Second, it recognizes that risk level reflects an interaction among a person's characteristics, background, and possible future situations that will affect whether the person engages in violent behaviour.

The process of risk assessment includes both a "prediction" and "management" component (Hart, 1998). The prediction component describes the probability that an individual will commit future criminal or violent acts. The focus of this component is on identifying the risk factors that are related to this likelihood of future violence. The management component describes the development of interventions to manage or reduce the likelihood of

future violence. The focus of this component is on identifying what treatment(s) might reduce the individual's level of risk or what conditions need to be implemented to manage the individual's risk. As described by Hart (1998), "the critical function of risk assessments is violence *prevention*, not violence *prediction*" (emphasis in the original; p. 123).

# RISK ASSESSMENTS: WHEN ARE THEY CONDUCTED?

Risk assessments are routinely conducted in civil and criminal contexts. Civil contexts refer to the private rights of individuals and the legal proceedings connected with such rights. Criminal contexts refer to situations in which an individual has been charged with a crime. Common to both contexts is a need for information that would enable legal judgments to be made concerning the probability of individuals committing some kind of act that would disrupt the peace and order of the state or individuals within the state.

## Civil Setting

A number of civil contexts require risk assessment:

- *Civil commitment* requires an individual to be hospitalized involuntarily if he or she has a mental illness and poses a danger to him- or herself or others. A mental health professional, usually a psychiatrist or psychologist, would need to know the probability of violence associated with various mental symptoms and disorders and be able to identify whether the circumstances associated with individual patients would affect the likelihood that they would harm others or themselves. In Canada, only a psychiatrist can civilly commit someone to a hospital.

- Assessment of risk in *child protection* contexts involves the laws that are in place to protect children from abuse. The risk of physical or sexual abuse or neglect is considered when a government protection agency, such as the Children's Aid Society, decides whether to temporarily remove a child from his or her home or to terminate parental rights. To provide assistance to protection agencies, professionals need to be familiar with the risk factors that predict childhood maltreatment.

- *Immigration* laws prohibit the admission of individuals into Canada if there are reasonable grounds for believing they will engage in acts of violence or if they pose a risk to the social, cultural, or economic functioning of Canadian society.

- *School* and *labour regulations* also provide provisions to prevent any kind of act that would endanger others.

- Other civil contexts include *duty to warn* and *limits of confidentiality*.

Mental health professionals are expected to consider the likelihood that their patients will act in a violent manner and to intervene to prevent such behaviour. The Canadian Psychological Association's Code of Ethics for Psychologists includes a guide to help psychologists decide the most ethical action for any potential dilemma.

## Criminal Settings

The assessment of risk occurs at nearly every major decision point in the criminal justice and forensic psychiatric systems, including pretrial, sentencing, and release. A person can be denied bail if there is a substantial likelihood that he or she will commit another criminal offence. In the case of adolescent offenders, the judge can decide to apply adult criminal sanctions depending on the age, type of offence, and risk level posed by the youth. Risk also plays a role in decisions about whether a youth should be sent to secure custody. For example, adolescent offenders should be committed to secure custody only if they are considered at high risk; if not, they should be placed in open custody or serve a probation term in the community.

An important issue in risk assessment in criminal settings is the disclosure of information about potential risk. This disclosure must be considered in light of the solicitor–client privilege that is fundamental to criminal proceedings. For lawyers to adequately represent their clients, they must be able to freely discuss the case with the clients.

This privilege is also extended to experts retained by lawyers. A case in Canada has clarified when solicitor–client privilege and doctor–patient confidentiality must be set aside for the protection of members of the public. *Smith v. Jones* (1999) involved a psychiatrist who was hired to aid a defence lawyer in preparing a case. The client was a man accused of aggravated sexual assault on a prostitute. The accused told the psychiatrist of his plans to kidnap, sexually assault, and kill prostitutes. The psychiatrist told the defence lawyer about his concerns that the accused was likely to commit future violent offences unless he received treatment. When the psychiatrist found out that the defence lawyer was not going to address his concerns at the sentencing hearing (the accused pled guilty to the charge of aggravated assault), he filed an affidavit providing his opinion about the level of risk posed by the accused. The trial judge ruled that because of concerns about public safety, the psychiatrist was duty-bound to disclose to the police and the Crown counsel the information he obtained. The case was appealed to the Supreme Court, which ruled that in cases where there is "clear, serious, and imminent danger," public safety outweighs solicitor–client privilege (*Smith v. Jones*, 1999, para. 87).

Although risk assessment is a routine component of many sentencing decisions, it is a critical component of certain kinds of sentencing decisions. For example, after 1947, when habitual criminal legislation was introduced, offenders could be sentenced to an indefinite period of incarceration. In 1977, dangerous offender legislation was enacted that requires mental health professionals to provide an assessment of risk for violence. Changes to the legislation in 1997 made indefinite incarceration the only option if an offender is found to be a dangerous offender (see Chapter 9 for more information about dangerous offenders). At the same time, a new category of dangerous persons was created, referred to as long-term offenders. To be declared a long-term offender, a person must pose a substantial risk for violently reoffending. Thus, risk assessment is also a core component of this legislation.

Risk assessment is also required for decisions concerning release from correctional and forensic psychiatric institutions, such as parole. If a person is sentenced to prison in Canada, he or she can apply to the NPB to get early release. Parole Board members use a variety of sources of information (including risk assessments provided by institutional psychologists) to decide the likelihood that the offender will commit another offence if released. Although most offenders get released on statutory release (after serving two-thirds of their sentences), statutory release can be denied if the offender is likely to commit further violent offences. Finally, a patient who has been found not criminally responsible on account of a mental disorder (see Chapter 8) can be released from a secure forensic psychiatric facility only if a risk assessment is completed.

Clearly, risk assessment plays an integral role in legal decision making, both in civil and criminal settings, allowing informed decisions that weigh the likelihood that an individual will engage in a dangerous or criminal act in the future. In the sections that follow, we will look at the predictive accuracy of these assessments, as well as the factors that actually predict violence.

# A HISTORY OF RISK ASSESSMENT

Before 1966, relatively little attention was paid to how well professionals could assess risk of violence. In the 1960s, civil rights concerns provided the rare opportunity to study the accuracy of mental health professionals to predict violence. In the case of *Baxstrom v. Herald* (1966), the U.S. Supreme Court ruled that the plaintiff Johnnie Baxstrom had been detained beyond his sentence expiry and was ordered released into the community. As a result of this case, more than 300 mentally ill offenders from the Dannemora State Hospital for the Criminally Insane and another state hospital were released into the community or transferred to less secure institutions. Steadman and Cocozza (1974) followed 98 of these patients who were released into the community but had been considered by mental health professionals as too dangerous to be released. Only 20 of these patients were arrested over a four-year period, and of these, only seven committed a violent offence.

In a larger study, Thornberry and Jacoby (1979) followed 400 forensic patients released into the community because of a similar civil rights case in Pennsylvania (*Dixon v. Attorney General of the Commonwealth of Pennsylvania*, 1971). During an average three-year follow-up period, 60 patients were either arrested or rehospitalized for a violent incident.

The two studies we have just described are known as the Baxstrom and Dixon studies. These cases and similar ones call into question the ability of mental health professionals to make accurate predictions of violence. Two key findings emerged from the research. First, the base rate for violence was relatively low. For example, in the Baxstrom study, 7 out of 98 (roughly 7%) violently reoffended, as did 60 out of 400 (15%) in the Dixon study. Second, the false positive rate was very high. In the Baxstrom and Dixon studies, the false positive rates were 86% and 85%, respectively. These findings indicate that in the past many mentally disordered forensic patients were needlessly kept in restrictive institutions based on erroneous judgments of violence risk.

Ennis and Litwack (1974) characterized clinical expertise in violence risk assessment as similar to "flipping coins in the courtroom" and argued that clinical testimony be barred from the courtroom. Other researchers have gone even further, concluding that "no expertise to predict dangerous behavior exists and . . . the attempt to apply this supposed knowledge to predict who will be dangerous results in a complete failure" (Cocozza & Steadman, 1978, p. 274).

This pessimism continued into the 1980s. John Monahan, a leading U.S. researcher, summarized the literature in 1981 and concluded that "psychiatrists and psychologists are accurate in no more than one out of three predictions of violent behavior over a several-year period among institutionalized populations that had both committed violence in the past (and thus had a high base rate for it) and who were diagnosed as mentally ill" (Monahan, 1981, p. 47).

Notwithstanding the above conclusion, both Canadian and U.S. courts have ruled that predictions of violence risk do not violate the basic tenets of fundamental justice, nor are they unconstitutional. In *Barefoot v. Estelle* (1983), the U.S. Supreme Court determined the constitutionality of a Texas death-penalty appeal decision. Thomas Barefoot burned down a bar and shot and killed a police officer. Barefoot was convicted of capital murder and, at the sentencing phase of the trial, testimony was presented from two psychiatrists (one being Dr. James Grigson, whom we will discuss later in the chapter) about the threat of future dangerousness posed by Thomas Barefoot. Both psychiatrists testified, based on a hypothetical fact situation, that the individual described would be a threat to society. The judge sentenced Barefoot to death. The U.S. Supreme Court rejected the defendant's challenge that psychiatrists were unable to make sufficient accurate predictions of violence and ruled that the use of hypothetical questions to establish future dangerousness was admissible. The court concluded that mental health professionals' predictions were "not always wrong . . . only most of the time" (p. 901).

Canadian courts have also supported the role of mental health professionals in the prediction of violent behaviour (*Re Moore v. the Queen*, 1984). For example, in a dangerous offender case, the issue of whether psychiatric testimony should be admitted as evidence was evaluated. The court concluded, "The test for admissibility is relevance, not infallibility . . . psychiatric evidence is clearly relevant to the issue whether a person is likely to behave in a certain way" (*R. v. Lyons*, 1987, para. 97).

## TYPES OF PREDICTION OUTCOMES

Predicting future events will result in one of four possible outcomes. Two of these outcomes are correct, and two are incorrect. The definitions provided below are stated in terms of predicting violent acts but could be used for any specific outcome:

**True positive:** A correct prediction that occurs when a person who is predicted to engage in some type of behaviour (e.g., a violent act) does so

**True negative:** A correct prediction that occurs when a person who is predicted not to engage in some type of behaviour (e.g., a violent act) does not

**False positive:** An incorrect prediction that occurs when a person is predicted to engage in some type of behaviour (e.g., a violent act) but does not

**False negative:** An incorrect prediction that occurs when a person is predicted not to engage in some type of behaviour (e.g., a violent act) but does

- A **true positive** represents a correct prediction and occurs when a person who is predicted to be violent engages in violence.

- A **true negative** is also a correct prediction and occurs when a person who is predicted not to be violent does not act violently.

- A **false positive** represents an incorrect prediction and occurs when a person is predicted to be violent but is not.

- A **false negative** is also an incorrect prediction and occurs when a person is predicted to be nonviolent but acts violently.

The two types of errors are dependent on each other. Minimizing the number of false positive errors results in an increase in the number of false negative errors. The implication of these errors varies depending on the decisions associated with them, and in many cases the stakes are high. A false positive error has implications for the individual being assessed (such as denial of freedom), whereas a false negative error has implications for society and the potential victim (such as another child victimized by a sexual offender). In some cases, it is perhaps tolerable to have a high rate of false positives if the consequences of such an error are not severe. For example, if the consequence of being falsely labelled as potentially violent is being supervised more closely while released on parole, the consequence may be acceptable. However, if the consequence of being falsely labelled as potentially violent contributes to a juror's decision to decide in favour of the death penalty, then this price is too high to pay. As in many legal settings, the consequences for the individual must be weighed in relation to the consequences for society at large.

## The Base Rate Problem

A problem with attempting to predict violence is determining base rates. The **base rate** represents the percentage of people within a given population who commit a criminal or violent act. It is difficult to make accurate predictions when the base rates are too high or too low. A problem that emerges when attempting to predict events that have a low base rate is that many false positives will occur. For example, the past decade has seen several high-profile school shootings. However, although these events generate much media coverage, they occur infrequently. Any attempt to predict which individual youths might engage in a school shooting would result in many youths being wrongly classified as potential shooters.

The base rate can vary dramatically depending on the group being studied, what is being predicted, and the length of the follow-up period over which the individual is monitored. For example, the base rate of sexual violence tends to be relatively low, even over extended follow-up periods, whereas the base rate for violating the conditions of a conditional release is very high. The base rate problem is not such a concern if predictions of violence are limited to groups with a high base rate of violence, such as incarcerated offenders. The general rule is that it is easier to predict frequent events than infrequent events.

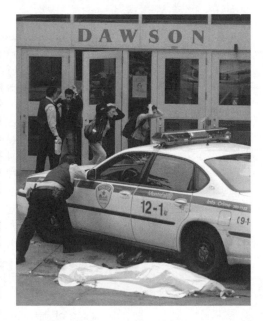

Deadly violence: Students escaping from a school shooter

**Base rate:** Represents the percentage of people within a given population who engage in a specific behaviour or have a mental disorder

## METHODOLOGICAL ISSUES

Risk assessment assumes that risk can be measured. Measurement, in turn, assumes that an instrument exists for the measurement of risk. What would be the ideal way to evaluate an instrument designed to measure risk? The way to proceed would be to assess a large number of offenders and then, regardless of their risk level, release them into the community. The offenders would then be tracked to see if they commit another criminal act. This way, the risk instrument could be evaluated to determine if it could accurately predict future criminal acts. However, although this is an ideal scenario from a research perspective, it is not ethically feasible to release high-risk individuals into the community. In reality, the sample available for evaluating a risk-assessment instrument is limited to those with a relatively low risk of reoffending. This constrains the kinds of conclusions that can be drawn when risk assessment is evaluated in the real world.

Monahan and Steadman (1994) have identified three main weaknesses of research on the prediction of violence. The first issue concerns the limited number of risk factors being studied. Violent behaviour is due to a complex interaction between individual dispositions and situational factors. In other words, people engage in violence for many different reasons. Thus, many risk factors are likely involved, including the person's background, social situation, and biological and psychological features. Many studies have focused on only a limited number of risk factors. Assessment of risk may be improved by measuring more of the reasons why people engage in violence.

The second issue concerns how the criterion variable (the variable you are trying to measure) is measured. Researchers have often used official criminal records as their criterion measure. However, many crimes may never be reported to police. Thus, many false positives may be undiscovered true positives. Even violent crimes may go undiscovered and many violent *sexual* crimes are recorded as simply *violent* in nature. Some research shows that the number of recorded violent crimes of sexual offenders is a better estimate of the number of sexual crimes they may have committed (Rice, Harris, Lang, & Cormier, 2006). In short, use of official records underestimates violence. When official records are combined with interviews with patients or offenders and with collateral reports (information from people or agencies who know the patient or offender), the rate of violence increases. The MacArthur Violence Risk Assessment Study (Steadman et al., 1998) illustrates the effect of using different measures. Using official agency records, the base rate for violence was 4.5%, but, when patient and collateral reports were added, the base rate increased to 27.5%, a rate of violence six times higher than the original base rate.

Finally, how the criterion variable is defined is a concern. In some studies researchers will classify their participants as having either engaged in violence or not. Monahan and Steadman (1994) recommend that researchers expand this coding to include the severity of violence (threatened violence versus severe violence), types of violence (spousal violence versus sexual violence), targets of violence (family versus stranger), location (institutions versus community), and motivation (reactive [unplanned violence in response to a provocation] versus instrumental [violence used as an instrument in the pursuit of some goal]). It is likely that some risk factors will be associated with certain forms of violence; for example, a history of sexual offences may predict future sexual offences but not future bank robberies.

## JUDGMENT ERROR AND BIASES

How do psychologists make decisions when conducting risk assessments? Researchers have identified the typical errors and biases in clinical decision making (Elbogen, 2002). The shortcuts people use to help to make decisions are called *heuristics* (Tversky & Kahneman, 1981). Some of these heuristics lead to inaccurate decisions. Clinicians may make several types of decision errors. Clinicians include traits they intuitively believe to be important or assume to be associated with the risk but that actually are not (Odeh, Zeiss, & Huss, 2006). Chapman and Chapman (1967) define an **illusory correlation** as the belief that a correlation exists between two events that in reality are either not correlated or correlated to a much lesser degree. For example, a clinician might assume a strong correlation between a diagnosis of mental disorder and high risk for violent behaviour. Although some forms of mental disorder are related to an increased risk, a relationship has not been consistently found (Monahan & Steadman, 1994). Clinicians also tend to ignore base rates of violence (Monahan, 1981). Clinicians working in prisons or forensic psychiatric facilities may not be aware of how often individuals with specific characteristics act violently. For example, the base rate for recidivism in homicide offenders is extremely low. Other investigators (Borum, Otto, & Golding, 1993) have noted the tendency to rely on highly salient or unique cues, such as bizarre delusions.

In general, people tend to be overconfident in their judgments (see Kahneman & Tversky, 1982). Clinicians who are very confident in their risk assessments will be more likely to recommend and implement intervention strategies. However, people can be very confident in their risk assessments but be completely wrong. Desmarais, Nicholls, Read, and Brink (2010) investigated the association between clinicians' confidence and accuracy of predicting short-term in-patient violence. Clinicians completed a structured professional

**Illusory correlation:** Belief that a correlation exists between two events that in reality are either not correlated or correlated to a much lesser degree

judgment measure designed to assess the likelihood of violent behaviour (i.e., verbal and physical aggression, self-harm) and indicated on a 5-point scale their level of confidence. Most clinicians were highly confident, however, the association between confidence and accuracy was minimal. The pattern of findings suggested clinicians tended to have an overconfidence bias.

# APPROACHES TO THE ASSESSMENT OF RISK

What are the existing methods of risk assessment? Three methods of risk assessment are most commonly described. **Unstructured clinical judgment** is characterized by a substantial amount of professional discretion and lack of guidelines. There are no predefined rules about what risk factors should be considered, what sources of information should be used, or how the risk factors should be combined to make a decision about risk. Thus, risk factors considered vary across clinicians and vary across cases (Grove & Meehl, 1996; Grove, Zald, Lebow, Snitz, & Nelson, 2000). Grove and Meehl (1996) have described this type of risk assessment as relying on an "informal, 'in the head,' subjective, impressionistic, subjective conclusion, reached (somehow) by a human clinical judge" (p. 294). See Box 10.1 for an example of a professional using this type of risk assessment.

> **Unstructured clinical judgment:** Decisions characterized by a substantial amount of professional discretion and lack of guidelines

In contrast, mechanical prediction involves predefined rules about what risk factors to consider, how information should be collected, and how information should be combined to make a risk decision. Thus, risk factors do not vary as a function of the clinician and the same risk factors are considered for each case. A common type of mechanical prediction is called **actuarial prediction**. With actuarial prediction, the risk factors used have been selected and combined based on their empirical or statistical association with a specific outcome (Grove & Meehl, 1996; Grove et al., 2000). In other words, a study has been done in which a number of risk factors have been measured, a sample of offenders have been followed for a specific period, and only those risk factors that were actually related to reoffending in this sample are selected (for an example of an actuarial scale, see the Violence Risk Appraisal Guide described later in this chapter).

> **Actuarial prediction:** Decisions are based on risk factors that are selected and combined based on their empirical or statistical association with a specific outcome

A debate in the literature exists concerning the comparative accuracy of unstructured clinical versus actuarial prediction. The first study to compare actuarial and unstructured clinical judgment was conducted by sociologist Ann Burgess in 1928. Burgess compared the accuracy of 21 objective risk factors (e.g., age, number of past offences, length of sentence) to clinical judgments of three psychiatrists in predicting parole failure in a sample of 3000 criminal offenders. The actuarial scale was markedly superior to the psychiatrists in identifying which offenders would fail on parole. In a review of 20 studies, Paul Meehl (1954) concluded that actuarial prediction was equal to or better than unstructured clinical judgment in all cases. A similar conclusion was reached almost 50 years later, when Meehl and his colleagues (Grove et al., 2000) conducted a meta-analysis of prediction studies for human health and behaviour (including criminal behaviour). In sum, the weight of the evidence clearly favours actuarial assessments of risk (Ægisdóttir et al., 2006; Mossman, 1994), even with samples of offenders with mental disorders (Bonta, Law, & Hanson, 1998; Phillips et al., 2005) and sex offenders (Hanson & Morton-Bourgon, 2009). A criticism of many actuarial assessments have been their sole reliance on static risk factors, which do not permit measuring changes in risk over time or provide information relevant for intervention (Wong & Gordon, 2006).

Box 10.1

# Dr. Death: A Legendary (Notorious) Forensic Psychiatrist

Dr. James Grigson was a Dallas psychiatrist who earned the nicknames *Dr. Death* and *the hanging shrink* because of his effectiveness at testifying for the prosecution in death-penalty cases. For nearly three decades, Dr. Grigson testified in death-penalty cases in Texas.

Death-penalty trials are divided into two phases. First, the defendant's guilt is decided. Next, if the defendant is guilty of a serious crime, the same judge and jury decide whether to impose life in prison or to sentence the defendant to die. One of the issues the jurors must decide on is "whether there is a probability that the defendant would commit criminal acts of violence that would constitute a continuing threat to society." Psychiatrists and psychologists are often hired to testify about the likelihood of future violence.

Dr. Grigson's testimony was very effective. He often diagnosed defendants as being sociopaths and stated with 100% certainty they will kill again. For example, in *Estelle v. Smith* (1981), Dr. Grigson testified on the basis of a brief examination that the defendant Smith was a "very severe sociopath," who, if given the opportunity, would commit another criminal act. The diagnosis of *sociopath* appears to have been based on the sole fact that Smith "lacked remorse."

Dr. Grigson has been proven wrong. In the case of Randall Dale Adams (documentarian Errol Morris made a movie about Adams's story in 1988, called *The Thin Blue Line*, which helped to get the case reopened), Dr. Grigson testified that Randall Adams was a "very extreme" sociopath and would continue to be a threat to society even if kept locked in prison. Dr. Grigson based his assessment on a 15-minute interview in which he asked about Adams's family background, had Adams complete a few items from a neuropsychological test designed to measure visual-motor functioning (Bender Gestalt Test), and asked Adams the

meaning of two proverbs: *A rolling stone gathers no moss* and *a bird in the hand is worth two in a bush*. Randall Adams was sentenced to death. However, after spending 12 years on death row, his conviction was overturned and he was released (another inmate confessed to the murder Adams had been charged for). It has been 13 years since Randall Adams has been released. He is now married, employed, and living a nonviolent life. Dr. Grigson was wrong in this case—and potentially in how many others?

In 1995, Dr. Grigson was expelled from the American Psychiatric Association (APA) for ethical violations. He was disqualified for claiming he could predict with 100% certainty that a defendant will commit another violent act (and, on at least one occasion, testifying that the defendant had a "1000%" chance of committing another violent act). The APA was also concerned that Dr. Grigson often testified in court based on hypothetical situations and diagnosed an individual without even examining the defendant. Dr. Grigson often diagnosed defendants as sociopaths on the basis of his own clinical opinion and not on any structured assessment procedures.

Dr. Grigson was also involved in the death-penalty case of Canadian Joseph Stanley Faulder, who was convicted and sentenced to death for the robbery and murder of Inez Phillips. Dr. Grigson testified that Stanley Faulder was an "extremely severe sociopath," that there was no cure, and that he would certainly kill again. We will never assess the accuracy of Dr. Grigson's predictions, since on June 17, 1999, after spending 22 years on death row, Stanley Faulder was executed. When Dr. Grigson died in 2004 at the age of 72, he had testified in 167 trials. How many of these defendants fell victim to Dr. Grigson and his misguided attempt to protect society is unknown.

**Structured professional judgment:** Decisions are guided by a predetermined list of risk factors that have been selected from the research and professional literature. Judgment of risk level is based on the evaluator's professional judgment

Arising from the limitations associated with unstructured clinical judgment and concern that the actuarial method did not allow for individualized risk appraisal or for consideration of the impact of situational factors to modify risk level, a new approach to risk assessment has emerged—**structured professional judgment** (SPJ) (Borum, 1996; Webster, Douglas, Eaves, & Hart, 1997). According to this method, the professional (the term *professional* is used to acknowledge that it is not only clinicians who make evaluations of risk but a diverse group, including law enforcement officers, probation officers, and social workers) is guided by a predetermined list of risk factors that have been selected

## Canadian Researcher Profile: Dr. Christopher Webster

Dr. Christopher Webster completed his undergraduate degree at the University of British Columbia, his master's at Queen's University, and his doctorate at Dalhousie University. His doctoral thesis focused on avoidance conditioning in guinea pigs. Currently, Dr. Webster is a consultant to various forensic mental health agencies and is professor emeritus with the Department of Psychiatry at the University of Toronto and the Department of Psychology at Simon Fraser University.

Dr. Webster's first position after graduating was as a research scientist at the Addiction Research Foundation in Toronto. Later he transferred to the Clarke Institute of Psychiatry (now the Centre for Addiction and Mental Health [CAMH]), where he established clinical and research programs for autistic children and their families. Later, at CAMH, he conducted fitness and criminal responsibility evaluations of defendants in court.

In the late 1970s, he accepted a position as senior research scientist with a new forensic program established by the Clarke Institute. He also began collaborating with practitioners and researchers from different disciplines and started conducting research on risk assessment and risk

management. Over the past three decades, Dr. Webster has made substantial contributions to the risk-assessment field, and his work has provided clinicians with essential ways to structure their risk assessments.

Dr. Webster notes that one of his favourite pieces of research was a study conducted with Robert Menzies (at that time a graduate student in sociology at the University of Toronto, now a professor at Simon Fraser University), identifying risk factors for violence in a large sample of offenders with mental disorders. In 1993, Dr. Webster joined and became chair of the Department of Psychology at Simon Fraser University. One of the many projects he worked on while there was the development of a structured professional judgment manual called the *HCR-20* (this was done in collaboration with Stephen Hart, Kevin Douglas, and Derek Eaves). Research that Dr. Webster finds particularly rewarding entails working with an interdisciplinary team and collaborating with researchers and clinicians from different countries. "Manualization" of violence risk is the essential theme of his work.

Dr. Webster has testified at dangerous offender hearings. He recently took part in an investigation of a released offender who subsequently committed a homicide. He is a member of the Ontario Review Board. This board makes decisions about the optimal ways to reintegrate forensic psychiatric patients into the community. This work is both important and rewarding since it has a vital effect on the patients' lives.

Of the many courses he has taught, Dr. Webster's two favourites are Psychology and the Law and Clinical Criminology. He thinks one important aspect of training future forensic researchers is having undergraduates involved in conducting research in forensic settings.

Dr. Webster owns a 1957 Triumph TRW motorcycle (military model). It came complete with an original manual, which should be helpful, as so far he has spent about as much time pushing it as riding it.

from the research and professional literature. The professional considers the presence and severity of each risk factor, but the final judgment of risk level is based on the evaluator's professional judgment. The reliability and predictive utility of these risk summary judgments are only beginning to be assessed. Dr. Christopher Webster, the Canadian researcher profiled in Box 10.2, has done extensive research on the use of SPJ.

# Types of Predictors

Clinicians and researchers might use hundreds of potential risk factors to predict antisocial and violent behaviour. A risk factor is a measurable feature of an individual that predicts the behaviour of interest, such as violence. Traditionally, risk factors were divided into two main types: static and dynamic.

**Static risk factors** are factors that do not fluctuate over time and are not changed by treatment. Age at first arrest is an example of a static risk factor, since no amount of time or treatment will change this risk factor. **Dynamic risk factors** fluctuate over time and are amenable to change. An antisocial attitude is an example of a dynamic risk factor, since it is possible that treatment could modify this variable. Dynamic risk factors have also been called *criminogenic needs* (see Chapter 9 for a discussion).

More recently, correctional researchers have begun to conceptualize risk factors as a continuous construct (Douglas & Skeem, 2005; Grann, Belfrage, & Tengström, 2000; Zamble & Quinsey, 1997). At one end of the continuum are the static risk factors described above. At the other end are acute dynamic risk factors. These risk factors change rapidly within days, hours, or minutes and often occur just prior to an offence. Factors at this end of the continuum include variables such as negative mood and level of intoxication. In the middle of the continuum are stable dynamic risk factors. These risk factors change but only over long periods of time, such as months or years, and are variables that should be targeted for treatment. These factors include criminal attitudes, coping ability, and impulse control.

Recent research has found that dynamic risk factors are related to the imminence of engaging in violent behaviour. Quinsey, Jones, Book, and Barr (2006) had staff make monthly ratings of dynamic risk factors in a large sample of forensic psychiatric patients. Changes in dynamic risk factors were related to the occurrence of violent behaviours.

# IMPORTANT RISK FACTORS

Since the late 1980s, a great deal of research has investigated what factors are associated with future violence. These can be classified into historical, dispositional, clinical, and contextual risk factors. **Historical risk factors** (sometimes called *static risk factors*) are events experienced in the past and include general social history and specific criminal history variables, such as employment problems and a history of violence. **Dispositional risk factors** are those that reflect the person's traits, tendencies, or style and include demographic, attitudinal, and personality variables, such as gender, age, criminal attitudes, and psychopathy. **Clinical risk factors** are the symptoms of mental disorders that can contribute to violence, such as substance abuse or major psychoses. **Contextual risk factors** (sometimes referred to as **situational risk factors**) are aspects of the individual's current environment that can elevate the risk, such as access to victims or weapons, lack of social supports, and perceived stress.

Some of these factors are likely relevant to risk assessment only, while others are relevant to both risk assessment and risk management. These factors vary in terms of how much they are subject to change. For example, some are fixed (e.g., gender), some cannot be undone (e.g., age of onset of criminal behaviour), and some may be resistant to change (e.g., psychopathy), whereas others (e.g., social support or negative attitudes) may be subject to intervention or may vary across time.

**Static risk factor:** Risk factor that does not fluctuate over time and is not changed by treatment (e.g., age at first arrest). Also known as a *historical risk factor*

**Dynamic risk factor:** Risk factors that fluctuate over time and are amenable to change

**Historical risk factor:** Risk factor that refers to events that have been experienced in the past (e.g., age at first arrest). Also known as *static risk factor*

**Dispositional risk factor:** Risk factors that reflect the individual's traits, tendencies, or styles (e.g., negative attitudes)

**Clinical risk factors:** Types and symptoms of mental disorders (e.g., substance abuse)

**Contextual risk factors:** Risk factors that refer to aspects of the current environment (e.g., access to victims or weapons). Sometimes called *situational risk factors*

**Situational risk factors:** Risk factors that refer to aspects of the current environment (e.g., access to victims or weapons). Sometimes called *contextual risk factors*

Several meta-analytic reviews have examined the predictors of general and violent recidivism in adult offenders, sexual offenders, and patients with mental disorders (Bonta, Law, et al., 1998; Gendreau, Little, & Goggin, 1996; Hanson & Morton-Bourgon, 2005). Two key findings have emerged. First, factors that predict general recidivism also predict violent or sexual recidivism. Second, predictors of recidivism in offenders with mental disorders overlap considerably with predictors found among offenders who do not have a mental disorder. A meta-analytic study examined the predictors of general recidivism in 23 studies of adolescent offenders (Cottle, Lee, & Heilbrun, 2001). The strongest predictors were age of first police contact, nonsevere pathology (e.g., stress or anxiety), family problems, conduct problems (e.g., presence of conduct disordered symptoms), ineffective use of leisure time, and delinquent peers.

## Dispositional Factors

**Demographics** Researchers in the 1970s identified young age as a risk factor for violence (Steadman & Cocozza, 1974): The younger the person is at the time of his or her first offence, the greater the likelihood that person will engage in criminal behaviour and violence. Dozens of studies have firmly established age of first offence as a risk factor for both general and violent recidivism in both offenders with mental disorders (Bonta, Law, et al., 1998) and offenders without mental disorders (Gendreau et al., 1996). Offenders who are arrested prior to age 14 tend to have more serious and more extensive criminal careers than those who are first arrested after age 14 (DeLisi, 2006; Piquero & Chung, 2001). Males are at higher risk than are females for general offending (Cottle et al., 2001; Gendreau et al., 1996). Notably, males engage in more serious violent acts, such as sexual assaults, homicides, and assaults causing bodily harm (Odgers & Moretti, 2002). Some studies using self-report measures have found that females engage in similar or even higher rates of less serious violence (Nichols, Graber, Brooks-Gunn, & Botvin, 2006; Steadman et al., 1994).

**Personality Characteristics** Two personality characteristics have been extensively examined: impulsiveness and psychopathy. Not being able to regulate behaviour in response to impulses or thoughts increases the likelihood of engaging in crime and violence (Webster & Jackson, 1997). Lifestyle impulsivity (being impulsive in most areas of life) distinguishes recidivistic rapists from nonrecidivistic rapists (Prentky, Knight, Lee, & Cerce, 1995).

Psychopathy is a personality disorder defined as a callous and unemotional interpersonal style characterized by grandiosity, manipulation, lack of remorse, impulsivity, and irresponsibility (see Chapter 11 for more information on psychopaths and the Hare Psychopathy Checklist-Revised [PCL-R], the most widely used measure of psychopathy). Given these features, it is not surprising that psychopathic individuals engage in diverse and chronic criminal behaviours. A recent meta-analysis has found that psychopathy is moderately related to general and

Psychologist conducting a risk-assessment interview

violent recidivism (Leisticio, Salekin, DeCoster, & Rogers, 2008) and moderately related to violence in a prison setting (Guy, Edens, Anthony, & Douglas, 2005). Psychopathy predicts reoffending across different countries (e.g., Canada, the United States, the United Kingdom, Belgium, Germany, the Netherlands, New Zealand, Sweden) (Hare, 2003), in both male and female offenders (Richards, Casey, & Lucente, 2003), offenders with mental disorders (Nicholls, Ogloff, & Douglas, 2004; Steadman et al., 2000; Strand, Belfrage, Fransson, & Levander, 1999), male adolescent offenders (Corrado, Vincent, Hart, & Cohen, 2004; Forth, Hart, & Hare, 1990; Gretton, Hare, & Catchpole, 2004; Murrie et al., 2004), and sexual offenders (Barbaree, Seto, Langton, & Peacock, 2001; Rice & Harris, 1997a). However, psychopathy may be weakly related or unrelated to violent reoffending in adolescent females (Odgers, Repucci, & Moretti, 2005; Schmidt, McKinnon, Chattha, & Brownlee, 2006; Vincent, Odgers, McCormick, & Corrado, 2008).

Several studies have found that the combination of psychopathy and deviant sexual arousal predicts sexual recidivism (Hildebrand, de Rutter, & de Vogel, 2004; Olver & Wong, 2006; Rice & Harris, 1997a). Deviant sexual arousal is defined as evidence that the sexual offender shows a relative preference for inappropriate stimuli, such as children or violent nonconsensual sex. For example, Rice and Harris (1997a) found that about 70% of sexual offenders with psychopathic features and evidence of deviant sexual arousal committed a new sexual offence, compared with about 40% of the other offender groups.

## Historical Factors

**Past Behaviour** The most accurate predictor of future behaviour is past behaviour. Past violent behaviour was first identified as a predictor in the 1960s and 1970s (see Cocozza, Melick, & Steadman, 1978) and has consistently been associated with future violence in diverse samples, including adolescents and adults, correctional offenders, mentally disordered offenders, and civil psychiatric patients (Farrington, 1991; McNiel et al., 1988; Phillips et al., 2005). Interestingly, it is not only past violent behaviour that predicts violence, but also past nonviolent behaviour (Harris, Rice, & Quinsey, 1993; Lipsey & Derzon, 1998). For example, offenders who have a history of break and enter offences are at an increased risk for future violence.

**Age of Onset** As noted earlier, individuals who start their antisocial behaviour at an earlier age are more chronic and serious offenders (Farrington, 1991; Tolan & Thomas, 1995). For example, Farrington (1991) found that 50% of the boys who committed a violent offence prior to age 16 were convicted of a violent offence in early adulthood. In another longitudinal study, Elliott (1994) reported that 50% of male youth who committed their first violent acts prior to age 11 continued their violent behaviour into adulthood, compared with 30% whose first violence was between the ages of 11 and 13, and only 10% of those whose first violent act occurred during adolescence. Age of onset is not as strong a predictor for female offenders (Piquero & Chung, 2001).

**Childhood History of Maltreatment** Having a history of childhood physical abuse or neglect is associated with increased risk for violence (Smith & Thornberry, 1995; Zingraff, Leiter, Johnsen, & Myers, 1994). In a large-scale study of childhood abuse, Widom (1989b) reported that victims of sexual abuse were no more likely than those who were not sexually abused to commit delinquent or violent offences. Those who were victims of physical abuse or who were victims of neglect were much more likely to commit criminal acts as compared with those who were not abused. Being abused in childhood predicts initiation into delinquency, but continued abuse predicts chronic offending (Lemmon, 2006). Physical abuse in adolescence is also directly related to adolescent offending and may be related to some types of offending in adulthood as well (Fagan, 2005; Smith, Ireland, & Thornberry, 2005).

## Clinical Factors

**Substance Use** Drug and alcohol use has been associated with criminal behaviour and violence. However, the drug-violence link is complex because of both direct effects (e.g., the pharmacological effects of the drugs) and indirect effects (e.g., the use of violence to obtain drugs; Hoaken & Stewart, 2003). The obvious link between drugs and crime is that the use, possession, and sale of illegal drugs are crimes. In some cases, the individual commits offences to support a drug habit (Klassen & O'Connor, 1994). For example, Chaiken and Chaiken (1983) found that severe drug users commit 15 times as many robberies and 20 times as many burglaries as compared with non-drug-using offenders. The drug that has been most associated with crime is heroin (Inciardi, 1986). A large study of 653 opiate users in Edmonton, Montreal, Quebec City, Toronto, and Vancouver concluded that individuals with greater heroin and crack use are at the greatest risk of committing property crimes (Manzoni, Brochu, Fischer, & Rehm, 2006). Not all classes of drugs are related to the same degree with criminal behaviour and violence, and in some cases the strength of the association depends on the amount of the drug used (Hoaken & Stewart, 2003).

Dowden and Brown (2002) conducted a meta-analysis of 45 studies to examine the association between substance abuse and recidivism. Alcohol and drug use problems were moderately related to general recidivism. Zanis et al. (2003) followed a sample of 569 offenders with a prior history of substance abuse or dependence for two years after release from prison on parole. Factors relating to a new conviction included the number of prior convictions, younger age, parole without treatment, and cocaine dependence.

Drug abusers also come in contact with antisocial people, thus leading to violent confrontations. Laboratory research (Taylor & Sears, 1988) has found that aggression displayed by intoxicated individuals is a joint function of the pharmacological effects of alcohol intoxication (disinhibition effects), expectancies, and the situation (what is happening in the environment). Neuropsychological deficits (i.e., executive functioning) also play a role in the effects of alcohol on aggression (Giancola, Parrott, & Roth, 2006).

In one of the largest surveys done, Swanson (1994) interviewed 7000 individuals in two U.S. cities (Durham and Los Angeles), asking about the presence of substance abuse, psychiatric disorders, and violent behaviour. Based on data from the previous year, less than 3% of men and women with no psychiatric diagnosis committed violence. However, for those with a diagnosis of substance abuse, the rates of violence for men and women were 22% and 17%, respectively.

**Mental Disorder** Much controversy exists over the connection between major mental disorder and violence. The general public believes that these two items are linked (Pescosolido, Monahan, Link, Stueve, & Kikuzawa, 1999). Although most people with mental disorders are not violent, a diagnosis of affective disorders and schizophrenia has been linked to higher rates of violence (Swanson, 1994). Hillbrand (1995) reported that in a sample of forensic psychiatric patients, those with a history of suicide attempts and engaging in self-harm behaviours were more likely to engage in verbal and physical aggression than were other patients.

Considerable research has investigated the link between psychotic symptoms (experiencing hallucinations and delusions) and violence (McNiel & Binder, 1994). Link and Steuve (1994) investigated the link between violence and specific types of psychotic symptoms. They proposed that symptoms overriding a person's self-control (i.e., feeling as if your mind is being dominated by forces beyond your control) or threatening a person's safety (i.e., thinking that someone is planning to hurt you) increase the likelihood of violence. They have labelled these types of symptoms "threat/control override" (TCO) symptoms. They compared these psychotic symptoms with other symptoms, such as having thoughts taken away, seeing visions, or hearing voices. TCO symptoms were strongly related to violence (hitting, fighting, and using weapons) in both patients and community controls. TCO symptoms were a significant predictor of violence even when the other psychotic symptoms were held constant. In a large study of more than 10 000 people (Swanson, Borum, Swartz, & Monahan, 1996), individuals with TCO symptoms were shown to be almost three times more likely to engage in violence. More recently, in a study of more than 35 000 people, Mojtabai (2006) found that the presence of any psychotic symptoms (not just TCO symptoms) was related to violence. Swanson et al. (1996) found that a combination of TCO symptoms and other mental disorder diagnoses are related to violence. The highest prevalence of violence was the combination of major mental disorder, substance abuse, and TCO symptoms, with an amazing 86% of such individuals reporting violence. For individuals with major mental disorders and TCO symptoms, the rate was 63%; for individuals with major mental disorders and no TCO symptoms, the rate dropped to 39%; and for individuals with no disorder and no TCO symptoms, the rate was 17%. Research has also examined the link between command hallucinations (hearing a voice telling you to harm yourself or others) and violence. Junginger (1990) reported a weak link between command hallucinations and dangerous behaviour. In a sample of 51 patients who reported experiencing command hallucinations, 20 (39%) complied with them but only 8 (17%) complied by committing acts that were a danger to themselves or others. A recent review has concluded that there are mixed, inconclusive results as to whether command hallucinations and violence are truly linked (Barrowcliff & Haddock, 2006). Other psychological processes appear to influence whether someone complies with the voice hallucinations, such as beliefs about what consequences will occur if they do not comply, as well as whether the individual recognizes the voice as a force of evil or good (Barrowcliff & Haddock, 2006).

In a recent meta-analysis of 204 studies, Douglas, Guy, and Hart (2009) concluded that psychosis was associated with between a 49% to 68% increase in the odds of violence. However, the strength of the psychosis–violence link depended on several factors, including study design (settings, comparison group), measurement (types of symptoms), and timing of the symptoms and the violence.

## Contextual Factors

**Lack of Social Support** This risk factor refers to the absence of strong support systems to help individuals in their day-to-day lives. Henggeler, Schoenwald, Borduin, Rowland, and Cunningham (1998) describe four kinds of support: (1) *instrumental*, "to provide the necessities of life"; (2) *emotional*, "to give strength to"; (3) *appraisal*, "to give aid

# Sex Offender Registry Missed Notorious Child Molester

The purpose of the Sex Offender Registry is to help police track high-risk sexual offenders. If a child is abducted, then the police need to know whether any high-risk child molesters are living or visiting where the abduction has occurred. The registry was launched in 2004, but one notorious child molester was missed. Peter Whitmore has a long history of sexually assaulting children. He is currently serving a life sentence without eligibility of parole for seven years for abduction and sexual assault. Although risk assessment is a challenging and complex process, there is consensus that Whitmore is a high-risk sexual offender. At his NPB hearing in March 2004, a psychological risk assessment noted he had "a 100 percent probability of recidivism." The NPB refused parole to Whitmore, and he was released after serving his entire sentence. The following points summarize the major events related to this case:

- 1993: Whitmore is convicted of abduction and five sexual offences involving four boys in Toronto. He is sentenced to one year and four months.

- 1995: Whitmore, who posed as a professional babysitter, sexually assaults an 8-year-old girl and a 9-year-old boy. He is sentenced to five years and banned from being near children under age 14 for the rest of his life.

- 2000: Less than one month after his prison release, Whitmore is found in a downtown Toronto motel with a 13-year-old boy. He is sentenced to one year in prison for breach of a court order.

- 2002: Police find Whitmore in the company of a 5-year-old boy, and Whitmore flees to B.C. A Toronto judge sentences him to three years for probation violations.

- March 2004: An NPB risk-assessment report notes a psychologist believes Whitmore has a "100 percent probability of recidivism."

- June 16, 2005: Whitmore is released from prison after serving his entire three year sentence and lives in Chilliwack, B.C.

- June 2, 2006: RCMP issues a press release stating Whitmore will be visiting Morinville, Alberta, for three days and states he is a "significant risk to male and female children."

- June 15, 2006: After returning to B.C., Whitmore returns to Morinville and tells the police he has come back. RCMP set up a court date so that Whitmore can legally extend his trip, but he does not show up for his court date.

- July 22, 2006: Whitmore shows up in Winnipeg and befriends a 14-year-old boy. He asks the boy's parents whether the boy can come with him to Brandon, Manitoba, to pick up a truck. When Whitmore and the boy fail to return, the boy's parents contact the police.

- July 30, 2006: RCMP issue an Amber Alert for a 10-year-old Saskatchewan boy believed to be abducted by Whitmore.

- July 31, 2006: A Canada-wide warrant is issued charging Whitmore with abduction.

- Aug. 1, 2006: A farmer notices a truck matching the description of Whitmore's truck outside an abandoned farm near Kipling, Saskatchewan. When the RCMP arrive, the 10-year-old victim runs out to meet them. Whitmore surrenders after a ten-hour standoff and the 14-year-old boy is rescued.

- Aug. 3, 2006: Whitmore is charged with abducting and sexually assaulting both boys.

- July 23, 2007: Whitmore pleads guilty and is sentenced to life in prison without eligibility for parole for seven years.

If Whitmore had been listed on the Sex Offender Registry, perhaps the abductions of these children could have been avoided.

Source: Friscolanti, M. (2008, January 9). 'A national embarrassment': Canada's sex offender registry is so flawed that hundreds of molesters and other criminals have gone missing. *Macleans*. Retrieved from http://www.macleans.ca/canada/national/article.jsp?content=20080109_90711_90711&page=1

or courage to"; and (4) *information*, "by providing new facts." Assessing the kinds and levels of support a person has and what types of support must be created will help to evaluate that person's level of risk. Klassen and O'Connor (1989) found that the current relationship an offender with a mental disorder has with his or her parents and siblings is related to violence.

**Access to Weapons or Victims** If the offender is released into an environment that permits easy access to weapons or victims, then the potential for another violent act increases. An offender who moves into a skid-row rooming house that houses many other antisocial individuals and provides easy access to drugs may start associating with antisocial people or using drugs (Monahan & Steadman, 1994). If the offender has engaged in violence with other associates or under the influence of substances, then releasing the offender to live in the same circumstances that led to past violence may induce future violence. In addition, if offenders who have assaulted their spouses and refused treatment for domestic violence return to live with their spouses, they have a much higher likelihood of violence than those who do not have easy access to a past victim. See the In the Media box for a profile of a high-risk child molester.

## RISK-ASSESSMENT INSTRUMENTS

Many of the factors affecting risk assessment that we've discussed above serve as the basis for various kinds of risk-assessment instruments. Some instruments have been developed to predict specific kinds of risk, while others utilize particular strategies outlined above, such as actuarial or structured clinical assessments. An example of an actuarial risk assessment and a structured professional judgment are described below. See Box 10.3 for a look at some other risk-assessment instruments.

An actuarial risk-for-violence instrument developed in Ontario is the Violence Risk Appraisal Guide (VRAG) (Harris, Rice, & Quinsey, 1993). The VRAG is an empirically derived 12-item measure designed to assess the long-term risk for violent recidivism in offenders with mental disorders. Researchers coded about 50 risk factors from institutional files in a sample of 618 male adult patients with mental disorders who had been transferred to less secure institutions or released into the community. Statistical analyses were used to select the 12 best predictors of violence from childhood history, adult adjustment, offence history, and assessment results. The 12 predictors varied in terms of how strongly they were related to violent recidivism and included the following (ordered from most to least predictive):

- Hare Psychopathy Checklist–Revised score
- Elementary school maladjustment
- Diagnosis of any personality disorder
- Age at index offence (young age, higher risk)
- Separation from biological parents prior to age 16
- Failure on prior conditional release
- Prior nonviolent offences
- Single marital status at time of offence
- Diagnosis of schizophrenia (lower risk)
- Victim injury (less injury, higher risk)
- History of alcohol problems
- Victim gender (female victim, lower risk)

Box 10.3

# Risk-Assessment Instruments

## Violence Risk Scale (VRS)

The VRS (Wong & Gordon, 2006) is a structured professional judgment tool designed to provide information on an offender's risk to reoffend while at the same time provide treatment targets to reduce the offender's risk. Canadian psychologists developed the VRS by using a sample of 918 male offenders. The VRS consists of 26 items, 6 static risk factors, and 20 dynamic risk factors. The static risk factors include the following:

- Age of first violent conviction
- Number of juvenile convictions
- Violence throughout life span
- Stability of family upbringing
- Prior release failures/escapes
- Current age

The dynamic risk factors are those that can be changed through treatment. Four examples of the 20 risk factors are listed below:

1. Emotional regulation/control (Is the individual able to control his or her emotions or is there a persistent relationship between inability to control emotions and violence?)

2. Insight into violence (Does the individual understand what factors are related to why he or she has committed violence or does the individual lack insight by denying responsibility, blaming others, or refusing recommended intervention?)

3. Impulsivity (Does the individual consider the consequences of his or her behaviour or is the individual still reacting impulsively?)

4. Work ethic (Does the individual want to work for a living or does the individual use violence or other socially inappropriate ways [e.g., pimping, drug dealing] of supporting him- or herself?)

The VRS predicts violent and nonviolent reoffending at a moderate level, and those offenders who score highest on the VRS reoffended the earliest when released.

## Spousal Assault Risk Assessment (SARA)

The SARA (Kropp, Hart, Webster, & Eaves, 1999) is a 20-item structured professional judgment scale designed to assess the risk for spousal violence. It consists of ten general violent risk factors (Part 1) and ten spousal violent risk factors (Part 2). Part 1 items code for past history of violence and substance use problems, as well as relationship and employment problems. Part 2 items code spousal assault incident, attitudes supporting of spousal assault, and violations of "no contact" orders. Researchers have often summed the individual risk factors to create a numerical total score. However, users are encouraged to make a summary risk judgment of low, moderate, or high. In a meta-analysis of 18 studies, Hanson, Helmus, and Bourgon (2007) found that the SARA total score and risk judgment was moderately related to spousal assault recidivism.

## Static-99

The Static-99 (Hanson & Thornton, 1999) is a ten-item actuarial scale designed to predict sexual recidivism. All items on this scale are static in nature. Scores on the Static-99 can range from 0 to 12, with scores being associated with four risk categories: low, moderate-low, moderate-high, and high. Items on the Static-99 include the following:

- Young age at time of release
- Ever lived with intimate partner
- Any prior nonsexual violent convictions
- Any index nonsexual violent convictions
- Number of prior sex offences
- Number of prior sentences
- Any male victims
- Any unrelated victims
- Any stranger victims
- Any noncontact sex offences

The Static-99 was tested on three development samples in Canada and a fourth cross-validation sample in the United Kingdom. The Static-99 showed good predictive validity in the combined sample of 1208, and the authors

(*continued*)

(continued)

provided observed recidivism rates for both violent and sexual reoffense at 5-, 10-, and 15-year intervals (Hanson & Thornton, 2000). More recently, the developers have provided a set of recidivism norms from larger and more geographically diverse samples (Helmus, Hanson, & Thornton, 2009). The developers have also developed the Static-2002 (Hanson & Thornton, 2003), which includes additional risk factors, such as persistence of sexual offending, deviant sexual interests, and general criminality.

A meta-analysis of the Static-99 (Hanson & Morton-Bourgon, 2009) reported moderate to strong predictive validity across more than 60 studies and 24 000 offenders.

Using scores on each of these risk factors, nine risk categories—or "bins"—were created. Each risk bin has a probability of violent recidivism within ten years ranging from 9% (bin 1), to 35% (bin 5), to 100% (bin 9).

The HCR-20 (Webster et al., 1997) was designed to predict violent behaviour in correctional and forensic psychiatric samples. The HCR-20 uses the structured professional judgment approach to risk assessment developed by a group of researchers in B.C. In this approach, the evaluator conducts a systematic risk assessment and refers to a list of risk factors, each having specific coding criteria and a demonstrated relationship with violent recidivism based on the existing professional and empirical literature. The HCR-20 stands for the list of 20 items organized into three main scales that align risk factors into past (historical), present (clinical), and future (risk management):

Historical (primarily static in nature):

■ Past violence
■ Age at first violent offence
■ Relationship instability
■ Employment instability
■ Relationship problems
■ Substance use problems
■ Major mental disorder
■ Psychopathy
■ Early maladjustment
■ Personality disorder
■ Prior supervision failure

Clinical (reflect current, dynamic risk factors):

■ Lack of insight
■ Negative attitudes
■ Active mental disorder symptoms
■ Impulsivity
■ Treatability

Risk management (future community or institutional adjustment of the individual):

■ Feasibility of plans
■ Exposure to destabilizers

**Table 10.1** The Predictive Accuracy of Different Risk-Assessment Measures

| Measure | Institutional Violence | Violent Recidivism |
|---|---|---|
| HCR-20 | 0.31 | 0.25 |
| LSI/LSI-R | 0.24 | 0.25 |
| PCL/PCL-R | 0.15 | 0.24 |
| VRAG | 0.27 | 0.27 |

Source: Campbell et al., 2009.

- Level of personal support
- Stress
- Likelihood of treatment compliance

Table 10.1 presents the results of a recent meta-analysis comparing the predictive effectiveness of several risk-assessment measures for institutional violence and violence recidivism (Campbell, French, & Gendreau, 2009). The values in the table are effect sizes. All the effect sizes are positive, indicating all the measures were predictive of institutional violence and violent reoffending. All the scales were equally predictive of violent recidivism, whereas the HCR-20 and Level of Supervision Inventory-Revised (LSI-R; Andrews & Bonta, 1995) were the most predictive of institutional violence.

## CURRENT ISSUES

## Where Is the Theory?

Much of the focus in risk-assessment research has been on perfecting the prediction of violence. This focus is especially true for actuarial methods of risk assessment in which risk factors are selected based on their statistical relation to a specific outcome. There is less attention as to *why* these risk factors are linked to violence. Understanding the causes of violence will aid in the development of prevention and intervention programs. Box 10.4 presents one model that explains criminal recidivism. Recently, Silver (2006) has recommended that researchers use criminological theories to help to guide "the next generation of empirical research in the area of mental disorder and violence" (p. 686).

## What about Female Offenders?

Most of the risk-assessment measures have been developed and validated with male offenders. How well these measures generalize to women is an empirical question. If the causes and explanations for female and male criminality are similar, then risk-assessment measures developed with male offenders likely can be used with female offenders. However, if there are important differences in male and female criminality, then it may be inappropriate to apply measures developed with male offenders to females. There are a number of gender differences in criminality. First, women engage is much less criminal

# Coping-Relapse Model of Criminal Recidivism

Zamble and Quinsey (1997) have attempted to explain why an individual will commit another offence after release. Figure 10.1 illustrates the recidivism process and how each level interacts. According to the model, the first event is some type of environmental trigger. What will be considered a trigger varies across individuals and can range from stressful life events, such as losing a job, having relationship problems, and financial difficulties, to more mundane daily events, such as being stuck in a traffic jam. Once the event has occurred, the individual will invoke both an emotional and cognitive appraisal of the event. If this appraisal process results in the experience of negative emotions (e.g., anger, hostility, fear) or elevated levels of stress, the individual will attempt to deal with these unpleasant feelings. If the individual does not possess adequate coping mechanisms, a worsening cycle of negative emotions and maladaptive cognitions occur, eventually resulting in criminal behaviour. The model also posits that how an individual perceives and responds to an environmental trigger is dependent on two factors: individual and response mechanisms.

Individual influences include factors such as criminal history and enduring personality traits (e.g., psychopathy, emotional reactivity). These factors influence how an individual will perceive an event and the likelihood that he or she will engage in criminal conduct, both of which are relatively stable. For example, research has found that psychopathic individuals are impulsive and more likely to interpret ambiguous events as hostile (Serin, 1991). These factors increase the likelihood of engaging in criminal behaviour.

Available response mechanisms also influence how an individual will perceive a situation, which, in turn, will mediate that person's response. These factors are considered to be more dynamic in nature and, thus, are important targets for intervention. Examples of these factors include coping ability, substance use, criminal attitudes and associates, and social supports. Imagine an individual who loses his job. He becomes angry and upset, and reverts to drinking to deal with these negative feelings. His drinking angers his intimate partner who becomes less and less supportive of him. These factors increase the likelihood that he will resume his criminal behaviour.

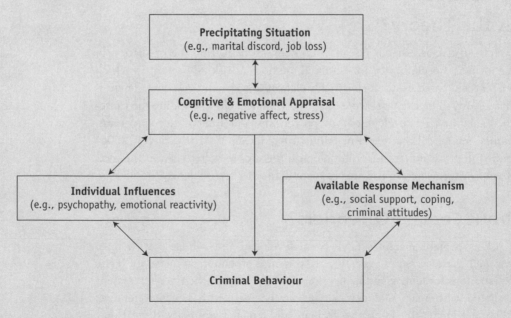

**Figure 10.1** The Recidivism Process

behaviour than men. In 2005, about 21% of people accused of a criminal offense were female (Kong & AuCoin, 2008). Women represented 6.5% of admissions to federal custody in 2008–2009 (Public Safety, 2010). In addition, women are arrested for different crimes than men. The only crime women commit more often than men is prostitution. When women engage in violence, they are more likely than men to target family members. Second, women reoffend at a lower rate than do men. In 2008–2009, the percentage of successful full paroles and statutory releases for women was higher than for men (76% versus 73% for full parole and 73% versus 59% for statutory release, Public Safety Canada, 2009). Third, childhood victimization is more prevalent in women offenders than men offenders. For example, 50% of incarcerated female offenders report childhood sexual abuse and 70% experienced childhood physical abuse (Shaw, 1994). Finally, female offenders are more likely to have a serious mental disorder, such as schizophrenia, bipolar disorder, depression, and anxiety disorders, than men are (Warren et al., 2002; Correctional Services Canada, 1998).

Gender-specific risk factors may exist; however, the research to date has found more similarities than differences in both adolescents and adults (Andrews & Bonta, 2006; Blanchette & Brown, 2006; Simourd & Andrews, 1994). Blanchette and Brown (2006) provide a review of static and dynamic risk factors in female offenders. They conclude that many of the static risk factors associated with recidivism in men, such as criminal history and age, are also predictors with women. Similar dynamic risk factors for women and men include substance abuse, antisocial attitudes, and antisocial associates. Evidence also suggests that women have further risk factors, such as a history of self-injury or attempted suicide, and self-esteem problems. Overall, additional research is needed to understand the static and dynamic risk factors for recidivism in women offenders. Further research is also needed to fully understand protective factors that may improve women's success in the community upon release from prison. For example, Benda (2005) found that being married was a protective factor for men but a risk factor for women.

How well do the risk-assessment instruments predict reoffending in female offenders? One risk-assessment scale that has been well researched with female offenders is the LSI-R. In a recent meta-analysis, Smith, Cullen, and Latessa (2009) reported that the LSI-R predicted general recidivism as well for women as for men (effect sizes of 0.27 and 0.26 for men and women, respectively). In addition, the LSI-R was also predictive of general recidivism in a sample of female offenders convicted of serious violent offences (Manchak, Skeem, Douglas, & Siranosian, 2009).

The predictive validity of the HCR-20 has been examined in several studies of female forensic psychiatric patients. Nicholls et al. (2004) reported the H subscale score and total score predicted any violence, physical violence, crime, and violent crime. In contrast, de Vogel and de Ruiter (2005), with their sample of female patients and ex-patients, found that neither the HCR-20 total score nor the subscale score showed any significant predictive value for violent outcome (i.e., violent recidivism and in-patient violence). Whether the HCR-20 has predictive validity with female offenders has yet to be established.

The above research indicates that some risk-assessment instruments developed and validated with male offenders may also be used with women. However, it is not appropriate to assume that this will always be the case, and a considerable amount of research still needs to be conducted.

## What about Protective Factors?

Various historical, dispositional, clinical, and contextual risk factors have been shown to have predictive utility. **Protective factors** are factors that mitigate or reduce the likelihood of antisocial acts or violence in high-risk offenders (Borum, 1996). Understanding the positive attributes could help to explain why some individuals with many risk factors do not become violent. For example, a youth may have antisocial parents at home (a risk factor) but also be strongly attached to school (a protective factor). Like risk factors, protective factors vary across time, and the impact they have depends on the situation. Most of the research on protective factors has been conducted with children and youth. The following factors have been identified as protective factors: prosocial involvement, strong social supports, positive social orientation (e.g., school, work), strong attachments (as long as attachment is not to an antisocial other), and intelligence (Caldwell, Silverman, Lefforge, & Silver, 2004; Caprara, Barbaranelli, & Pastorelli, 2001; Hoge, Andrews, & Leschied, 1996; Lipsey & Derzon, 1998). More research on protective factors in adult offenders is beginning. A variable identified as a potential protective factor for high-risk offenders is employment stability, whereas strong family connections appears to be a protective factor for lower-risk male offenders (DeMatteo, Heilbrun, & Marczyk, 2005). See the Case Study box to try to identify risk and protective factors for an offender applying for parole.

## CASE STUDY  YOU BE THE FORENSIC PSYCHOLOGIST

Jason Booth is a 23-year-old first-time federal offender currently serving a three-year sentence at a medium-security federal penitentiary for possession of property obtained by crime over $5000, carrying a concealed weapon, and failure to comply with a probation order. He pled guilty to all these charges. He has served one year of his sentence and has applied for full parole.

When Jason was arrested, he was driving a stolen car and had a handgun, and because he was on probation for a previous conviction at the time, his possession of both of these items constituted a breach of probation. He had been released from custody for his previous charge only two weeks prior to committing these offences.

Official records indicate that the courts have sentenced Jason ten times (seven times in youth court and three times in adult court) for a total of 17 convictions (ten in youth court and seven in adult court) for assault, assault with a weapon, carrying a concealed weapon, criminal harassment, obstructing a peace officer, breaking and entering, theft under $1000, theft under $5000, failure to attend court, unlawfully at large, and failure to comply with a probation order.

Jason has violated probation several times and has engaged in violence in institutions (e.g., spitting in a correctional officer's face, stabbing another inmate with a pen). He has also engaged in violence in the community (e.g., assaulting his girlfriend, threatening to kill a bouncer at a bar).

At his parole hearing, Jason explained that he committed the current offences because he had just been released from prison and would not be receiving any social assistance for two weeks. He seemed to feel that the only way to obtain money was to steal a car. He was unable to generate any prosocial alternatives by which he could have obtained assistance. In addition, Jason minimized his criminal history and the harm he has done to his victims. For example, he stated that one of his past victims, a woman who he had criminally harassed and threatened to kill, was "a spoiled brat who deserved what she got." Most of Jason's friends are criminals.

In the psychological report, Jason was described as hostile, arrogant, manipulative, impulsive, and remorseless. Jason denies any current problems with drugs or alcohol. Neither drugs nor alcohol have been involved in his current or past offences.

Jason was reportedly diagnosed with attention deficit hyperactivity disorder when he was 9 years old. He was never interested in school and was expelled numerous times. He completed Grade 9 but was absent for most of Grade 10. He dropped out of school when he was 16 years old. Jason's employment history consists of several short-term jobs, with the longest job lasting for one year. He has few employment skills and tends to get into altercations with his boss and other employees. He was fired from his last job for stealing merchandise from the company's warehouse. During his current incarceration, he has refused educational and vocational training.

Jason's biological father, who reportedly has been incarcerated himself, left Jason's mother when Jason was 3 years old. Jason was raised by his biological mother and an alcohol-abusing stepfather. His stepfather reportedly threw Jason out of the house when he was 13 years old because of his stealing and other disruptive behaviours. Jason was subsequently placed in a series of foster and group homes. He was often moved from home to home because of his aggressive and disruptive behaviour.

There is evidence that Jason has assaulted former intimate partners. Past reports indicate Jason can be jealous and overly controlling, having unreasonable expectations in relationships with women. He reportedly has two children of his own but does not maintain contact with either of them. At his parole hearing, Jason said that when he is released he and his ex-common-law spouse, a partner he assaulted in the past, plan to resume their relationship.

Jason plans to live with his mother when he is released, but she does not want him to stay with her. He typically lives on social assistance or obtains money from criminal behaviours when in the community.

There is no evidence that Jason has ever successfully completed either institutional or community programming. He is typically uncooperative with attempts at assessment and treatment. However, he has recently expressed an interest in treatment programs.

## Your Turn . . .

You are the forensic psychologist assessing Jason. What risk factors for future reoffending are present? Are there any protective factors present? How likely is Jason to commit another nonviolent or violent crime if he is released? Which risk-assessment instrument would you use to help determine Jason's risk for future crime and violence?

## Risk Assessment: Risky Business?

Risk assessments have limitations that forensic evaluators and decision makers need to be aware of (Glazebrook, 2010). Most actuarial risk-assessment measures provide probability statements about reoffending based on group data. However, currently there is no method of determining what the specific risk level is for an individual (see Hart, Michie, &

Cooke, 2008, for a review). In contrast to actuarial measures, structured professional judgment measures typically ask evaluators to state the level of risk in terms of low, moderate, or high. However, researchers have found that forensic evaluators do not agree on what is meant by low, moderate, or high risk (Hilton, Carter, Harris, & Sharpe, 2008; Mills & Kroner, 2006). Measures developed in one country or in one population may not generalize to another country or population (Austin, 2006). For example, Boccaccini, Murrie, Caperton, and Hawes (2009) reported that the Static-99 was not as predictive of sexual reoffending in a sample of sex offenders in the United States as compared with the published norms from Canada and the United Kingdom for this measure. Risk-assessment measures need to be validated in the community on which they will be used. Recently, some concerns have also been raised about the field reliability of risk-assessment measures. For example, researchers using the PCL-R have reported excellent inter-rater reliabilities. However, in a study comparing prosecution and defense PCL-R scores in an adversarial context (sexual violent predator evaluations), very poor agreement was found (Murrie, Boccaccini, Johnson, & Janke, 2008). Finally, clinicians who are writing risk-assessment reports or providing evidence to decision makers (e.g., an expert testifying in court) must ensure they use terminology that can be understood by the decision makers (e.g., juries, judges, lawyers, probation officers).

## Are Decision Makers Using the Scientific Research?

Despite the considerable strides that have been made in refining methods of violence prediction, many practitioners are not using these instruments. This gap in integrating science and clinical practice represents a significant challenge to this area. A survey by Boothby and Clements (2000) asked 820 correctional psychologists what tests they used in their assessments. The most commonly used test was the Minnesota Multiphasic Personality Inventory, which was used by 87% of the psychologists. Only 11% of the respondents mentioned using the Hare PCL-R, and less than 1% mentioned using the VRAG or the LSI-R. It is not clear why so few correctional psychologists are using these instruments. Research is needed to understand the obstacles to the adoption of new risk-assessment measures. One potential reason is that these newer instruments have not been part of the training programs for psychologists.

What impact do psychologists' recommendations have on forensic decision making? Past research has found that judicial decision making relies heavily on recommendations made by mental health professionals (Konecni & Ebbesen, 1984). In Canada, decisions to release forensic patients are strongly related to recommendations by clinicians (Quinsey & Ambtman, 1979), and reports by clinicians about treatment gains made by sex offenders strongly influence decisions about granting parole (Quinsey, Khanna, & Malcolm, 1998). Another related question is whether decision makers are relying on results of the newly developed actuarial risk instruments. Hilton and Simmons (2001) studied the influence of VRAG scores and clinical judgments on decisions made to transfer offenders with mental disorders in a maximum-security facility to less secure institutions. Review board decisions were not related to scores on the VRAG but to senior clinicians' testimony at the review board hearing. Patients who caused few institutional problems, who were compliant with medication, who were more physically attractive, and who had less serious criminal histories were more likely to be recommended by the clinician for transfer. Clinicians make more accurate decisions when they are given a statement that summarizes an individual's risk along with case information (i.e., "64% of people in Mr. Smith's risk category reoffended violently within 10 years after release") (Hilton, Harris, Rawson, & Beach, 2005). Clinicians also are able to make accurate decisions when they are provided with the information that relates to risk.

## Why Do Some Individuals Stop Committing Crimes?

Much of the research discussed in this chapter focuses on the risk factors related to engaging in crime and violence. However, if we want to prevent or reduce crime, knowledge about the factors relating to desistance from crime is probably equally important (Farrington, 2007). **Desistance** occurs when an individual who has engaged in criminal activities stops committing crime. Research even shows that a majority of offenders show large declines in their criminal activity in early adulthood (Blumstein & Cohen, 1987; Piquero et al., 2001). As many as 70% of offenders show significant declines in crime (and only a small percentage of offenders maintain criminal activity well into adulthood; Piquero et al., 2001). Yet, the reasons why offenders give up crime is poorly understood. Some research shows that the factors that relate to the onset of a criminal career do not necessarily explain desistance from crime (Stouthamer-Loeber, Wei, Loeber, & Masten, 2004). The desistance process occurs over time and may be related to such factors as "good" work or "good" marriages (Sampson & Laub, 2005; Maume, Ousey, & Beaver, 2005; Uggen, 1999). Age is strongly related to criminal behaviour, and the age-related

**Desistance:** The process of ceasing to engage in criminal behaviour

---

### Box 10.5

## Why Do High-Risk Violent Offenders Stop Offending?

In a study titled "Against All Odds: A Qualitative Follow-up of High-Risk Violent Offenders Who Were Not Reconvicted," Haggard, Gumpert, and Grann (2001) explored what factors were related to why repeat violent offenders stopped reoffending. To be eligible to participate in the study, the offender had to score high on the historical subscale of the HCR-20, to have been convicted of at least two violent crimes, and not to have been convicted for any crime for at least ten years. From a sample of 401 violent offenders, only six individuals were eligible to participate. Of these six, only four consented to be interviewed. The participants reported that the following factors are related to desistance. For each factor, a quotation from one of the participants is provided.

■ *Insight triggered by negative events connected to their criminal lifestyle.* "It grows within during a long time,

the insight, but you have to reach a point where it feels wrong. . . . To me, it was mostly due to the last time, when I was admitted to the forensic psychiatric hospital. The whole thing was crazy, and then I realized how off track I was—when you strike down a person with an axe because of a trivial thing . . . then you start wondering. I did anyway." (p. 1055)

■ *Social avoidance.* "I have a terrible temper and I can become violent, very violent. . . . You have to avoid different situations, you have to think about it all the time so that you don't put yourself in situations you can't handle." (p. 1057)

■ *Orientation to the family.* "After I served my sentence, I became more committed to my children. To help them not to make the same mistake I did." (p. 1057)

decline in criminal offending is connected to the maturation process (Menard & Huizinga, 1989). LeBlanc (1993) defines maturation as the "development of self- and social control" (p. 65). Shover and Thompson (1992) have suggested that as people age, they become less interested in a criminal lifestyle and are more able to understand and fear the consequences of engaging in crime. Recently, Serin and Lloyd (2009) have developed a model that proposes the transition between criminal offending and desistance is influenced by several intrapersonal moderators such as crime expectancies (what benefits do they see from not engaging in crime), beliefs about their ability to change (how hard will it be to change), and attributions for engaging in crime. See Box 10.5 for excerpts from a study that examines why high-risk offenders stop offending.

## SUMMARY

1. An assessment of risk requires two components: (1) an analysis of the likelihood of future criminal or violent acts, and (2) the development of strategies to manage or reduce the risk level.

2. Risk assessments are routinely conducted in the civil and criminal contexts. Risk assessments in civil contexts include civil commitments, child protection, immigration, and duty to warn. In criminal settings, the assessment of risk occurs at pretrial, sentencing, and release stages.

3. There are different types of errors when attempting to make predictions. Each of these errors has different consequences. False-positive errors affect the offender, whereas false-negative errors affect society and the victim.

4. Risk factors vary in terms of how fixed or changeable they are. Static factors either do not change or are highly resistant to change. Dynamic factors are changeable and are often targeted for intervention.

5. Various approaches have been developed to assess violent prediction. These include unstructured clinical judgment, actuarial prediction, and structured professional judgment. There are advantages and disadvantages to each approach.

6. Major risk factors can be classified into historical, dispositional, clinical, and contextual factors. Historical risk factors include general social history and specific criminal history variables, such as employment problems and past history of violence. Dispositional factors include demographic, attitudinal, and personality variables, such as gender, age, negative attitudes, and psychopathy. Clinical factors refer to those things that contribute to violence, such as substance abuse or major psychoses. Contextual factors refer to aspects of the individual's situation that can elevate the risk, such as access to victims or weapons, lack of social supports, or perceived stress.

### Discussion Questions

1. You have decided to take a summer job working at Correctional Service Canada. You are asked to help to devise a study to evaluate the accuracy of a new instrument designed to predict hostage-taking by federal offenders. How would you approach this task?

2. You think there should be more research on why offenders decide to stop offending. Describe a study you would conduct, focusing on the methodology and what factors you would measure that might relate to the desistance process.

3. Researchers have developed several risk-assessment instruments, but not all psychologists conducting risk assessments are using these scales. Why is this? What could be done to encourage forensic psychologists to start using these instruments?

4. A school board wants to know how to identify the next potential school shooter and has contacted you for your expertise. Describe what you know about problems with trying to identify low base-rate violent acts.

# Chapter 11
## Psychopaths

## Learning Objectives

■ Define psychopathy.

■ Outline the different assessment methods developed to measure psychopathy.

■ Describe the association between psychopathy and violence.

■ Describe the effectiveness of treatment programs for adult and adolescent psychopaths.

■ Identify the concerns associated with labelling a youth as a psychopath.

■ Explain the two main theories of psychopathy.

Jason Roach is a 19-year-old working in a convenience store. He dropped out of college and spends most of his time partying, and getting drunk and stoned. He decides that he does not want to spend the rest of his life working in a convenience store—a job he describes as "menial." One of his 16-year-old friends, Shawn, has been complaining about his parents and has started talking about wanting to "get rid of them." Jason offers to help, stating that if he helps he wants half of the insurance money. Jason convinces another 17-year-old friend with a car to help them with their murderous plan. Jason knows that they will need to have an alibi, so on the night of the murder they go to the nearby town to a strip club. Jason gets into an altercation with the bouncer to ensure the bouncer will remember them. Around midnight, armed with a baseball bat and a tire iron, they enter Shawn's house and beat his parents and his 14-year-old sister. While the beatings are taking place, Jason pours gasoline downstairs. As the offenders leave, Jason sets the house on fire. Two people die, and one is severely injured. Jason and his two friends are all charged and convicted of first-degree murder. At his trial, Jason describes himself as the "puppet master," appears proud of his ability to manipulate his younger friends, and shows no remorse for his actions.

**Psychopathy:** A personality disorder defined by a collection of interpersonal, affective, and behavioural characteristics, including manipulation, lack of remorse or empathy, impulsivity, and antisocial behaviours

Psychopaths have been called *intraspecies predators* (Hare, 1993). They seek vulnerable victims to use for their own benefit. Sometimes they get what they want by charming their victims, while at other times they use violence and intimidation to achieve their goals. Lacking a conscience and feelings for others, they satisfy their own selfish needs by preying on others. **Psychopathy** is a personality disorder defined by a collection of interpersonal, affective, and behavioural characteristics. Psychopaths are dominant, selfish, manipulative individuals who engage in impulsive and antisocial acts and who feel no remorse or shame for behaviour that often has a negative impact on others.

Descriptions of psychopathy exist in most cultures. Murphy (1976) found that the Inuit in Alaska use the term *kulangeta* to described an individual who "repeatedly lies and cheats and steals things and does not go hunting and, when the other men are out of the village, takes sexual advantage of many women—someone who does not pay attention to reprimands and who is always being brought to the elders for punishment" (p. 1026). When Murphy asked an Inuit elder what the group would typically do with a *kunlangeta*, he replied, "Somebody would have pushed him off the ice when nobody else was looking" (p. 1026).

In this chapter, we focus on methods for the assessment of psychopathy, how prevalent psychopathy is, its overlap with other disorders, the relationship between psychopathy and violence, and the effectiveness of treating psychopathy.

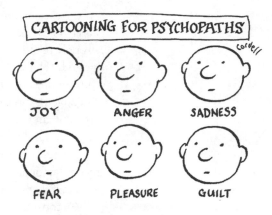

## ASSESSMENT OF PSYCHOPATHY

Hervey Cleckley (1976), a psychiatrist in Georgia, provided one of the most comprehensive clinical descriptions of the psychopath in his book *The Mask of Sanity*. Cleckley (1976) described 16 features, ranging from positive features (e.g., good intelligence, social charm, and absence of delusions and anxiety), emotional-interpersonal features (e.g., lack of remorse, untruthfulness, unresponsiveness in interpersonal relations), and behavioural problems (e.g., inadequately motivated antisocial behaviour, unreliability, failure to follow any life plan).

Currently, the most popular method of assessing psychopathy in adults is the **Hare Psychopathy Checklist–Revised** (PCL-R) (Hare, 1991, 2003). This assessment instrument was developed by Robert Hare at the University of British Columbia and is now being used around the world. The development of PCL-R was strongly influenced by the work of Hervey Cleckley. The PCL-R is a 20-item rating scale that uses a semi-structured interview and a review of file information to assess interpersonal (e.g., grandiosity, manipulativeness), affective (e.g., lack of remorse, shallow emotions), and behavioural (e.g., impulsivity, antisocial acts) features of psychopathy. Each item is scored on a 3-point scale: 2 indicates that the item definitely applies to the individual; 1 that it applies to some extent; and 0 indicates that the symptom definitely does not apply. The items are summed to obtain a total score ranging from 0 to 40. Researchers have often subdivided those administered the PCL-R into three groups: a high-PCL-R group (often called *psychopaths*), defined by a score of 30 or greater; a middle-scoring group (mixed group), with scores between about 20 and 30; and a low-scoring group (often called *nonpsychopaths*), with scores of below 20.

Initial factor analyses of the PCL-R indicated that it consisted of two correlated factors (Hare et al., 1990). Factor 1 reflects the combination of interpersonal and affective traits, whereas factor 2 is a combination of unstable and socially deviant traits. Researchers have examined the differential correlates of these two factors and found that factor 1 is more strongly related to predatory violence, emotional-processing deficits, and

**Hare Psychopathy Checklist–Revised:** The most popular method of assessing psychopathy in adults

poor treatment response (Hare, Clark, Grant, & Thornton, 2000; Patrick, Bradley, & Lang, 1993; Seto & Barbaree, 1999; Woodworth & Porter, 2002), whereas factor 2 is strongly related to reoffending, substance abuse, lack of education, and poor family background (Hare, 2003; Hemphill, Hare, & Wong, 1998; Porter, Birt, & Boer, 2001; Rutherford, Alterman, Cacciola, & McKay, 1997). Some researchers have argued for a three-factor model of psychopathy (Cooke & Michie, 2001). These three factors are (1) arrogant and deceitful interpersonal style, (2) deficient affective experience, and (3) impulsive and irresponsible behavioural style. This factor structure splits the original factor 1 into two factors and removes some of the antisocial items from factor 2. The most recent factor analysis of the PCL-R includes these three factors plus a fourth factor called *antisocial* that includes the antisocial items (Hare, 2003).

A considerable amount of research supports the use of the PCL-R in a range of samples, including male and female offenders, forensic psychiatric patients, sexual offenders, and substance abusers (Hare, 2003). Dr. Hare has been studying psychopaths for more than 35 years and is profiled in Box 11.1.

Another way of assessing for psychopathic traits is via self-report questionnaires. Using self-report measures has a number of advantages. First, they are able to measure those attitudes and emotions that are not easily observed by others (e.g., feelings of low self-esteem). Second, they are easy to administer (they can be administered on the web for research), quick to score, and relatively inexpensive. Third, it is not necessary to worry about inter-rater reliability since only the individual is completing the score. Finally, although there are concerns about psychopaths lying on self-report measures (see below), some questionnaires include measures of response styles to detect faking good or faking bad.

There are also a number of challenges with using self-report measures to assess for psychopathy (Lilienfeld & Fowler, 2006). First, as noted above, psychopaths often lie. Some psychopaths are "master manipulators" and will say whatever will be in their best interests. For example, they may malinger and claim they have a mental disorder to avoid facing more serious sanctions. Second, psychopaths may not have sufficient insight to accurately assess their traits. For example, psychopaths may not consider themselves as arrogant, dominant, or opinionated, whereas others might. Finally, it will likely be difficult for psychopaths to report on specific emotions if they have not experienced these emotions. For example, if asked if they feel remorse for the suffering they have caused others, they may mistake this feeling with the regret they feel for the consequences of getting caught.

**Psychopathic Personality Inventory:** A self-report measure of psychopathic traits

**Self-Report Psychopathy Scale:** A self-report measure of psychopathic traits

Two of the most widely used self-report scales are the **Psychopathic Personality Inventory-Revised** (PPI-R; Lilienfeld & Widows, 2005) and the **Self-Report Psychopathy Scale** (SRP; Paulhus, Hemphill, & Hare, in press). The PPI-R is a 154-item inventory designed to measure psychopathic traits in offender and community samples. It consists of eight content scales, two validity scales (to check for carelessness and positive or negative response styles), and measures two factors (fearless dominance and self-centred impulsivity). The SRP is a 64-item self-report measure designed to assess psychopathic traits in community samples. It consists of four factors: erratic lifestyle (e.g., "I'm a rebellious person"), callous affect (e.g., "I am more tough-minded than other people"), interpersonal manipulation (e.g., "I think I could 'beat' a lie detector"), and criminal tendencies (e.g., "I have been arrested by the police"). See Box 11.2 for research using self-report psychopathy scales in university students.

Box 11.1

## Canadian Researcher Profile: Dr. Robert Hare

Dr. Robert Hare is one of the world's leading authorities on psychopathy. Currently, he is a professor emeritus in the Department of Psychology at the University of British Columbia and an honorary professor of psychology at Cardiff University in Wales. Dr. Hare has a B.A. and M.A. from the University of Alberta and a Ph.D. from the University of Western Ontario.

Dr. Hare's more than 35-year career studying psychopathy began when he encountered a manipulative inmate while working as a prison psychologist between his M.A. and Ph.D. studies. Hervey Cleckley's book, *The Mask of Sanity*, played a pivotal role in his thinking about the clinical nature of psychopathy. Dr. Hare's early research focused on the use of theories, concepts, and procedures from learning, motivation, and psychophysiology in the laboratory study of psychopathy, with emphasis on information-processing and emotional correlates. However, a recurrent issue was the lack of a reliable, valid, and generally acceptable method for assessing the disorder. In the late 1970s, Dr. Hare, his students, and his colleagues began development of what was to become the Hare Psychopathy Checklist-Revised (PCL-R). The PCL-R is recognized worldwide as the leading instrument for the assessment of the disorder, both for scientific research and for practical applications in mental health and criminal justice.

Dr. Hare consistently acknowledges and praises the important contributions of his students to the theory and research on psychopathy, and he is pleased that many of his students have established themselves as major figures in the field. He describes the collaborative efforts with his former students as invigorating and fruitful, with major advances being made in the assessment of psychopathy, its

neurobiological nature, and its implications for the mental health and criminal justice systems. Currently, he is involved in a number of international research projects on assessment and treatment issues, risk for recidivism and violence, and functional neuroimaging. Although Dr. Hare has most often studied psychopaths in prison, he has recently begun to study them in a very different sphere— the corporate world.

He lectures widely about psychopathy and consults with law enforcement, including the FBI, the RCMP, and Her Majesty's Prison Service. He has been recognized worldwide for his research on psychopathy, receiving the Silver Medal of the Queen Sophia Center in Spain, three Canadian Psychological Association Awards (Award for Distinguished Scientific Applications of Psychology, Donald O. Hebb Award for Distinguished Contributions to Psychology as a Science, Distinguished Contributions to the International Advancement of Psychology), the Isaac Ray Award from the American Psychiatric Association, the American Academy of Psychiatry and Law Award for Outstanding Contributions to Forensic Psychiatry and Psychiatric Jurisprudence, and the B. Jaye Anno Award for Excellence in Communication from the National Commission on Correctional Health Care. He was the first recipient of the R.D. Hare Lifetime Achievement Award by the Society for the Scientific Study of Psychopathy.

Dr. Hare believes future forensic psychology researchers and clinicians should ensure that they are familiar with the important advances being made in cognitive/affective neuroscience and their implications for forensic psychology. The courses he most enjoyed teaching at the undergraduate level were Brain and Behaviour and Forensic Psychology.

Dr. Hare enjoys listening to jazz and blues and is an avid sailor. He credits his wife, Averil, whom he met in the back row of a course in abnormal psychology at the University of Alberta, with much of his success. In spite of a demanding professional career of her own, she found the time and energy to actively support and encourage his work. To this day, she remains his best friend and closest confidant. Their only child, Cheryl, died in 2005 after a long battle with multiple sclerosis and leukemia. Her courage and dignity in the face of adversity had a profound influence on their appreciation of the power of the human spirit.

Box 11.2

# Subclinical Psychopaths: University Samples

Psychopathic traits are dimensional, meaning that people vary on the number and severity of psychopathic features exhibited. Although most research has been conducted with offenders or forensic psychiatric patients, an increasing amount of research has examined people outside institutional settings. Much of this research has used self-report psychopathy measures. Several studies that investigated a range of different behaviours in university students are described below.

## Detecting Vulnerable Victims (Wheeler, Book, & Costello, 2009)

*Scenario:* University students were unknowingly videotaped walking down a hallway and were classified as being vulnerable or not based on their self-report of experienced victimization. Male university students were asked to pretend to be a mugger and rated the videotapes on vulnerability.

*Results:* Students with higher SRP scores were more accurate at detecting victim vulnerability.

## Defrauding a Lottery (Paulhus, Williams, & Nathanson, 2002)

*Scenario:* A student participates in a study and has a chance of winning $100. After the study has been completed, all study participants are sent an email in which the experimenter states that he has lost the information about who was supposed to receive the five $100 prizes. Participants are asked to email the experimenter to let him know it they had previously been a winner.

*Results:* Students scoring higher on the SRP were more likely to try and defraud the experimenter and claim they were the "true" winner.

## Cheating on Exams (Nathanson, Paulhus, & Williams, 2006)

*Scenario:* The experimenters obtained computerized multiple-choice exam answers and seating plans from the instructors of several large introductory psychology classes. The experimenters wanted to determine which personality traits were related to cheating.

*Results:* Four percent of students were identified as cheating pairs, in which one student copied the answers from an adjacent student. Psychopathic traits, as measured by the SRP, were the strongest predictors of cheating.

## Owning "Vicious" Dogs (Ragatz, Fremouw, Thomas, & McCoy, 2009)

*Scenario:* A large sample of 869 university students complete an anonymous online questionnaire assessing ownership of types of dog breeds, criminal behaviours, tolerance of animal abuse, and psychopathic traits. Owners of the following six breeds of dogs were classified as owning "vicious" dogs: Akita, chow, Doberman, pit bull, Rottweiler, and wolf-mix.

*Results:* Students classified as owning a "vicious" dog engaged in more criminal behaviours and scored higher on the primary psychopathy scale (measures of selfishness, carelessness, and manipulation) of the Levenson Primary and Secondary Psychopathy Scale (Levenson, Kiehl, & Fitzpatrick, 1995) but were not more tolerant of animal abuse than other students.

# PSYCHOPATHY AND ANTISOCIAL PERSONALITY DISORDER

**Antisocial personality disorder:** A personality disorder characterized by a history of behaviour in which the rights of others are violated

**Antisocial personality disorder** (APD) (American Psychiatric Association, 1994) refers to a personality disorder in which there is evidence for conduct disorder before age 15 and a chronic pattern of disregarding the rights of others since age 15. After age 15, a person diagnosed with APD would need to display three or more of the following symptoms:

- Repeatedly engaging in criminal acts
- Deceitfulness
- Impulsivity

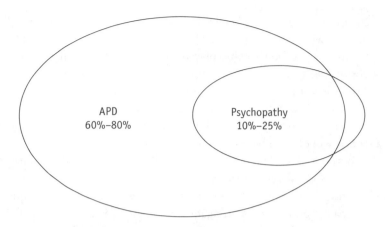

**Figure 11.1** DSM-IV Antisocial Personality Disorder and PCL-R Psychopathy: Construct Overlap

- Irritability
- Reckless behaviours
- Irresponsibility
- Lack of remorse

Additional confusion surrounds the diagnosis of APD and its relationship to both psychopathy and "**sociopathy**." The three terms are sometimes used interchangeably, whereas a general consensus among most researchers is that the constructs of APD, psychopathy, and "sociopathy" are related but distinct (Hare & Neumann, 2008). The term *sociopath* was coined in 1930 by Partridge to describe those people who had problems with or refused to adapt to society. Lykken (2006) proposed that sociopaths manifest similar traits as psychopaths but develop these traits as a result of poor parenting and other environmental factors, whereas psychopaths are genetically predisposed to a temperament that makes them difficult to socialize. The term *sociopath* is rarely used in the empirical literature, and no assessment instruments have been developed to identify this construct.

Although psychopathy and APD share some features, APD places more emphasis on antisocial behaviours than does the PCL-R. The prevalence of APD is very high in prisons, with up to 80% of adult offenders being diagnosed with this disorder (Hare, Forth, & Strachan, 1992; Motiuk & Porporino, 1991). Using a cut-off of 30 on the PCL-R, 10% to 25% of adult offenders can be classified as psychopaths (Hare, 2003). An asymmetrical relation exists between these two disorders: nearly all psychopathic offenders meet the diagnostic criteria for APD, but most offenders diagnosed with APD are not psychopaths. APD symptoms are most strongly related to the behavioural features of psychopathy and not to the interpersonal or affective features. Figure 11.1 illustrates the overlap between psychopathy and APD.

**Sociopathy:** A label used to describe a person whose psychopathic traits are assumed to be due to environmental factors

## FORENSIC USE OF PSYCHOPATHY

Several studies have surveyed the use of expert testimony regarding the assessment of psychopathy, sociopathy, or APD in criminal and civil court proceedings. Zinger and Forth (1998) reviewed cases in which an expert testified about psychopathy, sociopathy, or

APD, whereas in more recent studies by DeMatteo and Edens (2006) and Walsh and Walsh (2006) only cases in which the PCL-R was used by the expert were included. These researchers found that psychopathy has played a role in a diverse range of criminal cases, with the majority of testimony regarding psychopathy being associated with an increased severity of disposition. In Canada, psychopathy and associated constructs were used in making sentencing decisions: to support a case's transfer from youth to adult court, to contribute to dangerous offender hearings, to help to determine parole eligibility, and to assess mental state at time of offence hearings (Zinger & Forth, 1998). In the United States, the PCL-R was also used in sexual violent predator evaluations and death-penalty sentencing and in civil cases for child custody decisions. For example, in death-penalty hearings in the United States and dangerous offender proceedings in Canada, a diagnosis of psychopathy, sociopathy, and APD is an aggravating factor for the death penalty (in the United States), and considered to be associated with a higher risk of violent recidivism and a lack of treatment responsivity in dangerous offender hearings. With respect to the insanity defence, a diagnosis of psychopathy does fulfil the disease of the mind requirement, but it has never fulfilled the second requirement of not appreciating the nature or quality of the act or knowing that it is wrong.

## PSYCHOPATHY AND VIOLENCE

The characteristics that define psychopathy are compatible with a criminal lifestyle and a lack of concern for societal norms. Characteristics that ordinarily help to inhibit aggression and violence, such as empathy, close emotional bonds, and internal inhibitions, are lacking or relatively ineffective in psychopaths. Psychopathy is significant because of its association with criminal behaviour in general and violence in particular. Although psychopaths make up a relatively small proportion of the population, their involvement in serious repetitive crime and violence is out of proportion to their numbers. As stated by Hart (1998), "The two are so intimately connected that a full understanding of violence is impossible without consideration of the role played by psychopathy" (p. 367). See Box 11.3 for a description of a psychopath.

Psychopaths are high-density (prolific), versatile offenders. The crimes of psychopaths run the gamut from minor theft and fraud to "cold-blooded" murder. Compared to nonpsychopathic offenders, they start their criminal career at a younger age and persist longer, engage in more violent offences, commit a greater variety of violent offences, engage in more violence within institutions, and, as seen in Chapter 10, they are more likely to be violent after release (Hare, 2003).

The nature of psychopaths' violence also differs from other types: "Psychopathic violence is more likely to be predatory in nature, motivated by readily identifiable goals, and carried out in a callous, calculated manner without the emotional context that usually characterizes the violence of other offenders" (Hare, 2003, p. 136). Several studies have found that offenders who engage in instrumental violence (premeditated violence to obtain some goal) score significantly higher on measures of psychopathy than do offenders engaging in reactive violence (impulsive, unplanned violence that occurs in response to a provocation; Cornell et al., 1996; Walsh, Swogger, & Kosson, 2009). (Chapter 14 discusses instrumental and reactive violence in more detail.) One study by Williamson, Hare, and Wong (1987) found that when nonpsychopaths commit violence, they are likely to target

## Clifford Olson: A Predatory Psychopath

On August 22, 1997, a jury in Surrey, B.C., took just 15 minutes to reject Clifford Olson's bid for early parole. Olson is serving a life sentence for the murders of 11 children in 1980 and 1981. Clifford Olson is notorious, not only for being one of Canada's most prolific serial killers, but also for the deal he made with the police, what he calls his "cash for corpses" deal. Olson negotiated a payment of $10 000 for each body he uncovered for the RCMP. The money did not go to Olson but to a trust for Olson's wife. In total, $100 000 was paid to this trust fund.

According to section 745 of the Criminal Code of Canada, first-degree and second-degree murderers can apply for a judicial hearing to request an earlier parole eligibility date after serving 15 years. This provision has been called the *faint hope clause* and was introduced in 1976, when the death penalty was abolished and replaced by mandatory life sentences for first-degree and second-degree murder. The parole ineligibility period for first-degree murder was 25 years; for second-degree murder, it was 10 years, although the judge has the power to increase this period to up to 25 years. The underlying motivation for this clause was to provide murderers with an incentive to behave in prison, making prisons safer for correctional officers, and to motivate murderers to participate in rehabilitation.

Dr. Stanley Semrau, a forensic psychiatrist, was hired by the Crown prosecution to evaluate Olson for this judicial review hearing. Dr. Semrau assessed Olson on the Hare Psychopathy Checklist–Revised and gave him a score of 38

out of 40. At the judicial review hearing, he stated, "It's certainly the highest score I have ever given anyone" (Semrau & Gale, 2002, p. 273). Dr. Semrau also concluded that Olson was "completely untreatable" (Semrau & Gale, 2002, p. 286) and was more dangerous now than he was when arrested in 1981, since he currently sees himself as "the ultimate serial killer" (Semrau & Gale, 2002, p. 272).

In Dr. Semrau and Judy Gale's book, *Murderous Minds on Trial*, they devote a chapter to describing the evaluation Dr. Semrau conducted on Olson. In this chapter, he states, "I saw almost nothing that wasn't a perfect fit with the psychopath's cold, guilt-free use of others for his own ends, and chronically antisocial and deviant lifestyle" (Semrau & Gale, 2002, p. 289).

Partly in response to Olson's use of the faint hope clause, changes were made to section 745 of the Criminal Code. On January 1, 1997, these changes came into force. Multiple (including serial) murderers are now ineligible for a section 745 review. Olson currently remains incarcerated in the maximum-security prison in Quebec. He is in protective custody to safeguard him from other offenders. Olson is allowed out of his cell for one hour a day to participate in solitary exercise, to work alone as a cleaner, or to attend meetings. Olson was recently in the news bragging about receiving old age pension cheques from the government. After spending nearly 50 of his 70 years in prison he is receiving $1169.47 a month in pension. The government is now looking into denying pensions to violent offenders serving life sentences.

---

people they know and their violent behaviour is likely to occur in the context of strong emotional arousal. In contrast, psychopaths are more likely to target strangers and be motivated by revenge or material gain. Several studies of adolescent offenders have found that youth who engaged in instrumental violence were more psychopathic than other youth (Flight & Forth, 2007; Vitacco, Neumann, Caldwell, Leisticio & Van Rybroek, 2006).

Psychopaths' use of instrumental motives extends to homicide. Woodworth and Porter (2002) investigated the association between psychopathy and the nature of homicides committed by 135 Canadian offenders. Using PCL-R scores to divide the offenders into the three groups described above—nonpsychopaths (PCL-R scores of less than 20), medium scorers (PCL-R scores between 20 and 30), and psychopaths (PCL-R scores of 30 or greater)—the percentage of homicides that were primarily instrumental (planned and motivated by an external goal) were 28%, 67%, and 93%, respectively. The researchers

## Psychopathy in Animals?

Can you measure psychopathic traits in animals or is psychopathy unique to humans? Some researchers have speculated that certain breeds of dogs are more psychopathic than others. For example, Solomon (1960) compared dog breeds on being able to resist a tempting treat that was associated with punishment. In this study, 6-month-old puppies were placed in a room with two bowls of dog food, one containing boiled horsemeat, and the other dry dog food. When the puppies approached the bowl of horsemeat, they were swatted with a rolled-up newspaper on the rump. Most puppies quickly learned to stay away from the more desirable horsemeat and eat the bowl of dry dog food. However, certain breeds of dogs quickly learned to resist temptation (e.g., Shetland sheepdogs), whereas "Basenjis seem to be constitutional psychopaths and it is very difficult to maintain taboos in such dogs" (Eysenck & Gudjonnsson, 1989, p. 115). David Lykken (1995) describes the bull terrier as sharing similar features of human psychopaths, such as being fearless and immune to punishment.

The most detailed investigation into animal psychopathy has been a study by Lilienfeld and colleagues (1999) measuring psychopathic traits in chimpanzees. The Chimpanzee Psychopathy Measure (CPM) consists of 23 items rated on a 5-point scale, including items such as aggressive (causes harm to others), deceptive (is sneaky and manipulates others), greedy (takes more than fair share of food), confident (behaves in a positive, assured manner), boredom prone (stirs up excitement when nothing is happening), and dominant (demands submission of others). Six human raters rated 34 chimpanzees that were housed at the Yerkes Regional Primate Research Center in Georgia. There was strong agreement across the raters on the CPM. As in humans, there were sex differences, with male chimpanzees scoring higher on the CPM than female chimpanzees. The CPM was positively related to observer ratings of sexual activity, daring behaviours, teasing, bluff displays, and temper tantrums, and was negatively related to generosity.

concluded that psychopaths engage in "cold-blooded" homicides much more often than nonpsychopaths.

In a study of post-homicide behaviours, Häkkänen-Nyholm (2009) measured psychopathic traits in 546 Finnish homicide offenders. Higher PCL-R scores were found for cases with multiple versus single offenders, stranger victims, and male victims; for offenders who left the scene of the murder; and for offenders who denied responsibility for the murder. Rather than experiencing remorse for the murder they had committed, psychopathic offenders shifted the blame and focused on "saving their own skin." See Box 11.4 to see how some researchers have attempted to measure psychopathic traits in animals.

Recent evidence for psychopaths' ability to manipulate the criminal justice system comes from a study by Porter, ten Brinke, and Wilson (2009). Psychopathic offenders (both sexual and nonsexual offenders) were given early release from prison more often than nonpsychopathic offenders. However, when followed-up on, the psychopathic offenders were less successful than the nonpsychopathic offenders. It is critical that people making decisions about release be familiar with psychopathy and the psychopath's abilities to engage in impression management (i.e., telling people what they want to hear).

## PSYCHOPATHS IN THE COMMUNITY

Much of the research in community samples has used the Hare Psychopathy Checklist: Screening Version (PCL:SV; Hart, Cox, & Hare, 1995). This 12-item version takes less time to administer and places less emphasis on criminal behaviour for scoring than the

PCL-R. In the general population, psychopathy is rare. Coid, Yang, Ullrich, Roberts, and Hare (2009) assessed 301 male and 319 females in the community and found that only 0.6% of the sample had scores of 13 or greater on the PCL:SV (only one person scored above the cut-off score of 18), with 71% of the sample having no psychopathic traits (i.e., scoring 0 on the PCL:SV). In another community sample in the United States (Neumann & Hare, 2008), about 75% of the sample had scores of 2 or less and only 1.2% had scores in the "potential psychopathic" range (i.e., scores of 13 or greater on the PCL:SV). Regardless of sample, females consistently score lower than males on the PCL:SV and other psychopathy measures (Dolan & Völlm, 2009).

Not all psychopaths are violent, nor do they all end up in prison. As Hare (1993) notes, "[We] are far more likely to lose our life savings to an oily tongued swindler than our lives to a steely-eyed killer" (p. 6). Paul Babiak (2000), an organizational psychologist, consulted with six companies undergoing dramatic organizational change, such as merging and downsizing. In each of these companies, Babiak found employees with many psychopathic features to be at the root of some of the company problems. These employees were skilled at getting information on other employees, spreading unwarranted vicious rumours about others, and causing dissension among employees. What they were not doing was pulling their own weight on the job. They were particularly good at manipulating the key players in the organization (employees who can provide them with information or upper management) and blaming others for their failures (see Babiak [1995] for a case study of the corporate psychopath).

More recently, Babiak, Neumann, and Hare (2010) assessed psychopathic traits in a 203 corporate professionals. The average PCL-R score was 3.6; however, eight professionals (or 4.9%) scored above the 30-point cut-off for a diagnosis of psychopathy. The professionals with psychopathic traits were less likely to be team players, had poorer management skills, and had poorer performance appraisals than professionals with few psychopathic traits. However, the more psychopathic professionals were more creative, engaged in more strategic thinking, and had stronger communication skills than the less psychopathic professionals.

One area of research that has been vastly neglected is research with victims of psychopaths. To date there is only one published study exploring the experiences of victims of psychopaths. Through interviews with 20 female victims, Kirkman (2005) aimed to identify the behavioural and personality characteristics of nonincarcerated psychopathic males who may or may not have abused their partners. Eight characteristics of male psychopaths in heterosexual relationships were extracted from the interviews: (1) talking victim into victimization, (2) lying, (3) economic abuse, (4) emotional abuse/psychological torture, (5) multiple infidelities, (6) isolation and coercion, (7) assault, and (8) mistreatment of children. Future research using a larger, more diverse sample of victims needs to be conducted. See the In the Media box for how psychopaths are portrayed in the media.

## PSYCHOPATHY AND SEXUAL VIOLENCE

Psychopathy and sexual violence have been the focus of much research. As noted above, psychopathy is associated with violent offences. However, it is only weakly associated with sexual offences. For example, Brown and Forth (1997) reported that in a sample of 60 rapists, their PCL-R score was associated with their number of prior offences but not

# Mean on the Screen: Media's Portrayal of Psychopaths

When you think of the term *psychopath* who comes to mind? If you think of psychopaths in movies, the first character that most people think of is Hannibal Lector. This character was introduced in Thomas Harris's book *Red Dragon*, which was published in 1981. In 1988, the sequel was turned into the popular movie *Silence of the Lambs*, with actor Anthony Hopkins playing Hannibal Lector. Lector is a psychiatrist who happens also to be a cannibalistic serial killer who is in a secure forensic psychiatric institution. A trainee FBI agent is sent to interview Lector in hopes that he will help her capture another serial killer. The film revolves around Lector's manipulation of this agent and his escape. Although Lector has many psychopathic traits, most psychopaths are not serial killers, nor as intelligent or as successfully manipulative as Lector.

What about psychopaths on television shows? In recent years, the most popular psychopathic television character is Dexter Morgan. The *Dexter* series follows the day-to-day life of Dexter, a blood-spatter analyst who also happens to be a serial killer. However, Dexter is a serial killer with some morals, since he targets killers who have

escaped justice. In reality, most serial killers target vulnerable victims, such as children, sex-trade workers, runaways, or the homeless, not other violent criminals.

Both Hannibal Lector and Dexter Morgan experienced serious trauma in their early childhood. At age 8, Lector's parents are killed in an explosion and his sister is murdered and cannibalized in front of him. Lector is put in an orphanage and starts having deviant violent fantasies focused on avenging his sister's death.

Dexter witnessed the murder of his mother at age 3 and was adopted by Harry, a police officer. Harry recognizes Dexter's "psychopathic traits" and teaches him to channel his passion for killing to murder other killers. Harry also realizes that Dexter has no emotions and teaches Dexter to fake emotions.

Is experiencing a traumatic event in childhood related to the development of psychopathy? Although some psychopaths do experience trauma, many do not, which suggests that trauma is not a necessary precursor for psychopathy. Also, although these fictional psychopaths may have some characteristics associated with psychopathy, they are definitely not "typical" psychopaths.

the number of prior sexual offences. In a larger sample of offenders, Porter, Fairweather, et al. (2000) found that psychopaths engaged in significantly more violent offences than nonpsychopaths (7.3 versus 3.0, respectively) but engaged in fewer sexual offences (2.9 versus 5.9, respectively). One potential explanation for this finding is the high rate of sexual offending found in child molesters, who tend not to be psychopaths.

**Sexual homicide:** Homicides that have a sexual component

In general, offenders who commit **sexual homicides** (homicides that have a sexual component or in which sexual arousal occurs) are the most psychopathic, followed by mixed sexual offenders (those who sexually assault both children and adults), followed by

rapists, with the lowest psychopathy scores found among child molesters (Brown & Forth, 1997; Firestone, Bradford, Greenberg, & Larose, 1998; Porter, Fairweather, et al., 2000; Quinsey, Rice, & Harris, 1995).

Other studies have evaluated the motivations of psychopaths when committing sexual crimes. Brown and Forth (1997) examined specific motivations for psychopathic and nonpsychopathic rapists. The Massachusetts Treatment Center Rapist Typology (MTC: R3) (Knight & Prentky, 1990) identifies different types of rapists based on motivation and level of social competence. Brown and Forth reported that 81% of psychopathic rapists were opportunistic or vindictive, as compared with 56% of the nonpsychopathic rapists. Nonpsychopaths were more likely to report feelings of anxiety or alienation in the 24-hour period leading up to the rape, whereas psychopaths reported positive emotions. Porter, Woodworth, Earle, Drugge, and Boer (2003) investigated the relation between psychopathy and severity of violence in a sample of 38 sexual homicide offenders. Level of sadistic violence (evidence for overkill and that the offender obtained enjoyment from hurting the victim) was related to the PCL-R total scores and with the interpersonal and affective features of psychopathy.

In a recent study of 100 male German forensic patients (all sexual offenders), Mokros, Osterheider, Hucker, and Nitschke (2010) studied the association between psychopathy and **sexual sadism**. Sexual sadists are those people who are sexually aroused by fantasies, urges, or acts of inflicting pain, suffering, or humiliation on another human (American Psychiatric Association, 2000). PCL-R total scores, affective deficits facet, and antisocial facets were all related to sexual sadism.

**Sexual sadism:** People who are sexually aroused by fantasies, urges, or acts of inflicting pain, suffering, or humiliation on another human

## PSYCHOPATHY AND TREATMENT

Are psychopathic adults responsive to treatment? Most clinicians and researchers are pessimistic, although some (e.g., Salekin, 2002) are more optimistic. As Hare (1998) states, "Unlike most other offenders, they suffer little personal distress, see little wrong with their attitudes and behavior, and seek treatment only when it is in their best interests to do so (such as when seeking probation or parole)" (p. 202).

The best-known study of treatment outcome in psychopaths was a retrospective study by Rice, Harris, and Cormier (1992). These researchers investigated the effects of an intensive therapeutic treatment program on violent psychopathic and nonpsychopathic forensic psychiatric patients. Using a matched group design, forensic patients who spent two years in the treatment program (treated group) were paired with forensic patients who were assessed but not admitted to the program (untreated group). Using file information, all patients were scored on the PCL-R and were divided into psychopaths (scores of 25 or greater) and nonpsychopaths (scores of less than 25). Patients were followed for an average of ten years after release. The violent recidivism rate was 39% for untreated nonpsychopaths, 22% for treated nonpsychopaths, 55% for untreated psychopaths, and 77% for treated psychopaths. Treatment was associated with a reduction in violent recidivism among nonpsychopaths but an increase in violent recidivism among psychopaths. Some clinicians have concluded from the above study that we should not bother to treat psychopaths, since treatment will only make them worse: "This was the wrong program for serious psychopathic offenders" (Quinsey, Harris, Rice, & Cormier, 1998, p. 88).

Caution is required in interpreting the results of studies such as that carried out by Rice et al. (1992). Although at first glance such research implies that psychopaths are untreatable, an alternative but perhaps equally plausible account is that the treatments for psychopaths that have been tried so far have not worked (Hare et al., 2000; Richards, Casey, & Lucente, 2003; Seto & Barbaree, 1999). Reasons why a treatment may not work include the use of an inappropriate treatment and problems in implementing the treatment, such as inadequate training of those administering it or lack of support from management.

A more promising treatment outcome study has been reported by Olver and Wong (2009). These researchers found that although psychopathic sex offenders who dropped out of treatment were more likely to violently reoffend, those psychopathic sex offenders who stayed in treatment showed positive treatment gains and were less likely to violently reoffend. We hope that in the future, with better understanding of what causes psychopathy, treatment programs can be developed to target potentially changeable factors linked to why psychopaths engage in crime and violence.

## PSYCHOPATHY IN YOUTH

Research is increasingly focused on identifying the emergence of psychopathic traits in youth. The assumption is that psychopathy does not suddenly appear in adulthood but instead gradually develops from various environmental and biological antecedents. In line with this viewpoint, several measures have been recently developed to identify psychopathic traits early in development. Two assessment instruments have been adapted from the PCL-R: one for use with children and the other for adolescents. The **Antisocial Process Screening Device** (APSD) (Frick & Hare, 2001) is designed for assessing the precursors of psychopathic traits in children. The child is assigned a rating on various questions by parents or teachers. A self-report version of this scale also has been developed for use with adolescents. Frick, Bodin, and Barry (2000) found that the APSD has a three-dimensional structure consisting of a callous-unemotional factor, an impulsivity factor, and a narcissism factor. The **Hare Psychopathy Checklist: Youth Version** (PCL:YV) (Forth, Kosson, & Hare, 2003) is a rating scale designed to measure psychopathic traits and behaviours in male and female adolescents between the ages of 12 and 18.

Reservations have been raised concerning the appropriateness of applying the construct of psychopathy to children and adolescents (Edens, Skeem, Cruise, & Cauffman, 2001; Seagrave & Grisso, 2002; Zinger & Forth, 1998). One concern has been the use of the label *psychopath*, a label that has many negative connotations for the public and for mental health and criminal justice professionals. As stated by Murrie, Cornell, Kaplan, McConville, and Levy-Elkon (2004), "The use of the label 'psychopath' has ominous connotations that may adversely influence treatment decisions, social service plans, and juvenile justice determinations" (p. 64). Studies examining the effects of the *psychopathy* label in adults and juveniles are described in Box 11.5.

Psychopathy in adults is associated with violence, is assumed to be a stable trait, and is resistant to intervention attempts. Whether psychopathic traits in youth are stable has recently been studied. For example, a study using the APSD has indicated fairly high stability across a four-year period (Frick, Kimonis, Dandreaux, & Farell, 2003). The only longitudinal study to assess psychopathic traits in youth and to reassess for psychopathy in

**Antisocial Process Screening Device:** Observer rating scale to assess psychopathic traits in children

**Hare Psychopathy Checklist–Youth Version:** Scale designed to measure psychopathic traits in adolescents

Box 11.5

# Psychopathy Label: The Potential for Stigma

If an individual is called a *psychopath* in court, are judges and juries likely to be more punitive toward him or her? The results from mock juror decision-making trials have been mixed. Two studies examined the effect of the *psychopath* label in a death-penalty trial: one in which the defendant was an adult (Edens, Colwell, Deforges, & Fernandez, 2005) and one in which the defendant was a juvenile (Edens, Guy, & Fernandez, 2003). In both studies, undergraduates were presented with written descriptions of a defendant in a murder case. All aspects about the case presented to the students were the same except that the authors manipulated the diagnosis or personality traits of the defendant. In the Edens et al. (2005) study, the defendant was described as a psychopath, as psychotic, or as having no mental disorder. As can be seen in Figure 11.2, mock jurors were more likely to support the death penalty for the psychopathic defendant than for the psychotic or nondisordered defendant.

Edens et al. (2003), in a study that examined the influence of psychopathic traits, presented undergraduates with one of two versions of a modified newspaper clipping about a 16-year-old facing the death penalty. In one version, the juvenile defendant was described as having psychopathic traits; he was "the kind of teenager who did not feel remorse for his behavior or guilt when he got into trouble . . . a pathological liar who manipulated people . . .

arrogant" (p. 22). In contrast, the nonpsychopathic traits version described the youth as "the kind of teenager who felt remorseful and guilty when he got into trouble . . . a trustworthy adolescent who never conned people . . . modest and humble" (p. 22). In this study, the mock jurors presented with the psychopathic traits version were more likely to support the death penalty and to be less supportive of the defendant receiving intervention in prison. As can be seen in Figure 11.2, mock jurors also were less likely to support the death penalty for juveniles than for adults.

Murrie, Cornell, and McCoy (2005) investigated the potential influence of a diagnosis of psychopathy, conduct disorder, or no diagnosis with juvenile probation officers. In contrast to the above studies, the diagnostic label was not strongly related to probation officers' recommendations of type of sanction, risk level, or treatment amenability. Murrie et al. (2005) state, "There was little evidence that a specific diagnosis of psychopathy affected JPO [juvenile probation officer] judgments" (p. 338). Murrie and his colleagues have also studied the impact of the *psychopathy* label on juvenile court judges and clinicians (Murrie, Boccaccini, McCoy, & Cornell, 2007; Rockett, Murrie, & Boccaccini, 2007).

Source: Adapted from data from Edens et al. (2003) and Edens et al. (2005).

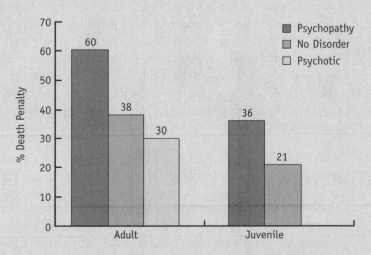

**Figure 11.2** Death-Penalty Verdicts Based on Mental Disorder of Offender and Age of Offender

adulthood was recently completed by Lynam, Caspi, Moffitt, Loeber, and Southamer-Loeber (2007). The results indicated that there was a moderate degree of stability in psychopathic traits from age 13 to age 24. Another concern that has been raised is whether "scores on measures of psychopathy arguably may be inflated by general characteristics of adolescence" (Edens et al. 2001, p. 59). Arguing against this last point are the few studies measuring psychopathic traits in community youth that have found the scores on psychopathy measures to be very low (Forth et al., 2003; Sevecke, Pukrop, Kosson, & Krischer, 2009).

Research has provided some support for extending the construct of psychopathy to youth. For example, boys who score high on the callous/unemotional dimension of the APSD have more police contacts, more conduct problems, and are more likely to have a parent with APD than are children who score low on this dimension. Research using the PCL:YV has found that adolescents with many psychopathic traits become involved in criminal behaviours at an earlier age, engage in more violence in institutions and in the community, and are at a higher risk of reoffending once released as compared with other adolescents (Corrado, Vincent, Hart, & Cohen, 2004; Forth et al., 2003; Kosson, Cyterski, Steuerwald, Neumann, & Walker-Matthews, 2002; Murrie et al., 2004). In contrast, however, more recent research has questioned the utility of the PCL:YV to predict violence in adolescent female offenders (Odgers, Reppucci, & Moretti, 2005; Schmidt, McKinnon, Chattha, & Brownlee, 2006). Research has also looked at the association between psychopathic traits and other symptoms in youth. For example, Campbell, Porter, and Santor (2004) found that psychopathic traits were related to delinquency and aggression but not to anxiety or depression symptoms in a sample of male and female adolescent offenders.

One aspect of psychopathy in youth that may differ from its adult counterpart is that youth with psychopathic traits may be more responsive to interventions (Salekin, Rogers, & Machin, 2001). In contrast, however, O'Neill, Lidz, and Heilbrun (2003) examined treatment outcome in a sample of 64 adolescent substance abusers and found that youth scoring high on the PCL:YV showed poor program attendance, poor quality of participation, and less clinical improvement, and were more likely to reoffend after completing the program. Caldwell, Skeem, Salekin, and Van Rybroek (2006) compared the treatment outcome of two groups of incarcerated youth, both with very high PCL:YV scores. Youth who were given intensive treatment at a juvenile treatment centre were compared with youth who were given treatment at a juvenile correctional centre. Youth who were released from the correctional centre violently reoffended at twice the rate in a two-year follow-up as compared with the youth receiving the intensive treatment at the treatment centre. These results suggest that with the appropriate intensive treatment, youth with many psychopathic traits are amenable to treatment (Caldwell, McCormick, Umstead, & Van Rybroek, 2007).

## PSYCHOPATHY: NATURE VERSUS NURTURE?

The nature versus nurture debate focuses on the relative importance of a person's innate characteristics (nature) as compared with his or her personal experiences (nurture). Growing evidence suggests a strong genetic contribution to psychopathy.

In all research designed to tease apart the role of genes (nature) and environment (nurture) in the development of psychological traits, investigators try to hold constant the effect of either genes or environment. Typically, this involves comparing individuals who have similar genes but who are raised in different environments. Variations on this basic idea can take several forms. Identical twins (who have identical genes) can be compared when raised apart from each other. This method holds genetic influences constant while allowing the environment to vary. In this kind of study, the twins are usually compared with randomly paired individuals. Also, fraternal twins (who share half their genes) raised together can be compared with identical twins (who share all their genes) raised together. Finally, biological siblings (who share half their genes) raised together can be compared with adoptive siblings (who share no genes but who are raised in the same environment).

To date, the only type of studies that have been done to measure the heritability of psychopathic traits are studies comparing identical and fraternal twins. Several twin studies have been done and all have yielded similar findings. In a study of adult male twins, Blonigen, Carlson, Krueger, and Patrick (2003) had each pair of identical and fraternal twins complete the Psychopathic Personality Inventory (PPI) (Lilienfeld & Andrews, 1996). Identical twins were much more similar in their PPI scores than were fraternal twins. Genetic influences accounted for between 29% and 59% of the variance for each of the different PPI subscales. In a recent adolescent twin study in Sweden, Larsson, Andershed, and Lichtenstein (2006) also found a strong genetic influence using the Youth Psychopathic Inventory (Andershed, Gustafson, Kerr, & Håkan, 2002). Finally, in a sample of 7-year-old twin pairs in the United Kingdom, Viding, Blair, Moffitt, and Plomin (2005) found that callous-unemotional traits were moderately to highly heritable. These studies point to the importance of genetic factors, but environmental factors, such as adverse family background, may influence how these innate traits are expressed.

## Does Family Matter?

The best research method to determine whether family experiences are related to the development of psychopathy is to do a prospective longitudinal study. Such research would study a group of young children and follow them through childhood, adolescence, and into adulthood, measuring family background variables and psychopathic traits. The strength of this type of study is that it allows researchers to avoid retrospective bias (the tendency to reconstruct past events so that they are consistent with an individual's current beliefs) and to establish causal order. Unfortunately, there are very few prospective longitudinal studies that specifically investigate the development of psychopathy.

The Cambridge Study in Delinquent Development is a 40-year prospective study of antisocial behaviour of 411 London boys who have been followed up from age 8 to age 48. At age 48, the men were assessed by using the PCL:SV (Hart, Cox, & Hare, 1995). Farrington (2006) reported that of those men scoring 10 or more, 97% had been convicted of an offence and 48.5% of these men were chronic offenders (i.e., convicted more than ten times). Measuring family background variables between ages 8 and 10, the best predictors of adult psychopathy were having a criminal father or mother, being a son whose father was uninvolved with him, having a low family income, coming from a disrupted family, and experiencing physical neglect.

In another longitudinal study, Weiler and Widom (1996) used court records to identify over 900 children who had been abused or neglected prior to age 11 and compared them with a control group matched on age, race, gender, elementary school class, and place of residence. Children were followed-up after 20 years and assessed on a modified PCL-R. Children who had been abused had slightly higher modified PCL-R scores as compared with the control sample.

Likely no single variable or combination of family background variables is responsible for the development of psychopathy. Current research is consistent with the view that there are multiple developmental pathways to the development of psychopathy, some of which involve family background and others in which psychopathy emerges irrespective of family background.

## PSYCHOPATHY AND LAW ENFORCEMENT

According to O'Toole (2007), "psychopathy can be described as one of law enforcement's greatest challenges" (p. 305). Psychopaths engage in high rates of crime, including violent offences. Thus, law enforcement personnel will often come into contact with psychopaths. In some cases, the contact can lead to lethal consequences. For example, Pinizzotto and Davis (1992) conducted a study of the characteristics of killers of police officers. Almost half of these killers had personality and behaviour features consistent with psychopathy. O'Toole (2007) describes the potential crime scene characteristics manifested by a psychopathic violent offender. For example, impulsivity (a feature of psychopathy) can be manifested at a crime scene by injury pattern to the victim, choice of weapon, and time and location of crime. Some psychopaths are charming and manipulative and will be more likely to use a con to minimize the threat they pose when approaching a victim. For example, a prolific serial killer convinced sex-trade workers that he was not a threat by having children's toys visible in his car and a photograph of his young son on the dashboard.

Another challenge for law enforcement personnel is to develop effective methods for interrogating psychopathic suspects. For example, when interrogating a suspected psychopathic serial killer, trying to get the suspect to confess by saying such things as "Think about the family of the victims" or "You will feel better if you tell us about it" will likely be counterproductive. Instead, appealing to the psychopath's sense of grandiosity and need for status might be more productive. Quayle (2008), a police officer in the United Kingdom, suggests that psychopathic suspects are likely to engage in the following types of behaviours during an interrogation:

■ Try to outwit the interrogator (they may consider the interrogation a "game" to win)

■ Enjoy being the focus of attention (they may act like they are holding a press conference)

■ Attempt to control the interrogation (they may attempt to "turn the tables" and become the interrogator)

■ Will not be fooled by bluffs (they are adept at conning others and may see through interrogators attempts to obtain a confession)

■ Attempt to shock (they may speak in a matter-of-fact manner about how they have treated other people)

Quayle (2008) has offered several suggestions for interviewing a psychopathic suspect including the following:

■ Case familiarity (interrogators should be extremely familiar with the evidence to counteract the psychopath's evasiveness and deceitfulness)

- Convey experience and confidence (interrogators need to be able to control the interview and create an atmosphere of authority)
- Show liking or admiration (psychopaths respond to thinking that interrogators want to learn from them; this apparent desire to learn encourages psychopaths to keep talking)
- Avoid criticism (psychopaths may become hostile and stop the interview)
- Avoid conveying emotions (interrogators should avoid conveying their own emotions about the offence or lack of progress in the case)

## WHAT MAKES THEM TICK? COGNITIVE AND AFFECTIVE MODELS OF PSYCHOPATHY

A number of theories have been proposed to help forensic psychologists to understand the development of psychopathy. Two of the most prominent theories of psychopathy place emphasis on either cognitive or affective processes. Newman, Brinkley, Lorenz, Hiatt, and MacCoon (2007) have proposed that psychopaths have a **response modulation deficit**. According to this theory, psychopaths fail to use contextual cues that are peripheral to a dominant response set to modulate their behaviour. In other words, if psychopaths are engaging in specific rewarded behaviour, they will not pay attention to other information that might inhibit their behaviour. This theory has been used to explain why psychopaths fail to learn to avoid punishment (i.e., have poor passive avoidance).

**Response Modulation Deficit Theory:** A theory that suggests that psychopaths fail to use contextual cues that are peripheral to a dominant response set to modulate their behaviour

The other theory proposes that psychopaths have a deficit in the experience of certain critical emotions that guide prosocial behaviour and inhibit deviance (Blair, 2006; Hare, 2007; Patrick, 2007). Hervey Cleckley (1976) was the first person to theorize that psychopaths had a deep-rooted emotional deficit that involved the disconnection between cognitive-linguistic processing and emotional experience. In one of the first experimental studies to measure this deficit, Williamson, Harpur, and Hare (1991) administered a lexical-decision task to psychopathic and nonpsychopathic offenders. In this task, emotional and neutral words and nonwords (e.g., *cancer, tree* versus *cercan, eter*) were presented briefly on a screen and participants indicated as quickly as possible whether what was on the screen was a word. When the word was emotional, nonpsychopaths were able to do this faster than if the word is neutral. However, psychopaths fail to show the normal, faster reaction time to emotional words. In addition, the study found that psychopaths' brain-wave activity does not differentiate between emotional and neutral words.

Researchers have used measured affective processing in a range of different paradigms. For example, Blair, Budhani, Colledge, and Scott (2005) asked children to identify the emotions in neutral words spoken with intonations conveying happiness, disgust, anger, sadness, and fear. Boys with many psychopathic traits were impaired at recognizing fearful vocal affect. In adults, Patrick, Bradley, and Lang (1993) compared startle reflexes of psychopathic and nonpsychopathic sexual offenders to slides of positive (e.g., puppies, babies, eroticism), neutral (e.g., table, glass), and negative (e.g., baby with tumour, injured kitten, homicide scene) stimuli. The startle-elicited blinks of nonpsychopathic offenders were smaller when watching positive slides, moderate when watching neutral slides, and enhanced when watching negative slides. In contrast, the psychopathic offenders' startle-elicited blink did not differ in magnitude across the different types of slides. See the Case Study box to try to design a study to further investigate emotional deficits in psychopaths.

## CASE STUDY YOU BE THE RESEARCHER

You have just finished reading Hervey Cleckley's book *The Mask of Sanity*. According to Cleckley, psychopaths are fundamentally deficient in the capacity for emotional experience. This lack of emotional response enables psychopaths to manipulate and exploit others without feeling any remorse for their actions. In Cleckley's view, the psychopath's characteristic "mask of sanity," results in the psychopath attempting to simulate emotional reactions to obtain what he or she wants. You are intrigued by Cleckley's ideas about the psychopath's core deficit in emotional experience and reactions.

### Your Turn . . .

Develop a study to test whether psychopaths have a core emotional deficit. First, decide what sample you will study and how you will measure psychopathic traits. Second, select what stimuli or task will you use (i.e., How will you try to elicit emotions?). Finally, decide how you will measure emotions (i.e., Will you ask them how they are feeling? Will you measure their physiological responses? Will you code their facial expressions?).

These findings of emotional deficits in psychopaths have led some researchers to propose an amygdala dysfunction theory (Blair, 2006, 2008). The amygdala is a small almond-shaped structure located in the medial temporal lobes. The amygdala is part of the limbic centre, which regulates the expression of emotion and emotional memory. It is linked to many other brain regions responsible for memory, control of autonomic nervous system, aggression, decision making, approach and avoidance behaviour, and defense reactions. Other researchers have proposed that other brain areas are implicated and have suggested a paralimbic model to explain the emotional deficits seen in psychopaths. Recently, Newman, Curtin, Bertsch, and Baskin-Sommers (2010) have argued that the emotional deficits seen in psychopaths can be explained by an attention deficit and are not due to an amygdala-mediated deficit.

Psychopathy is a complex disorder but one that causes a substantial amount of damage to society. Research over the past 30 years has led to many advances in researchers' knowledge about psychopathy's measurement, its associations with aggression, its genetic and environmental origins, and its treatment. Within the next few years, new research will provide further insights into how to prevent the development of this devastating disorder.

## SUMMARY

1. Psychopathy is a personality disorder defined by a cluster of interpersonal, affective, and behavioural features. Psychopathy, sociopathy, and antisocial personality disorder are overlapping but distinct constructs.

2. The Hare Psychopathy Checklist-Revised (PCL-R) is the most popular tool used to measure psychopathic traits in adults. The Hare Psychopathy Checklist: Youth

Version is an adaptation of the PCL-R for use with adolescents. Several self-report measures have been developed to assess psychopathic traits in community samples.

3. Psychopaths begin their criminal career earlier, persist longer, and are more violent and versatile than other offenders. Most of the murders committed by psychopaths are instrumental.

4. Psychopaths are difficult to treat. They are not motivated to change their behaviour and some research has shown that after treatment psychopaths were more likely to violently reoffend. However, some recent research has obtained more promising treatment outcome effects, especially with adolescent offenders with many psychopathic features.

5. Research is increasingly focused on identifying the emergence of psychopathic traits in youth, and assessment instruments have been developed to measure psychopathic traits in children and adolescents with some success. Concerns have been raised about the potential problems with labelling youth as psychopaths. These concerns have focused on (1) the issue of labelling a youth as a psychopath, (2) the stability of psychopathic traits from late childhood to early adulthood, and (3) the possibility that characteristics of psychopathy are common features of normally developing youth.

6. Two of the most prominent theories of psychopathy place emphasis on either cognitive or affective processes. Newman and his colleagues have proposed that psychopaths have a response modulation deficit. According to this theory, psychopaths fail to use contextual cues that are peripheral to a dominant response set to modulate their behaviour. The other theory proposes that psychopaths have a deficit in the experience of certain critical emotions that guide prosocial behaviour and inhibit deviance. This latter theory has been related to an amygdala dysfunction.

## Discussion Questions

1. Your friend has recently met a man via an online dating site. She has been dating him for a few months but is starting to feel uneasy about the stories he has been telling her. She knows you have been studying forensic psychology and asks you about psychopathy. Describe what you know about psychopathy and what red flags your friend might want to watch for.

2. The term *psychopath* has many negative connotations. What are the potential problems with using this label to identify youth?

3. You want to know how important childhood abuse and poor parenting is to the development of psychopathy. Describe the methodology you would use and the variables you would measure.

4. You have been hired by the police department to consult on a serial killing case. You suspect the serial killer might be a psychopath. Describe to the homicide investigators the key features of psychopathy, the potential crime scene characteristics of psychopathic serial killers, and any suggestions you have for the interrogation of this suspect.

# Chapter 12

## Assessment and Treatment of Young Offenders

## Learning Objectives

■ Describe the history of young offender legislation.

■ Identify the psychiatric diagnoses, and their trajectories, relevant to young offenders.

■ Differentiate between the theories of antisocial behaviour.

■ List the risk and protective factors associated with externalizing disorders in youth.

■ Distinguish between primary, secondary, and tertiary interventions for children, youth, and young offenders.

Seventeen-year-old Larry had been dating 16-year-old Tracy for four years. They lived in the same neighbourhood and were inseparable. For teenagers in love, Larry and Tracy had quite a volatile relationship, and they often had screaming matches in which objects were thrown. Following these arguments, the young couple would break up but not for long. Larry would often send Tracy emails and texts letting her know how sorry he was because the fights typically revolved around Larry's jealousy over Tracy's part-time job at a fast-food restaurant. Larry would claim that Tracy flirted with other boys who hung out at the fast-food restaurant after school. In their last fight, Larry punched Tracy in the face so that no one else would find her attractive. This violence was the final blow for Tracy: She ended her relationship with Larry for good. Unfortunately, Larry wanted Tracy back and felt that if he could not be with her, no one could. Later that night, Larry showed up at Tracy's house with a gun he had bought from a gang member he knew. Larry demanded that Tracy come down to see him. When Tracy's parents would not let Larry see Tracy, he started shooting. Tracy's father was killed and her mother was wounded. Larry left in a panic. Tracy had hid in the bathroom and called 911. Larry was arrested a block away from Tracy's home.

Did Larry have behavioural problems growing up? Did he have difficulties at school and in other relationships? Should teens be given adult sentences for violent crimes? In this chapter, we will focus on young offenders. We will consider the assessment and treatment of this group, along with the types of crimes they commit. We also will provide a discussion regarding the legal sanctions available to police and the justice system when dealing with this group.

Adolescents (i.e., older than age 12 and younger than age 18, generally) who come into contact with the criminal justice system pose several challenges to the adult-based system. Legislation has changed over the years in an attempt to address the special needs of adolescents. Moreover, it is critical to consider the developmental paths to youthful offending in order to prevent and rehabilitate. A number of treatment options have been developed for young offenders. Anyone younger than age 12 who engages in criminal acts is processed through family and social service agencies, usually under provincial or territorial legislation.

## HISTORICAL OVERVIEW

Youth who committed criminal acts in Canada during the seventeenth and eighteenth centuries were treated as adult offenders. The criminal justice system made no accommodations or considerations for how youth were charged, sentenced, or incarcerated. They were kept in the same facilities as adults while awaiting their trials, received the same penalties as adults, and served their sentences with adults. Even in cases involving the death penalty, youth were dealt with in a similar manner to adults.

Canada enacted the Juvenile Delinquents Act (JDA) in 1908, partly in response to the justice system's past disregard for the special population of youthful offenders. The JDA applied to children and youth between the ages of 7 and 16 (age 18 in some jurisdictions). Terminology was used to reflect a difference between youth and adults. For example, youth were called *delinquents* rather than *offenders*, and were considered to commit acts of delinquency, such as truancy, rather than criminal offences. A separate court system for youth was established, and it was suggested that court proceedings be as informal as possible in that delinquents were seen as misguided children in need of guidance and support. When possible, parents were encouraged to be part of the judicial process. In serious cases, the JDA made it possible for delinquents to be transferred to adult court. Punishments for delinquents were to be consistent with how a parent would discipline a child. For example, delinquents could be sentenced to an industrial school where they learned skills or a trade for future employment. Other dispositions for delinquents included adjournment without penalty, fines, probation, and foster care. Table 12.1 highlights the key changes to the Canadian criminal justice system under the JDA.

Many saw the JDA as a positive step toward youth justice. However, the JDA was not without critics. For example, the services to be provided to delinquents as outlined in the JDA were not always available. Also, given the informality of youth court, some youth

---

**Table 12.1** The Juvenile Delinquents Act's Key Changes to Canadian Criminal Justice

1. A separate court system for youth was established.
2. A minimum age (7 years old) was set for which a child could be charged with a criminal offence.
3. Judges had sentencing discretion and sentencing options increased (e.g., foster care, fines, and institutionalization).
4. Parents were encouraged to be part of the judicial process.

were denied their rights, such as the right to counsel and the right to appeal, and judges could impose open-ended sentences. Furthermore, the broad definition of delinquency included acts that were not illegal for adults.

The JDA was in effect until 1984, when it was replaced with the Young Offenders Act (YOA). The YOA represented a shift in how youth who broke the law were perceived. Youth were to be held responsible for their actions. However, the YOA acknowledged that youth were different from adults, having a different level of cognitive development, for example. The differences between youths and adults were to be recognized through the level of accountability and the consequences of the behaviour committed. The YOA also recognized the need to protect the public from young offenders. Lastly, the YOA recognized that youths should be afforded all the rights stated in the Canadian Charter of Rights and Freedoms (R.S.C., 1985, c. Y-1, s. 3).

Changes in the YOA included the age of criminal responsibility. Under the YOA, youth had to be at least 12 years old (and up to 18 years old) to be processed through the justice system. Children less than age 12 would be dealt with through child and family services. Some of the changes brought forward with the JDA remained with the YOA. For example, youth courts continued under the YOA. As with the JDA, for serious indictable offences, such as murder, youth could be transferred to adult courts, provided they were at least 14 years of age (R.S.C., 1985, c. Y-1, s. 16).

The YOA allowed for youth cases to be diverted. Diversion is a decision not to prosecute the young offender but rather have him or her undergo an educational or community service program. However, for diversion to be possible, the young offender would have to plead guilty (R.S.C., 1985, c. Y-1, s. 4). Other dispositions available for young offenders included absolute discharge (i.e., the young offender received no sentence other than a guilty verdict), fine, compensation for loss or damaged property, restitution to the victim, prohibition order (i.e., no weapons), community service, probation, and custody. Two types of custody are available: open (placing the youth in a community residential facility, group home, child-care facility, or wilderness camp) or secure (incarcerating the youth in a prison facility; R.S.C., 1985, c. Y-1, s. 20).

A number of amendments have been made to the YOA. For example, Bill C-106 section 16 (1986) required the youth court to consider whether the Crown or defence would like to make an application to transfer the case to adult court. This amendment was introduced to address the problem of defendants making guilty pleas to avoid transfers. Bill C-37 changed section 16 once again in 1995. With this amendment, 16- and 17-year-olds charged with murder, manslaughter, or aggravated sexual assault would go to adult court. On application, these cases could stay in youth court, if the youth court felt the objectives of rehabilitation and public protection could be reconciled. Also under Bill C-37, sentences for youth changed. For first-degree murder, a ten-year maximum, with a six-year maximum to be served incarcerated, was available. For second-degree murder, a seven-year maximum, with a four-year maximum to be served incarcerated, was available. Table 12.2 highlights the key changes to the Canadian criminal justice system under the YOA.

Overall, the YOA attempted to make youth more accountable for their behaviour, while supporting rehabilitation through treatment programs and providing alternatives to incarceration for less serious crimes. One of the major criticisms of the YOA was that serious, violent offences carried relatively short ("light") sentences. Other criticisms included

**Table 12.2** The Young Offenders Act's Key Changes to Canadian Criminal Justice

1. Youth are to be held accountable for their actions, however, not to the full extent that adults are.
2. The public has the right to be protected from young offenders.
3. Young offenders have legal rights and freedoms, including those described in the Canadian Charter of Rights and Freedoms.
4. Children have to be at least 12 years of age to be charged with a criminal offence.

disagreement over raising the minimum age of responsibility from age 7 to age 12. Also, the YOA allowed for discrepancies in the factors leading to transfer to adult court that suggested an arbitrariness in how cases were handled.

On April 1, 2003, the Youth Criminal Justice Act (YCJA) replaced the YOA. The three main objectives of the YCJA are the following:

1. To prevent youth crime
2. To provide meaningful consequences and encourage responsibility of behaviour
3. To improve rehabilitation and reintegration of youth into the community

With the YCJA, there is a movement to keep young offenders out of the court and out of custody. There is an onus on police to consider community outlets and less serious alternatives for youth before bringing them to the attention of youth court (Youth Criminal Justice Act, 2002, s. 7). These alternatives are called **extrajudicial** measures and include giving a warning or making a referral for treatment (with the consent of the youth; Youth Criminal Justice Act, 2002, s. 10).

**Extrajudicial:** Term applied to measures taken to keep young offenders out of court and out of custody (e.g., giving a warning or making a referral for treatment)

## Naming Youth

Under the current YCJA, the name of the youth cannot be reported to the public but, rather, can be released only under special circumstances. For instance, defendants between the ages of 14 and 17 who are convicted of serious, violent offences, such as murder and aggravated sexual assault, may have their names published and communicated to the public. Moreover, if the youth is considered dangerous, their photo also may be published. Also, an exception to releasing a youth's name and photo can be made if the youth has not yet been apprehended.

In a recent case that involved the murder of 14-year-old Stefanie Rengel of Toronto on January 1, 2008, the YCJA's "privacy clause" was put to the test. Within a few hours of the murder, the names of the victim and the two youths charged (David Bagshaw and Melissa Todorovic) were posted on the social network site Facebook. It should be noted that names of victims from youth crime also have their identities protected from publication until consent is provided. Although police and Facebook website staffers removed the prohibited information to comply with the privacy clause, the information was reposted shortly thereafter. It can be quite difficult to police the posts of individual users. See Box 12.1 to learn more about the Rengel case.

Box 12.1

# Sex, Text, and Murder

Fifteen-year-old Melissa Todorovic and 17-year-old David Bagshaw were two teens in love who had a mutual obsession and jealousy of each other. They began dating in March 2007. Bagshaw texted Todorovic over 3300 times in four months. Todorovic monitored Bagshaw's Facebook and MSN chats. She also seemed to be jealous of any former relationships that Bagshaw had had in the past. She seemed fixated on one particular former girlfriend, Stefanie Rengel. Rengel was 14 years old and had some of the same friends Bagshaw had. Rengel and Bagshaw's relationship was not sexual, and they had broken up after a few weeks. Neither of these things mattered to Todorovic however: She wanted Rengel dead. Todorovic demanded that Bagshaw kill Rengel. Todorovic taunted Bagshaw and said she would have sex with someone else if he didn't do what she wanted.

On January 1, 2008, Bagshaw took a kitchen knife to Rengel's home. Several phone calls occurred between Bagshaw and Todorovic on his way to Rengel's. Bagshaw then called Rengel and said he wanted her to come outside so they could talk. After Rengel went outside to talk to Bagshaw, he used the kitchen knife to stab Rengel six times. He then ran off, leaving Rengel to die in a snowbank. Later that evening, Bagshaw went to Todorovic's home to tell her he had killed Rengel. Bagshaw and Todorovic then had sex, which was Bagshaw's reward for killing his old girlfriend. Bagshaw was arrested at his home that evening.

Bagshaw pleaded guilty to the murder of Rengel and was sentenced as an adult, receiving life in prison with no chance of parole for ten years.

In a separate trial from Bagshaw's, Todorovic pleaded not guilty but was found guilty of first-degree murder. She was sentenced as an adult to life in prison, with no chance of parole for seven years, which is the maximum sentence allowed for a defendant who is under the age of 16. Todorovic was a few days shy of her sixteenth birthday when the murder occurred.

Sources: Rengel killer sentenced to life (2009, September 28). *CBC News.* Retrieved from http://www.cbc.ca/canada/toronto/story/2009/09/28/rengel-killer-sentencing265.html; Stefanie Rengel case statement of facts (2009, April 9). *CityNews.* Retrieved from http://www.citytv.com/toronto/citynews/news/local/article/10094–stefanie-rengel-case

Sentencing options have increased under the YCJA. Judges are able to provide a reprimand (i.e., lecture or warning to the youth), an intensive support and supervision order, an attendance order (i.e., youth must attend a specific program), a deferred custody and supervision order (i.e., youth can serve their sentence in the community as long as imposed conditions are met), and an intensive rehabilitative custody and supervision order (i.e., youth in custody receive intensive services and supervision) (Youth Criminal Justice Act, 2002, s. 42).

**Table 12.3** The Youth Criminal Justice Act's Key Changes to the Canadian Criminal Justice System

1. Less serious and less violent offences should be kept out of the formal court process.
2. The number of extrajudicial measures are increased.
3. There is a greater focus on prevention and reintegration into the community.
4. Transfers to adult court are removed; instead, youth court judges can impose adult sentences.
5. The interests and needs of victims are recognized.

In terms of transferring youth to adult court, the YCJA has made a number of changes from the process outlined in the YOA. Under the YCJA, the transfer process is eliminated. Rather, youth court determines whether the youthful defendant is guilty, and if so, the judge can impose an adult sentence with youth as young as 14 years old (this age can be set at 15 or 16 years of age). An adult sentence cannot be applied unless the Crown notifies the youth court that it will be seeking an adult sentence (Youth Criminal Justice Act, 2002, s. 61). A key issue in determining sentencing is that the sentence must be proportionate to the seriousness of the offence (Youth Criminal Justice Act, 2002, s. 38(2)(c)).

The YCJA has made a serious attempt at improving the interests of victims. Under the YCJA, victims are to be informed of the court proceedings and given an opportunity to participate. Victims also have the right to access youth court records. Moreover, victims can participate in community-based dispositions (Youth Criminal Justice Act, 2002, s. 3). Table 12.3 highlights the key changes to the Canadian criminal justice system under the YCJA. See the In the Media box to learn how the YCJA is perceived overseas.

## YOUTH CRIME RATES

Generally, the total number of crimes committed by youth has been decreasing for the past few years. This pattern also can be seen for violent offences. See Table 12.4 for a distribution of young offender cases by major crime category.

A youth vandalizes a wall in the community

Regarding sentencing in youth court, probation is the most frequent sentence imposed. In any given month during 2008 and 2009, 18 012 youth were on probation (www.statcan.gc.ca). This rate was stable from the previous year. Youth in custody during the 2008 to 2009 year decreased 8% from the previous year and decreased

**Table 12.4** Youth Accused of Selected Violations, Canada, 2007 and 2008

| Type of Violation | 2007 | 2008 | % Change in Rate 2007 to 2008 |
|---|---|---|---|
| Total Criminal Code violations (excluding traffic) | 177 397 | 166 561 | −5 |
| Total violent Criminal Code violations | 51 002 | 48 697 | −3 |
| Homicide | 77 | 56 | −26 |
| Total nonviolent Criminal Code violations (excluding traffic) | 126 395 | 117 864 | −6 |
| Breaking and entering | 13 034 | 11 311 | −12 |
| Total Criminal Code | | | |
| Traffic violations | 426 | 473 | 13 |
| Impaired driving | 143 | 176 | 25 |
| Total federal statute violations | 26 871 | 27 601 | 4 |
| Possession-cannabis | 13 712 | 14 063 | 4 |

Source: Wallace, M. (2009, July). Police-reported crime statistics in Canada, 2008 (Component of Statistics Canada catalogue No. 85-002-X). *Juristat, 29*(3).

42% from 2003 to 2004, when the YCJA was introduced (www.statcan.gc.ca). Examine the Case Study box to consider how you would deal with a youth engaged in unlawful behaviour.

# ASSESSMENT OF YOUNG OFFENDERS
## Assessing Those under Age 12

Often a clinician will obtain two levels of consent before assessing a child or adolescent. Because children and adolescents are not legally capable of providing consent, consent will be sought from parents or guardians. Following parental consent, assent or agreement to conduct the assessment will also be sought from the child or the adolescent. Although court-ordered assessments do not necessarily require consent or assent, clinicians often will seek it before commencing the assessment.

Broadly, children's and youth's emotional and behavioural difficulties can be categorized as internalizing or externalizing problems (Rutter, 1990). **Internalizing problems** are emotional difficulties such as anxiety, depression, and obsessions. **Externalizing problems** are behavioural difficulties such as delinquency, fighting, bullying, lying, and destructive behaviour. Externalizing problems have been considered more difficult to treat and more likely to have long-term persistence (Ebata, Peterson, & Conger, 1990; Robins, 1986).

**Internalizing problems:** Emotional difficulties such as anxiety, depression, and obsessions experienced by a youth

**Externalizing problems:** Behavioural difficulties such as delinquency, fighting, bullying, lying, or destructive behaviour experienced by a youth

## CASE STUDY YOU BE THE POLICE OFFICER

Jimmy Jones is the neighbourhood "bad boy." He and his mom have lived in one of the government-subsidized housing units since Jimmy was 4 years old. Now, he is 14. Jimmy is well-known at school and in his neighbourhood. As a young boy, Jimmy would take toys from other children and often would become aggressive if he didn't get his way. His school-teachers called Mrs. Jones on a weekly basis because they could not manage Jimmy's aggression and tantrums. Jimmy bullied other kids and was cruel to his pet dog.

Jimmy's problems just seemed to keep escalating. As he got older, he started hanging around with some older teenaged boys known to belong to a local street gang. Jimmy liked how the gang boys always had money. He soon began selling drugs for the gang leader. At first, Jimmy was selling drugs at the high schools in the neighbourhood. The high schools were visited by police officers who were trying to work with the drug dealers to change their ways. The police knew Jimmy well.

One night, Jimmy's gang leader said he needed Jimmy to do him a favour. A rival gang had set up shop in an abandoned warehouse and was trying to get in on the drug dealing. Jimmy was asked to set fire to the warehouse to burn it down. Jimmy knew that if he could do this successfully he would be rewarded financially and would move up in the gang hier-archy. He agreed to set the fire. Although Jimmy did not want to hurt anyone, some of the rival gang members were in the warehouse when he started the fire, and three rival gang members received serious burns. Police were informed that Jimmy set the fire.

### Your Turn . . .

You are a police officer dealing with Jimmy's case. How should you handle it? Should you keep Jimmy out of the criminal justice system? Should Jimmy be dealt with using extraju-dicial measures? If so, which ones?

Externalizing disorders have been known to be quite stable, though symptoms often peak in teenage years and decrease in the late 20s (Rutter, 1995). Males are more likely to have externalizing difficulties than females, with a ratio of about 10:1 (Barkley, 1997; Rutter, 1990). It should be noted that internalizing problems might co-occur with externalizing difficulties that should also be assessed and treated.

To assess externalizing problems, multiple informants are necessary to obtain an accu-rate assessment because the child or youth may not be aware of his or her behaviour or the influence it has on others (McMahon, 1994). Parents, teachers, and peers may be interviewed or asked to rate the child or adolescent. Also, it is important that behaviour be viewed within a developmental context. For example, rebelling against rules set by par-ents may be normative for adolescents but worrisome if younger children are oppositional and continually refuse to comply with parents' requests. The duration, severity, and frequency of troublesome behaviours should be measured.

Three childhood psychiatric diagnoses occur with some frequency in young offenders: **attention deficit hyperactivity disorder** (ADHD), **oppositional defiant disorder** (ODD), and **conduct disorder** (CD). ADHD is described in the DSM-IV as an inattention and

**Attention deficit hyperactivity disorder:** A disorder in a youth characterized by a persistent pattern of inattention and hyperactivity or impulsivity

**Oppositional defiant disorder:** A disorder in a youth characterized by a persistent pattern of negativis-tic, hostile, and defiant behaviours

**Conduct disorder:** A disorder characterized by a persistent pattern of behaviour in which a youth violates the rights of others or age-appropriate societal norms or rules

restlessness (APA, 1994). Some examples of features associated with ADHD include the following: does not appear to listen when spoken to, has difficulty with organization, loses items, fidgets, and talks excessively. To qualify for an ADHD diagnosis, a number of symptoms must be present, occur in two or more settings, and persist for at least six months. When making an ADHD diagnosis, it is important to consider the age of the child. In young children, many of the symptoms of ADHD are part of normal development and behaviour and may not lead to criminal activity later on. However, there may be some hyperactive-impulsive or inattentive symptoms before the age of 7 that cause impairment. Many children with ADHD also receive diagnoses of ODD or CD (Barkley, 1991).

ODD is described as a "pattern of negativistic, hostile, and defiant behaviour" (APA, 1994, p. 93). Some examples of features associated with ODD include loses temper, deliberately annoys others, and is vindictive. Approximately 40% of children with ODD develop CD (Loeber et al., 1993). If a child with ODD qualifies for a CD diagnosis, an ODD diagnosis is not used. Some examples of features associated with CD include initiates physical fights, is physically cruel to animals, sets fires, lies for gain, and is a truant before age 13. Approximately 50% of children meeting criteria for CD go on to receive diagnoses of antisocial personality disorder in adulthood (APA, 1994; Loeber & Farrington, 2000). Thus, CD often is the precursor to antisocial personality disorder. ODD and CD are not diagnosed if the individual is more than 18 years old (the individual may meet criteria for antisocial personality disorder).

## Assessing the Adolescent

Once an adolescent's antisocial behaviour receives the attention of the courts, a court-ordered assessment may be issued. In such cases, the adolescent does not need to provide consent/assent. The issue for the courts is to determine what level of risk the young person poses for reoffending. In other words, will having this young offender in the community pose a risk for others? Does the young offender have the potential to change in a positive manner? Young offenders are assessed so that resources can be used effectively and the risk to the community is reduced.

The instruments used to assess a young offender's risk generally include a "checklist," where items are scored on a scale, the points are summed, and a cut-off value is set for either detaining or releasing the young offender. Risk-assessment instruments collect information about a set of factors, both static (i.e., factors that cannot change, such as age of first arrest) and dynamic (i.e., factors that can change, such as antisocial attitudes). Interviews with the young offender as well as case files and histories may be used to complete a risk assessment. A total risk score is then obtained. Generally, the notion is that the more relevant risk factors that are present, the more likely the youth will reoffend. Any number of professionals (front-line staff in institutions, probation staff, credentialed professionals) may be responsible for conducting the risk assessment.

The task of identifying risk factors for young offenders who will reoffend is different than for adults (Mulvey, 2005). For example, history of behaviour often is considered in the risk assessment of adult offenders. This information may be limited and ambiguous for young offenders. Young offenders simply do not have the years behind them that can be examined. Child and adolescent behaviour may be more influenced by context than enduring character. Children and adolescents may display behaviour that is adaptive to the environment they are in rather than a behaviour that demonstrates their character across all situations (Masten & Coatsworth 1998). A child who is disruptive in one school may not be disruptive in another—so interpreting a behaviour problem may be inaccurate. Children and adolescents experience more developmental and character changes than adults. It is a challenge to separate developmental issues from persistent personality and character for the prediction of future offending. Some researchers argue further that risk assessment may differ between adolescent boys and girls (Odgers, Moretti, & Reppucci 2005).

Box 12.2 provides a list of risk-assessment tools used with young offenders in Canada.

## Rates of Behaviour Disorders in Youth

It has been estimated that approximately 5% to 15% of children display severe behavioural problems (Rutter, 1990). This estimate may, however, be too low. Notably, in the Ontario Child Health Study in 1987, approximately 18% of children between the ages of 4 and 16 were found to experience conduct disorder, hyperactivity, emotional disturbance, or a combination of these (Offord et al., 1987). Researchers have found that behavioural disorders commonly co-occur. For example, 20% to 50% of children with ADHD also have symptoms consistent with CD or ODD (Offord, Lipman, & Duku, 2001).

## Trajectories of Youthful Offenders

When examining the aggressive histories of young offenders, two categories emerge. Young offenders may be categorized as those who started with social transgressions and behavioural problems in very early childhood (child-onset, life-course persistent) or those whose problem behaviours emerged in the teen years (adolescent-onset, adolescent limited; Moffitt, 1993). Thus, two developmental pathways to youthful antisocial behaviour have been suggested: childhood onset versus adolescent onset.

Age of onset is a critical factor in the trajectory to adult offending. A number of researchers have found that early onset of antisocial behaviour is related to more serious and persistent antisocial behaviour later in life (Fergusson & Woodward, 2000; Loeber & Farrington, 2000). Those with a childhood onset also may have a number of other difficulties, such as ADHD, learning disabilities, and academic difficulties (Hinshaw, Lahey, & Hart, 1993). The childhood-onset trajectory is a less frequent occurrence than adolescent onset, with about 3% to 5% of the general population showing a childhood-onset trajectory (Moffitt, 1993). It is important to remember, however, that most young children with behavioural difficulties do not go on to become adult offenders (or even young offenders for that matter).

The adolescent-onset pattern occurs in about 70% of the general population (Moffitt, 1993). Many young people engage in social transgressions during their adolescence, but adolescents who engage in only a few antisocial acts do not qualify for a CD diagnosis. Although it is more common for adolescent-onset youth to desist their antisocial behaviour in their early adulthood than for those with a childhood onset, some of these adolescent-onset youth continue to engage in antisocial acts in adulthood (Moffitt et al., 2002).

In a study by Brame, Nagin, and Tremblay (2001), a group of boys from Montreal were followed from the time they entered kindergarten through to their late teen years. The researchers found that participants' overall level of aggression decreased as they got older,

Box 12.2

# Risk-Assessment Tools Used with Young Offenders in Canada

### Adolescent Chemical Dependency Inventory (ACDI)—Corrections Version II

This instrument is designed for 14- to 17-year-olds to screen for substance (alcohol and other drugs) use and abuse, overall adjustment, and issues for troubled youth. Young offenders respond to 140 items that constitute seven scales: (1) truthfulness, (2) violence, (3) adjustment, (4) distress, (5) alcohol, (6) drugs, and (7) stress and coping abilities.

### HCR-20

The HCR-20 takes its name from the three scales it assesses—historical, clinical, and risk management—and from the number of items. It examines risk and violence broadly, including risk factors from the past, present, and future. The scale consists of ten historical factors, five clinical items that reflect current factors related to violence, and five risk-management items that focus attention on situational post-assessment factors that may aggravate or mitigate risk.

### Offender Risk Assessment and Management System (ORAMS)

ORAMS is a set of tools developed by Manitoba Corrections to assess the different risks offenders pose. Two scales can be used with young offenders: Inmate Security Assessment and Primary Risk Assessment.

1. **Inmate Security Assessment (ISA)—Young Offenders**
The objective of the ISA is to obtain information to assess a young offender's threat to him- or herself and others in an institution. Dangerous behaviour includes suicide, assaults on other inmates or staff, and escape risk. This scale is completed once an offender has been admitted into an institution for security reasons and also assists decisions relating to institutional placement or transfer.

2. **Primary Risk Assessment (PRA)—Young Offenders**
This scale is a modified version of the Youthful Offender—Level of Service Inventory (YO-LSI). It is used to predict a young offender's risk to reoffend in any type of offence (as opposed to specific types of offences, such as sexual assault). This information is then used to determine the degree and type of supervision needed and to assist in the formulation of a case plan.

### Structured Assessment of Violence Risk in Youth (SAVRY) (Borum, Bartel, & Forth, 2002)

The SAVRY is used to make assessments and recommendations about the nature and degree of risk that a youth may pose for future violence. Twenty-four risk factors and six protective factors are considered.

### Youth Level of Service/Case Management Inventory (YLS/CMI) (Hoge & Andrews, 2002)

This standardized instrument includes a 42-item checklist for use by professional workers in assessing risk of future violence, need for correctional programs to reduce future violence, and responsivity factors that have an impact on case plan goals. A detailed survey of youth risk and needs factors is produced that can be used to create a case plan. The instrument contains seven sections: (1) assessment of risk and need; (2) summary of risk/need factors; (3) assessment of other needs/special considerations; (4) assessment of the client's general risk/need level; (5) contact level; (6) case management plan; and (7) case management review.

### Youthful Offender—Level of Service Inventory (YO-LSI)

The YO-LSI is a risk/needs assessment instrument used to classify and assess a young offender's overall risk level and to identify and target areas of criminogenic need. The YO-LSI consists of 82 static and dynamic predictors of criminal risk/needs that are grouped into the following seven categories: (1) criminal history, (2) substance abuse, (3) educational/employment problems, (4) family problems, (5) peer relation problems, (6) accommodation problems, (7) and psychological factors.

Source: Hannah-Moffat and Maurutto (2003).

regardless of how high it was when the participants were youngsters. It was notable, however, that for a small proportion of youngsters with high levels of aggression, these high levels continued into their teen years. A much larger proportion of youngsters with high levels of aggression reported little to no aggression in their teen years. Thus, for a small group of youngsters with high levels of aggression, these levels will continue into later years.

# THEORIES TO EXPLAIN ANTISOCIAL BEHAVIOUR

## Biological Theories

To explain why some youth engage in antisocial acts, researchers have examined the relation between frontal lobe functioning and antisocial behaviour. The frontal lobe is responsible for the planning and inhibiting of behaviour. Moffit and Henry (1989) have found that conduct-disordered youth have less frontal lobe inhibition of behaviour. Thus, the likelihood that these youth will act impulsively is increased, making it more likely that they will make poor behavioural choices.

Physiologically, conduct-disordered youth have been found to have slower heart rates than youth who do not engage in antisocial behaviour (Wadsworth, 1976). Genetic studies have found a relation between paternal antisocial behaviour and child offspring antisocial behaviour (Frick et al., 1992). Moreover, adoption and twin studies also find a biological link to youthful offending. That is, children who have an antisocial biological father are more likely to engage in antisocial behaviour, even when raised apart from the biological father (Cadoret & Cain, 1980; Jarey & Stewart, 1985). Overall, the research explaining the relation among biology, physiology, genetics, and behaviour is preliminary at this point.

## Cognitive Theories

Kenneth Dodge and his colleagues proposed a model of conduct-disordered behaviour that focuses on the thought processes that occur in social interactions (Crick & Dodge, 1994; Dodge, 2000). Thought processes start when individuals pay attention to and interpret social and emotional cues in their environment. The next step in the model is to consider alternative responses to the cues. Finally, a response is chosen and performed. Conduct-disordered youth demonstrate cognitive deficits and distortions (Fontaine, Burks, & Dodge, 2002). These youth often attend to fewer cues and misattribute hostile intent to ambiguous situations. Moreover, conduct-disordered youth demonstrate limited problem-solving skills, producing few solutions to problems, and these solutions are usually aggressive in nature. Cognitive deficits are likely to be present in early childhood and may contribute to child-onset conduct disorder (Coy, Speltz, DeKlyen, & Jones, 2001).

Dodge and his colleagues also have distinguished between two types of aggressive behaviour: reactive aggression and proactive aggression (Dodge, 1991; Schwartz et al., 1998). Reactive aggression is described as an emotionally aggressive response to a perceived threat or frustration. In contrast, proactive aggression is aggression directed at achieving a goal or receiving positive reinforcers. Referring to Dodge's model, deficiencies in the process occur at different points for reactive and proactive aggression. Reactively aggressive youth are likely to demonstrate deficiencies early in the cognitive process, such as focusing on only a few social cues and misattributing hostile intent to ambiguous situations. In contrast, proactive aggressive youth are likely to have deficiencies in generating alternative responses and often choose an aggressive response. Furthermore, reactive and proactive aggressors tend to have different trajectories. Reactive aggressors tend to have an earlier onset of problems than proactive aggressors (Dodge, Lochman, Harnish, Bate, & Pettit, 1997).

## Social Theories

**Social learning theory:** A theory of human behaviour based on learning from watching others in the social environment and reinforcement contingencies

Bandura's (1965) **social learning theory** suggests that children learn their behaviour from observing others. Children are more likely to imitate behaviour that receives positive reinforcement than behaviour that receives negative reinforcement or punishment. As children are developing, numerous models are available to imitate, including parents, siblings, peers, and media figures. Studies have found that children who are highly aggressive and engage in antisocial behaviour often have witnessed parents, siblings, or grandparents engage in aggression and antisocial behaviour (Farrington, 1995; Waschbusch, 2002). In this pattern of intergenerational aggression, one aggressive generation produces the next aggressive generation (Glueck & Glueck, 1968; Huesmann, Eron, Lefkowitz, & Walder, 1984).

Watching extremely violent television and movies in which actors are rewarded for their aggression also increases children's likelihood of acting aggressively (Bushman & Anderson, 2001). In addition, playing aggressive video games presents a forum for children and youth to be reinforced for their aggression and, in turn, may increase the likelihood of children and youth acting aggressively in real life (Anderson & Dill, 2000). Moreover, some data find a link between violent video exposure and aggressive behaviour to brain processes believed to be associated with desensitization to real-world violence (Barthlow, Bushman, & Sestir, 2006).

## RISK FACTORS

A number of individual and social factors place children at increased risk for developmental psychopathology, such as emotional and behavioural problems (Coie et al., 1992; Fitzpatrick, 1997; Jessor, Turbin, & Costa, 1998; Rutter, 1988, 1990; Wasserman & Saracini, 2001; Werner & Smith, 1992). It is important to remember that it is not just one risk factor but rather multiple risk factors that can lead to negative child outcomes (Rutter, 1979).

## Individual Risk Factors

A variety of genetic or biological factors have been linked to behavioural problems. Even before a child is born, factors can operate to increase the likelihood for later behavioural difficulties. For example, a parent's own history of ADHD or behavioural difficulties are known risk factors for their offspring, especially for sons (Cohen, Adler, Kaplan, Pelcovitz, & Mandel, 2002; National Crime Prevention Council, 1995, 1997).

A pregnant woman's use of drugs and alcohol can place the fetus at risk for later behavioural problems (Cohen et al., 2002). Once the child is born, diet and exposure to high levels of lead are risk factors for externalizing disorders (Cohen et al., 2002; National Crime Prevention Council, 1995, 1997).

A child's temperament also can be a risk factor. For example, children who are difficult to soothe or who have a negative disposition can be at risk for later behavioural difficulties (Farrington, 1995). It also has been found that impulsive children are at risk for behavioural problems (Farrington, 1995).

## Familial Risk Factors

Parents play a critical role in the development of their children. Children of parents who are neglectful (Shaw, Keenan, & Vondra, 1994) or children who do not attach securely to their parents are at risk for later behavioural problems (Fagot & Kavanagh, 1990). Divorce and familial conflict are risk factors for children (Amato & Keith, 1991; Cummings, Davies, & Campbell, 2000). Parenting style also can be problematic. For example, inconsistent and overly strict parents who apply harsh discipline pose a risk to the child (Dekovic, 1999). In addition, not properly supervising a child presents a risk factor to the child for later behavioural problems (Dekovic, 1999; Farrington, 1995; Hoge, Andrews, & Leschied, 1996; National Crime Prevention Council, 1995, 1997; Patterson, Reid, & Dishion, 1998; Rutter, 1990).

It has been suggested that parents who drink heavily are less likely to respond appropriately to their children's behaviour, thus increasing the likelihood of future negative behaviour (Lahey, Waldman, & McBurnett, 1999). Also, heavy drinking has been implicated in inept monitoring of children and less parental involvement, both being familial risk factors (Lahey et al., 1999).

Consequences of child abuse may be psychological, physical, behavioural, academic, sexual, interpersonal, self-perceptual, or spiritual (Health Canada, 2003). Boys, in particular, may respond to abuse by acting aggressively and later engaging in spousal abuse (Fergusson & Lynskey, 1997; Health Canada, 2003; Loos & Alexander, 1997). Cohen et al. (2002) found that physical abuse experienced during adolescence increases the risk for developing lifetime mental health difficulties and behaviour problems.

Numerous other family variables have been reported as risk factors, including low socioeconomic status, large family size, and parental mental health problems (Frick, 1994; Patterson, Reid, & Dishion, 1998; Waschbusch, 2002).

## School and Social Risk Factors

Having trouble reading and having a lower intelligence are both risk factors for antisocial behaviour (Elkins, Iacono, Doyle, & McGue, 1997; Rutter, 1990). The school environment also provides an opportunity for peer influences on behaviour. Young children who play with aggressive peers at an early age are at risk for externalizing behaviour (Fergusson & Horwood, 1998; Laird, Jordan, Dodge, Petit, & Bates, 2001). Children with early CD symptoms who do not end up with CD tend to associate with less delinquent peers compared with children who later qualify for a CD diagnosis (Fergusson & Horwood, 1996). As children get older, they may get involved in gangs. See Box 12.3 for a discussion of youth gangs.

Social disapproval and being rejected are likely to occur with aggressive children and adolescents (Coie, Belding, & Underwood, 1988; Ebata et al., 1990; Rutter, 1990), and

Box 12.3

# Running Around with the Wrong Crowd: A Look at Gangs

The National Crime Prevention Centre (NCPC) of Public Safety Canada is the federal organization responsible for providing direction on how to deal with the problem of youth gangs in Canada. There are three key elements to a youth gang:

1. The individuals involved must identify themselves as a group (e.g., they may have a group name and group colours).
2. Other people see the members as a distinct group.
3. Group members commit "delinquent" acts, often imposing on the rights of others in the community.

Although anyone can be a gang member, gangs are often composed of individuals from lower socioeconomic backgrounds who belong to a minority ethnic group. In Canada, the largest proportion of youth gang members are African-Canadian, at 25%, then First Nations at 21%, and Caucasian at 18%. An overwhelming proportion of gang members are male (approximately 94%). However, the trend of female Aboriginal gang membership in Western Canada is increasing. In addition, it is not uncommon for gang members to have a pre-existing substance abuse problem and to have engaged in violent young offending prior to joining the gang. The motivation to join a gang often involves a desire to attain prestige, status, protection, and an opportunity to make money.

A Canadian police survey conducted in 2002 estimated that there are approximately 434 youth gangs in Canada with a total membership slightly over 7000. The top three provinces with absolute number of gangs and gang membership (not taking population into account) are Ontario, Saskatchewan, and British Columbia. Table 12.5 illustrates youth gang numbers and membership as a function of province/territory.

Erickson and Butters (2006) examined the relationship between gangs, guns, and drugs in Toronto and Montreal. A total of 904 male high school students, school dropouts, and young offenders were interviewed. The researchers found that as gang presence in schools increased, so did the number of guns and amount of drugs. Almost 19% of boys aged 14 to 17 in Toronto and 15% in Montreal brought a gun to school. Dropouts who sell drugs are more likely to be engaged in gun violence than dropouts who do not sell drugs.

**Table 12.5** Youth Gang Numbers in Canada

| Province | No. of Youth Gangs | No. of Gang Members | Youth Gang Members per 1000 |
|---|---|---|---|
| British Columbia | 102 | 1027 | 0.26 |
| Alberta | 42 | 668 | 0.22 |
| Saskatchewan | 28 | 1315 | 1.34 |
| Manitoba | 15 | 171 | 0.15 |
| Ontario | 216 | 3320 | 0.29 |
| Quebec* | 25 | 533 | 0.07 |
| Nova Scotia | 6 | 37 | 0.04 |
| Prince Edward Island | 0 | 0 | 0 |
| Newfoundland and Labrador | 0 | 0 | 0 |
| Yukon | 0 | 0 | 0 |
| Northwest Territories | 0 | 0 | 0 |
| Nunavut | 0 | 0 | 0 |

*Data were obtained from only four police agencies and should be interpreted cautiously; figures may not be representative of the province.

these rejected, aggressive children are at risk for behavioural problems (Parker & Asher, 1987; Rudolph & Asher, 2000).

# PROTECTIVE FACTORS

Although children may experience a similar environment and adversity, children's responses and outcomes vary, with some children prevailing and prospering, and others having a number of difficulties and negative outcomes. The child who has multiple risk factors but who can overcome them and prevail has been termed **resilient**. Resilience has been described as the ability to overcome stress and adversity (Winfield, 1994).

**Resilient:** Characteristic of a child who has multiple risk factors but who does not develop problem behaviours or negative symptoms

It has been suggested that resilient children may have protective factors that allow them to persevere in the face of adversity. The notion of protection and protective factors was introduced in the early 1980s (Garmezy, 1985). Garmezy (1991) identified a number of areas in which protectiveness can be present: genetic variables, personality dispositions, supportive family environments, and community supports. There is some debate over the definition of protective factors and how protective factors work. Many agree, however, that protective factors help to improve or sustain some part of an individual's life (Leadbeater, Kuperminc, Blatt, & Hertzog, 1999). Rutter (1990) identifies four ways that protective factors are effective:

1. Protective factors reduce negative outcomes by changing the risk level of the child's exposure to a risk factor.
2. They change the negative chain reaction following exposure to risk.
3. They help to develop and maintain self-esteem and self-efficacy.
4. They provide opportunities to children that they would not otherwise have.

Protective factors can be grouped into three categories: (1) individual, (2) familial, and (3) social/external factors (Grossman et al., 1992).

## Individual Protective Factors

Protective factors that reside within the individual, known as resilient temperaments (Hoge, 1999), include exceptional social skills, child competencies, confident perceptions, values, attitudes, and beliefs within the child (Vance, 2001).

Work from twin studies has suggested that social support may have a heritable component, which is influenced by personality. For example, likeable children may respond to good role models in a positive manner, thus promoting a positive and continuing relationship.

## Familial Protective Factors

Protective familial factors are those positive aspects of the child's parents/guardians and home environment. For example, a child who has a positive and supportive relationship with an adult may display less negative behaviour. Thus, a good parent/adult–child relationship is a protective factor for the child who is growing up in an underprivileged community.

## Social/External Protective Factors

Peer groups can have a strong effect on child outcomes (Vance, 2001). Associating with deviant peers is a risk factor for antisocial behaviour. The converse is a protective factor. That is, associating with prosocial children is a protective factor against antisocial behaviour (Fergusson & Horwood, 1996).

Just as there are risk factors leading to increased negative outcomes, there are also protective factors that may reduce negative outcomes in the presence of risk factors (Grossman et al., 1992; Masten, Best, & Garmezy, 1990). Protective factors may counteract risk (Loeber & Farrington, 1998b; Rutter, 1988). Further research is necessary to understand the role protective factors play in positive outcomes.

## PREVENTION, INTERVENTION, AND TREATMENT OF YOUNG OFFENDING

Prevention, intervention, and treatment of young offending can be conceptualized as occurring at three levels: primary, secondary, and tertiary (DeMatteo & Marczyk 2005; Flannery & Williams 1999; Mulvey et al., 1993). **Primary intervention strategies** are strategies that are implemented prior to any violence occurring, with the goal of decreasing the likelihood that violence will occur later on. **Secondary intervention strategies** are strategies that attempt to reduce the frequency of violence. **Tertiary intervention strategies** are strategies that attempt to prevent violence from reoccurring.

## Primary Intervention Strategies

At the primary level of intervention, the goal is to identify groups (of children) that have numerous risk factors for engaging in antisocial behaviour later on. The belief is that if the needs of these children are addressed early, before violence has occurred, then the likelihood that they will go on to become young offenders is reduced. Because "groups" (rather than specific individuals) are targeted, often these intervention strategies occur at broad levels such as in the family, at school, and in the community (Mulvey et al., 1993). The following strategies are examples of primary intervention approaches.

**Family-Oriented Strategies** Targeting the family may be an effective means of preventing young offending, given that family poses a number of risk factors (Kumpfer & Alvarado, 2003). According to Mulvey et al., (1993), family-based intervention efforts can generally be classified as either parent-focused or family-supportive. **Parent-focused interventions** are interventions directed at assisting parents to recognize warning signs for later youth violence and/or training parents to effectively manage any behavioural problems that arise. **Family-supportive interventions** are interventions that connect at-risk families to various support services (e.g., child care, counselling, medical assistance) that may be available in their community.

An example of a family-oriented strategy is a popular parent-education program known as The Incredible Years Parenting Program, a 12-week training program that starts with building a strong emotional bond between parent(s) and child, and then teaches parents how to set behavioural expectations for their children, to monitor children's behaviour, to reinforce positive behaviour, to provide consequences for inappropriate behaviour, and to develop and use effective communication skills (Webster-Stratton, 1992). Videos are used to demonstrate parenting techniques and enhance parent learning. Although parent-focused approaches have shown some success in the shorter term, the most common research finding is that parents of high-risk children tend to discontinue the training at rates that may exceed 50% (Mulvey et al., 1993). With such high attrition rates, particularly among families with the greatest need for these services, it is unlikely that parent-focused approaches are a reliable mechanism for preventing youth violence. Parenting programs usually are not "stand alone" and are part of more comprehensive programs that may involve a child component, school component, and/or community program.

**School-Oriented Strategies** Given the amount of time children spend in school and the number of difficulties that can arise there, school is a common environment for primary prevention strategies. School-based prevention programs include preschool programs (e.g., Project Head Start, which incorporates The Incredible Years Parenting Program); social skills training for children, which may include cognitive behavioural therapy; and broad-based social interventions, which are designed to alter the school environment (Mulvey et al., 1993; Loeber & Farrington, 1998a).

Project Head Start is designed for children from low socioeconomic backgrounds. A number of social services are provided to these children and families (e.g., nutrition, structured activities, academic tutoring, medical services) to reduce disadvantages that may interfere with learning. Preschool programs can produce some positive outcomes in the short term; however, the positive effects at reducing antisocial behaviour over the long term are questionable (Mulvey et al., 1993; Loeber & Farrington, 1998a).

It is not uncommon to recommend a social skills program to children showing some early signs of interpersonal and behavioural difficulties. Social skills training may involve a structured program with a limited number of sessions (e.g., 12), teaching alternative methods for conflict resolution, adjusting social perceptions (recall that a cognitive theory approach suggests that aggressive children may interpret ambiguous situations aggressively [e.g., Lochman, Whidby, & FitzGerald, 2000]), managing anger, and developing empathy. Cognitive behavioural therapy usually is a component of social skills programs. The cognitive behavioural component focuses on children's thought processes and social interactions. Concrete strategies for handling interpersonal conflict are outlined, which children practise through role-playing and modelling with others in the class. Program evaluations have suggested that social skills training with cognitive behaviour therapy can be beneficial in the short term, although long-term follow-up suggests that the effects on reducing antisocial behaviour may be small (e.g., Denham & Almeida, 1987). Larger effects may be obtained if social skills programs are combined with others, such as parent education (Webster-Stratton & Hammond, 1997).

Social process intervention is another school-based approach that alters the school environment (Gauce, Comer, & Schwartz, 1987; Mulvey et al., 1993). Changes include increasing the connection among students with learning problems, assisting the transition from elementary school to high school, improving the perception of safety in school, and providing students with experiences in the community (Mulvey et al., 1993). Although these efforts may improve academic success, their influence on reducing the likelihood of young offending is unclear.

**Community-Wide Strategies** Community approaches include providing structured community activities for children and increasing a community's cohesion. Few community-based programs exist for children younger than age 12 who are at risk for future young offending. One such program, developed in Canada in 1985, is known as the SNAP Under 12 Outreach Project (ORP).

The ORP is a standardized 12-week outpatient program with five key components:

1. The SNAP Children's Club—a structured group that teaches children a cognitive-behavioural self-control and problem-solving technique called SNAP (Stop Now And Plan) (Earlscourt Child and Family Centre, 2001a)

2. A concurrent SNAP parenting group that teaches parents effective child management strategies (Earlscourt Child and Family Centre, 2001b)

3. One-on-one family counselling based on SNAP parenting (Levene, 1998)

4. Individual befriending for children who are not connected with positive structured activities in their community and require additional support

5. Academic tutoring to assist children who are not performing at an age-appropriate grade level

Recently, the ORP's effectiveness was assessed in Toronto by Augimeri, Farrington, Koegl, and Day (2007). Sixteen pairs of children were matched on age, sex, and severity of delinquency (e.g., theft, fighting, severe defiance at home, vandalism, assault, arson, trespassing, public mischief) and then randomly assigned to the ORP or to a control program that received a less-intensive version of ORP (i.e., arts and crafts and cooperative game activities). Data were collected at five intervals: Time 1 (pretreatment); Time 2 (post-treatment—at least three months after Time 1); Time 3 (three months after Time 2); Time 4 (six months after Time 3); and Time 5 (six months after Time 4). A national criminal record search was conducted between each participant's twelfth and eighteenth birthday. Results indicated a significant decrease in externalizing behaviours for children in the ORP group compared with those in the control program. These gains were sustained over the one-year follow-up period. Although children in the ORP group had fewer official contacts with the criminal justice system between the ages of 12 and 18 than the control group, this difference was not significant. Multifaceted interventions with cognitive behavioural skills training along with parent training may have produced positive effects for children under the age of 12 displaying antisocial behaviours.

# Secondary Intervention Strategies

Secondary intervention strategies are directed at young offenders who have either had contact with the police or criminal justice system or have demonstrated behavioural problems at school. The goal of these strategies is to provide social and clinical services so that young offenders do not go on to commit serious violence. Many of the same approaches used in primary intervention strategies are used here. One of the main differences is the target (i.e., which children are involved in the program) rather than the content of the intervention. Common secondary intervention strategies include diversion programs, alternative and vocational education, family therapy, and skills training (see Mulvey et al., 1993).

Diversion programs "divert" youth offenders from the young justice system into community- or school-based treatment programs. The belief is that the justice system may cause more harm than good in reducing offending. Intervention and treatment in the community may be more successful at reducing the likelihood that the young offender will escalate their offending. Alternative and vocational education programs offer the option of mainstream schooling. Family therapy and skills-training programs incorporate the youth and family. Diversion and certain school-, family-, and community-based interventions have shown some success at reducing antisocial behaviour in youth (e.g., Davidson & Redner, 1988; Kazdin, 1996).

One particular secondary intervention program that has undergone considerable evaluation is Multisystemic Therapy (MST). MST examines a child across the contexts or "systems" in which they live: family, peers, school, neighbourhood, and community (Henggeler & Borduin, 1990; Henggeler, Melton, & Smith, 1992; Henggeler, Schoenwald, & Pickrel, 1995; Henggeler et al., 1998). MST has been implemented in various parts of Canada and the United States. To evaluate its effectiveness, a four-year randomized study was conducted across four Ontario communities: London, Mississauga, Simcoe County, and Ottawa (Leschied & Cunningham, 2002). Approximately 200 families received MST from 1997 to 2001. During the same period, another 200 families (acting as the comparison group) were asked to access the services that were available through their local youth justice and social service organizations. These services included probation and specialized programs. All families underwent psychological testing at the start of the study and then again at the end. The psychological testing included measures to assess family functioning, caregiver depression, the youth's social skills, procriminal attitudes, and behavioural problems. Based on this assessment, the youth and families in the MST group were provided services and had access to a case manager 24 hours a day, 7 days a week. Areas that may be targeted in MST treatment include family communication, parent management, and cognitive-behavioural issues. All youth were followed for three years after the end of treatment (until 2004). Overall, MST was not found to be more effective than the typical services available in Ontario. For example, after the three-year follow-up, 68% of the participants in the MST group had at least one conviction, compared with 67% of those in the comparison group. The average number of days to reconviction for the MST group was about 283, compared with 310 for the control group (this difference was not statistically significant). It is important to note, however, that MST may have benefited youth and their families on factors that were not measured. Interestingly, some studies evaluating MST in the United States have found it more effective than incarceration, individual counselling, and probation (Henggeler et al., 1986, 1992, 1995). Perhaps the quantity and quality of programs available in various parts of the United States differ from those in Canada—accounting for some of the differing results between the two countries. Dr. Alan Leschied has been involved in MST evaluation, among other programs, for youth and legislation involving youth. See Box 12.4 to learn more about Dr. Leschied.

Box 12.4

## Canadian Researcher Profile: Dr. Alan Leschied

Dr. Alan Leschied's research interests are in the areas related to the assessment and treatment of youth at risk, as well as with children's legislation and how policies and services promote the welfare of children and families. Of note have been his books *The Young Offenders Act: A Revolution in Canadian Young Justice* (1991); *Offender Rehabilitation in Practice: Implementing and Evaluating Effective Programs* (2001), and *Research and Treatment for Aggression with Adolescent Girls* (2002). More recently, Dr. Leschied's specific research interests have included studies related to youth justice and children's mental health outcomes, the completion of an assessment of Multisystemic Therapy funded by the National Crime Prevention Centre, and the examination of factors related to increases in the demand for child welfare services.

Dr. Leschied says that his introduction to working with youth in the justice system was a matter of happenstance. In the late 1970s, during his time as a graduate student at the University of Western Ontario, the Family Court Clinic (also in London, Ontario) was looking for someone to work part-time to provide assessments of youth coming into contact with the criminal justice system by using

psychological tests alongside social workers who were providing a social history of the youth. At the time, Dr. Leschied and his colleagues made a commitment to research everything they could involving youth and the criminal justice system—this commitment began a tradition of integrating clinical practice with research. Dr. Leschied's approach was truly groundbreaking when one considers that in the 1980s there was very little published research to support what was going on in the youth justice system. Through this work, Dr. Leschied was able to become part of the larger dialogue on youth justice practice, legislation, and policy.

Dr. Leschied's favourite study is the one he co-authored in 1986 with Paul Gendreau titled "The Declining Role of Rehabilitation in Canadian Young Justice: Implications of Underlying Theory in the Young Offenders Act (YOA)," which was published in the *Canadian Journal of Criminology*. This paper was particularly special to Dr. Leschied because it started a collaboration with Paul Gendreau that turned into a treasured professional relationship and personal friendship. This paper was the first to review the YOA and address the imbalance of the law toward deterrence and away from rehabilitation, which was reflected in the high rates of the use of custody. With this paper, Dr. Leschied realized that data could address policy within legislation.

After almost 30 years of research, Dr. Leschied feels that Canadians should be proud that Canada has some of the most forward-thinking youth justice legislation in the world. In looking forward, Dr. Leschied suggests that researchers turn their attentions to how the four service delivery systems for youth—namely education, child welfare, children's mental health, and justice—need to better coordinate their services to meet the needs of the highest risk cases that come through the youth justice system. "Most of the extreme cases that are before a youth court judge represent youth who have experienced some form of violence in their lives, either directly through maltreatment or exposure through interparental assault, unsuccessful academically, or who have been the recipient of some form of bullying or school-based violence, and have been diagnosed with a serious mental health disorder," says Dr. Leschied. "Eventually, these young people make their way into the justice system where the need to coordinate services and expertise from the various service delivery sectors is sorely lacking."

Following an almost 20-year career at the Family Court Clinic, Dr. Leschied moved to the University of Western Ontario on a full-time basis in 1998, where, as a professor, he teaches primarily in the graduate program of counselling psychology. Dr. Leschied's dedication and commitment to youth justice was made possible by a very supportive family by his side and a house full of dogs that keep him grounded.

## Tertiary Intervention Strategies

Tertiary intervention strategies are aimed at youth who have engaged in criminal acts and who may have already been processed through formal court proceedings (Flannery & Williams, 1999). As such, these intervention efforts are actually more "treatment" than prevention, and the recipients are often chronic and serious young offenders. The goal of tertiary intervention strategies is to minimize the impact of existing risk factors and foster the development of protective factors, which may reduce the likelihood that the at-risk adolescent will engage in future offending.

Tertiary intervention strategies include in-patient treatment (i.e., institutional, residential) and community-based treatment (Mulvey et al., 1993). The approach can be one of retribution or rehabilitation. For those who favour retribution, they believe that young offenders should be held accountable for their actions, punished accordingly, and separated from society. Treatment for these young offenders should be provided in an institutional setting (e.g., youth detention centre) By contrast, those who favour rehabilitation believe that treatment based in the community is a more effective way to reduce the likelihood of reoffending. One meta-analysis reported that shorter stays (rather than longer stays) in institutional settings and greater involvement with community services are more effective for violent young offenders (Wooldredge, 1988). See Box 12.5 to read about a very novel tertiary intervention.

## Box 12.5

## Let the Music Play: An Alternative to Offending

Rap lyrics often speak of crime and offending. What if working in the rap music world could be used as an alternative to offending? A rapper named Rochester from the Toronto area performed at the Brookside youth jail in Cobourg, Ontario, giving some of the inmates the idea of creating their own music and music videos by using basic recording equipment at the youth facility. Rochester was impressed with their efforts and decided to give them some professional equipment to allow them to produce their own songs. A pilot project was launched where five teens from the facility would be selected to spend one-day a week to produce

two singles with original lyrics and cover art. The teens also will learn marketing and distribution. The plan is to have the singles released, although this may prove challenging because young offenders have their identities protected. Perhaps once the teens are released from the facility they will enter the music industry rather than reoffend. Let the music play . . .

Source: Mendleson, R. (2010, January 21). Hip hop helps young offenders. *Macleans.ca*. Retrieved from http://www2.macleans.ca/2010/01/21/hip-hop-helps-young-offenders/

# SUMMARY

1. The Juvenile Delinquents Act (JDA) in 1908 was the first piece of legislation in Canada to address youthful offenders. In 1984, the Young Offender's Act (YOA) replaced the JDA with several notable changes to youth justice. Although the YOA underwent several amendments, it was eventually replaced in 2003 with the Youth Criminal Justice Act (YCJA).

2. Three common disorders are diagnosed in youthful offenders: attention-deficit hyperactivity disorder (ADHD), oppositional defiant disorder (ODD), and conduct disorder (CD). Young children diagnosed with conduct disorder are at greatest risk for youthful and adult criminal offending.

3. Biological theories focus on genetic and physiological differences between young offenders and those who do not behave antisocially. Cognitive theories propose a model of antisocial behaviour that focuses on thought processes that occur in social interactions. Social theories are based in social learning theory, which proposes that children learn behaviour from observing others and through reinforcement contingencies.

4. Risk factors increase the likelihood of behavioural (and emotional) disorders in children and youth. Protective factors provide a buffer against the risk factors children and youth may experience.

5. Primary intervention strategies are implemented prior to any violence occurring, with the goal of decreasing the likelihood that violence will occur later on. Secondary intervention strategies attempt to reduce the frequency of violence. Tertiary intervention strategies attempt to prevent violence from reoccurring.

## Discussion Questions

1. Fifteen-year-old Andrew Smith is appearing before Judge Brown in youth court for the third time in two years. Andrew's most current offences are robbery and possession of a handgun. Given the objectives of the Youth Criminal Justice Act, discuss the sentencing options available to Judge Brown. Consider which option is most appropriate in this case. Why?

2. In your opinion, what factors should the courts consider when determining whether a young offender should be given an adult sentence?

3. Various unconventional treatment approaches have been proposed as a way of dealing with young offenders. For example, young offenders have been taken to prison to witness the prison environment first-hand and they have been taken to the morgue. Do you think these sorts of approaches will successfully rehabilitate young offenders? Why or why not?

4. You decide to volunteer at the local Boys and Girls Club on Saturday mornings. You participate in a program for 4- to 6-year-olds. You notice that a few of the children in the group are showing early signs of aggressive behaviour. Design a program to reduce young children's aggression. Each program runs for eight-weeks. What elements would you include in your program? Why?

# Chapter 13
## Domestic Violence

## Learning Objectives

■ Differentiate between the different forms of abuse, and outline the prevalence of domestic violence.

■ Explain why some women remain in, or return to, abusive relationships.

■ Outline how social learning theory has been used to explain domestic violence.

■ Describe the various types of male batterers.

■ Outline the effectiveness of domestic violence offender treatment.

■ Define stalking, and identify the various types of stalkers.

Mohadeseh Farias is serving a federal sentence for criminal harassment, threatening, and assault causing bodily harm. His abusive behaviour started when his wife, Fatima, was pregnant with their first child. He engaged in verbally abusive behaviour, calling Fatima names and threatening to use violence against her. After the baby was born, the verbal abuse escalated and he started physically abusing his wife (i.e., slapping her, shoving her into walls, punching her). After the birth of their second child, he became very controlling and refused to allow Fatima to have contact with her family or friends unless he was present.

After a particularly brutal beating, Fatima left him and took the children to her sister's home and told Mohadeseh she wanted a divorce. For three weeks, Mohadeseh phoned her and on several occasions he showed up at the home demanding to see his wife and children. The police were called and Mohadeseh was charged with criminal harassment. One evening Mohadeseh broke into the house, threatened to kill his brother-in-law, and repeatedly punched his wife. He was arrested and charged with threatening and assault causing bodily harm. He was sentenced to four years in prison and has been attending the high-risk domestic violence treatment program for the past two months. The program consists of individual and group therapy. One therapist thinks Mohadeseh is making considerable progress in treatment, whereas the other therapist is less optimistic. In group therapy, Mohadeseh is evasive when challenged, has been vindictive toward other group members, and is continually testing boundaries. The therapist who has been concerned with Mohadeseh's attitudes and behaviour thinks that Mohadaseh is not genuinely interested in changing.

Violence occurring within the family has a major impact on victims and society. Violence and its aftermath is also a major focus of forensic psychology, with psychologists involved in developing assessment and intervention programs for victims and offenders. Reading the opening vignette raises a number of questions. How common is this sort of behaviour? Why would someone hurt a person he or she claims to love? After being caught, does the violence stop? What can be done to prevent the development of attitudes supportive of abuse? Are treatment programs effective at reducing risk for future violence? We shall address these and other questions in this chapter.

**Domestic violence:** Any violence occurring between family members

The term **domestic violence** refers to any violence occurring between family members. Domestic violence typically occurs in private settings. Although not necessarily condoned, historically it was tolerated and was not subject to effective legal sanctions. Reasons for this were varied, but religious and cultural attitudes generally positioned women and children in deferential roles within families. In Canada, little attention was paid to domestic violence prior to the 1980s. It was the women's liberation movement and the growth of feminism that gave women the courage to speak out against such violence. Since that time, domestic violence has become a major focus of research and legal action.

**Spousal violence:** Any violence occurring between intimate partners who are living together or separated. Also known as *intimate partner violence*

**Intimate partner violence:** Any violence occurring between intimate partners who are living together or separated. Also known as *spousal violence*

In this chapter, we will focus on violence occurring between intimate partners who are living together or separated (called **spousal violence** or **intimate partner violence**). Abuse and aggression within intimate relationships has a long history and is, unfortunately, still common. We will review the different types of abuse experienced and the prevalence of intimate partner violence. We will present theories that attempt to explain why some people engage in violence against their partners. Research examining the different types of domestically violent men will be provided. In addition, some of the major approaches to treatment will be presented and research on their effectiveness will be reviewed. Finally, research examining the prevalence of stalking and types of stalkers will be summarized.

## TYPES OF VIOLENCE AND MEASUREMENT

Violence against partners is varied in terms of types and severity and includes physical (e.g., hitting, punching, stabbing, burning), sexual, financial (e.g., restricting access to personal funds, forcing complete financial responsibility, theft of paycheques), and emotional abuse (e.g., verbal attacks, degradation, threats about hurting family members or pets, isolation from family members, unwarranted accusations about infidelity).

A victim of domestic violence

The scale most commonly used to measure domestic assault has been the Conflict Tactics Scale (CTS) (Straus, 1979). This scale consists of 18 items intended to measure how the person and his or her partner resolve conflict. The items range from constructive problem solving (e.g., discuss the item calmly) to verbal or indirect aggression (e.g., swearing or threatening to hit) to physical aggression (e.g., slapping or using a gun). Respondents are asked how frequently they have engaged in the behaviour and how often they have experienced these acts. Box 13.1 describes some of the myths associated with domestic violence.

Box 13.1

# Myths and Realities Concerning Domestic Violence

Domestic violence is associated with many myths. A list of these myths appear below, accompanied by facts that challenge these false beliefs.

### Myth 1: Domestic violence is not a common problem.

Because of the private nature of domestic violence and the shame and embarrassment that inhibits many victims from talking about the issue, it is impossible to determine exactly how many people are subject to violence. In Canada, about one in eight women are abused by their partners. You likely know someone who has been assaulted by his or her partner or who is currently in an abusive relationship. Highest rates of domestic violence are experienced by women between the ages of 15 and 25.

### Myth 2: Only heterosexual women get battered. Men are not victims, and women never batter.

Such myths ignore and deny the realities of violent relationships. Men can be and are victims of domestic violence. Women can be and are batterers. Even when two people are of the same gender, in a same-sex relationship, abuse can and does occur.

### Myth 3: When a woman leaves a violent relationship, she is safe.

The most dangerous time for a battered spouse is after separation. Of all spousal homicides, 75% occur after separation. At this time, the abusive partner is losing control, which may cause an escalation of abuse in an attempt to regain control.

### Myth 4: Alcohol and/or drugs cause people to act aggressively.

Although abuse of alcohol or drugs is often present in incidents of spousal abuse, it is not the alcohol or drug that causes the violence. However, people will often use this excuse to rationalize their behaviour by saying, "I wasn't myself" or "I hit you because I was drunk." Blaming alcohol or drugs takes the responsibility away from the abusive person and can prevent that person from changing.

### Myth 5: When a woman gets hit by her partner, she must have provoked him in some way.

No one deserves to be hit. Whether or not there was provocation, violence is always wrong. It never solves problems, although it often silences the victim.

### Myth 6: Maybe things will get better.

Once violence begins in a relationship, it usually gets worse without some kind of intervention. Waiting and hoping the abusive partner will change is not a good strategy. Partners in an abusive relationship need help to break out of the abusive pattern.

Archer (2002) conducted a meta-analysis of 48 studies by using the CTS and found that females are more likely to engage in minor physical aggression, such as slapping, kicking, or hitting with an object, whereas men are more likely to beat up or choke their partners. Large differences were found when comparing community, university student, and treatment samples (couples in treatment for domestic violence). Within treatment samples, men engage in much higher rates of minor and severe physical violence compared with students and community samples. Within community and university student samples, males and females commit equal amounts of violence. Comparing self- and partner reports, respondents report fewer violent acts than their partners, and men are more likely to under-report than women.

Although commonly used, the CTS is often criticized for a number of reasons (Dobash & Dobash, 1979; Ratner, 1998):

1. The way it is introduced to respondents has been criticized. Respondents read the following: "No matter how well a couple get along, there are times when they disagree,

get annoyed with the other person or just have spats or fights because they're in a bad mood or for some other reason. They also use many different ways of trying to settle their differences" (Straus, 1990, p. 33). The introduction to a questionnaire is crucial since it provides respondents with information on what to focus on. In the case of the CTS, its focus is on how couples settle disputes. However, some acts of violence are not precipitated by an argument and therefore the respondent may not report these.

2. The CTS does not include the full range of potential violent acts. For example, sexual aggression is not included.

3. It is likely that different results would be found if acts such as kicking, biting, and punching were not combined into one item.

4. The CTS does not take into account the different consequences of the same act for men and women. For example, treating a punch by a woman and a man as equivalent ignores the difference in the injury that might be inflicted (Nazroo, 1995). Surveys have consistently shown that women are more likely than men are to suffer both physical and psychological consequences from domestic violence (Saunders, 2002). Tjaden and Thoennes (2001) reported an injury rate of 42% for women versus 19% for men in the most recent violent episode. Canadian women reported that they had been physically injured in 44% of all cases of intimate violence, and in 13% of cases they sought and received medical care.

5. The CTS does not assess motive for violence and therefore offensive violence is treated as equal to a defensive response. For example, consider the case of a couple arguing. If he threatens to punch her, and she pushes him away from her, both acts would be included on the CTS.

6. Items on the CTS may be interpreted differently depending on the gender of the respondent.

In response to these and other criticisms, Straus, Hamby, Boney-McCoy, and Sugarman (1996) revised the CTS (CTS2), deleting some items and adding new items. For example, physically aggressive acts, such as slamming a person against a wall, burning them on purpose, and sexual aggression, have been included. The verbal aggression scale was renamed *psychological aggression* and additional items were added (e.g., did something to spite partner). Moreover, the consequence (physical injury) has also been added. Researchers are using the CTS2 in studies of domestic violence. Box 13.2 provides more details about the prevalence and severity of mutual violence, as well as gender-specific differences.

## Intimate Partners: A Risky Relationship

In the 1993 Statistics Canada Violence Against Women Survey, 51% of women reported at least one incident of physical or sexual violence since the age of 16 (Johnson, 1996). The most recent Canadian survey on intimate partner assault was conducted by Statistics Canada in 2004 (Statistics Canada, 2006a). This survey used a modified CTS to measure psychological, physical, and sexual violence in intimate relationships. Large samples of men (10 604) and women (13 162) from all provinces and territories were asked questions about their experiences with various forms of intimate partner violence, ranging from threats to sexual assault, in the last 12 months and the past 5 years. In the year preceding the survey, 2% of men and women experienced physical and/or sexual

# Husband Battering Does Exist

Domestic violence is certainly not exclusively initiated by men. However, some researchers have minimized the impact of such abuse. For example, Berk, Berk, Loseke, and Rauma (1983) note that "While there are certainly occasional instances of husbands being battered, it is downright pernicious to equate their experiences with those of the enormous number of women who are routinely and severely victimized" (p. 210). In a review of the literature on women as perpetrators of intimate violence, Carney, Buttell, and Dutton (2007) address the following questions.

■ Is domestic violence invariably male-initiated?

The answer is "no." It appears that women engage in the same amount of violence as men, and some studies found that women engaged in more minor violence then men (Archer, 2002). Williams and Frieze (2005) analyzed the different violence patterns of 3519 couples and found that the most common type of violence was mutual mild violence, followed by mutual severe violence. Thus, the long-assumed gender gap does not exist. As Carney et al. (2007) conclude, "Female violence is common, [and] occurs at the same rate as male violence" (p. 113).

■ Do males suffer any serious consequences of female-initiated violence?

The answer is "yes." Felson and Cares (2005) reported that in intimate partner violence, men were more likely than women to suffer serious injuries. In a recent reanalysis of the Canadian General Social Survey data, Laroche (2005) found that 83% of men "feared for their life," as compared with 77% of women, when being unilaterally terrorized by their partners. Rates of domestic terrorism were similar for men and women across several measures. Men and women who were victims of intimate partner violence received medical care (84% for both men and women), sought psychological counselling (62% of men and 63% of women), and reported everyday routines being disrupted (80% of men and 74% of women). Based on their review of the literature, Carney et al. (2007) conclude, "(1) women are injured more than men but (2) men are injured as well and are not immune to being seriously injured." (p. 110).

■ Is there a gender bias in police responses to domestic violence?

The limited research indicates the answer is "yes." Brown (2004) studied differences in arrest rates in cases of injury and no-injury assaults. When the female partner was injured, the male was charged in 91% of the cases; however, when the male was injured, the female was charged 60% of the time. When no injury occurred, the female was charged in 13% of cases as compared with 52% of the time for males.

■ Do the courts treat men and women charged with domestic violence the same way?

The answer is "no." Women are more likely to have the charges against them dropped by prosecutors and are less likely to be found guilty. For example, Brown (2004) reported that in severe injury cases, 71% of men and 22% of women defendants were found guilty. A major factor for why such a low percentage of women were found guilty was that the male victim was not willing to testify.

assault. Seven percent of female and 6% of male respondents reported having experienced physical and/or sexual assault between 1999 and 2004. Table 13.1 presents the percentage of men and women experiencing different types of violence in the past five years. The results indicate that both men and women experience violence, although women report experiencing more severe forms of violence (i.e., being choked, sexually assaulted, or threatened by a partner with a knife or gun). Respondents were asked about whether the violence was reported to police. Violence against women was more likely to be reported to the police (36%) than was violence against men (17%).

**The prevalence of dating violence in university students** The International Dating Violence Study (Chan, Strauss, Brownridge, Tiwari, & Leung, 2008) examined the prevalence of dating violence in 14 252 university students across 32 countries. The

**Table 13.1** Types of Relationship Violence Experienced over the Past Five Years

| Type of Violence | Men (%) | Women (%) |
|---|---|---|
| Threw something | 49 | 44 |
| Pushed, shoved | 48 | 81 |
| Threatened to hit | 53 | 61 |
| Slapped | 57 | 36 |
| Hit with object | 23 | 23 |
| Kicked, bit, hit | 40 | 27 |
| Beat up | 8 | 19 |
| Forced sex | — | 16 |
| Choked | 5 | 19 |
| Threatened to use/used gun or knife | 9 | 11 |

Note: — = data not available

Source: Statistics Canada, 2006a.

CTS-2 scale was administered, asking students whether they had engaged in any physical and sexual violence with their dating partner and whether they had experienced any physical and sexual violence by their dating partners. Students responded to items about any assaults, including violence ranging from minor (e.g., having something that could hurt them thrown at them, being slapped, having their arm twisted) to serious (e.g., being choked, being beaten up, being threatened by a knife or a gun). Rates of perpetration and victimization of sexual coercion, from minor acts (e.g., was made to have sex without a condom, partner insisted on sex when they did not want to) to more severe acts (e.g., was forced to have oral or anal sex, had sex because of partner threats), were measured. Table 13.2 presents the perpetration and victimization results across male and female students in Canada. Female students were less likely to be perpetrators of serious assaults and

**Table 13.2** Rates of Violence as Reported by Canadian University Students

| Measure | Total (%) | Men (%) | Women (%) |
|---|---|---|---|
| Perpetration of any assault | 24.0 | 25.1 | 23.6 |
| Victim of any assault | 22.2 | 8.3 | 19.5 |
| Perpetration of serious assault | 6.9 | 15.5 | 3.0 |
| Victim of serious assault | 7.3 | 15.3 | 3.7 |
| Perpetration of sexual coercion | 24.3 | 32.4 | 20.7 |
| Victim of sexual coercion | 28.4 | 27.9 | 28.6 |

Source: Chan et al., 2008.

sexual coercion as compared with male students. The median rates across all the countries of having physically assaulted their partners was 29.8% for any assaults, 5.8% for serious assaults, and 21.5% for any sexual coercive acts. Canadian dating physical violence rates were in the lower half of countries surveyed; about one in five Canadian university students reported having experienced physical assault by their dating partner in the last 12 months. However, Canada had higher rates of sexual coercion as compared with many other countries. These findings suggest that dating violence is a substantial problem. Moreover, if university students are engaging in dating violence, this violence will likely continue in future intimate relationships.

## THEORIES OF INTIMATE VIOLENCE

Some researchers believe that a patriarchal society contributes to the domestic assault of women by men (e.g., Dobash & Dobash, 1979; Ellis, 1989; Straus, 1977). The theory of patriarchy was first described in the 1970s and is often associated with sociology and feminism. **Patriarchy** refers to a broad set of cultural beliefs and values that support the male dominance of women. As stated by Dobash and Dobash (1979), "the seeds of wife beating lie in the subordination of females and in their subjection to male authority and control" (p. 33). Smith (1990) has proposed a distinction between "social" patriarchy (male domination at the social level) and "familial" patriarchy (male domination within the family). To study the association between patriarchy and spousal abuse, Yllo and Straus (1990) compared the rates of spousal abuse across American states with the degree to which each state was characterized by patriarchal structure. States with male-dominant norms had much higher rates of spousal assault than those with more egalitarian norms.

**Patriarchy:** Broad set of cultural beliefs and values that support the male dominance of women

Patriarchy likely influences the development of individual expectations about the appropriate level of authority within intimate relationships. One difficulty for patriarchal accounts of domestic violence is that it does not predict which individuals within a system will engage in intimate violence. Other factors operating within the community (e.g., work, peers), family (e.g., communication level between partners), and individual (e.g., coping skills, empathy) are needed to provide an explanation (Dutton, 1995). For example, consider two men who are raised to value the same cultural beliefs, who have similar social supports and identical levels of conflict in the home; one man may react with violence, whereas the other does not.

Social learning theory was developed by Bandura (1973) to explain aggression and has been applied by Dutton (1995) to explain spousal assault. There are three main components to social learning theory: origins of aggression, instigators of aggression, and regulators of aggression. One way people acquire new behaviours is via **observational learning**. Bandura (1973) describes three major sources for observational learning: family of origin, the subculture the person lives in, and televised violence. Studies of the family background of male batterers have found they are much more likely to have witnessed parental violence than are nonviolent men (Kalmuss, 1984; Straus, Gelles, & Steinmetz, 1980). Not all behaviour that is observed, however, will be practised. Social learning theory posits that for a person to acquire a behaviour, it must have functional value for him or her. Behaviour that is rewarded increases in likelihood of occurrence, and behaviour that is punished decreases in likelihood of occurrence.

**Observational learning:** Learning behaviours by watching others perform these behaviours

The next requirement is that even acquired behaviours are manifested only if an appropriate event in the environment acts as a stimulus for the behaviour. These events are called **instigators**. Dutton (1995) describes two types of instigators in domestic assault: aversive instigators and incentive instigators. Aversive instigators produce emotional arousal, and how a person labels that emotional arousal will influence how he or she responds. Studies with male batterers have found that they tend to label many different emotional states as anger (Gondolf [1985] labels this the *male-emotional funnel system*). Incentive instigators are perceived rewards for engaging in aggression. When people believe they can satisfy their needs by using aggression, they may decide to be violent.

Social learning theory assumes that behaviour is regulated by its consequences. Two types of **regulators** include external punishment and self-punishment. An example of external punishment would be if the person was arrested for engaging in violence. An example of self-punishment would be if the person felt remorse for engaging in violence. If the consequences outweigh the rewards for engaging in the behaviour and if alternatives are provided to cope with instigators, the likelihood of violence should diminish.

Another helpful way to conceptualize the interaction among factors related to violence within intimate relationships is in terms of the nested ecological model first proposed by Dutton (1995). This model focuses on the relationship among the multiple levels that influence intimate violence, such as the following:

- *Macrosystem.* This level considers the broad sets of societal and cultural beliefs and attitudes. For example, patriarchy and social norms that condone or promote gender inequality, male domination, and aggression.

- *Exosystem.* This level considers the social structures that connect the individual to the wider society (e.g., social supports, employment, friends), which can influence the likelihood of intimate violence. For example, job stress or unemployment can increase the likelihood of violence, whereas family or friends who provide emotional support or corrective feedback can decrease the likelihood of violence.

- *Microsystem.* This level focuses on the immediate environment in which abuse occurs. For example, the couple's pattern of communication or level of conflict, or each spouse's method of coping with conflict.

- *Ontogenic level.* This level focuses on the psychological and biological features of the individual. For example, the individual's abuse history, exposure to violent models, and abilities to manage emotions.

Dutton's model is useful because it recognizes the importance of various levels of explanation and acknowledges the importance of the interactions that can occur among levels. See Box 13.3 for more information on Dr. Donald Dutton.

## WHY DO BATTERED WOMEN STAY?

One of the more perplexing questions is, "If a woman is in an abusive relationship, why doesn't she just leave?" Although intimate violence is no longer sanctioned by society, negative myths and stereotypes concerning battered woman still prevail. These myths include that a battered woman has a masochistic desire to be beaten, that she is emotionally

## Canadian Researcher Profile: Dr. Donald Dutton

The research of Dr. Donald Dutton is an amazing blend of basic and applied research. He has contributed greatly to the understanding of why men engage in domestic violence while showing how to apply this knowledge to real-world situations. Dr. Dutton completed his degrees at the University of Toronto, focusing on social psychology. Currently, he is a professor of psychology at the University of British Columbia, where he conducts research on domestic violence, spousal homicide, and other forms of extreme violence, such as genocide.

In a recent review of his more than 30 years of research on domestic violence, Dutton (2008) describes how he became interested in the topic:

> I started by riding on police patrol and asking the police what part of their job they felt the least equipped to handle. The answer was "domestic disturbances." I developed a police training manual and was then asked to assist with police intervention (p. 1).

Dr. Dutton recognized early on in his career that to protect victims from future violence, a treatment program was needed. He and his colleagues developed a court-mandated cognitive-behavioural treatment (CBT) program in the early 1980s. This program and subsequent CBT programs have been found to be the most effective type of treatment for reducing future spousal assaults.

In response to a question about what keeps him interested in research, Dr. Dutton replied, "Curiosity." He is intrigued with the question of why someone would kill someone they love or how "ordinary men" become cruel and sadistic in war situations. He uses a range of methodologies in his research, from laboratory studies to field studies, and more recently, to forensic ethology. Forensic ethology is a perspective that examines the details of real-world events to understand the motivation of individual perpetrators.

Dr. Dutton's favourite research topic is also the title of his book, *The Abusive Personality*, which was first published in 2003. In it, he describes abusive personalities as constellations of traits that lead people to become easily threatened and jealous, and to mask these feelings with anger and control behaviours. In the second edition of his book in 2007, Dr. Dutton extended the concept to explain women's use of violence in intimate relationships. He encourages students interested in domestic violence to become familiar with the considerable amount of research conducted on the psychology of domestic violence. He is frustrated by the focus of policy makers and treatment providers on attempting to explain domestic violence on male dominance and society's acceptance of violence. He believes that the causes of intimate violence are complex, that both men and women engage in this form of violence, and that a multi-faceted treatment approach is needed.

Dr. Dutton was called to testify at one of the most high-profile criminal trials in U.S. history—the O.J. Simpson murder trial. His expertise in the areas of spousal violence and homicide were particularly relevant to the case.

Dr. Dutton enjoys teaching forensic psychology, social psychology, and a graduate course titled Nested Ecology of Violence. He recently published a book, *The Psychology of Genocide, Massacres, and Extreme Atrocities*, which he dedicated to his dog. When asked why, Dr. Dutton stated, "Dogs are inherently nicer than humans"—a statement many dog-lovers would agree with.

disturbed, that the violence cannot be as bad as she claims, and that the woman is partially to blame for her victimization (Ewing & Aubrey, 1987; Harrison & Esqueda, 1999; Walker, 1979).

The extent to which people believe such myths varies (Ewing & Aubrey, 1987; Greene, Raitz, & Lindblad, 1989). To examine myths about battered women, Ewing and

Aubrey (1987) gave community samples a hypothetical scenario about a couple having ongoing marital problems, including a description of an incident in which the husband assaulted his wife (the husband accused his wife of cheating on him and then grabbed her and threw her to the floor). The percentage of males and females agreeing with each statement are shown in parentheses:

■ The female victim "bears at least some responsibility." (Males = 47%; Females = 30%)

■ The battered woman could simply leave her battering husband. (Males = 57%; Females = 71%)

■ The battered woman who stays is "somewhat masochistic." (Males = 24%; Females = 50%)

■ The woman can prevent battering by seeking counselling. (Males = 86%; Females = 81%)

■ Battering is an isolated event. (Males = 40%; Females = 27%)

■ The woman can rely on the police to protect her. (Males = 18%; Females = 15%)

Researchers have asked victims of domestic violence why they stay in abusive relationships, and for those who returned after separating, why they did so. The decision to stay with, to leave, or to return to an abusive partner is complex. According to the Violence Against Women Survey (Johnson, 1996), 42% of women left their abusive partners for a short while or permanently. The primary reasons given for leaving were related to experiencing an increase in the severity of the violence (e.g., if they feared for their lives or were physically injured), having children witness the violence, and reporting the abuse to the police. Seventy percent of women who left their abusive partners returned home at least once. The most common reasons for returning were

■ for the sake of the children (31%)

■ to give the relationship another chance (24%)

■ the partner promised to change (17%)

■ lack of money or a place to go (9%)

Similar findings have been reported by Anderson et al. (2003) in a study of victims of intimate violence. In this study, 400 women who sought help from a domestic violence advocacy centre were asked, "If you never left your mate or returned to your mate after separating, check those factors that affected your decision" (p. 152). Thirty-two potential factors were listed and most women endorsed several different reasons. The reasons included

■ mate promised to change (71%)

■ lack of money (46%)

■ mate needed me (36%)

■ nowhere to go or stay (29%)

■ threats of mate to find me and kill me (22%)

■ children [with me] wanted to go back (19%)

■ shelter was full (5%)

This study and others point to the environmental, social, and psychological barriers that exist for victims. For a woman to leave, she needs resources such as money, a place

Box 13.4

# Woman's Best Friend: Pet Abuse and Intimate Violence

Only recently have researchers started to investigate the link between animal maltreatment and violence against women (Ascione, 1998; Ascione, Weber, Thompson, Heath, Maruyama, & Hayashi, 2007; Faver & Strand, 2003). In a study of women in domestic violence shelters, Ascione (1998) reported that 72% said their partners had either threatened to harm or actually had harmed their pets. Moreover, 54% reported that their pets had actually been injured or killed by their abusive partners. Compared with women who said they had not experienced *intimate violence*, Ascione et al. (2007) found that women in domestic violence shelters were 11 times more likely to indicate that their partners had hurt or killed pets. Faver and Strand (2003) questioned 50 abused women who owned pets and found that 49% reported their partners had threatened their pets and 46% indicated that their partners had actually harmed their pets.

Flynn (2000) asked a series of questions about the women's experiences with their pets:

1. In dealing with the abuse, how important has your pet been as a source of emotional support?
2. Has your partner ever threatened to harm your pet, actually harmed your pet, or killed your pet?
3. Where is your pet now?
4. Did concern about your pet's safety keep you from seeking shelter sooner?

Flynn divided the sample of 42 battered women into a pet-abuse group ($n = 20$) and the no-pet-abuse group ($n = 22$). Ninety percent of the women in the pet-abuse group considered their pet a source of emotional support, compared with 47% of the no-pet-abuse group. About half of the pets in both groups were left with the abusive partner. In light of the partner's history of pet abuse, it is not surprising that 65% of the women in the pet-abuse group worried about the safety of their pets, whereas only 15% of the women in the no-pet-abuse group were concerned. Eight women actually delayed leaving their abusive partners out of concern for their pets' safety, with five of these women reporting that they delayed leaving for more than two months. Flynn concluded that "efforts to prevent and end such violence must not only recognize the interconnections, but grant legitimacy to all victims, human and animal" (p. 176).

A recent study of 860 university students found a robust overlap among experiencing childhood abuse, witnessing animal abuse, and witnessing domestic violence. The researchers concluded, "There is a significant overlap between these various forms of abuse within the home and that, in particular, the identification of animal cruelty in a home (perpetrated by parents or children) may serve as a reliable red flag for the presence of child maltreatment or severe domestic violence" (DeGue & DiLillo, 2009, p. 1053).

to go, and support from the criminal justice system (examples of environmental barriers). Women are socialized to be the primary caretaker in relationships and appear to place a high value on the promises of the abuser to change. In addition, they return because they do not want their children to suffer (35%). Psychological barriers also exist. Some victims reported that they felt safer remaining in the relationship than leaving, because they knew what the abuser was doing (22%).

Recently, researchers have begun to study the link between family violence and animal maltreatment. Growing evidence suggests that batterers often threaten or harm their partners' pets and that one reason women delay leaving is out of concern for the welfare of their animals (Ascione, 1998; Faver & Strand, 2003; Flynn, 2000). Box 13.4 describes one such study. Although a link between maltreatment of animals and domestic violence may appear insignificant in relation to other factors, it underscores the complexity of the variables associated with remaining in a violent relationship.

# A HETEROGENEOUS POPULATION: TYPOLOGIES OF MALE BATTERERS

An increasing body of empirical research demonstrates that not all batterers are alike. Categories of male batterers have been developed to help understand the causes of intimate violence. Holtzworth-Munroe and Stuart (1994) divided male batterers into three types based on severity of violence, generality of violence, and personality disorder characteristics: family only, dysphoric/borderline, and generally violent/antisocial.

The **family-only batterer**

**Family-only batterer:** A male spousal batterer who is typically not violent outside the home, does not show much psychopathology, and does not possess negative attitudes supportive of violence

- of all types of batterers, engages in the least amount of violence
- typically neither is violent outside the home nor engages in other criminal behaviours
- does not show much psychopathology, and if a personality disorder is present, it would most likely be passive-dependent personality
- does not report negative attitudes supportive of violence and has moderate impulse-control problems
- typically displays no disturbance in attachment to his partner

The **dysphoric/borderline batterer**

**Dysphoric/borderline batterer:** A male spousal batterer who exhibits some violence outside the family, is depressed, has borderline personality traits, and has problems with jealousy

- engages in moderate to severe violence
- exhibits some extra-familial violence and criminal behaviour
- of all types of batterers, displays the most depression and borderline personality traits, and has problems with jealousy
- has moderate problems with impulsivity and alcohol and drug use
- has an attachment style that would be best described as preoccupied

The **generally violent/antisocial batterer**

**Generally violent/antisocial batterer:** A male spousal batterer who is violent outside the home, engages in other criminal acts, has drug and alcohol problems, has impulse-control problems, and possesses violence-supportive beliefs

- engages in moderate to severe violence
- of all types of batterers, engages in the most violence outside of the home and in criminal behaviour
- has antisocial and narcissistic personality features
- likely has drug and alcohol problems
- has high levels of impulse-control problems and many violence-supportive beliefs
- shows a dismissive attachment style

Several studies have provided support for this typology both in offender and community samples of male batterers (Tweed & Dutton, 1998; Waltz, Babcock, Jacobson, & Gottman, 2000). See the Case Study box for a profile of a domestic violence victim who knew her abuser.

# CRIMINAL JUSTICE RESPONSE

For centuries, wife battering was seen as a private family matter and police were reluctant to become involved (Dobash & Dobash, 1979). When called to a domestic violence scene, police would attempt to calm the people involved and, once order was restored,

# CASE STUDY YOU BE THE RESEARCHER

On March 11, 1982, Jane Hurshman-Corkum shot and killed her husband, Billy Stafford, when he had passed out after drinking all evening. Stafford was killed by a single shot to his head. For five years, Hurshman-Corkum had experienced regular beatings by her husband. Stafford had shot at her, held a knife to her throat, raped her, and forced her to engage in bizarre sexual acts. Stafford also directed his violence toward his son, Darren.

Stafford was known and feared in the Bangs Falls area of Nova Scotia by both community members and the RCMP. He had a violent temper, was unpredictable, and would physically attack others. He was often drunk and would regularly get into fights at bars.

Stafford's two previous partners left after being abused by him. Hurshman-Corkum described feeling totally trapped with nowhere and no one to turn to. Stafford had threatened to track her down and kill her, her sons, and her family if she ever tried to leave him.

On that fateful day, Stafford had said that he planned to set fire to his neighbour's trailer and to "deal" with Hurshman-Corkum's 16-year-old son Allen who was temporarily living with them. Hurshman-Corkum finally decided that she had had enough and killed Stafford.

Hurshman-Corkum was charged with first-degree murder. At her first trial, her lawyer argued that she had acted in self-defence. The jury agreed, and she was found not guilty. The courtroom applauded when the verdict was announced. The Crown appealed, and 15 months later, on the advice of her lawyer, Hurshman-Corkum pleaded guilty to the charge of manslaughter. She was sentenced to six months in jail and two years' probation.

After her release from jail, Hurshman-Corkum became a vocal advocate for battered women. She lobbied for the establishment of transition houses for battered women and became a symbol of hope and resistance in the fight against domestic violence.

Hurshman-Corkum never got over the trauma of the abuse. She was often depressed and was embarrassed by her kleptomania (an uncontrollable urge to steal that led to several shoplifting convictions). On February 22, 1992, she was found dead in her car in Halifax. The autopsy report ruled that Hurshman-Corkum died from a point-blank bullet wound to her chest that was consistent with suicide.

## Your Turn . . .

What type of male batterer was Stafford? Why do you think Hurshman-Corkum did not leave Stafford? What triggered her to commit homicide?

they would leave (Jaffe, Hastings, Reitzel, & Austin, 1993). Since the 1980s, however, mandatory charging policies have been in effect in Canada and in most jurisdictions in the United States. **Mandatory charging policies** give police the authority to lay charges against a suspect when there are reasonable and probable grounds to believe that an assault has occurred. Prior to mandatory charging, women were required to bring charges against their husbands. Women were often too intimidated to do so as they feared further violence; as a result, charges were usually not laid.

The first experimental study to examine the specific deterrence effect of arrest on spousal violence was conducted by Sherman and Berk (1984) in Minneapolis. This study

**Mandatory charging policies:** Policies that give police the authority to lay charges against a suspect where there is reasonable and probable grounds to believe a domestic assault has occurred

involved the random assignment of 314 domestic assault calls to three police responses: separation (order for suspect to leave premises for at least eight hours), mediation (provide advice to victim), or arrest. A six-month follow-up of the men was conducted by using both police reports and victim reports. Figure 13.1 presents the recidivism rates across the groups for both police and victim reports. The recidivism rates for the arrested men were much lower than those of men in the separation or mediation groups. Attempts to replicate this finding have met with mixed results. Tolman and Weisz (1995) also found a deterrent effect for arrest, whereas Hirschell, Hutchinson, and Dean (1990) did not. In an attempt to replicate their findings, Sherman, Schmidt, and Rogan (1992) randomly assigned police calls of domestic violence to nonarrest or arrest. Using police and victim reports, lower rates of recidivism were reported in the short term (30 days after police contact) for both arrest and nonarrest groups. However, in the long-term follow-up (seven to nine months after police contact) the arrest group had slightly higher rates of recidivism than did the nonarrest group. The authors found that arrest did not work for those offenders who were unemployed. In other words, arrest worked as a deterrent only for those men who had something to lose.

Do mandatory arrest policies increase the probability of domestic abusers being arrested? Arrest rates for intimate partner violence have increased dramatically since mandatory arrest policies were implemented. For example, in the 1970s and 1980s, arrest rates in Canada and the United States ranged from 7% to 15%, whereas more recent rates of 30% to 75% have been reported. However, one unanticipated outcome of these policies has been an increase in dual arrests (Hirschel & Buzawa, 2002). If the police are unable to determine the identity of the primary aggressor, and if there are minor injuries to both parties, then the police will charge both the man and the woman.

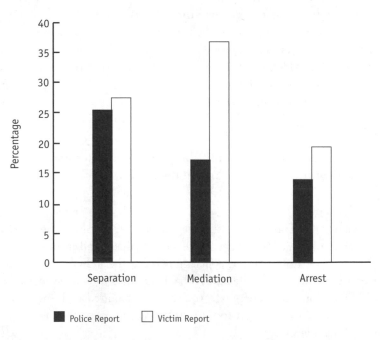

**Figure 13.1** Rates of Recidivism for Different Police Responses

Source: Sherman and Berk, 1984.

Another consequence of the increase in the number of arrests for domestic assault has been the dramatic increase in the number of men who are court-mandated to attend treatment. Since most batterers are not motivated to attend treatment programs, having judges impose a treatment order forces men to obtain treatment. If the man fails to attend treatment, then the judge can impose a prison term. The use of court-mandated treatment is based on the belief that it is possible to treat male batterers. However, the effectiveness of treatment for batterers is still very much in question.

## Does Treatment of Male Batterers Work?

A number of different procedures have been developed to treat male batterers. The two most common forms of intervention are feminist psychoeducational group therapy (also referred to as the Duluth model, since the treatment was designed at the Duluth Domestic Abuse Intervention Project in Minnesota) and cognitive-behavioural group therapy. According to the Duluth model (Pence & Paymar, 1993), the primary cause of domestic violence is patriarchal ideology. Group therapy in this model focuses on challenging the man's perceived right to control his partner. The atmosphere in treatment often has a blaming, punitive orientation, which can result in very high drop-out rate (up to 75%).

The Duluth model has been criticized on several grounds. First, the entire focus is on violence done by men to women. This restricted gendered approach limits its usefulness for dealing with women's use of violence (which is common) against men, and women to women and men to men violence within in same-sex relationships. Second, violence is viewed as one-sided and not as an interaction between people. Much of violence in relationships is mutual. For the treatment to be effective, it cannot be only the man in these relationships who needs to change. Third, the focus of the Duluth model is on shaming the man and therapists fail to establish a therapeutic bond with their clients. Finally, there is a limited focus on changing the man's attitudes about power and control in relationships. The cause of domestic violence is multi-determined and focusing solely on power and control is not sufficient to effect change. In a review of the effectiveness of the Duluth model, Dutton and Corvo (2006) concluded this model has "negligible success in reducing or eliminating violence among perpetrators" (p. 462).

The other, more common, treatment program is cognitive-behavioural therapy, which subscribes to the beliefs that violence is a learned behaviour and that use of violence is reinforcing for the offender because he or she obtains victim compliance and reduces feelings of tension (Sonkin, Martin, & Walker, 1985). Cognitive-behavioural therapy focuses on the costs of engaging in violence. Alternatives to violence are taught, such as anger-management and communication-skills training. Some cognitive-behavioural treatment programs also address perpetrators' attitudes about control and dominance. The rationale for using group therapy is to help to break through the barriers of denial and

Group therapy for male batterers

minimization. The Correctional Service of Canada has developed a family violence program which is described in more detail in Box 13.5.

Babcock, Green, and Robie (2004) conducted a meta-analysis of 22 studies to evaluate the efficacy of treatment for male batterers. Studies were included only if the outcome was measured by either police reports or partner reports of violence (i.e., studies using only batterer self-report were not included). Studies were also divided into three types of treatment: the Duluth model, cognitive-behavioural, and other (e.g., couples therapy). There were no differences in efficacy among the three treatment types in terms of recidivism rates. Based on partner reports, the effect size for quasi-experimental studies was $d = 0.34$, and for experimental studies, it was $d = 0.09$. The authors conclude that "regardless of reporting method, study design, and type of treatment, the effect on recidivism rates remains in the small range" (p. 1044). Based on experimental studies and the use of partner reports, these results mean there is a 5% increase in success rate because of treatment. This small effect does not mean we should abandon attempts to treat batterers. As stated by the authors, "a 5% decrease in violence. . . in [the] United States. . . would equate to approximately 42,000 women per year no longer being battered" (p. 1044). Although the effects appear to be small, they are similar to treatment effects for alcohol abuse when abstinence from alcohol is the outcome (Agosti, 1995).

Recent research, however, is more optimistic about the promise of domestic violence treatment. Bennett, Stoops, Call, and Flett (2007) found that even when controlling for differences in the history of violence, personality, demographic variables, and motivation, men who completed treatment were less than half as likely to be re-arrested for domestic violence than those who did not finish the intervention program. Bowen and Gilchrist (2006) identified participant characteristics that predict program attrition, including youthful age, having served a previous prison sentence, and self-reporting a low level of partner violence. The researchers recommended using these static factors to tailor domestic violence treatment and prevent program attrition so that participants can benefit from treatment. In another study, Lee, Uken, and Sebold (2007) recommended the inclusion of more self-determined goals for offenders in treatment, based on their study of 88 male perpetrators of domestic violence participating in court-mandated treatment. They found that goal specificity and the facilitator's agreement with the participant's goals positively predicted offenders' confidence to achieve their goals, which in turn had a negative relationship with recidivism.

Future research should examine the treatment response of specific subsamples, such as types of batterers (e.g., family-only, borderline/dysphoric, and generally violent/antisocial), batterers with substance abuse problems, and batterers at different levels of motivation. As Saunders (2001) has asserted, "The best intervention outcomes for men who batter may be obtained when the type of offender is matched to the type of treatment" (p. 237). Failure to match a batterer to treatment services may lead to a batterer completing a program that does not meet his or her specific treatment needs. Cavanaugh and Gelles (2005) point out that a victim could thus be led to having a "false sense of security, with the belief that she is now safer when, in fact, she is not." (p. 162). According to Gondolf and Fisher (1988), the variable most predictive of whether a woman will return to a violent partner after a shelter stay is if the batterer has sought treatment. In addition, future research needs to focus on women's use of violence and to develop interventions for domestically violent women.

Box 13.5

# The Correctional Service of Canada's Family Violence Prevention Programs

The Correctional Service of Canada's (CSC) National Family Violence Prevention Programs are primarily focused on male offenders who have been abusive in their intimate relationships with female partners or ex-partners. These programs include a moderate-intensity program for offenders with less extensive histories of partner abuse, a high-intensity program for higher risk offenders, a high-intensity program for higher risk Aboriginal offenders, a maintenance program for offenders who have completed the programs, and a treatment primer designed to enhance motivation of potential participants.

## Philosophy

The programs are based on a social learning model that conceptualizes violence against women as a learned pattern of behaviour that can be modified. These programs teach offenders to understand the dynamics of their abusive relationships by using cognitive-behavioural techniques. These techniques allow them to identify their abusive behaviours and replace them with alternative skills and behaviours that help them form positive nonabusive relationships.

The High Intensity Family Violence Prevention Program (HIFVPP, established in 2001) provides intervention to federal offenders who are assessed as high risk to be violent in their intimate relationships. This program is only offered in institutions. It consists of about seventy-five 2.5 hour group sessions, delivered over a period of about 15 weeks. There are also eight to ten individual counselling sessions scheduled with each participant's primary counsellor. The program is delivered by a team made up of a psychologist and a qualified program officer.

The Moderate Intensity Family Violence Prevention Program (MIFVPP, established in 2001) is intended to help offenders who are at a moderate risk to engage in future violence in their intimate relationships. This program is offered in the community and institutions. It consists of twenty-four 2.5 hour group sessions, delivered two to five times per week over a period of between 5 to 13 weeks. There are also three individual counselling sessions. The program is delivered by two training program facilitators.

The Aboriginal High Intensity Family Violence Prevention Program is similar to the HIFVPP, but the process

and method of delivery reflects the teachings, traditions, and cultural values of Aboriginal people. The program was approved by Aboriginal Elders, and Elders are involved in the delivery of the program; they provide counselling and conduct ceremonies. This program was established in 2004.

The programs include the following components:

- *Motivation*. Addresses the offender's level of motivation to change
- *Education*. Provides information about the prevalence of intimate violence and the range of abusive behaviours
- *Attitudes*. Recognizes the attitudes and beliefs that condone abusive patterns
- *Management of emotions*. Provides skills training in controlling feelings of jealousy, anger, and fear of relationship loss
- *Skills building*. Provides training on the social and communication skills that underlie healthy relationships, such as negotiation and responding appropriately to criticism
- *Relapse prevention*. Develops avoidance strategies to sidestep high-risk situations and coping plans for use when the high-risk situation cannot be avoided

## Effectiveness

Stewart, Gabora, Kropp, and Lee (2005) conducted a preliminary evaluation of the high and moderate family violence prevention programs. A sample of 572 male offenders were assessed prior to and after completing the program. Moderate to strong treatment effects were found; offenders who completed treatment showed lower levels of jealousy, fewer negative attitudes about relationships, better recognition of relapse prevention skills, and more respect and empathy for their partners. Feedback from parole officers who supervised program completers reported positive attitudes and behaviours while under supervision. Participants also reported they felt the program was useful and reported they were able to use the skills they learned. A six-month follow-up study was conducted comparing 160 offenders who completed the treatment program (high and moderate intensity program) and 86 offenders who dropped out of treatment or who

*(continued)*

did not participate in the treatment. Figure 13.2 presents the six-month recidivism for another arrest for spousal assault, any violent offense, or any infractions across treated and untreated groups. Treated offenders were less likely to engage in spousal assault or violent reoffending as compared with the untreated group. There was no group difference in rates of any infractions. Whether these treatment gains will continue after a longer period needs to be determined. In addition, recidivism was based on official statistics and not on self-report from the offender or the offender's intimate partner. However, the preliminary results are promising, suggesting that the treatment programs are targeting the criminogenic needs of male batterers.

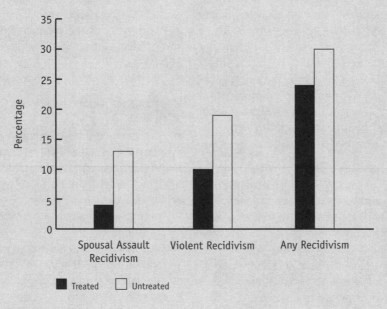

**Figure 13.2** Recidivism Rates for Treated and Untreated Groups

## STALKING

Interest in stalking has increased dramatically over the past decade. Often, it has been the cases of celebrity stalking that have caught the attention of the media. However, celebrities aren't the only people who get stalked. Stalking can occur when an abusive relationship ends. Stalking is a form of violence that is known in Canadian criminal law as criminal harassment. According to section 264 of the Criminal Code of Canada, **criminal harassment** can involve repeatedly following, communicating with, watching, and/or threatening a person either directly or through someone a person knows. The person being stalked must fear for his or her own safety or the safety of someone they know for the police to charge someone.

The prevalence of stalking can be measured via official statistics or by victimization studies. In 2008, there were 18 347 charges of criminal harassment in Canada. The largest victimization study to be done in Canada was done by Statistics Canada in 2004 (see description by AuCoin, 2005). As part of the General Social Survey (GSS) a sample of 24 000 men and women were asked, "In the past 5 years, have you been the subject of repeated and unwanted attention that caused you to fear for your safety or the safety of someone known to you?" Participants were asked about receiving repeated unwanted phone calls, being

**Criminal harassment:** Crime that involves repeatedly following, communicating with, watching, or threatening a person directly or indirectly

followed, having someone wait outside their home, school, or work place, and receiving unwanted gifts or letters. Women were more likely to be victims of stalking than men. More than one in ten women (11%) reported being stalked over the past five years in a way that caused them to fear for their safety, as compared with 7% of men. In total, over 2.3 million Canadians were stalked. Young women between the ages of 15 to 24 have the highest stalking rates. Prevalence of stalking is more common in university students than the general public. Studies measuring stalking in students have found rates of between 9% and 30% for university females and between 11% and 17% for university males (Bjerregaard, 2002; Fremouw, Westrup, & Pennypacker, 1997). The prevalence rates vary depending on the definition of stalking used and the time period (e.g., last 12 months versus ever).

Most stalking victims know their stalkers. In a meta-analysis of 175 studies of stalking, Spitzberg and Cupach (2007) reported that 79% of stalking victims knew their stalkers. The most common type of relationship was romantic (49%)—that is, the stalking occurred after a romantic relationship between the stalker and the stalking victim had ended. According to the GSS, most of the stalkers were male (80%) and the victims were female. The most common gender pattern was a male stalker and a female victim (53% of the cases). However, in 5% of the cases, the stalker was a female and the victim a male. Some researchers have suggested that more males are actually stalked by ex-intimates than the surveys indicated (Kropp et al., 2002). However, these men do not report they have been stalked since the behaviour does not cause them to fear for their safety.

If you are a victim of criminal harassment, one of the most important questions to ask is, "What is the likelihood of being a victim of a violent act?" A meta-analysis has attempted to differentiate stalkers who represent a significant risk of violence from those who pose less of a risk (Rosenfeld, 2004). Rosenfeld analyzed 10 studies that included 1055 stalking offenders. Violence occurred in 38.6% of the cases. The following variables were significantly related to violence:

■ *Clinical variables.* Substance-abuse disorder, personality disorder, and the absence of a psychotic disorder predicted violence.

■ *Case-related variables.* A former intimate relationship between offender and victim and threats toward the victim predicted violence.

Stalking offenders who are at the greatest risk for continuing stalking behaviour after release from prison are those who have both a personality disorder and a history of substance abuse (Rosenfeld, 2004).

Imagine being in constant fear of what might happen to you. Stalking victims suffer intense stress, anxiety, sleep problems, and depression, as well as disruptions in social functioning and work. Overall, victims of stalking experience a decrease in the quality of their lives (Davis & Frieze, 2000; Fisher, Cullen, & Turner, 2002; Spitzberg & Cupach, 2007). In the GSS study, about a third of stalking victims feared their lives were in danger. When the stalker is an ex-spouse, 60% of women victims reported being afraid they may be killed. McFarlane, Campbell, and Watson (2002) examined the prevalence and type of stalking behaviours 12 months prior to an attempted or actual murder or assault by an ex-partner. This study consisted of 821 women, 174 who had survived an attempt on their lives by their intimate partners (attempted femicides), 263 who had been killed by their intimate partners (actual femicides), and 384 who had been physically abused or threatened with physical harm but no attempt on their lives had been made (controls).

Stalking was more common in the attempted/actual femicide group (68%) than in the controls (51%). Women who were spied on or followed were twice as likely to become attempted or actual homicide victims. In addition, in cases in which threats of harm were made to children, if the woman did not go back to having a relationship with the stalker, the likelihood of attempted or actual homicide increased by nine times. This study suggests that certain types of stalking behaviours are associated with increased risk of lethal violence, and stalking victims and police need to be aware of these risk factors.

Stalking victims often change their behaviours to try to protect themselves. In the GSS survey, most often victims avoided certain places or people, followed by getting an unlisted phone number or call display, and about a third of the victims would not leave their homes alone. Only 37% of the stalking victims contacted the police, and charges were laid against the stalker in 23% of the cases (the most common charge was criminal harassment). In 11% of cases, victims received restraining orders in an attempt to stop their stalkers from contacting them. Of those victims who secured a restraining order against their stalkers, just under half (49%) of these orders were violated—that is, the stalker contacted the victim.

Categories of stalkers have been developed to help to understand the causes of stalking. Kropp, Hart, and Lyon (2002) formulated a typology that classifies stalkers into four categories based on their relationships with their victims.

### The **ex-intimate stalker**

- is the most common type

- engages in stalking after an intimate relationship breaks up

- is an individual who is disgruntled or estranged, and unable to let go of his or her partner

- has a history of domestic violence in intimate relationships

### The **love-obsessional stalker**

- is a rare type

- is an individual who has never had an intimate relationship with the victim but has been an acquaintance or co-worker

- has intense emotional feelings for the victim

- does not have symptoms of depression or psychosis

### The **delusional stalker**

- is a rare type

- is an individual who has never had any relationship with the victim, but the delusional stalker believes that a relationship exists

- sometimes targets a celebrity, media figure, or politician

- is often diagnosed with delusional disorders, schizophrenia, or bipolar disorder

### The **grudge stalker**

- is a rare type

- is an individual who knows the victim but has not had an intimate relationship with the victim

- is an angry individual seeking revenge for a perceived injustice

**Ex-intimate stalker:** A stalker who engages in stalking after an intimate relationship breaks up

**Love-obsessional stalker:** A stalker who has intense emotional feelings for the victim but who has never had an intimate relationship with the victim

**Delusional stalker:** A stalker who suffers from delusions and wrongly believes he or she has a relationship with the victim

**Grudge stalker:** A stalker who knows and is angry at the victim for some perceived injustice

# Dangerous Fixations: Celebrity Stalkers

Although most stalking takes place in the context of ex-partners or prior acquaintances, it is the stalking of celebrities that catches the attention of the media. It was the stalking of celebrities that prompted several countries to introduce criminal code offences. In 1990, California was the first state to introduce antistalking laws in the aftermath of the Rebecca Schaffer murder. In 1993, Canada introduced the new offence of criminal harassment. Three high-profile cases of celebrity stalkers are described below.

## Rebecca Schaffer

Born in 1967, Rebecca Schaffer was the only child of a clinical psychologist and a writer. She lived in Los Angeles and starred in the TV series *My Sister Sam*. In 1986, John Bardo (born in 1970), who was working as a fast-food cook living in Tuscon, Arizona, developed an obsession with Schaffer and started sending her letters. She responded to these fan letters and sent him a response signed "with love Rebecca." In 1987, he travelled to Burbank Studios with a teddy bear and a bouquet of roses and demanded to see Schaffer. The security guards refused to allow him entrance. Bardo sent hundreds of letters to Schaffer and his bedroom was decorated with dozens of photos of her. At the age of 21, Bardo saw Schaffer in the movie *Scenes from the Class Struggle in Beverly Hills* in which Schaffer was shown in a sex scene with a male actor. Bardo was extremely upset and asked his older brother to buy him a gun. Bardo sent his older sister a letter, which stated that if he could not have Rebecca no one could. In July 1989, he travelled to Hollywood and hired a private investigator to find out where Schaffer lived. On the morning of July 18, 1989, he rang her doorbell. When she answered the door, he told her he was her biggest fan. She asked him to leave. He returned an hour later and shot her twice, killing her. Bardo was convicted of capital murder and was sentenced to life without eligibility of parole. He is currently serving his sentence at a maximum-security prison in California. On July 27, 2007, Bardo was stabbed 11 times by another inmate but survived.

## David Letterman

Margaret Ray (born 1958) developed an obsession with David Letterman in the mid-1980s after the break-up of her marriage. Ray was diagnosed with schizophrenia. She was first arrested in 1988 when she stole Letterman's Porsche and was caught driving it with her 3-year-old son. She told the police that she was Letterman's wife and the child was Letterman's son. Over the next few years, Ray repeatedly showed up at Letterman's house, leaving letters, books, and cookies. She was charged with trespassing eight times. In the early 1990s, she served a ten-month prison sentence for harassing Letterman. After her release, she shifted her obsession to astronaut Story Musgrave. In 1998, Ray committed suicide by kneeling in front of a train. Both Letterman and Musgrave expressed sympathy upon her death.

## Jodie Foster

In 1976, John Hinckley (born 1955) watched the movie *Taxi* in which Jodie Foster played a child prostitute. Hinckley became obsessed with Foster. When Foster when to Yale University, Hinckley followed her there, called her, and left messages and poems in her mailbox. These attempts failed to get Foster to notice him. Hinckley then planned to get her attention by assassinating the president of United States. He spent a couple of months trailing President Jimmy Carter but was stopped at the Nashville airport for carrying handguns in his luggage. He was fined and released. On March 30, 1981, he fired six shots at President Ronald Reagan, injuring him and three others. Just prior to the shooting, he sent a letter to Foster stating,

> As you well know by now I love you very much. Over the past seven months I've left you dozens of poems, letters and love messages in the faint hope that you could develop an interest in me. Although we talked on the phone a couple of times I never had the nerve to simply approach you and introduce myself.... the reason I'm going ahead with this attempt now is because I cannot wait any longer to impress you.

Hinckley was found not guilty by reason of insanity and was sent to a secure forensic psychiatric hospital. In 1999, he was allowed supervised visits to his parents' house. However, in 2004, these visits were halted because he smuggled materials about Foster back into the hospital. In 2009, he was allowed to visit his mother for nine days at a time.

Some stalkers may fall into several categories. For example, an ex-intimate stalker may be motivated by a grudge relating to a child custody dispute.

Because of their high-profile, politicians are more vulnerable to being stalked than the general population. In a recent survey of 424 Canadian federal and provincial politicians, Adams, Hazelwood, Pitre, Bedard, and Landry (2009) reported that 30% of participants had experienced harassment. The most common communication was telephone calls or emails, the most common theme was threats, and a small portion (about 8%) were declarations of love. Of those politicians harassed, 60% were personally approached, with 24% having some form of physical contact with their stalker and 6% being physically assaulted. See the In the Media box for a description of some high-profile celebrity stalking cases.

## SUMMARY

1. The prevalence rates of domestic violence are difficult to estimate accurately since the violence often occurs in private. Domestic violence can be classified into the following types: physical abuse, sexual abuse, financial abuse, and emotional abuse.

2. Abused women remain in, or return to, abusive relationships for a number of reasons. Environmental, socialization, and psychological barriers exist that make it difficult for abused women to leave these relationships.

3. Social learning theory has been used to explain domestic violence. There are three main components to social learning theory: origins of aggression, instigators of aggression, and regulators of aggression. One way people acquire new behaviours is via observational learning. Instigators are events in the environment that act as stimuli for the behaviour, and behaviour is regulated by the prospect of its consequences. Behaviours that are rewarded increase in frequency, and behaviours that are punished decrease in frequency.

4. Holtzworth-Munroe and Stuart (1994) divided male batterers into three types based on severity of violence, generality of violence, and personality disorder characteristics: family only, dysphoric/borderline, and generally violent/antisocial.

5. Treatment for domestically violent offenders involves modifying attitudes that condone violence; enhancing conflict-resolution skills; learning to mange emotions; and developing relapse-prevention plans. The effectiveness of treatment programs for male batterers varies, with some cognitive-behavioural treatment programs showing promising results.

6. Research on stalking has found (a) most stalkers know their victims, (b) males are more likely to be stalkers and females are more likely to be victims, (c) spying, following, and making threats of violence are related to an increased risk for lethal violence, and (d) the most common type of stalker is the ex-intimate stalker.

### Discussion Questions

1. What are the barriers to some battered women leaving an abusive relationship? What could be done at both an individual and a societal level to help battered women?

2. You are having a discussion with your friends about dating-related violence and one of them states that women engage solely in self-defence violence. Describe the data that calls your friend's statement into question.

3. You are interested in doing a study on the association between animal abuse and domestic violence. Describe the methodology you would use and what variables you would measure.

4. Your friend has recently broken up with her boyfriend. She tells you that her boyfriend falsely accused her of cheating on him and had become very controlling. She left her boyfriend after he had punched her for failing to call him when he told her to. She tells you that he has been sending her repeated email messages and calling her cellphone daily. What advice can you give her?

# Chapter 14
## Sexual and Homicidal Offenders

## Learning Objectives

- List the different typologies of rapists and child molesters.

- Outline the treatment targets for sexual offenders.

- Describe the effectiveness of treatment for sexual offenders.

- Describe the characteristics of homicide in Canada.

- Differentiate between instrumental and reactive homicide.

- Describe different types of murderers.

- Describe the effectiveness of treatment for violent offenders.

Trevor Cook was 26 years old when the police finally caught up with him. For years, he had been terrorizing women in the city where he lived. Throughout his teenage years, Trevor was known as a womanizer and a con man who was always trying to make a quick buck. The first of Trevor's crimes could be traced back to when he was 16 years old. He had just started dating a 17-year-old girl and they were sexually active. One night, his girlfriend wasn't feeling well and denied his sexual advances. Upset at being rejected, Trevor pushed her onto the bed and held her down as he forced her to have intercourse. Similar incidents occurred with several other girlfriends, and Trevor's behaviour toward women quickly became more parasitic and aggressive. He regularly stole money from his girlfriends, and in addition to frequently cheating on them, he was emotionally and verbally abusive.

By the time he was in his early 20s, Trevor's behaviour had escalated to the point where he was committing sexual assaults against women he met while at bars. He would spot a young woman he thought was attractive and would follow her home. The first few times Trevor attacked a woman, he put on a ski mask, fondled the woman, and ran away. However, that didn't satisfy him for long and, when he was 23 years old, Trevor raped and beat one of the women he followed home in a back alley outside of her house. He would commit more rapes that year, with each rape being more vicious than the previous one. Trevor's crimes ended when one of his victims finally got away before he could attack her. This woman had ripped Trevor's ski mask off him and gotten a good look at his face. The description she gave to the police ultimately led to his arrest. The police had been searching for Trevor for more than five years. By the time he was arrested at the age of 26, Trevor had raped 12 women. Given the escalation of his behaviour, the police are confident that Trevor would have eventually gone on to kill.

Violence of the sort displayed by Trevor in the opening vignette has a major impact on victims and society. For example, the victims of such crimes can be scarred for life and the family members of these victims sometimes fare no better. In addition, the media often focuses on violent crimes and, as a consequence, violence is on the minds of the Canadian public. Indeed, when pollsters ask the public about the concerns we have, fear of violent crime is a common response (Roberts, 2001). Unsurprisingly, given this response, our politicians also talk about violent crime a great deal. They "play the crime card" in an attempt to get elected and, once elected, they devote a large amount of energy to showing the country how they are dealing with the violent crime problem.

Violence and its aftermath is also a major focus of forensic psychology. For example, many forensic psychologists are involved in developing theories to explain why people become violent. They conduct research to understand the nature of this violence and develop procedures to assess and programs to rehabilitate violent offenders. This chapter discusses some of this work. In the first part of the chapter, we cover sexual violence; in the second part, we examine acts of homicide.

## SEXUAL OFFENDERS

## Nature and Extent of Sexual Violence

Sexual violence is on par with homicide in terms of how perpetrators are vilified by society. In 2008, just over 20 992 sexual assaults were reported to the police in Canada (Statistics Canada, 2009). The rate per 100 000 population was 63, a slight drop compared with previous years. However, official statistics do not provide an accurate measure of the true incidence of this type of crime, since the majority of victims do not report the crime to the police (Yurchesyn, Keith, & Renner, 1992). Victims do not report sexual offences for the following reasons: victims often don't feel that the matter is important enough; they believe the matter has already been dealt with; they feel the matter is too personal; or they simply don't want to involve the police (Brennan & Taylor-Butts, 2008).

Sexual assault affects a large percentage of the population. High victimization rates are reported among children and youth (roughly 1 in 12 in the United States; Finkelhor, Ormrod, Turner, & Hamby, 2005), and adult women (10% to 20% report being raped; Johnson & Sacco, 1995; Koss, 1993). In a review of community samples, Gorey and Leslie (1997) calculated the prevalence of childhood sexual abuse as 17% for females and 8% for males. Given the large number of victims, it is not surprising that sexual offenders admit to having many victims. For example, Abel, Becker, Mittelman, and Cunningham-Rathner (1987) investigated the number of victims reported by 127 rapists, 224 female-victim child molesters, and 153 male-victim child molesters. High victim rates were reported, with rapists having on average 7 victims, female-victim child molesters having 20 victims, and male-victim child molesters averaging 150 victims. In studies of community samples (e.g., university students) in which the respondent was assured there would be no negative consequences of reporting, 10% to 20% of men admit to sexually assaulting women or children (Hanson & Scott, 1995; Lisak & Roth, 1988).

# Definition of Sexual Assault

In Canada, the definition of sexual assault has undergone substantial change over the past 25 years. Prior to 1983, a number of different offences were lumped together under the label of *rape*. According to the Criminal Code of Canada at that time, "a male person commits rape when he has sexual intercourse with a female person who is not his wife . . . without her consent" (section 143). In response to criticism, and to make the definition more inclusive of diverse sexual relationships and more representative of the nature of sexual assault, rape was reclassified. Sexual assault became defined as any nonconsensual sexual act by either a male or female person to either a male or female person, regardless of the relationship between the people involved. Sexual assault, like physical assault, was divided into three levels based on severity issues. Each level comes with different maximum penalties: simple sexual assault (maximum sentence: 10 years), sexual assault with a weapon or causing bodily harm (maximum sentence: 14 years), and aggravated sexual assault (maximum sentence: life imprisonment).

# Consequences for Victims

Sexual aggression has serious psychological and physical consequences for victims. For example, child victims of sexual abuse develop a wide range of short- and long-term problems. In the year following disclosure of abuse, up to 70% of children experience significant psychological symptoms. Longer-term problems can include substance abuse, depression, eating disorders, and prostitution (Hanson, 1990).

Victims of rape also report high levels of stress and fear that often disrupts social, sexual, and occupational functioning, while also generating high levels of anxiety and depression (Hanson, 1990). Physically, Koss (1993) reports that up to 30% of rape victims contract sexually transmitted diseases, and pregnancy results in about 5% of cases. Psychologically, a wide range of negative consequences have been reported, as discussed below.

**Rape trauma syndrome:** A group of symptoms or behaviours that are frequent after-effects of having been raped

In 1974, Burgess and Holmstrom first proposed the term **rape trauma syndrome** to describe the psychological after-effects of rape. Burgess and Holmstrom interviewed 92 women who had been raped. The first interview took place within 30 minutes of the women's arriving at the hospital and the second interview took place one month later. The effects of rape identified by the researchers were divided into two phases: an acute crisis phase and a long-term reactions phase.

According to Burgess and Holmstrom (1974), the acute crisis phase lasts for a few days to several weeks and the symptoms are often quite severe. These symptoms can include very high levels of fear, anxiety, and depression. Victims of rape also often ask questions about why the rape happened to them, and they commonly engage in self-blame (Janoff-Bulman, 1979), which is perhaps unsurprising given the common myth that rape victims sometimes "ask for it" by the way they dress or act (see Box 14.1 for a discussion of other rape myths). Heightened levels of distrust and self-doubt are also common reactions.

The second phase is more protracted, lasting anywhere from a few months to several years. A quarter of women who have been raped do not significantly recover, even after several years (Resick, 1993). Long-term reactions include the development of phobias, such as a fear of being left alone or a fear of leaving the house. Another long-term reaction is the development of sexual problems and depression. Often, victims make dramatic changes in their lifestyles.

Box 14.1

# Sexual Assault: Discounting Rape Myths

Rape myths are stereotypic ideas that people have about rape (Burt, 1980). Rape myths appear to be accepted across many levels of society (Gylys & McNamara, 1996, Kershner, 1996; Szymanski, Devlin, Chrisler, & Vyse, 1993), though men appear to be more accepting of rape myths than women are (Bohner et al., 1998). The following list of some of the many myths associated with sexual assault or rape includes facts that challenge these false beliefs.

### Myth 1: Sexual assault is not a common problem.

One in every four women and one in every six men have experienced some type of sexual assault. You likely know someone who has been sexually assaulted.

### Myth 2: Sexual assault is most often committed by strangers.

Women face the greatest risk of sexual assault from men they know, not from strangers. About half of all rapes occur in dating relationships. In about 80% of cases, victims of sexual assault knew the attacker.

### Myth 3: Women who are sexually assaulted "ask for it" by the way they dress or act.

Victims of sexual assault range across the age span (from infants to elderly), and sexual assaults can occur in almost any situation. No woman "deserves" to be sexually assaulted, regardless of what she wears, where she goes, or how she acts. Blaming sexual assault on how a victim behaves would be like blaming a mugging on a person for carrying a wallet.

### Myth 4: Avoid being alone in dark, deserted places, such as parks or parking lots, and this will protect you from being sexually assaulted.

Most sexual assaults occur in a private home and many in the victim's home.

### Myth 5: Women derive pleasure from being a victim.

Sexual assault is associated with both short- and long-term serious problems. High rates of anxiety, fear, depression, and post-traumatic stress disorder are seen in survivors of sexual assault. Some women are physically injured during assaults.

### Myth 6: Women lie about sexual assault.

False accusations happen but are very rare. Sexual assault is a vastly under-reported crime, and most sexual assaults are not reported to the police.

---

The psychological consequences of rape victimization also include **post-traumatic stress disorder** (PTSD). The *DSM-IV* (American Psychiatric Association, 1994) defines PTSD as an anxiety disorder that can develop in response to exposure to an extremely traumatic event. PTSD symptoms include frequent, distressing, and intrusive memories of the event, avoidance of stimuli associated with the traumatic event, and persistent anxiety or increased arousal symptoms.

Rothbaum, Foa, Riggs, Murdock, and Walsh (1992) assessed the PTSD symptoms in 95 female rape victims over a nine-month follow-up period. One month after the rape, 65% of victims were diagnosed with PTSD and, at nine months, 47% were classified as having PTSD. Some victims continue to experience PTSD symptoms years after the rape. In one study, 16.5% of rape victims had PTSD 15 years after the rape (Kilpatrick, Saunders, Veronen, Best, & Von, 1987). Fortunately, effective treatment programs have been developed to help rape victims overcome the emotional suffering caused by this trauma (Foa & Rothbaum, 1998).

**Post-traumatic stress disorder:** Anxiety disorder that can develop in response to exposure to an extremely traumatic event. Symptoms include frequent, distressing, and intrusive memories of the event, avoiding stimuli associated with the traumatic event, and persistent anxiety or increased arousal symptoms

# Classification of Sexual Offenders

Sexual offenders are usually divided into categories based on the type of sexually deviant behaviour they exhibit, the relationship between victim and offender, and the age of the victim. **Voyeurs** obtain sexual gratification by observing unsuspecting people, usually strangers, who are naked, in the process of undressing, or engaging in sexual activity. **Exhibitionists** obtain sexual gratification by exposing their genitals to strangers. These two types of sexual offenders are sometimes referred to as hands-off or no-contact sexual offenders.

**Rapists** are offenders who sexually assault victims aged 16 years or older. The term *pedophilia* means "love of children." Thus, the term **pedophile** is often used to refer to an adult whose primary sexual orientation is toward children. Other researchers use the term **child molester** to refer to individuals who have actually sexually molested a child. Child molesters are also divided into two types: intra-familial and extra-familial. **Intra-familial child molesters** (also called **incest offenders**) are those who sexually abuse their own biological children or children for whom they assume a parental role, such as a stepfather or live-in boyfriend. **Extra-familial child molesters** sexually abuse children outside the family.

## Rapist Typologies

As highlighted in Box 14.2, it is important to understand that rapists are not part of a homogeneous group and do not all engage in sexual assault for the same reasons. Several different rapist typologies have been proposed. During the 1990s, an ambitious project was undertaken at the Massachusetts Treatment Center to develop and empirically validate a typology for rapists. The resulting classification system, *The Revised Rapist Typology, Version 3* (MTC:R3; Knight & Prentky, 1990), consists of five primary subtypes of rapists based on motivational differences:

1. The opportunistic type commits sexual assault that is generally impulsive, void of sexual fantasies, controlled primarily by situational or contextual factors, and void of gratuitous violence. These offenders often engage in other criminal behaviours. For example, a rapist who breaks into a home with the intention of stealing but who rapes the female occupant could be classified as opportunistic.

2. The pervasively angry type has a high level of anger that is directed toward both men and women. These offenders tend to be impulsive, use unnecessary force, cause serious victim injury, and be void of sexual fantasies.

3. The sexual type is distinguished from the other types in that these offenders' crimes are primarily motivated by sexual preoccupation or sexual fantasies.

4. The sadistic type is differentiated from the sexual type in that there must be a sadistic element to the offence.

5. The fifth type is labelled vindictive. In contrast to the pervasively angry type, the vindictive rapist's anger is focused solely on women. These offenders are not impulsive, nor are they preoccupied by sexual fantasies. The goal of this type of rapist is to demean and degrade the victim.

The opportunistic, sexual, and vindictive subtypes are further subdivided based on their level of social competence. The sadistic type is also further subdivided into overt or muted sadists based on the presence or absence of gratuitous violence (Knight & Prentky, 1990). Research using the MTC:R3 has found that these types differ on prevalence of

**Voyeur:** People who obtain sexual gratification by observing unsuspecting people, usually strangers, who are either naked, in the process of undressing, or engaging in sexual activity

**Exhibitionist:** Someone who obtains sexual gratification by exposing his or her genitals to strangers

**Rapist:** Person who sexually assaults victims over 16 years of age

**Pedophile:** Person whose primary sexual orientation is toward children

**Child molester:** Someone who has actually sexually molested a child

**Intra-familial child molesters:** People who sexually abuse their own biological children or children for whom they assume a parental role, such as a stepfather or live-in boyfriend. Also known as *incest offenders*

**Incest offenders:** People who sexually abuse their own biological children or children for whom they assume a parental role, such as a stepfather or live-in boyfriend. Also known as *intra-familial child molesters*

**Extra-familial child molester:** Someone who sexually abuses children not related to him or her

psychopathy (Barbaree, Seto, Serin, Amos, & Preston, 1994; Brown & Forth, 1997), rates of sexual recidivism (Knight, Prentky, & Cerce, 1994), and treatment needs (Knight, 1999). Knight and Guay (2006) describe a restructuring of the MTC:R3 in which the muted sadistic type of sexual offender has been dropped since the existence of this type of sexual offender has not been supported by research.

Another typology that uses motivations to classify rapists was proposed by Groth (1979). Groth suggested that rapists can be divided into three main types: anger rapists, power rapists, and sadistic rapists.

The features of the **anger rapist** include

- the use of more force than necessary to obtain compliance and engagement in a variety of sexual acts to degrade the victim
- high levels of anger directed solely toward women
- not being motivated primarily by sexual gratification

Most of these rapes are precipitated by conflict or perceived humiliation by some significant woman, such as the offender's wife, mother, or boss. Approximately 50% of rapists fit this type.

The features of the **power rapist** include

- the intention to assert dominance and control over the victim
- variation in the amount of force used, depending on the degree of submission shown by the victim
- not being motivated primarily by sexual gratification
- frequent rape fantasies

About 40% of rapists fit into this category.

The features of the **sadistic rapist** include

- obtaining sexual gratification by hurting the victim
- high levels of victim injury, including torture and sometimes death
- frequent violent sexual fantasies

Approximately 5% of rapists fit this type.

There is considerable overlap between the MTC:R3 and Groth typologies. Both typologies describe a sadistic rapist. The vindictive rapist is similar to the anger rapist and the pervasively angry rapist shares some of the features of the power rapist.

### Child Molester Typologies

With respect to child molesters, the most widely used typology is Groth's typology of the fixated and regressed child molester (Groth, Hobson, & Gary, 1982). Groth developed his typology based on research with incarcerated child molesters.

**Fixated child molesters** tend to have the following features:

- Their primary sexual orientation is toward children, and they have little or no sexual contact with adults.
- Their sexual interest in children begins in adolescence and is persistent.
- Male children are their primary targets.
- Precipitating stress is not evident.

**Anger rapist:** A rapist, as defined by Groth, who uses more force than necessary to obtain compliance from the victim and who engages in a variety of sexual acts to degrade the victim

**Power rapist:** A rapist, as defined by Groth, who seeks to establish dominance and control over the victim

**Sadistic rapist:** A rapist, as defined by Groth, who obtains sexual gratification by hurting the victim

**Fixated child molester:** A child molester, as defined by Groth, who has a long-standing, exclusive sexual preference for children

## Is Resisting a Sexual Attack a Good Idea?

One question often posed by women is, "If attacked, should I fight back or not?" Responses to this answer are common and websites abound where advice is given to women so that they can prevent themselves from being victimized. Unfortunately, the answer to the question is complicated, for reasons discussed below. For example, based on the typologies described above, the answer to the question will likely depend on the type of rapist under consideration.

Research with incarcerated rapists indicates that they search for vulnerable victims in certain areas and attack women who they believe cannot or will not resist the attack (Stevens, 1994). That being said, many women do resist their attackers, and research has shown that, compared with the use of nonresistance strategies, such as pleading with the offender, crying, or reasoning, victims who use forceful measures to resist their attacker (either verbal or physical) are more likely to avoid being raped (Ullman & Knight, 1993; Zoucha, Jensen, & Coyne, 1993).

However, the association between victim injury and resistance is inconclusive at present. For example, Zoucha-Jensen and Coyne (1993) found no association between victim resistance and injury. In contrast, Ullman and Knight (1993) found that if the offender had a weapon, which is probably more common with certain types of rapists, women who resisted the rape suffered more physical injury than those who did not resist.

In a review of universities' sexual assault prevention programs, Söchting, Fairbrother, and Koch (2004) conclude that the most promising prevention program is teaching self-defence skills. This strategy is also the one recommended by many agencies in Canada that provide advice to women on how to better protect themselves against rapists (e.g., Toronto Rape Crisis Centre).

- Their offences are planned.
- They are emotionally immature, have poor social skills, and are usually single.
- They usually have no history of alcohol or drug abuse.
- They often feel no remorse or distress over their behaviour.

**Regressed child molester:** A child molester, as defined by Groth, whose primary sexual orientation is toward adults, but whose sexual interests revert to children after a stressful event or because of feelings of inadequacy

**Regressed child molesters** usually have the following characteristics:

- Their primary sexual orientation is toward adults.
- Their sexual interest in children begins in adulthood and is episodic.
- Female children are their primary targets.
- Precipitating stress and feelings of inadequacy are usually present.
- Their offences are more impulsive.
- They are often married and are having marital problems.
- Many of their offences are related to alcohol use.
- They are more likely to report feeling remorse for their behaviour.

Groth also subdivided child molesters into two types based on the type of coercion they used. The *sex-pressure* child molester uses persuasion or entrapment to make the child feel obligated to participate in sexual acts. For example, this type of child molester may buy the child gifts or take the child on fun outings. The *sex-force* child molester threatens or uses physical force to overcome any resistance by the child. This latter group has been divided into the exploitative type who uses the threat of force to obtain compliance and the sadistic type who obtains gratification from hurting a child. The sadistic type of child molester is, fortunately, very rare.

## Adolescent Sexual Offenders

Prior to the 1980s, sexually aggressive behaviour by adolescents was not deemed serious and was discounted by some as normal experimentation. However, crime reports and victimization surveys indicate that about 20% of rapes and between 30% and 50% of child sexual abuse is committed by adolescents (Davis & Leitenberg, 1987). In Canada, 1630 adolescents were tried in youth court for sexual assault in 2004 (Public Safety and Emergency Preparedness Canada, 2006).

Like their adult counterparts, adolescent sexual offenders consistently report having been victims of sexual abuse themselves. The prevalence rate for sexual abuse committed against adolescent sexual offenders ranges from about 40% to 80% (Friedrich & Luecke, 1988; Ryan, Miyoshi, Metzner, Krugman, & Fryer, 1996). However, although early sexual victimization and later sexual offending are related, the majority of sexually abused children do not go on to become adolescent or adult sexual offenders and prior history of childhood sexual victimization is not related to sexual recidivism in samples of adult sexual offenders (Hanson & Bussière, 1998) or samples of adolescent sexual offenders (Worling & Curwen, 2000). Clearly, being the victim of sexual abuse is only one factor that affects later sexual offending. Rasmussen, Burton, and Christopherson (1992) suggest that in addition to sexual abuse, other factors such as social inadequacy, lack of intimacy, and impulsiveness also play a role.

In a national sample of adolescent sex offenders undergoing treatment, Ryan et al. (1996) investigated victim characteristics and found that adolescent sexual offenders tend to sexually abuse young female victims. Notably, the researchers found that 63% of the adolescent sexual offenders' victims were younger than age 9.

## Female Sexual Offenders

Research on female sexual offenders is limited. This relative lack of attention is probably because only 2% to 5% of incarcerated sex offenders are female. However, some researchers have suggested that sexual abuse of children by women is more prevalent than previously believed.

The rates of sexual abuse by females vary dramatically, depending on the definition used. For example, should a female be classified as a sexual abuser if she knew that her husband was sexually abusing their child and did nothing to stop the abuse? Does a mother sleeping with her child constitute sexual abuse in the absence of sexual touching? What if the child is a teenager who becomes sexually aroused by sleeping with his mother? Most people would agree that it is sexual abuse for a 20-year-old to have sexual contact with an 8-year-old boy, but not if the boy is 16. But what if the boy is 14? If the 14-year-old boy initiates the sexual act and views it positively, should this be classified as sexual abuse?

Retrospective surveys of university students have found that a large percentage of perpetrators are females. For example, Fritz, Stoll, and Wagner (1981) reported that of the 5% of college men who were molested as children, 60% were molested by females, most being older female adolescents. In a large survey of 2972 university students that used broad criteria for sexual abuse, Risin and Koss (1987) reported that 7.3% were abused. They found that almost half of the perpetrators were female (43%), and of these, almost half were female adolescent babysitters. Similar to other studies, about half of the male respondents reported that they participated in the sexual acts voluntarily and did not feel victimized. In contrast to these studies, fewer female perpetrators have been reported by other researchers (Finkelhor, 1984; Reinhart, 1987). For example, Finkelhor (1984) found that only 6% of university women and 16% of university men who reported childhood sexual abuse indicated that the offender was a woman.

Some researchers have speculated that the rate of sexual abuse by females is underestimated. Some reasons include the following (Banning, 1989; Groth, 1979):

- Women are able to mask their sexually abusive behaviours through caregiving activities and thus are more difficult to recognize.

- Women sexual offenders are more likely to target their own children, who are less likely to disclose the abuse.

- Boys are more frequent targets than girls, and boys are less likely to disclose abuse.

Research designed to determine the characteristics of female sexual offenders has generally been plagued with very small sample sizes. Whether the findings will generalize to larger samples of female sexual offenders remains to be investigated. Keeping this limitation in mind, Atkinson (1996) suggests there are four types of female sexual offenders:

1. *Teacher/lover*. These offenders initiate sexual abuse of a male adolescent that they relate to as a peer. The offender is often in a position of authority or power. It is unknown how common this type of female sex offender is because the victim rarely reports the abuse to authorities. This type has not likely experienced childhood sexual abuse, although substance-use problems are common. These offenders often are not aware that their behaviour is inappropriate. Teacher/lovers often describe themselves as being "in love" with the victim. Victims often report they participated voluntarily and do not feel victimized.

2. *Male-coerced*. These offenders are coerced or forced into sexual abuse by an abusive male. Often the victim is the female offender's own daughter. These offenders are unassertive, dependent on men, and are relatively passive partners in the abuse.

3. *Male-accompanied*. These offenders also engage in sexual abuse with a male partner. However, they are more willing participants than are the male-coerced type. Victims are both inside and outside the family.

4. *Predisposed*. This offender initiates the sexual abuse alone. She has often experienced severe and persistent childhood sexual abuse and has been a victim of intimate violence. This type often reports having deviant sexual fantasies, the offences are more violent and bizarre, and they typically involve younger children. Victims are often their own children, and they also frequently physically abuse and neglect the victim.

In a study of 40 female sexual offenders, Faller (1987) reported that most had significant psychological and social functioning problems. Most of the offenders (29 out of the 40, or 73%) were classified as engaging in poly-incestuous abuse, which involved two perpetrators and generally two or more victims. The male offender usually instigated the sexual abuse, while the women played a secondary role.

In another study, Vandiver and Teske (2006) compared 61 juvenile female sex offenders with 122 juvenile male sex offenders, using sex offender registration data and criminal records. The female offenders were found to be younger than their male counterparts at the time of their arrest. The female offenders also had younger victims and chose both male and female victims equally while male offenders chose female victims more often.

## Theories of Sexual Aggression

It is important that we understand why child molestation and rape occurs, and a number of theories have been proposed to account for these forms of antisocial behaviour. One of the most popular and widely cited theories is Finkelhor's precondition model (1984) of child molestation. Finkelhor's theory of child molesting proposes that four preconditions must be met for the sexual abuse to occur:

1. The offender must be motivated to sexually abuse. Motivation is due to three factors: (1) emotional congruence, which is the offender's desire for the child to satisfy an emotional need; (2) sexual attraction to the child; and (3) blockage of emotional outlets for the offender to meet his sexual and emotional needs.

2. The next precondition relates to the offender's lack of internal inhibitions. For example, alcohol and impulse-control problems can weaken the offender's ability to restrain the behaviours that lead to abuse.

3. The offender must overcome external inhibitors for the abuse to occur. For example, the offender might need to create opportunities to be alone with the child.

4. The offender must overcome the child's resistance. Offenders will reward the child with attention or bribes to encourage the child to cooperate. Alternatively, some offenders will use the threat of harm to intimidate the child.

Marshall and Barbaree (1990) have proposed an integrated model of sexual aggression that includes biological factors, childhood experiences, sociocultural influences, and situational events. They argue that males normally learn to inhibit sexually aggressive behaviour via a socialization process that promotes the development of strong, positive attachments. The authors suggest that sexual offenders fail to acquire effective inhibitory control because they experienced childhood abuse (emotional, physical, or sexual abuse) or because they were raised in extremely dysfunctional families (e.g., harsh and inconsistent punishment, lack of supervision, hostility). They also acknowledged the importance of the structure of society that reinforces the use of aggression and the acceptance of negative attitudes toward women.

More recently, Ward and Siegert (2002) have proposed a pathway model of child sexual abuse that integrates Finkelhor's precondition model, Marshall and Barbaree's integrated model, and Hall and Hirschman's quadripartite model (Hall & Hirschman's model is not discussed here; for more information on their model, see Hall & Hirschman, 1992). The pathway model proposes that there are different causal pathways, each having its own set of dysfunctional mechanisms, including inappropriate emotions, deviant sexual arousal, cognitive distortions, and intimacy deficits. For example, one pathway, labelled *emotional dysregulation*, focuses on individuals who have problems controlling their emotions and who use sex as an emotional coping strategy. For these offenders, the association between sex and negative emotions increases the probability they will sexually molest a child.

A number of theorists have also applied evolutionary theory to sexual offending (Quinsey & Lalumière, 1995; Thornhill & Palmer, 2000). Evolutionary theories focus on how behaviour is the product of our ancestral history and how features that are related to reproductive success become more frequent. Quinsey (2002) provides a clear example of a mating strategy that would not be very successful. "Consider a man in an ancestral environment who preferred trees as sexual partners. We can surmise that this man is very unlikely to be among our ancestors if his tree preference was caused by genes, because these genes would decrease in frequency over generations" (p. 2). Quinsey and others view rape as a consequence of a mating strategy that was selected for because it resulted in a reproductive advantage for males (Lalumière, Harris, Quinsey, & Rice, 2005). Evolutionary theories of sexual aggression have been criticized both for having a limited scope and lacking explanatory depth (see Ward & Siegert, 2002, for a detailed criticism).

## Assessment and Treatment of Sexual Offenders

Researchers assess sexual offenders to help to determine future risk for reoffending, to identify treatment needs, and to evaluate whether the treatment has had the desired effect. The focus of this section will be on the assessment of treatment needs and the effectiveness of treatment programs.

Most treatment programs are designed to address the following: denial, minimizations and cognitive distortions, victim empathy, modification of deviant sexual interest, enhanced social skills, substance-abuse problems, and the development of relapse-prevention plans (Marshall, 1999).

**Denial, Minimizations, and Cognitive Distortions** As is clearly illustrated in the Case Study box, sex offenders often deny (i.e., they claim they didn't do what they are accused of or that the victim consented) or fail to take full responsibility for their sexual offending (Barbaree, 1991). Often, blame is shifted to someone else, including the victim or some external factor. For example, sex offenders will often say, "The victim wanted to have sex with me" or "I was drunk and didn't know what I was doing." Assessments of denial and acceptance of responsibility are most often done through self-report questionnaires, such as the Clarke Sex History Questionnaire (Langevin, Handy, Paitich, & Russon, 1985), or by a comparison of police and victim reports with what the offenders admit in interviews. Most research has not found a link between denial and sexual recidivism. Recently, however, Nunes et al. (2007) have found that in low-risk sexual offenders and incest offenders denial is related to increased sexual recidivism.

**Cognitive distortions:** Deviant cognitions, values, or beliefs that are used to justify or minimize deviant behaviours

**Cognitive distortions** are deviant cognitions, values, and beliefs that the sexual offender uses to justify deviant behaviours. For example, a child molester might state, "Having sex with a child in a loving relationship is a good way to teach a child about sex," or an incest offender might claim, "It was better for her to have her first sexual experience with me since I love her, rather than with some teenager who would just want to use her." Both these child molesters are reporting cognitive distortions that are self-serving and inhibit them from taking full responsibility for their offences.

Some treatment programs refuse to accept deniers because a person who refuses to admit to having committed a sexual offence cannot fully participate in the treatment, since the focus is on sexual offending. In treatment, offenders are asked to disclose in detail what happened before, during, and after the sexual abuse. The therapist has access

## CASE STUDY  YOU BE THE FORENSIC PSYCHOLOGIST

You have just been hired as a psychologist at a forensic psychiatric hospital. Larry Wilkins is a child molester who has been at the hospital for some time. He has just been assigned to your caseload, and you are now responsible for developing a treatment plan for Larry and working with him to address his serious offending problem.

Most of Larry's victims have been very young girls. When you talk to Larry, he doesn't seem to see anything wrong with the fact that he regularly engages in sexual interactions with these girls. Usually, the encounters involve just touching the girls, he says, and not much else. In fact, he thinks he has been a good influence on many of the girls and says that they rarely resist his advances.

In fact, he says that occasionally the girls make the first move and they are usually very affectionate toward him. He assures you that he never actually hurts the girls. In fact, he says he does just the opposite. He frequently buys them presents, takes them on nice outings, and always says nice things to them.

Larry also says he is aware of research that indicates sexual relations between men and children may be healthy for kids because it provides them with a sense of belonging and shows them that they are loved. Before being caught by the police, he actually belonged to an organization that promotes sexual relations between adults and kids and he assures you that many men think the same way he does. He has heard them say so at meetings.

### Your Turn . . .

As the psychologist working with Larry, what are some of the issues you would need to deal with? How would you proceed with your assessment of Larry and his treatment?

to the police and victim reports in order to challenge an offender who is denying or minimizing aspects of the event. Other group members are encouraged to also challenge what the offender discloses.

**Empathy** Although some sex offenders have a general deficit in empathy (e.g., psychopathic sex offenders), most have a specific deficit in empathy toward their victims (Marshall, Barbaree, & Fernandez, 1995). Empathy is the ability to perceive others' perspectives and to recognize and respond in a compassionate way to the feelings of others. Cognitive distortions can cause empathy problems in sexual offenders. Because they minimize the amount of harm they have done, they do not think the victim has suffered, and therefore they do not empathize with the victim. Measures of empathy have focused on self-report scales, such as the Rape Empathy Scale (Deitz, Blackwell, Daley, & Bentley, 1982), and interviews.

Empathy training typically focuses on getting the offender to understand the impact of the abuse on the victim and the pain caused, and to develop feelings such as remorse. Offenders read survivor accounts of rape and child abuse and compare these accounts with how their victim likely felt. Videos of victims describing the emotional damage they have suffered and the long-term problems they experience are often used. Some therapy programs use role-playing, with the offender taking the part of the victim. Finally, although controversial, some programs may have sexual offenders meet with adult survivors of rape or child sexual abuse. Only those sexual offenders who are demonstrating empathy are permitted to take part in these meetings.

**Social Skills** Sexual offenders lack a variety of social skills, including self-confidence in interpersonal relations, capacity for intimacy, assertiveness, and dealing with anger (Bumby & Hansen, 1997; Marshall, Anderson, & Champagne, 1997; Marshall et al., 1995). Self-report questionnaires, interviews, and responses to scenarios have all been developed to assess social-skill deficits (see Marshall, 1999, for a review). Treatment programs for sexual offenders vary in terms of which social-skill deficits are targeted. Some programs focus on anger and communication skills (Pithers, Martin, & Cumming, 1989), whereas others target relationship skills, anger control, and self-esteem (Marshall et al., 1997).

**Substance Abuse** Substance abuse problems are common in nonsexual offenders and sexual offenders (Lightfoot & Barbaree, 1993). It is likely that some sexual offenders use alcohol to facilitate offending by reducing their inhibitions. Self-report measures are often used to assess problems with alcohol and drugs.

Sexual offenders with substance-abuse problems are often referred to substance-abuse programs. These programs are usually based on the relapse-prevention model developed by Marlatt and his colleagues, which is described in more detail below (Marlatt & Gordon, 1985).

**Deviant Sexual Interests** Deviant sexual interests motivate some sexual offenders. However, many other salient motives also play a role, including power and control over others, anger toward others, and desire for emotional intimacy. One of the most popular methods to assess deviant sexual interests is the use of **penile phallometry**. Penile phallometry involves placing a measurement device around the penis to measure changes in sexual arousal. To measure deviant sexual interests in child molesters, photos of naked male and female children and adults are presented, as well as rapists' recorded descriptions of nondeviant and deviant sexual behaviour. Phallometric assessments have been used to differentiate extra-familial child molesters from nonoffenders. However, most intra-familial child molesters do not differ in their phallometric responses from nonoffenders (see Marshall, 1999, for review). Research with rapists is mixed. Some studies have found differences between rapists and nonrapists (Quinsey, Chaplin, & Upfold, 1984), whereas others have not (Marshall & Fernandez, 2003).

Many different techniques have been developed to train offenders to eliminate deviant thoughts and interests and to increase the frequency of appropriate sexual thoughts and interests. For example, in **aversion therapy**, the offender is sometimes given an aversive substance to smell (e.g., ammonia) whenever he has a deviant sexual fantasy. The underlying goal is to reduce the attractiveness of these deviant fantasies by pairing them with a negative event.

Another approach is called *masturbatory satiation*. In this treatment, the offender is told to masturbate to ejaculation to a nondeviant fantasy. After ejaculation, he is told to switch to a deviant fantasy, thus pairing the inability to become aroused to this deviant fantasy. The effectiveness of these techniques to change deviant sexual interests has been questioned by several researchers (Quinsey & Earls, 1990).

Pharmacological interventions appear to be effective at suppressing deviant sexual desires (Bradford & Pawlak, 1993). Drugs used in the past acted to suppress all sexual

**Penile phallometry:** A measurement device placed around the penis to measure changes in sexual arousal

**Aversion therapy:** The pairing of an aversive stimuli with a deviant fantasy for the purpose of reducing the attractiveness of these deviant fantasies

interests and compliance was a serious problem (Langevin, 1979). The use of selective serotonin-reuptake inhibitors (SSRIs) has shown to be effective at controlling deviant sexual fantasies and not eliminating all sexual functioning (Federoff & Federoff, 1992).

**Relapse Prevention** Sexual offenders need to identify their offence cycle (e.g., emotional states and stress factors that put them at risk; grooming strategies) and develop ways to avoid these problems or to deal with them.

Programs with a **relapse prevention** (RP) component usually consist of two main parts. First, offenders are asked to list emotional and situational risk factors that lead to either fantasizing about sexual abuse or actually committing the abuse. For example, for a rapist, perhaps feelings of anger toward women would be a risk factor; for a child molester, perhaps feeling lonely and sitting on a bench, watching children in a playground would be a risk factor. Second, offenders need to develop plans to deal more appropriately with their problems (e.g., meeting their emotional needs in a prosocial way) and ways to avoid or cope with high-risk situations. Box 14.3 describes in more detail how the relapse prevention model has been applied with sexual offenders.

**Relapse prevention:** A method of treatment designed to prevent the occurrence of an undesired behaviour (e.g., sexual assault)

## Effectiveness of Treatment for Sexual Offenders

If we are going to treat sexual offenders, it is important to know whether the treatment actually works. There is a lack of consensus about whether sex offender treatment is effective.

### Box 14.3

## Relapse Prevention with Sexual Offenders

Relapse prevention (RP) is a self-control program designed to teach sexual offenders to recognize risky situations that could lead to reoffending and to learn coping and avoidance strategies to deal with those situations. The RP model was initially developed for the treatment of addictive behaviours, such as smoking, alcohol abuse, and overeating (Marlatt & Gordon, 1985). Sexual offenders are asked to develop a personalized sexual offence cycle that identifies their pre-offence thoughts, feelings, and behaviours. At each step of the cycle, the offender generates options or alternative behaviours that interrupt the offence cycle. RP is not considered a cure, but it helps the sexual offender manage the urge to offend sexually. RP is a way of teaching sexual offenders to think and look ahead to prevent committing another sexual offence. For RP to be successful, the sexual offender must be motivated to stop offending.

The following are some relevant terms (used in Figure 14.1) associated with relapse prevention:

- *Lapse:* Any occurrence of fantasizing about sexual offending or engaging in behaviours in the offence cycle

- *Relapse:* Occurrence of a sexual offence

- *High-risk situation:* Any situation that increases the likelihood of a lapse or a relapse

- *Apparently irrelevant decisions:* Conscious or unconscious decisions made by offenders that put them in high-risk situations

- *Coping response:* Development of avoidance strategies to sidestep high-risk situations and escape plans if the high-risk situation cannot be avoided

- *Abstinence violation effect:* Refers to how the offender reacts to a lapse. Both cognitive reactions (e.g., lack of willpower) and emotional states (e.g., feeling guilty) are considered. If the offender views the lapse as an irreversible failure, then this can promote a relapse. Alternatively, if the lapse is seen as a reasonable mistake in a learning process, the offender can become more confident in his ability to avoid or handle future lapses.

Figure 14.1 presents the sequences of events that may lead to a relapse in a child molester.

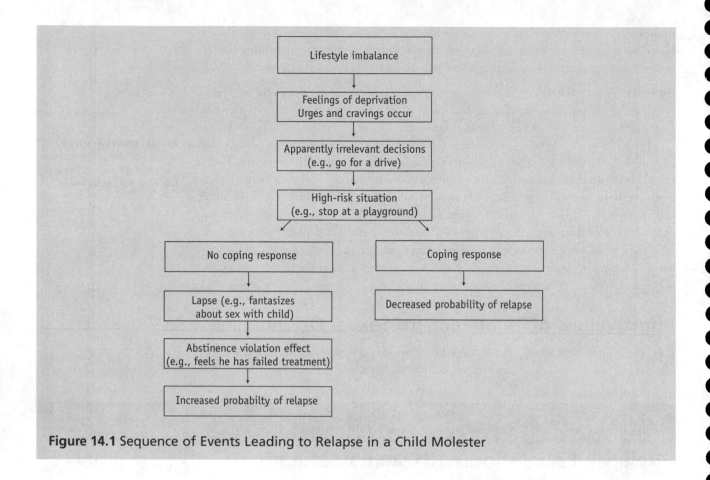

**Figure 14.1** Sequence of Events Leading to Relapse in a Child Molester

Some researchers argue that treatment does not work (Quinsey, Harris, Rice, & Lalumière, 1993), whereas others are more optimistic (Marshall, Eccles, & Barbaree, 1991).

What we do know is that incarceration does not appear to be a deterrent for sexual or other offenders. Nunes, Firestone, Wexler, Jensen, and Bradford (2007) reported that there was no association between incarceration and sexual recidivism rates in a sample of 627 Canadian adult male sexual offenders. Certainly, incarceration may be the only effective method for handling high-risk sexual offenders. However, for the majority of sexual offenders, community alternatives may be a more effective and less expensive option.

Numerous problems face researchers wanting to evaluate the effectiveness of sexual offender treatment programs. The main problem is that it is unethical to carry out the ideal controlled study. The optimal design would randomly assign motivated sexual offenders (i.e., offenders all wanting treatment) to either treatment or no treatment. Then, both treated and untreated sexual offenders would be released at the same time, followed up for several years, and rates of reoffending would be measured. Most treatment outcome studies have not used this design (see Marques, 1999, for one of the few studies to use random assignment). It is unlikely that many sexual offenders would agree to participate in this ideal study since untreated sexual offenders are held in custody longer than treated offenders.

Another challenge for researchers has been the relatively low base rates of sexual recidivism, even in untreated offenders (Barbaree, 1997). On average, only 15% of sex offenders are detected committing a new sexual offence after five years and 20% after ten years (Hanson & Bussière, 1998; Hanson & Thornton, 2000). Thus, for researchers to detect any differences between treatment groups, they need to wait many years. As a way of trying to deal with this problem, some researchers have begun to use unofficial data, such as child protection agency files, or self-reports to detect reoffending (see Marshall & Barbaree, 1988).

Despite the challenges described above, a number of meta-analyses of sexual offender treatment programs have been published (e.g., Alexander, 1999; Gallagher, Wilson, Hirschfield, Coggeshall, & MacKenzie, 1999; Hall, 1995; Hanson et al., 2002; Lösel & Schmucker, 2005). For example, in one well-cited meta-analytic study, Hanson et al. (2002) examined 42 separate studies with a total of 5078 treated sex offenders and 4376 untreated sex offenders. Averaged across the different types of treatment, the sexual recidivism rate was 12.3% for the treated sex offenders and 16.8% for the untreated sexual offenders. The following results were found:

- Sexual offenders who refused treatment or who dropped out of treatment had higher sexual recidivism rates compared with those who completed the treatment.
- Treatment effects were equally effective for adolescent and adult sex offenders.
- Both institutional treatment and community treatment were associated with reductions in sexual recidivism.

Based on their findings, Hanson et al. (2002) concluded that "The treatments that appeared most effective were recent programs providing some form of cognitive-behavioral treatment, and, for adolescent sex offenders, systemic treatment aimed at a range of current life problems (e.g., family, school, peers)" (p. 187). In contrast, the treatment approach that Lösel and Schmucker (2005) reported to be the most effective was surgical castration. However, this form of treatment has been considered by some to be unethical. In addition, the sexual offenders willing to participate in this form of intervention are a very select group and highly motivated.

However, as noted above, not all studies have reported positive effects of sexual offender treatment. For example, Hanson, Broom, and Stephenson (2004) compared the sexual recidivism rates of 403 treated sexual offenders with 321 untreated sexual offenders. In a 12-year follow-up, the rates of sexual reoffending were almost identical—21.1% for the treated group and 21.8% for the untreated group.

## HOMICIDAL OFFENDERS

The ultimate violent act is homicide. Although the homicide rate in Canada, the United States, and the United Kingdom has been dropping over the past decade, communities demonstrate substantial fear and fascination about homicide. As illustrated by the case of Colonel Russell Williams, which is discussed in the In the Media box, newspapers and television shows focus on homicides, particularly those that are bizarre or involve several victims. As a consequence, the public believes homicide is more common than it actually is (Stein, 2001).

## The Double Life of Col. Russell Williams

The media often reports on offenders who seem to live a double life—people who commit horrendous acts of violence, yet are known by all around them as decent people. For example, while committing some of the worst crimes in American history, serial killer Ted Bundy was also contributing positively to his community and was viewed with respect by those who interacted with him. Recently, Canadians have been exposed to one of these offenders, in the form of Colonel Russell Williams.

After many years of committing crimes, Williams was eventually charged with almost 100 counts of breaking and entering, forcible confinement, sexual assault, and the murders of 38-year-old Cpl. Marie-France Comeau and 27-year-old Jessica Elizabeth Lloyd. After confessing to the crimes and pleading guilty to 88 charges, Williams was formally sentenced on October 21, 2010. He received two terms of life sentence for his murders, with no chance of parole for 25 years, plus extra prison time for each of the lesser charges.

All this is hard to believe given that Williams was a highly respected military officer with previous responsibilities as a flight instructor at various Canadian Forces training schools and as a pilot for high-profile government officials. Perhaps even more unimaginable is that Williams was also the Commander of CFB Trenton during the time that many of his crimes were committed, including the two murders that he pled guilty to.

Sources: Appleby, 2010; CBC News, 2010; Hendry, 2010; Ontario Provincial Police, 2010; Rankin & Contenta, 2010.

## Nature and Extent of Homicidal Violence

Canadian criminal law recognizes four different types of homicide: first-degree murder, second-degree murder, manslaughter, and infanticide (the killing of a baby). Different penalties are imposed for each type, with a maximum of five years for infanticide and life in prison for the other three. In considering the different kinds of homicide, it should be noted that some killing is exempt from penalties, such as killing during war or killing in self-defence.

First-degree murder includes all murder that is planned and deliberate. It also includes the murder of a law enforcement officer or correctional staff member, or a murder occurring during the commission of another violent offence (e.g., sexual assault, kidnapping), regardless of whether the murder was unplanned or deliberate.

All murder that is not considered first-degree murder is classified as second-degree murder. Manslaughter is unintentional murder that occurs during the "heat of passion" or because of criminal negligence. For example, if a man returned home unexpectedly from a business trip and found his wife in bed with her lover, and during the ensuing altercation he grabbed a rifle and shot and killed the lover, the man would be charged with manslaughter.

As illustrated in Figure 14.2, Canada's homicide rate peaked in the 1970s and gradually declined from 1975 to 2003, when it reached a 30-year low. The homicide rate increased in 2004 and 2005, reaching its highest point in nearly a decade (Statistics Canada, 2006b), but appears to be generally decreasing again (Statistics Canada, 2009a), despite a slight 2% increase from 2007 to 2008 (Statistics Canada, 2009b). Although the

rate of homicide is substantially higher in the United States, the homicide rate in that country has also been steadily declining (Department of Justice, 2009).

Additional details relating to homicide in Canada include the following (Statistics Canada, 2009a):

■ Canada is seeing a steady rise in gang-related homicides. For example, 138 homicides in 2008 were classified as gang-related, compared with 118 in 2007. Most of these gang-related homicides occur in major metropolitan areas, such as Toronto and Calgary.

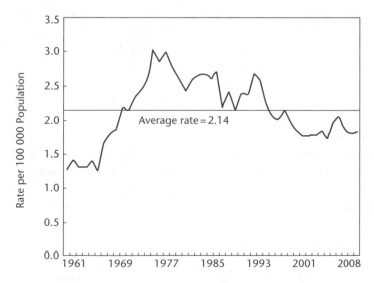

**Figure 14.2** Homicide Rate in Canada, 1961–2008
Source: Statistics Canada, 2009a.

- Gun-related homicides have also been on the rise since 2002. In 2008, 200 homicides resulted from the use of firearms, mostly handguns (61%).

- The rate of female homicide victims is decreasing. In fact, the rate of females killed because of homicide (0.87 per 100 000 population) is the lowest since 1961. The decrease in spousal homicides over this period (where the wife is typically the victim) probably accounts for some of this.

- Homicides are more likely to occur in the Western provinces than the Eastern provinces. In 2008, Manitoba reported the highest homicide rate out of any province (4.47 per 100 000 population) and New Brunswick reported the lowest rate (0.40 per 100 000 population). The territories report much higher homicide rates than any province. For example, the homicide rate in Nunavut in 2008 was 12.72 per 100 000 population.

## Bimodal Classification of Homicide

Over the past few decades, a number of researchers have attempted to characterize aggression in animals and humans in a bimodal manner. For example, Kingsbury, Lambert, and Hendrickse (1997) proposed a bimodal classification scheme for the study of aggression and homicide in humans, in which homicides are classified as **reactive** (or **affective**) **aggression** and **instrumental** (or **predatory**) **aggression**. Reactive homicide is defined as impulsive, unplanned, immediate, driven by negative emotions, and occurring in response to some perceived provocation. Instrumental homicide is defined as proactive rather than reactive, and is a premeditated, calculated behaviour, motivated by some goal. This goal could be to obtain money, power, control, or even the gratification of sadistic fantasies (Meloy, 1997).

Reactive homicide occurs more often among relatives, and instrumental homicide among strangers (Daly & Wilson, 1982). In a large-scale study, Miethe and Drass (1999) coded 34 329 single-victim, single-offender homicides in the United States between 1990 and 1994. Eighty percent were classified as reactive, and 20% as instrumental. In this study, the victim–offender relationship was divided into three categories: strangers, acquaintances, and family members/intimates. Most of the homicides involved acquaintances (55%), with most of these being classified as reactive (80%). Family members and intimate partners accounted for 28% of the cases, with nearly all these homicides being classified as reactive (93%). Finally, in 17% of the cases, the victim was a stranger, with 52% being classified as reactive.

In a Canadian study, Woodworth and Porter (2002) used a continuum of violence—from purely reactive, reactive-instrumental, instrumental-reactive, to purely instrumental—to code homicides committed by 125 adult male offenders. In this sample, 12.8% were coded as purely reactive, 23.2% as reactive-instrumental, 20% as instrumental-reactive, and 36% as purely instrumental (8% of the sample could not be coded).

## Filicide: When Parents Kill

The killing of a child by a parent is difficult to understand. The term **filicide** refers to the killing of children by their biological parents or step-parents and includes neonaticide (killing a baby within 24 hours of birth) and infanticide (killing a baby within the first

**Reactive aggression:** Violence that is impulsive, unplanned, immediate, driven by negative emotions, and occurring in response to some perceived provocation. Also known as *affective violence*

**Affective violence:** Violence that is impulsive, unplanned, immediate, driven by negative emotions, and occurring in response to some perceived provocation. Also known as *reactive aggression*

**Instrumental aggression:** Violence that is premeditated, calculated behaviour, motivated by some goal. Also known as *predatory aggression*

**Predatory aggression:** Violence that is premeditated, calculated behaviour, motivated by some goal. Also known as *instrumental aggression*

**Filicide:** The killing of children by their biological parents or step-parents; includes neonaticide (killing a baby within 24 hours of birth) and infanticide (killing a baby within the first year of life)

year of life). Attitudes toward parents killing their children vary across cultures and time. For example, in ancient Rome, a father had a right to kill his children (Finkel, Burke, & Chavez, 2000). A few cultures have also sanctioned the gender-based killing of children. Notably, in China and India, female children are more likely to be killed than male children because of the greater value these societies place on male children. In the past, certain Inuit and African societies killed infants that had birth defects or killed one infant when twins were born (Garber, 1947; Stewart, 2000).

Child murder in Canada is uncommon. In 2004, 55 children and youth under the age of 18 were killed (including 30 male victims and 25 female victims). This rate is the lowest since the first recording of these rates in 1974, but the murder of children and youth still accounted for about 9% of national homicides in 2004. The majority (62%) of these homicides were perpetrated by family members, and 85% of these homicides were committed by a parent. The father was the perpetrator in 59% of homicides against children by a family member between 1995 and 2004, while 32% involved the mother. Overall, it is more common for a father to be accused of killing his child than for a mother to be so accused, but the difference is not apparent for infants (Statistics Canada, 2006b).

Some studies have found that stepfathers are more likely to kill a child than are biological fathers (Daly & Wilson, 1996). However, a study in Sweden failed to replicate this finding (Temrin, Buchmayer, & Enquist, 2000). In Canada, the proportion of step-parents accused of killing a stepchild in their family has increased in the last decade, with 14% of all parents accused of killing their child between 1995 and 2004 being the child's stepfather or stepmother. Infants have consistently been at higher risk of homicide by a family member, and baby boys are at higher risk than baby girls, although as children age and their overall risk decreases, the gender difference also disappears (Statistics Canada, 2006b).

**Mothers Who Kill** Why would a mother kill her child? Several studies have classified maternal filicides (Cheung, 1986; Resnick, 1970). Stanton and Simpson (2002) reviewed these and other studies of child murder and concluded that there are three broad types of maternal filicides: (1) neonaticides, (2) those committed by battering mothers, and (3) those committed by mothers with mental illnesses.

The neonaticide group, those who kill their children within 24 hours of birth, are typically young, unmarried women with no prior history of mental illness, who are not suicidal, and who have concealed their pregnancies, fearing rejection or disapproval from their families. Battering mothers have killed their children impulsively in response to the behaviour of the child. These mothers have the highest rates of social and family stress, including marital stress and financial problems. The group with mental disorders tend to be older and married. They are likely to have killed older children, to have multiple victims, and to be diagnosed with a psychosis or depression. They are also the group that is most likely to attempt suicide after the murder. Some researchers have used the term *altruistic filicide* (Resnick, 1969) to describe mothers who kill out of love. In these cases, the murder is in response to the mother's delusional beliefs that the child's death will somehow protect the child.

**Infanticide and Mental Illness** Does childbirth trigger mental illness? The assumption underlying the offence of infanticide is that women who kill their infants are suffering from a mental illness related to childbirth. Three types of mental illness have been identified during the postpartum period (period after childbirth): postpartum blues, postpartum depression, and postpartum psychosis.

# From Devotion to Depression: Mothers Who Kill

Postpartum depression affects about 10% of new mothers; this rate increases to about 20% to 30% for those who have had previous depressive episodes. If a mother has experienced postpartum depression with one child, she has about a 50% chance of developing postpartum depression if she has another baby.

Postpartum psychosis is the rarest but also the most severe postpartum mental illness. It afflicts about 1 in 1000 mothers within six months of birth. Symptoms include hearing voices, seeing things, and feeling an irrational guilt that they have somehow done something wrong. Without treatment, women may try to harm themselves or their infants. The following two cases illustrate the potential lethality of postpartum depression and psychosis.

## Suzanne Killinger Johnson

Suzanne Killinger Johnson was a physician with a psychotherapy practice in Toronto. She had a history of depression while in medical school at the University of Western Ontario. She had a successful marriage, flourishing career, and supportive family and friends. In February 2000, she gave birth to a son named Cuyler. Sometime after the birth, Killinger Johnson started to become more and more obsessive about caring for Cuyler. By the spring, she started to see a therapist and was taking medication for depression. In July, she stopped taking her antidepressants because she was worried about the effects of the medicine in her breast milk. Subsequently, she avoided her friends and missed her therapy appointments. Her husband, family, and friends attempted to help her. However, at 6:30 a.m. on August 11, while her father had left her alone for a few minutes, she took her son, drove to a nearby subway station, and with Cuyler in her arms, jumped in front of a train. Cuyler died instantly and his mother died eight days later on August 19, 2000.

## Andrea Yates

Andrea Yates had been diagnosed with postpartum depression after the birth of her fourth son, Paul. She had attempted suicide twice, was hospitalized, and was given antidepressant medication. After the birth of her daughter, Mary, Yates experienced severe postpartum depression again, was hospitalized twice, and was given antidepressants. According to her defence lawyers and mental health experts, Andrea Yates was not only experiencing postpartum depression but also postpartum psychosis.

On June 20, 2001, after her husband had left to go to work and prior to her mother arriving to help her, Andrea Yates drowned each of her five children—Noah (age 7), John (age 5), Luke (age 3), Paul (age 2), and Mary (6 months)—in a bathtub at their family home. According to the defence lawyers, Yates was delusional when she murdered her children, believing that she had to murder them to save them from Satan. The prosecution agreed that Andrea Yates had a mental illness but that she knew what she was doing and knew that killing them was wrong.

In March 2002, it took a jury four hours to reject Andrea Yates's insanity plea and find her guilty of capital murder. A week later, the same jury took 40 minutes to both reject the death penalty and sentence Yate's to life in prison. In 2005, the Texas Court of Appeals reversed Yates's convictions because of false testimony given by a psychiatrist witness for the prosecution. A new trial ended on July 26, 2006, when Yates was found not guilty by reason of insanity and committed to a state mental hospital.

Treatment of postpartum depression and postpartum psychosis is possible. However, in both of these cases, the women had sought medical intervention, but the treatment had limited success. Continuing research holds the promise of improved treatment and, ultimately, the prevention of these devastating illnesses.

The most common type of mental illness is postpartum blues (experienced by up to 85% of women), which includes crying, irritability, and anxiety, beginning within a few days of childbirth and lasting from a few hours to days but rarely continuing past day 12 (Affonso & Domino, 1984; O'Hara, 1995). Given the onset and short time span of postpartum blues, it has not been considered a causal factor in either neonaticide or filicide.

Postpartum depression (experienced by 7% to 19% of women) occurs within the first few weeks or months after birth and usually lasts for several months (O'Hara, 1995). The symptoms are identical to clinical depression and include depressed mood, loss of appetite, concentration and sleep problems, and suicidal thoughts. Recent studies have found that postpartum depression is not a mental illness that occurs as a consequence of childbirth (O'Hara, 1995).

The most severe and rare type of mental illness that has been associated with childbirth is postpartum psychosis (occurring in 1 or 2 of every 1000 births). Postpartum psychosis usually involves delusions, hallucinations, and suicidal or homicidal thoughts within the first three months after childbirth (Millis & Kornblith, 1992). Research does support a link between childbirth and postpartum psychosis (Kendell, Chalmers, & Platz, 1987). Box 14.4 describes the case of Andrea Yates, the Houston mother who killed her five children, and the case of Suzanne Killinger Johnson, who jumped in front of a Toronto subway train holding her infant son. These cases illustrate the potential lethality of postpartum psychosis.

**Fathers Who Kill** Fathers rarely commit neonaticide. In contrast to maternal filicides, paternal filicides are often described as fatal child abuse (Brewster, Nelson, & Hymel, 1998). Fathers have lower rates of psychotic disorder but higher rates of alcohol abuse and previous criminality. Within the past decade, a history of family violence was twice as likely to be present in cases in which a father has killed a child (36%) than in cases in which a mother is accused (18%) (Statistics Canada, 2006b).

**Familicide** occurs when a spouse and children are killed. It is almost always committed by a man, and is often accompanied by a history of spousal and child abuse prior to the offence. Wilson, Daly, and Daniele (1995) examined 109 Canadian and British cases and found that in about half of the cases the killer committed suicide. They also found that those who killed their spouse and their own children (i.e., genetic offspring) had a greater likelihood of committing suicide than those who killed their spouse and their stepchildren. Wilson et al. (1995) also described two types of familicide murderers: the despondent nonhostile killer and the hostile accusatory killer. The despondent nonhostile killer is depressed and worried about an impending disaster for himself or his family. He kills his family and then commits suicide. Past acts of violence toward children and spouse are not characteristic of this type of killer. The hostile accusatory killer, however, expresses hostility toward his wife, often related to alleged infidelities or her intentions to terminate the relationship. A past history of violent acts is common for this type of killer.

**Familicide:** The killing of a spouse and children

## Youth Who Kill

Eighty-three youths aged 12 to 17 were accused of homicide in Canada in 2006 (Statistics Canada, 2008). The juvenile homicide rate in Canada has remained relatively stable over the past decade. Researchers have searched for distinguishing characteristics among youth who commit murder. Although the number of homicides by youth is approximately one-tenth that of the total number of homicides in Canada, homicide by youth holds a particular fascination in the mind of the public. What motivates youth to kill? What factors underlie homicide by youth?

Corder, Ball, Haizlip, Rollins, and Beaumont (1976) compared three groups of youths: ten youths charged with killing parents, ten youths charged with killing relatives or acquaintances, and ten youths charged with killing strangers. Youth charged with parricide (killing parents) were more likely to have been physically abused, to have witnessed spousal abuse, and to report amnesia for the murders, compared with the other youth who committed murder. More recently, Darby, Allan, Kashani, Hartke, and Reid (1998) examined the association between family abuse and suicide attempts in a sample of 112 adolescents convicted of homicide. Abused youth were younger, more often Caucasian, and more likely to have attempted suicide prior to the homicide than nonabused youth.

Cornell, Benedek, and Benedek (1987) developed a typology of juvenile homicide offenders based on the circumstances of the offence. The types of homicide were labelled *psychotic* (youth who had symptoms of severe mental illness at the time of the murder), *conflict* (youth who were engaged in an argument or conflict with the victim when the killing occurred), and *crime* (youth who killed during the commission of another crime, such as robbery or sexual assault). When the classification system was applied to 72 juveniles charged with murder, 7% were assigned to the psychotic subgroup, 42% to the conflict subgroup, and 51% to the crime subgroup. Differences across these homicide subgroups in family background, criminal history, and psychopathology have been reported (Greco & Cornell, 1992).

## Spousal Killers

**Femicide:** The killing of women

During the period from 1974 to 1983 in Canada, 812 wives and 248 husbands were killed by their spouses (Daly & Wilson, 1988). As this statistic makes clear, husbands are much more likely to kill their wives than wives are to kill their husbands. **Femicide** is the general term applied to the killing of women, *uxoricide* is the more specific term denoting the killing of a wife by her husband, and *mariticide* is the term denoting the killing of a husband by his wife.

In 2008, 62 spousal homicides occurred in Canada, with women's victimization rates three times higher than men's (Statistics Canada, 2009). A married woman in Canada is about nine times more likely to be killed by her partner than by a stranger (Wilson & Daly, 1993). In a study of 896 femicides in Ontario between 1974 and 1990, Crawford and Gartner (1992) found that 551 (62%) of the femicides were uxoricides. A consistent finding concerning uxoricide is the high incidence of perpetrator suicide following the murder (Crawford & Gartner, 1992). Offenders rarely commit suicide after killing acquaintances or strangers (Stack, 1997).

Why do men kill their spouses? Crawford and Gartner (1992) found that the most common motive for uxoricide (in 43% of cases) was the perpetrators' anger over either estrangement from their partners or sexual jealously about perceived infidelity. Comparing police records in Canada, Australia, and the United States, Wilson and Daly (1993) found that recent or imminent departure by the eventual victim was associated only with a husband killing his wife and not with a wife killing her husband. A study of risk factors for femicide in abusive relationships by Campbell, Webster, and Koziol-McLain (2003) found the following factors increased the risk for homicide: offender access to a gun, previous threats with a weapon, estrangement, and the victim having left for another partner.

## Serial Murderers: The Ultimate Predator

**Serial murder:** The killing of a minimum of three people over time. The time interval between the murders varies and has been called a *cooling-off period*. Subsequent murders occur at different times, have no apparent connection to the initial murder, and are usually committed in different locations

The term **serial murder** was first coined in the early 1980s, and there is a considerable amount of disagreement regarding its definition. Researchers trying to establish a definition debate the answers to the following questions: How many victims are required? Should the motive for killing matter? Should the relationship between the murderer and the victim be considered? Most definitions of serial murder include the criterion that a minimum of three people are killed over time. The time interval between the murders varies and has been called a *cooling-off period*. Subsequent murders occur at different times, have no apparent connection to the initial murder, and are usually committed in different locations.

**Characteristics of Serial Murderers** Although they belong to a heterogeneous group, many serial killers appear to have certain characteristics in common (Hickey, 2006). These include the following:

- Most serial murderers are male. For example, in a review of 399 serial murderers in the United States between 1825 and 1995, Hickey (2006) reported that 83% were male and 17% were female.

- Most serial murderers operate on their own. However, there are team murders that are committed by two or more offenders working together. Between 1875 and 1995, there were 47 serial killer teams in the United States (Hickey, 2006). For example, the Hillside Stranglers were Kenneth Bianchi and his cousin Angelo Buono. In Canada, the most notorious team killers are Paul Bernardo and Karla Homolka, who together killed three young women, including Homolka's younger sister.

- Most serial murderers in the United States are Caucasian. Hickey (2006), in his review, reported that 73% of serial murderers were Caucasian and 22% African-American.

- Victims of serial murderers are usually young females who are not related to the murderer. However, the age and sex of the victim can vary. For example, Dr. Harold Shipman, England's most prolific known serial murderer, is suspected of having killed 215 people, mostly elderly women who were his patients. Other serial killers, such as the Chicago-based John Wayne Gacy, kill young men.

**Female Serial Murderers** Like female offenders in general, female serial murderers have not been the focus of much research. One reason for this is because serial killing by females is extremely rare. Most female serial killers are either "black widows," those who kill husbands or family members for financial gain, or "angels of death," nurses who kill their patients. For example, Dorothea Puente was charged with nine murders of her tenants and, in 1993, convicted of three of the murders. The murders were supposedly done in order for Puente to collect the tenants' social security cheques. Puente claims that the seven people whose bodies were found in her yard had all died of natural causes and that she is innocent.

Aileen Wuornos is one of the few female serial murderers who did not kill family members or kill for financial gain (although she stole cash, belongings, and some of the victims' cars). In 1989 and 1990, she killed seven men she had agreed to have sex with. Initially, Wuornos claimed that she had killed each of them in self-defence because they had become violent with her. Wuornos was executed in Florida in 2002.

Table 14.1 summarizes the differences between male and female serial murders. As compared with male serial murderers, female serial murders are more likely to have no prior criminal record, have an accomplice, use poison, kill for money, and kill a family member or someone they know (Hickey, 2006).

**Table 14.1** Differences between Male and Female Serial Murderers

| Point of Comparison | Male Serial Murderers | Female Serial Murderers |
|---|---|---|
| Prior criminal history | Males tend to have a prior criminal history. | Females tend not to have a prior criminal history. |
| Accomplice | Only about 25% of males have an accomplice. | About 50% of females have an accomplice. |
| Murder method[a] | Males are more likely to use a firearm or to strangle or stab their victims. | Females are much more likely to use poison. |
| Murder motive[b] | Males are more likely to kill for sexual gratification or control. | Females are more likely to kill for money. |
| Victim type[c] | Males are more likely to kill strangers. | Females are much more likely to kill family members. |
| Geographic type | Males tend to be more geographically mobile. | Females are more likely to be place specific (i.e., to carry out all killings in one location). |

[a]Hickey (2006) reported that 35% of female serial murderers killed by using poison, as compared with only 5% of male serial murderers.

[b]Hickey (2006) reported that in 74% of female serial murders, money played a role, as compared with only 26% of male serial murders. In contrast, he reported that sexual gratification played a role in 55% of male serial murders, as compared with only 10% of female serial murders.

[c]Hickey (2006) found that 50% of female serial murderers had killed at least one family member, as compared with 1% of males.

Source: Hickey, 2006.

**Visionary serial murderer:** A murderer who kills in response to voices or visions telling him or her to kill

**Mission-oriented serial murderer:** A murderer who targets individuals from a group that he or she considers to be "undesirable"

**Hedonistic serial murderer:** A murderer who is motivated by self-gratification. This type of killer is divided into three subtypes: lust, thrill, and comfort

**Power/control serial murderer:** A murderer who is motivated not by sexual gratification but by wanting to have absolute dominance over the victim

**Lust serial murderer:** A murderer who is motivated by sexual gratification

**Thrill serial murderer:** A murderer who is motivated by the excitement associated with the act of killing

**Comfort serial murderer:** A murderer who is motivated by material or financial gain

**Typologies of Serial Murderers** A number of classification systems have been developed to classify serial murderers, although most have yet to be subjected to empirical verification. One typology that focuses on crime scenes and offenders is the organized-disorganized model proposed by the FBI in the 1980s. This typology was described in Chapter 3.

In 1998, Holmes and Holmes proposed another typology. They used 110 case files of serial murderers to develop a classification system based on victim characteristics and on the method and location of the murder. They proposed four major types of serial murders: (1) **visionary**, (2) **mission-oriented**, (3) **hedonistic**, and (4) **power/control oriented**.

The visionary serial murderer kills in response to voices or visions telling him or her to kill. This type of serial murderer would most likely be diagnosed as delusional or psychotic. The mission-oriented serial murderer believes there is a group of undesirable people who should be eliminated, such as homeless people, sex-trade workers, or a specific minority group. Hedonistic serial murderers are motivated by self-gratification. These killers have been divided into three subtypes based on the motivation for killing: **lust murderer, thrill murderer,** or **comfort murderer**. The lust serial murderer is motivated by sexual gratification and becomes stimulated and excited by the process of killing. The thrill murderer derives excitement from seeing his or her victims experience terror or pain. The comfort serial murderer is motivated by material or financial gain. The power/control serial murderer is not motivated by sexual gratification but by wanting to have absolute dominance over the victim.

The above typology is compelling but has been criticized for the following reasons. First, there is considerable overlap among categories. For example, lust, thrill, and power/control murders are all characterized by a controlled crime scene, a focus on process (i.e., an enjoyment of the act of killing), and a selection of specific victims. Second, the typology's developers have failed to test it empirically. Recently, Canter and Wentink (2004) tested whether the characteristics within each type would tend to co-occur in 100 U.S. serial murderers. The researchers failed to find support for the proposed typologies. One reason for the lack of support for this typology is that murderers' motives may change over the course of their killings.

Keppel and Walter (1999) applied the motivational rapist typology proposed by Groth, Burgess, and Holmstrom (1977) to classify sexual murder. They proposed two types of sexual murders that reflect the theme of power (power-assertive and power-reassurance) and two types reflecting the theme of anger (anger-retaliation and anger-excitation). The authors describe how these types differ with regard to crime scene characteristics. For example, the power-reassurance type commits a planned rape that escalates to an unplanned overkill of the victim. In contrast, the anger-excitation type commits a planned rape and murder of the victim. Using prison files from the Michigan Department of Corrections, Keppel and Walter (1999) classified 2475 sexual homicide offenders as follows: 38% power-assertive, 34% anger-retaliation, 21% power-reassurance, and 7% anger-excitation.

How well this typology will apply to serial sexual murders and whether it will help with the identification of serial sexual homicides remains to be tested.

**How Many Serial Murderers Are There?** Based on statistics from the United States, it appears that there has been an increase in the number of serial murderers over time. However, it is difficult to know the true prevalence rate of serial murderers. For example, the apparent increase in the number of serial murderers may be due to better police investigation and communication among law enforcement agencies, which has led to better detection. What is clear from official statistics is that the percentage of murder victims killed by strangers or unknown persons has increased dramatically in the United States. For example, in 1965, only 5% of murders were committed by strangers or unknown persons, whereas in 1999, 51% of murders were committed by strangers or unknown persons. Egger (1999) has suggested that some of this increase is due to an increase in the number of drug-related murders, but that at least part of it is the result of an increase in serial murder.

The rates of male serial killers appear to have regional differences. For example, DeFronzo, Ditta, Hannon, and Pruchrow (2007) measured the rate of serial killers per 10 million in various U.S. locations and found 18.6 in California, 10.3 in Florida, 7.0 in Texas, 6.3 in New York, and 3.0 in Pennsylvania. The researchers propose that sociocultural factors may help to explain these differential rates. For example, cultures that are supportive of violence appear to have higher rates of serial homicide.

# Mass Murderers

**Mass murder** is defined as the killing of three or more victims at a single location during one event with no cooling-off period. School shootings such as those at Columbine and,

**Mass murder:** The killing of three or more victims at a single location during one event with no cooling-off period

Memorial for victims of violent crime

more recently, Virginia Tech are examples of mass murder. In the classic mass murder, an individual goes to a public place and kills strangers at that location. In contrast, in a family mass murder, three or more family members are killed, usually by another family member. Mass murderers are much more likely to commit suicide or get killed by police during the killing rampage than are serial murderers. Mass murders can also occur when the murderer intends to kill a specific person but, in doing so, kills others, as illustrated by the case of Joseph-Albert Guay. Guay placed a bomb on a Canadian Pacific Airlines flight between Quebec City and Baie-Comeau on September 9, 1949, to kill his wife, Rita. In the ensuing explosion over Sault-au-Cochon, not only was his wife killed, but 22 others were killed also.

Mass murderers are not all motivated by the same reasons, but the outcome is always the same: the deaths of many innocent people. Mass murderers are often depressed, angry, frustrated individuals who believe they have not succeeded in life. They are often described as socially isolated and lacking in interpersonal skills. In some cases, the murder is triggered by what they perceive as a serious loss. In most cases, these offenders select targets that represent who they hate or blame for their problems. They often feel rejected by others and come to regard suicide and homicide as justified acts of revenge. Most mass murderers plan their crimes and obtain semi-automatic guns in order to maximize the number of deaths. In other words, they do not "just snap" but in fact display warning signs that, if recognized by others, may help to prevent tragedies. In addition, mass murderers often plan to commit suicide or get killed by law enforcement officers.

To date, the most deadly mass murder in the United States occurred on April 16, 2007, when Seung-Hui Cho killed 32 people (27 students and 5 faculty members) at the Virginia Tech campus before committing suicide. Cho, a 23-year-old student majoring in English at Virginia Tech, was described as being a loner. Professors had encouraged him to seek counselling because of the violent themes in his writing, and he had been investigated for stalking two female students. In the suicide note he left, Cho expressed his hatred of wealthy students. In the United States, the Virginia Tech shooting has raised a fierce debate over the importance of civil liberty on the one hand and public safety on the other in domains including media coverage (i.e., whether to show the videos made by Cho), mental health treatment, and firearms regulations. Canada's deadliest mass murder is described in Box 14.5.

## Theories of Homicidal Aggression

**Trauma-control model of serial murder:** The model suggesting that a multitude of factors are involved in predicting who may be predisposed to commit serial murder

While numerous theories have been proposed to explain the emergence of specific forms of aggression (e.g., Hickey's, 2006, **trauma-control model** to explain why serial murderers kill), most of our thinking about homicidal aggression is guided by general theories of aggression. Although many theories of aggression exist (see Anderson & Bushman, 2002), we will focus on just three theories that have been particularly influential in the field of forensic psychology: social learning theory, evolutionary theory, and the general aggression model.

# Canada's Deadliest Mass Murder

On December 6, 1989, 25-year-old Marc Lépine walked into a classroom at the Montreal engineering school École Polytechnique, fired a shot into the ceiling and said, "Separate. The girls on the left and the guys on the right." He told the men to leave. He then stated, "I am fighting feminism." One of the nine women left behind responded, "I am not a feminist." All nine of the women were shot (six died and three were injured). Lépine then moved to other parts of the school, where he shot and killed others. In total, 14 women were killed, and 10 women and 4 men were injured that day at École Polytechnique. The killing ended when Lépine committed suicide.

What prompted Lépine to commit this massacre, and why did he target women? According to media reports, Lépine's father had little respect for women and was verbally and physically abusive toward both his wife and their two children (Lépine and his sister). Lépine's parents separated when he was 7 years old and divorced when he was 12. He graduated from high school and attended CEGEP but dropped out during his last term. In 1986, he applied to study engineering at École Polytechnique and was offered admission conditional on completing two courses at CEGEP. Lépine has been described as quiet and shy, as showing little emotion, and as having problems with accepting authority. He had no history of alcohol or drug problems or prior criminal behaviour. Lépine was apparently uncomfortable around women and expressed his dislike of career women and women who held jobs in traditionally male occupations, such as the police force and the military. He applied to the military but was not accepted.

Lépine applied for a firearm's acquisition in September and received his permit in October 1989. On November 21, 1989, he purchased a Ruger Mini-14 semi-automatic rifle, which he used in the shootings. A suicide note found on Lépine's body stated, "The feminists have always enraged me. They want to keep the advantages of women (e.g., cheaper insurance, extended maternity leave preceded by a preventative leave, etc.) while seizing for themselves those of men."

It is unlikely that we will ever be able to predict a tragedy such as the one that occurred on December 6, 1989. Lépine was similar to other mass murderers: socially isolated, equipped with poor interpersonal skills, frustrated and angry, and targeting a group that he blamed for the lack of success in his personal life.

A memorial plaque outside École Polytechnique lists the names of the 14 women whose lives were lost:

Geneviève Bergeron (21 years)—civil engineering student
Hélène Colgan (23 years)—mechanical engineering student
Nathalie Croteau (23 years)—mechanical engineering student
Barbara Daigneault (22 years)—mechanical engineering student
Anne-Marie Edward (21 years)—chemical engineering student
Maud Haviernick (29 years)—material engineering student
Maryse Laganière (25 years)—budget clerk
Maryse Leclair (23 years)—materials engineering student
Anne-Marie Lemay (22 years)—mechanical engineering student
Sonia Pelletier (28 years)—mechanical engineering student
Michèle Richard (21 years)—materials engineering student
Annie St-Arneault (23 years)—mechanical engineering student
Annie Turcotte (20 years)—material engineering student
Barbara Klucznik-Widajewicz (31 years)—nursing student

Each year on December 6, Canadians mark the day with a National Day of Remembrance and Action on Violence Against Women.

According to social learning theorists (e.g., Akers, 1973), aggressive behaviour is learned the same way non-aggressive behaviour is, through a process of reinforcement. Specifically, the likelihood of engaging in aggressive behaviour is thought to increase as a function of how rewarding aggressive behaviour has been in an individual's past. Rewards for aggressive behaviour are often experienced directly, such as when an individual beats up a schoolmate and experiences an increase in status among his friends (as "tough" or "cool"). However, social learning theorists also place a great deal of emphasis on rewards that are not experienced directly, but vicariously, as a result of observing others. Social learning theory highlights several major sources that can influence behaviour in this

Box 14.6

# Canadian Researcher Profile: Dr. Martin Daly

Dr. Martin Daly may be viewed by some as a strange person to profile in a book about forensic psychology. After all, to earn his Ph.D. at the University of Toronto, he studied the effect of rearing environment on the behaviour and development of golden hamsters. Even his post-doctoral work focused on animal behaviour, and this focus is true of much of his academic work since that time. Yet, although not a forensic psychologist by training, Dr. Daly's name is well-known to forensic psychologists. Indeed, one could argue that his name is almost synonymous with the study of homicide in Canada. He, together with his wife and long-time collaborator, Margo Wilson, has contributed substantially to our understanding of homicide, particularly from an evolutionary perspective.

Dr. Daly's interest in homicide sprang from an interest in the evolution of social behaviour more generally (i.e., not just in humans). In the 1970s, he and Dr. Wilson, who unfortunately passed away in 2009, were struck with the idea that studying homicides might reveal something about human interpersonal conflict and permit tests of evolution-minded hypotheses about the different sorts of conflicts that characterize different relationships (e.g., between same-sex rivals, romantic partners, and parents and

offspring). Dr. Daly says that once he and his wife got started with this line of research, they just couldn't stop . . . and here we are over 30 years later.

Much of the research conducted by Drs. Daly and Wilson has focused on explaining variability in homicide rates between places and over time. For the most part, they have used evolutionary theory to understand the patterns that emerge. For example, some of their research focuses on the notion that inequitable access to resources inspires escalated competition. In one of Daly's favourite studies, published in the Canadian Journal of Criminology, Drs. Daly and Wilson demonstrated that a single variable—local levels of income inequality—is sufficient to explain the Canada–United States difference in homicide rates.

Dr. Daly's preferred approach to research is to conduct epidemiological analyses, which involves combining multiple sources of information in an attempt understand a specific phenomenon. In an attempt to understand variability in homicide rates, the data he draws on could come from the census, governmental or police homicide archives, income surveys, and so on. He also emphasizes the importance of interdisciplinary research and training, and the importance of combining knowledge and approaches from various disciplines, such as psychology, sociology, anthropology, and biology, rather than being restricted by disciplinary loyalties.

As a professor in the Department of Psychology, Neuroscience, and Behaviour at McMaster University in Hamilton, Ontario, Dr. Daly teaches a number of courses, including Evolution and Human Behaviour. Set to retire in the next two years, Dr. Daly, who is an avid bird watcher, will be able to dedicate more time to his early passion of studying nonhuman animal behaviour. Fortunately, for all of us, he also plans to continue his studies of homicide, which will include new research examining the homicide problem in Brazil, a country with almost unrivalled economic inequality.

indirect fashion, including the family circle, the peer group, and the mass media. Aggressive behaviour can be common in each of these settings and research has confirmed that observing aggressive behaviour being reinforced in each context can increase the likelihood that the observer will model that aggressive behaviour (e.g., Anderson et al., 2003; Loeber & Stouthamer-Loeber, 1986; Pratt & Cullen, 2000).

As mentioned above, evolutionary theories of crimes, including violent crimes such as homicide, are also popular. The focus in evolutionary theories is on how crime can be thought of as adaptive behaviour, developed as a means for people to survive (and pass on genes) in their ancestral environment (Daly & Wilson, 1988). In an ancestral environment characterized by recurring challenges or conflicts, such as finding mates, securing shelter, and/or establishing status, certain physiological, psychological, and behavioural characteristics became associated with reproductive success. From an evolutionary perspective, homicide emerged as one approach to best competitors who were competing for limited resources, and modern humans have simply inherited this strategy from their successful ancestors (Buss & Shackelford, 1997). Notwithstanding criticisms made against this theory, a growing body of research is exploring these ideas and showing how they can be used to account for different forms (and rates) of homicide (e.g., Daly & Wilson, 1990). Much of this research is being conducted by Dr. Martin Daly of McMaster University, who is profiled in Box 14.6.

The General Aggression Model (GAM) is one of the more recent theories of aggression (Anderson & Bushman, 2002). As its name implies, the GAM is a general theory of human aggression in that it integrates a number of domain-specific theories to explain the emergence of all types of aggression. The model is complex and a full discussion of it is beyond the scope of this book. However, we will discuss its main components, which are highlighted in Figure 14.3.

The first component is referred to as inputs, which refer to biological, environmental, psychological, and social factors that influence aggression in a specific social encounter. Inputs are categorized into person factors (e.g., traits, attitudes, genetic predispositions) and situation factors (e.g., incentives, provocation, frustration). According to the GAM, inputs influence behaviour via the internal states that they create within an individual. Specifically, input variables are thought to influence cognitions (e.g., hostile thoughts), emotions (e.g., anger), and arousal, and these three routes are also thought to influence one another (e.g., hostile thoughts can lead to increases in anger). These internal states in turn influence behavioural outcomes through a variety of appraisal and decision

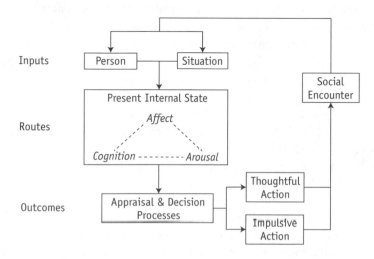

**Figure 14.3** The General Aggression Model

Source: Anderson & Bushman, 2002.

processes. Some of the outcomes reflect relatively automatic, impulsive actions, whereas other actions are heavily controlled and thoughtful in nature. These outcomes influence the social encounter, which has an impact on the inputs in the next social encounter. Research supports many of the links proposed in the GAM (e.g., see Anderson & Bush, 2002), and the model appears useful, not only for understanding human aggression, but also for developing interventions to reduce aggression.

## Treatment of Homicidal Offenders

The treatment of homicidal offenders has not received the same degree of attention as the treatment of sexual offenders (Serin, Gobeil, & Preston, 2009). While this may be unsurprising in the case of serial or mass murderers, given the very long sentences these offenders will likely receive and their low potential for rehabilitation, it is more surprising for other types of homicide offenders. Indeed, given the serious consequences of their actions, it is remarkable that so little attention has been given to the development and evaluation of treatment programs for violent offenders, including offenders who have committed homicide.

Like sexual offending, nonsexual violent offending has a multitude of interacting causes and these causes inform treatment programs for violent offenders. While there is no such thing as a "typical" treatment program for violent offenders, many treatment programs are designed to target some or all of the following factors: anger (and emotions) management, self-regulation (i.e., self-control), problem solving, interpersonal skills, and social attitudes (e.g., beliefs supporting violence; Polaschek & Collie, 2004).

Given these factors, it makes sense that some of the intervention programs used for sexual offenders (e.g., relapse prevention programs) are sometimes also used to treat nonsexual violent offenders. However, a wide variety of other programs are also used to intervene with violent offenders (see Jolliffe & Farrington, 2007; Polaschek & Collie, 2004). When it comes to the effectiveness of these treatment programs, there are few well-controlled evaluations (Polaschek & Collie, 2004). That being said, there have been some attempts recently to fill this gap using meta-analysis techniques.

For example, the recent meta-analysis by Jolliffe and Farrington (2007) was designed to evaluate treatment effectiveness for violent (male) offenders specifically (the study was not restricted to homicide offenders, but it excluded domestic and sexual offenders). These researchers included eight studies in which treated and untreated violent offenders were compared and they calculated an effect size to determine the impact of treatment. In each of these studies, violent reoffending (in addition to general reoffending) was used as the outcome measure of interest.

In this study, positive effect sizes indicated lower rates of reoffending in the treated group and negative effect sizes indicated higher rates of reoffending in the treated group. Jolliffe and Farrington (2007) found the average effect to be about 0.13 when comparing the reoffending rates of violent offenders who did, or did not, participate in treatment. Thus, their results indicate that the treatment programs that they examined were effective to some extent, though the effect certainly wasn't very large.

Like the meta-analysis by Hanson et al. (2002) that we previously described, where various moderators of effectiveness for sexual offender treatment were identified, Jolliffe and Farrington (2007) also found that not all violent offender treatment programs were equally effective. Whether a treatment program resulted in reductions in violent reoffending depended partially on what the treatment program targeted. For example, on the one hand, treatment programs that targeted anger control were associated with an average effect size of 0.14. On the other hand, treatment programs that provided empathy training were associated with an average effect size of –0.05 (i.e., reoffending actually increased).

Beyond the content of the intervention, other factors that had an impact on the effectiveness of treatment included features of the study (e.g., providing longer treatment sessions increased effectiveness), the delivery of the intervention (e.g., having the intervention delivered by correctional staff versus a rehabilitation professional increased effectiveness), and the methodology of the study (e.g., restricting the samples to only offenders who completed the treatment increased effectiveness).

## SUMMARY

1.  Rapists are offenders who sexually assault adults, and child molesters are offenders who sexually assault children. Typologies of both rapists and child molesters have been proposed that focus on the motives for sexual abuse. Rapists have been classified into the following five primary types based on research by Knight and Prentky (1990): (1) opportunistic, (2) pervasively angry, (3) sexual, (4) sadistic, and (5) vindictive. Groth (1979) proposed a different rapist typology, consisting of the following three types: (1) angry, (2) power, and (3) sadistic. Groth et al. (1982) proposed that child molesters be classified into two main types: (1) regressed and (2) fixated.

2.  Treatment for sexual offenders involves recognizing denial, minimizations, and cognitive distortions; gaining victim empathy; modifying deviant sexual interest; enhancing social skills; dealing with substance-abuse problems; and developing relapse-prevention plans.

3.  Meta-analyses of sexual offender treatment programs have found the following: (1) sexual offenders who complete treatment have lower rates of sexual recidivism than do dropouts or treatment refusers, (2) treatment is effective for both adolescent and adult sexual offenders, (3) both institutional and community treatment programs are associated with reductions in sexual recidivism, and (4) cognitive-behavioural treatments are more effective than other forms of treatment.

4.  Although homicide receives extensive media coverage, it occurs relatively infrequently in Canada. Certain trends are present in homicide statistics: gang-related homicides appear to be on the increase, as do homicides involving firearms; the likelihood of females being homicide victims continues to decrease potentially because of a decrease in spousal murders; and homicide rates vary across regions in Canada, with higher rates in the Western provinces than in the Eastern provinces (and the highest rates in the territories).

5.  Reactive homicide is defined as impulsive, unplanned, immediate, driven by negative emotions, and occurring in response to some perceived provocation. Instrumental homicide is defined as proactive rather than reactive and is a premeditated, calculated behaviour, motivated by some goal.

6.  Different types of homicides can be identified, based largely on who the victims and offenders are. Some murders include multiple victims. Serial murder is the killing of

at least three people over time, with an emotional cooling-off period between each murder. Mass murder is the killing of three or more victims at a single location during one event, with no cooling-off period.

7. Compared with studies that have examined the effectiveness of sexual offender treatment programs, less research has been conducted to examine the effectiveness of treatment programs for other violent offenders, such as homicidal offenders. However, recent meta-analytic studies suggest that existing programs may have a small, but significant impact on these offenders such that they are less likely to reoffend violently after taking part in treatment.

## Discussion Questions

1. You are interested in doing a study on the association between childhood sexual abuse and sexual offending later in life. Describe the methodology you would use and what variables you would measure.

2. Several typologies have been proposed for child molesters and rapists. What are the similarities and differences?

3. The Correctional Service of Canada has proposed a new treatment program for sexual offenders. You have been hired to develop an evaluation of the program to determine whether it would be effective. Describe how you plan to evaluate this program.

4. Your friend has been following the Robert Pickton serial murder case in the newspaper and realizes that she has heard of hardly any female serial killers. She knows you have been studying forensic psychology and asks you about female serial killers. Describe the characteristics associated with male and female serial killers.

5. Homicide offenders have been classified into instrumental and reactive types. What are the treatment implications for these two types of murderers?

# Glossary

**Aboriginal overrepresentation** The discrepancy between the relatively low proportion of Aboriginal people in the general Canadian population and the relatively high proportion of Aboriginal people involved in the criminal justice system

**Absolute discharge** The defendant is released into the community without restrictions to his or her behaviour

**Absolute judgment** Witness compares each lineup member to his or her memory of the culprit to decide whether the lineup member is the culprit

**Actuarial prediction** Decisions are based on risk factors that are selected and combined based on their empirical or statistical association with a specific outcome

**Actus reus** A wrongful deed

**Adjournment** Delaying the trial until sometime in the future

**Affective violence** Violence that is impulsive, unplanned, immediate, driven by negative emotions, and occurring in response to some perceived provocation. Also known as *reactive aggression*

**Anatomically detailed dolls** A doll, sometimes like a rag doll, that is consistent with the male or female anatomy

**Anger rapist** A rapist, as defined by Groth, who uses more force than necessary to obtain compliance from the victim and who engages in a variety of sexual acts to degrade the victim

**Antisocial personality disorder** A personality disorder characterized by a history of behaviour in which the rights of others are violated

**Antisocial process screening device** Observer rating scale to assess psychopathic traits in children

**Assessment centre** A facility in which the behaviour of police applicants can be observed in a number of situations by multiple observers

**Attention deficit hyperactivity disorder** A disorder in a youth characterized by a persistent pattern of inattention and hyperactivity or impulsivity

**Automatism** Unconscious, involuntary behaviour such that the person committing the act is not aware of what he or she is doing

**Aversion therapy** The pairing of an aversive stimuli with a deviant fantasy for the purpose of reducing the attractiveness of these deviant fantasies

**Base rate** Represents the percentage of people within a given population who engage in a specific behaviour or have a mental disorder

**Biased lineup** A lineup that "suggests" who the police suspect and thereby who the witness should identify

**Black sheep effect** When evidence is strong, similarity between defendant and jury leads to punitiveness

**Capping** Notion introduced through Bill C-30 where there is a maximum period of time a person with a mental illness could be affected by their disposition

**Challenge for cause** An option to reject biased jurors

**Change of venue** Moving a trial to a community other than the one in which the crime occurred

**Child molester** Someone who has actually sexually molested a child. See also *pedophile*

**Classic trait model** A model of personality that assumes the primary determinants of behaviour are stable, internal traits

**Clinical forensic psychologists** Psychologists who are broadly concerned with the assessment and treatment of mental health issues as they pertain to the law or legal system

**Clinical risk factors** Types and symptoms of mental disorders (e.g., substance abuse)

**Coerced-compliant false confessions** A confession that results from a desire to escape a coercive interrogation environment or gain a benefit promised by the police

**Coerced-internalized false confessions** A confession that results from suggestive interrogation techniques, whereby the confessor actually comes to believe he or she committed the crime

**Cognitive ability tests** Procedure for measuring verbal, mathematical, memory, and reasoning abilities

**Cognitive distortions** Deviant cognitions, values, or beliefs that are used to justify or minimize deviant behaviours

**Cognitive interview** Interview procedure for use with eyewitnesses based on principles of memory storage and retrieval

**Comfort serial murderer** A murderer who is motivated by material or financial gain

**Community service** A sentence that involves the offender performing a duty in the community, often as a way of paying off a fine

**Community treatment order** Sentence that allows the mentally ill offender to live in the community, with the stipulation that the person will agree to treatment or detention in the event that his or her condition deteriorates

**Comparison Question Test** Type of polygraph test that includes irrelevant questions that are unrelated to the crime, relevant questions concerning the crime being investigated, and control questions concerning the person's honesty and past history prior to the event being investigated

**Competency inquiry** Questions posed to child witnesses under the age of 14 to determine whether they are able to communicate the evidence and understand the difference between the truth and a lie, and, in the circumstances of testifying, to see if they feel compelled to tell the truth

**Compliance** A tendency to go along with demands made by people perceived to be in authority, even though the person may not agree with them

**Concealed Information Test** Type of polygraph test designed to determine if the person knows details about a crime

**Conditional discharge** A defendant is released; however, release carries certain conditions (e.g., not to possess firearms) that the defendant must meet. Failure to meet the conditions imposed with a conditional discharge may result in the defendant being incarcerated or sent to a psychiatric facility

**Conditional sentence** A sentence served in the community

**Conduct disorder** A disorder characterized by a persistent pattern of behaviour in which a youth violates the rights of others or age-appropriate societal norms or rules

**Confabulation** The reporting of events that never actually occurred

**Contextual risk factors** Risk factors that refer to aspects of the current environment (e.g., access to victims or weapons). Sometimes called *situational risk factors*

**Countermeasures** As applied to polygraph research, techniques used to try to conceal guilt

**Criminal harassment** Crime that involves repeatedly following, communicating with, watching, or threatening a person directly or indirectly

**Criminal profiling** An investigative technique for identifying the major personality and behavioural characteristics of an individual based upon an analysis of the crimes he or she has committed (Douglas et al., 1986)

**Criterion-based content analysis** Analysis that uses criteria to distinguish truthful from false statements made by children

**Cross-race effect** The phenomenon of witnesses remembering own-race faces with greater accuracy than faces from other races. Also known as the *other-race effect* and the *own-race bias*

**Cue-utilization hypothesis** Proposed by Easterbrook (1959) to explain why a witness may focus on the weapon rather than other details. The hypothesis suggests that when emotional arousal increases, attentional capacity decreases

**Culprit** The guilty person who committed the crime

**Dangerous offender** A label attached to offenders who are proven to constitute a significant danger to others

***Daubert* criteria** A standard for accepting expert testimony, which states that scientific evidence is valid if the research on which it is based has been peer reviewed, is testable, has a recognized rate of error, and adheres to professional standards

**Day parole** A form of parole that allows the offender to enter the community for up to one day (e.g., for the purpose of holding down a job)

**Deception detection** Detecting when someone is being deceptive

**Deductive criminal profiling** Profiling the background characteristics of an unknown offender based on evidence left at the crime scenes by that particular offender

**Defensiveness** Conscious denial or extreme minimization of physical or psychological symptoms

**Deliberation** When jury members discuss the evidence privately among themselves to reach a verdict that is then provided to the court

**Delusional stalker** A stalker who suffers from delusions and wrongly believes he or she has a relationship with the victim

**Desistance** The process of ceasing to engage in criminal behaviour

**Direct question recall** Witnesses are asked a series of specific questions about the crime or the culprit

**Dispositional risk factor** Risk factors that reflect the individual's traits, tendencies, or styles (e.g., negative attitudes)

**Disputed confessions** A confession that is later disputed at trial

**Distractors** Lineup members who are known to be innocent for the crime in question. Also known as *foils*

**Diversion** A decision not to prosecute a young offender but rather have him or her undergo an educational or community-service program. Also an option for the courts dealing with offenders with mental illnesses who are facing minor charges. The court can divert the offender directly into a treatment program rather than have him or her go through the court process

**Domestic violence** Any violence occurring between family members

**Dynamic risk factor** Risk factors that fluctuate over time and are amenable to change

**Dysphoric/borderline batterer** A male spousal batterer who exhibits some violence outside the family, is depressed, has borderline personality traits, and has problems with jealousy

**Elimination lineup** Lineup procedure for children that first asks them to pick out the person who looks most like the culprit from the photos displayed. Next, children are asked whether the most similar person selected is in fact the culprit

**Emotional maltreatment** Acts or omissions by caregivers that cause or could cause serious behavioural, cognitive, emotional, or mental disorders

**Enhanced cognitive interview** Interview procedure that includes various principles of social dynamics in addition to the memory retrieval principles used in the original cognitive interview

**Estimator variables** Variables that are present at the time of the crime and that cannot be changed

**Event-related brain potentials** Brain activity measured by placing electrodes on the scalp and by recording electrical patterns related to presentation of a stimulus

**Ex-intimate stalker** A stalker who engages in stalking after an intimate relationship breaks up

**Exhibitionist** Someone who obtains sexual gratification by exposing his or her genitals to strangers

**Experimental forensic psychologists** Psychologists who are broadly concerned with the study of human behaviour as it relates to the law or legal system

**Expert witness** A witness who provides the court with information (often an opinion on a particular matter) that assists the court in understanding an issue of relevance to a case

**Externalizing problems** Behavioural difficulties such as delinquency, fighting, bullying, lying, or destructive behaviour experienced by a youth

**Extra-familial child molester** Someone who sexually abuses children not related to him or her

**Extrajudicial** Term applied to measures taken to keep young offenders out of court and out of custody (e.g., giving a warning or making a referral for treatment)

**Fabricating** Making false claims

**Factitious disorder** A disorder in which the person's physical and psychological symptoms are intentionally produced and are adopted to assume the role of a sick person

**Fair lineup** A lineup where the suspect does not stand out from the other lineup members

**False confession** A confession that is either intentionally fabricated or is not based on actual knowledge of the facts that form its content

**False memory syndrome** Term to describe clients' false beliefs that they were sexually abused as children, having no memories of this abuse until they enter therapy to deal with some other psychological problem, such as depression or substance abuse

**False negative** An incorrect prediction that occurs when a person is predicted not to engage in some type of behaviour (e.g., a violent act) but does

**False positive** An incorrect prediction that occurs when a person is predicted to engage in some type of behaviour (e.g., a violent act) but does not

**Familicide** The killing of a spouse and children

**Family-only batterer** A male spousal batterer who is typically not violent outside the home, does not show much psychopathology, and does not possess negative attitudes supportive of violence

**Family-supportive interventions** Interventions that connect at-risk families to various support services

**Femicide** The killing of women

**Filicide** The killing of children by their biological parents or step-parents and includes neonaticide (killing a baby within 24 hours of birth) and infanticide (killing a baby within the first year of life)

**Fine** A sentence where the offender has to make a monetary payment to the courts

**Fixated child molester** A child molester, as defined by Groth, who has a long-standing, exclusive sexual preference for children

**Foils** Lineup members who are known to be innocent for the crime in question. Also known as *distractors*

**Forensic psychiatry** A field of medicine that deals with all aspects of human behaviour as it relates to the law or legal system

**Forensic psychology** A field of psychology that deals with all aspects of human behaviour as it relates to the law or legal system

**Free narrative** Witnesses are asked to either write or orally state all they remember about the event without the officer (or experimenter) asking questions. Also known as *open-ended recall*

**Full parole** A form of parole that allows the offender to serve the remainder of his or her sentence under supervision in the community

**Fundamental principle of sentencing** Belief that sentences should be proportionate to the gravity of the offence and the degree of responsibility of the offender

**General acceptance test** A standard for accepting expert testimony, which states that expert testimony will be admissible in court if the basis of the testimony is generally accepted within the relevant scientific community

**General deterrence** Sentencing to reduce the probability that members of the general public will offend in the future

**Generally violent/antisocial batterer** A male spousal batterer who is violent outside the home, engages in other criminal acts, has drug and alcohol problems, has impulse-control problems, and possesses violence-supportive beliefs

**Geographic profiling systems** Computer systems that use mathematical models of offender spatial behaviour to make predictions about where unknown serial offenders are likely to reside

**Geographic profiling** An investigative technique that uses crime scene locations to predict the most likely area where an offender resides

**Ground truth** As applied to polygraph research, the knowledge of whether the person is actually guilty or innocent

**Grudge stalker** A stalker who knows and is angry at the victim for some perceived injustice

**Hare Psychopathy Checklist–Revised** The most popular method of assessing psychopathy in adults

**Hare Psychopathy Checklist–Youth Version** Scale designed to measure psychopathic traits in adolescents

**Hedonistic serial murderer** A murderer who is motivated by self-gratification. This type of killer is divided into three subtypes: lust, thrill, and comfort

**Heuristics** Simple general rules of thumb that can be used to make decisions and solve problems. In some instances, a reliance on heuristics can result in biased decisions. In other cases, heuristics can result in reasonably accurate decisions

**Historic child sexual abuse (HCSA)** Allegations of child abuse having occurred several years, often decades, from when they are being prosecuted

**Historical risk factor** Risk factor that refers to events that have been experienced in the past (e.g., age at first arrest). Also known as *static risk factor*

**Hung jury** A jury that cannot reach a unanimous verdict

**Illusory correlation** Belief that a correlation exists between two events that in reality are either not correlated or correlated to a much lesser degree

**Impartiality** A characteristic of jurors who are unbiased

**Imprisonment** A sentence served in prison

**In need of protection** A term used to describe a child's need to be separated from his or her caregiver because of maltreatment

**Incest offenders** People who sexually abuse their own biological children or children for whom they assume a parental role, such as a stepfather or live-in boyfriend. Also known as *intra-familial child molesters*

**Incidence** Number of new child-maltreatment cases in a specific population occurring in a given time period, usually a year

**Inductive criminal profiling** Profiling the background characteristics of an unknown offender based on what we know about other solved cases

**Insanity** Impairment of mental or emotional functioning that affects perceptions, beliefs, and motivations at the time of the offence

**Instigators** In social learning theory, these are events in the environment that act as a stimulus for acquired behaviours

**Instrumental aggression** Violence that is premeditated, calculated behaviour, motivated by some goal. Also known as *predatory violence*

**Internalization** The acceptance of guilt for an act, even if the person did not actually commit the act

**Internalizing problems** Emotional difficulties such as anxiety, depression, and obsessions experienced by a youth

**Intimate partner violence** Any violence occurring between intimate partners who are living together or separated. Also known as *spousal violence*

**Intra-familial child molesters** People who sexually abuse their own biological children or children for whom they assume a parental role, such as a stepfather or live-in boyfriend. Also known as *incest offenders*

**Investigator bias** Bias that can result when police officers enter an interrogation setting already believing that the suspect is guilty

**Inwald Personality Inventory** An assessment instrument used to identify police applicants who are suitable for police work by measuring their personality attributes and behaviour patterns

**Job analysis** A procedure for identifying the knowledge, skills, and abilities that make a good police officer

**Juries Act** Provincial and territorial legislation that outlines the eligibility criteria for jury service and how prospective jurors must be selected

**Jury nullification** Occurs when a jury ignores the law and the evidence, rendering a verdict based on some other criteria

**Jury summons** A court order that states a time and place to go for jury duty

**Known-groups design** As applied to malingering research, involves comparing genuine patients and malingerers attempting to fake the disorder the patients have

**Leniency bias** When jurors move toward greater leniency during deliberations

**Lineup** A set of people presented to the witness who must state whether the culprit is present and, if so, which one

**Linkage blindness** An inability on the part of the police to link geographically dispersed serial crimes committed by the same offender because of a lack of information sharing among police agencies

**Long-term offender** A label attached to offenders who are proven to be a high risk for reoffending

**Love-obsessional stalker** A stalker who has intense emotional feelings for the victim but who has never had an intimate relationship with the victim

**Lust serial murderer** A murderer who is motivated by sexual gratification

**Malingering** Intentionally faking psychological or physical symptoms for some type of external gain

**Mandatory charging policies** Policies that give police the authority to lay charges against a suspect where there is reasonable and probable grounds to believe a domestic assault has occurred

**Mass murder** The killing of three or more victims at a single location during one event with no cooling-off period

**Maximization techniques** Scare tactics used by police interrogators that are designed to intimidate a suspect believed to be guilty

**Memory impairment hypothesis** Explanation for the misinformation effect where the original memory is replaced with the new, incorrect, information

**Mens rea** Criminal intent

**Minimization techniques** Soft sell tactics used by police interrogators that are designed to lull the suspect into a false sense of security

**Minnesota Multiphasic Personality Inventory** An assessment instrument for identifying people with psychopathological problems

**Misinformation acceptance hypothesis** Explanation for the misinformation effect where the incorrect information is provided because the witness guesses what the officer or experimenter wants the response to be

**Misinformation effect** Phenomenon where a witness who is presented with inaccurate information after an event will incorporate that "misinformation" in a subsequent recall task. Also known as *post-event information effect*

**Mission-oriented serial murderer** A murderer who targets individuals from a group that he or she considers to be "undesirable"

***Mohan* criteria** A standard for accepting expert testimony, which states that expert testimony will be admissible in court if the testimony is relevant, necessary for assisting the trier of fact, does not violate any exclusionary rules, and is provided by a qualified expert

**Munchausen syndrome** A rare factitious disorder in which a person intentionally produces a physical complaint and constantly seeks physician consultations, hospitalizations, and even surgery to treat the nonexistent illness

**Narrative elaboration** An interview procedure whereby children learn to organize their story into relevant categories: participants, settings, actions, conversation/affective states, and consequences

**National Parole Board** The organization in Canada responsible for making parole decisions

**Need principle** Principle that correctional interventions should target known criminogenic needs (i.e., factors that relate to reoffending)

**Neglect/failure to provide** When a child's caregivers do not provide the requisite attention to the child's emotional, psychological, or physical development

**Observational learning** Learning behaviours by watching others perform these behaviours

**Occupational stressors** In policing, stressors relating to the job itself

**Open-ended recall** Witnesses are asked to either write or orally state all they remember about the event without the officer (or experimenter) asking questions. Also known as a *free narrative*

**Oppositional defiant disorder** A disorder in a youth characterized by a persistent pattern of negativistic, hostile, and defiant behaviours

**Organizational stressors** In policing, stressors relating to organizational issues

**Organized-disorganized model** A profiling model used by the FBI that assumes that the crime scenes and backgrounds of serial offenders can be categorized as *organized* or *disorganized*

**Other-race effect** Phenomenon of witnesses remembering own-race faces with greater accuracy than faces from other races. Also known as the *cross-race effect* and the *own-race bias*

**Own-race bias** Phenomenon of witnesses remembering own-race faces with greater accuracy than faces from other races. Also known as the *cross-race effect* and the *other-race effect*

**Parent-focused interventions** Interventions directed at assisting parents to recognize warning signs for later youth violence and/or training parents to effectively manage any behavioural problems that arise

**Parole** The release of offenders from prison into the community before their sentence term is complete

**Patriarchy** Broad set of cultural beliefs and values that support the male dominance of women

**Pedophile** Person whose primary sexual orientation is toward children. See also *child molester*

**Penile phallometry** A measurement device placed around the penis to measure changes in sexual arousal

**Physical abuse** The deliberate application of force to any part of a child's body that results in or may result in a nonaccidental injury

**Polarization** When individuals tend to become more extreme in their initial position following a group discussion

**Police discretion** A policing task that involves discriminating between circumstances that require absolute adherence to the law and circumstances where a degree of latitude is justified

**Police interrogation** A process whereby the police interview a suspect for the purpose of gathering evidence and obtaining a confession

**Police selection procedures** A set of procedures used by the police to either screen out undesirable candidates or select in desirable candidates

**Polygraph** A device for recording an individual's autonomic nervous system responses

**Polygraph disclosure tests** Polygraph tests that are used to uncover information about an offender's past behaviour

**Post-event information effect** Phenomenon where a witness who is presented with inaccurate information after an event will incorporate that "misinformation" in a subsequent recall task. Also known as the *misinformation effect*

**Post-traumatic stress disorder** Anxiety disorder that can develop in response to exposure to an extremely traumatic event. Symptoms include frequent, distressing, and intrusive memories of the event, avoiding stimuli associated with the traumatic event, and persistent anxiety or increased arousal symptoms

**Power/control serial murder** A murderer who is motivated not by sexual gratification but by wanting to have absolute dominance over the victim

**Power rapist** A rapist, as defined by Groth, who seeks to establish dominance and control over the victim

**Predatory aggression** Violence that is premeditated, calculated behaviour, motivated by some goal. Also known as *instrumental aggression*

**Prevalence** In the study of child abuse, the proportion of a population at a specific point in time that was maltreated during childhood

**Prima facie case** Case in which the Crown prosecutor must prove there is sufficient evidence to bring the case to trial

**Primary intervention strategies** Strategies that are implemented prior to any violence occurring, with the goal of decreasing the likelihood that violence will occur later on

**Protective factors** Factors that mitigate or reduce the likelihood of a negative outcome (e.g., aggression, psychopathology)

**Psychology *and* the law** The use of psychology to examine the operation of the legal system

**Psychology *in* the law** The use of psychology in the legal system as that system operates

**Psychology *of* the law** The use of psychology to examine the law itself

**Psychopathic Personality Inventory** A self-report measure of psychopathic traits

**Psychopathy** A personality disorder defined by a collection of interpersonal, affective, and behavioural characteristics, including manipulation, lack of remorse or empathy, impulsivity, and antisocial behaviours

**Racial bias** The disparate treatment of racial out-groups

**Rape trauma syndrome** A group of symptoms or behaviours that are frequent after-effects of having been raped

**Rapist** People who sexually assault victims over 16 years of age

**Reactive aggression** Violence that is impulsive, unplanned, immediate, driven by negative emotions, and occurring in response to some perceived provocation. Also known as *affective violence*

**Recall memory** Reporting details of a previously witnessed event or person

**Recognition memory** Determining whether a previously seen item or person is the same as what is currently being viewed

**Regressed child molester** A child molester, as defined by Groth, whose primary sexual orientation is for adults, but whose sexual interests revert to children after a stressful event or because of feelings of inadequacy

**Regulators** In social learning theory, these are consequences of behaviours

**Reid model** A nine-step model of interrogation used frequently in North America to extract confessions from suspects

**Relapse prevention** A method of treatment designed to prevent the occurrence of an undesired behaviour (e.g., sexual assault)

**Relative judgment** Witness compares lineup members to one another and the person that looks most like the culprit is identified

**Reparations** A sentence where the offender has to make a monetary payment to the victim or the community

**Representativeness** A jury composition that represents the community where the crime occurred

**Resilient** Characteristic of a child who has multiple risk factors but who does not develop problem behaviours or negative symptoms

**Resolution conference** Involves an offender and his or her family coming together with the victim and the police in an attempt to solve a problem

**Response Modulation Deficit Theory** A theory that suggests that psychopaths fail to use contextual cues that are peripheral to a dominant response set to modulate their behaviour

**Responsivity principle** Principle that correctional interventions should match the general learning style of offenders

**Restitution** A sentence where the offender has to make a monetary payment to the victim or the community; see *reparations*

**Restorative justice** An approach for dealing with the crime problem that emphasizes repairing the harm caused by crime. Based on the philosophy that when victims, offenders, and community members meet voluntarily to decide how to achieve this, transformation can result

**Retracted confessions** A confession that the confessor later declares to be false

**Review boards** Legal bodies mandated to oversee the care and disposition of defendants found unfit and/or not criminally responsible on account of a mental disorder

**Risk factor** A factor that increases the likelihood for emotional and/or behavioural problems; in terms of a predictor: a measurable feature of an individual that predicts the behaviour of interest (e.g., violence or psychopathology)

**Risk principle** Principle that correctional interventions should target offenders who are at high risk to reoffend

**Sadistic rapist** A rapist, as defined by Groth, who obtains sexual gratification by hurting the victim

**Secondary intervention strategies** Strategies that attempt to reduce the frequency of violence

**Selection interview** In recruiting police officers, an interview used by the police to determine the extent to which an applicant possesses the knowledge, skills, and abilities deemed important for the job

**Self-Report Psychopathy Scale** A self-report measure of psychopathic traits

**Sentencing disparity** Variations in sentencing severity for similar crimes committed under similar circumstances

**Sentencing guidelines** Guidelines that are intended to reduce the degree of discretion that judges have when handing down sentences

**Sequential lineup** Alternative lineup procedure where the lineup members are presented serially to the witness, and the witness must make a decision as to whether the lineup member is the culprit before seeing another member. Also, a witness cannot ask to see previously seen photos and the witness is unaware of the number of photos to be shown

**Serial murder** The killing of a minimum of three people over time. The time interval between the murders varies and has been called a *cooling-off period*. Subsequent murders occur at different times, have no apparent connection to the initial murder, and are usually committed in different locations

**Sexual abuse** When an adult or youth uses a child for sexual purposes

**Sexual homicide** Homicides that have a sexual component

**Sexual sadism** People who are sexually aroused by fantasies, urges, or acts of inflicting pain, suffering, or humiliation on another human

**Showup** Identification procedure that shows one person to the witness; the suspect

**Simultaneous lineup** A common lineup procedure that presents all lineup members at one time to the witness

**Situational risk factors** Risk factors that refer to aspects of the current environment (e.g., access to victims or weapons). Sometimes called *contextual risk factors*

**Situational test** A simulation of a real-world policing task

**Social learning theory** A theory of human behaviour based on learning from watching others in the social environment and reinforcement contingencies

**Sociopathy** A label used to describe a person whose psychopathic traits are assumed to be due to environmental factors

**Somatoform disorders** A disorder in which physical symptoms suggest a physical illness but have no known underlying physiological cause and the symptoms are not intentionally produced

**Source misattribution hypothesis** Explanation for the misinformation effect—where the witness has two memories, the original and the misinformation; however, the witness cannot remember where each memory originated or the source of each

**Specific deterrence** Sentencing to reduce the probability that an offender will reoffend in the future

**Spousal violence** Any violence occurring between intimate partners who are living together or separated. Also known as *intimate partner violence*

**Statement validity analysis** A comprehensive protocol to distinguish truthful or false statements made by children containing three parts: (1) a structured interview of the child witness, (2) a systematic analysis of the verbal content of the child's statements (criterion-based content analysis), and (3) the application of the statement validity checklist

**Static risk factor** Risk factor that does not fluctuate over time and is not changed by treatment (e.g., age at first arrest). Also known as *historical risk factor*

**Statutory release** The release of offenders from prison after they have served two-thirds of their sentences

**Step-wise interview** Interview protocol with a series of "steps" designed to start the interview with the least leading and directive type of questioning, and then proceed to more specific forms of questioning, as necessary

**Structured professional judgment** Decisions are guided by a predetermined list of risk factors that have been selected from the research and professional literature. Judgment of risk level is based on the evaluator's professional judgment

**Supreme Court of Canada** Created in 1875, the Supreme Court of Canada consists of eight judges plus the chief justice, who are all appointed by the federal government. The Supreme Court is the final court of appeal in Canada, and lower Canadian courts are bound by its rulings. The Supreme Court also provides guidance to the federal government on law-related matters, such as the interpretation of the Canadian constitution.

**Suspect** A person the police "suspect" committed the crime, who may be guilty or innocent for the crime in question

**System variables** Variables that can be manipulated to increase (or decrease) eyewitness accuracy

**Systematic disparity** Consistent disagreement among judges about sentencing decisions because of factors such as how lenient judges think sentences should be

**Target-absent lineup** A lineup that does not contain the culprit but contains innocent suspects

**Target-present lineup** A lineup that contains the culprit

**Temporary absence** A form of parole that allows the offender to enter the community on a temporary basis (e.g., for the purpose of attending correctional programs)

**Tertiary intervention strategies** Strategies that attempt to prevent violence from reoccurring

**Thrill serial murderer** A murderer who is motivated by the excitement associated with the act of killing

**Trauma-control model of serial murder** The model suggesting that a multitude of factors are involved in predicting who may be predisposed to commit serial murder

**True negative** A correct prediction that occurs when a person who is predicted not to engage in some type of behaviour (e.g., a violent act) does not

**True positive** A correct prediction that occurs when a person who is predicted to engage in some type of behaviour (e.g., a violent act) does so

**Truth-bias** The tendency of people to judge more messages as truthful than deceptive

**Unstructured clinical judgment** Decisions characterized by a substantial amount of professional discretion and lack of guidelines

**Unfit to stand trial** Refers to an inability to conduct a defence at any stage of the proceedings on account of a person's mental disorder

**Unsystematic disparity** Inconsistencies in a judge's sentencing decisions over time when judging the same type of offender or crime because of factors such as the judge's mood

**Unwarranted sentencing disparity** Variations in sentencing severity for similar crimes committed under similar circumstances that result from reliance by the judge on legally irrelevant factors

**Use of force continuum** A model that is supposed to guide police officer decision making in use-of-force situations by providing the officer with some guidance as to what level of force is appropriate given the suspect's behaviour and other environmental conditions

**VICLAS** The Violent Crime Linkage Analysis System, which was developed by the RCMP to collect and analyze information on serious crimes from across Canada

**Visionary serial murderer** A murderer who kills in response to voices or visions telling him or her to kill

**Voluntary false confession** A false confession that is provided without any elicitation from the police

**Voyeurs** People who obtain sexual gratification by observing unsuspecting people, usually strangers, who are either naked, in the process of undressing, or engaging in sexual activity

**Walk-by** Identification procedure that occurs in a naturalistic environment. The police take the witness to a public location where the suspect is likely to be. Once the suspect is in view, the witness is asked whether he or she sees the culprit

**Weapon focus** Term used to describe the phenomenon of a witness's attention being focused on the culprit's weapon rather than on the culprit

# References

Aamodt, M.G. (2004). *Research in law enforcement selection.* Boca Raton, FL: Brown Walker Press.

Aamodt, M.G., & Stalnaker, N.A. (2006). *Police officer suicide: Frequency and officer profiles.* Retrieved from PoliceOne.com website: http://www.policeone.com/health-fitness/articles/137133-Police-Officer-Suicide-Frequency-and-officer-profiles/

Aamondt, M.G., & Custer, H. (2008). Who can best catch a liar? A meta-analysis of individual differences in detecting deception. *The Forensic Examiner, 15.1,* 6–11.

Abdollahi, M.K. (2002). Understanding police stress research. *Journal of Forensic Psychology Practice, 2,* 1–24.

Abel, G.G., Becker, J.V., Mittelman, M., & Cunningham-Rathner, J. (1987). Self-reported sex crimes of nonincarcerated paraphiliacs. *Journal of Interpersonal Violence, 2,* 3–25.

Abootalebi, V., Moradi, M.H., & Khalilzadeh, M.A. (2006). A comparison of methods for ERP assessment in a P300-based GKT. *International Journal of Psychophysiology, 62,* 309–320.

Aboriginal Justice Inquiry of Manitoba. (2009). *Report of the Aboriginal Justice Inquiry of Manitoba.* Retrieved from http://www.ajic.mb.ca/volume.html

Aboriginal Legal Services of Toronto. (2001). *Gladue (Aboriginal persons) court. Ontario Court of Justice—Old City Hall. Fact sheet.* Retrieved from http://www.aboriginallegal.ca/docs/apc_factsheet.htm.

Aboriginal Task Force. (1989). *Task force on Aboriginal peoples in federal corrections: Final report.* Ottawa, ON: Solicitor General of Canada.

Ackerman, M.J. (1999). *Forensic psychological assessment.* New York, NY: John Wiley & Sons.

Adams, K. (1999). *What we know about police use of force.* Washington, DC: U.S. Department of Justice.

Adams, S.M., Hazelwood, T.E., Pitre, N.L., Bedard, T.E., & Landry, S.E. (2009). Harassment of members of parliament and the legislative assemblies in Canada by individuals believed to be mentally disordered. *The Journal of Forensic Psychiatry & Psychology, 20,*801–814.

Adams-Tucker, C. (1982). Proximate effects of sexual abuse in childhood: A report on 28 children. *American Journal of Psychiatry, 139,* 1252–1256.

Adler, F. (1975). *Sisters in crime: The rise of the new female criminal.* New York, NY: McGraw-Hill.

Ægisdóttir, S., White, M.J., Spengler, P.M., Maugherman, A.S., Anderson, L.A., Cook, R.S., . . . Rush, J.D. (2006). The meta-analysis of clinical judgment project: Fifty-six years of accumulated research on clinical versus statistical prediction. *The Counseling Psychologist, 34,* 341–382.

Affonso, D.D., & Domino, G. (1984). Postpartum depression: A review. *Birth: Issues in Perinatal Care and Education, 11,* 231–235.

Aglionby, J. (2006). Thai police hold maid for JonBenet murder. *Guardian.co.uk.* Retrieved from http://www.guardian.co.uk/world/2006/aug/17/usa.johnaglionby

Agosti, V. (1995). The efficacy of treatments in reducing alcohol consumption: A meta-analysis. *International Journal of the Addictions, 30,* 1067–1077.

Ainsworth, P.B. (1993). *Psychological testing and police applicant selection: Difficulties and dilemmas.* Paper presented to the European Conference on Law and Psychology, Oxford, England.

Aitken, C.C.G., Connolly, T., Gammerman, A., Zhang, G., Bailey, D., Gordon, R., & Oldfield, R. (1996). Statistical modelling in specific case analysis. *Science & Justice, 36,* 245–256.

Alarid, L.F., Burton, V.S. Jr., & Cullen, F.T. (2000). Gender and crime among felony offenders: Assessing the generality of social control and differential association theories. *Journal of Research in Crime and Delinquency, 37,* 171–199.

Aldridge, N. (1998). Strengths and limitations of forensic child sexual abuse interviews with anatomical dolls: An empirical review. *Journal of Psychopathology and Behavioral Assessment, 20,* 1–41.

Alexander, D.A., Innes, G., Irving, B.L., Sinclair, S.D., & Walker, L.G. (1991). *Health, stress and policing: A study in Grampian policing.* London, England: The Police Foundation.

Alexander, M.A. (1999). Sexual offender treatment efficacy revisited. *Sexual Abuse: Journal of Research and Treatment, 11,* 101–116.

Alison, L.J., Bennell, C., Mokros, A., & Ormerod, D. (2002). The personality paradox in offender profiling: A theoretical review of the processes involved in deriving background characteristics from crime scene actions. *Psychology, Public Policy, and Law, 8,* 115–135.

Alison, L.J., Goodwill, A.M., Almond, L., van den Heuvel, C., & Winter, J. (2010). Pragmatic solutions to offender profiling and behavioural investigative advice. *Legal & Criminological Psychology, 15,* 115–132.

Alison, L.J., Smith, M., & Morgan, K. (2003). Interpreting the accuracy of offender profiles. *Psychology, Crime and Law, 9,* 185–195.

Alison, L.J., Smith, M., Eastman, O., & Rainbow, L. (2003). Toulmin's philosophy of argument and its relevance to offender profiling. *Psychology, Crime and Law, 9*, 173–183.

Allan, A., Dawson, D., & Allan, M.M. (2006). Prediction of the risk of male sexual reoffending in Australia. *Australian Psychologist, 41*, 60–68.

Allen, J.J. & Iacono, W.G. (1997). A comparison of methods for the analysis of event-related potentials in deception detection. *Psychophysiology, 34*, 234–240.

Almond, L., Alison, L., & Porter, L. (2007). An evaluation and comparison of claims made in behavioural investigative advice reports compiled by the National Policing Improvements Agency in the United Kingdom. *Journal of Investigative Psychology & Offender Profiling, 4*, 71–83.

Alpert, G.P., & Dunham, R. (1999). *The force factor: Measuring and assessing police use of force and suspect resistance.* Washington, DC: U.S. Department of Justice.

Amato, P.R. (2000). The consequences of divorce for adults and children. *Journal of Marriage and the Family, 62*, 1269–1287.

Amato, P.R., & Keith, B. (1991). Parental divorce and the well being of children: A meta-analysis. *Psychological Bulletin, 110*, 26–46.

American Board of Forensic Psychology & American Psychology-Law Society. (1995). *Petition for the recognition of a specialty in professional psychology.* Retrieved from University of Nebraska-Lincoln website: http://www.unl.edu/ap-ls/petition.pdf

American Psychiatric Association (1994). *Diagnostic and statistical manual of mental disorders* (4th ed.). Washington, DC: Author.

American Psychological Association. (2007). *Psychology and the law: Jenkins v. United States.* Retrieved from http://www.apa.org/psyclaw/jenkins.html

Ammerman, R.T., Cassisi, J.E., Hersen M., & Van Hasselt, V.B. (1986). Consequences of physical abuse and neglect in children. *Clinical Psychology Review, 6*, 291–310.

Andershed, H.A., Gustafson, S.B., Kerr, M., & Hakån, S. (2002). The usefulness of self-reported psychopathy-like traits in the study of antisocial behaviour among non-referred adolescents. *European Journal of Personality, 16*, 383–402.

Anderson, C.A., & Bushman, B.J. (2002). Human aggression. *Annual Review of Psychology, 53*, 27–51.

Anderson, C.A., & Dill, F.E. (2000). Video games and aggressive thoughts, feelings, and behavior in the laboratory and in life. *Journal of Personality and Social Psychology, 78*, 772–790.

Anderson, M., Gillig, P.M., Sitaker, M., McCloskey, K., Malloy, K., & Grigsby, N. (2003). "Why doesn't she just leave?": A descriptive study of victim reported impediments to her safety. *Journal of Family Violence, 18*, 151–155.

Andrews, D. (2001). Principles of effective correctional programs. In L. Motiuk and R. Serin (Eds.), *Compendium 2000 on effective correctional programming* (pp. 9–17). Ottawa, ON: Correctional Service Canada.

Andrews, D., Dowden, C., & Gendreau, P. (1999). *Clinically relevant and psychologically informed approaches to reduced re-offending: A meta-analytic study of human service, risk, need, responsivity, and other concerns in justice contexts.* Unpublished manuscript, Carleton University, Ottawa, ON.

Andrews, D., Robblee, M., & Saunders, R. (1984). *The sentencing factors inventory.* Toronto, ON: Ontario Ministry of Correctional Services.

Andrews, D.A., & Bonta, J. (1998). *The psychology of criminal conduct* (2nd ed.). Cincinnati, OH: Anderson Publishing Co.

Andrews, D.A., & Bonta, J. (2006). *The psychology of criminal conduct* (4th ed.). Cincinnati, OH: Anderson Publishing.

Andrews, D.A., & Dowden, C. (2006). Risk principle of case classification in correctional treatment: A meta-analytic investigation. *International Journal of Offender Therapy and Comparative Criminology, 50*, 88–100.

Andrews, D.A., Zinger, I., Hoge, R.D., Bonta, J., Gendreau, P., & Cullen, F.T. (1990). Does correctional treatment work? A clinically relevant and psychologically informed meta-analysis. *Criminology, 28*, 369–404.

Anshel, M.H. (2000). A conceptual model and implications for coping with stressful events in police work. *Criminal Justice and Behavior, 27*, 375–400.

Anson, R.H., & Bloom, M.E. (1988). Police stress in an occupational context. *Journal of Police Science and Administration, 16*, 229–235.

Antonowicz, D., & Ross, R. (1994). Essential components of successful rehabilitation programs for offenders. International *Journal of Offender Therapy and Comparative Criminology, 38*, 97–104.

Appleby, T. (2010). Russell Williams faces 82 more burglary-related charges. *The Globe and Mail.* Retrieved from http://www.theglobeandmail.com/news/national/toronto/russell-williams-faces-82-more-burglary-related-charges/article1550700/

Archer, J. (2002). Sex differences in physically aggressive acts between heterosexual partners: A meta-analytic review. *Aggression and Violent Behavior, 7*, 313–351.

Archer, R.P., Buffington-Vollum, J.K., Stredny, R.V., & Handel, R.W. (2006). A survey of psychological test use patterns among forensic psychologists. *Journal of Personality Assessment, 87*, 84–94.

Arditti, J.A. (1999). Rethinking relationships between divorced mothers and their children: Capitalizing on family strengths. *Family Relations, 48*, 109–119.

Artwohl, A. (2002, October). Perceptual and memory distortion during officer-involved shootings. *FBI Law Enforcement Bulletin*, 18–24.

Ascione, F.R. (1998). Battered women's reports of their partners' and their children's cruelty to animals. *Journal of Emotional Abuse, 1,* 119–133.

Ascione, F.R., Weber, C.V., Thompson, T.M., Heath, J. Maruyama, M., & Hayashi, K. (2007) Battered pets and domestic violence: Animal abuse reported by women experiencing intimate violence and by nonabused women. *Violence Against Women, 13,* 354–373.

Ash, P., Slora, K.B., & Britton, C.F. (1990). Police agency officer selection practices. *Journal of Police Science and Administration, 17,* 258–269.

Atkinson, J.L. (1996). Female sex offenders: A literature review. *Forum on Corrections Research, 8,* 39–43.

AuCoin, K. (2005). Family violence in Canada: A statistical profile. Ottawa, ON: Statistics Canada.

Augimeri, L., Farrington, D., Koegl, C., & Day, D. (2007). The SNAP under 12 outreach project: Effects of a community based program for children with conduct problems. *Journal of Child and Family Studies, 16,* 799–807.

Austin, J. (2006). How much risk can we take? The misuse of risk assessment in corrections. *Federal Probation, 70,* 58–63.

Babcock, J.C., Green, C.E., & Robie, C. (2004). Does batterers' treatment work? A meta-analytic review of domestic violence treatment. *Clinical Psychology Review, 23,* 1023–1053.

Babiak, P. (1995). When psychopaths go to work: A case study of an industrial psychopath. *Applied Psychology: An International Review, 44,* 171–188.

Babiak, P. (2000). Psychopathic manipulation at work. In C.B. Gacono (Ed.), *Clinical and forensic assessment of psychopathy: A practitioner's guide* (pp. 287–311). Mahwah, NJ: Lawrence Erlbaum Associates.

Babiak, P., Neumann, C.S., & Hare, R.D. (2010). Corporate psychopathy: Talking the walk. *Behavioral Sciences and the Law, 28,* 174–193.

Baer, R.A., Wetter, M.W., & Berry, D.T.T. (1995). Sensitivity of MMP-2 validity scales to underreporting of symptoms. *Psychological Assessment, 7,* 419–423.

Bagby, R.M., Nicholson, R.A., Bacchiochi, J.R., Ryder, A.B., & Bury, A.S. (2002). The predictive capacity of MMPI-2 and PAI validity scales and indexes of coached and uncoached feigning. *Journal of Personality Assessment, 78,* 69–86.

Bala, N. (1999a). Child witnesses in the Canadian criminal courts. *Psychology, Public Policy, and Law, 5,* 323–354.

Bala, N. (1999b). *The best interests of the child in the post-modern era: A central but paradoxical concept.* Paper presented at the Law Society of Upper Canada Special lectures 2000: Family Law, Toronto, ON.

Bala, N., Lindsay, R.C.L., Lee, K., & Talwar, V. (2002, September). The legal competence of child witnesses: Assessing present practices and the need for law reform. Paper presented at the Faculty of Law, Queen's University, Kingston, ON. Retrieved from http://qsilver.queensu.ca/law/witness/childcompsept20001_files.

Ball, E.M., Young, D., Dotson, L.A., & Brothers, L.T. (1994). Factors associated with dangerous behavior in forensic inpatients: Results from a pilot study. *Bulletin of the American Academy of Psychiatry and the Law, 22,* 605–620.

Bandura, A. (1965). Influence of models' reinforcement contingencies on the acquisition of imitative responses. *Journal of Personality and Social Psychology, 1,* 589–595.

Bandura, A. (1973). *Aggression: A social learning analysis.* Englewood Cliffs, NJ: Prentice-Hall.

Banning, A. (1989). Mother–son incest: Confronting a prejudice. *Child Abuse and Neglect, 13,* 563–570.

Barbaree, H. (1997). Evaluating treatment efficacy with sexual offenders: The insensitivity of recidivism studies to treatment effects. *Journal of Research and Treatment, 9,* 111–128.

Barbaree, H.E. (1991). Denial and minimization among sex offenders: Assessment and treatment outcome. *Forum on Corrections Research, 3,* 300–333.

Barbaree, H.E., Langton, C.M., & Peacock, E.J. (2006). The factor structure of static actuarial items: Its relation to prediction. *Sexual Abuse: A Journal of Research and Treatment, 18,* 207–226.

Barbaree, H.E., Seto, M.C., Langton, C.M., & Peacock, E.J. (2001). Evaluating the predictive accuracy of six risk assessment instruments for adult sex offenders. *Criminal Justice and Behavior, 28,* 490–521.

Barbaree, H.E., Seto, M.C., Serin, R., Amos, N., & Preston, D. (1994). Comparisons between sexual and nonsexual rapist subtypes: Sexual arousal to rape, offense precursors, and offense characteristics. *Criminal Justice and Behavior, 21,* 95–114.

Barkley, R.A. (1991). Attention deficit hyperactivity disorder. *Psychiatric Annals, 21,* 725–733.

Barkley, R.A. (1997). Attention-deficit/hyperactivity disorder. In E.J. Mash & L.G. Terdal (Eds.), *Assessment of childhood disorders* (pp. 71–129). New York, NY: Guilford Press.

Baron, R.A., & Bryne, D. (1991). *Social psychology: Understanding human interaction* (6th ed.). Toronto, ON: Allyn & Bacon.

Barrowcliff, A.L., & Haddock, G. (2006). The relationship between command hallucinations and factors of compliance: A critical review of the literature. *The Journal of Forensic Psychiatry & Psychology, 17,* 266–298.

Barthlow, B.D., Bushman, B.J., & Sestir, M.A. (2006). Chronic violent video game exposure and desensitization to violence: Behavioral and event-related brain potential data. *Journal of Experimental Social Psychology, 42,* 532–539.

Bartol, C.R., & Bartol, A.M. (1994). *Psychology and law* (2nd ed.). Pacific Grove, CA: Brooks/Cole Publishing Company.

Bartol, C.R., & Bartol, A.M. (2004). *Introduction to forensic psychology*. London, England: Sage Publications.

Bartol, C.R., & Bartol, A.M. (2006). History of forensic psychology. In I.B. Weiner & A. Hess (Eds.), *Handbook of forensic psychology* (3rd ed., pp. 3–27). New York, NY: John Wiley & Sons.

Bartosh, D.L., Garby, T., Lewis, D., & Gray, S. (2003). Differences in the predictive validity of actuarial risk assessments inn relation to sex offender type. International *Journal of Offender Therapy and Comparative Criminology, 47*, 422–438.

Beck, A.J., & Marushak, L.M. (2001, June). *Mental health treatment in state prisons, 2000*. (NCJ Publication No. 188215). Bureau of Justice Statistics.

Beck, K.A., & Ogloff, J.R.P. (1995). Child abuse reporting in British Columbia: Psychologists' knowledge of and compliance with the reporting law. *Professional Psychology: Research and Practice, 26*, 245–251.

Beck, N.C., Menditto, A.A., Baldwin, L., Angelone, E., & Maddox, M. (1991). Reduced frequency of aggressive behavior in forensic patients in a social learning program. *Hospital and Community Psychiatry, 42*, 750–752.

Becker, H. S. (1963). *Outsiders: Studies in the sociology of deviance*. London, England: Macmillan.

Behrman, B.W., & Davey, S.L. (2001). Eyewitness identification in actual criminal cases: An archival analysis. *Law and Human Behavior, 25*, 475–491.

Bekerian, D.A., & Dennett, J.L. (1993). The cognitive interview technique: Reviving the issues. *Applied Cognitive Psychology, 7*, 275–298.

Benaquisto, L. (2000). Inattention to sanctions in criminal conduct. In R. Silverman, T. Teevan, & V. Sacco (Eds.), *Crime in Canadian society* (pp. 203–215). Toronto, ON: Harcourt Brace and Co.

Benda, B.B. (2005). Gender differences in life-course theory of recidivism: A survival analysis. *International Journal of Offender Therapy and Comparative Criminology, 49*, 325–342.

Benjamin, L.T., & Crouse, E.M. (2002). The American Psychological Association's response to Brown v. Board of Education: The case of Kenneth B. Clark. *American Psychologist, 57*, 38–50.

Bennell, C., & Canter, D.V. (2002). Linking commercial burglaries by modus operandi: Tests using regression and ROC analysis. *Science & Justice, 42*, 153–164.

Bennell, C., & Jones, N.J. (2005). Between a ROC and a hard place: A method for linking serial burglaries using an offender's modus operandi. *Journal of Investigative Psychology and Offender Profiling, 2*, 23–41.

Bennell, C., Jones, N.J., Taylor, P.J., & Snook, B. (2006). Validities and abilities in criminal profiling: A critique of the studies conducted by Richard Kocsis and his colleagues. *International Journal of Offender Therapy and Comparative Criminology, 50*, 344–360.

Bennell, C., Taylor, P.J., & Snook, B. (2007). Clinical versus actuarial geographic profiling strategies: A review of the research. *Police Practice and Research, 8*, 335–345.

Bennett, L.W., Stoops, C., Call, C., & Flett, H. (2007). Program completion and re-arrest in a batterer intervention system. *Research on Social Work Practice, 17*(1), 42–54.

Ben-Porath, Y.S. (1994). The ethical dilemma of coached malingering research. *Psychological Assessment, 6*, 14–15.

Ben-Shakhar, G., & Elaad, E. (2003). The validity of psychophysiological detection of information with the guilty knowledge test: A meta-analytic review. *Journal of Applied Psychology, 88*, 131–151.

Ben-Shakhar, G., & Furedy, J. J. (1990). *Theories and applications in the detection of deception: Psychophysiological and cultural perspectives*. New York, NY: Springer-Verlag.

Benton, T., Ross, D.F., Bradshaw, E., Thomas, W., & Bradshaw, G. (2006). Eyewitness memory is still not common sense: Comparing jurors, judges, and law enforcement to eyewitness experts. *Applied Cognitive Psychology, 20*, 115–130.

Berk, R.A., Berk, S.F., Loseka, O.R., & Rauma, D. (1983). Mutual combat and other family violence myths. In D. Finkelhor, R.J. Gelles, G.T. Hotaling, & M.A. Straus, (Eds.), *The darker side of families: Current family violence research* (pp. 197–212). Beverly Hills, LA: Sage.

Binet, A. (1900). *La suggestibilité*. Paris, France: Schleicher Freres.

Birch, D.E. (1992). Duty to protect: Update and Canadian perspective. *Canadian Psychology, 33*, 94–101.

Birkenmayer, A., & Roberts, J.V. (1997). Sentencing in adult provincial courts. *Juristat, 17*, 1–15.

Bittner, E. (1967). Police discretion in emergency apprehension of mentally ill persons. *Social Problems, 14*, 278–292.

Bjerregaard, B. (2002). An empirical study of stalking victimization. In K.E. Davis, I.H. Frieze, & R.D. Maiuro (Eds.), *Stalking: Perspectives on victims and perpetrators* (pp. 112–137). New York, NY: Springer Publishing Company, Inc.

Blackman, J. (1990). Emerging images of severely battered women and the criminal justice system. *Behavioral Sciences and the Law, 8*, 121–130.

Blair, R.J.R. (2006). Subcortical brain systems in psychopathy: The amygdala and associated structures. In C.J. Patrick (Ed.), *Handbook of psychopathy* (pp. 296–312). New York, NY: Guilford Press.

Blair, R.J.R. (2006). The emergence of psychopathy: Implications for the neuropsychological approach to developmental disorders. *Cognition, 101*, 414–442.

Blair, R.J.R. (2008). The cognitive neuroscience of psychopathy and implications for judgments of responsibility. *Neuroethics, 1*, 149–157.

Blair, R.J.R., Budhani, S., Colledge, E., & Scott, S. (2005). Deafness to fear in boys with psychopathic tendencies. *Journal of Child Psychology and Psychiatry, 46,* 327–336.

Blanchette, K. (2001). *Classifying female offenders for effective intervention: Application of the case-based principles of risk and need.* Unpublished comprehensive paper, Carleton University, Ottawa, ON.

Blanchette, K.D., & Brown, S. L. (2006). The assessment and treatment of women offenders: An integrative perspective. Chichester, England: John Wiley & Sons.

Bland, R.C., & Orn, H. (1986). Family violence and psychiatric disorder. Canadian Journal of Psychiatry, 31, 129–137.

Bland, R., Orn, H., & Newman, S. (1988). Lifetime prevalence of psychiatric disorders in Edmonton. *Acta Psychiatrica Scandinavica, 77,* 24–32.

Blatchford, C. (2002, April 19). Dooley parents convicted of murder. *National Post.* Retrieved from http://www.canada.com/national/features/dooleytrial/index.html

Blonigen, D.M., Carlson, S.R., Krueger, R.F., & Patrick, C.J. (2003). A twin study of self reported psychopathic personality traits. *Personality and Individual Differences, 35,* 179–197.

Blonigen, D.M., Hicks, B.M., Krueger, R.F., Patrick, C.J. & Iacono, W.G. (2005). Psychopathic personality traits: Heritability and genetic overlap with internalizing and externalizing psychopathology. *Psychological Medicine, 35,* 637–648.

Bloom, H., & Schneider, R.D. (2007). *Mental health courts: Decriminalizing the mentally ill.* Toronto, ON: Irwin Law.

Blumstein, A., & Cohen, J. (1987). Characterizing criminal careers. *Science, 237,* 985–991.

Boccaccini, M.T., Murrie, D.C., & Duncan, S.A. (2006). Screening for malingering in a criminal-forensic sample with the Personality Assessment Inventory. *Psychological Assessment, 18,* 415–423.

Boccaccini, M.T., Murrie, D.C., Caperton, J.D., & Hawes, S.W. (2009). Field validity of the Static-99 and MnSORT-R among sex offenders evaluated for civil commitment as sexually violent predators. *Psychology, Public Policy, and Law, 15,*278–314.

Bohner, G., Siebler, F., Sturm, S., Effler, D., Litters, M., Reinhard, M., & Rutz, S. (1998). Rape myth acceptance and accessibility of the gender category. *Group Processes and Intergroup Relations, 1,* 67–79.

Bohus, M., Haaf, B., Stiglmayr, C., Pohl, U., Boehme, R., & Linehan, M.M. (2000). Evaluation of behavioral therapy for borderline personality disorder: A prospective study. *Behavior Research & Therapy, 38,* 875–887.

Bonazzoli, M.J. (1998). Jury selection and bias: Debunking invidious stereotypes through science. *Quinnipiac Law Review, 18,* 247–305.

Bond, C.F., & DePaulo, B.M. (2006). Accuracy of deception judgments. *Personality and Social Psychology Review, 10,* 214–234.

Bond, C.F., & DePaulo, B.M. (2008). Individual differences in judging deception: Accuracy and bias. *Psychological Bulletin, 134,* 477–492.

Bonnie, R.J., & Grisso, T. (2000). Adjudicative competence and youthful offenders. In T. Grisso & R.G. Schwartz (Eds.), *Youth on trial: A developmental perspective on juvenile justice* (pp. 73–103). Chicago, IL: University of Chicago Press.

Bonta, J. (2002). Offender risk assessment: Guidelines for selection and use. *Criminal Justice and Behavior, 29,* 355–379.

Bonta, J., Pang, B., & Wallace-Capretta, S. (1995). Predictors of recidivism among incarcerated female offenders. *Prison Journal, 75,* 277–294.

Bonta, J.L., Harman, W.G., Hann, R.G., & Cormier, R.B. (1996). The prediction of recidivism among federally sentenced offenders: A re-validation of the SIR scale. *Canadian Journal of Criminology, 38,* 61–79.

Bonta, J.L., Law, M., & Hanson, R.K. (1998). The prediction of criminal and violent recidivism among mentally disordered offenders: A meta-analysis. *Psychological Bulletin, 123,* 123–142.

Boothby, J. & Clements, C.B. (2000). A national survey of correctional psychologists. *Criminal Justice and Behavior, 27,* 715–731.

Borduin, C.M., Henggeler, S.W., Blaske, D.M., & Stein, R. (1990). Multisystemic treatment of adolescent sexual offenders. *International Journal of Offender Therapy and Comparative Criminology, 34,* 105–113.

Borum, R. (1996). Improving the clinical practice of violence risk assessment: Technology, guidelines and training. *American Psychologist, 51,* 945–956.

Borum, R., Otto, R., & Golding, S. (1993). Improving clinical judgment and decision making in forensic evaluation. *Journal of Psychiatry and Law, 21,* 35–76.

Bowen, E., & Gilchrist, E. (2006). Predicting dropout of court-mandated treatment in a British sample of domestic violence offenders. *Psychology, Crime and Law, 12,* 573–587.

Bowker, L. (1993). A battered woman's problems are social, not psychological. In R. Gelles & D. Loseke (Eds.), *Current controversies on family violence* (pp. 154–165). Newbury Park, CA: Sage.

Bowlby, J. (1944). Forty-four juvenile thieves. *International Journal of Psychoanalysis, 25,* 1–57.

Boyd, C. (2003, July 17). Girl's abduction exposes extent of internet luring. *The Globe and Mail.*Retrieved from http://www.globeandmail.com.

Bradfield, A., & McQuiston, D. (2004). When does evidence of eyewitness confidence inflation affect judgments in a criminal trial? *Law and Human Behavior, 28,*369–387.

Bradfield, A.L., Wells, G.L., & Olson, E.A. (2002). The damaging effect of confirming feedback on the relation between eyewitness certainty and identification accuracy. *Journal of Applied Psychology, 87,* 112–120.

Bradford, J.M., & Pawlak, A. (1993). Effects of cyproterone acetate on sexual arousal patterns of pedophiles. *Archives of Sexual Behavior, 22,* 629–641.

Brainerd C.J., & Reyna, V.F. (2004). Fuzzy-trace theory and memory development. *Developmental Review, 24,* 396–439.

Brainerd, C., & Reyna, V. (1996). Mere testing creates false memories in children. *Developmental Psychology, 32,* 467–476.

Brame, B., Nagin, D.S., & Tremblay, R.E. (2001). Developmental trajectories of physical aggression from school entry to late adolescence. *Journal of Child Psychology and Psychiatry, 42,* 503–512.

Brennan, S., & Taylor-Butts, A. (2008). *Sexual assaults in Canada: 2004 and 2007.* Ottawa, ON: Canadian Centre for Justice Statistics.

Breslin, N.A. (1992). Treatment of schizophrenia: Current practice and future promise. *Hospital and Community Psychiatry, 43,* 877–885.

Brewer, N., Potter, R., Fisher, R.P., Bond, N., & Luszcz (1999). Beliefs and data on the relationship between consistency and accuracy of eyewitness testimony. *Applied Cognitive Psychology, 13,* 297–313.

Brewster, A.L., Nelson, J.P., & Hymel, K.P. (1998). Victim, perpetrator, family, and incident characteristics of 32 infant maltreatment deaths in the United States Air Force. *Child Abuse and Neglect, 22,* 91–101.

Brigham, J.C. (1999). What is forensic psychology, anyway? *Law and Human Behavior, 23,* 273–298.

British Columbia Ministry of Attorney General. (2004). *Policy on the criminal justice system response to violence against women and children: Violence against women in relationships policy.* Victoria, BC: Author.

Brodsky, S. (1991). *Testifying in court: Guidelines and maxims for the expert witness.* Washington, DC: American Psychological Association.

Brodsky, S. (1999). *The expert witness: More maxims and guidelines for testifying in court.* Washington, DC: American Psychological Association.

Brooks, N. (1983). *Police guidelines: Pretrial identification procedures.* Ottawa, ON: Law Reform Commission.

Brooks-Gordon, B., Bilby, C., & Wells, H. (2006). A systematic review of psychological interventions for sexual offenders I: Randomised control trials. *Journal of Forensic Psychiatry and Psychology, 17,* 442–466.

Brown, D., & Pipe, M-E. (2003). Variations on a technique: Enhancing children's recall using narrative elaboration training. *Applied Cognitive Psychology, 17,* 377–399.

Brown, D., Scheflin, A.W., & Hammond, D.C. (1998). *Memory, trauma treatment, and the law.* New York, NY: Norton.

Brown, G.R. (2004). Gender as a factor in the response of the law-enforcement systems to violence against partners. *Sexuality and Culture, 9,* 1–87.

Brown, J.M., & Campbell, E.A. (1994). *Stress and policing: Sources and strategies.* New York, NY: John Wiley & Sons.

Brown, S.L., & Forth, A.E. (1997). Psychopathy and sexual assault: Static risk factors, emotional precursors, and rapist subtypes. *Journal of Consulting and Clinical Psychology, 65,* 848–857.

Browne, A. (1987). *When battered women kill.* New York, NY: Free Press.

Browne, A., & Finkelhor, D. (1986). Impact of child sexual abuse: A review of the research. *Psychological Bulletin, 99,* 66–77.

Browne, A., Miller, B., & Maguin, E. (1999). Prevalence and severity of lifetime physical and sexual victimization among incarcerated women. *International Journal and Psychiatry, 22,* 301–322.

Bruce, V., Henderson, Z., Newman, C., & Burton, A.M. (2001). Matching identities of familiar and unfamiliar faces caught on CCTV images. *Journal of Experimental Psychology: Applied, 7,* 207–218.

Bruck, M., & Ceci, S.J. (1999). The suggestibility of children's memory. *Annual Review of Psychology, 50,* 419–439.

Brzozowski, J., Taylor-Butts, A., & Johnson, S. (2006). Victimization and offending among the Aboriginal population in Canada. *Juristat, 26.*

Buck, S.M., Warren, A.R., Betman, S., & Brigham, J.C. (2002). Age differences in Criteria-Based Content Analysis scores in typical child sexual abuse interviews. *Journal of Applied Developmental Psychology, 23,* 267–283.

Bull, R., & Clifford, B.R. (1984). Earwitness voice recognition accuracy. In G. Wells, & E. Loftus (Eds.), *Eyewitness testimony, psychological perspectives* (pp. 92–123). Cambridge, England: Cambridge University Press.

Bumby, K.M. & Hansen, D.J. (1997). Intimacy deficits, fear of intimacy, and loneliness among sexual offenders. *Criminal Justice and Behavior, 24,* 315–331.

Burgess, A.W., & Holmstrom, L.L. (1974). Rape trauma syndrome. *American Journal of Psychiatry, 131,* 981–986.

Burke, R.J. (1993). Work–family stress, conflict, coping, and burnout in police officers. *Stress Medicine, 9,* 171–180.

Burt, M.R. (1980). Cultural myths and supports for rape. *Journal of Personality and Social Psychology, 38,* 217–230.

Bushman, B.J., & Anderson, C.A. (2001). Media violence and the American public: Scientific facts versus media misinformation. *American Psychologist, 56,* 477–489.

Butcher, J.N., Dahlstrom, W.G., Graham, J.R., Tellegen, A., & Kaemmer, B. (1989). *MMPI-2: Manual for administration and scoring.* Minneapolis, MN: University of Minnesota Press.

Butler, C. (2009). *The use of force model and its application to operational law enforcement—Where have we been and where are we going?* Retrieved from Canadian Association for Civilian Oversight of Law Enforcement website: http://www.cacole.ca/resource%20library/conferences/2009%20Conference/Chris%20Butler.pdf

Butler, C., & Hall, C. (2008). *Public police interaction and its relation to use of force by police and resulting injuries to subjects and officers*. Retrieved from International Council of Police Representative Associations website: http://www.icpra.org/home/reading_2/Calgary_Police_Service_Study_Police_Public_Interaction_and_Use_of_Force.pdf

Cadoret, R.J., & Cain, C. (1980). Sex differences in predictors of antisocial behavior in adoptees. *Archives of General Psychiatry, 37*, 1171–1175.

Caldwell, M.F., McCormick, D.J., Umstead, D., & Van Rybroek, G.J. (2007). Evidence of treatment progress and therapeutic outcomes among adolescents with psychopathic features. *Criminal Justice and Behavior, 34*, 573–587.

Caldwell, M.F., Skeem, J., Salekin, R. & Van Rybroek, G. (2006). Treatment response of adolescent offenders with psychopathy-like features. *Criminal Justice and Behavior, 33, 5*, 571–596.

Caldwell, R.M., Silverman, J., Lefforge, N., & Silver, N.C. (2004). Adjudicated Mexican American adolescents: The effects of familial emotional support on self-esteem, emotional well-being, and delinquency. *The American Journal of Family Therapy, 32*, 55–69.

Campbell, C. (1976). Portrait of a mass killer. *Psychology Today, 9*, 110–119.

Campbell, C., Mackenzie, D., & Robinson, J. (1987). Female offenders: Criminal behaviour and gender-role identity. *Psychological Reports, 60*, 867–873.

Campbell, D. (2004, April 24). Sportscaster's killer wants release from custody. *Ottawa Citizen*, pp. E1–E2.

Campbell, J.C. (1986). Nursing assessment for risk of homicide with battering women. *Advances in Nursing Science, 8*, 36–51.

Campbell, J.C., Webster, D., & Koziol-McLain, J. (2003). Risk factors for femicide in abusive relationships: Results from a multisite case control study. *American Journal of Public Health, 93*, 1089–1097.

Campbell, M.A., French, S., & Gendreau, P. (2009). The prediction of violence in adult offenders: A meta-analytic comparison of instruments and methods of assessment. *Criminal Justice and Behavior, 36*, 567–590.

Campbell, M.A., Porter, S., & Santor, D. (2004). Psychopathic traits in adolescent offenders: An evaluation of criminal history, clinical, and psychosocial correlates. *Behavioral Sciences and the Law, 22*, 23–47.

Campion, M.A., Palmer, D.K., & Campion, J.E. (1997). A review of structure in the selection interview. *Personnel Psychology, 50*, 655–702.

Canadian Association of Chiefs of Police. (2007). *The national use of force framework*. Retrieved from http://www.cacp.ca/english/committees/download.asp?id=169.

Canadian Centre for Justice Statistics. (1997, February). Sentencing in adult provincial courts—A study of nine Canadian jurisdictions. *Juristat, 17*.

Canadian Mental Health Association, Citizens for Mental Health (2004). *Backgrounder: Justice and mental health*. Retrieved from http://www.cmha.ca/citizens/justice.pdf

Canadian Psychological Association. (2010). *Provincial and territorial licensing requirements*. Retrieved from http://www.cpa.ca/psychologyincanada/psychologyintheprovincesandterritories/provincialandterritoriallicensingrequirements/

Canter, D.V. & Youngs, D. (2009) Investigative psychology: Offender profiling and the analysis of criminal action. Chichester, England: Wiley.

Canter, D.V. (1994). *Criminal shadows*. London, England: HarperCollins.

Canter, D.V. (2000). Offender profiling and criminal differentiation. *Legal and Criminological Psychology, 5*, 23–46.

Canter, D.V., & Alison, L.J. (Eds.) (1999). *Interviewing and deception*. Aldershot, UK: Ashgate Publishing.

Canter, D.V., & Wentink, N. (2004). An empirical test of Holmes and Holmes's serial murder typology. *Criminal Justice and Behavior, 31*, 489–515.

Canter, D.V., Alison, L.J., Wentink, N., & Alison, E. (2004). The organized/disorganized typology of serial murder: Myth or model? *Psychology, Public Policy, and Law, 10*, 293–320.

Canter, D.V., Coffey, T., Huntley, M., & Missen, C. (2000). Predicting serial killers' home base using a decision support system. *Journal of Quantitative Criminology, 16*, 457–478.

Canter. D.V. (2005). Confusing operational predicaments and cogntiive explorations: Comments on Rossmo and Snook et al. *Applied Cognitive Psychology, 19*, 663–668.

Caprara, G.V., Barbaranelli, C., & Pastorelli, C. (2001). Facing guilt: Role of negative affectivity, need for reparation, and fear of punishment in leading to prosocial behaviour and aggression. *European Journal of Personality, 15*, 219–237.

Carney, M., Buttell, F., & Dutton, D. (2007). Women who perpetrate intimate partner violence: A review of the literature with recommendations for treatment. *Aggression and Violent Behavior, 12*, 108–115.

Carrington, P.J., & Schulenberg, J.L. (2003). Police discretion with young offenders. Ottawa, ON: Department of Justice Canada.

Cassell, P.G. (1998). Protecting the innocent from false confessions and lost confessions—and from Miranda. *Journal of Criminal Law and Criminology, 88*, 497–556.

Cattell, J.M. (1895). Measurements of the accuracy of recollection. *Science, 2*, 761–766.

Cavanaugh, M.M. & Gelles, R.J. (2005). The utility of male domestic violence offender typologies: New directions for research, policy, and practice. *Journal of Interpersonal Violence, 20*, 155–166.

CBC News, (2007, August 28), *Defence arguments in Pickton trial delayed until Sept. 4*. Author. Retrieved from http://www.cbc.ca/canada/british-columbia/story/2007/08/28/bc-pickton.html

CBC News. (2010a). *Pardon me: A guide to federal clemency*. Retrieved from http://www.cbc.ca/canada/story/2010/05/11/f-background-pardons.html

CBC News (2010b). *Williams gets 2 life sentences for 'despicable crimes.'* Retrieved from http://www.cbc.ca/canada/story/2010/10/21/russell-williams-day-four.html

Ceci, S.J., & Bruck, M. (1993). The suggestibility of the child witness: A historical review and synthesis. *Psychological Bulletin, 113,* 403–439.

Cervone, D., & Shoda, Y. (Eds.) (1999). *The coherence of personality: Social-cognitive bases of consistency, variability and organization*. New York, NY: Guilford Press.

Chadee, D. (1996). Race, trial evidence and jury decision making. *Caribbean Journal of Criminology and Social Psychology, 1,* 59–86.

Chaiken, J.M, & Chaiken, M.R. (1983). Crime rates and the active offender. In J.Q. Wilson (Ed.), *Crime and public policy* (pp. 203–229). New Brunswick, OH: Transaction Books.

Chan, K.L., Strauss, M.R., Brownridge, D.A., Tiwari, A., & Leung, W.C. (2008). Prevalence of dating partner violence and suicidal ideation among male and female university students worldwide. *Journal of Midwifery & Women's Health, 53,* 529–537.

Chandler, R.K., Peters, R.H., Field, G., & Juliano-Bult, D. (2004). Challenges in implementing evidence-based treatment practices for co-occurring disorders in the criminal justice system. *Behavioral Science and the Law, 22,* 431–448.

Chapman, L.J., & Chapman, J.P. (1967). Genesis of popular but erroneous psychodiagnostic observations. *Journal of Abnormal Psychology, 74,* 193–204.

Cheung, P.T.K. (1986). Maternal filicide in Hong Kong. *Medicine, Science, and Law, 26,* 185–192.

Chibnall J.T., & Detrick P. (2003). The NEO PI-R, Inwald Personality, Inventory, and MMPI-2 in the prediction of police academy performance: A case of incremental validity. *American Journal of Criminal Justice, 27,* 224–233.

Chiroro, P., & Valentine, T. (1995). An investigation of the contact hypothesis of the own-race bias in face recognition. *Quarterly Journal of Experimental Psychology, 48,* 879–894.

Cirincione, C., Steadman, H.J., Clark-Robbins, P.C., & Monahan, J. (1992). Schizophrenia as a contingent risk factor for criminal violence. *International Journal of Law and Psychiatry, 15,* 347–358.

City of Vancouver Police Department. (2010). *The job*. Retrieved from http://vancouver.ca/police/recruiting/police-officers/policing.html

Clark, S.E. (2005). A re-examination of the effects of biased lineup instructions in eyewitness identification. *Law and Human Behavior, 29,* 575–604.

Clark, S.E., & Wells, G.L. (2008). On the diagnosticity of multiple-witness identifications. *Law and Human Behavior, 32,* 406–422.

Cleckley, H.R. (1976). *The mask of sanity* (5th ed.). St. Louis, MO: Mosby.

Clifford, B.R. (1980). Voice identification by human listeners: On earwitness reliability. *Law and Human Behavior, 4,* 373–394.

CNN. (2006). *No DNA match, no JonBenet charges*. Retrieved from http://www.cnn.com/2006/LAW/08/28/ramsey.arrest/

Cochrane, R.E., Tett, R.P., & Vandecreek, L. (2003). Psychological testing and the selection of police officers: A national survey. *Criminal Justice and Behavior, 30,* 511–537.

Cocozza, J.J., & Steadman, H.J. (1978). Prediction in psychiatry: An example of misplaced confidence in experts. *Social Problems, 25,* 265–276.

Cocozza, J.J., Melick, M.E., & Steadman, H.J. (1978). Trends in violent crime among ex-mental patients. *Criminology: An Interdisciplinary Journal, 16,* 317–334.

Cohen, A.J., Adler, N., Kaplan, S.J., Pelcovitz, D., & Mandel, F.G. (2002). Interactional effects of marital status and physical abuse on adolescent psychopathology. *Child Abuse and Neglect, 26,* 277–288.

Cohn, E.S., Buccolo, D., Pride, M., & Sommers, S.R. (2009). Reducing White juror bias: The role of race salience and racial attitudes. *Journal of Applied Social Psychology, 39,* 1953–1973.

Coid, J., Yang, M., Ullrich, S., Roberts, A., & Hare, R.D. (2009). Prevalence and correlates of psychopathic traits in the household population of Great Britain. *International Journal of Law and Psychiatry, 32,* 65–73.

Coie, J.D., Belding, M., & Underwood, M. (1988). Aggression and peer rejection in childhood. In B.B. Lahey & A.E. Kazdin (Eds.), *Advances in clinical child psychology* (Vol. II, pp. 125–158). New York, NY: Plenum.

Coie, J.D., Lochman, J.E., Terry, R., & Hyman, C. (1992). Predicting early adolescent disorder from childhood aggression and peer rejection. *Journal of Consulting and Clinical Psychology, 60,* 783–792.

Cole, W.G., & Loftus, E.F. (1979). Incorporating new information into memory. *American Journal of Psychology, 92,* 413–425.

Collins, P.I., Johnson, G.F., Choy, A., Davidson, K.T., & Mackay, R.E. (1998). Advances in violent crime analysis and law enforcement: The Canadian violent crime linkage analysis system. *Journal of Government Information, 25,* 277–284.

Commission for Public Complaints Against the RCMP. (2010). *RCMP taser policy a positive development*. Retrieved from http://www.cpc-cpp.gc.ca/nrm/nr/2010/20100504-eng.aspx

Conaway, L.P., & Hansen, D.J. (1989). Social behavior of physically abused and neglected children: A critical review. *Clinical Psychology Review, 9,* 627–652.

Connolly, D.A., & Read, J.D. (2006). Delayed prosecutions of historic child sexual abuse: Analyses of 2064 Canadian criminal complaints. *Law and Human Behavior, 30,* 409–434.

Cook, S., & Wilding, J. (1997). Earwitness testimony 2: Voices, faces, and context. *Applied Cognitive Psychology, 11,* 527–541.

Cooke, D.J., & Michie, C. (2001). Refining the construct of psychopathy: Towards a hierarchical model. *Psychological Assessment, 13,* 171–188.

Copson, G. (1995). *Coals to Newcastle? Part 1: A study of offender profiling.* London, England: Home Office.

Corder, B.F., Ball, B.C., Haizlip, T.M., Rollins, R., & Beaumont, R. (1976). Adolescent parricide: A comparison with other adolescent murder. *American Journal of Psychiatry, 133,* 957–961.

Cornell, D.G., & Hawk, G.L. (1989). Clinical presentation of malingerers diagnosed by experienced forensic psychologists. *Law and Human Behavior, 13,* 374–383.

Cornell, D.G., Benedek, E.P., & Benedek, D.M. (1987). Characteristics of adolescents charged with homicide: Review of 72 cases. *Behavioral Sciences and the Law, 5,* 11–23.

Cornell, D.G., Warren, J., Hawk, G., Stafford, E., Oram, G., & Pine, D. (1996). Psychopathy in instrumental and reactive violent offenders. *Journal of Consulting and Clinical Psychology, 64,* 783–790.

Corrado, R.R., Vincent, G.M., Hart, S.D., & Cohen, I.M. (2004). Predictive validity of the Psychopathy Checklist: Youth Version for general and violent recidivism. *Behavioral Sciences and the Law, 22,* 5–22.

Correctional Service Canada. (1989). *Mental health survey of federally sentenced female offenders at Prison for Women.* Unpublished raw data.

Cortina, J.M., Goldstein, N.B., Payne, S.C., Davison, H.K., & Gilliland, S.W. (2000). The incremental validity of interview scores over and above cognitive ability and conscientiousness scores. *Personnel Psychology, 53,* 325–351.

Cortina, L.M., & Kubiak, S.P. (2006). Gender and posttraumatic stress: Sexual violence as an explanation for women's increased risk. *Journal of Abnormal Psychology, 115,* 753–759.

Cottle, C.C., Lee, R.J., & Heilbrun, K. (2001). The prediction of criminal recidivism in juveniles: A meta-analysis. *Criminal Justice and Behavior, 28,* 367–394.

Cotton, D., & Coleman, T. (2008). *Contemporary policing guidelines for working with the mental health system.* Retrieved from Canadian Association of Chiefs of Police website: https://www.cacp.ca/media/committees/efiles/2/458/Guidelines_for_Police_-_2008_(2).pdf

Coulson, G., Ilacqua, G., Nutbrown, V., Giulekas, D., & Cudjoe, F. (1996). Predictive utility of the LSI for incarcerated female offenders. *Criminal Justice and Behavior, 23,* 427–439.

Coy, E., Speltz, M.L., DeKlyen, M., & Jones, K. (2001). Social-cognitive processes in preschool boys with and without oppositional defiant disorder. *Journal of Abnormal Child Psychology, 29,* 107–119.

Craig, L.A., Browne, K.D., & Stringer, I. (2004). Comparing sex offender risk assessment measures on a UK sample. *International Journal of Offender Therapy and Comparative Criminology, 48,* 7–27.

Craissati, J., & Beech, A. (2005). Risk prediction and failure in a complete urban sample of sex offenders. *The Journal of Forensic Psychiatry & Psychology, 16,* 24–40.

Crawford, M., & Gartner, R. (1992). *Women killing: Intimate femicide in Ontario, 1974–1990.* Women's Directorate, Ministry of Social Services, Toronto, ON.

Crick, N.R., & Dodge, K.A. (1994). A review and reformulation of social information-processing mechanisms in children's social adjustment. *Psychological Bulletin, 115,* 74–101.

Crocker, A. G., Hartford, K., & Heslop, L. (2009). Gender differences in police encounters among persons with and without serious mental illness. *Psychiatric Services, 60,* 86–93.

Cross, J.F., Cross, J., & Daly, J. (1971). Sex, race, age, and beauty as factors in recognition of faces. *Perception and Psychophysics, 10,* 393–396.

Cross, T.P., & Saxe, L. (2001). Polygraph testing and sexual abuse: The lure of the magic lasso. Child Maltreatment: *Journal of the American Professional Society of the Abuse of Children, 6,* 195–206.

Cullen, F., & Gendreau, P. (2000). Assessing correctional rehabilitation: Policy, practice, and prospects. In J. Horney (Ed.), *NIJ Criminal justice 2000: Changes in decision-making and discretion in the criminal justice system* (pp. 109–175). Washington, DC: U.S. National Institute of Justice.

Cummings, E.M., Davies, P.T., & Campbell, S.B. (2000). *Developmental psychopathology and family process: Theory, research, and clinical implications.* New York, NY: The Guilford Press.

Cutler, B.L., & Penrod, S.D. (1989a). Forensically relevant moderators of the relationship between eyewitness identification accuracy and confidence. *Journal of Applied Psychology, 74,* 650–652.

Cutler, B.L., & Penrod, S.D. (1989b). Moderators of the confidence-accuracy relation in face recognition: The role of information processing and base rates. *Applied Cognitive Psychology, 3,* 95–107.

Cutler, B.L., Fisher, R.P., & Chicvara, C.L. (1989). Eyewitness identification from live versus videotaped lineups. *Forensic Reports, 2,* 93–106.

Dahle, K.P. (2006). Strengths and limitations of actuarial prediction of criminal reoffence in a German prison sample: A comparative study of LSI-R, HCR-20 and PCL-R. *International Journal of Law and Psychiatry, 29,* 431–442.

Dalby, J.T. (2006). The case of Daniel McNaughton: Let's get the story straight. *American Journal of Forensic Psychiatry, 27*, 17–32.

Daly, M., & Wilson, M. (1988). Evolutionary social psychology and family homicide. *Science, 242*, 519–524.

Daly, M., & Wilson, M.I. (1982). Homicide and kinship. *American Anthropologist, 84*, 372–378.

Daly, M., & Wilson, M.I. (1996). Violence against stepchildren. Current Directions in Psychological *Science, 5*, 77–81.

Dando, C., Wilcock, R., & Milne, R. (2009). The cognitive interview: The efficacy of a modified mental reinstatement of context procedure for frontline police investigators. *Applied Cognitive Psychology, 23*, 138–147.

Darby, P.J., Allan, W.D., Kashani, J.H., Hartke, K.L., & Reid, J.C. (1998). Analysis of 112 juveniles who committed homicide: Characteristics and a closer look at family abuse. *Journal of Family Violence, 13*, 365–375.

Davies, G., & Thasen, S. (2000). Closed-circuit television: How effective an identification aid. *British Journal of Psychology, 91*, 411–426.

Davies, G., Tarrant, A., & Flin, R. (1989). Close encounters of the witness kind: Children's memory for a simulated health inspection. *British Journal of Psychology, 80*, 415–429.

Davies, G.M., Stevenson-Robb, Y., & Flin, R. (1988). Telling tales out of school: Children's memory for an unexpected event. In M. Gruneberg, P. Morris, & R. Sykes (Eds.), *Practical aspects of memory* (pp. 122–127). Chichester, England: John Wiley & Sons.

Davis, G.E., & Leitenberg, H. (1987). Adolescent sex offenders. *Psychological Bulletin, 101*, 417–427.

Davis, K.E., & Frieze, I.H. (2000). Research on stalking: What do we know and where do we go? *Violence and Victims, 15*, 473–487.

de Vogel, V., & de Ruiter, C. (2006). Structured professional judgment of violence risk in forensic clinical practice: A prospective study into the predictive validity of the Dutch HCR-20. *Psychology, Crime & Law, 12*, 321–336.

de Vogel, V., de Ruiter, C., van Beek, D., & Mead, G. (2004). Predictive validity of the SVR-20 and Static-99 in a Dutch sample of treated sex offenders. *Law and Human Behavior, 28*, 235–251.

Decaire, M. (1999). *A quick A–Z guide to the forensic specialties.* Retrieved from Suite101.com website: http://www.suite101.com/article.cfm/forensic_psychology/19346

DeFronzo, J., Ditta, A., Hannon, L., & Prochnow, J. (2007). Male serial homicide: The influence of cultural and structural variables. *Homicide Studies: An Interdisciplinary & International Journal, 11*, 3–14.

DeGue, S., & DiLillo, D. (2009). Is animal cruelty a "red flag" for family violence? Investigating the co-occurring violence toward children, partners, and pets. *Journal of Interpersonal Violence, 24*, 1036–1056.

Deitz, S.R., Blackwell, K.T., Daley, P.C., & Bentley, B.J. (1982). Measurement of empathy toward rape victims and rapists. *Journal of Personality and Social Psychology, 43*, 372–384.

DeKeseredy, W.S., & Kelley, K. (1993). The incidence and prevalence of woman abuse in Canadian university and college dating relationships. *The Canadian Journal of Sociology, 18*, 57–159.

Dekovic, M. (1999). Risk and protective factors in the development of problem behavior during adolescence. *Journal of Youth and Adolescence, 28*, 667–685.

DeLisi, M. (2006). Zeroing in on early arrest onset: Results from a population of extreme career criminals. *Journal of Criminal Justice, 34*, 17–26.

DeLoache, J.S., & Marzolf, D.P. (1995). The use of dolls to interview young children: Issues of symbolic representation. *Journal of Experimental Child Psychology, 60*, 155–173.

Delveaux, K., Blanchette, K., & Wickett, J. (2005). *Employment, needs, interests, and programming for women offenders* (Research Report No. R-166). Ottawa, ON. Correctional Services of Canada.

DeMateo, D., & Marczyk, G. (2005). Risk factors, protective factors, and the prevention of antisocial behavior among juveniles. In K. Heilbrun, N. Goldstein, & R. Redding (Eds.), *Juvenile delinquency: Prevention, assessment, and intervention* (pp. 19–44). New York, NY: Oxford University Press.

DeMatteo, D., & Edens, J.F. (2006). The role and relevance of the Psychopathy Checklist-Revised in court: A case law survey of U.S. courts (1991–2004). *Psychology, Public Policy, and Law, 12*, 214–241.

DeMatteo, D., Heilbrun, K., & Marczyk, G. (2005). Psychopathy, risk of violence, and protective factors in a noninstitutionalized and noncriminal sample. *International Journal of Forensic Mental Health, 4*, 147–157.

Demo, D.H., & Acock, A.C. (1988). The impact of divorce on children. *Journal of Marriage and the Family, 50*, 619–648.

Dempsey, J.L. & Pozzulo, J.D. (2008). Identification accuracy of eyewitnesses for a multiple perpetrator crime: Examining the simultaneous and elimination lineup procedures. *American Journal of Forensic Psychology, 26*, 67–81.

Denham, S., & Almeida, M. (1987). Children's social problem solving skills, behavioral adjustment, and interventions: A meta-analysis evaluating theory and practice. *Journal of Applied Developmental Psychology, 8*, 391–409.

Department of Justice (1990, May). *Evaluation of the Divorce Act. Phase II: Monitoring and Evaluation.* Retreived from http://dsp-psd.pwgsc.gc.ca/Collection-R/LoPBdP/CIR/963-e.htm

Department of Justice Canada. (2010a). *Youth justice.* Retrieved from http://www.justice.gc.ca/eng/pi/yj-jj/index.html

Department of Justice Canada. (2010b). *Canada's court system.* Retrieved from http://www.justice.gc.ca/eng/dept-min/pub/ccs-ajc/page3.html

Department of Juvenile Justice. (2010). *Restorative justice*. Retrieved from Health & Social Services, State of Alaska website: http://www.hss.state.ak.us/djj/restorative.htm

DePaulo, B.M., & Kirkendol, S.E. (1989). The motivational impairment effect in the communication of deception. In Y.C. Yuille (Ed.), *Credibility assessment* (pp. 51–70). Dordrecht, the Netherlands: Kluwer.

DePaulo, B.M., & Pfeifer, R.L. (1996). On-the-job experience and skill at detecting deception. *Journal of Applied Social Psychology, 16*, 249–267.

DePaulo, B.M., Charlton, L., Cooper, H., Lindsay, J.J., & Muhlenbruck, L. (1997). The accuracy-confidence correlation in the detection of deception. *Personality and Social Psychology Review, 1*, 346–357.

DePaulo, B.M., Kashy, D.A., Kirkendol, S.E., Wyer, M.M., & Epstein, J.A. (1996). Lying in everyday life. *Journal of Personality and Social Psychology, 70*, 979–995.

DePaulo, B.M., Lassiter, G.D., & Stone, J.I. (1982). Attentional determinants of success at detecting deception and truth. *Personality and Social Psychology Bulletin, 8*, 273–279.

DePaulo, B.M., LeMay, C.S., & Epstein, J.A. (1991). Effects of importance of success and expectations for success on effectiveness at deceiving. *Personality and Social Psychology Bulletin, 17*, 14–24.

DePaulo, B.M., Lindsay, J.J., Malone, B.E., Muhlenbruck, L., Charlton, K., & Cooper, H. (2003). Cues to deception. *Psychological Bulletin, 129*, 74–118.

Deregowski, J.B., Ellis, HD., & Shepherd, J.W. (1975). Descriptions of White and Black faces by White and Black subjects. *International Journal of Psychology, 10*, 119–123.

Desmarais, S.L., Nicholls, T.L., Read, D., & Brink, J. (2010). Confidence and accuracy in assessments of short-term risks presented by forensic psychiatric patients. *The Journal of Forensic Psychiatry & Psychology, 21*, 1–22.

Devine, D.J., Clayton, L.D., Dunford, B.B., Seying, R., & Pryce, J. (2001). Jury decision making: 45 years of empirical research on deliberating groups. *Psychology, Public Policy, and Law, 7*, 622–727.

Devlin, K., & Lorden, G. (2007). *The numbers behind numb3rs: Solving crime with mathematics*. New York, NY: Plume.

Diamond, S.S., & Zeisel, H. (1975). Sentencing councils: A study of sentencing disparity and its reduction. *University of Chicago Law Review, 43*, 109–149.

Dickinson, J., Poole, D., & Bruck, M. (2005). Back to the future: A comment on the use of anatomical dolls in forensic interviews. *Journal of Forensic Psychology Practice, 5*, 63–74.

Dobash, R., & Dobash, R.E. (1979). *Violence against women*. New York, NY: Free Press.

Dodge, K.A. (1991). The structure and function of reactive and proactive aggression. In D. Pepler & K. Rubin (Eds.), *The development and treatment of childhood aggression* (pp. 201–218). Hillsdale, NJ: Earlbaum.

Dodge, K.A. (2000). Conduct disorder. In A.J. Sameroff, M. Lewis, & S.M. Miller (Eds.), *Handbook of developmental psychopathology* (2nd ed., pp. 447–463). New York, NY: Kluwer Academic/Plenum Publishers.

Dodge, K.A., Lochman, J.E., Harnish, J.D., Bates, J.E., & Pettit, G.S. (1997). Reactive and proactive aggression in school children and psychiatrically impaired chronically assaultive youth. *Journal of Abnormal Psychology, 106*, 37–51.

Doehring, D.G., & Ross, R.W. (1972). Voice recognition by matching the sample. *Journal of Psycholinguistic Research, 1*, 233–242.

Doerner, W.G. (1997). The utility of the oral interview board in selecting police academy admissions. *Policing: An International Journal of Police Strategies & Management, 20*, 777–785.

Dolan, M., & Khawaja, A. (2004). The HCR-20 and post-discharge outcome in male patients discharged from medium security in the UK. *Aggressive Behavior, 30*, 469–483.

Dolan, M., & Völlm, B. (2009). Antisocial personality disorder and psychopathy in women: A literature review on the reliability and validity of assessment instruments. *International Journal of Law and Psychiatry, 32*, 2–9.

Doob, A.N. (1985). The many realities of crime. In A.N. Doob & E.L. Greenspan (Eds.), *Perspectives in criminal law* (pp. 103–122). Aurora, ON: Canada Law Book.

Doob, A.N., & Roberts, J.A. (1988). Public punitiveness and knowledge of the facts: Some Canadian surveys. In N. Walker and M. Hough (Eds.), *Public attitudes to sentencing: Surveys from five countries* (pp. 111–133). Aldershot: Gower.

Doren, D.M. (2004). Stability of the interpretative risk percentages for the RRASOR and Static-99. *Sexual Abuse: A Journal of Research and Treatment, 16*, 25–36.

Douglas, J. (2010). *John Douglas*. Retrieved from http://www.johndouglasmindhunter.com/bio.php

Douglas, J.E., & Burgess, A.W. (1986). Criminal profiling: A viable investigative tool against violent crime. *FBI Law Enforcement Bulletin, 12*, 9–13.

Douglas, J.E., & Olshaker, M. (1995). *Mindhunter: Inside the FBI's elite serial crime unit*. New York, NY: Charles Scribner's.

Douglas, J.E., Burgess, A.W., Burgess, A.G., & Ressler, R.K. (1992). *Crime classification Manual*. New York, NY: Lexington Books.

Douglas, J.E., Ressler, R.K., Burgess, A.W., & Hartman, C.R. (1986). Criminal profiling from crime scene analysis. *Behavioral Sciences and the Law, 4*, 401–421.

Douglas, K.S., & Ogloff, J.R.P. (2003). The impact of confidence on the accuracy of structured professional and actuarial violence risk judgments in a sample of forensic psychiatric patients. *Law and Human Behavior, 27*, 573–587.

Douglas, K.S., & Skeem, J.L. (2005). Violence risk assessment: Getting specific about being dynamic. *Psychology, Public Policy, and Law, 11*, 347–383.

Douglas, K.S., & Webster, C.D. (1999). Predicting violence in mentally and personality disordered individuals. In R. Roesch, S.D. Hart, & J.P. Ogloff (Eds.), *Psychology and the law: The state of the discipline* (pp. 175–239). New York, NY: Kluwer Academic/Plenum.

Douglas, K.S., Guy, L.S., & Hart, S.D. (2009). Psychosis as a risk factor for violence to others: A meta-analysis. *Psychological Bulletin, 135*, 679–706.

Douglas, K.S., Yeomans, M., & Boer, D.P. (2005). Comparative validity analysis of multiple measures of violence risk inn a sample of criminal offenders. *Criminal Justice and Behavior, 32*, 479–510.

Douglass, A.B., & Steblay, N. (2006). Memory distortion in eyewitnesses: A meta-analysis of the post-identification feedback effect. *Applied Cognitive Psychology, 20*, 859–869.

Dowden, C., & Andrews, D.A. (1999). What works for female offenders: A meta- analytic review. *Crime & Delinquency, 45*, 438–452.

Dowden, C., & Brown, S.L. (2002). The role of substance abuse factors in predicting recidivism: A meta-analysis. *Psychology, Crime, and Law, 8*, 243–264.

Doyle, A. (2003). *Arresting images: Crime and policing in front of the television camera*. Toronto, ON: University of Toronto Press.

Doyle, M., Lewis, G., & Brisbane, M. (2008). Implementing the Short-Term Assessment of Risk and Treatability (START) in a forensic mental health service. *Psychiatric Bulletin, 32*, 406–408.

Dube, S.R., Anda, R.F., Whitfield, C.L., Brown, D.W., Felitti, V.J., Dong, M., & Giles, W. (2005). Long-term consequences of childhood sexual abuse by gender of victim. *American Journal of Preventive Medicine, 28*, 430–438.

Ducro, C., & Pham, T. (2006). Evaluation of the SORAG and the Static-99 on Belgian sex offenders committed to a forensic facility. *Sexual Abuse: A Journal of Research and Treatment, 18*, 15–26.

Dutton, D.G. (1995). *The domestic assault of women: Psychological and criminal justice perspectives*. Vancouver, BC: University of British Columbia Press.

Dutton, D.G., & Corvo, K. (2006). Transforming a flawed policy: A call to revive psychology and science in domestic violence research and practice. *Aggression and Violent Behavior, 11*, 457–483.

Duxbury, L., & Higgins, C. (2003). *Work-life conflict in Canada in the new millennium: A status report*. Ottawa, ON: Health Canada.

Duxbury, L., Higgins, C., & Coghill, D. (2003). *Voices of Canadians: Seeking work-life balance*. Ottawa, ON: Human Resources Development Canada.

Dysart, J.E., Lindsay, R.C.L., & Dupuis, P. (2006). Showups: The critical issue of clothing bias. *Applied Cognitive Psychology, 20*, 1009–1023.

Earlscourt Child and Family Centre (2001a). *SNAP children's group manual*. Toronto, ON: Author.

Earlscourt Child and Family Centre (2001b). *SNAP parent group manual*. Toronto, ON: Author.

Easterbrook, J.A. (1959). The effect of emotion on cue utilization and the organization of behavior. *Psychological Review, 66*, 183–201.

Eastwood, J., & Snook, B. (2010). Comprehending Canadian police cautions: Are the rights to silence and legal counsel understandable? *Behavioral Sciences and the Law, 28*, 366–377.

Ebata, A.T., Peterson, A.C., & Conger, J.J. (1990). The development of psychopathology in adolescence. In J. Rolf, A.S. Masten, D. Cicchetti, K. Nuechterlein, & S. Weintraub (Eds.), *Risk and protective factors in the development of psychopathology* (pp. 308–333). Cambridge, MA: Cambridge University Press.

Ebbesen, E.G., & Konecni, V.J. (1997). Eyewitness memory research: Probative versus prejudicial value. *Expert Evidence, 5*, 2–28.

Eberhardt, J.L., Davies, P.G., Purdie-Vaughns, V.J., & Johnson, S.L. (2006). Looking deathworthy: Perceived stereotypicality of Black defendants predicts capital-sentencing outcomes. *Psychological Science, 17*, 383–386.

Edens, J. F., Poythress, N. G., & Watkins-Clay, M.M. (2007). Detection of malingering in psychiatric unit and general population prison inmates: A comparison of the PAI, SIMS, and SIRS. *Journal of Personality Assessment, 88*, 33–42.

Edens, J.F., Colwell, L.H., Desforges, D.M. & Fernandez, K. (2005). The impact of mental health evidence on support for capital punishment: Are defendants labeled psychopathic considered more deserving of death. *Behavioral Sciences and the Law, 23*, 603–625.

Edens, J.F., Guy, L.S. & Fernandez, K. (2003). Psychopathic traits predict attitudes toward a juvenile capital murderer. *Behavioral Sciences & the Law, 21*, 807–828.

Edens, J.F., Skeem, J.L., & Douglas, K.S. (2006). Incremental validity analyses of the violence risk appraisal guide and the Psychopathy Checklist: Screening Version in a civil psychiatric sample. *Assessment, 13*, 368–374.

Edens, J.F., Skeem, J.L., Cruise, K.R., & Cauffman, E. (2001). Assessment of "Juvenille Psychopathy" and its association with violence: A critical review. *Behavioral Sciences and the Law, 19*, 53–80.

Edwards, G., & Mazzuca, J. (1998). Sixty-one percent support death penalty for murder. *The Gallup Poll, 58*, 68.

Egeth, H.E. (1993). What do we not know about eyewitness identification. *American Psychologist, 48*, 577–580.

Egger, S.A. (1999). Psychological profiling: Past, present and future. *Journal of Contemporary Criminal Justice, 15,* 242–261.

Egger, S.A. (2002). *The serial killers among us: An examination of serial murder and its investigation* (2nd ed.). Upper Saddle River, NJ: Prentice Hall.

Eisendrath, S.J. (1996). Current overview of physical factitious disorders. In M.D. Feldman & S.J. Eisendrath (Eds.), *The spectrum of factitious disorders* (pp. 21–36). Washington DC: American Psychiatric Association.

Ekman, P. (1992). *Telling lies: Clues to deceit in the marketplace, politics, and marriage.* New York, NY: W. W. Norton.

Ekman, P., & Friesen, W.V. (1974). Detecting deception from the body or face. *Journal of Personality and Social Psychology, 29,* 288–298.

Ekman, P., & O'Sullivan, M. (1991). Who can catch a liar? *American Psychologist, 46,* 913–920.

Ekman, P., & O'Sullivan, M., & Frank, M.G. (1999). A few can catch a liar. *Psychological Science, 10,* 263–266.

Elaad, E. (1990). Detection of guilty knowledge in real-life criminal applications. *Journal of Applied Psychology, 75,* 521–529.

Elaad, E., Ginton, A., & Jungman, N. (1992). Detection measures in real-life criminal guilty knowledge tests. *Journal of Applied Psychology, 77,* 757–767.

Elbogen, E.B. (2002). The process of violence risk assessment: A review of descriptive research. *Aggression and Violent Behavior, 7,* 591–604.

Elbogen, E.B., Williams, A.L., Kim, D., Tomkins, A.J., & Scalora, M.J. (2001). Gender and perceptions of dangerousness in civil psychiatric patients. *Legal and Criminological Psychology, 6,* 215–228.

Elkins, I.J., Iacono, W.G., Doyle, A.E., & McGue, M. (1997). Characteristics associated with the persistence of antisocial behavior: Results from recent longitudinal research. *Aggression and Violent Behavior, 2,* 102–124.

Elliott, D. (1994). Serious violent offenders: Onset, development course, and termination. The American Society of Criminology 1993 presidential address. *Criminology, 32,* 1–21.

Ellis, D. (1989). Male abuse of a married or cohabiting female partner: The application of sociological theory to research findings. *Violence and Victims, 4,* 235–255.

Ellis, H.D., Shepherd, J.W., & Davies, G.M. (1980). The deterioration of verbal descriptions of faces over different delay intervals. *Journal of Police Science and Administration, 8,* 101–106.

Ellsworth, P.C., & Mauro, R. (1998). Psychology and law. In D.T. Gilbert, S.T. Fiske, & G. Lindzey. *The handbook of social psychology* (pp. 684–732). New York, NY: Aronson.

Ennis, B. J., & Litwack, T.R. (1974). Psychiatry and the presumption of expertise: Flipping coins in the courtroom. *California Law Review, 62,* 693–752.

Erickson, P.G., & Butters, J.E. (2006). Youth, weapons, and violence in Toronto and Montreal. Report prepared for Public Safety and Emergency Preparedness Canada, Ottawa, ON.

Ewing, C. (1987). *Battered women who kill: Psychological self-defence as legal justification.* Lexington, MA: Lexington Books.

Ewing, C.P., & Aubrey, M. (1987). Battered woman and public opinion: Some realities about the myths. *Journal of Family Violence, 2,* 257–264.

Ex-marine jailed for abduction. (2004, April 2). *This is London.* Retrieved from http://www.thisislondon.com

Ex-marine: No sex with girl. (2003, July 17). *CBS News.* Retrieved from http://www.cbsnews.com

Eysenck, H.J. (1964). *Crime and personality* (1st ed.). London, England: Methuen.

Eysenck, H.J., & Gudjonsson, G.H. (1989). The causes and cures of criminality: Perspectives on individual differences. New York, NY: Plenum Press.

Fabricatore, J.M. (1979). Pre-entry assessment and training: Performance evaluation of police officers. In C.D. Speilberger (Ed.), *Police selection and evaluation: Issues and techniques* (pp. 77–86). New York, NY: Praeger Publishers.

Fagan, A.A. (2005). The relationship between adolescent physical abuse and criminal offending: Support for an enduring and generalized cycle of violence. *Journal of Family Violence, 20,* 279–290.

Fagot, B.I., & Kavanagh, K. (1990). The prediction of antisocial behavior from avoidant attachment classifications. *Child Development, 61,* 864–873.

Faigman, D.L., & Wright, A.J. (1997). The battered woman syndrome in the age of science. *Arizona Law Review, 39,* 67–115.

Falkenberg, S., Gaines, L.K., & Cordner, G. (1991). An examination of the constructs underlying police performance appraisals. *Journal of Criminal Justice, 19,* 151–160.

Faller, K.C. (1987). Women who sexually abuse children. *Violence and Victims, 2,* 263–276.

Farkas, G.M., DeLeon, P.H., & Newman, R. (1997). Sanity examiner certification: An evolving national agenda. *Professional Psychology: Research and Practice, 28,* 73–76.

Farrington, D. (2006). Family background and psychopathy. In C.J. Patrick (Ed.), *Handbook of psychopathy* (pp. 229–250). New York, NY: Guilford Press.

Farrington, D.P. (1989). Early predictors of adolescent aggression and adult violence. *Violence and Victims, 4,* 79–100.

Farrington, D.P. (1989). Early predictors of adolescent aggression and adult violence. *Violence and Victims, 4,* 79–100.

Farrington, D.P. (1991). Psychological contributions to the explanation of offending. *Issues in Criminological and Legal Psychology, 1,* 7–19.

Farrington, D.P. (1995). The development of offending and antisocial behavior from childhood: Key findings from the

Cambridge Study in Delinquent Development. *Journal of Child Psychology and Psychiatry, 36*, 929–964.

Farrington, D.P. (2007). Advancing knowledge about desistance. *Journal of Contemporary Criminal Justice, 23*, 125–134.

Farrington, D.P., & Hawkins, D. (1991). Predicting participation, early onset and later persistence in officially recorded offending. *Criminal Behavior and Mental Health, 1*, 1–33.

Farrington, D.P., (1995). The development of offending and antisocial behavior from childhood: Key findings from the Cambridge Study in Delinquent Development. *Journal of Child Psychology and Psychiatry, 36*, 929–964.

Farwell, L.A., & Donchin, E. (1991). The truth will out: Interrogative polygraphy ("lie detection") with event-related brain potentials. *Psychophysiology, 28*, 531–547.

Fast facts about the Pickton trial. (2007, January 22). *Ottawa Citizen*, p. A3.

Faver, C.A., & Strand, E.B. (2003). To leave or to stay? Battered women's concern for vulnerable pets. *Journal of interpersonal violence, 18*, 1367–1377.

Federoff, J.P., & Federoff, I.C. (1992). Buspirone and paraphilic sexual behavior. *Journal of Offender Rehabilitation, 18*, 89–108.

Feinman, S., & Entwisle, D.R. (1976). Children's ability to recognize other children's faces. *Child Development, 47*, 506–510.

Felner, R.D., & Terre, L. (1987). Child custody dispositions and children's adaptation following divorce. In L.A. Weithorn (Ed.), *Psychology and child custody determinations: Knowledge, roles, and expertise* (pp. 106–153). Lincoln, NE: University of Nebraska Press.

Felson, R.B. & Cares, A.C. (2005). Gender and the seriousness of assaults on intimate partners and other victims. *Journal of Marriage and Family, 67*, 182–195.

Fergusson, D.M., & Horwood, L.J. (1996). The role of adolescent peer affiliations in the continuity between childhood behavioral adjustment and juvenile offending. *Journal of Abnormal Child Psychology, 24*, 205–221.

Fergusson, D.M., & Horwood, L.J. (1998). Early conduct problems and later life opportunities. *Journal of Child Psychology and Psychiatry, 39*, 1097–1108.

Fergusson, D.M., & Lynskey, M.T. (1997). Early reading difficulties and later conduct problems. *Journal of Child Psychology and Psychiatry, 38*, 899–907.

Fergusson, D.M., & Woodward, L.J. (2000). Educational, psychological, and sexual outcomes of girls with conduct problems in early adolescence. *Journal of Child Psychology and Psychiatry, 41*, 779–792.

Fiedler, K., & Walka, I. (1993). Training lie detectors to use nonverbal cues instead of global heuristics. *Human Communication Research, 20*, 199–223.

Finkel, N.J., Burke, J.E., & Chavez, L.J. (2000). Commonsense judgments of infanticide: Murder, manslaughter, madness, or miscellaneous? Psychology, *Public Policy, and Law, 6*, 1113–1137.

Finkelhor, D. (1984). *Child sexual abuse: New theory and research*. New York, NY: Free Press.

Finkelhor, D., & Browne, A. (1985). The traumatic impact of child sexual abuse: A conceptualization. *American Journal of Orthopsychiatry, 55*, 530–541.

Finkelhor, D., Hotaling, G., Lewis, I.A., & Smith, C. (1990). Sexual abuse in a national survey of adult men and women: Prevalence, characteristics, and risk factors. *Child Abuse and Neglect, 14*, 19–28.

Finkelhor, D., Ormrod, R., Turner, H., & Hamby, S. (2005). The victimization of children and youth: A comprehensive, national survey. *Child Maltreatreatment, 10*, 5–25.

Finn, P., & Tomz, J.E. (1996). *Developing a law enforcement stress program for officers and their families*. Washington, DC: U.S. Department of Justice.

Firestone, P., Bradford, J.M., Greenberg, D.M., & Larose, M.R. (1998). Homicidal sex offenders: Psychological, phallometric, and diagnostic features. *Journal of theAmerican Academy of Psychiatry and the Law, 26*, 537–552.

Fisher, B.S., Cullen, F.T., & Turner, M.G. (2002). Being pursued: Stalking victimization in a national study of college women. *Criminology and Public Policy, 1*, 257–308.

Fisher, K., Vidmar, N., & Ellis, R. (1993). The culture of battering and role of mediation in domestic violence cases. *SMU Law Review, 46*, 2117–2173.

Fisher, R.P. (1995) Interviewing victims and witnesses of crime. *Psychology, Public Police, and Law, 1*, 732–764.

Fisher, R.P., & Geiselman, R.E. (1992). *Memory-enhancing techniques for investigative interviewing*. Springfield, IL: Charles C. Thomas.

Fisher, R.P., Geiselman, R.E., & Raymond, D.S. (1987). Critical analysis of police interviewing techniques. *Journal of Police Science and Administration, 15*, 177–185.

Fitzpatrick, K.M. (1997). Fighting among America's youth: A risk and protective factors approach. *Journal of Health and Social Behavior, 38*, 131–148.

Flannery, D.J., & Williams, L. (1999). Effective youth violence prevention. In T. Gullotta & S.J. McElhaney (Eds.), *Violence in homes and communities: Prevention, intervention, and treatment*. Thousand Oaks, CA: Sage.

Flight, J., & Forth, A.E. (2007). Instrumentally violent youth: The roles of psychopathic traits, empathy, and attachment. *Criminal Justice and Behavior, 34*, 721–738.

Flynn, C.P. (2000). Woman's best friend: Pet abuse and the role of companion animals in the lives of battered women. *Violence against women, 6*, 162–177.

Foa, E.B., & Rothbaum, B.O. (1998). *Treating the trauma of rape: Cognitive-behavioral therapy for PTSD*. New York, NY: Guilford.

Fontaine, R.G., Burks, V.S., & Dodge, K.A. (2002). Response decision processes and externalizing behavior problems in adolescents. *Development and Psychopathology, 14,* 107–122.

Forcese, D. (1999). *Policing Canadian society.* Scarborough, ON: Prentice Hall.

Forero, C.G., Gallardo-Pujol, D., Maydeu-Olivares, A., Andres-Pueyo, A. (2009). A longitudinal model for predicting performance of police officers using personality and behavioral data. *Criminal Justice and Behavior, 36,* 591–606.

Forrest, J.A., & Feldman, R.S. (2000). Detecting deception and judge's involvement: Lower task involvement leads to better lie detection. *Personality and Social Psychology Bulletin, 26,* 118–125.

Forth, A.E., Hart, S.D., & Hare, R.D. (1990). Assessment of psychopathy in male young offenders. *Psychological Assessment: A Journal of Consulting and Clinical Psychology, 2,* 342–344.

Forth, A.E., Kosson, D.S., & Hare, R.D. (2003). *The Psychopathy Checklist: Youth Version manual.* Toronto, ON: Multi-Health Systems.

Frank, M.G., & Ekman, P. (1997). The ability to detect deceit generalizes across different types of high-stake lies. *Journal of Personality and Social Psychology, 72,* 1429–1439.

Franke, W.D., Collins, S.A., & Hinz, P.N. (1998). Cardiovascular disease morbidity in an Iowa law enforcement cohort, compared with the general population. *Journal of Occupational and Environmental Medicine, 40,* 441–444.

Frederick, R.I., Crosby, R.D., & Wynkoop, T.F. (2000). Performance curve classification of invalid responding on the Validity Indicator Profile. *Archives of Clinical Neuropsychology, 15,* 281–300.

Fremouw, W.J., Westrup, D., & Pennypacker, J. (1997). Stalking on campus: The prevalence and strategies for coping with stalking. *Journal of Forensic Science, 42,* 666–669.

Frick, P.J. (1994). Family dysfunction and the disruptive disorders: A review of recent empirical findings. In T.H. Ollendick & Prinz, R.J. (Eds.), Advances in clinical child psychology. (Vol. 16) New York, NY: Plenum Press.

Frick, P.J., & Hare, R.D. (2001). *Antisocial Process Screening Device.* Toronto, ON: Multi-Health Systems.

Frick, P.J., Bodin, S.D., & Barry, C.T. (2000). Psychopathic traits and conduct problems in community and clinic-referred samples of children: Further development of the Psychopathy Screening Device. *Psychological Assessment, 12,* 382–393.

Frick, P.J., Kimonis, E.R., Dandreaux, D.M., & Farell, J.M. (2003). The 4 year stability of psychopathic traits in non-referred youth. *Behavioral Sciences and the Law, 21,* 713–736.

Frick, P.J., Lahey, B.B., Loeber, R., Stouthamer, M., Christ, M.A.G., & Hanson, K. (1992). Familial risk factors to oppositional defiant disorder and conduct disorder: parental psychopathology and maternal parenting. *Journal of Consulting and Clinical Psychology, 60,* 49–55.

Friedrich, W.N., & Luecke, W.J. (1988). Young school-age sexually aggressive children. Professional Psychology: *Research and Practice, 19,* 155–164.

Friscolanti, M. (2008, January 9). 'A national embarrassment': Canada's sex offender registry is so flawed that hundreds of molesters and other criminals have gone missing. *Macleans.* Retrieved from http://www.macleans.ca/canada/national/article.jsp?content=20080109_90711_90711&page=1

Fritz, G., Stoll, K., & Wagner, N. (1981). A comparison of males and females who were sexually molested as children. *Journal of Sex and Marital Therapy, 7,* 54–58.

Fukuda, K. (2001). Eye blinks: New indices for the detection of deception. International *Journal of Psychophysiology, 40,* 239–245.

Fulero, S.M., & Everington, C. (2004). Mental retardation, competency to waive Miranda rights, and false confessions. In G.D. Lassiter (Ed.), *Interrogations, confessions, and entrapment* (pp. 163–179). New York, NY: Kluwer Academic.

Furedy, J.J. (1996). The North American Polygraph and psychophysiology: Disinterested, uninterested, and interested perspectives. *International Journal of Psychophysiology, 21,* 97–105.

Fyfe, J.J. (1979). Administrative interventions on police shooting discretion: An empirical examination. *Journal of Criminal Justice, 7,* 309–324.

Gallagher, C.A., Wilson, D.B., Hirschfield, P., Coggeshall, M.B., & MacKenzie, D.L. (1999). A quantitative review of the effects of sex offender treatment of sexual reoffending. *Corrections Management Quarterly, 3,* 19–29.

Gamer, M., Rill, H.-G., Vossel, G., & Gödert, H.W. (2005). Psychophysiological and vocal measures in the detection of guilty knowledge. *International Journal of Psychophysiology, 60,* 76–87.

Ganis, G., Kosslyn, S.M., Stose, S., Thompson, W.L., & Yurgelun-Todd, D.A. (2003). Neural correlates of different types of deception: An fMRI investigation. *Cerebral Cortex, 13,* 830–836.

Gardner, J., Scogin, F., Vipperman, R., & Varela, J.G. (1998). The predictive validity of peer assessment in law enforcement: A 6-year follow-up. *Behavioral Sciences and the Law, 16,* 473–478.

Garmezy, N. (1985). Stress-resistant children: The search for protective factors. In J.E. Stevenson (Ed.), *Recent research in developmental psychopathology* (pp. 213–233). New York, NY: Pergamon.

Garmezy, N. (1991). Resilience in children's adaptation to negative life events and stressed environments. *Pediatric Annuals, 20,* 460–466.

Gauce, A.M., Cormer, J.P., & Schwartz, D. (1987). Long term effects of a systems oriented school prevention program. *American Journal of Orthopsychiatry, 57,* 125–131.

Geberth, V.J. (1990). *Practical homicide investigation: Tactics, procedures, and forensic techniques* (2nd ed.). New York, NY: Elsevier.

Geiselman, R.E., Fisher, R.P., Firstenberg, I., Hutton, L.A., Sullivan, S., Avetissian, I., & Prosk, A. (1984). Enhancement of eyewitness memory: An empirical evaluation of the cognitive interview. *Journal of Police Science and Administration, 12,* 74–80.

Geiselman, R.E., Fisher, R.P., MacKinnon, D.P., & Holland, H.L. (1985). Eyewitness memory enhancement in the police interview: Cognitive retrieval mnemonics versus hypnosis. *Journal of Applied Psychology, 70,* 401–412.

Geller, W., & Scott, M.S. (1992). *Deadly force: What we know.* Washington, DC: Police Executive Forum.

Gellespie, C. (1989). *Justifiable homicide.* Columbus, OH: Ohio State University Press.

Gendreau, P., Goggin, C., & Smith, P. (2002). Is the PCL-R really the "unparalleled" measure of offender risk? A lesson in knowledge cumulation. *Criminal Justice and Behavior, 29,* 397–426.

Gendreau, P., Goggin, C., Cullen, F., & Andrews, D. (2001). The effects of community sanctions and incarceration of recidivism. In L. Motiuk and R. Serin (Eds.), *Compendium 2000 on effective correctional programming* (pp. 18–21). Ottawa, ON: Correctional Service Canada.

Gendreau, P., Little, T., & Goggin, C. (1996). A meta-analysis of the predictors of adult offender recidivism: What works! *Criminology, 34,* 575–607.

Gentry, A.L., Dulmus, C.N., & Theriot, M.T. (2005). Comparing sex offender risk classification using the Static-99 and LSI-R assessment instruments. *Research on Social Work Practice, 15,* 557–563.

Giancola, P.R., Parrott, D.J., & Roth, R.M. (2006). The influence of difficult temperament on alcohol-related aggression: Better accounted for by executive functioning? *Addictive Behaviors, 31,* 2169–2187.

Gibbs, J.L., Ellison, N.B., & Heino, R.D. (2006). Self-presentation in online personals: The role of anticipated future interaction, self-disclosure, and perceived success in Internet dating. *Communication Research, 33,* 1–25.

Glazebrook, S. (2010). Risky business: Predicting recidivism. *Psychiatry, Psychology, & Law, 17,* 88–120.

Glendinning, S. (2010). Behind the blue line: Policing in Vancouver blog. Retrieved from http://www.behindtheblueline.ca/blog/blueline/about/

Glover, A.J.J., Nicholson, D.E., & Hemmati, T. (2002). A comparison of predictors of general and violent recidivism among high-risk federal offenders. *Criminal Justice and Behavior, 29,* 235–249.

Glueck, S., & Glueck, E.T. (1968). *Delinquents and nondelinquents in perspective.* Cambridge, MA: Harvard University Press.

Gobeil, R., & Serin, R. (2009). Preliminary evidence of adaptive decision making techniques used by parole board members. *International Journal of Forensic Mental Health, 8,* 97–104.

Golding, S.L. (1993). *Training manual: Interdisciplinary fitness interview revised.* Department of Psychology, University of Utah.

Golding, S.L., Roesch, R., & Schreiber, J. (1984). Assessment and conceptualization of competency to stand trial. Preliminary data on the interdisciplinary fitness interview. *Law and Human Behavior, 8,* 321–334.

Goldstein, A.G. (1979). Race-related variation of facial features: Anthropometric data I. *Bulletin of the Psychonomic Society, 13,* 187–190.

Gondolf, E., & Fisher, E. (1988). *Battered women as survivors: An alternative to treating learned helplessness.* Lexington, MA: Lexington Books.

Gondolf, E.W. (1985). *Men who batter: An integrated approach for stopping wife abuse.* Holmes Beach, CA: Learning Publications.

Gondolf, E.W. (1988). Who are these guys? Towards a behavioral typology of batterers. *Violence and Victims, 3,* 187–202.

Gonzalez, R., Ellsworth, P., & Pembroke, M. (1993). Response biases in lineups and showups. *Journal of Personality and Social Psychology, 64,* 525–537.

Goodman, G.S., Pyle-Taub, E.P., Jones, D.P.H., England, P., Port, L.K., Rudy, L., & Prado, L. (1992). Testifying in court: The effects on child sexual assault victims. *Monographs of the Society for Research in Child Development, 57* (Serial No. 229), 1–163.

Goodman, G.S., Quas, J.A., Batterman-Faunce, J.M., Riddlesberger, M., & Kuhn, J. (1997). Children's reactions to and memory for a stressful event: Influences of age, anatomical dolls, knowledge, and parental attachment. *Applied Developmental Science, 1,* 54–75.

Gordon, N.J., Mohamed, F.B., Faro, S.H., Platek, S.M., Ahmad, H., & Williams, J.M. (2006). Integrated zone comparison polygraph technique accuracy with scoring algorithms. *Physiology & Behavior, 87,* 251–254.

Gorey, K., & Leslie, D. (1997). The prevalence of child sexual abuse: Integrative review adjustment for potential response and measurement bias. *Child Abuse and Neglect, 21,* 391–398.

Gottfredson, M.R., & Hirschi, T. (1990). *A general theory of crime.* Palo Alto, CA: Stanford University Press.

Gowan, M.A., & Gatewood, R.D. (1995). Personnel selection. In N. Brewer & C. Wilson (Eds.), *Psychology and policing* (pp. 177–204). Hillsdale, NJ: Lawrence Erlbaum Associates.

Graham, J.R. (1999). *MMPI-2: Assessing personality and psychopathology* (3rd ed.). New York, NY: Oxford University Press.

Granger, C. (1996). *The criminal jury trial in Canada*. Toronto, ON: Carswell.

Grann, M., & Wedin, I. (2002). Risk factors for recidivism among spousal assault and spousal homicide offenders. *Psychology, Crime and Law, 8*, 5–23.

Grann, M., Belfrage, H., & Tengström, A. (2000). Actuarial assessment of risk for violence: Predictive validity of the VRAG and the historical part of the HCR-20. *Criminal Justice and Behavior, 27*, 97–114.

Gray, N.S., Snowden, R.J., MacCulloch, S., Phillips, H., Taylor, J., & MacCulloch, M.J. (2004). Relative efficacy of criminological, clinical, and personality measures of future risk of offending in mentally disordered offenders: A comparative study of HCR-20, PCL:SV, and OGRS. *Journal of Consulting and Clinical Psychology, 72*, 523–530.

Greco, C.M., & Cornell, D.G. (1992). Rorschach object relations of adolescents who committed homicide. *Journal of Personality Assessment, 59*, 574–583.

Greene, E., Raitz, A., & Lindblad, H. (1989). Jurors' knowledge of battered women. *Journal of Family Violence, 4*, 105–125.

Gretton, H.M., Hare, R.D., & Catchpole, R.E.H. (2004). Psychopathy and offending from adolescence to adulthood: A 10-year follow-up. *Journal of Consulting and Clinical Psychology, 72*, 636–645.

Greve, K.W., & Bianchini, K.J. (2006). Should the retention trial of the test of memory malingering be optional? *Archives of Clinical Neuropsychology, 21*, 117–119.

Grisso, T. (1981). *Juveniles' waiver of rights: Legal and psychological competence*. New York, NY: Plenum.

Grossman, F.K., Beinashowitz, J., Anderson, L., Sakurai, M., Finnin, L., & Flaherty, M. (1992). Risk and resilience in young adolescents. *Journal of Youth and Adolescence, 21*, 529–550.

Groth, A.N. (1979). *Men who rape: The psychology of the offender*. New York, NY: Plenum.

Groth, A.N., Burgess, A.W. & Holmstrom, L.L. (1977). Rape: Power, anger, and sexuality. *American Journal of Psychiatry, 134*, 1239–1243.

Groth, A.N., Hobson, W.F., & Gary, T.S. (1982). The child molester: Clinical observations. *Journal of Social Work and Human Sexuality, 1*, 129–144.

Grove, W., & Meehl, P (1996). Comparative efficiency of informal (subjective, impressionistic) and formal (mechanical, algorithmic) prediction procedures: The clinical-statistical controversy. *Psychology, Public Policy and Law, 2*, 293–323.

Grove, W.M., Zald, D.H., Lebow, B.S., Snitz, B.E., & Nelson, C. (2000). Clinical versus mechanical prediction: A meta-analysis. *Psychological Assessment, 12*, 19–30.

Guardian, The. (1988, October 28). Police set up unit for stress crisis.

Gudjonsson, G.H. (1992). Interrogation and false confessions: Vulnerability factors. British Journal of Hospital *Medicine, 47*, 597–599.

Gudjonsson, G.H. (2003). *The psychology of interrogations, confessions, and testimony*. Chichester, England: John Wiley & Sons.

Gudjonsson, G.H., & MacKeith, J.A.C. (1988). Retracted confessions: Legal, psychological and psychiatric aspects. *Medicine, Science, and the Law, 28*, 187–194.

Gudjonsson, G.H., & Sigurdsson, J.F. (1994). How frequently do false confessions occur? An empirical study among prison inmates. *Psychology, Crime and Law, 1*, 21–26.

Gudjonsson, G.H., Clare, I.C.H., & Cross, P. (1992). The revised PACE "Notice to Detained Persons": How easy is it to understand? *Journal of the Forensic Science Society, 32*, 289–299.

Gureje, O., Simon, G.E., Ustun, T.B., & Goldberg, D.P. (1997). Somatization in cross-cultural perspective: A world health organization study in primary care. *American Journal of Psychiatry, 154*, 989–995.

Guy, L.S., & Miller, H.A. (2004). Screening for malingered psychopathology in a correctional setting: Utility of the Miller-Forensic Assessment of Symptoms Test (M-FAST). *Criminal Justice and Behavior, 31*, 695–716.

Guy, L.S., Edens, J.F., Anthony, C., & Douglas, K.S. (2005). Does psychopathy predict institutional misconduct among adults? A meta-analytic investigation. *Journal of Consulting and Clinical Psychology, 73*, 1056–1064.

Guy, L.S., Kwartner, P.P., & Miller, H.A. (2006). Investigating the M-FAST: Psychometric properties and utility to detect diagnostic specific malingering. *Behavioral Sciences & the Law, 24*, 687–702.

Gylys, J.A., & McNamara, J.R. (1996). Acceptance of rape myths among prosecuting attorneys. *Psychological Reports, 79*, 15–18.

Hadjistavropoulos, T., & Malloy, D.C. (2000). Making ethical choices: A comprehensive decision-making model for Canadian psychologists. *Canadian Psychology, 41*, 104–115.

Haggard, U., Gumpert, C.H., & Grann, M. (2001). Against all odds: A qualitative follow-up study of high-risk violent offenders who were not reconvicted. *Journal of Interpersonal Violence, 16*, 1048–1065.

Häkkänen-Nyholm, H., & Hare, R.D. (2009). Psychopathy, homicide, and the courts: Working the system. *Criminal Justice and Behavior, 36*, 761–777.

Hall, G.C. (1995). Sexual offender recidivism revisited: A meta-analysis of recent treatment studies. *Journal of Consulting and Clinical Psychology, 63*, 802–809.

Hall, G.C.N., & Hirschman, R. (1992). Sexual aggression against children: A conceptual perspective of etiology. *Criminal Justice and Behavior, 19*, 8–23.

Hallett, B. (2000). *Aboriginal people in Manitoba 2000.* Winnipeg, MB: Human Resources Development Canada.

Halman, L. (2001). The European values study: A third wave (Sourcebook of the 1999/2000 European values study). Tilburg, NL: Tilburg University.

Hamilton Police Service. (2010). Essential competency interview. Retrieved from http://www.hamiltonpolice.on.ca/HPS/Careers/Sworn/EssentialCompetencyInterview.htm

Hamilton, G. & Sutterfield, T. (1997). Comparison of women who have and have not murdered their abusive partners. *Women & Therapy, 20*, 45–55.

Hanes, A. (2004, April 28). Charge dropped for father who forgot child in car for 8 hours. *National Post.* Retrieved from http://www.canada.com.

Haney, C. (1980). Psychology and legal change: On the limits of a factual jurisprudence. *Law and Human Behavior, 17*, 371–398.

Haney, J., & Kristianson, C. M. (1997). An analysis of the impact of prison on women survivors of childhood sexual abuse. *Women & Therapy, 20*, 29–44.

Hannah-Moffat, K., & Maurutto, P. (2003). *Youth risk/need assessment: An overview of issues and practices.* Ottawa, ON: Department of Justice Canada, Research and Statistics Division.

Hans, V.P., & Doob, A.N. (1976). Section 12 of the Canada Evidence Act and the deliberation of simulated juries. *Criminal Law Quarterly, 18*, 235–253.

Hanson, K.R., & Bourgon-Morton, K.E. (2009). The accuracy of fecidivism risk assessments for sexual offenders: A meta-analysis of 118 prediction studies. *Psychological Assessment, 21*, 1–21.

Hanson, K.R., Helmus, L., & Bourgon, G. (2007). The validity of risk assessment measures for intimate partner violence: A meta-analysis. Public Safety Canada, 2007-07. Retrieved from http://www.publicsafety.gc.ca/res/cor/rep/vra_ipv_200707-eng.aspx

Hanson, R.K. (1990). The psychological impact of sexual assault on women and children: A review. *Annuals of Sex Research, 3*, 187–232.

Hanson, R.K. (1997). Invoking sympathy-assessment and treatment of empathy deficits among sexual offenders. In B.K. Schwartz & H.R. Cellini (Eds.), *The sex offender: New insights, treatment innovations and legal developments* (pp. 1.1–1.12). Kingston, NJ: Civic Research Institute.

Hanson, R.K., & Bussière, M.T. (1998). Predicting relapse: A meta-analysis of sexual offender recidivism studies. *Journal of Consulting and Clinical Psychology, 66*, 348–362.

Hanson, R.K., & Harris, A.J. (2000). Where should we intervene? Dynamic predictors of sexual offense recidivism. *Criminal Justice and Behavior, 27*, 6–35.

Hanson, R.K., & Morton-Bourgon, K.E. (2005). The characteristics of persistent sexual offenders: A meta-analysis of recidivism studies. *Journal of Consulting and Clinical Psychology, 73*, 1154–1163.

Hanson, R.K., & Scott, H. (1995). Assessing perspective-taking among sexual offenders, nonsexual criminals, and offenders. *Sexual Abuse: Journal of Research and Treatment, 7*, 259–277.

Hanson, R.K., & Thornton, D. (1999). *Static-99: Improving actuarial risk assessment for sexual offenders.* Ottawa, ON: Department of Solicitor General.

Hanson, R.K., & Thornton, D. (2000). Improving risk assessments for sex offenders: A comparison of three actuarial scales. *Law and Human Behavior, 24*, 119–136.

Hanson, R.K., Broom, I., & Stephenson, M. (2004). Evaluating community sex offender treatment programs: A 12-year follow-up of 724 offenders. *Canadian Journal of Behavioural Sciences, 36*, 85–94.

Hanson, T.L. (1999). Does parental conflict explain why divorce is negatively associated with child welfare. *Social Forces, 77*, 1283–1316.

Hare, R.D. (1991). *The Hare Psychopathy Checklist–Revised.* Toronto, ON: Multi-Health Systems.

Hare, R.D. (1993). *Without conscience: The disturbing world of the psychopaths among us.* New York, NY: Pocket Books.

Hare, R.D. (1998). The Hare PCL-R: Some issues concerning its use and misuse. *Legal and Criminological Psychology, 3*, 99–119.

Hare, R.D. (2003). *The Hare Psychopathy Checklist–Revised.* (2nd ed.). Toronto, ON: Multi-Health Systems.

Hare, R.D. (2007). Forty years aren't enough: Recollections, prognostications, and random musings. In H. Hervé & J.C. Yuille (Eds.), *The psychopath: Theory, research and practice* (pp. 3–28). Mahway, NJ: Erlbaum.

Hare, R.D., & Neumann, C.S. (2008). Psychopathy as a clinical and empirical construct. *Annual Review of Clinical Psychology, 4*, 217–246.

Hare, R.D., Clark, D., Grant, M., & Thornton, D. (2000). Psychopathy and the predictive validity of the PCL-R: An international perspective. *Behavioral Sciences and the Law, 18*, 623–645.

Hare, R.D., Forth, A.E., & Strachan, K.E. (1992). Psychopathy and crime across the life span. In R.D. Peters & R.J. McMahon (Eds.), *Aggression and violence throughout the life span* (pp. 285–300). Thousand Oaks, CA: Sage Publications Inc.

Hare, R.D., Harpur, T.J., Hakstian, A.R., Forth, A.E., Hart, S.D., & Newman, J.P. (1990). The Revised Psychopathy Checklist: Reliability and factor structure. *Psychological Assessment: A Journal of Consulting and Clinical Psychology, 2*, 338–341.

Hargrave, G.E., & Hiatt, D. (1987). Law enforcement selection with the interview, MMPI, and CPI: A study of reliability and validity. *Journal of Police Science and Administration, 15*, 110–117.

Harris, G.T., Rice, M.E., & Camilleri, J.A. (2004). Applying a forensic actuarial assessment (the Violence Risk Appraisal Guide) to nonforensic patients. *Journal of Interpersonal Violence, 19*, 1063–1074.

Harris, G.T., Rice, M.E., & Quinsey, V.L. (1993). Violent recidivism of mentally disordered offenders: The development of a statistical prediction instrument. *Criminal Justice and Behavior, 20*, 315–335.

Harris, R.D., Rice, M.E., & Cormier, C.A. (2002). Prospective replication of the Violence Risk Appraisal Guide in predicting violent recidivism among forensic patients. *Law and Human Behavior, 26*, 377–394.

Harrison, L.A., & Esqueda, C.W. (1999). Myths and stereotypes of actors involved in domestic violence: Implications for domestic violence culpability attributions. *Aggression and Violent Behavior, 4*, 129–138.

Harrison, S. (1993). *Diary of Jack the Ripper: The discovery, the investigation, the debate.* New York, NY: Hyperion.

Hart, S.D. (1998). The role of psychopathy in assessing risk for violence: Conceptual and methodological issues. *Legal and Criminological Psychology, 3*, 121–137.

Hart, S.D., Cox, D.N., & Hare, R.D. (1995). *Manual for the Psychopathy Checklist: Screening Version (PCL: SV).* Toronto, ON: Multi-Health Systems.

Hart, S.D., Kropp, P.R., & Hare, R.D. (1988). Performance of male psychopaths following conditional release from prison. *Journal of Consulting and Clinical Psychology, 56*, 227–232.

Hart, S.D., Michie, C., & Cooke, D. J. (2007). Precision of actuarial risk assessment instruments: Evaluating the 'margins of error' of group v. individual predictions of violence. *British Journal of Psychiatry, 190*, 60–65.

Hartford, K., Heslop, L., & Stitt, L. (2005). Design of an algorithm to identify persons with mental illness in a police administrative database. International Journal of Law and Psychiatry, 28, 1–11.

Hartley, J. (2002). Notetaking in non-academic settings: A review. *Applied Cognitive Psychology, 16*, 559–574.

Hartley, T. A., Burchfiel, C. M., & Violanti, J. M. (2010). Police and stress. Retrieved from Centers for Disease Control and Prevention website: http://www.cdc.gov/niosh/blog/nsb063008_policestress.html

Haslip, S. (2001). Conditional sentencing and the overrepresentation of Aboriginal offenders in penal institutions. *Gonzaga Journal of International Law, 5*, 1–40.

Hastie, R. (Ed.). (1993). Inside the juror: *The psychology of juror decision making.* New York, NY: Cambridge University Press.

Hastie, R., Penrod, S.D., & Pennington, N. (1983). *Inside the jury.* Cambridge, MA: Harvard University Press.

Hathaway, S.R., & McKinley, J.C. (1942). *The Minnesota Multiphasic Personality Inventory Manual.* New York, NY: Psychological Corporation.

Hay Group. (2007). *A national diagnostic on human resources in policing.* Ottawa, ON: Hay Group.

Hazelwood, R.R., & Douglas, J.E. (1980). The lust murderer. *FBI Law Enforcement Bulletin, 50*, 18–22.

Health Canada. (2003). *The consequences of child maltreatment: A reference guide for health practitioners.* Report prepared by Jeff Latimer. Ottawa, ON: Health Canada.

Heinrick, J. (2006, Fall). *Everyone's an expert: The CSI effect's negative impact on juries.* Arizona State University: The Triple Helix.

Hemphill, J. F., Hare, R.D., & Wong, S. (1998). Psychopathy and recidivism: A review. *Legal and Criminological Psychology, 3*, 139–170.

Hemphill, J. F., Templeman, R., Wong, S., & Hare, R.D. (1998). Psychopathy and crime: Recidivism and criminal careers. In D.J. Cooke, A.E. Forth, & R.D. Hare (Eds.) *Psychopathy: Theory, Research and implications for society* (pp. 375–398). Boston, MA: Kluwer.

Hendry, L (2010). About Col. Russell Williams. *The Intelligencer.* Retrieved from http://www.intelligencer.ca/ArticleDisplay.aspx?e=2440501

Henggeler, S.W. (1991). Multidimensional causal models of delinquent behaviour and their implications of treatment. In R. Cohen & A.W. Siegel (Eds.), *Context and development* (pp. 211–231). Hillsdale, NJ: Lawrence Erlbaum Associates.

Henggeler, S.W., & Borduin, C.M. (1990). *Family therapy and beyond: A multisystemic approach to treating the behavior problems of children and adolescents.* Pacific Grove, CA: Brooks/Cole.

Henggeler, S.W., Melton, G.B., & Smith, L.A. (1992). Family preservation using multisystemic therapy: An effective alternative to incarcerating serious juvenile offenders. *Journal of Consulting and Clinical Psychology, 60*, 953–961.

Henggeler, S.W., Schoenwald, S.K. Borduin, C.M., Rowland, M.D., & Cunningham, P.B. (1998). *Multisystemic treatment of antisocial behavior in children and adolescents.* New York, NY: Guilford Press.

Henggeler, S.W., Schoenwald, S.K., & Pickrel, S.A.G. (1995). Multisystemic therapy: Bridging the gap between university and community baed treatment. *Journal of Consulting and Clinical Psychology, 63*, 709–717.

Henggeler, S.W., Schoenwald, S.K., & Pickrel, S.A.G. (1995). Multisystemic therapy: Bridging the gap between university and community-based treatment. *Journal of Consulting and Clinical Psychology, 63*, 709–717.

Henggeler, S.W., Schoenwald, S.K., Borduin, C.M., Rowland, M.D., & Cunningham, P.B. (1998). *Multisystemic treatment of antisocial behavior in children and adolescents.* New York, NY: Guilford Press.

Hess, A.K. (1987). Dimensions of forensic psychology. In I.B. Weiner & A.K. Hess (Eds.), *The handbook of forensic psychology* (1st ed.) (pp. 22–49). New York, NY: John Wiley & Sons.

Hess, A.K. (1999). Defining forensic psychology. In A.K. Hess & I.B. Weiner (Eds.), *The handbook of forensic psychology* (2nd ed.) (pp. 24–47). New York, NY: John Wiley & Sons.

Heuer, L., & Penrod, S. (1994). Juror note taking and question asking during trials: A national field experiment. *Law and Human Behavior, 18,* 121–150.

Hickey, E. W. (2006). Serial murderers and their victims. Belmont, CA: Wadsworth.

Hicks, S.J., & Sales, B.D. (2006). *Criminal profiling: Developing an effective science and practice.* Washington, DC: American Psychological Association.

Hildebrand, M., de Ruiter, C., & de Vogel, V. (2004). Psychopathy and sexual deviance in treated rapists: Association with sexual and nonsexual recidivism. *Sexual Abuse: A Journal of Research and Treatment, 16,* 1–24.

Hillbrand, M. (1995). Aggression against self and aggression against others in violent psychiatric patients. *Journal of Consulting and Clinical Psychology, 63,* 668–671.

Hilton, N.Z., & Simmons, J.L. (2001). The influence of actuarial risk assessment in clinical judgments and tribunal decisions about mentally disordered offenders in maximum security. *Law and Human Behavior, 25,* 393–408.

Hilton, N.Z., Carter, A.M., Harris, G.T., & Sharpe, A.J.B. (2008). Does use of nonnumerical terms to describe risk aid violence risk communication? Clinician agreement and decision making. *Journal of Interpersonal Violence, 23,* 171–188.

Hilton, N.Z., Harris, G.T., Rawson, K., & Beach, C.A. (2005). Communicating violence risk information to forensic decision makers. *Criminal Justice and Behavior, 32,* 97–116.

Hinshaw, S.P., Lahey, B.B., & Hart, E.L. (1993). Issues of taxonomy and comorbidity in the development of conduct disorder. *Development and Psychopathology, 5,* 31–49.

Hirschell, D., & Buzawa, E. (2002). Understanding the context of dual arrest with directions for future research. *Violence Against Women, 8,* 1449–1473.

Hirschell, D.J., Hutchison, I.W., & Dean, C.W. (1990). The failure of arrest to deter spouse abuse. *Journal of Research in Crime and Delinquency, 29,* 7–33.

Hirsh, H.R., Northrop, L.C., & Schmidt, F.L. (1986). Validity generalization for law enforcement occupations. *Personnel Psychology, 39,* 399–420.

Ho, T. (1999). Assessment of police officer applicants and testing instruments. *Journal of Offender Rehabilitation, 29,* 1–23.

Hoaken, P.N.S., & Stewart, S.H. (2003). Drugs of abuse and elicitation of human aggressive behavior. *Addictive Behaviors, 28,* 1533–1554.

Hoch, J.S., Hartford, K., Heslop, L., & Stitt, L. (2009). Mental illness and police interactions in a mid-sized Canadian city: What the data do and do not say. *Canadian Journal of Community Mental Health, 28,* 49–66.

Hodgins, S. (1992). Mental disorder, intellectual deficiency and crime: Evidence from a birth cohort. *Archives of General Psychiatry, 49,* 476–483.

Hodgins, S. (Ed.) (1993). The criminality of mentally disordered person. In S. Hodgins (Ed.), *Mental disorder and crime* (pp. 3–21). Newbury Park, CA: Sage.

Hogarth, J. (1971). *Sentencing as a human process.* Toronto, ON: University of Toronto Press.

Hoge, R.D. (1999). *Assessing adolescents in educational, counselling, and other settings.* Mahwah, NJ: Lawrence Erlbaum Associates.

Hoge, R.D., & Andrews, D.A. (1996). *Assessing the youthful offender: Issues and techniques.* New York, NY: Plenum.

Hoge, R.D., Andrews, D.A., & Lescheid, A.W. (1996). An investigation of risk and protective factors in a sample of youthful offenders. *Journal of Child Psychology and Psychiatry and Allied Disciplines, 37,* 419–424.

Hoge, R.D., Andrews, D.A., & Leschied, A.W. (1996). An investigation of risk and protective factors in a sample of youthful offenders. *Journal of Child Psychology and Psychiatry, 37,* 419–424.

Hoge, S., Poythress, N., Bonnie, R., Monahan, J., Eisenberg, M., & Feucht-Haviar, T. (1997). The MacArthur Adjudication Competence Study: Diagnosis, psychopathology, and adjudicative competence-related abilities. *Behavioral Sciences and the Law, 15,* 329–345.

Hoge, S.K., Bonnie, R.J., Poythress, N., & Monahan, J. (1992). Attorney–client decision-making in criminal cases: Client competence and participation as perceived by their attorneys. *Behavioral Sciences and the Law, 10,* 385–394.

Holliday, R.E., & Albon, A. (2004). Minimizing misinformation effects in young children with cognitive interview mnemonics. *Applied Cognitive Psychology, 18,* 263–281.

Hollin, C.R., & Palmer, E.J. (2006). The Level of Service Inventory-Revised profile of English prisoners: Risk and reconviction analysis. *Criminal Justice and Behavior, 33,* 347–366.

Holmes, R.M., & Holmes, S.T. (1998). *Serial murder* (2nd ed.). Thousand Oaks, CA: Sage.

Holmes, R.M., & Holmes, S.T. (2002). *Profiling violent crimes: An investigative tool* (3rd ed.). Thousand Oaks, CA: Sage.

Holsinger, A.M., Lowenkamp, C.T., & Latessa, E.J. (2006). Exploring the validity of the Level of Service Inventory-Revised with Native American offenders. *Journal of Criminal Justice, 34,* 331–337.

Holtfreter, K., Reisig, M. D., & Morash, M. (2004). Poverty, state capital, and recidivism among women offenders. *Criminology and Public Policy, 3,* 185–208.

Holtzworth-Munroe, A., & Stuart, G.L. (1994). Typologies of male batterers: Three subtypes and the differences among them. *Psychological Bulletin, 116,* 476–497.

Homant, R.J., & Kennedy, D.B. (1998). Psychological aspects of crime scene profiling: Validity research. *Criminal Justice and Behavior, 25,* 319–343.

Home Office (1998). *Statistics on race and the criminal justice system.* London, England: Home Office.

Honts, C.R., & Raskin, D.C. (1988). A field study of the validity of the directed lie control question. *Journal of Police Science and Administration, 16,* 56–61.

Honts, C.R., & Schweinle, W. (2009). Information gain of psychophysiological detection of deception in forensic and screening settings. *Applied Psychophysiology Biofeedback, 34,* 161–172.

Honts, C.R., Raskin, D.C., & Kircher, J.C. (1994). Mental and physical countermeasures reduce the accuracy of polygraph tests. *Journal of Applied Social Psychology, 79,* 252–259.

Horner, J.J. (2007). *Canadian law and the Canadian legal system.* Toronto, ON: Pearson Canada.

Horowitz, I.A., & Seguin, D.G. (1986). The effects of bifurcation and death qualification on assignment of penalty in capital crimes. *Journal of Applied Social Psychology, 16,* 165–185.

Horselenberg, R., Merckelbach, H., & Josephs, S. (2003). Individual differences and false confessions: A conceptual replication of Kassin and Kiechel (1996). *Psychology, Crime & Law, 9,* 1–8.

Hubbard, K.L., Zapf, P.A., & Ronan, K.A. (2003). Competency restoration: An examination of the differences between defendants predicted restorable and not restorable to competency. *Law and Human Behavior, 27,* 127–139.

Huesmann, L.R., Eron, L.D., Lefkowitz, M.M., & Walder, L.O. (1984). Stability of aggression over time and generations. *Developmental Psychology, 20,* 1120–1134.

Huff, C.R., Rattner, A., & Sagarin, E. (1996). *Convicted but innocent: Wrongful conviction and public policy.* Thousand Oaks, CA: Sage.

Hughes, M., & Grieve, R. (1980). On asking children bizarre questions. *First Language, 1,* 149–160.

Humm, D.G., & Humm, K.A. (1950). Humm-Wadsworth temperament scale appraisals compared with criteria of job success in the Los Angeles Police Department. *The Journal of Psychology, 30,* 63–57.

Hung, K., & Bowles, S. (1995). Public perceptions of crime. *Juristat, 15.*

Hunter, S., & Baron, E. (2006, December). A daunting task for Pickton jury. *Ottawa Citizen,* p. A3.

Hurley, W., & Dunne, M. (1991). Psychological distress and psychiatric morbidity in women prisoners. *Australia and New Zealand Journal of Psychiatry, 25,* 461–470.

Huurre, T., Junkkari, H., & Hillevi, A. (2006). Long-term psychosocial effects of parental divorce. *European Archives of Psychiatry and Clinical Neuroscience, 256,* 256–263.

Iacono, W.G., & Lykken, D.T. (1997). The validity of the lie detector: Two surveys of scientific opinion. *Journal of Applied Psychology, 82,* 426–433.

Iacono, W.G., & Patrick, C. J. (1988). Polygraphy techniques. In R. Rogers (Ed.), *Clinical assessment of malingering and deception* (2nd ed., pp. 252–281). New York, NY: Guilford Press.

Iacono, W.G., & Patrick, C.J. (1999). Polygraph ("lie detector") testing: The state of the art. In A.K. Hess & I.B. Weiner (Eds.), *The handbook of forensic psychology* (2nd ed., pp. 440–473). New York, NY: John Wiley & Sons.

Iacono, W.G., & Patrick, C.J. (2006). Polygraph ("lie detector") testing: Current status and emerging trends. In I.B. Weiner & A. Hess (Eds.), *Handbook of forensic psychology* (3rd ed., pp. 552–588). New York, NY: John Wiley & Sons.

Iacono, W.G., Cerri, A.M., Patrick, C.J., & Fleming, J.A.E. (1992). Use of antianxiety drugs as countermeasures in the detection of guilty knowledge. *Journal of Applied Psychology, 77,* 60–64.

Ilacqua, G.E., Coulson, G.E., Lombardo, D., & Nutbrown, V. (1999). Predictive validity of the Young Offender Level of Service Inventory for criminal recidivism of male and female young offenders. *Psychological Reports, 84,* 1214–1218.

Inbau, F.E., Reid, J.E., Buckley, J.P., & Jayne, B.C. (2004). *Criminal interrogation and confessions*(4th ed.). Boston, MA: Jones and Bartlett.

Inciardi, J.A. (1986). Getting busted for drugs. In G. Beschner & A.S. Friedman (Eds.), *Teen drug use* (pp. 63–83). Lexington, MA: Lexington Books.

Inwald, R.E. (1992). *Inwald personality inventory technical manual* (Rev. ed.). Kew Gardens, NY: Hilson Research.

Inwald, R.E., & Shusman, E.J. (1984). The IPI and MMPI as predictors of academy performance for police recruits. *Journal of Police Science and Administration, 12,* 1–11.

Izzett, R.R., & Leginski, W. (1974). Group discussion and the influence of defendant characteristics in a simulated jury setting. *The Journal of Social Psychology, 93,* 271–279.

Izzo, R.L., & Ross, R.R. (1990). Meta-analysis of rehabilitation programs for juvenile delinquents. *Criminal Justice and Behavior, 17,* 134–142.

Jackiw, L.B., Arbuthnott, K.D., Pfeifer, J.E., Marcon, J.L., & Meissner, C.A. (2008). Examining the cross-race effect in lineup identification using Caucasian and First Nations samples. *Canadian Journal of Behavioral Science, 40,* 52–57.

Jackson, J.L., Sijlbing, R., & Thiecke, M.G. (1996). The role of human memory processes in witness reporting. *Expert Evidence, 5,* 98–105.

Jackson, J.L., van Koppen, P.J., & Herbrink, J. (1993). An expert/novice approach to offender profiling. Paper presented at the First NISCALE Workshop on Criminality and Law Enforcement, Leiden.

Jackson, R.L., Rogers, R., & Sewell, K.W. (2005). Forensic application of the Miller Forensic Assessment of Symptoms Test (MFAST): Screening for feigned disorders in competency to stand trial evaluations. *Law and Human Behavior, 29*, 199–210.

Jacobs, P.A., Brunton, M., Melville, M.M., Brittain, M.M., & McClemonts, W.F. (1965). Aggressive behaviour, mental subnormality, and the XYY male. *Nature, 208*, 351–352.

Jaffe, P., Hastings, E., Reitzel, D., & Austin, G. (1993). The impact of police laying charges. In Z. Hilton (Ed.) *Legal responses to wife assault: Current trends and evaluation* (pp. 62–95). Newbury Park, CA: Sage.

Janoff-Bulman, R. (1979). Characterological versus behavioral self-blame: Inquiries into depression and rape. *Journal of Personality and Social Psychology, 37*, 1798–1809.

Jarey, M.L., & Stewart, M.A. (1985). Psychiatric disorder in the parents of adopted children with aggressive conduct disorder. *Neuropsychobiology, 13*, 7–11.

Jayne, B.C. (1986). The psychological principles of criminal interrogation: An appendix. In F.E. Inbau, J.E. Reid, & J.P. Buckley (Eds.), *Criminal interrogation and confessions* (3rd ed., pp. 327–347). Baltimore, MD: Williams and Williams.

Jenkins, P. (1988). Myth and murder: The serial killer panic of 1983–1985. *Criminal Justice Research Bulletin, 3*, 1–7.

Jessor, R., Turbin, M.S., & Costa, F. (1998). Risk and protection in successful outcomes among disadvantaged adolescents. *Applied Developmental Science, 2*, 194–208.

John Howard Society. (1999). *Sentencing in Canada.* Toronto, ON: John Howard Society.

John Howard Society. (2007). *The death penalty: Any nation's shame.* Retrieved from http://www.johnhoward.on.ca/Library/death/1mar01.htm.

Johnson, H. (1996). *Dangerous domains: Violence against women in Canada.* Scarborough, ON: Nelson.

Johnson, H., & Sacco, V.F. (1995). Researching violence against women: Statistics Canada's national survey. *Canadian Journal of Criminology, 37*, 281–304.

Johnston, J.C. (2000). Aboriginal federal offender surveys: A synopsis. *Forum on Corrections Research, 12*, 25–27.

Jokinen, A., Santilla, P., Ravaja, N., & Puttonen, S. (2006). Salience of guilty knowledge test items affects accuracy in realistic mock crimes. *International Journal of Psychophysiology, 62*, 175–184.

Jolliffe, D., & Farrington, D.P. (2007) *A systematic review of the national and international evidence on the effectiveness of interventions with violent offenders* (Research Series 16/07). Retrieved from Ministry of Justice website: http://www.justice.gov.uk/docs/review-evidence-violent.pdf

Jones, A.B., & Llewellyn, J. (1917). *Malingering.* London, England: Heinemann.

Jones, W.D. (1997). *Murder of justice: New Jersey's greatest shame.* New York, NY: Vantage Press.

Jordan, B.K., Schlenger, W.E., Fairbank, J.A., & Caddell, J.M. (1996). Prevalence of psychiatric disorders among incarcerated women II. Convicted felons entering prison. *Archives of General Psychiatry, 53*, 513–519.

Junginger, J. (1990). Predicting compliance with command hallucinations. *American Journal of Psychiatry, 147*, 245–247.

Kahneman, D., & Tversky, A. (1982). Variants of uncertainty. *Cognition, 11*, 143–157.

Kalmuss, D.S. (1984). The intergenerational transmission of marital aggression. *Journal of Marriage and the Family, 46*, 11–19.

Kalvern, H., & Zeisel, H. (1966). *The American jury.* Boston, MA: Little, Brown.

Kanas, N. & Barr, M.A. (1984). Self-control of psychotic productions in schizophrenics [Letter to the editor]. *Archives of General Psychiatry, 41*, 919–920.

Karl, S. (2009, December 21). On memory: Hypnotically refreshed memory. *National Post.* Retrieved from www.nationalpost.com/story.html?id=2368653

Kask, K., Bull, R., & Davies, G. (2006). Trying to improve young adults' person descriptions. *Psychiatry, Psychology, and Law, 13*, 174–181.

Kassin, S.M. (1997). The psychology of confession evidence. *American Psychologist, 52*, 221–233.

Kassin, S.M. (1998). Eyewitness identification procedures: The fifth rule. *Law and Human Behavior, 22*, 649–653.

Kassin, S.M. (2008). False confessions: Causes, consequences, and implications for reform. *Current Directions in Psychological Science, 17*, 249–253.

Kassin, S.M., & Gudjonsson, G.H. (2004). The psychology of confessions: A review of the literature and issues. *Psychological Science in the Public Interest, 5*, 33–67.

Kassin, S.M., & Kiechel, K.L. (1996). The social psychology of false confessions: Compliance, internalization, and confabulation. *Psychological Science, 7*, 125–128.

Kassin, S.M., & Sommers, S.R. (1997). Inadmissible testimony, instructions to disregard, and the jury: Substantive versus procedural considerations. *Personality and Social Psychology Bulletin, 23*, 1046–1054.

Kassin, S.M., & Sukel, H. (1997). Coerced confessions and the jury: An experimental test of the "harmless error" rule. *Law and Human Behavior, 21*, 27–46.

Kassin, S.M., & Wrightsman, L.S. (1985). Confession evidence. In S.M. Kassin & L.S. Wrightsman (Eds.), *The psychology of evidence and trial procedures* (pp. 67–94). London, England: Sage.

Kassin, S.M., Ellsworth, P., & Smith, V.L. (1989). The "general acceptance" of psychological research on eyewitness testimony. *American Psychologist, 49*, 878–893.

Kassin, S.M., Goldstein, C.C., & Savitsky, K. (2003). Behavioral confirmation in the interrogation room: On the dangers of presuming guilt. *Law and Human Behavior, 27,* 187–203.

Kassin, S.M., Leo, R.A., Meissner, C.A., Richman, K.D., Colwell, L.H., Leach, A-M., & La Fon, D. (2007). Police interviewing and interrogation: A self-report survey of police practices and beliefs. *Law and Human Behavior, 31,* 381–400.

Kassin, S.M., Tubb, V., Hosch, H.M., & Memon, A. (2001). On the "general acceptance" of eyewitness testimony research. *American Psychologist, 56,* 405–416.

Katz, R.S. (2000). Explaining girls' and women's crime and desistance in the context of their victimization experiences: A developmental test of revised strain theory and the life course perspective. *Violence Against Women, 6,* 633–660.

Kaufman, J., & Zigler, E. (1987). Do abused children become abusive parents? *American Journal of Orthopsychiatry, 57,* 186–192.

Kazdin, A.E. (1996). *Conduct disorders in childhood and adolescence* (2nd ed.). Thousand Oaks, CA: Sage.

Kazdin, A.E., Kraemer, H.C., Kessler, R.C., Kupfer, D.J., & Offord, D.R. (1997). Contributions of risk factor research to developmental psychopathology. *Clinical Psychology Review, 17,* 375–406.

Kebbell, M.R., & Wagstaff, G.F. (1998). Hypnotic interviewing: The best way to interview eyewitnesses. *Behavioural Sciences and the Law, 16,* 115–129.

Kendall-Tackett, K.A., Williams, L.M., & Finkelhor, D. (1993). Impact of sexual abuse in children: A review and synthesis of recent empirical studies. *Psychological Bulletin, 113,* 164–180.

Kendell, R.E., Chalmers, J.C., & Platz, C.L. (1987). Epidemiology of puerperal psychoses. *British Journal of Psychiatry, 150,* 662–673.

Keppel, R.D., & Walter, R. (1999). Profiling killers: A revised classification model for understanding sexual murder. *International Journal of Offender Therapy and Comparative Criminology, 43,* 417–437.

Kershner, R. (1996). Adolescent attitudes about rape. *Adolescence, 31,* 29–33.

Kerstholt, J.H., Jansen, N.J.M., Van Amelsvoort, A.G., & Broeders, A.P.A. (2006). Earwitnesses: Effects of accent, retention, and telephone. *Applied Cognitive Psychology, 20,* 187–197.

Kiehl, K.A. (2006). A cognitive neuroscience perspective on psychopathy: Evidence for paralimbic system dysfunction. *Psychiatry Research, 142,* 107–128.

Kilpatrick, D.G., Saunders, B.E., Veronen, L.J., Best, C.L., & Von, J.M. (1987). Criminal victimization: Lifetime prevalence, reporting to police, and psychological impact. *Crime and Delinquency, 33,* 479–489.

Kim, Y.S., Barak, G., & Shelton, D.E. (2009). Examining the CSI-effect in the cases of circumstantial evidence and eyewitness testimony: Multivariate and path analyses. *Journal of Criminal Justice, 37,* 452–460.

Kind, S.S. (1987). Navigational ideas and the Yorkshire ripper investigation. *Journal of Navigation, 40,* 385–393.

King, L., & Snook, B. (2009). Peering inside the Canadian interrogation room: An examination of the Reid model of interrogation, influence tactics, and coercive strategies. *Criminal Justice and Behavior, 36,* 674–694.

Kingsbury, S.J., Lambert, M.T., & Hendrickse, W. (1997). A two-factor model of aggression. *Psychiatry: Interpersonal and Biological Processes, 60,* 224–232.

Kircher, J.C., & Raskin, D.C. (1988). Human vs. computerized lie detection. *Journal of Applied Psychology, 73,* 291–302

Kirkman, C.A. (2005). From soap opera to science: Towards gaining access to the psychopaths who live amongst us. *Psychology and Psychotherapy: Theory, Research and Practice, 78,* 379–396.

Klassen, D., & O'Connor, W.A. (1989). Assessing the risk of violence in released mental patients: A cross-validation study. *Psychological Assessment, 1,* 75–81.

Klassen, D., & O'Connor, W.A. (1994). Demographic and case history variables in risk assessment. In J. Monahan & H.J. Steadman (Eds.), *Violence and mental disorder: Developments in risk assessment* (pp. 229–257). Chicago, IL: University of Chicago Press.

Kleinman, L., & Gordon, M. (1986). An examination of the relationship between police training and academy performance. *Journal of Police Science and Administration, 14,* 293–299.

Kleinmuntz, B., & Szucko, J.J. (1984). Lie detection in ancient and modern times: A call for contemporary scientific study. *American Psychologist, 39,* 766–776.

Knight, R.A, & Guay, J.P. (2006). The role of psychopathy in sexual coercion against women. In C.J. Patrick (Ed.), *Handbook of psychopathy* (pp. 512–532). New York, NY: Guilford.

Knight, R.A. (1999). Validation of a typology for rapists. *Journal of Interpersonal Violence, 14,* 303–330.

Knight, R.A., & Prentky, R.A. (1990). Classifying sexual offenders: The development and corroboration of taxonomic models. In W.L. Marshall & D.R. Laws (Eds.), *Handbook of sexual assault: Issues, theories, and treatment of the offender* (pp. 23–52). New York, NY: Plenum Press.

Knight, R.A., Prentky, R.A., & Cerce, D.D. (1994). The development, reliability, and validity of an inventory for the multidimensional assessment of sex and aggression. *Criminal Justice and Behavior, 21,* 72–94.

Kocsis, R.N. (2003). Criminal psychological profiling: Validities and abilities. *International Journal of Offender Therapy and Comparative Criminology, 47,* 126–144.

Kocsis, R.N. Irwin, H.J., Hayes, A.F., & Nunn, R. (2000). Expertise in psychological profiling: A comparative assessment. *Journal of Interpersonal Violence, 15,* 311–331.

Köehnken, G. (1987). Training police officers to detect deceptive eyewitness statements. Does it work? *Social Behavior, 2,* 1–17.

Köehnken, G. (1995). Interviewing adults. In R. Bull and D. Carson (Eds.), *Handbook of psychology in legal contexts* (pp. 215–233). Toronto, ON: John Wiley & Sons.

Kohnken, G., Milne, R., Memon, A., & Bull, R. (1999). The cognitive interview: A meta-analysis. The cognitive interview: Current research and applications [Special Issue]. *Psychology, Crime & Law, 5,* 3–27.

Konecni, V.J., & Ebbesen, E.B. (1984). The mythology of legal decision making. *International Journal of Law and Psychiatry, 7,* 5–18.

Kong, R., & AuCoin, K. (2008). Female offenders in Canada (Statistics Canada, Catalogue No. 85-022-XIE). *Juristat.*

Koocher, G.P., Goodman, G.S., White, C.S., Friedrich, W.N., Sivan, A.B., & Reynolds, C.R. (1995). Psychological science and the use of anatomically detailed dolls in child sexual-abuse assessments. *Psychological Bulletin, 118,* 199–222.

Koons, B.A., Burrow, J.D., Morash, M., & Bynum, T. (1997). Expert and offender perceptions of program elements linked to successful outcomes for incarcerated women. *Crime & Delinquency, 43,* 512–532.

Koss, M.P. (1993). Detecting the scope of rape: A review of the prevalence research methods. *Journal of Interpersonal Violence, 8,* 198–222.

Kosson, D.S., Cyterski, T.D., Steuerwald, B.L., Neumann, C.S., & Walker-Matthews, S. (2002). Reliability and validity of the Psychopathy Checklist: Youth Version (PCL:YV) in nonincarcerated adolescents males. *Psychological Assessment, 14,* 97–109.

Kozel, F.A., Johnson, K.A., Mu, Q., G35enesko, E.L., Laken, S.J., & George, M.S. (2005). Detecting deception using functional magnetic resonance imaging. *Biological Psychiatry, 58,* 605–613.

Kramer, G.P., Kerr, N.L., & Carroll, J.S. (1990). Pretrial publicity, judicial remedies, and jury bias. *Law and Human Behavior, 14,* 409–438.

Krantz, S.E. (1988). The impact of divorce on children. In S.M. Dornbusch & M.H. Strober (Eds.), *Feminism, children, and the new families* (pp. 249–273). New York, NY: Guilford Press.

Krauss, D.A., Sales, B.D., Becker, J.V., & Figueredo, A.J. (2000). Beyond prediction to explanation in risk assessment research: A comparison of two explanatory theories of criminality and recidivism. *International Journal of Law and Psychiatry, 23,* 91–112.

Kroes, W.H., Margolis, B.L., & Hurrell, J.J. (1974). Job stress in policemen. *Journal of Police Science and Administration, 2,* 145–155.

Kroner, D.G., & Mills, J.F. (2001). The accuracy of five risk appraisal instruments in predicting institutional misconduct and new convictions. *Criminal Justice and Behavior, 28,* 471–489.

Kropp, P.R., & Hart, S.D. (2000). The Spousal Assault Risk Assessment (SARA) Guide: Reliability and validity in adult male offenders. *Law and Human Behavior, 24,* 101–118.

Kropp, P.R., Hart, S., Webster, C., & Eaves, D. (1999). *Manual for the spousal assault risk assessment guide* (3rd ed). Toronto, ON: Multi-Health Systems.

Kropp, R., Hart, S. & Lyon, D. (2002). Risk assessment of stalkers: Some problems and potential solutions. *Criminal Justice and Behavior, 29,* 590–616.

Kumpfer, K.L., & Alvarado, R. (2003). Family-strengthening approaches for the prevention of youth problem behaviors. *American Psychologist, 58,* 457–465.

Kurdek, L.A. (1981). An integrative perspective on children's divorce adjustment. *American Psychologist, 26,* 856–866.

Laboratory of Community Psychiatry, Harvard Medical School. (1973). *Competency to stand trial and mental fitness* (DHEW Pub. No. ADM-77-103). Rockville, MD: Department of Health, Education, and Welfare.

Lahey, B.B., Waldman, I.D., & McBurnett, K. (1989). The development of antisocial behaviour: An integrative causal model. *Journal of Child Psychology and Psychiatry, 40,* 669–682.

Laird, R.D., Jordan, K.Y., Dodge, K.A., Petit, G.S., & Bates, J.E. (2001). Peer rejection in childhood, involvement with antisocial peers in early adolescence and the development of externalizing behavior problems. *Development and Psychopathology, 13,* 337–354.

Laliumière, M., Harris, G., Quinsey, V., & Rice, M. (2005). *The causes of rape: Understanding individual differences in male propensity for sexual aggression.* Washington, DC: American Psychological Association.

Lamb, M., Hershkowitz, I., Orbach, Y., & Esplin, P. (2008). Tell me what happened: Structured investigative interviews of child victims and witnesses. West Sussex, England: John Wiley and Sons.

Lamphear, V.S. (1985). The impact of maltreatment on children's psychosocial adjustment: A review of the research. *Child Abuse and Neglect, 9,* 251–263.

Langevin, R. (1979). The effect of assertiveness training, Provera and sex of therapist in the treatment of genital exhibitionism. *Journal of Behavior Therapy and Experimental Psychiatry, 10,* 275–282.

Langevin, R., Handy, L., Paitich, D., & Russon, A. (1985). A new version of the Clarke Sex History Questionnaire for Males. In R. Langevin (Ed.), *Erotic preference, gender identity, and aggression in men: New research studies* (pp. 287–306). Hillsdale, NJ: Erlbaum.

Langleben, D.D., Loughead, J.W., Bilker, W.B., Ruparel, K., Childress, A.R., Busch, S.I., & Gur, R.C. (2005). Telling truth from lie in individual subjects with fast event-related fMRI. *Human Brain Mapping, 26,* 262–272.

Langleben, D.D., Schroeder, L., Maldjian, J.A., Gur, R.C., McDonald, S., Ragland, J.D., . . . Childress, A.R. (2002). Brain activity during simulated deception: An event-related functional magnetic resonance study. *Neuroimage, 15,* 727–732.

Langström, N. (2004). Accuracy of actuarial procedures for assessment of sexual offender recidivism risk may vary across ethnicity. *Sexual Abuse: A Journal of Research and Treatment, 16,* 107–120.

LaPrairie, C. (1992). Aboriginal crime and justice: Explaining the present, exploring the future. *Canadian Journal of Criminology, 34,* 281–298.

LaPrairie, C. (1996). *Examining Aboriginal corrections.* Ottawa, ON: Solicitor General of Canada, Corrections Branch.

Laroche, D. (2005). Aspects of the context and consequences of domestic violence: Situational couple violence and intimate terrorism in Canada in 1999. Quebec City, QC: Government of Quebec.

Larson, J.A. (1921). Modification of the Marston deception test. *Journal of the American Institute of Criminal Law and Criminology, 12,* 391–399.

Larsson, A.S., & Lamb, M.E. (2009). Making the most of information-gathering interviews with children. *Infant and Child Development, 18,* 1–16.

Larsson, H., Andershed, H. & Lichtenstein, P. (2006). A genetic factor explains most of the variation in the psychopathic personality. *Journal of Abnormal Psychology, 115,* 221–230.

Latimer, J., & Lawrence, A. (2006). *The Review Board systems in Canada: An overview of results from the mentally disordered accused data collection study.* Research and Statistics Division, Department of Justice, Ottawa, ON.

Laub, J.H., Nagin, D.S., & Sampson, R.J. (1998). Trajectories of change in criminal offending: Good marriages and the desistance process. *American Sociological Review, 63,* 225–238.

Law Courts Education Society of B.C. (2009). *Gladue and Aboriginal sentencing.* Retrieved from http://www.justiceeducation.ca/research/aboriginal-sentencing/gladue-sentencing

Leach, A.-M., Talwar, V., Lee, K., Bala, N., & Lindsay, R.C.L. (2004). "Intuitive" lie detection of children's deception by law enforcement officials and university students. *Law and Human Behavior, 28,* 661–685.

Leadbeater, B.J., Kuperminc, G.P., Blatt, S.J., & Hertzog, C. (1999). A multivariate model of gender differences in adolescents' internalizing and externalizing problems. *Developmental Psychology, 35,* 1268–1282.

Leblanc, M. (1993). Late adolescent deceleration of criminal activity and development of self- and social control. *Studies on Crime and Crime Prevention, 2,* 51–68.

Lee, M.Y., Uken, A., & Sebold, J. (2007). Role of self-determined goals in predicting recidivism in domestic violence offenders. *Research on Social Work Practice, 17,* 30–41.

Lees-Haley, P.R. (1997). MMPI-2 base rates for 492 personal injury plaintiffs: Implications and challenges for forensic assessment. *Journal of Clinical Psychology, 53,* 745–755.

Leichtman, M.D., & Ceci, S.J. (1995). The effects of stereotypes and suggestions on preschoolers' reports. *Developmental Psychology, 31,* 568–578.

Leippe, M.R. (1995). The case for expert testimony about eyewitness memory. *Psychology, Public Policy, and Law, 1,* 909–959.

Leistico, A.R., Salekin, R.T., DeCoster, J., & Rogers, R. (2008). A large-scale meta-analysis relating the Hare measures of psychopathy to antisocial conduct. *Law and Human Behavior, 32,* 28–45.

Lemmon, J.H. (2006). The effects of maltreatment recurrence and child welfare services on dimensions of delinquency. *Criminal Justice Review, 31,* 5–32.

Leo, R.A. (1992). From coercion to deception: The changing nature of police interrogation in America. *Crime, Law and Social Change, 18,* 35–39.

Leo, R.A. (1996). Inside the interrogation room. *Journal of Criminal Law and Criminology, 86,* 266–303.

Leo, R.A. (1996a). Miranda's revenge: Police interrogation as a confidence game. *Law and Society Review, 30,* 259–288.

Leo, R.A. (1996b). Inside the interrogation room. *The Journal of Criminal Law and Criminology, 86,* 266–303.

Leo, R.A., & Ofshe, R.J. (1998). The consequences of false confessions: Deprivations of liberty and miscarriages of justice in the age of psychological interrogation. *The Journal of Criminal Law and Criminology, 88,* 429–496.

Leschied, A.W., & Cunningham, A. (2002). *Seeking effective interventions for serious young offenders: Interim results of a four-year randomized study of multisystemic therapy in Ontario, Canada.* London, ON: Centre for Children and Families in the Justice System.

Leshied, A., & Cunningham, A. (February, 2002). Seeking effective interventions for serious young offenders: Interim results of a four-year randomized study of multisystemic therapy in Ontario, Canada. Centre for Children & Families in the Justice System, London.

Levenson, M.R., Kiehl, K.A., & Fitzpatrick, C.M. (1995). Assessing psychopathic attributes in a noninstitutionalized population. *Journal of Personality and Social Psychology, 68,* 151–158.

Levett, L.M., & Kovera, M.B. (2009). Psychological mediators of the effects of opposing expert testimony on juror decisions. *Psychology, Public Policy, and Law, 15,* 124–148.

Levine, N. (2007). CrimeStat: A spatial statistics program for the analysis of crime incident locations. Washington, DC: National Institute of Justice.

Lidz, C.W., Mulvey, E.P., & Gardner, W. (1993). The accuracy of predictions of violence to others. *Journal of the American Medical Association, 269,* 1007–1011.

Lieberman, J.D., & Sales, B.D. (1997). What social science teaches us about the jury instruction process. *Psychology, Public Policy, and Law, 3,* 589–644.

Lightfoot, L.O., & Barbaree, H.E. (1993). The relationship between substance use and abuse and sexual offending in adolescents. In H.E. Barbaree & W.L. Marshall (Eds.), *Juvenile sex offender* (pp. 203–224). New York, NY: Guilford Press.

Lilienfeld, S.O. & Andrews, B.P. (1996). Development and preliminary validation of a self-report measure of psychopathic personality traits in noncriminal populations. *Journal of Personality Assessment, 66,* 488–524.

Lilienfeld, S.O., Gershon, J., Duke, M., Marino, L., de Waal, F.B.M. (1999). A preliminary investigation of the construct of psychopathic personality (psychopathy) in chimpanzees (Pan troglodytes). *Journal of Comparative Psychology, 113,* 365–375.

Lindberg, M., Chapman, M.T., Samsock, D., Thomas, S.W., & Lindberg, A. (2003). Comparisons of three different investigative interview techniques with young children. *The Journal of Genetic Psychology, 164,* 5–28.

Lindsay, D.S. (1994). Memory source monitoring and eyewitness testimony. In D.F. Ross, J.D. Read, & M.P. Toglia (Eds.), *Adult eyewitness testimony: Current trends and development* (pp. 27–55). New York, NY: Cambridge University Press.

Lindsay, D.S., & Read, J.D. (1995). "Memory work" and recovered memories of childhood sexual abuse: Scientific evidence and public, professional, and personal issues. *Psychology, Public Policy, and Law, 1,* 846–909.

Lindsay, P.S. (1977). Fitness to stand trial in Canada: An overview in light of the recommendations of the law reform commission of Canada. *Criminal Law Quarterly, 19,* 303–348.

Lindsay, R.C.L., & Wells, G.L. (1985). Improving eyewitness identification from lineups: Simultaneous versus sequential lineup presentations. *Journal of Applied Psychology, 70,* 556–564.

Lindsay, R.C.L., Lea, J.A., & Fulford, J.A. (1991). Sequential lineup presentation: Technique matters. *Journal of Applied Psychology, 76,* 741–745.

Lindsay, R.C.L., Mansour, J.K., Beaudry, J.L., Leach, A., & Bertrand, M.I. (2009). Sequential lineup presentation: Patterns and policy. *Legal and Criminological Psychology, 14,* 13–24.

Lindsay, R.C.L., Martin, R., & Webber, L. (1994). Default values in eyewitness descriptions: A problem for the match-to-description lineup foil selection strategy. *Law and Human Behavior, 18,* 527–541.

Lindsay, R.C.L., Wallbridge, H., & Drennan, D. (1987). Do clothes make the man? An exploration of the effect of lineup attire on eyewitness identification accuracy. *Canadian Journal of Behavioural Science, 19,* 463–478.

Linehan, M.M., Schmidt, H., Dimeff, L.A., Craft, J.C., Kanter, J., & Comtois, K.A. (1999). Dialectical behavior therapy for patients with borderline personality disorder and drug-dependence. *American Journal of Addictions, 8,* 279–292.

Link, B.G., & Steuve, A. (1994). Psychotic symptoms and the violent/illegal behavior of mental patients compared to community controls. In J. Monahan & H. J. Steadman (Eds.), *Violence and mental disorder: Developments in risk assessment* (137–159). Chicago, IL: University of Chicago Press.

Lipsey, M.W. (1992). Juvenile delinquency treatment: A meta-analytic inquiry into the variablilty of effects. In T.D. Cook, H. Cooper, D.S. Corday, H. Hartmann, L.V. Hedges, R.J. Light, . . . F. Mosteller (Eds.), *Meta-analysis for explanation* (pp. 83–127). New York, NY: Sage.

Lipsey, M.W., & Derzon, J.H. (1998). Predictors of violent or serious delinquency in adolescence and early adulthood: A synthesis of longitudinal research. In R. Loeber & D.P. Farrington (Eds.), *Serious and violent juvenile offenders: Risk factors and successful interventions* (pp. 86–105). Thousand Oaks, CA: Sage Publications.

Lipsitt, P.D., Lelos, D., & McGarry, L. (1971). Competency to stand trial: A screening instrument. *American Journal of Psychiatry, 128,* 104–109.

Lisak, D., & Roth, S. (1988). Motivational factors in nonincarcerated sexually aggressive men. *Journal of Personality and Social Psychology, 55,* 795–802.

Lochman, J.E., Whidby, J.M., & Fitzgerald, D.P. (2000). Cognitive-behavioural assessment and treatment with aggressive children. In P. Kendall (Ed.), *Child and adolescent therapy: Cognitive behavioural procedures* (2nd ed., pp. 31–87). New York, NY: Guilford Press.

Loeber, R., & Farrington, D.P. (1998a). Never too early, never too late: Risk factors and successful interventions for serious and violent juvenile offenders. *Studies on Crime and Crime Prevention, 7,* 7–30.

Loeber, R., & Farrington, D.P. (1998b). *Serious and violent juvenile offenders: Risk factors and successful interventions.* Thousand Oaks, CA: Sage.

Loeber, R., & Farrington, D.P. (2000). Young children who commit crime: Epidemiology, developmental origins, risk factors, early interventions, and policy implications. *Development and Psychopathology, 12,* 737–762.

Loeber, R., & Farrington, D.P. (Eds.). (2001). *Child delinquents: Development, intervention, and service needs.* Thousand Oaks, CA: Sage.

Loeber, R., Keenan, K., Lahey, B.B., Green, S.M., & Thomas, C. (1993). Evidence for developmentally based diagnoses of Oppositional Defiant Disorder and Conduct Disorder. *Journal of Abnormal Psychology, 100,* 379–390.

Loftus, E., & Palmer, J.C. (1974). Reconstructions of automobile destruction: An example of the interaction between language and memory. *Journal of Verbal Learning and Verbal Behavior, 12,* 585–589.

Loftus, E.F. (1975). Leading questions and the eyewitness report. Cognitive Psychology, 7, 560–572.

Loftus, E.F. (1979a). Reactions to blatantly contradictory information. Memory and Cognition, 7, 368–374.

Loftus, E.F. (1979b). The malleability of human memory. American Scientist, 67, 312–320.

Loftus, E.F. (1983). Silence is not golden. American Psychologist, 38, 564–572.

Loftus, E.F., Altman, D., & Geballe, R. (1975). Effects of questioning upon a witness' later recollections. Journal of Police Science and Administration, 3, 162–165.

Loftus, E.G., Miller, D.G., & Burns, H.J. (1978). Semantic integration of verbal information into a visual memory. Journal of Experimental Psychology. Human Learning and Memory, 4, 19–31.

Loh, J. (1994, January 23). Keeping the job from becoming a killer: Counselors fight rising police suicide rate. Fort Worth Star-Telegram, p. A4.

Lombroso, C., & Ferrero, W. (1895). The female offender. London, England: Fisher Unwin.

London Family Court Clinic (1993). Three years after the verdict: A longitudinal study of the social and psychological adjustment of child witnesses referred to the child witness project (FVDS #4887-06-91-026). London, ON: London Family Court Clinic Inc.

Loo, R. (1994). Burnout among Canadian police managers. The International Journal of Organizational Analysis, 2, 406–417.

Looman, J. (2006). Comparison of two risk assessment instruments for sexual offenders. Sexual Abuse: A Journal of Research and Treatment, 18, 193–206.

Loos, M.E., & Alexander, P.C. (1997). Differential effects associated with self-reported histories of abuse and neglect in a college sample. Journal of Interpersonal Violence, 12, 340–360.

Lösel, F. & Schmucker, M. (2005). The effectiveness of treatment for sexual offenders: A comprehensive meta-analysis. Journal of Experimental Criminology, 1, 117–146.

Loucks, A.D., & Zamble, E. (2000). Predictors of criminal behavior and prison misconduct in serious female offenders. Empirical and Applied Criminal Justice Review, 1, 1–47.

Lowenkamp, C.T., Holsinger, A.M., & Latessa, E.J. (2001). Risk/need assessment, offender classification, and the role of childhood abuse. Criminal Justice and Behavior, 28, 543–563.

Lowry, P.E. (1996). A survey of the assessment center process in the public sector. Public Personnel Management, 25, 307–321.

Luus, C.A.E., & Wells, G.L. (1991). Eyewitness identification and the selection of distractors for lineups. Law and Human Behavior, 15, 43–57.

Luus, C.A.E., & Wells, G.L. (1994). The malleability of eyewitness confidence: Co-witness and perseverance effects. Journal of Applied Psychology, 79, 714–723.

Lykken, D.L. (2006). Psychopathic personality: The scope of the problem. In C.J. Patrick (Ed.), Handbook of psychopathy (pp. 3–13). New York, NY: Guilford Press.

Lykken, D.T. (1960). The validity of the guilty knowledge technique: The effects of faking. Journal of Applied Psychology, 44, 258–262.

Lykken, D.T. (1998). A tremor in the blood. Uses and abuses of the lie detector. New York, NY: Plenum.

Lynam, D.R., Caspi, A., Moffitt, T.E., Loeber, R., & Stouthamer-Loweber, M. (2007). Longitudinal evidence that psychopathy scores in early adolescence predict adult psychopathy. Journal of Abnormal Psychology, 116, 155–165.

Maccoby, E.E., & Mnookin, R.H. (1992). Dividing the child: Social and legal dilemmas of custody. Cambridge, England: Harvard University Press.

MacCoun, R.J., & Kerr, N.L. (1988). Asymmetric influence in mock deliberation: Jurors' bias for leniency. Journal of Personality and Social Psychology, 54, 21–33.

MacDonald, J.M., Manz, P.W., Alpert, G.P., & Dunham, R.G. (2003). Police use of force: Examining the relationship between calls for service and the balance of police force and suspect resistance. Journal of Criminal Justice, 31, 119–127.

MacMillan, H.L. (2000). Child maltreatment: What we know in the year 2000. Canadian Journal of Psychiatry, 45, 702–709.

MacMillan, H.L., Fleming, J.E., Streiner, D.L., Lin, E., Boyle, M.H., Jamieson, E., . . . Beardslee, W.R. (2001). Childhood abuse and lifetime psychopathology in a community sample. American Journal of Psychiatry, 158, 1878–1883.

Malinosky-Rummell, R., & Hansen, D.J. (1993). Long-term consequences of childhood physical abuse. Psychological Bulletin, 114, 68–79.

Malpass, R.S., & Devine, P.G. (1981). Eyewitness identification: Lineup instructions and the absence of the offender. Journal of Applied Psychology, 66, 482–489.

Malpass, R.S., Tredoux, C.G., & McQuiston-Surrett, D. (2009). Response to Lindsay, Mansour, Beaudry, Leach, and Bertrand's Sequential lineup presentation patterns and policy. Legal and Criminological Psychology, 14, 25–30.

Manchak, S.M., Skeem, J.L., Douglas, K.S., & Siranosian, M. (2009). Does gender moderate the predictive utility of the Level of Service Inventory-Revised (LSI-R) for serious violent offenders? Criminal Justice and Behavior, 36, 425–442.

Mann, S., Vrij, A., & Bull, R. (2004). Detecting true lies: Police officers' ability to detect suspects' lies. Journal of Applied Psychology, 89, 137–149.

Manson, A. (2006). Fitness to be sentenced: A historical, comparative and practical review. International Journal of Law and Psychiatry, 29, 262–280.

Manzoni, P., Brochu, S., Fischer, B., & Rehm, J. (2006). Determinants of property crime among illicit opiate users outside of treatment across Canada. *Deviant Behavior, 27,* 351–376.

Marcus, K.D., Lyons Jr., P.M., & Guyton, M.R. (2000). Studying perceptions of juror influence In Vivo: A social relations analysis. *Law and Human Behavior, 24,* 173–186.

Mark, V.H., & Ervin, F.R. (1970). *Violence and the brain.* New York, NY: Harper and Row.

Marques, J.K. (1999). How to answer the questions "Does sexual offender treatment work?" *Journal of Interpersonal Violence, 14,* 437–451.

Marshall, W.L. (1999). Current status of North American assessment and treatment programs for sexual offenders. *Journal of Interpersonal Violence, 14,* 221–239.

Marshall, W.L., & Barbaree, H.E. (1988). An outpatient treatment program for child molesters. *Annals of the New York Academy of Sciences, 528,* 205–214.

Marshall, W.L., & Barbaree, H.E. (1990). An integrated theory of the etiology of sexual offending. In W.L. Marshall & D.R. Laws (Eds.), *Handbook of sexual assault: Issues, theories, and treatment of the offender* (pp. 257–275). New York, NY: Plenum Press.

Marshall, W.L., & Fernandez, Y.M. (2003). Sexual preferences are they useful in the assessment and treatment of sexual offenders? *Aggression and Violent Behavior, 8,* 131–143.

Marshall, W.L., Anderson, D., & Champagne, F. (1997). Self-esteem and its relationship to sexual offending. *Psychology, Crime and Law, 3,* 161–186.

Marshall, W.L., Barbaree, H.E., & Fernandez, Y.M. (1995). Some aspects of social competence in sexual offenders. *Sexual Abuse: Journal of Research and Treatment, 7,* 113–127.

Marshall, W.L., Eccles, A., & Barbaree, H.E. (1991). The treatment of exhibitionists: A focus on sexual deviance versus cognitive and relationship features. *Behavior Research and Therapy, 29,* 129–135.

Martineau, M., & Corey, S. (2008). Investigating the reliability of the violent crime linkage analysis system (ViCLAS) crime report. *Journal of Police and Criminal Psychology, 23,* 51–60.

Martinson, R. (1974). What works? Questions and answers about prison reform. *The Public Interest, 35,* 22–54.

Martlatt, G.A., & Gordon, J.R. (Eds.) (1985). *Relapse prevention: Maintenance strategies in the treatment of addictive behaviors.* New York, NY: Guilford.

Masten, A., & Coatsworth, J. (1998). The development of competence in favourable and unfavourable environments: Lessons from research on successful children. *American Psychologist, 53,* 205–220.

Masten, A.S., Best, K.M., & Garmezy, N. (1990). Resilience and development: Contributions from the study of children who overcome adversity. *Development and Psychopathology, 2,* 425–444.

Maume, M.O., Ousey, G.C., & Beaver, K. (2005). Cutting the grass: A reexamination of the link between marital attachment, delinquent peers and desistance from marijuana use. *Journal of Quantitative Criminology, 21,* 27–53.

McCann, J.T. (1998). A conceptual framework for identifying various types of confessions. *Behavioral Sciences and the Law, 16,* 441–453.

McCloskey, M., & Egeth, H. (1983). Eyewitness identification: What can a psychologist tell a jury? *American Psychologist, 38,* 550–563.

McCloskey, M., & Zaragoza, M. (1985). Misleading post event information and memory for events: Arguments and evidence against memory impairment hypothesis. *Journal of Experimental Psychology: General, 114,* 1–16.

McCormick, C.T. (1972). *Handbook of the law of evidence* (2nd ed.). St. Paul, MN: West.

McCoy, S.P., & Aamodt, M.G. (2010). A comparison of law enforcement divorce rates with those of other occupations. *Journal of Police and Criminal Psychology, 25,* 1–16.

McCraty, R., Tomasino, D., Atkinson, M., & Sundram, J. (1999). *Impact of the HeartMath self-management skills program on physiological and psychological stress in police officers.* Boulder Creek, CA: HeartMath Research Center, Institute of HeartMath.

McCreary, D.R., & Thompson, M.M. (2006). Development of two reliable and valid measures of stressors in policing: The Operational and Organizational Police Stress Questionnaires. *International Journal of Stress Management, 13,* 494–518.

McDaniel, M.A., Whetzel, D.L., Schmidt, F.L., & Maurer, S.D. (1994). The validity of employment interviews: A comprehensive review and meta-analysis. *Journal of Applied Psychology, 79,* 599–616.

McDonagh, D., Taylor, K., & Blanchette, K. (2002). Correctional adaptation of dialectical behaviour therapy (DBT) for federally sentenced women. *Forum on Corrections, 14,* 36–39.

McFarlane, J., Campbell, J.C., & Watson, K. (2002). Intimate partner stalking and femicide: Urgent implications for women's safety. *Behavioral Sciences and the Law, 20,* 51–68.

McFatter, R.M. (1986). Sentencing disparity. *Journal of Applied Social Psychology, 16,* 150–164.

McIntyre, M. (2009, March 5). Victim's family incensed as beheading killer avoids jail time. *National Post.* Retrieved from http://www.nationalpost.com/related/topics/story.html?id=1356797

McKenna, P.F. (2002). *Police powers.* Toronto, ON: Prentice Hall.

McMahon, M. (1999). Battered women and bad science: The limited validity and utility of battered women syndrome. *Psychiatry, Psychology, and Law, 6,* 23–49.

McMahon, R.J. (1994). Diagnosis, assessment, and treatment of externalizing problems in children: The role of longitudinal data. *Journal of Consulting and Clinical Psychology, 62,* 901–917.

McNiel, D.E., & Binder, R.L. (1994). The relationship between acute psychiatric symptoms, diagnosis, and short-term risk of violence. *Hospital and Community Psychiatry, 45,* 133–137.

McNiel, D.E., Sandberg, D.A., & Binder, R.L. (1998). The relationship between confidence and accuracy in clinical assessment of psychiatric patients' potential for violence. *Law and Human Behavior, 22,* 655–669.

McQuinston-Surrett, D., Malpass, R.S., & Tredoux, C.G. (2006). Sequential vs. simultaneous lineups: A review of methods, data, and theory. *Psychology, Public Policy, and Law, 12,* 137–169.

Meadow, R. (1977). Munchausen syndrome by proxy: The hinterland of child abuse. *Lancet, 2,* 343–345.

Meehl, P.E. (1954). *Clinical vs. statistical prediction.* Minneapolis, MN: University of Minnesota Press.

Meissner, C.A., & Brigham, J.C. (2001). Thirty years of investigating the own-race bias in memory for faces: A meta-analytic review. *Psychology, Public Policy, and Law, 7,* 1–35.

Meissner, C.A., & Russano, M.B. (2003). The psychology of interrogations and false confessions: Research and recommendations. *The Canadian Journal of Police and Security Services: Practice, Policy and Management, 1,* 53–64.

Meissner, C.A., Brigham, J.C., & Pfeifer, J.E. (2003). Jury nullification: The influence of judicial instruction on the relationship between attitudes and juridic decision making. *Basic and Applied Social Psychology, 25,* 243–254.

Meissner, D. (2000, March 5). *Reena Virk murder trial set to begin this week. Canadian Press.* Retrieved from Canoe website: http://acmi.canoe.ca/CNEWSLaw0003/13_virk6.html

Melnyk, L., Crossman, A., & Scullin, M. (2006). The suggestibility of children's memory. In M. Toglia, J.D. Read, D. Ross, & R.C.L. Lindsay (Eds.), *The handbook of eyewitness psychology: Vol 1. Memory for events* (pp. 401–427). Mahwah, NJ: Lawrence Erlbaum Associates.

Meloy, J.R. (1997). Predatory violence during mass murder. *Journal of Forensic Sciences, 42,* 326–329.

Melton, G., Petrila, J., Poythress, N.G., & Slobogin, C. (1997). Competency to stand trial. In *Psychological evaluations for the court: A handbook for mental health professionals and lawyers* (2nd ed., pp. 119–155). New York, NY: Guilford Press.

Melton, H.C. (1999). Police response to domestic violence. *Journal of Offender Rehabilitation, 29,* 1–21.

Memon, A., & Bull, R. (1991). The cognitive interview: Its origins, empirical support, evaluation and practical implications. *Journal of Community and Applied Social Psychology, 1,* 291–307.

Memon, A., & Gabbert, G. (2003). Improving the identification accuracy of senior witnesses: Do prelineup questions and sequential testing help? *Journal of Applied Psychology, 88,* 341–347.

Memon, A., Holliday, R., & Hill, C. (2006). Pre-event stereotypes and misinformation effects in young children. *Memory, 14,* 104–114.

Memon, A., Vrij, A., & Bull, R. (2003). *Psychology and law: Truthfulness, accuracy, and credibility.* London, England: Jossey-Bass.

Menard, S., & Huizinga, D. (1989). Age, period, and cohort size effects on self-reported alcohol, marijuana, and polydrug use: Results from the National Youth Survey. *Social Science Research, 18,* 174–194.

Mendleson, R. (2010, January 21). Hip hop helps young offenders. *Macleans.ca.* http://www2.macleans.ca/2010/01/21/hip-hop-helps-young-offenders/

Mental Health, Law, and Policy Institute, Department of Psychology, Simon Fraser University. (2010). *SFU—Mental Health Law and Policy Institute.* Retrieved September 27th, 2010 from http://www.sfu.ca/mhlpi

Merton R.K. (1938). Social structure and anomie. *American Sociological Review, 3,* 672–682.

Messman-Moore, T.L., & Long, P.J. (2003). The role of childhood sexual abuse sequelae in the sexual revictimization of women: An empirical review and theoretical reformulation. *Clinical Psychology Review, 23,* 537–571.

Miethe, T.D., & Drass, K.A. (1999). Exploring the social context of instrumental and expressive homicides: An application of qualitative comparative analysis. *Journal of Quantitative Criminology, 15,* 1–21.

Miller, H.A. (2001). M-FAST: *Miller Forensic Assessment of Symptoms Test and professional manual.* Odessa, FL: Psychological Assessment Resources.

Miller, H.A. (2005). The Miller-Forensic Assessment of Symptoms Test (M-FAST): Test generalizability and utility across race, literacy, and clinical opinion. *Criminal Justice and Behaviour, 32,* 591–611.

Millis, J.B., & Kornblith, P.R. (1992). Fragile beginnings: Identification and treatment of postpartum disorders. *Health and Social Work, 17,* 192–199.

Mills, J.F., & Kroner, D.G. (2006). The effect of base-rate information on the perception of risk for reoffense. *American Journal of Forensic Psychology, 24,* 45–56.

Mills, J.F., Jones, M.N., & Kroner, D.G. (2005). An examination of the generalizability of the LSI-R and VRAG probability bins. *Criminal Justice and Behavior, 32,* 565–585.

Milne, R., & Bull, R. (1999). *Investigative interviewing: Psychology and practice.* Chichester, UK: Wiley.

Mischel, W. (1968). *Personality and assessment.* New York, NY: Lawrence Erlbaum.

Mitchell, K.J., Finkelhor, D., & Wolak, J. (2001). Risk factors for and impact of online sexual solicitation of youth. *Journal of the American Medical Association, 285,* 3011–3014.

Mitchell, K.J., Livosky, M., & Mather, M. (1998). The weapon focus effect revisited: The role of novelty. *Legal and Criminological Psychology, 3,* 287–303.

Mitchell, T.L., Haw, R.M., Pfeifer, J.E., & Meissner, C.A. (2005). Racial bias in mock juror decision-making: A meta-analytic review of defendant treatment. *Law and Human Behavior, 29,* 621–637.

Moffitt, T.E. (1993). Adolescence-limited and life-course persistent antisocial behaviour: A developmental taxonomy. *Psychological Review, 100,* 674–701.

Moffitt, T.E., & Henry, B. (1989). Neurological assessment of executive functions in self-reported delinquents. *Developmental and Psychopathology, 1,* 105–118.

Moffitt, T.E., Caspi, A., Harrington, H., & Milne, B.J. (2002). Males on the life-course persistent and adolescence limited antisocial pathways: Follow-up at age 26 years. *Development and Psychopathology, 14,* 179–207.

Mojtabai, R. (2006). Psychotic-like experiences and interpersonal violence in the general population. *Social Psychiatry and Psychiatric Epidemiology, 41,* 183–190.

Mokros, A., Osterheider, M., Hucker, S.J., & Nitschke, J. (2010). Psychopathy and Sexual Sadism. *Law and Human Behavior.* Retrieved from http://www.springerlink.com/content/121631662p604u2u/fulltext.html

Monahan, J. (1981). *Predicting violent behavior: An assessment of clinical techniques.* Beverly Hills, CA: Sage.

Monahan, J., & Steadman, H.J. (1994). *Violence and mental disorder: Developments in risk assessment.* Chicago, IL: University of Chicago Press.

Monahan, J., Steadman, H.J., Appelbaum, P., Grisso, T., Mulvey, E. P., Roth, L., . . . Silver, E. (2006). Classification of violence risk. *Behavioral Sciences and the Law, 24,* 721–730.

Monahan, J., Steadman, H.J., Appelbaum, P.S., Robbins, P.C., Mulvey, E.P., Silver, E., et al. (2000). Developing a clinically useful actuarial tool for assessing violence risk. *British Journal of Psychiatry, 176,* 312–319.

Monahan, J., Steadman, H.J., Robbins, P.C., Appelbaum, P., Banks, S., Grisso, T., Heilbrun, K., Mulvey, E.P., Roth, L., & Silver, E. (2005). An actuarial model of violence risk assessment for persons with mental disorders. *Psychiatric Services, 56,* 810–815.

Moore, T.E., & Gagnier, K. (2008). "You can talk if you want to": Is the police caution on the 'right to silence' understandable? *Criminal Reports, 51,* 233–249.

Moran, R. (1985). The modern foundation for the insanity defense: The cases of James Hadfield (1800) and Daniel M'Naughten (1843). *Annals of the American Academy of Political and Social Science, 477,* 31–42.

Mossman, D. (1994). Assessing predictions of violence: Being accurate about accuracy. *Journal of Consulting and Clinical Psychology, 62,* 783–792.

Motiuk, L., & Nafekh, M. (2001). Using reintegration potential at intake to better identify safe release candidates. *Forum on Corrections Research, 13,* 11–13.

Motiuk, L.L., & Porporino, F.J. (1991). *The prevalence, nature, and severity of mental health problems among federal male inmates in Canadian penitentiaries* (Research Report No. 24). Ottawa, ON: Correctional Service of Canada.

Motiuk, L.L., & Serin, R.C. (2001). *Compendium 2000 on effective correctional programming.* Ottawa, ON: Correctional Service of Canada.

Mulvey, E. (2005). Risk assessment in juvenile justice policy and practice. In K. Heilbrun, N. Goldstein, & R. Redding (Eds.), *Juvenile delinquency: Prevention, assessment, and intervention* (pp. 209–231). New York, NY: Oxford University Press.

Mulvey, E.P., Arthur, M.W., & Reppucci, N.D. (1993). The prevention and treatment of juvenile delinquency: A review of the research. *Clinical Psychology Review, 13,* 133–167.

Munsterberg, H. (1908). *On the witness stand.* Garden City, New York, NY: Doubleday.

Murphy, J.M. (1976). Psychiatric labelling in cross-cultural perspective: Similar kinds of behaviour appear to be labelled abnormal in diverse cultures. *Science, 191,* 1019–1028.

Murrie, D.C., Boccaccini, M.T., Johnson, J.T., & Janke, C. (2008). Does interrater (dis)agreement on Psychopathy Checklist score in sexually violent predator trials suggest partisan allegiance in forensic evaluations? *Law and Human Behavior, 32,* 352–362.

Murrie, D.C., Boccaccini, M.T., McCoy, W. & Cornell, D.G. (2007). Diagnostic labels in juvenile court: How do descriptions of psychopathy and conduct disorder influence judges? *Journal of Clinical Child and Adolescent Psychology, 36,* 288–291.

Murrie, D.C., Cornell, D.G. & McCoy, W. (2005). Psychopathy, conduct disorder, and stigma: Does diagnostic language affect juvenile probation officer recommendations. *Law and Human Behavior, 29,* 323–342.

Murrie, D.C., Cornell, D.G., Kaplan, S., McConville, D., & Levy-Elkon, A. (2004). Psychopathy scores and violence among juvenile offenders: A multi-measure study. *Behavioral Sciences and the Law, 22,* 49–67.

Nafekh, M. & Motiuk, L. (2002). *The Statistical Information on Recidivism—Revised 1 (SIR-R1) Scale: A psychometric examination* (Research Report R-126). Ottawa, ON: Correctional Service Canada.

Nafekh, M. (2003). Using proxy measures for correctional research [Electronic version]. *Forum on Corrections Research, 15,* 41–43.

Narby, D.J., Cutler, B.L., & Moran, G. (1993). A meta-analysis of the association between authoritarianism and jurors' perceptions of defendant culpability. *Journal of Applied Psychology, 78,* 34–42.

Nathanson, C., Paulhus, D.L., & Williams, K.M. (2006). Predictors of a behavioral measure of scholastic cheating: Personality and competenence but not demographics. *Contemporary Educational Psychology, 31,* 97–122.

National Crime Prevention Council (1995). *Risk or threat to children.* Ottawa, ON: Author.

National Crime Prevention Council (1997). *Preventing crime by investing in families and communities: Promoting positive outcomes in youth twelve- to eighteen-years-old.* Ottawa, ON: Author.

National Crime Prevention Council. (1995). *Risk or threat to children.* Ottawa, ON: National Crime Prevention Council.

National Crime Prevention Council. (1997). *Preventing crime by investing in families and communities: Promoting positive outcomes in youth twelve- to eighteen-years-old.* Ottawa, ON: National Crime Prevention Council.

National Parole Board. (2006). *2005–2006 performance monitoring report.* Ottawa, ON: National Parole Board.

National Parole Board. (2009). *Policy manual.* Retrieved from http://www.npb-cnlc.gc.ca/infocntr/policym/polman-eng.shtml#a420

National Parole Board. (2010a). *History of parole in Canada.* Retrieved from http://www.npb-cnlc.gc.ca/about/hist-eng.shtml

National Parole Board. (2010b). *Mission.* Retrieved from http://www.npb-cnlc.gc.ca/about/miss-eng.shtml

National Parole Board. (2010c). *Parole decision-making: Myths and realities.* Retrieved from http://www.npb-cnlc.gc.ca/infocntr/myths_reality-eng.shtml

National Parole Board. (2010d). *The decision process.* Retrieved from http://www.npb-cnlc.gc.ca/infocntr/parolec/pdec-eng.shtml

National Parole Board. (2010e). *Types of release.* Retrieved from http://www.npb-cnlc.gc.ca/infocntr/factsh/rls-eng.shtml

National Parole Board. (2010f). *Pardons.* Retrieved from http://www.npb-cnlc.gc.ca/infocntr/factsh/pardon-eng.shtml

National Research Council (2003). *The polygraph and lie detection.* Washington, DC: National Academies Press.

Navon, D. (1990). How critical is the accuracy of eyewitness memory? Another look at the issue of lineup diagnosticity. *Journal of Applied Psychology, 75,* 506–510.

Nazroo, J. (1995). Uncovering gender differences in the use of marital violence: The effect of methodology. *Sociology, 29,* 475–494.

Nemeth, M. (1996, May 20). Joudrie not guilty. *Maclean's.* Retrieved from http://thecanadianencyclopedia.com/index.cfm?PgNm=TCE&Params=M1ARTM001067.

Neumann, C.S., & Hare, R.D. (2008). Psychopathic traits in a large community sample: Links to violence, alcohol use, and intelligence. *Journal of Consulting and Clinical Psychology, 76,* 893–899.

Newhill, C.E., Mulvey, E.P., & Lidz, C.W. (1995). Characteristics of violence in the community by female patients seen in a psychiatric emergency service. *Psychiatric Services, 46,* 785–789.

Newman, J.P., Brinkley, C.A., Lorenz, A.R., Hiatt, K.D., & MacCoon, D.G. (2007). Psychopathy as psychopathology: Beyond the clinical utility of the Psychopathy Checklist-Revised. In H. Hervé & J.C. Yuille (Eds.), The *psychopath: Theory, research and practice*(pp. 173–206). Mahway, NJ: Erlbaum.

Newman, J.P., Curtin, J.J., Bertsch, J.D., & Baskin-Sommers, A.R. (2010). Attention moderates the fearlessness of psychopathic offenders. *Biological Psychiatry, 67,* 66–70.

Ng, W., & Lindsay, R.C.L. (1994). Cross-race facial recognition: Failure of the contact hypothesis. *Journal of Cross-Cultural Psychology, 25,* 217–232.

Nicholls, T.L., Brink, J., Desmarais, S.L., Webster, C.D., & Martin, M. (2006). The Short-Term Assessment of Risk and Treatability (START): A prospective validation study in a forensic psychiatric sample. *Assessment, 13,* 313–327.

Nicholls, T.L., Ogloff, J.R.P., & Douglas, K.S. (2004). Assessing risk for violence among male and female civil psychiatric patients: The HCR-20, PCL:SV, and VSC. *Behavioral Sciences and the Law, 22,* 127–158.

Nichols, T.R., Graber, J.A., Brooks-Gunn, J., & Botvin, G.J. (2006). Sex differences in overt aggression and delinquency among urban minority middle school students. *Applied Developmental Psychology, 27,* 78–91.

Nicholson, R.A., & Kugler, K. (1991). Competent and incompetent criminal defendants: A quantitative review of comparative research. *Psychological Bulletin, 109,* 355–370.

Niedermeier, K.E., Horowitz, I.A., & Kerr, N.L. (1999). Informing jurors of their nullification power: A route to a just verdict or judicial chaos? *Law and Human Behavior, 23,* 331–351.

Nisbett, R.E., & Wilson, T.D. (1977). Telling more than we can know: Verbal reports on mental processes. *Psychological Review, 84,*231–259.

Note. (1953). Voluntary false confessions: A neglected area in criminal investigation. *Indiana Law Review, 28,* 374–392.

Nuffield, J. (1982). *Parole decision-making in Canada.* Ottawa, ON: Solicitor General of Canada.

Nunes, K.L., Firestone, P., Bradford, J.M., Greenberg, D.M., & Broom, I. (2002). A comparison of modified versions of the Static-99 and the Sex Offender Risk Appraisal Guide. *Sexual Abuse: A Journal of Research and Treatment, 14,* 253–269.

Nunes, K.L., Firestone, P., Wexler, A., Jensen, T.L., & Bradford, J.M. (2007). Incarceration and recidivism among sexual offenders. *Law and Human Behavior, 31,* 305–318.

Nunes, K.L., Hanson, K., Firestone, P., Moulden, H.M., Greenberg, D.M., & Bradford, J. M. (2007). Denial predicts recidivism for some sexual offenders. *Sexual Abuse: A Journal of Research and Treatment, 19*, 91–106.

O'Bryant, S.E., & Lucas, J.A. (2006). Estimating the predictive value of the test of memory malingering: An illustrative example for clinicians. *The Clinical Neuropsychologist, 20*, 533–540.

O'Hara, M.W. (1995). Childbearing. In M.W. O'Hara, R.C. Reiter, S.R. Johnson, A. Milburn, & J. Engeldinger (Eds.), *Psychological aspects of women's reproductive health* (pp. 26–48). New York, NY: Springer Publishing Co.

O'Keefe, M., & Schnell, M.J. (2007). Offenders with mental illness in the correctional system. *Mental Health Issues in the Criminal Justice System, 45*, 81–104. Retrieved from http://jor.haworthpress.com

O'Malley, M., & Wood, O. (2003). Cruel & unusual: The law and Latimer. *CBC News*. Retrieved from http://www.cbc.ca/news/background/latimer.

O'Neill, M.L., Lidz, V., & Heilbrun, K. (2003). Adolescents with psychopathic characteristics in a substance abusing cohort: Treatment process and outcomes. *Law and Human Behavior, 27*, 299–313.

O'Toole, M. (2007). Psychopathy as a behavior classification system for violent and serial crime scenes. In H. Hervé & J.C. Yuille (Eds.), *The psychopath: Theory, research and practice* (pp. 301–325). Mahway, NJ: Erlbaum.

Oberlander, L.B., & Goldstein, N.E. (2001). A review and update on the practice of evaluating Miranda comprehension. *Behavioral Sciences and the Law, 19*, 453–471.

Odeh, M.S., Zeiss, R.A., & Huss, M.T. (2006). Cues they use: Clinicians' endorsement of risk cues in predictions of dangerousness. *Behavioral Sciences and the Law, 24*, 147–156.

Odgers, C.L., & Moretti, M.M. (2002). Aggressive and antisocial girls: Research update and challenges. *International Journal of Forensic Mental Health, 1*, 103–119.

Odgers, C.L., Moretti, M.M., & Reppucci, N.D. (2005). Examining the science and practice of violence risk assessment with female adolescents. *Law and Human Behavior, 29*, 7–27.

Odgers, C.L., Reppucci, N.D., & Moretti, M.M. (2005). Nipping psychopathy in the bud: An examination of the convergent, predictive, and theoretical utility of the PCL-YV among adolescent girls. *Behavioral Sciences and the Law, 23*, 743–763.

Office of Juvenile Studies and Delinquency Prevention. (1992). *Juvenile justice bulletin: OJJDP update on statistics*. Washington, DC: Author.

Offord, D.R., Boyle, M.H., Szatmari, P., Rae Grant, J.L., Links, P.S., Cadman, D.T., Byles, J.A., Crawford, J.W., Blum, H.M., Byrne, C., Thomas, H., & Woodward, C.A. (1987). Ontario Child Health Study: II Six month prevalence of disorder and rates of service utilization. *Archives of General Psychiatry, 44*, 832–836.

Offord, D.R., Lipman, E.L., & Duku, E.K. (2001). Epidemiology of problem behaviour up to age 12 years. In R. Loeber & D.P. Farrington (Eds.), *Child delinquents* (pp. 95–134). Thousand Oaks, CA: Sage Publications.

Ofshe, R.J. (1989). Coerced confessions: The logic of seemingly irrational action. *Journal of Cultic Studies, 6*, 1–15.

Ofshe, R.J., & Leo, R.A. (1997). The social psychology of police interrogation: The theory and classification of true and false confessions. *Studies in Law, Politics, and Society, 16*, 189–251.

Ofshe, R.J., & Watters, E. (1994). *Making monsters: False memories, psychotherapy, and sexual hysteria*. New York, NY: Charles Scribner's.

Ogloff, J.R.P. (Ed.). (2002). *Taking psychology and law into the 21st century*. New York, NY: Kluwer Academic.

Ogloff, J.R.P., & Cronshaw, S.F. (2001). Expert psychological testimony: Assisting or misleading the trier of fact. *Canadian Psychology, 42*, 87–91.

Ogloff, J.R.P., & Vidmar, N. (1994). The effect of pretrial publicity on jurors: A study to compare the relative effects of television and print media in a child sex abuse case. *Law and Human Behavior, 18*, 507–525.

Ogloff, J.R.P., Schweighofer, A., Turnbull, S., & Whittemore, K. (1992). Empirical research and the insanity defense: How much do we really know? In J.R.P. Ogloff (Ed.), *Psychology and law: The broadening of the discipline* (pp. 171–210). Durham, NC: Carolina Academic Press.

Ogloff, J.R.P., Wallace, D.H., & Otto, R.K. (1991). Competencies in the criminal process. In D. K. Kagehiro & W.S. Laufer (Eds.), *Handbook of psychology and law* (pp. 343–360). New York, NY: Springer Verlag.

Olczak, P.V., Kaplan, M.F., & Penrod, S. (1991). Attorneys' lay psychology and its effectiveness in selecting jurors: Three empirical studies. *Journal of Social Behavior and Personality, 6*, 431–452.

Olio, K.A., & Cornell, W.F. (1998). The façade of scientific documentation: A case study of Richard Ofshe's analysis of the Paul Ingram case. *Psychology, Public Policy, and Law, 4*, 1182–1197.

Olver, M.E., & Wong, S.C.P. (2006). Psychopathy, sexual deviance, and recidivism among sex offenders. *Sexual Abuse: A Journal of Research and Treatment, 18*, 65–82.

htmlOntario Provincial Police. (2010). *Williams faces additional charges*. Retrieved from http://www.opp.ca/ecms/index.php?id=405&nid=233

Orchard, T.L., & Yarmey, A.D. (1995). The effects of whispers, voice-sample duration, and voice distinctiveness on criminal speaker identification. *Applied Cognitive Psychology, 9*, 249–260.

Ormerod, D. (1999). Criminal profiling: Trial by judge and jury, not criminal psychologist. In D.V. Canter & L.J. Alison

(Eds.), *Profiling in policy and practice* (pp. 207–261). Aldershot, England: Ashgate.

Otto, R., & Heilbrun, K. (2002). The practice of forensic psychology: A look toward the future in light of the past. *American Psychologist, 57*, 5–19.

Paglia, A., & Schuller, R.A. (1998). Jurors' use of hearsay evidence: The effects of type and timing of instructions. *Law and Human Behavior, 22*, 501–518.

Palys, T.S., & Divorski, S. (1986). Explaining sentencing disparity. *Canadian Journal of Criminology, 28*, 347–362.

Pankratz, L. (1988). Malingering on intellectual and neuropsychological measures. In R. Rogers (Ed.), *Clinical assessment of malingering and deception* (1st ed., pp. 168–192). New York, NY: Guilford Press.

Paolucci, E., Genuis, M., & Violato, C. (2001). A meta-analysis of the published research on the effects of child sexual abuse. *Journal of Psychology, 135*, 17–36.

Parker, A.D., & Brown, J. (2000). Detection of deception: Statement Validity Analysis as a means of determining truthfulness or falsity of rape allegations. *Legal and Criminological Psychology, 5*, 237–259.

Parker, J. (1995). Age differences in source monitoring of performed and imagined actions. *Journal of Experimental Child Psychology, 60*, 84–101.

Parker, J.G., & Asher, S.R. (1987). Peer relations and later personal adjustment: Are low accepted children at risk? *Psychological Bulletin, 102*, 357–389.

Partial court victory for Muslim woman over niqab (2009, May 1). *Ctvtoronto.ca* Retrieved from http://montreal.ctv.ca/servlet/an/local/CTVNews/20090501/niqab_ruling_090501?hub=MontrealHome

Parwatikar, S.D., Holcomb, W.R., & Menninger, K.A., II. (1985). The detection of malingered amnesia in accused murders. *Bulletin of American Academy of Psychiatry and Law, 13*, 97–103.

Patrick, C.J. (2006). *Handbook of psychopathy.* New York, NY: Guilford Press.

Patrick, C.J., & Iacono, W.G. (1989). Psychopathy, threat, and polygraph test accuracy. *Journal of Applied Psychology, 74*, 347–355.

Patrick, C.J., & Iacono, W.G. (1991). Validity of the control question polygraph test: The problem of sampling bias. *Journal of Applied Social Psychology, 76*, 229–238.

Patrick, C.J., Bradley, M.M. & Lang, P.J. (1993). Emotion in the criminal psychopath: Startle reflex modulation. *Journal of Abnormal Psychology, 102*, 82–92.

Patrick, C.P. (2007). Getting to the heart of psychopathy. In H. Hervé & J.C. Yuille (Eds.), The psychopath: Theory, research and practice (pp. 207–252). Mahway, NJ: Erlbaum.

Patry, M.W. Attractive but guilty: Deliberation and the physical attractiveness bias. *Psychological Reports, 102*, 727–733.

Patterson, G.R., Reid, J.B., & Dishion, T.J. (1998). *Antisocial boys.* Eugene, OR: Castalia.

Paul, G.L., & Lentz, R.J. (1977). *Psychosocial treatment of chronic mental patients: Milieu versus social learning programs.* Cambridge, MA: Harvard University Press.

Paulhus, D.L., Williams, K.M., & Nathanson, C. (2002). The Dark Triad revisited. Presented at the 3rd annual meeting of the Society for Personality and Social Psychology, Savannah, GA.

Pavlidis, I., Eberhardt, N.L., & Levine, J.A. (2002). Seeing though the face of deception. *Nature, 415*, 35.

Pearson, F.S., Lipton, D.S., & Cleland, C.M. (1996, November 20). Some preliminary findings from the CDATE project. Paper presented at the Annual Meeting of the American Society of Criminology, Chicago, IL.

Pence, E., & Paymar, M. (1993). *Education groups for men who batter: The Duluth model.* New York, NY: Springer Publishing Co.

Pennington, N., & Hastie, R. (1986). Evidence evaluation in complex decision making. *Journal of Personality and Social Psychology, 51*, 242–258.

Pennington, N., & Hastie, R. (1988). Explanation-based decision making: Effects of memory structure on judgement. *Journal of Experimental Psychology: Learning, Memory, and Cognition, 14*, 521–533.

Penrod, S.D., & Cutler, B. (1995). Witness confidence and witness accuracy: Assessing their forensic relation. *Psychology, Public Policy, and Law, 1*, 817–845.

Penrod, S.D., & Heuer, L. (1997). Tweaking commonsense: Assessing aids to jury decision making. *Psychology, Public Policy, and Law, 3*, 259–284.

Perez, D.A., Hosch, H.M., Ponder, B., & Trejo, G.C. (1993). Ethnicity of defendants and jurors as influences on jury decisions. *Journal of Applied Social Psychology, 23*, 1249–1262.

Perfect, T., Wagstaff, Moore, D., Andrews, B., Cleveland, Newcombe, S., . . . Brown, L. (2008). How can we help witnesses to remember more? It's an (Eyes) open and shut case. *Law and Human Behavior, 32*, 314–324.

Perreault, S. (2009). *The incarceration of Aboriginal people in adult correctional services.* Retrieved from http://www.statcan.gc.ca/pub/85-002-x/2009003/article/10903-eng.htm

Peters, M. (2001). Forensic psychological testimony: Is the courtroom door now locked and barred? *Canadian Psychology, 42*, 101–108.

Peterson, C., & Biggs, M. (1997). Interviewing children about trauma: Problems with "specific" questions. *Journal of Traumatic Stress, 10*, 279–290.

Pezdek, K., Morrow, A., Blandon-Gitlin, I., Goodman, G., Quas, J.A., Saywitz, K., . . . Brodie, L. (2004). Detecting deception in children: Event familiarity affects criterion-based content analysis ratings. *Journal of Applied Psychology, 89*, 119–126.

Pham, T.H., Ducro, C., Marghem, B., & Réveillère, C. (2005). Prediction of recidivism among prison inmates and forensic patients in Belgium. Annales Médico Psychologiques, 163, 842–845.

Phillips, H.K., Gray, N.S., MacCulloch, S.I., Taylor, J., Moore, S.C., Huckle, P., & MacCulloch, M.J. (2005). Risk assessment in offenders with mental disorders: Relative efficacy of personal demographic, criminal history and clinical variables. Journal of Interpersonal Violence, 20, 833–847.

Picard, A., (2003, July 22). Grieving mother's farewell: "Adieu, my little flower." The Globe and Mail. Retrieved from http://www.globeandmail.com

Pickel, K.L. (1998). Unusualness and threat as possible causes of weapon focus. Memory, 6, 277–295.

Pickel, K.L. (1999). The influence of context on the "weapon focus" effect. Law and Human Behavior, 23, 299–311.

Pickel, K.L., Karam, T.J., & Warner, T.C. (2009). Jurors' responses to unusual inadmissible evidence. Criminal Justice and Behavior, 36, 466–480.

Pickel, K.L., Ross, S.J., & Truelove, R.S. (2006). Do weapons automatically capture attention? Applied Cognitive Psychology, 20, 871–893.

Pinizzotto, A.J., & Davis, E.F. (1992). Killed in the line of duty. Washington, DC: Department of Justice, FBI Uniform Crime Reporting Program.

Pinizzotto, A.J., & Finkel, N.J. (1990). Criminal personality profiling: An outcome and process study. Law and Human Behavior, 14, 215–233.

Piquero, A.R., & Chung, H.L. (2001). On the relationships between gender, early onset, and the seriousness of offending. Journal of Criminal Justice, 29, 189–206.

Piquero, A.R., Blumstein, A., Brame, R., Haapanen, R., Mulvey, E.P., & Nagin, D.S. (2001). Assessing the impact of exposure time and incapacitation on longitudinal trajectories of criminal offending. Journal of Adolescent Research, 16, 54–74.

Pithers, W.D., Martin, G.R., & Cumming, G.F. (1989). Vermont Treatment Program for Sexual Aggressors. In R.D. Laws (Ed.), Relapse prevention with sex offenders (pp. 292–310). New York, NY: Guilford Press.

Platz, S.J., & Hosch,.M. (1988). Cross-racial/ethnic eyewitness identification: A field study. Journal of Applied Social Psychology, 18, 972–984.

Polaschek, D.L.L., & Collie, R.M. (2004). Rehabilitating serious adult violent offenders: An empirical and theoretical stock-take. Psychology, Crime & Law, 10, 321–334.

Police Sector Council. (2005). Results from Ipsos-Reid's reconnecting government with youth 2005. Ottawa, ON: Police Sector Council.

Police Sector Council. (2006). Police environment 2005: Update of the 2000 sector study and implications for HR planning and management today and into the future. Ottawa, ON: Police Sector Council.

Pollina, D.A., Dollins, A.B., Senter, S.M., Krapohl, D.J., & Ryan, A.H. (2004). Comparison of polygraph data obtained from individuals involved in mock crime and actual criminal investigations. Journal of Applied Psychology, 89, 1099–1105.

Pope, H.G., Jonas, J.M., & Jones, B. (1982). Factitious psychosis: Phenomenology, family history, and long-term outcome of nine patients. American Journal of Psychiatry, 139, 1480–1483.

Porporino, F.J., & Motiuk, L.L. (1995). The prison careers of mentally disordered offenders. International Journal of Law and Psychiatry, 18, 29–44.

Porter, S. & ten Brinke, L. (2008). Reading between the lies: Identifying concealed and falsified emotions in universal facial expressions. Psychological Science, 19, 508–514.

Porter, S., & Birt, A.R. (2001). Is traumatic memory special? A comparison of traumatic memory characteristics with memory for other emotional life experiences. Applied Cognitive Psychology, 15, S101–S117.

Porter, S., Birt, A., & Boer, D.P. (2001). Investigation of the criminal and conditional release profiles of Canadian federal offenders as a function of psychopathy and age. Law and Human Behavior, 25, 647–661.

Porter, S., Campbell, M.A., Stapleton, J., & Birt, A.R. (2002). The influence of judge, target, and stimulus characteristics on the accuracy of detecting deceit. Canadian Journal of Behavioural Science, 34, 172–185.

Porter, S., Doucette, N.L., Woodoworth, M., Earle, J., & MacNeil, B. (2008). "Halfe the world knows not how the other halfe lies": Investigation of verbal and non-verbal signs of deception exhibited by criminal offenders and non-offenders. Legal and Criminological Psychology, 13, 27–38.

Porter, S., Fairweather, D., Drugge, J., Herve, H., Birt, A., & Boer, D.P. (2000). Profiles of psychopathy in incarcerated sexual offenders. Criminal Justice and Behavior, 27, 216–233.

Porter, S., Juodis, M., ten Brinke, L., Klein, R. & Wilson, K. (2010). Evaluation of a brief deception detection training program. Journal of Forensic Psychiatry & Psychology, 21, 66–76.

Porter, S., ten Brinke, L., & Wilson, K. (2009). Crime profiles and conditional release performance of psychopathic and nonpsychopathic offenders. Legal and Criminological Psychology, 14, 109–118.

Porter, S., Woodworth, M., & Birt, A. (2000). Truth, lies, and videotape: An investigation of the ability of federal parole officers to detect deception. Law and Human Behavior, 24, 643–658.

Porter, S., Woodworth, M., Earle, J., Drugge, J., & Boer, D. (2003). Characteristics of sexual homicides committed by psychopathic and nonpsychopathic offenders. Law and Human Behavior, 27, 459–470.

Powell, B. (2009, February 2). Order to take off niqab pits law against religion. TheStar.com. Retrieved from http://www.thestar.com/printarticle/580790.

Pozzulo, J.D., & Balfour, J. (2006). The impact of change in appearance on children's eyewitness identification accuracy: Comparing simultaneous and elimination lineup procedures. *Legal and Criminological Psychology, 11*, 25–34.

Pozzulo, J.D., & Crescini, C. (2007). *Preschoolers' person description and identification accuracy: A comparison of the simultaneous and elimination lineup procedures*. Unpublished manuscript.

Pozzulo, J.D., & Lindsay, R.C.L. (1998). Identification accuracy of children versus adults: A meta-analysis. *Law and Human Behavior, 22*, 549–570.

Pozzulo, J.D., & Lindsay, R.C.L. (1999). Elimination lineups: An improved identification procedure for child eyewitnesses. *Journal of Applied Psychology, 84*, 167–176.

Pozzulo, J.D., & Warren, K.L. (2003). Descriptions and identifications of strangers by youth and adult eyewitnesses. *Journal of Applied Psychology, 88*, 315–323.

Pozzulo, J.D., Dempsey, J., & Crescini, C. (2009). Preschoolers' person description and identification accuracy: A comparison of the simultaneous and elimination lineup procedures. *Journal of Applied Developmental Psychology, 30*, 667–676.

Pozzulo, J.D., Dempsey, J., Corey, S., Girardi, A., Lawandi, A., & Aston, C. (2008). Can a lineup procedure designed for child witnesses work for adults: Comparing simultaneous, sequential, and elimination lineup procedures. *Journal of Applied Social Psychology, 38*, 2195–2209.

Pozzulo, J.D., Dempsey, J., Maeder, E., & Allen, L. (2010). The effects of victim gender, defendant gender, and defendant age on juror decision making. *Criminal Justice and Behavior, 37*, 47–63.

Prentky, R.A., Knight, R.A., Lee, A.F.S., & Cerce, D.D. (1995). Predictive validity of lifestyle impulsivity for rapists. *Criminal Justice and Behavior, 22*, 106–128.

Pryke, S., Lindsay, R.C.L., Dysart, J.E., & Dupuis, P. (2004). Multiple independent identification decisions: A method of calibrating eyewitness identifications. *Journal of Applied Psychology, 89*, 73–84.

Public Safety and Emergency Preparedness Canada. (2006). *Corrections and conditional release statistical overview: Annual report 2006*. Public Safety and Emergency Preparedness Canada.

Pugh, G. (1985a). The California Psychological Inventory and police selection. *Journal of Police Science and Administration, 13*, 172–177.

Pugh, G. (1985b). Situation tests and police selection. *Journal of Police Science and Administration, 13*, 31–35.

Putnam, F.W. (2003). Ten-year research update review: Child sexual abuse. Journal of the American Academy of Child Adolescent Psychiatry, 42, 269–278.

Pynes, J., & Bernardin, H.J. (1992). Entry-level police selection: The assessment centre as an alternative. *Journal of Criminal Justice, 20*, 41–52.

Quann, N. & Trevethan, S. (2000). *Police-reported Aboriginal crime in Saskatchewan*.Ottawa, ON: Statistics Canada.

Quas, J., Schaaf, J., Alexander, K., & Goodman, G. (2000). Do you really remember it happening or do you only remember being asked about it happening. Children's source monitoring in forensic contexts. In K.P. Roberts & M. Blades (Eds.), *Children's source monitoring* (pp. 197–226). Mahwah, NJ: Lawrence Erlbaum Associates.

Quayle, J. (2008). Interviewing a psychopathic suspect. *Journal of Investigative Psychology and Offender Profiling, 5*, 79–91.

Quinsey, V.L. (2002). Evolutionary theory and criminal behaviour. *Legal and Criminological Psychology, 7*, 1–13.

Quinsey, V.L., & Ambtman, R. (1979). Variables affecting psychiatrists' and teachers' assessments of the dangerousness of mentally ill offenders. *Journal of Consulting and Clinical Psychology, 47*, 353–362.

Quinsey, V.L., & Earls, C.M. (1990). The modification of sexual preferences. In W.L. Marshall & D.R. Laws, *Handbook of sexual assault: Issues, theories, and treatment of the offender* (pp. 279–295). New York, NY: Plenum Press.

Quinsey, V.L., & Lalumière, M. L. (1995). Evolutionary perspectives on sexual offending. *Sexual Abuse: Journal of Research and Treatment, 7*, 301–315.

Quinsey, V.L., & Maguire, A. (1983). Offenders remanded for a psychiatric examination: Perceived treatability and disposition. *International Journal of Law and Psychiatry, 6*, 193–205.

Quinsey, V.L., Jones, G.B., Book, A.S., & Barr, K.N. (2006). They dynamic prediction of antisocial behavior among forensic psychiatric patients: A prospective field study. *Journal of Interpersonal Violence, 21*, 1539–1565.

Quinsey, V.L., Chaplin, T.C., & Upfold, D. (1984). Sexual arousal to nonsexual violence and sadomasochistic themes among rapists and non-sex-offenders. *Journal of Consulting and Clinical Psychology, 52*, 651–657.

Quinsey, V.L., Harris, G.T., Rice, M.E., & Cormier, C. (1998). *Violent offenders: Appraising and managing risk*. Washington, DC: American Psychological Association.

Quinsey, V.L., Harris, G.T., Rice, M.E., & Lalumière, M.L. (1993). Assessing the treatment efficacy in outcome studies of sex offenders. *Journal of Interpersonal Violence, 8*, 512–523.

Quinsey, V.L., Khanna, A., & Malcolm, P.B. (1998). A retrospective evaluation of the regional treatment centre sex offender treatment program. *Journal of Interpersonal Violence, 13*, 621–644.

Quinsey, V.L., Rice, M.E., & Harris, G.T. (1995). Actuarial prediction of sexual recidivism. *Journal of Interpersonal Violence, 10*, 85–105.

Ragatz, L., Fremouw, W., Thomas, T., & McCoy, K. (2009). Vicious dogs: The antisocial behaviors and psychological characteristics of owners. *Journal of Forensic Science, 54*, 699–703.

Rankin, J., & Contenta, S. (2010, April 30). The frantic life of Col. David Russell Williams. *TheStar.com*. Retrieved from http://www.thestar.com/news/ontario/article/803220—the-frantic-life-of-col-david-russell-williams

Raskin, D.C., & Esplin, P.W. (1991). Statement validity assessment: Interview procedures and content analysis of children's statements of sexual abuse. *Behavioral Assessment, 12*, 265–291.

Raskin, D.C., & Hare, R.D. (1978). Psychopathy and detection of deception in a prison population. *Psychophysiology, 15*, 126–136.

Raskin, D.C., Honts, C.R., & Kircher, J.C. (1997). The scientific status of research on polygraph techniques: The case for polygraph tests. In D.L. Faigman, D. Kaye, M.J. Saks, & J. Sanders (Eds.), *Modern scientific evidence: The law and science of expert testimony* (pp. 565–582). St. Paul, MN: West.

Rasmussen, L.A., Burton, J.E., & Christopherson, B.J. (1992). Precursors to offending and the trauma outcome process in sexually reactive children. *Journal of Child Sexual Abuse, 1*, 33–48.

Ratner, P.A. (1998). Modeling acts of aggression and dominance as wife abuse and exploring their adverse health effects. *Journal of Marriage and the Family, 60*, 453–465.

Read, J.D. (1999). The recovered/false memory debate: Three steps forward, two steps back? *Expert Evidence, 7*, 1–24.

Read, J.D., & Desmarais, S.L. (2009). Lay knowledge of eyewitness issues: A Canadian evaluation. *Applied Cognitive Psychology, 23*, 301–326.

Read, J.D., Connolly, D.A., & Welsh, A. (2006). An archival analysis of actual cases of historic child sexual abuse: A comparison of jury and bench trials. *Law and Human Behavior, 30*, 259–285.

Rees, L.M., Tombaugh, T.N., Gansler, D.A., & Moczynski, N.P. (1998). Five validation experiments of the Test of Malingered Memory (TOMM). *Psychological Assessment, 10*, 10–20.

Reifman, A., Gusick, S.M., & Ellsworth, P.C. (1992). Real jurors' understanding of the law in real cases. *Law and Human Behavior, 16*, 539–554.

Reinhart, M.A. (1987). Sexually abused boys. *Child Abuse and Neglect, 11*, 229–235.

Reiser, M. (1982). *Police psychology: Collected papers*. Los Angeles, CA: LEHI.

Reiser, M. (1989). Investigative hypnosis. In D. Raskin (Ed.), *Psychological methods in criminal investigation and evidence* (pp. 151–190). New York, NY: Springer.

Rengel killer sentenced to life (2009, September 28). *CBC News.*Retrieved from http://www.cbc.ca/canada/toronto/story/2009/09/28/rengel-killer-sentencing265.html

Resick, P.A. (1993). The psychological impact of rape. *Journal of Interpersonal Violence, 8*, 223–255.

Resnick, P.J. (1969). Child murder by parents: A psychiatric review of filicide. *American Journal of Psychiatry, 126*, 325–334.

Resnick, P.J. (1970). Murder of the newborn: A psychiatric review of neonaticide. *American Journal of Psychiatry, 126*, 1414–1420.

Resnick, P.J. (1997). Malingered psychosis. In R. Rogers (Ed.), *Clinical assessment of malingering and deception* (2nd ed., pp. 47–67). New York, NY: Guilford Press.

Ressler, R.K., Burgess, A.W., Douglas, J.E., Hartman, C.R., & D'Agostino, R.B. (1986). Sexual killers and their victims: Identifying patterns through crime scene analysis. *Journal of Interpersonal Violence, 1*, 288–308.

Reuter, R.P. (1995, July 25). Consider "9 days of deceit" prosecutors urge Smith jury. *Toronto Star*, p. A4.

Rice, M.E., & Harris, G.T. (1990). The predictors of insanity acquittal. *International Journal of Law and Psychiatry, 13*, 217–224.

Rice, M.E., & Harris, G.T. (1992). A comparison of criminal recidivism among schizophrenic and nonschizophrenic offenders. *International Journal of Law and Psychiatry, 15*, 397–406.

Rice, M.E., & Harris, G.T. (1997). Cross validation and extension of the Violence Risk Appraisal Guide with child molesters and rapists. *Law and Human Behavior, 21*, 231–241.

Rice, M.E., & Harris, G.T. (1997). The treatment of mentally disordered offenders. *Psychology, Public Policy, and Law, 3*, 126–183.

Rice, M.E., Harris, G.T., & Cormier, C.A. (1992). An evaluation of a maximum security therapeutic community for psychopaths and other mentally disordered offenders. *Law and Human Behaviour, 16*, 399–412.

Rice, M.E., Harris, G.T., Lang, C., & Cormier, C. (2006). Violent sex offenses: How are they best measured from official records? *Law and Human Behavior, 30*, 525–541.

Richards, H.J., Casey, J.O., & Lucente, S.W. (2003). Psychopathy and treatment response in response to incarcerated female substance abusers. *Criminal Justice and Behavior, 30*, 251–276.

Rind, B., Jaeger, M., & Strohmetz, D.B. (1995). Effect of crime seriousness on simulated jurors' use of inadmissible evidence. *Journal of Social Psychology, 135*, 417–424.

Risin, L.I., & Koss, M.P. (1987). The sexual abuse of boys: Prevalence and descriptive characteristics of childhood victimizations. *Journal of Interpersonal Violence, 2*, 309–323.

Robert Baltovitch: Not guilty. (2008, April 22). *CBC News.*Retrieved from http://www.cbc.ca/news/background/baltovich_robert/

Roberts, A.R. (1996). Battered women who kill: A comparative study of incarcerated participants with a community sample of battered women. *Journal of Family Violence, 11*, 291–304.

Roberts, J. (2001). *Fear of crime and attitudes to criminal justice in Canada: A review of recent trends 2001–2002*. Ottawa, ON: Public Safety Canada.

Roberts, J. (2007). Public attitudes to sentencing in Canada: Exploring recent findings. *Canadian Journal of Criminology and Criminal Justice, 49,* 75–107.

Roberts, J.V. & Birkenmayer, A. (1997). Sentencing in adult provincial courts. *Juristat, 17.*

Roberts, J.V. (1991). Sentencing reform: The lessons of psychology. *Canadian Psychology, 32,* 466–477.

Roberts, J.V., & Melchers, R. (2003). The incarceration of Aboriginal offenders: Trends from 1978 to 2001. *Canadian Journal of Criminology and Criminal Justice, 45,* 211–242.

Roberts, K. & Lamb, M. (1999). Children's responses when interviewers distort details during investigative interviews. *Legal and Criminological Psychology, 4,* 23–31.

Roberts, K., Lamb, M., & Sternberg, K. (2004). The effects of rapport-building style on children's reports of a staged event. *Applied Cognitive Psychology, 18,* 189–202.

Robins, L.N. (1986). The consequences of conduct disorder in girls. In D. Olweus, J. Block, & M. Radke-Yarrow (Eds.), *Development of antisocial and prosocial behavior* (pp. 385–408). New York, NY: Academic Press.

Rockett, J.L., Murrie, D.C., & Boccaccini, M.T. (2007). Diagnostic labeling in juvenile justice settings: Do psychopathy and conduct disorder findings influence clinicians? *Psychological Services, 4,*107–122

Roebers, C.M., Bjorklund, D.F., Schneider, W., & Cassel, W.S. (2002). Differences and similarities in event recall and suggestibility between children and adults in Germany and the United States. *Experimental Psychology, 49,* 132–140.

Roesch, R., Eaves, D., Sollner, R., Normandin, M., & Glackman, W. (1981). Evaluating fitness to stand trial: A comparative analysis of fit and unfit defendants. *International Journal of Law and Psychiatry, 4,* 145, 157.

Roesch, R., Ogloff, J.R.P., Hart, S.D., Dempster, R.J., Zapf, P.A., & Whittemore, K.E. (1997). The impact of Canadian Criminal Code changes on remands and assessments of fitness to stand trial and criminal responsibility in British Columbia. *Canadian Journal of Psychiatry, 42,* 509–514.

Roesch, R., Zapf, P.A., Eaves, D., & Webster, C.D. (1998). The Fitness Interview Test (rev. ed.) [Interview test]. Mental Health Law, and Policy Institute, Simon Fraser University, Burnaby, BC.)

Rogers, R. (1984). *Rogers Criminal Responsibility Assessment Scales.* Psychological Assessment Resources. Odessa, FL.

Rogers, R. (1986). *Conducting insanity evaluations.* New York, NY: Van Nostrand Reinhold.

Rogers, R. (1988). Structured interviews and dissimulation. In R. Rogers (Ed.), *Clinical assessment of malingering and deception* (1st ed., pp. 250–268). New York, NY: Guilford Press.

Rogers, R. (1990). Models of feigned mental illness. *Professional Psychology, 21,* 182–188.

Rogers, R. (1997). Structured interviews and dissimulation. In R. Rogers (Ed.), *Clinical assessment of malingering and deception* (2nd ed., pp. 301–327). New York, NY: Guilford Press.

Rogers, R. (2008). *Clinical assessment of malingering and deception* (3rd ed.). New York, NY: Guilford Press.

Rogers, R., & Ewing, C.P. (1992). The measurement of insanity: Debating the merits of the R-CRAS and its alternatives. *International Journal of Law and Psychiatry, 15,* 113–123.

Rogers, R., & Sewell, K.W. (1999). The R-CRAS and insanity evaluations: A reexamination of construct validity. *Behavioral Sciences and the Law, 17,* 181–194.

Rogers, R., Bagby, R.M., & Dickens, S.E. (1992). *Structured Interview of Reported Symptoms (SIRS) and professional manual.* Odessa, FL: Psychological Assessment Resources.

Rogers, R., Sewell, K.W., & Goldstein, A.M. (1994). Explanatory models of malingering: A prototypical analysis. *Law and Human Behavior, 18,* 543–552.

Rogers, R., Sewell, K.W., Martin, M.A., & Vitacco, J.J. (2003). Detection of feigned mental disorders: A meta-analysis of the MMPI-2 and malingering. *Assessment, 10,* 160–177.

Rogers, R., Ustad, K.L., & Salekin, R.T. (1998). Convergent validity of the Personality Assessment Inventory: A study of emergency referrals in a correctional setting. *Assessment, 5,* 3–12.

Rosenberg, D.A. (1987). A web of deceit: A literature review of Munchausen syndrome by proxy. *Child Abuse & Neglect, 11,* 547–563.

Rosenfeld, B. (2003). Recidivism in stalking and obsessional harassment. *Law and Human Behavior, 27,* 251–265.

Rosenfeld, B. (2004). Violence risk factors in stalking and obsessional harassment: A review and preliminary meta-analysis. *Criminal Justice and Behavior, 31,* 9–36.

Rosenfeld, J.P., Angell, A., Johnson, M., & Qian, J. (1991). An ERP-based, control-question lie detector analog: Algorithms for discriminating effects within individuals' average waveforms. *Psychophysiology, 38,* 319–335.

Rosenfeld, J.P., Nasman, V.T., Whalen, R., Cantwell, B., & Mazzeri, L. (1987). Late vertex positivity in event-related potentials as a guilty knowledge indicator: A new method of lie detection. *Polygraph, 16,* 223–231.

Rosenfeld, J.P., Soskins, M., Bosh, G., & Ryan, A. (2004). Simple, effective countermeasures to P300-based tests of detection of concealed information. *Psychophysiology, 41,* 205–219.

Rosenhan, D.L. (1973). On being sane in insane places. *Science, 179,* 250–257.

Rossmo, D.K. (1995). Place, space and police investigations: Hunting serial violent criminals. In J.E. Eck & D. Weisburd (Eds.), *Crime and place* (pp. 217–235). Monsey, NY: Criminal Justice Press.

Rossmo, D.K. (2000). *Geographic profiling*. Boca Raton, FL: CRC Press.

Rossmo, D.K. (2005). Cognitive heuristics or shortcuts to failure: Response to Snook et al. *Applied Cognitive Psychology, 19*, 65–654.

Rossmo, D.K. (2005). Geographic heuristics or shortcuts to failure? A response to Snook et al. (2004). *Applied Cognitive Psychology, 19*, 651–654.

Rotenberg, K.J., Hewlet, M.G., & Siegwart, C.M. (1998). Principled moral reasoning and self-monitoring as predictors of jury functioning. *Basic and Applied Social Psychology, 20*, 167–173.

Rothbaum, B.O., Foa, E.B., Riggs, D., Murdock, T., & Walsh, W. (1992). A prospective examination of post-traumatic stress disorder in rape victims. *Journal of Traumatic Stress, 5*, 455–475.

Royal Canadian Mounted Police. (2010a). *Cadet selection process*. Retrieved from http://www.rcmp-grc.gc.ca/recruiting-recrutement/selection/process-processus-eng.htm

Royal Canadian Mounted Police. (2010b). *The RCMP police aptitude test—RPAT*. Retrieved from http://www.rcmp-grc.gc.ca/recruiting-recrutement/selection/rpat-tatpg-eng.htm

Ruby, C.L., & Brigham, J.C. (1997). The usefulness of the criteria-based content analysis technique in distinguishing between truthful and fabricated allegations: A critical review. *Psychology, Public Policy, and Law, 3*, 705–727.

Rudin, J. (2006). *Aboriginal peoples and the criminal justice system*. Retrieved from http://www.attorneygeneral.jus.gov.on.ca/inquiries/ipperwash/policy_part/research/pdf/Rudin.pdf

Rudolph, K.D., & Asher, S.R. (2000). Adaptation and maladaptation in the peer system: Developmental processes and outcomes. In A.J. Sameroff, M. Lewis, & S.M. Miller (Eds.), *Handbook of developmental psychopathology* (2nd ed., pp. 157–175). New York, NY: Kluwer Academic/Plenum Publishers.

Rugge, T. (2006). *Risk assessment of male Aboriginal offenders: A 2006 perspective*. Ottawa, ON: Public Safety and Emergency Preparedness Canada.

Russano, M.B., Meissner, C.A., Narchet, F.M., & Kassin, S.M. (2005). Investigating true and false confessions within a novel experimental paradigm. *Psychological Science, 16*, 481–486.

Rutherford, M.J., Alterman, A.I., Cacciola, J.S., & McKay, J.R. (1997). Validity of the psychopathy checklist-revised in male methadone patients. *Drug and Alcohol Dependence, 44*, 143–149.

Rutter, M. (1979). Protective factors in children's responses to stress and disadvantage. In M.W. Kent & J.E. Rolf (Eds.), *Primary Prevention of Psychopathology, Vol. 3: Social Competence in Children* (pp. 49–74). Hanover, NH: University Press of New England.

Rutter, M. (1988). Studies of psychosocial risk: The power of longitudinal data. Cambridge, MA: Cambridge University Press.

Rutter, M. (1990). Psychosocial resilience and protective mechanisms. In J. Rolf, A.S. Masten, D. Cicchetti, K. Nuechterlein, & S. Weintraub (Eds.), *Risk and protective factors in the development of psychopathology* (pp. 181–214). Cambridge, MA: Cambridge University Press.

Rutter, M. (Ed.). (1995). Psychosocial disturbances in young people: Challenges for prevention. Cambridge, MA: Press Syndicate of the University of Cambridge.

Ruva, C.L., & McEvoy, C. (2008). Negative and positive pretrial publicity affect juror memory and decision making. *Journal of Experimental Psychology: Applied, 14*, 226–235.

Ryan, G., Miyoshi, T.J., Metzner, J.L., Krugman, R.D., & Fryer, G.E. (1996). Trends in a national sample of sexually abusive youths. *Journal of the American Academy of Child and Adolescent Psychiatry, 35*, 17–25.

Saks, M.J., & Marti, M.W. (1997). A meta-analysis of the effects of jury size. *Law and Human Behavior, 21*, 451–466.

Salekin, R.T. (2002). Factor-analysis of the Millon Adolescent Clinical Inventory in a juvenile offender population: Implications for treatment. *Journal of Offender Rehabilitation, 34*, 15–29.

Salekin, R.T., Rogers, R., & Machin, D. (2001). Psychopathy in youth: Pursuing diagnostic clarity. *Journal of Youth and Adolescence, 30*, 173–195.

Salekin, R.T., Rogers, R., & Sewell, K.W. (1996). A review and meta-analysis of the Psychopathy Checklist and Psychopathy Checklist-Revised: Predictive validity of dangerousness. *Clinical Psychology: Science and Practice, 3*, 203–215.

Salekin, R.T., Rogers, R., & Sewell, K.W. (1997). Construct validity of psychopathy in female offender sample: A multitrait-multimethod evaluation. *Journal of Abnormal Psychology, 106*, 576–585.

Salekin, R.T., Rogers, R., Ustad, K.L., & Sewell, K.W. (1998). Psychopathy and recidivism among female inmates. *Law and Human Behavior, 22*, 109–128.

Sampson, R.J., & Laub, J.H. (2005). A life-course view of the development of crime. *Annals of the American Academy of Political and Social Science, 602*, 12–45.

Sanders, B.A. (2003). Maybe there's no such thing as a "good cop": Organizational challenges in selecting quality officers. *Policing: An International Journal of Police Strategies and Management, 26*, 313–328.

Sanders, B.A. (2008). Using personality traits to predict police officer performance. *Policing: An International Journal of Police Strategies and Management, 31*, 129–147.

Sandys, M., & Dillehay, R.C. (1995). First ballot votes, predeliberation dispositions and final verdicts in jury trials. *Law and Human Behavior, 19*, 175–195.

Saslove, H., & Yarmey, A.D. (1980). Long-term auditory memory: Speaker identification. *Journal of Applied Psychology*, 65, 111–116.

Saunders, D.G. (2001). Developing guidelines for domestic violence offenders: What can we learn from related fields and current research? In R.A. Geffner & A. Rosenbaum (Eds.), *Domestic violence offenders: Current interventions, research, and implications for policies and standards* (pp. 235–248). New York, NY: Haworth.

Saunders, D.G. (2002). Are physical assaults by wives and girlfriends a major social problem? A review of the literature. *Violence Against Women*, 8, 1424–1448.

Saunders, J.W.S. (2001). Experts in court: A view from the bench. *Canadian Psychology*, 42, 109–118.

Saunders, P., & Thompson, J. (2002, February 7). The missing women of Vancouver. *CBC News*. Retrieved from http://www.cbc.ca/news/features/bc_missingwomen.html

Saywitz, K., Goodman, G.S., Nicholas, E., & Moan, S. (1991). Children's memories of physical examinations involving genital touch: Implications for reports of child sexual abuse. *Journal of Consulting and Clinical Psychology*, 59, 682–691.

Saywitz, K.J., & Snyder, L. (1996). Narrative elaboration: Test of a new procedure for interviewing children. *Journal of Consulting and Clinical Psychology*, 64, 1347–1357.

Scheck, B. Neufeld, P., & Dwyer, J. (2000). *Actual innocence*. Garden City, NY: Doubleday.

Schmidt, F., McKinnon, L., Chattha, H.K., & Brownless, K. (2006). Concurrent and predictive validity of the Psychopathy Checklist: Youth Version across gender and ethnicity. *Psychological Assessment*, 18, 393–401.

Schneider, E.M. (1986). Describing and changing: Women's self-defence work and the problem of expert testimony on battering. *Women's Rights Law Reports*, 9, 195–222.

Schneider, R.D., Bloom, H., & Heerema, M. (2007). *Mental health courts: Decriminalizing the mentally ill*. Toronto, ON: Irwin Law.

Schuller, R.A. (1992). The impact of battered woman syndrome evidence on jury decision processes. *Law and Human Behavior*, 16, 597–620.

Schuller, R.A. (1995). Expert evidence and hearsay: The influence of "secondhand" information on jurors' decisions. *Law and Human Behavior*, 19, 345–362.

Schuller, R.A., & Hastings, P. (1996). Trials of battered women who kill: The impact of alternative forms of expert evidence. *Law and Human Behavior*, 20, 167–187.

Schuller, R.A., & Hastings, P.A. (2002). Complainant sexual history evidence: Its impact on mock jurors' decisions. *Psychology of Women Quarterly*, 26, 252–261.

Schuller, R.A., & Ogloff, J.R.P. (2001). *Introduction to psychology and law: Canadian perspectives*. Toronto, ON: University of Toronto Press.

Schuller, R.A., & Rzepa, S. (2002). Expert testimony pertaining to battered woman syndrome: Its impact on jurors' decisions. *Law and Human Behavior*, 26, 655–673.

Schuller, R.A., Smith, V.L., & Olson, J.M. (1994). Jurors' decisions in trials of battered women who kill: The role of prior beliefs and expert testimony. *Journal of Applied Social Psychology*, 24, 316–337.

Schuller, R.A., Terry, D., & McKimmie, B. (2005). The impact of expert testimony on jurors' decisions: Gender of the expert and testimony complexity. *Journal of Applied Social Psychology*, 6, 1266–1280.

Schwartz, D., Dodge, K.A., Coie, J.D., Hubbard, J.A., Cillessen, A.H.N., Lemerise, E.A., & Bateman, H. (1998). Social-cognitive and behavioral correlates of aggression and victimization in boys' play groups. *Journal of Abnormal Child Psychology*, 26, 431–440.

Scogin, F., Schumacher, J., Gardner, J., & Chaplin, W. (1995). Predictive validity of psychological testing in law enforcement settings. *Professional Psychology: Research and Practice*, 26, 68–71.

Seagrave, D., & Grisso, T. (2002). Adolescent development and the measurement of juvenile psychopathy. *Law and Human Behavior*, 26, 219–239.

Sear, L., & Williamson, T. (1999). British and American interrogation strategies. In D.V. Canter and L.J. Alison (Eds.), Interviewing and deception (pp. 67–81). Aldershot, England: Ashgate Publishing.

Seligman, M.E. (1975). *Helplessness: On depression, development, and death*. San Francisco, CA: W.H. Freeman.

Seltzer, R. (2006). Scientific jury selection: Does it work? *Journal of Applied Social Psychology*, 36, 2417–2435.

Semrau, S., & Gale, J. (2002). *Murderous minds on trials: Terrible tales from a forensic psychiatrist's case book*. Toronto, ON: Dundurn Press.

Serin, R., Forth, A., Brown, S., Nunes, K., Bennell, C., & Pozzulo, J. (2009). *Psychology of criminal behaviour: A Canadian perspective*. Toronto, ON: Pearson Education Canada.

Serin, R.C. (1991). Psychopathy and violence in criminals. *Journal of Interpersonal Violence*, 6, 423–431.

Serin, R.C., & Amos, N.L. (1995). The role of psychopathy in the assessment of dangerousness. *International Journal of Law and Psychiatry*, 18, 231–238.

Serin, R.C., & Lloyd, C. (2009). Examining the process of offender change: The transition to crime desistance. *Psychology, Crime, & Law*, 15, 347–364.

Serin, R.C., Gobeil, R., & Preston, D. (2009). Evaluation of the persistently violent offender treatment program. *International Journal of Offender Therapy and Comparative Criminology*, 53, 57–73.

Serota, K.B., Levine, T.R., & Boster, F.J. (2010). The prevalence of lying in America: Three studies of self-reported lies. *Human Communication Research*, 36, 2–25.

Seto, M.C., & Barbaree, H.E. (1999). Psychopathy, treatment behavior, and sex offender recidivism. *Journal of Interpersonal Violence, 14*, 1235–1248.

Sevecke, K., Pukrop, R., Kosson, D.S., & Krischer, M.K. (2009). Factor structure of the Hare Psychopathy Checklist: Youth version in German female and male detainees and community adolescents. *Psychological Assessment, 21*, 45–56.

Seymour, T.L., Seifert, C.M., Shafto, M.G., & Mosmann, A.L. (2000). Using response time measures to assess "guilty knowledge." *Journal of Applied Psychology, 85*, 30–37.

Shaw, D.S., Keenan, K., & Vondra, J.I. (1994). Developmental precursors of externalizing behaviour: Ages 1 to 3. *Developmental Psychology, 30*, 355–364.

Shaw, J.S., III (1996). Increases in eyewitness confidence resulting from postevent questioning. *Journal of Experimental Psychology: Applied, 12*, 126–146.

Shaw, J.S., III, & McClure, K.A. (1996). Repeated postevent questioning can lead to elevated levels of eyewitness confidence. *Law and Human Behavior, 20*, 629–654.

Shaw, M. (1994). Women in prison: A literature review. *Forum on Corrections Research, 6*, 13–18.

Sheehan, P.W., & Tilden, J. (1984). Real and simulated occurrences of memory distortion in hypnosis. *Journal of Abnormal Psychology, 93*, 47–57.

Sheehan, R., & Cordner, G.W. (1989). *Introduction to police administration* (2nd ed.). Cincinnati, OH: Anderson Publishing Co.

Sheldon, D.H., & Macleod, M.D. (1991). From normative to positive data: Expert psychological evidence re-examined. *Criminal Law Review*, 811–820.

Sheldon, W.H. (1949). *Varieties of delinquent youths: A psychology of constitutional differences*. New York, NY: Harper & Row.

Shepherd, J.W. (1981). Social factors in face recognition. In G. Davies, H. Ellis, & J. Shepherd (Eds.), *Perceiving and remembering faces* (pp. 55–79). London, England: Academic Press.

Shepherd, J.W., & Deregowski, J.B. (1981). Races and faces: A comparison of the responses of Africans and Europeans to faces of the same and different races. *British Journal of Social Psychology, 20*, 125–133.

Sheridan, M.S. (2003). The deceit continues: An updated literature review of Munchausen syndrome by proxy. *Child Abuse & Neglect, 27*, 431–451.

Sherman, L.W., & Berk, R.A. (1984). The specific deterrent effects of arrest for domestic assault. *American Sociological Review, 49*, 261–272.

Sherman, L.W., Schmidt, J.D., & Rogan, D.P. (1992). *Policing domestic violence: Experiments and dilemmas*. New York, NY: Free Press.

Shover, N., & Thompson, C.Y. (1992). Age differential expectations, and crime desistance. *Criminology, 30*, 89–104.

Siegal, L., & Senna, J. (1994). *Juvenile delinquency: Theory, practice and law* (5th ed.). St. Paul, MN: West Publishing Company.

Silver, E. (2006). Understanding the relationship between mental disorder and violence: The need for a criminological perspective. *Law and Human Behavior, 30*, 685–706.

Simourd, D.J. (2004). Use of dynamic risk/need assessment instruments among long-term incarcerated offenders. *Criminal Justice and Behavior, 31*, 306–323.

Simourd, D.J., & Malcolm, P.B. (1998). Reliability and validity of the Level of Service Inventory-Revised among federally incarcerated sex offenders. *Journal of Interpersonal Violence, 13*, 261–274.

Simourd, D.J., Hoge, R.D., Andrews, D.A., & Leschied, A.W. (1994). An empirically based typology of male young offenders. *Canadian Journal of Criminology, 36*, 447–461.

Simourd, L., & Andrews, D.A. (1994). Correlates of delinquency: A look at gender differences. *Forum on Corrections Research, 6*, 26–31.

Sin, L. (2006, December 6). By the numbers. *Ottawa Citizen*, p. A3.

Sioui, R., & Thibault, J. (2001). *Pertinence of cultural adaptation of Reintegration Potential Reassessment (RPR) scale to Aboriginal context* (Research Report No. R-109). Ottawa, ON: Correctional Service Canada.

Sjöstedt, G., & Langström, N. (2002). Assessment of risk for criminal recidivism among rapists: A comparison of four different measures. *Psychology, Crime & Law, 8*, 25–40.

Skeem, J.L., Mulvey, E.P., Odgers, C., Schubert, C., Stowman, S., Gardner, W., & Lidz, C. (2005). What do clinicians expect? Comparing envisioned and reported violence for male and female patients. *Journal of Consulting and Clinical Psychology, 73*, 599–609.

Skelton, C. (2010, August 5). Crown drops 20 murder charges against Picton. *Times Colonist*. Retrieved from http://www.timescolonist.com/news/Crown+drops+murder+charges+against+Picton/3362068/story.html

Skilling, T.A., Quinsey, V.L., & Craig, W.M. (2001). Evidence of a taxon underlying serious antisocial behavior in boys. *Criminal Justice and Behavior, 28*, 450–470.

Slone, A.E., Brigham, J.C., & Meissner, C.A. (2000). Social and cognitive factors affecting the own-race bias in Whites. *Basic and Applied Social Psychology, 22*, 71–84.

Smith, C., & Thornberry, T.P. (1995). The relationship between childhood maltreatment and adolescent involvement in delinquency. *Criminology, 33*, 451–481.

Smith, C.A., Ireland, T.O., & Thornberry, T.P. (2005). Adolescent maltreatment and its impact on young adult antisocial behavior. *Child Abuse & Neglect, 29*, 1099–1119.

Smith, D.W., Letourneau, E.J., Saunders, B.E., Kilpatrick, D.G., Resnick, H.S., & Best, C.L. (2000). Delay in disclosure of childhood rape: Results from a national survey. *Child Abuse & Neglect, 24,* 273–287.

Smith, M.D. (1990). Patriarchal ideology and wife beating: A test of a feminist hypothesis. *Violence and Victims, 5,* 257–273.

Smith, P. Cullen, F.T., & Latessa, E.J. (2009). Can 14,373 women be wrong? A meta-analysis of the LSI-R and recidivism for female offenders. *Criminology and Public Policy,* 8,183–208.

Smith, S.M., Patry, M., & Stinson, V. (2008). Is the CSI effect real? If it is, what is it? In G. Bourgon, R.K. Hanson, J.D. Pozzulo, K.E. Morton Bourgon, & C.L. Tanasichuk (Eds.), *Proceedings of the 2007 North American Correctional & Criminal Justice Psychology Conference* (User Report). Ottawa, ON: Public Safety Canada.

Smith, S.M., Stinson, V., & Patry, M.W. (2009). Using the "Mr. Big" technique to elicit confessions: Successful innovation or dangerous development in the Canadian legal system. *Psychology, Public Policy, and Law, 15,* 168–193.

Snook, B., Eastwood, J., Gendreau, P, Goggin, C., & Cullen, R.M. (2007). Taking stock of criminal profiling: A narrative review and meta-analysis. *Criminal Justice and Behavior, 34,* 437–453.

Snook, B., Eastwood, J., Stinson, M., Tedeschini, J., & House, J.C. (2010). Reforming investigative interviewing in Canada. *Canadian Journal of Criminology and Criminal Justice, 52,*203–217.

Snook, B., Haines, A., Taylor, P.J., & Bennell, C. (2007). Criminal profiling belief and use: A survey of Canadian police officer opinion. *Canadian Journal of Police and Security Services, 5,* 169–179.

Snook, B., Taylor, P.J., & Bennell, C. (2004). Geographic profiling: The fast, frugal and accurate way. *Applied Cognitive Psychology, 18,* 105–121.

Snook, B., Taylor, P.J., & Bennell, C. (2005). Shortcuts to geographic profiling success: A reply to Rossmo. *Applied Cognitive Psychology, 19,*1–7.

Snook, B., Zito, M., Bennell, C., & Taylor, P. J. (2005). On the complexity and accuracy of geographic profiling strategies. *Journal of Quantitative Criminology, 21,* 1–26.

Söchting, I., Fairbrother, N., & Koch, W. J. (2004). Sexual assault of women: Prevention efforts and risk factors. *Violence Against Women, 10,* 73–93.

Solomon, R.L. (1960). Letter quoted by O.H. Mowrer. Learning theory and the symbolic processes. (pp. 399–404). New York, NY: Wiley.

Sonkin, D.J., Martin, D., & Walker, I.E. (1985). *The male batterer: A treatment approach.* New York, NY: Springer.

Soothill, K., Harman, J., Francis, B., & Kirby, S. (2005). Identifying future repeat danger from sexual offenders against children: A focus on those convicted and those strongly suspected of such crime. *The Journal of Forensic Psychiatry & Psychology, 16,* 225–247.

Spanos, N.P., DuBreuil, S.C., & Gwynn, M.I. (1991–1992). The effects of expert testimony concerning rape on the verdicts and beliefs of mock jurors. *Imagination, Cognition, and Personality, 11,* 37–51.

Sparwood Youth Assistance Program. (2007). *Sparwood youth assistance program.* Retrieved from http://www.sparwood .bc.ca/syap-out.htm.

Spitzberg, B.H., & Cupach, W.R. (2007). The state of the art of stalking: Taking stock of the emerging literature. *Aggression and Violent Behavior, 12,* 64–86.

Sporer S.L., & Schwandt, B. (2007). Moderators of non-verbal indicators of deception: A meta-analytic synthesis. *Psychology, Public Policy, and Law, 13,* 1–34.

Sporer, S.L. & Schwandt, B. (2006). Paraverbal indicators of deception: A meta-analytic synthesis. *Applied Cognitive Psychology, 20,* 421–446.

Sporer, S.L. (1996). Psychological aspects of person descriptions. In S. Sporer, R. Malpass, & G. Köehnken (Eds.), *Psychological issues in eyewitness identification* (pp. 53–86). Mahwah, NJ: Erlbaum.

Sporer, S.L., Penrod, S.D., Read, D., & Cutler, B.L. (1995). Choosing confidence and accuracy: A meta-analysis of the confidence-accuracy relations in eyewitness identification studies. *Psychological Bulletin, 118,* 315–327.

Sprott, J.B., & Doob, A. (1997). Fear, victimization, and attitudes to sentencing, the courts, and the police. *Canadian Journal of Criminology, 39,* 275–291.

Stack, S. (1997). Homicide followed by suicide: An analysis of Chicago data. *Criminology, 35,* 435–453.

Stadtland, C., Hollweg, M., Kleindienst, N., Dietl, J., Reich, U., & Nedopil, N. (2005). Risk assessment and prediction of violent and sexual recidivism in sex offenders: Long-term predictive validity of four assessment instruments. *The Journal of Forensic Psychiatry & Psychology, 16,* 92–108.

Stanton, J., & Simpson, A. (2002). Filicide: A review. *International Journal of Law and Psychiatry, 25,* 1–14.

Statistics Canada, Health Statistics Division. (1999). Divorces, 1996 and 1997 (Cat. No. 84F0213XPB). Ottawa, ON: Author.

Statistics Canada, Health Statistics Division. (2003, September 3). Canadian Community Health Survey: Mental health and well-being. *The Daily,* Ottawa, ON: Author.

Statistics Canada. (2003a). *Table: Court, youth cases by decision (total all decisions).* Retrieved from http://www40.statcan. ca/l01/cst01/legal25a.htm

Statistics Canada. (2003b). *Table: Court, youth cases by type of sentence, by province and territory (Canada).* Retrieved from http://www40.statcan.ca/l01/cst01/legal40a.htm

Statistics Canada. (2003c, June 20). Youth court statistics. *The Daily.* Retrieved from http://www.statcan.ca/Daily/English/030620/d030620d.htm

Statistics Canada. (2004a, March 12). Youth court statistics. *The Daily*. Retrieved from http://www.statcan.ca/Daily/English/040312/d040312c.htm

Statistics Canada. (2004b, October 13). Youth custody and community services. *The Daily*. Retrieved from http://www.statcan.ca/Daily/English/041013/d041013c.htm

Statistics Canada. (2005a). *CANSIM Table 252-0030: Youth court survey, number of cases by type of decision, annual, 1991 to 2003* (Cat. No. 85-002-X). Retrieved from http://www.statcan.ca/Daily/English/050624/d050624c.htm

Statistics Canada. (2005b, December 1). Youth correctional services: Key indicators. *The Daily*. Retrieved from http://www.statcan.ca/Daily/English/051201/d051201a.htm

Statistics Canada. (2006a). *Family violence in Canada: A statistical profile*. Ottawa, ON: Minister of Industry.

Statistics Canada. (2006b). *Homicides, 2005*. Retrieved from http://www.statcan.gc.ca/daily-quotidien/061108/dq061108b-eng.htm

Statistics Canada. (2006c). *Report on the demographic situation in Canada 2003 and 2004* (Cat. No. 91-209-X1E). Ottawa, ON. Author.

Statistics Canada. (2008). *Youth crime*. Retrieved from http://www.statcan.gc.ca/daily-quotidien/080516/dq080516a-eng.htm

Statistics Canada. (2009). *Homicides in Canada, 2008*. Retrieved from http://www.statcan.gc.ca/daily-quotidien/091028/dq091028a-eng.htm

Statistics Canada. (2009). *Police-reported crime statistics, 2008*. Retrieved from http://www.statcan.gc.ca/daily-quotidien/090721/t090721a1-eng.htm

Steadman, H.J. (2000). From dangerousness to risk assessment of community violence: Taking stock at the turn of the century. *Journal of the American Academy of Psychiatry and the Law, 28*, 265–271.

Steadman, H.J., & Cocozza, J. (1974). Careers of the criminally insane. Lexington, MA: Lexington Books.

Steadman, H.J., McGreevy, M.A., Morrissey, J.P., Callahan, L.A., Robbins, P.C., & Cirincione, C. (1993). *Before and after Hinckley: Evaluating insanity defense reform*. New York, NY: Guilford Press.

Steadman, H.J., Monahan, J., Appelbaum, P.S., Grisso, T., Mulvey, E.P., Roth, L.H., . . . D. Klassen. (1994). Designing a new generation of risk assessment research. In J. Monahan & H. J. Steadman (Eds.), Violence and mental disorder: Developments in risk assessment (297–318). Chicago, IL: University of Chicago Press.

Steadman, H.J., Mulvey, E.P., Monahan, J., Robbins, P.C., Appelbaum, P.S., Grisso, T., . . . Silver, E. (1998). Violence by people discharged from acute psychiatric inpatient facilities and by others in the same neighborhoods. *Archives of General Psychiatry, 55*, 393–401.

Steadman, H.J., Silver, E., Monahan, J., Appelbaum, P.S., Robbins, P.C., Mulvey, E.P., . . . Banks, S. (2000). A classification tree approach to the development of actuarial violence risk assessment tools. *Law and Human Behavior, 24*, 83–100.

Steblay, N., Dysart, J.E., Fulero, S., & Lindsay, R.C.L. (2003). Eyewitness accuracy rates in police showup and lineup presentations: A meta-analytic comparison. *Law and Human Behavior, 27*, 523–540.

Steblay, N.M. & Bothwell, R.B. (1994). Evidence for hypnotically refreshed testimony: The view from the laboratory. *Law and Human Behavior, 18*, 635–651.

Steblay, N.M. & Bothwell, R.B. (1994). Evidence for hypnotically refreshed testimony: The view from the laboratory. *Law and Human Behavior, 18*, 635–651.

Steblay, N.M. (1992). A meta-analytic review of the weapon focus effect. *Law and Human Behavior, 16*, 413–424.

Steblay, N.M. (1997). Social influence in eyewitness recall: A meta-analytic review of lineup instruction effects. *Law and Human Behavior, 21*, 283–298.

Steblay, N.M., Besirevic, J., Fulero, S.M., & Jimenez-Lorente, B. (1999). The effects of pretrial publicity on juror verdicts: A meta-analytic review. *Law and Human Behavior, 23*, 219–235.

Steblay, N.M., Dysart, J., Fulero, S., & Lindsay, R.C.L. (2001). Eyewitness accuracy rates in sequential and simultaneous lineup presentations: A meta-analytic comparison. *Law and Human Behavior, 25*, 459–474.

Stefanie Rengel case statement of facts (2009, April 9). *CityNews*. Retrieved from http://www.citytv.com/toronto/citynews/news/local/article/10094—stefanie-rengel-case

Stein, K. (2001). *Public perceptions of crime and justice in Canada: A review of opinion polls*. Ottawa, ON: Department of Justice Canada.

Stein, M., Koverola, C., Hanna, C., Torchia, M., & McClarry, B. (1997). Hippocampal volume in woman victimized by childhood sexual abuse. *Psychological Medicine, 27*, 951–959.

Stellar, M. (1989). Recent developments in statement analysis. In J.C. Yuille (Ed.), *Credibility assessment* (pp. 135–154). Dordrecht, the Netherlands: Kluwer.

Stellar, M. & Kohnken, G. (1989). Statement analysis: Credibility assessment of children's testimonies in sexual abuse cases. In D. C. Raskin (Ed.), *Psychological methods in criminal investigation and evidence* (pp. 217–245). New York, NY: Springer.

Stern, W. (1910). Abstracts of lectures on the psychology of testimony and on the study of individuality. *American Journal of Psychology, 21*, 270–282.

Sternberg, K., Lamb, M., Esplin, P., Orbach, Y, & Hershkowitz, I. (2002). Using a structure interview protocol to improve the quality of investigative interviews. In M. Eisen, J. Quas, & G. Goodman (Eds.), *Memory and suggestibility in the forensic interview. Personality and clinical psychology series* (pp. 409–436). Mahwah, NJ: Lawrence Erlbaum Associates.

Stewart, L., Gabora, N., Kropp, R., & Lee, Z. (2005). *Family violence programming: Treatment outcome for Canadian federally sentenced offenders*. Ottawa, ON: Correctional Service of Canada.

Storm, J., & Graham, J.R. (2000). Detection of coached general malingering on the MMPI-2. *Psychological Assessment, 12,* 158–165.

Stouthamer-Loeber, M., Wei, E., Loeber, R., & Masten, A.S. (2004). Desistance from persistent serious delinquency in the transition to adulthood. *Development and Psychopathology, 16,* 897–918.

Strand, S., & Belfrage, H. (2001). Comparison of HCR-20 scores in violent mentally disordered men and women: Gender differences and similarities. *Psychology, Crime, & Law, 7,* 71–79.

Strand, S., Belfrage, H., Fransson, G., & Levander, S. (1999). Clinical and risk management factors in risk prediction of mentally disordered offenders—more important than historical data? A retrospective study of 40 mentally disordered offenders assessed with the HCR-20 violence risk assessment scheme. *Legal and Criminological Psychology, 4,* 67–76.

Straus, M.A. (1977). Wife beating: How common and why? *Victimology, 2,* 443–458.

Straus, M.A. (1979). Measuring family conflict and violence: The Conflict Tactics Scale. *Journal of Marriage and the Family, 41,* 75–88.

Straus, M.A. (1990). Measuring intrafamily conflict and violence: The Conflict Tactics (CTS) Scales. In M. Straus & R. Gelles (Eds.), *Physical violence in American families: Risk factors and adaptations to violence in 8,145 families* (pp. 29–47). New Brunswick, NJ: Transaction.

Straus, M.A., Gelles, R. J., & Steinmetz, S. (1980). *Behind closed doors: Violence in the American family.* Garden City, NY: Anchor/Doubleday.

Straus, M.A., Hamby, S.L., Boney-McCoy, S., & Sugarman, D.B. (1996). The revised Conflict Tactics Scales (CTS2): Development and preliminary psychometric data. *Journal of Family Issues, 17,* 283–316.

Strier, F. (1999). Whither trial consulting? Issues and projections. *Law and Human Behavior, 23,* 93–115.

Strömwall, L.A., Hartwig, M., & Granhag, P.A. (2006). To act truthfully: Nonverbal behaviour and strategies during a police interrogation. *Psychology, Crime & Law, 12,* 207–219.

Sue, S., Smith, R.E., & Caldwell, C. (1973). Effects of inadmissible evidence on the decisions of simulated jurors: A moral dilemma. *Journal of Applied Social Psychology, 3,* 345–353.

Sundby, S.E. (1997). The jury as critic: An empirical look at how capital juries perceive expert and lay testimony. *Virginia Law Review, 83,* 1109–1188.

Supreme Court of Canada. (2010). *About the court.* Retrieved from http://www.scc-csc.gc.ca/court-cour/index-eng.asp

Suspect in bus killing delivered newspapers, worked at McDonald's: employer (2008, August 1). *CBC News.* Retrieved from http://www.cbc.ca/canada/story/2008/08/01/stabbing-victim.html

Sutherland, E.H. (1939). *Principles of criminology.* Philadelphia, PA: J.B. Lippincott Company.

Swanson, J.W. (1994). Mental disorder, substance abuse, and community violence: An epidemiological approach. In J. Monahan & H. J. Steadman (Eds.), *Violence and mental disorder: Developments in risk assessment* (101–137). Chicago, IL: University of Chicago Press.

Swanson, J.W., Borum, R., Swartz, M.S., & Monahan, J. (1996). Psychotic symptoms and disorders and the risk of violent behavior in the community. *Criminal Behavior and Mental Health, 6,* 317–338.

Swanson, J.W., Borum, R., Swartz, M.S., Hiday, V.A., Wagner, H.R., & Burns, B.J. (2001). Can involuntary outpatient commitment reduce arrests among persons with severe mental illness? *Criminal Justice and Behavior, 28,* 156–189.

Swanson, J.W., Holzer, C.E., Ganju, V.K., & Jono, R.T. (1990). Violence and psychiatric disorder in the community: Evidence from the epidemiologic catchment area surveys. *Hospital and Community Psychiatry, 41,* 761–770.

Sykes, J.B. (Ed.). (1982). *The Concise Oxford Dictionary* (7th ed.). Oxford: Oxford University Press.

Szymanski, L.A., Devlin, A.S., Chrisler, J.C., & Vyse, S.A. (1993). Gender role and attitudes toward rape in male and female college students. *Sex Roles, 29,* 37–57.

Taylor, A., & Bennell, C. (2006). Operational and organizational police stress in an Ontario police department: A descriptive study. *Canadian Journal of Police and Security Services, 4,* 223–234.

Taylor, S.P., & Sears, J.D. (1988). The effects of alcohol and persuasive social pressure on human physical aggression. *Aggressive Behavior, 14,* 237–243.

Teasdale, B., Silver, E., & Monahan, J. (2006). Gender, threat/control-override delusions and violence. *Law and Human Behavior, 30,* 649–658.

Technical Working Group for Eyewitness Evidence. (1999). *Eyewitness evidence: A guide for law enforcement* (NCJ 178240). Washington, DC: United States Department of Justice, Office of Justice Programs. Retrieved from www.ojp.usdoj.gov

Temrin, H., Buchmayer, S., & Enquist, M. (2000). Step-parents and infanticide New data contradict evolutionary predictions. *Proceedings of the Royal Society of London, Series B: Biological Sciences, 267,* 943–945.

Teplin, L.A. (1984). Criminalizing mental disorder: The comparative arrest rate of the mentally ill. *American Psychologist, 39,* 784–803.

Teplin, L.A. (1986). Keeping the peace: The parameters of police discretion in relation to the mentally disordered. Washington, DC: U.S. Department of Justice.

Teplin, L.A. (2000, July). Keeping the peace: Police discretion and mentally ill persons. *National Institute of Justice Journal,* 8–15.

Teplin, L.A. Abram, K.M., & McClelland, G.M. (1994). Does psychiatric disorder predict violent crime among released jail detainees? *American Psychologist, 49*, 335–342.

Teplin, L.A., Abram, K.M., & McClelland, G.M. (1996). Prevalence of psychiatric disorders among incarcerated women I. Pretrial jail detainees. *Archives of General Psychiatry, 53*, 505–512.

Terman, L.M. (1917). A trial of mental and pedagogical tests in a civil service examination for policemen and firemen. *Journal of Applied Psychology, 1*, 17–29.

Terrance, C. & Matheson, K. (2003). Undermining reasonableness: Expert testimony in a case involving a battered woman who kills. *Psychology of Women Quarterly, 27*, 37–45.

Territo, L., & Sewell, J.D. (2007). *Stress management in law enforcement* (2nd edition). Durham, NC: Carolina Academic Press.

Test, M.A., (1992). Training in community living. In R.P Liberman (Ed.), *Handbook of psychiatric rehabilitation* (pp. 153–170). New York, NY: Macmillan.

Thierry, K.L., Lamb, M.E., Orbach, Y., & Pipe, M. (2005). Developmental differences in the function and use of anatomical dolls during interviews with alleged sexual abuse victims. *Journal of Counsulting and Clinical Psychology, 73*, 1125–1134.

Thonney, J., Kanachi, M., Sasaki, H., & Hatayama, T. (2005). Eye blinking as a lie-detection index in an emotionally arousing context. *Tohoku Psychologica Folia, 64*, 58–67.

Thornhill, R., & Palmer, C.T. (2000). *A natural history of rape: Biological bases of sexual coercion.* Cambridge, MA: MIT Press.

Tibbetts, J. (2003, July 21). Divorce courts shift to parallel parenting. *Ottawa Citizen*, p. A5.

Tibbetts, J. (2009, November 10). Canada's youth crime laws hailed as success. *National Post.* http:www.nationalpost.com/story.html?id=2207627

Tjaden, P., & Thoennes, N. (1998). *Stalking in America: Findings from the National Violence Against Women Survey.* Washington, DC: American Psychological Association.

Tjaden, P.G., & Thoennes, N. (2001). Coworker violence and gender: Findings from the National Violence Against Women Survey. *American Journal of Preventive Medicine, 20*, 85–89.

Tolan, P., & Thomas, P. (1995). The implications of age of onset for delinquency risk: II. Longitudinal data. *Journal of Abnormal Child Psychology, 23*, 157–181.

Tolman, R.M., & Weisz, A. (1995). Coordinated community intervention for domestic violence: The effects of arrest and prosecution on recidivism of woman abuse perpetrators. *Crime and Delinquency, 41*, 481–495.

Toma, C.L., Hancock, J.T., & Ellison, N.B. (2008). Separating fact from fiction: An examination of deceptive self-presentation in online dating profiles. *Personality and Social Bulletin, 34*, 1023–1036.

Tombaugh, T.N. (1996). *Test of Malingered Memory (TOMM).* Toronto, ON: Multi-Health Systems.

Tombaugh, T.N. (2002). The Test of Memory Malingering (TOMM) in forensic psychology. *Journal of Forensic Neuropsychology, 2*, 69–96.

Toomey, J.A., Kucharski, L.T., & Duncan, S. (2009). The utility of the MMPI-2 Malingering Discriminant Function Index in the detection of malingering: A study of criminal defendants. *Assessment, 16*, 115–121.

Trager, J., & Brewster, J. (2001). The effectiveness of psychological profiles. *Journal of Police and Criminal Psychology, 16*, 20–28.

Trice, A.D., & Lamb, M. (1996). Sex-role orientation among incarcerated women. *Psychological Reports, 79*, 92–94.

Trocme, N., Fallon, B., MacLaurin, B., Daciuk, J., Felstiner, C., Black, T., . . . Cloutier, R., (2005). *Canadian Incidence Study of Reported Child Abuse and Neglect 2003: Major Findings.* Ottawa, ON: Minister of Public Works and Government Services Canada.

Trupin, E.W., Stewart, D.G., Beach, B., & Boesky, L. (2002). Effectiveness of a Dialectical Behaviour Therapy Program for incarcerated female juvenile offenders. *Child and Adolescent Mental Health, 7(3)*, 121–127.

Tufts, J. (2000) Public attitudes toward the criminal justice system. *Juristat, 20.*

Turtle, J.W., Lindsay, R.C.L., & Wells, G.L. (2003). Best practice recommendations for eyewitness evidence procedures: New ideas for the oldest way to solve a case. *The Canadian Journal of Police and Security Services, 1*, 5–18.

Turvey, B. (2002). *Criminal profiling: An introduction to behavioral evidence analysis* (2nd ed.). San Diego, CA: Academic Press.

Tversky, A., & Kahneman, D. (1981). The framing of decisions and the psychology of choice. *Science, 211*, 453–458.

Tweed, R.G., & Dutton, D.G. (1998). A comparison of impulsive and instrumental subgroups of batters. *Violence and Victims, 13*, 217–230.

U.S. Bureau of Justice Statistics. (2005). *Contacts between police and the public: Findings from the 2002 national survey.* Washington, DC: U.S. Bureau of Statistics.

U.S. Department of Justice (2001). *Internet crimes against children.* Office for victims of Crime Bulletin. Washington, DC: Author.

Uggen, C. (1999). Ex-offenders and the conformist alternative: A job quality model of work and crime. *Social Problems, 46*, 127–151.

Ullman, S.E., & Knight, R.A. (1993). The efficacy of women's resistance strategies in rape situations. *Psychology of Women Quarterly, 17*, 23–38.

Ulmer, J.T. (1997). *Social worlds of sentencing: Court communities under sentencing guidelines.* Albany, NY: State University of New York Press.

Undeutsch, U. (1989). The development of statement reality analysis. In J.C. Yuille (Ed.), *Credibility assessment* (pp. 101–121). Dordrecht, the Netherlands: Kluwer Academic Publishers.

United States Department of Justice (2010). *2008 crime in the United States*. Retrieved from Federal Bureau of Investigation website: http://www.fbi.gov/ucr/cius2008/data/table_01.html

Urbaniok, F., Noll, T., Grunewald, S, Steinbach, J., & Endrass, J. (2006). Prediction of violent and sexual offences: A replication study of the VRAG in Switzerland. *The Journal of Forensic Psychiatry & Psychology, 17*, 23–31.

Vallée, B. (1998). *Life and death with Billy*. Toronto, ON: Random House.

Van Koppen, P.J., & Lochun, S.K. (1997). Portraying perpetrators: The validity of offender descriptions by witnesses. *Law and Human Behavior, 21*, 661–685.

Vance, J.P. (2001). Neurobiological mechanisms of psychosocial resiliency. In J.M. Richman & M.W. Fraser (Eds.), *The context of youth violence: Resilience, risk, & protection* (pp. 43–81). Westport, CN: Praeger.

Vandiver, D.M., & Teske, R.J. (2006). Juvenile female and male sex offenders: A comparison of offender, victim and judicial processing characteristics. *International Journal of Offender Therapy and ComparativeCriminology, 50*, 148–165.

Varendonck, J. (1911). Les temoignages d'enfants dans un proces retentisaant. *Archives de Psycholgie, 11*, 129–171.

Viding, E., Blair, R.J., Moffitt, T.E. & Plomin, R. (2005). Evidence for substantial genetic risk for psychopathy in 7-year-olds. *Journal of Child Psychology and Psychiatry and Allied Disciplines, 46*, 592–597.

Viljoen, J.L. & Zapf, P.A. (2002). Fitness to stand trial evaluations: A comparison of referred and non-referred defendants. *International Journal of Forensic Mental Health, 1*, 127–138.

Viljoen, J.L., Roesch, R., Ogloff, J.R.P., & Zapf, P.A. (2003). The role of Canadian psychologists in conducting fitness and criminal responsibility evaluations. *Canadian Psychology, 44*, 369–381.

Vincent, G.M., Odgers, C.L., McCormick, A.V., & Corrado, R.R. (2008). The PCL:YV and recidivism in male and female juveniles: A follow-up into young adulthood. *International Journal of Law and Psychiatry, 31*, 287–296.

Vingoe, F.J. (1995). Beliefs of British law and medical students compared to expert criterion group on forensic hypnosis. *Contemporary Hypnosis, 12*, 173–187.

Violanti, J.M., Marshall, J.R., & Howe, B. (1985). Stress, coping and alcohol use: The police connection. *Journal of Police Science and Administration, 31*, 106–110.

Violanti, J.M., Vena, J.E., & Marshall, J.R. (1986). Disease risk and mortality among police officers: New evidence and contributing factors. *Journal of Police Science and Administration, 14*, 17–23.

Vitacco, M.J., Neumann, C.S., Caldwell, M.F., Leistico, A. & Van Rybroek, G.J. (2006). Testing four models of the Psychopathy Checklist: Youth Version and their association with instrumental aggression. *Journal of Personality Assessment, 87*, 74–83.

Vitale, J.E., Smith, S.S., Brinkely, C.A., & Newman, J.P. (2002). The reliability and validity of the Psychopathy Checklist-Revised in a sample of female offenders. *Criminal Justice and Behavior, 29*, 202–231.

Vizard, E., & Trantor, M. (1988). Helping young children to describe experiences of child sexual abuse: General issue. In A. Bentovim, A., Elton, J. Hilderbrand, M. Tranter, & E. Vizard (Eds.), *Child sexual abuse within the family: Assessment and treatment* (pp. 84–104). Bristol, England: John Wright.

Vrij, A. (1994). The impact of information and setting on detection of deception by police detectives. *Journal of Nonverbal Behavior, 18*, 117–127.

Vrij, A. (1995). Behavioural correlates of deception in simulated police interview. *Journal of Psychology: Interdisciplinary and Applied, 129*, 15–29.

Vrij, A. (1998). Nonverbal communication and credibility. In A. Memon, A. Vrij, & R. Bull (Eds.), *Psychology andlaw: Truthfulness, accuracy, and credibility* (pp. 32–58). London, England: McGraw-Hill.

Vrij, A. (2000). *Detecting lies and deceits: The psychology of lying and the implications for professional practice*. Chichester, England: John Wiley & Sons.

Vrij, A. (2005). Criteria-Based Content Analysis: A qualitative review of the first 37 studies. *Psychology, Public Policy, and Law, 11*, 3–41.

Vrij, A. (2008). *Detecting lies and deceit: Pitfalls and opportunities* (2nd ed.). Chichester, England: Wiley.

Vrij, A., & Mann, S. (2001). Who killed my relative? Police officers' ability to detect real-life high-stake lies. *Psychology, Crime, and Law, 7*, 119–132.

Vrij, A., & Semin, G.R. (1996). Lie experts' beliefs about nonverbal indicators of deception. *Journal of Nonverbal Behavior, 20*, 65–80.

Vrij, A., Akenhurst, L., Soukara, S., & Bull, R. (2002). Will the truth come out?: The effect of deception, age, status, coaching, and social skills on CBCA scores. *Law and Human Behavior, 26*, 261–284.

Vrij, A., Edward, K., Roberts, K.P., & Bull, R. (2000). Detecting deceit via analysis of verbal and nonverbal behaviour. *Journal of Nonverbal Behaviour, 24*, 239–263.

Wadsworth, M.E.J. (1976). Delinquency, pulse rates, and early emotional deprivation. *British Journal of Criminology, 16*, 245–256.

Wagstaff, G.F., MacVeigh, J., Boston, R., Scott, L., Brunas-Wagstaff, J., & Cole, J. (2003). Can laboratory findings on eyewitness testimony be generalized to the real world? An archival analysis of the influence of violence, weapon presence, and age on eyewitness accuracy. *The Journal of Psychology, 137*, 17–28.

Waite, S., & Geddes, A. (2006). Malingered psychosis leading to involuntary psychiatric hospitalization. *Australian Psychiatry, 14*, 419–421.

Wakefield, H., & Underwager, R. (1998). Coerced or nonvoluntary confessions. *Behavioral Sciences and the Law, 16*, 423–440.

Walker, L. (1979). *The battered woman*. New York, NY: Harper Perennial.

Walker, L.E. (1984). *The battered woman syndrome*. New York, NY: Springer.

Walker, L.E. (1993). Battered woman as defendants. In N.Z. Hilton (Ed.), *Legal response to wife assault: Current trends and evaluation* (pp. 233–257). Thousand Oaks, CA: Sage.

Wallace, H.S. (1993). Mandatory minimums and the betrayal of sentencing reform: A legislative Dr. Jekyll and Mr. Hyde. *Federal Probation, 57*, 9.

Wallace, M. (2003). Crime statistics in Canada. *Juristat, 23*.

Wallace, M. (2009 July). Police-reported crime statistics in Canada, 2008 (Statistics Canada Catalogue, No. 85-002-X). *Juristat, 29*(3).

Walma, M.W., & West. L. (2002). *Police powers and procedures*. Toronto, ON: Emond Montgomery Publications Limited.

Walsh, T., & Walsh, Z. (2006). The evidentiary introduction of Psychopathy Checklist-Revised assessed psychopathy in U.S. Courts: Extent and appropriateness. *Law and Human Behavior, 30*,493–507.

Walsh, Z., Swogger, M.T., & Kosson, D.S. (2009). Psychopathy and instrumental violence: Facet level relationships. *Journal of Personality Disorders, 23*, 416–424.

Walters, G.D. (2003). Predicting institutional adjustment and recidivism with the psychopathy checklist factor scores: A meta-analysis. *Law and Human Behavior, 27*, 541–558.

Waltz, J., Babcock, J.C., Jacobson, N.S., & Gottman, J.M. (2000). Testing a typology of batterers. *Journal of Consulting and Clinical Psychology, 68*, 658–669.

Ward. T., & Siegert, R. (2002). Rape and evolutionary psychology: A critique of Thornhill and Palmer's theory. *Aggression and Violent Behavior, 7*, 145–168.

Warick, J. (1997, November 29). Power in the spirit: Okimaw Ohci Healing Lodge. *The Saskatchewan Star Phoenix*, p. C1.

Warick, J. (2003 July, 5). Saskatchewan considers racially balanced juries. *Ottawa Citizen*, p. A16.

Warmington, J. (2007, December 6). Schizophrenic killer wandering around unmonitored. *Toronto Sun*. Retrieved from Canoe website: http://cnews.canoe.ca/CNEWS/MediaNews/2007/12/06/4710576-sun.html

Warren, J.L., Burnette, M., South, C.S., Chauhan, P., Bale, R., & Friend, R. (2002). Personality disorders and violence among female prison inmates. *Journal of the American Academy of Psychiatry and the Law, 30*, 502–509.

Warren, J.L., Burnette, M., South, C.S., Chauhan, P., Bale, R., Friend, R., & Van Patten, I. (2003). Psychopathy in women: Structural modelling and co-morbidity. *International Journal of Law and Psychiatry, 26*, 223–242.

Warren, J.L., South, S.C., Burnette, M.L., Rogers, A., Friend, R., Bale, R., & Van Patten, I. (2005). Understanding the risk factors for violence and criminality in women: The concurrent validity of the PCL-R and HCR-20. *International Journal of Law and Psychiatry, 28*, 269–289.

Waschbusch, D.A. (2002). A meta-analytic examination of comorbid hyperactive-impulsive-attention problems and conduct problems. *Psychological Bulletin, 128*, 118–150.

Wasserman, G.A., & Saracini, A.M. (2001). Family risk factors and interventions. In R. Loeber, & D.P. Farrington (Eds.), *Child delinquents: Development, intervention, and service needs* (pp. 165–190). Thousand Oaks, CA: Sage.

Waterman, A., Blades, M., & Spencer, C. (2004). Indicating when you do not know the answer: The effect of question format and interviewer knowledge on children's 'don't know' response. *British Journal of Developmental Psychology, 22*, 135–148.

Webb, A.K., Honts, C.R., Bernhardt, P., & Cook, A.E. (2009). Effectiveness of pupil diameter in a probable-lie comparison questions test for deception. *Legal and Criminological Psychology, 14*, 279–292.

Webster, C.D., & Jackson, M.A. (Eds.), (1997) *Impulsivity: Theory, assessment, and treatment*. New York, NY: Guilford.

Webster, C.D., Douglas, K., Eaves, D., & Hart, S. (1997). *HCR-20: Assessing risk for violence, Version 2*. Burnaby, British Columbia: Simon Fraser University and Forensic Psychiatric Services Commission of British Columbia.

Webster, C.D., Martin, M.L., Brink, J., Nicholls, T.L., & Middleton, C. (2004). *Manual for the Short-Term Assessment of Risk and Treatability (START), Version 1.0 (consultation ed.)*. St. Joseph's Healthcare Hamilton, Ontario—Forensic Psychiatric Services Commission: Port Coquitlam, B.C.

Webster, C.D., Menzies, R.S., Butler, B.T., & Turner, R.E. (1982). Forensic psychiatric assessment in selected Canadian cities. *Canadian Journal of Psychiatry, 27*, 455–462.

Webster, C.D., Nicholls, T.L., Martin, M., Desmarais, S.L., & Brink, J.L. (2006). Short-Term Assessment of Risk and Treatability (START): The case for a new structured professional judgment scheme. *Behavioral Sciences and the Law, 24*, 747–766.

Webster-Stratton, C. (1992). The incredible years: A trouble shooting guide for parents of children ages 3–8 years. Toronto, ON: Umbrella Press.

Webster-Stratton, C., & Hammond, M. (1997). Treating children with early-onset conduct problems: A comparison of child and parenting training interventions. *Journal of Consulting and Clinical Psychology, 65*, 93–109.

Weiler, B.L. & Widom, C.S. (1996). Psychopathy and violent behaviour in abused and neglected young adults. *Criminal Behaviour and Mental Health, 6*, 253–271.

Weinrath, M. (2007). Sentencing disparity: Aboriginal Canadian, drunk driving, and age. *Western Criminology Review, 8*, 16–28.

Wells, G.L. (1978). Applied eyewitness- testimony research: System variables and estimator variables. *Journal of Personality and Social Psychology, 12*, 1546–1557.

Wells, G.L. (1993). What do we know about eyewitness identification? *American Psychologist, 48*, 553–571.

Wells, G.L., & Bradfield, A.L. (1998). "Good, you identified the suspect": Feedback to eyewitnesses distorts their reports of the witnessing experience. *Journal of Applied Psychology, 83*, 366–376.

Wells, G.L., & Olson, E.A. (2003). Eyewitness testimony. *Annual Psychology Review, 54*, 277–295.

Wells, G.L., & Turtle, J.W. (1986). Eyewitness identification: The importance of lineup models. *Psychological Bulletin, 99*, 320–329.

Wells, G.L., Leippe, M.R., & Ostrom, T.M. (1979). Guidelines for empirically assessing the fairness of a lineup. *Law and Human Behavior, 3*, 285–293.

Wells, G.L., Malpass, R.S., Lindsay, R.C.L., Turtle, J.W., & Fulero, S.M. (2000). From the lab to the police station: A successful application of eyewitness research. *American Psychologist, 55*, 581–598.

Wells, G.L., Rydell, S.M., & Seelau, E.P. (1993). On the selection of distractors for eyewitness lineups. *Journal of Applied Psychology, 78*, 835–844.

Wells, G.L., Small, M., Penrod, S., Malpass, R.S., Fulero, S.M., & Brimacombe, C.A.E. (1998). Eyewitness identification procedures: Recommendations for lineups and photo spreads. *Law and Human Behavior, 22*, 603–647.

Werner, E.E., & Smith, R.S. (1992). *Overcoming the odds: High-risk children from birth to adulthood*. Ithaca, NK: Cornell University Press.

Wetter, M.W., & Corrigan, S.K. (1995). Providing information to clients about psychological tests: A survey of attorneys' and law students' attitudes. *Professional Psychology: Research and Practice, 26*, 474–477.

Wheeler, S., Book, A., & Costello, K. (2009). Psychopathic traits and perceptions of victim vulnerability. *Criminal Justice and Behavior, 36*, 635–648.

Whipple, G.M. (1909). The observer as reporter: A survey of "the psychology of testimony." *Psychological Bulletin, 6*, 153–170.

Whipple, G.M. (1910). Recent literature on the psychology of testimony. *Psychological Bulletin, 7*, 365–368.

Whipple, G.M. (1911). The psychology of testimony. *Psychological Bulletin, 8*, 307–309.

Whipple, G.M. (1912). The psychology of testimony and report. *Psychological Bulletin, 9*, 264–269.

White, M.D. (2001). Controlling police discretion to use deadly force: Re-examining the importance of administrative policy. *Crime and Delinquency, 47*, 131–151.

Widom, C., & Ames, M. (1994). Criminal consequences of childhood sexual victimization. *Child Abuse and Neglect, 18*, 303–318.

Widom, C.S. (1989a). Does violence beget violence? A critical examination of the literature. *Psychological Bulletin, 106*, 2–28.

Widom, C.S. (1989b). The cycle of violence. *Science, 244*, 160–166.

Wigmore, J.H. (1909). Professor Munsterberg and the psychology of testimony. *Illinois Law Review, 3*, 399–434.

Williams, K., & Houghton, A. (2004). Assessing risk of domestic violence reoffending: A validation study. *Law and Human Behavior, 28*, 437–455.

Williams, S.L. & Frieze, I.H. (2005). Patterns of violent relationship, psychological distress, and marital satisfaction in national sample of men and women. *Sex Roles, 52*, 771–785.

Williamson, S., Hare, R.D., & Wong, S. (1987). Violence: Criminal psychopaths and their victims. *Canadian Journal of Behavioral Science, 19*, 454–462.

Williamson, S., Harpur, T., & Hare, R. (1991). Abnormal processing of affective words by psychopaths. *Psychophysiology, 28*, 260–273.

Willing, J. (2009, September 9). Arenburg back in Canada. *Ottawa Sun*. Retrieved from http://www.ottawasun.com/news/ottawa/2009/09/08/10789686.html

Wilson, J.Q., & Herrnstein, R. J. (1985). *Crime and human nature*. New York, NY: Simon and Schuster.

Wilson, M., & Daly, M. (1993). Spousal homicide risk and estrangement. *Violence and Victims, 8*, 3–16.

Wilson, M., Daly, M., & Daniele, A. (1995). Familicide: The killing of spouse and children. *Aggressive Behavior, 21*, 275–291.

Wilson, P., Lincoln, R., & Kocsis, R. (1997). Validity, utility and ethics of profiling for serial violent and sexual offenders. *Psychiatry, Psychology and Law, 4*, 1–12.

Winfield, L. (1994). *NCREL Monograph: Developing resilience in urban youth*. NCREL: Urban Education Monograph Series.

Wong, S.C.P., & Gordon, A. (2006). The validity and reliability of the violence risk scale: A treatment-friendly violence risk assessment tool. *Psychology, Public Policy, and Law, 12*, 279–309.

Woodsworth, M., & Porter, S. (1999). Historical foundations and current applications of criminal profiling in violent crime investigations. *Expert Evidence, 7*, 241–264.

Woodworth, M., & Porter, S. (2002). In cold blood: Characteristics of criminal homicides as a function of psychopathy. *Journal of Abnormal Psychology, 111*, 436–445.

Wooldredge, J.D. (1988). Differentiating the effects of juvenile court sentences on eliminating recidivism. *Journal of Research in Crime and Delinquency, 25*, 264–300.

Worling, J.R., & Curwen, T. (2000). Adolescent sexual offender recidivism: Success of specialized treatment and implications for risk prediction. *Child Abuse and Neglect, 24*, 965–982.

Wright, A.M., & Holliday, R.E. (2007). Enhancing the recall of young, young-old, and old-old adults with cognitive interviews. *Applied Cognitive Psychology, 21*, 19–43.

Wrightsman, L.S. (2001). *Forensic psychology.* Belmont, CA: Wadsworth.

Yarmey, A.D. (2001). Expert testimony: Does eyewitness memory research have probative value for the courts? *Canadian Psychology, 42*, 92–100.

Yarmey, A.D., & Jones, H.P.T. (1983). Is the psychology of eyewitness identification a matter of common sense? In S. Lloyd-Bostock & B.R. Clifford (Eds.), *Evaluating witness evidence* (pp. 13–40). Chichester, England: John Wiley & Sons.

Yarmey, A.D., Jacob, J., & Porter, A. (2002). Person recall in field settings. *Journal of Applied Social Psychology, 32*, 2354–2367.

Yarmey, A.D., Yarmey, M.J., & Yarmey, A.L. (1996). Accuracy of eyewitness identifications in showups and lineups. *Law and Human Behavior, 20*, 459–477.

Yllo, K., & Straus, M. (1990). Patriarchy and violence against wives: The impact of structural and normative factors. In M. Straus & R. Gelles (Eds.), *Physical violence in American families* (pp. 383–399). New Brunswick, NJ: Transaction.

Yuille, J.C., Hunter, R., Joffe, R., & Zaparniuk, J. (1993). Interviewing children in sexual abuse cases. In G. Goodman, & B. Bottoms, (Eds.), *Child victims, child witnesses: Understanding and improving testimony* (pp. 95–115). New York, NY: Guilford Press.

Yurchesyn, K.A., Keith, A., & Renner, K.E. (1992). Contrasting perspectives on the nature of sexual assault provided by a service for sexual assault victims and by the law courts. *Canadian Journal of Behavioral Science, 24*, 71–85.

Zamble, E., & Quinsey, V.L. (1997). *The criminal recidivism process.* Cambridge, England: Cambridge University Press.

Zanis, D.A., Mulvaney, F., Coviello, D., Alterman, A.I., Savitz, B., & Thompson, W. (2003). The effectiveness of early parole to substance abuse treatment facilities on 24-month criminal recidivism. *Journal of Drug Issues, 33*, 223–236.

Zapf, P., & Roesch, R. (1998). Fitness to stand trial: Characteristics of remands since the 1992 criminal code amendments. *Canadian Journal of Psychiatry, 43*, 287–293.

Zill, N., Morrison, D.R., & Coiro, M.J. (1993). Long-term effects of parental divorce on parent-child relationships, adjustment, and achievement in young adulthood. *Journal of Family Psychology, 7*, 91–103.

Zinger, I., & Forth, A. (1998). Psychopathy and Canadian criminal proceedings: The potential for human rights abuses. *Canadian Journal of Criminology, 40*, 237–276.

Zinger, I., & Forth, A.E. (1998). Psychopathy and Canadian criminal proceedings: The potential for human rights abuses. *Canadian Journal of Criminology, 40*, 237–276.

Zingraff, M.T., Leiter, J., Johnsen, M.C., & Myers, K.A. (1994). The mediating effect of good school performance on the maltreatment delinquency relationship. *Journal of Research in Crime and Delinquency, 31*, 62–91.

Zoucha-Jensen, J.M., & Coyne, A. (1993). The effects of resistance strategies on rape. *American Journal of Public Health, 83*, 1633–1634.

# Credits

## Text Credits

**p. 11**, From Ceci, S.J. & Bruck, M. (1993). Suggestibility of the child witness: A historical review and synthesis. *Psychological Bulletin*, 113, 403–439. (p. 406) © 1993 by the American Psychological Associations, Adapted with permission. **p. 27**, Excerpt from http://vancouver.ca/police/recruiting/police-officers/index.html, Vancouver Police Department, © City of Vancouver. **p. 33**, Doerner, W.G. (1997). The utility of the oral interview board in selecting police academy admissions. *Policing: An International Journal of Police Strategy and Management*, 20, 777–785. Republished with the permission of Emerald Group Publishing Limited http://www.emeraldinsight.com. **p. 39**, *Police discretion with young offenders*. Ottawa, ON: Department of Justice Canada. © HER MAJESTY THE QUEEN IN RIGHT OF CANADA (2003). **p. 41**, From Hoch et al. (2009), Figure 1B (p. 54). Hoch, J.S., Hartford, K., Heslop, L., & Stitt, L. (2009). Mental illness and police interactions in a mid-sized Canadian city: What the data do and do not say. *Canadian Journal of Community Mental Health*, 28, 49–66. Reprinted with permission of *Canadian Journal of Community Mental Health*. **p. 47**, Walma, M.W. & West, L. (2002). *Police powers and procedures*. Toronto, ON: Emond Montgomery Publications Limited. Reprinted with permission. **pp. 47–48**, Canadian Association of Chiefs of Police. (2000), The National Use of Force Framework. www.cacp.ca/english.committees/download.asp?id=170. Reprinted with permission of CACP. **p. 49**, Teplin, L.A. (2000). Keeping the peace: Police discretion and mentally ill persons. *National Institute of Justice Journal*, July, 8–15. **p. 50**, Adapted from Taylor and Bennell, *Canadian Journal of Police & Security Services*. **p. 62**, King, L., & Snook, B. (2009). Peering inside the Canadian interrogation room: An examination of the Reid model of interrogation, influence tactics, and coercive strategies. *Criminal Justice and Behavior*, 36. **p. 64**, Eastwood, J., & Snook, B. (2009). Comprehending Canadian police cautions: Are the rights to silence and legal counsel understandable? *Behavioral Sciences and the Law*. **p. 72**, Kassin, S.M & Kiechel, K.L. (1996). The social psychology of false confessions: Compliance, internalization, and confabulation. *Psychological Science*. 7(3), 125–128. Reprinted with permission of Blackwell Publishing. **p. 84**, Kocsis, R.N., Irwin, H.J., Hayes, A.F. & Nunn, R. (2000). Expertise in psychological profiling: A comparative assessment. *Journal of Interpersonal Violence*, 13, 311–331. © 2000 by Sage Publications. Reprinted by permission of Sage Publications. **pp. 96–97**, National Research Council (2003). *The polygraph and its detection*. Washington, DC. National Academies Press. Reprinted with permission. **p. 126**, From Fisher, R.P., & Geiselman, R.E., *Memory-enhancing techniques for investigative interviewing*, 1992. Courtesy of Charles C. Thomas Publisher, Ltd., Springfield, Illinois. **p. 153**, From "Statement Validity Assessment: Interview Procedures and Content Analysis of Children's Statements of Sexual Abuse," by D.C. Raskin and P.W. Esplin, 1991, *Behavioural Assessment*, 12, p. 279. **p. 156**, From Saywitz, K.J., & Snyder, L. (1996). Narrative Elaboration: Test of a new procedure for interviewing children. *Journal of Consulting and Clinical Psychology*, 64, 1347–1357 © 1996 by the American Psychological Association. Reprinted with permission. **p. 170**, From MacMillan, H.L. (2000). Child maltreatment: What we know in the year 2000. *Canadian Journal of Psychiatry*, 45, p. 704. Reprinted with permission of the Canadian Psychiatric Association. **p. 181**, Hunter, S. & Baron, E. (2006, December). A daunting task for Pickton jury. *The Ottawa Citizen*. **p. 186**, From Penrod, S.D. & Heuer, L. (1997). Tweaking commonsense: Assessing aids to jury decision making. *Psychology, Public Policy, and Law*, 3, 259–284 (pp. 271 and 280). **p. 204**, The Review Board Systems in Canada: An Overview of Results from the Mentally Disordered Accused Date Collection Study, http://www.justice.gc.ca/en/ps/rs/rep/2006/rr06-1/index.html. **p. 206**, *International Journal of Forensic Mental Health* 2002, Vol. 1, No. 2, pages 127–138, Copyright © IAFMHS. **pp. 207–208**, From Ackerman, M.J. *Forensic Psychological Assessment*. © 1999 John Wiley & Sons. Reprinted with permission of John Wiley & Sons, Inc. **p. 215**, The Review Board Systems in Canada: An Overview of Results form the Mentally Disordered Accused Data Collection Study, www.justice.gc.ca. **p. 218**, Adapted from "Special study on mentally disordered accused and the criminal justice system," Catalogue no. 85-559, Figure 3.2, pg. 15, January 2003, available at www.statcan.ca/english/freepub/85-559-XIE/85-559-XIE00201.pdf. **p. 219**, Nemeth, M. (1996, May 20). Joudrie not guilty. *Maclean's*. **p. 231**, Canada's System of Justice, Figure: Outline of Canada's Court System, http://canada.justice.gc.ca/eng/dept-min/pub/just/07.html. Department of Justice Canada, 2005. Reproduced with the permission of the Minister of Public Works and Government Services Canada, 2010. **p. 234**, Trevethan, S., Moore, J. & Rastin, C.J. (2002). A profile of Aboriginal offenders in federal facilities and serving time in the community. *Forum on Corrections Research*, 124, 17–19. Reproduced with the permission of the Minister of Public Works and Government Services of Canada, 2004. **p. 236**, Taken from the Department of Juvenile Justice website. Department of Juvenile Justice (2010). Restorative justice. http://www.hss.state.ak.us/djj/restorative.htm. **p. 242**, Reprinted with permission from *Journal of Applied Social Psychology*, 1986, vol. 15, No. 2, pp. 150–164. © V.H. Winston & Son, Inc., 260 South Ocean Boulevard, Palm Beach, FL 33480. All rights reserved. **p. 243**, Reprinted with permission from *Journal of Applied Social Psychology*, 1986, vol. 15, No. 2, pp. 150–164. © V.H. Winston & Son, Inc., 260 South Ocean Boulevard, Palm Beach, FL 33480. All rights reserved. **p. 246**, From Gendreau, P., Goggin, C., Cullen, F. & Andrews, D. (2001). The effects of community sanctions and incarceration of recidivism. In L. Motiuk and R. Serin (Eds.), *Compendium 2000 on effective correctional programming* (pp. 18–21). Ottawa: Correctional Service Canada - constructed from Table 3.1, p. 19, and Table 3.2, p. 20. Reproduced with the permission of the Minister of Public Works and Government Services of Canada, 2004. **p. 249**, National Parole Board Website: http://www.npb-cnlc.gc.ca/infocntr/myths_reality_e.htm Adapted with permission of the National Parole Board. **p. 253**, Taken from National Parole Board (2009). http://www.npb-cnlc.gc.ca/rprts/pmr/pmr_2008_2009/2008-2009-eng.pdf. © Minister of Public Works and Government Services of Canada, 2000 (Figure 9.4 and Figure 9.5). **p. 255**, Roberts, J. (2007). Public confidence in criminal justice in Canada: A comparative and contextual analysis. *Canadian Journal of Criminology and Criminal Justice*, 49, 153–184. **p. 275**, Adapted from August 4, 2006 The Canadian Press; The Canadian Encyclopaedia, 2010. **p. 276**, Adapted from Harris, G.T., Rice, M.E. and Quinsety, V.L. (1993). Violent recidivism of mentally disordered offenders: The development of a statistical instrument. *Criminal Justice and Behavior*, 20, 315–335, p. 324. **p. 277**, Adapted from Webster, C.D., Douglas, K.S., Eaves, D., & Hart, S.D. (1997). *HCR-20 Assessing risk for violence* (Version 2). Vancouver, Canada: Mental Health, Law and Policy Institute, Simon Fraser University, pg. 11. Reprinted with permission. **p. 278**, Campbell, M.A., French, S., & Gendreau, P. (2009). The prediction of violence in adult offenders: A meta-analytic comparison of instruments and methods of assessment. *Criminal Justice and Behavior*, 36, 567–590. **p. 278**, Wong, S.C.P., & Gordon, A. (2006). The validity and reliability of the violence risk scale: A treatment-friendly violence risk assessment tool. *Psychology, Public Policy, and Law*, 12, 279–309. **p. 314**, Taken from Wallace, M. (July, 2009). Police-reported crime statistics in Canada, 2008. *Juristat Article*, Vol. 29, no. 3. Component of Statistics Canada catalogue, no. 85-002-X. **p. 322**, Results of the 2002 Canadian Police Survey on Youth Gangs (Astwood Strategy Corporation, 2004). © Her Majesty the Queen in Right of Canada, represented by the Solicitor General of Canada (Minister of Public Safety and Emergency Preparedness), 2004. All rights reserved. **p. 336**, Adapted from Stats Canada publication *Family Violence in Canada*," Catalogue 85-224, July 25, 2005, Table 1.1, p. 28, available at http://www.statcan.ca/englishfreepub/85-224-XIE/85-224-XIE2005000.pdf. **p. 336**, Reprinted from Chan, K.L., Strauss, M.R., Brownridge, D.A., Tiwari, A., & Leung, W.C. (2008). Prevalence of dating partner violence and suicidal ideation among male and female university students worldwide. *Journal of Midwifery & Women's Health*, 53, 529–537. With permission from Elsevier. **p. 344**, From Sherman & Berk (1984)–Sherman, L.W., & Berk, R.A. (1984). The specific deterrent effects of arrest for domestic assault. *American Sociological Review*, 49, 261–272. **p. 348**, Adapted from Stewart, L., Gabora, N., Kropp, R., & Lee, Z. (2005). *Family violence programming: Treatment outcome for Canadian federally sentenced offenders*. Ottawa, ON: Correctional Service of Canada. **p. 371**, Taken from Statistics Canada (2009a). Statistics Canada (2009), Homicides in Canada, 2008, Retrieved on June 17, 2010, from http://www.statcan.gc.ca/daily-quotidien/091028/dq091028a-eng.htm. **p. 378**, Table extracted from *Serial Murderers and Their Victims*, 4th edition by Eric W. Hickey. Copyright 2006 by Wadsworth Publishing Company (a division of Cengage Learning).

# Photo Credits

**p. 2,** Monarchy/Regency/The Kobal Collection/Zade Rosenthal. **p. 12,** Illustration by Lyrl Ahern. **p. 15,** Gordon Parks, Photographer/Library of Congress Prints and Photographs Division. **p. 17,** Courtesy of the Victorian Institute of Forensic Mental Health, Monash University. **p. 29,** Regina Leader Post/Roy Antal. **p. 42,** Courtesy of Dr. Dorothy Cotton. **p. 46,** Reuters/Landov. **p. 50,** AP Photo/Ed Andrieski. **p. 59,** © Shout Pictures. **p. 69,** © Bettmann/CORBIS. **p. 86,** Don Anders, Media Relations and Publications. Courtesy of Texas State University. **p. 90,** Don Anders, Media Relations and Publications. Courtesy of Texas State University. **p. 98,** © Wolfgang Flamish/zefa/Corbis. **p. 107,** Courtesy of Dr. Stephen Porter. **p. 119,** © David Young-Wolff/PhotoEdit. **p. 132,** Photo by Monica Hurt, Queen's University. Courtesy of Dr. Roderick C.L. Lindsay. **p. 133,** Carlos Serrao/Getty Images. **p. 150,** Courtesy of Johns Hopkins Children's Centre. **p. 152,** © Custom Medical Stock Photo. **p. 165,** Courtesy of the Ministry of the Attorney-General of British Columbia, Criminal Justice Branch. **p. 185,** Courtesy of Joanna Pozzulo. **p. 190,** CP PHOTO/Jane Wolsak. **p. 198,** Courtesy of Regina Schuller. **p. 221,** Willy McElligott. **p. 226,** Photo courtesy of MHCP. **p. 227,** Photograph by Trent Maracle, Courtesy of Marnie Rice, Mental Health Centre Penetanguishene. **p. 232,** Shutterstock. **pp. 241, 244,** © Correctional Service Canada, 2004. Reprinted with permission. **p. 252,** THE CANADIAN PRESS/Bill Becker. **p. 254,** Courtesy of Centre for Criminology, University of Oxford. **p. 260,** © Copyright Sidney Harris, ScienceCartoonsPlus.com. **p. 265,** CP PHOTO/Peter McCabe. **p. 269,** Photo by Chris Koegl. Courtesy of Dr. Chris Webster. **p. 271,** © Helen King/CORBIS. **p. 289,** Tim Cordell/www.cartoonstock.com. **p. 291,** Courtesy of Dr. Robert D. Hare **p. 298** (left), MGM/UNIVERSAL/DE LAURENTIIS/THE KOBAL COLLECTION. **p. 298** (right), SHOWTIME/THE KOBAL COLLECTION/LITTLEJOHN, DAN. **p. 313,** Dimitrisurkov/Dreamstime.com. **p. 328,** Courtesy of Dr. Alan Leschied/University of Western Ontario. **p. 332,** Shutterstock. **p. 339,** Courtesy of University of British Columbia, Department of Psychology. **p. 345,** © Mark Richards/PhotoEdit. **p. 370,** BILL TREMBLAY/NORTHUMBERLAND NEWS FILE PHOTO. **p. 371,** Magic1/Dreamstime.com. **p. 380,** CP PHOTO/Toronto Star - Tony Bock. **p. 382,** Courtesy of Dr. Martin Daly.

# Case Index

## B

Barefoot v. Estelle, 463 U.S. 880 (1983), 263

Baxtrom v. Herald, 383 U.S. 107 (1966), 263

Bill C-106. (1986). Proposed Amendments (YOA). Ottawa: Queen's Printer., 310

Bill C-15A. (2002). An Act to amend the Criminal Code and to amend other Acts (protecting children from sexual exploitation). Ottawa: Queen's Printer, 170

Bill C-30 (1991). An Act to amend the Criminal Code (Mental Disorder) and to amend the National Defense Act and Young Offender Act in consequence thereof (as passed by the House of Commons November 21, 1991). Ottawa: Queen's Printer., 202, 203, 213, 217

Bill C-37. (2005). An Act to amend the Telecommunications Act. Ottawa: Queen's Printer., 310

Bill C-41. (1995). An Act to amend the Criminal Code of Canada (Sentencing). Ottawa, ON: Queen's Printer., 234, 238

Bill C-72. (1995). An Act to amend the Criminal Code (Self-Induced Intoxication). Ottawa: Queen's Printer., 220

Brian's Law. (Mental Health Legislative Reform). 2000. S.O. 2000, c. 9 (formerly Bill 68), online: Ontario Legislative Library http://www.ontla.on.ca/library/bills/68371.htm, 214

Brown v. Board of Education, 347 U.S. 483 (1954), 14

## C

Canada Evidence Act, R.S.C. (1985), (2006), s. 16.1, 164

Canadian Charter of Rights and Freedoms, 38, 45, 63, 166, 202, 211, 213

Canadian Foundation for Children, Youth, and the Law v. Canada (Attorney General) (2004) 234 D.L.R. (4th) 257, 166

Canadian Human Rights Act, R.S.C. (1985), c. H-6, 252

Child and Family Services Act, R.S.O. 1990, c. C. 11, 167

Criminal Code, R.S.C. (1985), C-34, s. 172, 171

Criminal Code, R.S.C. (1985), C-34, s. 43, 166

Criminal Code, R.S.C. (1985), C-46, s. 2; 1992, c. 20, s. 216, c. 51, s. 32, 202, 203

Criminal Code, R.S.C. (1985), C-46, s. 16; 1985, c. 27 (1st Supp.), s. 185F; 1991, c. 43, s. 2, 213, 215

Criminal Code, R.S.C. (1985), C-46, s. 25, 43

Criminal Code, R.S.C. (1985), C-46, s. 143, 356

Criminal Code, R.S.C. (1985), C-46, s. 264; 1985, c. 27 (1st Supp.), s. 37; 1993, c. 45, s. 2; 1997, c. 16, s. 4, c. 16, s. 9; 2002, c. 13, s. 10, 348

Criminal Code, R.S.C. (1985), C-46, s. 272; 1995, c. 39, s. 145, 177

Criminal Code, R.S.C. (1985), C-46, s. 276; 1992, c. 38, s. 2, 194, 195

Criminal Code, R.S.C. (1985), C-46, s. 343; 1995, c. 44, s. 302, 177

Criminal Code, R.S.C. (1985), C-46, s. 433; 1990, c. 15, s. 1, 177

Criminal Code, R.S.C. (1985), C-46, s. 469; c. 27 (1st Supp.), s. 62; 2000, c. 24, s. 44, 177

Criminal Code, R.S.C. (1985), C-46, s. 473, 176

Criminal Code, R.S.C. (1985), C-46, s. 553; c. 27 (1st Supp.), s. 104; 1992, c. 1, s. 58; 1994, c. 44, s. 27; 195, c. 2, s. 2; 1996, c. 19, s. 72; 1997, c. 18, s. 66; 1999, c. 3, s. 37; 2000, c. 25, s. 4, 176, 177

Criminal Code, R.S.C. (1985), C-46, s. 599; c. 1, (4th Supp.), s. 16, 180

Criminal Code, R.S.C. (1985), C-46, s. 649; 1998, c. 9, s. 7, 184

Criminal Code, R.S.C. (1985), C-46, s. 672.1; 1991, c. 43, s. 4, 204

Criminal Code, R.S.C. (1985), C-46, s. 672.15; 1991, c. 43, s. 4, 203

Criminal Code, R.S.C. (1985), C-46, s. 672.22; 1991, c. 43, s. 4, 203

Criminal Code, R.S.C. (1985), C-46, s. 672.23(2); 1991, c. 43, s. 4, 203

Criminal Code, R.S.C. (1985), C-46, s. 672.28; 1991, c. 43, s. 4, 210

Criminal Code, R.S.C. (1985), C-46, s. 672.29; 1991, c. 43, s. 4, 210–211

Criminal Code, R.S.C. (1985), C-46, s. 672.43; 1991, c. 43, s. 4; 2005, c. 22, s. 42(F), 210

Criminal Code, R.S.C. (1985), C-46, s. 672.47; 1991, c 4.3, s. 4, 210

Criminal Code, R.S.C. (1985), C-46, s. 672.54; 1991, c.43, s. 4, 216

Criminal Code, R.S.C. (1985), C-46, s. 672.58; 1991, c. 43, s. 4, 209

Criminal Code, R.S.C. (1985), C-46, s. 672.81; 1991, c.43, s. 4, 216

Criminal Code, R.S.C. (1985), C-46, s. 718, 236

Criminal Code, R.S.C. (1985), C-46, s. 718.1, 234, 237

Criminal Code, R.S.C. (1985), C-46, s. 718.2(e), 234, 235

Criminal Code, R.S.C. (1985), C-46, s. 745, 295

Criminal Code, R.S.C. (1985), C-46, s. 753.1, 239

Criminal Code, R.S.C. (1985), C-46, s. 781.1, 176

Criminal Lunatics Act (1800), 39 & 40, Geo. 333, c. 94 (U.K.), 211

## D

Daubert v. Merrell Dow Pharmaceuticals, Inc., 509 U.S. 579 (1993), 20, 97

Dixon v. Attorney General of Commonwealth of Pennsylvania, 325 F.Supp. 966 (M.D. Pa. 1971), 263

## E

Employee Polygraph Protection Act of 1988, Pub. L. 100-347, 102 Stat. 646, 29 U.S.C. 2001-2009., 91

Ernst v. Quinonez (2003), O.J. No. 3781 (Ont. Sup. Ct.), 44

Estelle v. Smith, 451, U.S. 454 (1981), 268

## F

Frye v. United States, 293 F.1013 (1923), 90, 97

Frye v. United States, 293 F.1013 (DC Cir. 1923), 20

## H

Health Care Consent Act, R.S.O. (1996), c. 2, Sched. A, s. 25, 214

## J

Jackson v. Indiana (1972), 406 U.S. 715, 209

Jenkins v. United States, 307 F.2d 637 (D.C. Court of Appeals, 1962), 14

Juries Act, R.S.O. (1990), J3; S.O. 1994, c. 27; 1997, c. 4, 177

Juvenile Delinquents Act (1908), c. 40, 309, 309t

## K

Kumho Tire Company v. Carmichael, 526 U.S. 137 (1999), 21, 97

## M

Mental Health Act, R.S.O. (1990), c. M.7; 2000, c. 9, s. 33.1, 214

## N

National Defence Act, R.S.O. (1985), c. N-5, 232, 245

Neil v. Biggers, 409 U.S. 188 (1972), 135

## P

Police Services Act, R.S.O. (1990), c. P.15, 45

## R

R. v. Andrade (1985), 18 C.C.C. 3d 41 (Ont. CA), 186

R. v. Arenburg,(1997), O.J. No. 2386, 214

R. v. Balliram (2003), 173, C.C.C. (3d) 547, 202

R. v. Beland (1987), 2 S.C.R. 398, 97

R. v. Brown (2005), S.J. No. 43, 179

R. v. Budai, Gill & Kim (2001), 154 C.C.C. (3d) 289, 179

R. v. Darrach (2000), 2 S.C.R. 443, 196

R. v. Daviault (1994), 93 C.C.C. 3d 21, 220

R. v. Demers (2004), 2 S.C.R. 489, 2004, SCC 46, 211

R. v. Gayme (1991), 7 C.R.D. 725, 194

R. v. Gill (2002), B.C.J. No. 1473, 179

R. v. Gladue (1999), 1.S.C.R. 688, 16, 234, 235

R. v. Guess (1998), B.C.J. No. 1989, 179

R. v. Henderson (2009), 44 O.R. (3d) 628, 140

R. v. Hoilett (1999), 136 C.C.C. (3d) 449, 65, 66

R. v. Hubbert (1975), 29 C.C.C. (2d) 279, 31 C.R.N.S. 27, 11 O.R. (2d) 464 (C.A.), 16

R. v. Kliman (1998), No. 49 B.C.J. (Quicklaw), 158

R. v. L.T.H. (2008), 2 S.C.R. 739, 2008 S.C.C. 49, 16

R. v. Latimer (2001), 1 S.C.R. 3, 183

R. v. Lavallee (1990), 1 S.C.R. 852, 16

R. v. Levogiannis (1993), 4 S.C.R. 475, 160 N.R. 1, C.R. (4th) 325, 85 C.C.C. (3d) 327, 18 C.R.R. (2d) 242, 16

R. v. Lyons (1987), 44 D.L.R. (4th) 193, 264

R. v. M.J.S. (2000), Alta.P.C. 44, 70

R. v. McIntosh and McCarthy (1997), 117 C.C.C. (3d) 385 (Ont. C.A.), 23, 140

R. v. McIntosh and McCarthy (1997), 117 C.C.C. 56 (B.C.A.A.), 23

R. v. McLeod (2005), ABQB 946, 181

R. v. McNaughton (1843), 8 Eng. Rep. 718, 211

R. v. Mohan (1994), 89 C.C.C. (3d) 402 (S.C.C.), 16, 21

R. v. Morgentaler (1988), 1 S.C.R. 30, 183

R. v. Nepoose (1991), 85 Alta. LR (2d) 8 (Q.B.), 178

R. v. Oickle (2000), S.C.C. 38, 16, 65

R. v. Parks (1992), 2 S.C.R. 871, 217

R. v. Poulin (2002), 169 C.C.C. (3d) 378, 166

R. v. Prichard (1836), 7. Car, 202

R. v. Seaboyer (1991), 2 S.C.R. 577, 195

R. v. Sherratt (1991), 1 S.C.R. 509, 178

R. v. Sophonow (1986), 50 CR (3d) 193 (Man. CA), 16, 142, 143

R. v. Sterling (1995), 102 C.C.C. (3d) 481, 148

R. v. Stone (1999), 2 S.C.R. 290, 217, 219

R. v. Swain (1991), 63 C.C.C. (3d) 481 (S.C.C.), 13, 16, 212, 213, 218

R. v. Symes (2005), O.J. No. 6041, 172

R. v. Taylor (1992), 77 C.C.C. (3d) 551 (Ont.. C.A.), 203

R. v. Williams (1998), 1 S.C.R. 1128, 16

Re Moore and the Queen, 10 C.C.C. (3d) 306 (1984), 264

Roe v. Wade (1973), 410 U.S. 113, 183

## S

Smith v. Jones (1999), 1 S.C.R. 455, 262

Starson v. Swayze (1999), O.J. No. 4483, 210

Starson v. Swayze (2003), 1 S.C.R. 722, 210

State v. Driver, 88 W. Va. 479, 107 S.E. 189 (1921), 12, 14

State v. Harrington, 659 N. W. 2d 509 (2003), 99

## T

Ticket of Leave Act (1899), 247

## U

U.S. v. Scheffer, 140L. Ed. 2d 413 (1998), 97

## W

Wenden v. Trikha (1991), 116 A.R. 81 (Q.B.), 16

Winko v. British Columbia (1999), 2 S.C.R. 625, 213

## Y

Young Offenders Act, R.S.C. (1985), Y-1, s. 3, 310

Young Offenders Act, R.S.C. (1985), Y-1, s. 4, 310

Young Offenders Act, R.S.C. (1985), Y-1, s. 16, 310

Young Offenders Act, R.S.C. (1985), Y-1, s. 20, R.S., 1985, c. 27 (1st Supp.), s. 187, c. 24 (2nd Supp.), s. 14, c. 1 (4th Supp.), s. 38; 1992, c. 11, s. 3; 1993, c. 45, s. 15; 1995, c. 19, s. 3, c. 22, ss. 16, 17, 25, c. 39, s. 178, 310

Young Offenders Act, R.S.C. (1985), Y-1, s. 38(2)(c), 313

Youth Criminal Justice Act (2002), c. 1, s. 1, 311

Youth Criminal Justice Act (2002), c. 1, s. 3, 313

Youth Criminal Justice Act (2002), c. 1, s. 7, 311

Youth Criminal Justice Act (2002), c. 1, s. 10, 311

Youth Criminal Justice Act (2002), c. 1, s. 141(10), 210

Youth Criminal Justice Act (2002), c. 1, s. 42, 312

Youth Criminal Justice Act (2002), c. 1, s. 61, 313

# Name Index

## A

Aamodt, M. G., 34–35, 36, 103
Abel, G. G., 355
Abram, K. M., 223
Adams, Randall Dale, 268
Adams, S. M., 352
Ainsworth, P. B., 30
Aitken, C. C. G., 79
Alexander, D. A., 52
Alison, L. J., 81, 82
Allan, W. D., 376
Allen, L., 194
Allen, Robb, 313
Almond, L., 81
Alpert, G. P., 44
Andershed, H., 303
Anderson, C. A., 383
Anderson, M., 340
Andrews, D. A., 247
Anshel, M. H., 54
Appleby, T., 370
Arboleda-Floez, Dr. J., 219
Archer, J., 333
Arenburg, Jeffrey, 214
Arnold, Terry, 143
Ascione, F. R., 341
Atkinson, J. L., 362
Aubrey, M., 340
Augimeri, L., 326

## B

Babcock, J. C., 346
Babiak, Paul, 297
Bagby, R. M., 111
Bagshaw, David, 311, 312
Bain, Elizabeth, 126
Bala, Professor Nicholas, 165
Balfour, J., 163
Ball, B. C., 375–376
Baltovich, Robert, 126
Bandura, A., 320, 337
Barak, G., 188
Baranovski, Matti, 191
Barbaree, H. E., 363
Bardo, John, 351
Barefoot, Thomas, 264
Barr, K. N., 270
Barry, C. T., 300
Bartol, A. M., 4, 12, 14
Bartol, C. R., 4, 12, 14

Baskin-Sommers, A. R., 306
Batterman-Faunce, J. M., 152
Baxtrom, Johnnie, 263
Beaumont, R., 375
Beck, K. A., 167–168
Becker, J. V., 13, 355
Bedard, T. E., 352
Bekerian, D. A., 126
Ben-Porath, Y. S., 111
Benda, B. B., 281
Benedek, D. M., 376
Benedek, E. P., 376
Bennell, C., 50, 85
Bennett, L. W., 346
Berk, R. A., 335, 344
Berk, S. F.,., 335
Bernardin, H. J., 36
Bernardo, Paul, 126, 377
Bertsch, J. D., 306
Besirevic, J., 180
Best, C. L., 159
Bianchi, Kenneth (a.k.a Hillside
    Stranglers - with Angelo Buono), 377
Binet, Alfred, 9, 10
Birkenmayer, A., 238
Birt, A. R., 104, 106, 158
Blades, Mark, 149
Blair, R. J. R., 303, 305
Bland, R. C., 221
Blatchford, C., 168
Blonigen, D. M., 303
Boccaccini, M. T., 284
Bodin, S. D., 300
Boer, D., 298
Bond, C. F. Jr., 106
Boney-McCoy, S., 334
Bonnie, R. J., 203
Bonta, J. L., 224, 247, 259
Book, A. S., 270
Boothby, J., 284
Borduin, C. M., 274
Boston, R., 127
Bourgon, G., 188, 277
Bowen, E., 346
Bowlby, John, 13
Bradfield, A. L., 136
Bradford, J. M., 368
Bradley, M. M., 305
Brame, B., 317
Brigham, J. C., 7, 137, 154, 183

Brimacombe, C. A. E., 136
Brinckley, C. A., 305
Brink, J., 266
Brittan, R. R., 13
Broeders, A. P. A., 134
Brooks, Adrian, 180
Brooks, Neil, 142
Broom, I., 369
Brown, C. L., 273
Brown, D., 156
Brown, G. R., 335
Brown, J. M., 51, 53
Brown, Jeffrey, 179
Brown, S. L., 297, 299
Bruck, Dr. Maggie, 9, 11, 147, 150
Brunas-Wagstaff, J., 127
Brunton, M., 13
Brussel, Dr. James, 77
Bucolo, D., 192
Budhani, S., 305
Bull, R., 105, 128
Bundy, Ted, 370
Buono, Angelo (a.k.a. Hillside Stranglers
    with Kenneth Bianchi), 377
Burchfiel, C., 53
Burgess, A. W., 353, 356
Burgess, Ann, 259
Burke, R. J., 53
Burton, J. E., 361
Bushman, B. J., 383
Butler, B. T., 203
Butler, C., 45
Buttell, F., 335
Butters, J. E., 322

## C

Caldwell, M. F., 302
Call, C., 346
Campbell, E. A., 51, 53
Campbell, J. C., 349–350, 376
Campbell, M. A., 106, 279, 302
Canter, D. V., 379
Canter, David, 77, 79, 87
Caperton, J. D., 284
Cares, A. C., 335
Carlson, S. R., 303
Carney, M., 6, 335
Carter, Jimmy, 351
Caspi, A., 302
Cattell, James McKeen, 9

Cavanagh, Patrick, 150
Cavanaugh, M. M., 346
Ceci, Dr. Steve J., 9, 11, 147, 150, 161
Cerri, A. M., 96
Chaiken, J. M., 273
Chaiken, M. R., 273
Chan, K. L., 336
Chapman, J. P., 266
Chapman, L. J., 266
Chapman, M. T., 154
Charlton, K., 106
Cheeseman, Dennis, 58
Chicvara, C. L., 131
Cho, Seung-Hui, 380
Christopherson, B. J., 361
Chung, Christopher, 181
Cirincione, C., 224
Clark, Kenneth, 14
Clark-Robbins, P. C., 224
Cleckley, Hervey, 4, 289, 305, 306
Clements, C. B., 284
Clinton, Bill, 104
Cochrane, Lee, 191
Cochrane, R. E., 29, 35
Cocozza, J., 263
Cohen, A. J., 321
Cohn, E. S., 192
Coid, J., 297
Coleman, T. G., 40
Colledge, E., 305
Collins, S. A., 51
Comeau, Marie-France, 370
Conlon, Gerry, 69
Connolly, D. A., 159, 161
Conradt, Louis, 172
Cook, S., 134
Cooper, H., 106
Corder, B. F., 376
Cordner, G. W., 37, 38
Cormier, C. A., 299
Cornell, D. G., 112, 300, 301, 376
Cornell, W. F., 71
Corvo, K., 345
Cory, Supreme Court Justice Peter, 142
Cotton, Dr. Dorothy H., 40, 42
Coyne, A., 360
Crawford, M., 376
Cronshaw, S. F., 18
Crosby, R. D., 109
Crossman, A. M., 149–150
Cullen, F. T., 247, 281
Cunningham, P. B., 274
Cunningham-Rathner, J., 355
Cupach, W. R., 349

Curtin, J. J., 306
Custer, H., 104
Cutler, B. L., 131, 193

D
Daly, Dr. Martin, 375, 376, 382, 383
Daniele, A., 375
Darby, P. J., 376
Darrach, Andrew, 196
Daubert, William, 3, 20
Daviault, Henri, 220
Davies, G., 128, 160, 161
Davies, Justice Barry, 179
Davies, P. G., 192
Davis, E. F., 304
Day, D., 326
Day-Lewis, Daniel, 69
de Ruiter, C., 281
de Vogel, V., 281
Dean, C. W., 344
Decaire, M. W., 6
DeFronzo, J., 379
DeLeon, P. H., 204
DeLoache, J. S., 152
DeMatteo, D., 294
Dempsey, J., 194
Dennett, J. L., 126
DePaulo, B. M., 100, 101–102, 105, 106
Desmarais, S. L., 140, 266
Devine, D. J., 193–194
Diamond, S. S., 242
Ditta, A., 379
Dixon, Donald, 263
Dobash, R. E, 337
Dobash, R., 337
Dodge, Kenneth, 319
Doerner, W. G., 33, 34
Donchin, E., 98
Doob, A. N., 256, 257
Dooley, Marcia, 168
Dooley, Randal, 168
Dooley, Teego, 168
Dooley, Tony, 168
Douglas, John, 75, 76
Douglas, K. S., 274
Douglas, Kevin, 269
Dowden, C., 273
Doyle, Aaron, 3
Drass, K. A., 372
Drugge, J., 298
Drummond, Edmund, 211, 213
Dubbé, Sylvie, 167
DuBreuil, S. C., 193
Duffy, John (a.k.a. Railway Rapist), 77

Dunham, R. G., 44
Dunning, D., 138
Dupuis, P., 134
Dutton, Dr. Donald G., 107, 335, 337, 338, 339, 345
Dwyer, J., 67
Dyck, R. J., 221
Dysart, J. E., 133, 134
Dziekanski, Robert, 46

E
Earle, J., 298
Easterbrook, J. A., 138
Eastman, O., 82
Eastwood, J., 63, 64
Eaves, Derek, 269
Ebbesen, E. G., 139
Eberhardt, J. L., 192
Eberhardt, N. L., 96
Edens, J. F., 293–294, 301
Edmonson, Dean, 179
Egger, S. A., 379
Ekman, P., 100, 104, 112
Elaad, E., 95
Ellard, Kelly, 180
Elliott, D., 272
Ellison, N., 103
Ellsworth, P. C., 133, 189
Ennis, B. J., 263
Epstein, J. A., 100
Erickson, P. G., 322
Ernst, Edward, 44
Ervin, F. R., 13
Esplin, P. W., 152, 153
Ewaschuk, Superior Court Justice Eugene, 168
Ewing, C. P., 339
Eysenck, Hans J., 13

F
Fairbrother, N., 360
Fairweather, D., 298
Faller, K. C., 362
Farkas, G. M., 204
Farrington, D. P., 272, 303, 326, 384
Farwell, Lawrence A., 98, 99
Faulder, Joseph Stanley, 268
Faver, C. A., 341
Felson, R. B., 335
Finkel, N. J., 78–79
Finkelhor, D., 171, 354, 363
Finlay, P., 172
Finn, P., 49
Firestone, P., 368

Fisher, E., 346
Fisher, R. P., 122, 125, 126, 131
Fleming, J. A. E., 96
Flett, H., 346
Flin, R., 160, 161
Flynn, C. P., 341
Foa, E. B., 357
Forth, A. E., 294, 297, 299
Foster, Jodie, 351
Frank, M. G., 104, 112
Franke, W. D., 51
Frederick, R. I., 109
Frick, P. J., 300
Friesen, W. V., 100
Frieze, I. H., 335
Friscolanti, Michael, 252, 275
Fritz, G., 361
Frye, James Alphonzo, 20, 97
Fulero, S. M., 133, 136, 180
Fyfe, J. J., 45

## G

Gabbert, G., 137
Gabora, N., 347
Gacy, John Wayne, 377
Gaill, Peter, 179
Gale, Judy, 295
Ganis, G., 98
Garmezy, N., 323
Gartner, R., 376
Gein, Ed, 76
Geiselman, R. E., 125, 126
Gelb, Dr. Ed, 104
Gelles, R. J., 346
Gendreau, Paul, 245, 246, 247, 328
Giese, Keith, 106
Gilchrist, E., 346
Ginton, A., 95
Gladue, Jamie Tanis, 235
Glendinning, Sandra, 28
Glenn, Scott, 76
Gobeil, R., 250
Goldstein, A. M., 110, 137
Gondolph, E. W., 346
Gonzalez, R., 133
Goodman, G. S., 152
Goodwill, M., 81
Gorey, K., 355
Gottfredson, M. R., 13
Graham, J. R., 116
Granhag, P. A., 101
Grann, M., 285
Green, C. E., 346
Grieve, R., 151

Grigson, Dr. James (a.k.a. Dr. Death),
    264, 268
Grisso, T., 203
Groth, A. N., 359, 360, 379
Grove, W., 267
Guay, J. P., 359
Guay, Joesph-Albert, 380
Gudjonsson, Dr. Gisli H., 68, 70
Guess, Gillian, 179
Gumpert, C. H., 285
Gusick, S. M., 189
Guy, L. S., 274
Guyton, M. R., 193
Gwynn, M. I., 193

## H

Hadfield, James, 211
Haggard, U., 285
Haizlip, T. M., 375
Häkkänen-Nyholm, H., 296
Hall, Dr. C., 45
Hall, G. C. N., 363
Hamby, S. L., 334
Hancock, J., 103
Haney, Craig, 7
Hannah-Moffat, K., 318
Hannon, L., 353
Hans, Valerie, 198
Hansen, D. J., 170
Hanson, R. Karl, 188, 224, 277, 369, 384
Hare, Dr. Robert D., 107, 289, 290, 291,
    295, 297, 299, 305
Harper, Stephen, 313
Harpur, T., 305
Harrington, Terry, 99
Harris, Dr. Grant T., 225–226, 227, 272,
    299
Harris, Thomas, 76, 298
Hart, Stephen D., 203, 260, 269, 274,
    294, 350
Hartford, K., 40
Hartke, K. L., 376
Hartley, J., 186
Hartley, T., 53
Hartwig, M., 101
Hastie, R., 190, 191–192
Hastings, Patricia A., 195, 198
Hauptman, Bruno Richard, 68, 134
Haw, R. M., 192
Hawes, S. W., 284
Hawk, G. L., 112
Hayes, A. F., 83
Hazelwood, T. E., 352
Heilbrun, K., 2, 302

Heinrick, Jeffrey, 188
Helmus, L., 277
Henderson, John William, 140
Hendrickse, W., 372
Hendry, L., 370
Henggeler, S. W., 274
Hennessey, Shawn, 58
Henry, B., 319
Heslop, L., 40
Hess, A. K., 19
Heuer, L., 186, 187
Hewlett, M. G., 193
Hiatt, K. D., 305
Hickey, E. W., 377, 378, 380
Hill, C., 161
Hilton, N. Z., 284–285
Hinckley, John, Jnr., 17, 351
HInz, P. N., 51–52
Hirschell, D. J., 344
Hirschi, T., 13
Hirschman, R., 363
Hirsh, H. R., 34
Hoch, J., 40, 41
Hodgins, S., 224
Hogarth, J., 239
Hogben, Alia, 197
Hoge, R. D., 247
Hoilett, C., 66
Holland, H. L., 125
Holliday, R. E., 161
Holmes, R. M., 378
Holmes, S. T., 378
Holmstrom, L. L., 356, 379
Holtzworth-Munroe, A., 342
Homolka, Karla, 377
Honts, C. R., 96
Hopkins, Anthony, 298
Hosch, H. M., 139, 192
Howitt, D., 74
Hubbard, K. L., 208
Hucker, S. J., 299
Hughes, Kevin, 99
Hughes, M., 151
Hurrell, J. J., 51
Hurshman-Corkum, Jane, 343
Hutchinson, I. W., 344

## I

Iacono, Dr. William G., 93, 94, 95,
    96, 112
Inbau, F. E., 59, 60, 61
Ingram, Paul, 71
Innes, G., 52
Inwald, R. E., 35

Irving, B. L., 52
Irwin, H. J., 83
Izzett, R. R., 194

**J**

Jack the Ripper, 76, 77
Jacob, J., 127
Jacobs, P. A., 13
Jacoby, J. E., 263
James, Graham, 252
Jansen, N. J. M., 134
Jenkins, Vincent E., 14
Jensen, T. L., 368
Jiminez-Lorente, B., 180
Johnson, S. L., 192
Johnson, Suzanne Killinger, 374, 375
Jolliffe, D., 384
Jonas, J. M., 111
Jones, A. B., 113
Jones, B., 111–112
Jones, G. B., 270
Jones, H. P. T., 23
Jones, Paula, 104
Joudrie, Dorothy, 219
Joudrie, Earl, 219
Junginger, J., 274
Jungman, M., 95

**K**

Kaplan, S., 300
Karam, T. J., 189
Karl, S., 126
Karr, John Mark, 68
Kashani, J. H., 376
Kashy, D. A., 100
Kask, K., 128
Kassin, Dr. Saul M., 61, 64, 65, 68,
    69–70, 71, 72, 72t, 74, 139, 142, 187,
    188
Kebbell, M. R., 125
Kendall-Tackett, K. A., 171
Keppel, W. D., 379
Kerr, N. L., 191
Kerstholt, J. H., 134
Kiechel, K. L., 71, 72–73, 72t
Kilpatrick, D. G., 159
Kim, Y., 188
Kindrat, Jeffrey, 179
King George III, 211
King, L., 61, 62
Kingsbury, S. J., 372
Kircher, J. C., 96
Kirkendol, S. E., 100
Kirkman, C. A., 297

Klassen, D., 275
Kliman, Michael, 158
Knight, R. A., 359, 360
Koch, W. J., 360
Kocsis, R. N., 83, 84
Koegl, C., 326
Kohnken, G., 152
Konecni, V. J., 139
Koss, M. P., 356, 361–362
Kozel, F. A., 99
Koziol-McLain, J., 376
Kroes, W. H., 51
Kropp, R., 347, 350
Krueger, R. F., 303
Kugler, K., 206
Kuhn, J., 152

**L**

Lamb, Dr. Michael E., 152, 157
Lambert, M. T., 372
Landry, S. E., 352
Lang, P. J., 305
Laroche, D., 335
Larsson, H., 303
Lassiter, G. D., 100
Latessa, E. J., 281
Latimer, J., 204, 215
Latimer, Robert, 183
Latimer, Tracy, 183
Laurier, Sir Wilfrid, 248
Law, M., 225
Lawrence, A., 204, 215
Leblanc, M., 285–286
Lee, M. Y., 346
Lee, Z., 347
Lees-Haley, P. R., 109
Leginski, W., 194
Leichtman, M. D., 161
Leippe, M. R., 139–140
Leo, R. A., 61
Lépine, Marc, 381
Leschied, Dr. Alan, 327, 328–329
Leslie, D., 355
Letourneau, E. J., 159
Letterman, David, 351
Levine, J. A., 96
Levy-Elkon, A., 300
Li, J. C., 138
Li, Vincent, 225
Lichtenstein, P., 303
Lidz, V., 302
Lieberman, J. D., 189
Lilienfeld, S. O., 296
Lindberg, A., 154
Lindberg, M., 154

Lindbergh, Charles, 68, 74, 134
Lindbergh, Charles, Jr., 68, 74
Lindsay, Dr. Rod C. L., 127, 129, 131,
    132, 133, 134, 138, 159, 162, 163
Lindsay, J. J., 105–106
Link, B. G., 274
Litwack, T. R., 263
Llewellyn, L. J., 113
Lloyd, C., 286
Lloyd, Jessica Elizabeth, 370
Lochun, S. K., 127
Loeber, R., 302
Loftus, Elizabeth F., 122, 123, 124, 143,
    157, 158
Long, P. J., 171
Lorenz, A. R., 305
Loseka, O. R., 335
Lösel, F., 369
Lucas, Arthur, 245
Luus, C. A. E., 129
Lykken, David T., 93, 293, 296
Lynam, D. R., 302
Lyon, D., 350
Lyons, P. M. Jr., 193

**M**

MacCoon, D. G., 305
MacCoun, R. J., 191
MacDonald, J. M., 44
MacKinon, D. P., 125
Macleod, M. D., 19
MacMillan, H. L., 170
MacVeigh, J., 127
Maeder, E., 194
Malinosky-Rummell, R., 170
Malpass, R. S., 136, 138
Mann, S., 105, 106
Manz, P. W., 44
Marcus, K. D., 193
Margolis, B. L., 51
Mariani, Meir, 191
Mark, V. H., 13
Marrocco, Justice Frank, 197
Marshall, Donald, 141
Marshall, J. R., 52
Marshall, W. L., 363
Marston, William, 90
Marti, M. W., 191
Martin, Dominic, 167
Martin, R., 127
Marzolf, D. P., 152
Mauro, R., 189
Maurutto, P., 318
McCarthy, Paul, 23
McClelland, G. M., 223

McClemont, W. E., 13
McConville, D., 300
McCoy, W., 301
McCraty, R., 51
McCreary, D. R., 50
McEvoy, C., 180
McFarlane, J., 349
McFatter, R. M., 241, 242
McGhee, Curtis, 99
McIntosh, Owen, 23
McIntyre, M., 225
McKenna, P. E., 37
McKimmie, B., 196
McLachlan, Chief Justice
    Beverley, 233
McLean, Tim, 225
McLeod, Germaine, 181
McNaughton, Daniel, 211, 213
Meadow, S. R., 108
Meehl, Paul, 267
Meissner, C. A., 66, 137, 183, 192
Melcher, R., 234
Melnyk, L., 149
Melton, H. C., 41, 43
Melville, M. M., 13
Memon, A., 137, 139, 161
Mendleson, R., 329
Menzies, Robert S., 203, 269
Merton, R. K., 13
Messman-Moore, T. L., 171
Metesky, George (a.k.a. Mad
    Bomber), 77
Miethe, T. D., 372
Milgaard, David, 141
Mitchell, T. L., 192
Mittelman, M., 355
Moan, S., 152
Moffitt, T. E., 302, 303, 319
Mohan, Dr. C., 21
Mojtabai, R., 274
Mokros, A., 299
Molloy, Justice Ann, 210
Monahan, John, 224, 263,
    265, 266
Moore, J., 234
Moran, G., 193
Morgan, K., 82
Morgentaler, Dr. Henry,
    183
Morin, Guy Paul, 141
Morris, Errol, 268
Morton, K. E., 188
Motiuk, L. L., 223, 244
Muhlenbruck, L., 106
Munsterberg, Hugo, 12

Murdock, T., 357
Murphy, J. M., 289
Murrie, D. C., 284, 300, 301
Musgrave, Story, 351

N
Nagin, D. S., 317–319
Narby, D. J., 193
Nemeth, M., 219
Neufeld, P., 67
Neumann, C. S., 297
Newman, J. P., 305, 306
Newman, R., 204, 221
Ng, W., 138
NIcholas, E., 152
Nicholls, T. L., 266, 281
Nicholson, R. A., 206–208
Nisbett, R. E., 182
Nitschke, J., 299
Northrop, L. C., 34
Nunes, K. L., 364, 368
Nunn, R., 83

O
O'Connor, W. A., 275
O'Neill, M. L., 302
O'Sullivan, M., 104
O'Toole, M., 304
Ofshe, Dr. Richard J., 67, 71
Ogloff, Dr. James R. P., 15, 17–18, 168,
    203, 215
Oickle, Richard, 65
Olio, K. A., 71
Olson, Clifford, 295
Olson, J. M., 199
Olver, M. E., 300
Orbach, Y., 152
Orchard, T. L., 134
Orn, H., 221
Osterheider, M., 299
Otto, R. K., 2

P
Palmer, J. C., 122
Parks, Kenneth, 217
Partridge, G. E., 293
Patrick, Dr. Christopher J., 93, 94, 95,
    96, 112, 303, 305
Patry, Dr. M., 188, 194
Pavlidis, I., 96
Peel, Robert, 211, 213
Pembroke, M., 133
Pennington, N., 190, 191
Penrod, S. D., 136, 186, 187, 191

Perez, D. A., 192
Pezdek, K., 154
Pfeifer, J. E., 183, 192
Pfeifer, R. L., 105
Phillip, Dr. George, 77
Phillips, Inez, 268
Picard, A., 167
Picasso, Pablo, 79
Pickel, K. L., 139, 189
Pickton, Robert, 180, 181
Pinizzotto, A. J., 78–79, 304
Pipe, M., 152, 156
Pitre, N. L., 352
Plomin, R., 303
Ponder, B., 192
Pope, H. G., 111
Porporino, F. J., 223
Porter, A., 127
Porter, Dr. Stephen, 78, 101, 104,
    106, 107
Porter, S., 158, 296, 298, 299, 302, 372
Posner, Dr. Paul, 210
Poulin, Lucille, 166
Powell, B., 197
Pozzulo, J. D., 160, 161, 162, 163,
    188, 194
Pride, M., 192
Prochnow, J., 379
Pryke, S., 134–135
Puente, Dorothea, 377
Pugh, G., 30
Purdie-Vaughns, V., 192
Putnam, F. W., 171
Pynes, J., 36, 66

Q
Quan, D., 222
Quas, J. A., 152
Quayle, J., 304
Quinsey, Dr. Vern L., 227, 270, 280, 364

R
Rainbow, L., 82
Ramsey, JonBenet, 68, 74
Raskin, D. C., 96, 152, 153
Rasmussen, L. A., 361
Rastin, C. J., 234
Rauma, D., 335
Ray, Margaret, 351
Read, D., 266
Read, J. D., 140, 159
Reagan, Ronald, 17, 351
Reid, J. C., 376
Reid, John E., 59
Reifman, A., 189

Rengel, Stephanie, 311, 312
Reno, Janet, 141
Resnick, H. S., 159
Resnick, P. J., 113, 114
Ressler, R. K., 80
Rice, Dr. Marnie E., 225–226, 227, 272, 299, 300
Riddlesberger, M., 152
Riggs, D., 357
Risin, L. I., 361–362
Roberts, A., 297
Roberts, Dr. Julian V., 234, 235, 238, 239, 243, 253–255
Roberts, Dr. Kim, 157
Robie, C., 346
Roesch, Dr. Ron, 203, 204, 208
Rogan, D. P., 344
Rogers, Richard, 109, 110
Rollins, R., 375
Ronan, K. A., 208
Rosenberg, D. A., 108
Rosenfeld, B., 349
Rosenham, David, 113
Ross, S. J., 139
Rossmo, Dr. Kim, 76, 85, 86
Roszko, James, 58
Rotenberg, K. J., 193
Rothbaum, B. O., 357
Rowland, M. D., 274–275
Ruby, C. L., 154
Russano, M. B., 66, 73
Rutter, M., 323
Ruva, C. L., 180
Ryan, G., 361

S

Saks, M. J., 191
Salekin, R. T., 109, 302
Sales, B. D., 189
Samsock, D., 154
Santor, D., 302
Sapers, Howard, 222
Saunders, B. E., 159
Saunders, D. G., 346
Saywitz, K. J., 152, 155, 156
Schaffer, Rebecca, 351
Scheck, B., 67
Schmidt, F. L., 34
Schmidt, J. D., 344
Schmucker, M., 369
Schoenwald, S. K., 274
Schrenck-Notzing, Albert von, 11, 118
Schuller, Dr. Regina A., 15, 196, 198, 199
Schwandt, B., 102

Schweer, John, 99
Schweighofer, A., 215
Scogin, F., 35
Scott, L., 127
Scott, S., 305
Scullin, M. H., 149–150
Sebold, J., 346
Semin, G. R., 105
Semrau, Dr. Stanley, 295
Senna, J., 38
Serin, R. C., 244, 250, 286
Sewell, K. W., 110
Sheehan, R., 37, 38
Sheldon, W. H., 13, 19
Shelton, D., 188
Sheridan, M. S., 108
Sherman, L. W., 344
Shipman, Dr. Harold, 377
Shover, N., 285
Siegal, L., 38
Siegert, R., 363
Siegwart, C. M., 193
Silver, E., 279
Simmons, J. L., 284
Simpson, A., 373
Simpson, O. J., 339
Sinclair, S. D., 52
Skeem, J., 302
Slade, Michael, 86
Small, M., 136
Smith, Ashley, 222
Smith, Brian, 214
Smith, D. W., 159
Smith, Dr. S. M., 188
Smith, Ernest Benjamin, 268
Smith, M. D., 337
Smith, M., 82
Smith, P., 281
Smith, S. M., 58
Smith, Susan, 106
Smith, V. L., 199
Snook, B., 61, 62, 63, 64, 86
Snyder, L., 155, 156
Söchting, I., 360
Solomon, Enver, 313
Solomon, R. L., 296
Sommers, S. R., 187, 188, 192
Sophonow, Thomas, 16, 142, 143
Southamer-Loweber, W., 300–302
Spanos, N. P., 193
Spencer, C. P., 149
Spitzberg, B. H., 349
Sporer, S. L., 102
Sprott, J. B., 256
Stafford, Billy, 343

Stanton, J., 373
Stapleton, J., 106
Starson, Scott (a.k.a. Scott Jeffrey Schutzman), 210
Steadman, H. J., 224, 263, 265, 266
Steblay, N., 133, 180
Stein, K., 255
Stellar, M., 152
Stephenson, M., 369
Sterling, Linda, 148
Sterling, Ronald, 148
Sterling, Travis, 148
Stern, William, 10
Steuve, A., 274
Stevenson-Robb, Y., 161
Steves, Jason, 44
Stewart, L., 347
Stinson, Dr. V., 188
Stitt, L., 40
Stoll, K., 361
Stone, Bert, 219
Stone, J. I., 100
Stoops, C., 346
Stoppel, Barbara, 142, 143
Storm, J., 116
Strand, E. B., 341
Straus, M. A., 314, 334
Strömwall, L. A., 101
Stuart, G. L., 342
Sugarman, D. B., 334
Sukel, H. L., 73
Sundby, S. E., 197
Sutcliffe, Peter (a.k.a. Yorkshire Ripper), 74, 85
Sutherland, E. H., 13
Swanson, J. W., 273, 274
Swayze, Dr. Ian, 210
Symes, Kenneth, 172

T

Tanasichuk, C. L., 188
Tarrant, A., 160
Taylor, A., 50, 86
ten Brinke, Leanne, 101, 296
Teplin, L. A., 223
Terman, Lewis, 28
Terry, D., 196
Teske, R. J., 363
Thierry, K. L., 152
Thoennes, N., 334
Thomas, Justice J., 97
Thomas, S. W., 154
Thompson, C. Y., 285–286
Thompson, M. M., 50
Thornberry, T., 263

Tibbetts, J., 313
Tjaden, P. G., 334
Todorovic, Melissa, 311, 312
Toews, Vic, 222
Tolman, R. M., 344
Toma, C., 103
Tomz, J. E., 49
Trejo, D. C., 192
Tremblay, R. E., 317
Trevethan, S., 234
Trocme, N., 120, 169
Truelove, R. S., 139
Tubb, V., 139
Turnbull, S., 215
Turner, R. E., 203
Turpin, Robert, 245
Turtle, J. W., 141
Tyler, Tom, 198

**U**

Uken, A., 346
Ullman, S. E., 314
Ullrich, S., 297
Ulmer, J. T., 239
Undeutsch, Udo, 152
Ustad, K. L., 109

**V**

Van Amelsvoort, A. G., 134
van den Heuvel, C., 81
Van Koppen, P. J., 127
Van Ryebroek, G., 302
Vandiver, D. M., 363
Varendonck, Julian, 11
Vena, J. E., 52
Viding, E., 303
Vidmar, Neil, 198
Viljoen, J. L., 205, 206, 208

Violanti, Dr. John M., 52, 53
Virk, Reena, 180
Vrij, A., 102, 105, 106

**W**

Wagner, N., 361
Wagstaff, G. E., 125, 127
Waima, M. W., 45, 47
Walker, S., 52
Wallace, M., 314
Walma, M. W., 37
Walsh, T., 294
Walsh, W., 357
Walsh, Z., 294
Walter, R., 379
Ward, T., 363
Warner, T. C., 189
Warren, Chief Justice Earl, 14
Warren, K. L., 160, 161
Waterman, A. H., 149
Watson, K., 349–350
Webber, L., 127
Webster, D., 376
Webster, Dr. Christopher D., 203, 269
Weiler, B. L., 303–304
Weisman, Justice Norris, 197
Weisz, A., 344
Wells, Gary L., 120–121, 129, 130, 131, 132, 135, 136, 141
Welsh, A., 159
Wentink, N., 379
West, L., 37, 45, 47
Wexler, A., 368
White, M. D., 46
Whitmore, Peter, 275
Whittemore, K. E., 203, 215
Widom, C. S., 272, 303

Wigmore, John Henry, 12
Wilding, J., 134
Williams, Colonel Russell, 369, 370
Williams, L. M., 171
Williams, S. L., 335
Williamson, S., 294, 305
Wilson, Dr. Margo, 375, 376, 382
Wilson, K., 296
Wilson, T. D., 182
Winter, J., 81
Wong, S. C. P., 300
Wong, S., 294
Woodworth, Mike, 8, 78, 104, 107, 298, 372
Wrightsman, L. S., 68, 69–70
Wundt, Wilhelm, 9, 12
Wuornos, Aileen, 377
Wyer, M. M., 100
Wynkoop, T. F., 109

**Y**

Yang, M., 297
Yarmey, A. L., 104
Yarmey, Dr. A. Dan, 23, 104, 127, 134, 140
Yarmey, M. J., 133
Yates, Andrea, 374, 375
Yllo, K., 337
Yuille, Dr. John, 107, 148, 154, 155, 158

**Z**

Zamble, E., 280
Zanis, D. A., 273
Zapf, P. A., 203, 204, 205, 206, 208
Zeisel, H., 242
Zinger, I., 247, 294
Zoucha-Jensen, J. M., 360

# Subject Index

Page numbers followed by italic *f* indicate figures, and those followed by italics *t* indicate tables.

## Numbers/Symbols

*60 Minutes* (television series), 99

## A

Aboriginal courts, 233–234
Aboriginal High Intensity Family
    Violence Prevention Program, 347
Aboriginal overrepresentation (in criminal
    justice system), 233
  causes of, 233–234
  Gladue courts and, 235
  legislation to help reduce, 234–235
absolute discharge, 216, 238
*Abusive Personality, The*, 339
Acadia University, 107
ACDI. *See* Adolescent Chemical
    Dependency Inventory (ACDI):
    Corrections Version II
Action for Child Protection, West
    Virginia, 154
actuarial prediction, 267
  distinctions between unstructured
    clinical judgment and, 267
*actus rea* (wrongful deed), 202
Addiction Research Foundation, 269
ADHD. *See* attention deficit hyperactivity
    disorder (ADHD)
administrative tribunals, 232
Adolescent Chemical Dependency
    Inventory (ACDI): Corrections
    Version II, 318
Alberta Court of Queen's Bench rules, 16
American Bar Foundation, 198
American Polygraph Association, 90
American Psychiatric Association, 291
American Psychological Association
    (APA), 2, 15, 268
American Psychology-Law Society
    (AP-LS), 15, 18
anger rapist, 359
antisocial personality disorder (APD), 292
  expert testimony and, 293–294
  psychopathy and, 293, 293*f*
  symptoms, 292–293
Antisocial Process Screening Device
    (APSD), 300, 302
AP-LS. *See* American Psychology-Law
    Society (AP-LS)
APA. *See* American Psychological
    Association (APA)

APD. *See* antisocial personality disorder
    (APD)
APSD. *See* Antisocial Process Screening
    Device (APSD)
*Arresting Images: Crime and Policing in
    Front of the Television Camera*, 3
Association for the Defence of the
    Wrongly Convicted, 141
attention deficit hyperactivity disorder
    (ADHD), 315–316, 317, 320
automatism, 217, 219
  NCRMD and, 220
  noninsane, 217, 219
  processes for defences of, 217
aversion therapy, 366

## B

battered women's syndrome, 197
  expert testimony on, 198, 199
Baxtrom study, 263
BCOPS Study. *See* Buffalo Cardio-
    Metabolic Occupational Police
    Stress (BCOPS) Study
Becker's labelling theory (of crime), 13
*Behavioral Assessment*, 153
Behavioral Sciences Unit of FBI, 77
Bender Gestalt Test, 268
black-sheep effect, 192
*Blueline* magazine, 42
Bowlby's maternal deprivation theory (of
    crime), 13
Brain Fingerprinting Laboratories, 99
brain fingerprinting, 99
British Columbia Court of Appeal, 235
Buffalo Cardio-Metabolic Occupational
    Police Stress (BCOPS) Study, 53
*Burnt Bones*, 86

## C

CACP. *See* Canadian Association of
    Chiefs of Police (CACP)
CAI. *See* Competency to Stand Trial
    Assessment Instrument (CAI)
Calgary Police Service, 45
Cambridge Study in Delinquent
    Development, 303
CAMH. *See* Centre for Addiction and
    Mental Health (CAMH) (prev.
    Clarke Institute of Psychiatry)
Canada,
  categories of child maltreatment in, 169*f*

child murder in, 373
children testifying in, 163–164
courts in, 176, 231*f*
dating violence in universities in,
    336–337, 337*t*
fitness to stand trial standards in,
    202–203
guidelines for eyewitness evidence
    in, 142
HCSA in, 159
homicide rate in, 370–371, 371*f*
NCRMD cases in, 215*t*
noninsane automatism cases in,
    219–220
offences n, 176–177
polygraph evidence in, 97
stalking rates in, 348–349
use of force by police in, 45
youth crime in, 38–313*t*
youth gangs in, 322*t*
Canadian Association of Chiefs of Police
    (CACP), 42
  national use-of-force-model,
    47, 48*f*
Canadian Council of Muslim
    Women, 197
Canadian Foundation for Children,
    Youth, and the Law, 166
Canadian Incidence Study of Reported
    Child Abuse and Neglect, 168
*Canadian Journal of Behavioural
    Science*, 254
*Canadian Journal of Criminology*, 254,
    328, 382
Canadian Mental Health
    Association, 222
Canadian Police College, 90
Canadian Psychological Association
    (CPA), 15, 18, 42, 132, 291
  Code of Ethics, 261
Canadian Security Intelligence Service
    (CSIS), 91
Canadian Sentencing Commission, 254
capping, 217
Cardiff University, Wales, 291
Carleton University, 3, 188
CBCA. *See* criterion-based content
    analysis (CBCA)
CBT program. *See* cognitive-behavioural
    treatment (CBT) program

CD. *See* conduct disorder (CD)

celebrity stalkers, 351

Centre for Addiction and Mental Health (CAMH) (prev. Clarke Institute of Psychiatry), 209, 269

Child Maltreatment Section (CMS) of Health Canada, 165

child maltreatment, 165
  categories of, 169f
  emotional maltreatment, 166
  government agencies and, 167–168
  incidences of, 168–169
  internet luring and, 171, 172
  long-term effects of, 170, 171
  neglect/failure to provide, 166
  outcomes, 171–173
  physical abuse, 165
  prevalence of, 168–169
  reasons for, 168
  reporting, 169
  risk factors for, 169, 169t
  sexual abuse, 166
  short-term effects of, 170, 171

child molesters, 358
  typologies, 359–360

child psychiatric disorders, 315–316
  rates of, 317

child witnesses, 147
  anatomically detailed dolls and, 151, 152
  CBCA and, 152–153
  cognitive interviews of, 157
  court procedures for, 163–164
  courtrooms for, 164, 165
  culprit descriptions by, 160–162
  culprit recognition by, 162
  developmental differences and, 151
  elimination lineups and, 163
  event recall by, 147–148
  false memory syndrome and, 157
  free recall *versus* direct questioning of, 148–150
  identification procedures for, 162–163
  lineups and, 162
  narrative elaboration for, 155–156
  negative attitudes towards, 147
  NICHD protocol and, 156–157
  research into, 147
  social pressure on, 151
  step-wise interview for, 154–155, 154t
  traumatic memories and, 157–159

Children's Aid Society, 261

Chimpanzee Psychopathy Measure (CPM), 296

CIT. *See* Concealed Information Test (CIT) (polygraph type) (prev. Guilty Knowledge Test)

Clarke Sex History Questionnaire, 364

classic trait model of personality, 81–82

clinical forensic psychologists, 4–5
  Canadian license requirements for, 5
  concerns of, 4–5
  training for, 7

clinical risk factors, 270

CMS. *See* Child Maltreatment Section (CMS) of Health Canada

cognitive distortions, 364

cognitive interview, 125–126
  child witnesses and, 157
  enhanced, 126–127
  use of, 127

cognitive-behavioural treatment (CBT) program, 339
  male batterers and, 345–346

College of Psychologists of Ontario, 42

Columbine High School shootings, 379

Commission on Law Enforcement and Administration of Justice (1967, U.S.), 28

community service, 238

community treatment order, 226

community-wide strategies (against youth violence), 326

Comparison Question Test (CQT) (polygraph type), 91–92
  accuracy of, 94–95, 95t
  typical questions in, 92t

competency inquiry, 163

Competency Screening Test (CST), 207

Competency to Stand Trial Assessment Instrument (CAI), 207

Concealed Information Test (CIT) (polygraph type) (prev. Guilty Knowledge Test), 93
  accuracy of, 94, 95
  ERPs and, 98

conditional discharge, 216, 238

conditional sentence, 238

conduct disorder (CD), 315–316, 317, 321

confession evidence,
  courts and, 65
  disputed, 67
  false, 67
  retracted, 67

Conflict Tactics Scale (CTS), 332, 333, 334
  criticisms of, 333–334

Conflict Tactics Scale 2 (CTS2), 334, 336

*Contemporary Policing Guidelines for Working with the Mental Health System*, 42

contextual risk factors, 270

coping-relapse model of criminal recidivism, 280

*Cops* (television series), 3

corporal punishment, 166

correctional intervention, 246
  principles for effective, 246–247

Correctional Service of Canada (CSC), 42, 251, 346
  mentally disordered defendants and, 222
  National Violence Prevention Programs, 347–348

Court Martial Appeal Court, 233

court system, 231–232, 231f, 233

CPA. *See* Canadian Psychological Association (CPA)

CPM. *See* Chimpanzee Psychopathy Measure (CPM)

CQT. *See* Comparison Question Test (CQT) (polygraph type),

crime,
  biological theories of, 13
  psychological theories of, 13
  sociological theories of, 13

crime-based reality television, 3

criminal harassment (stalking), 348
  categories of, 350–352
  prevalence of, 348–349
  *see also* individual types of stalkers

*Criminal Interrogation and Confessions*, 62

*Criminal Justice in Canada: A Reader*, 254

*Criminal Minds* (television series), 1

criminal profiling, 75
  accuracy of, 83–84
  ambiguous profiles and, 82–83
  classic trait model of personality as basis for, 81–82
  deductive method of, 79
  early attempts at, 77
  FBI and, 77
  Hollywood versions of, 76
  inductive method of, 79–80
  investigative psychology and, 77–78
  linkage blindness and, 78
  organized-disorganized model of, 80, 80t
  process of, 78–79
  purposes of, 75
  reliability of, 81

criteria, 19

criterion-based content analysis (CBCA), 152
  criteria for, 153*t*
  criticism of, 154
cross-race (other-race) effect, 137
  attitude as explanation for, 137
  interracial contact as explanation for, 138
  physiognomic homogeneity as explanation or, 137
CSC. *See* Correctional Service of Canada (CSC)
CSI (television series), 1, 176, 187, 188
CSIS. *See* Canadian Security Intelligence Service (CSIS)
CST. *See* Competency Screening Test (CST)
CTS *See* Conflict Tactics Scale (CTS)
CTS2. *See* Conflict Tactics Scale 2 (CTS2)
cue-utilization hypothesis, 138
culprit, 128

## D

Dalhousie University, 107, 269
dangerous offender, 239
  conditions to be, 239
*Dateline NBC* (television series), 172
dating violence, 335–337, 337*t*
*Daubert* criteria (for expert testimony), 20, 21
death penalty, 245
  Dr. Death and, 268
deception detection, 62
  brain fingerprinting and, 99
  ERPs and, 97–98
  factors affecting abilities in, 105–106
  fMRI and, 98–99
  measurement of, 96
  non-verbal cues for, 100–101, 101*t*
  professional abilities in, 104–105, 105*t*
  stereotypes and, 103–104
  verbal cues for, 101–102
deception disorders, 108–109
  ethical research into, 112
  *see also* defensiveness; factitious disorder; Munchausen syndrome; somatoform disorders
deDelley Foundation for Life, 225
defensiveness, 109
delusional stalker, 350
desistance (from crime), 285
deviance, 13
*Dexter* (television series), 298

*Diagnostic and Statistical Manual of Mental Disorders*, Fourth Edition (*DSM-IV*), 108, 315
  malingering and, 109–110
  PTSD and, 357
direct question recall, 121
dispositional risk factors, 270
diversion, 226
Dixon study, 263
DNA evidence, 141
  exoneration cases in Canada, 142
  exoneration cases in U.S., 141*t*
domestic violence, 41–43, 332
  animal maltreatment and, 341
  battered women myths, 338–341
  characteristics of, 335*t*–336*t*
  criminal justice system and, 342–344
  mandatory charging policies and, 343–344
  measurements for, 332
  myths, 333
  nested ecological model and, 338
  patriarchy as cause of, 337
  rates of, 334–335
  reasons for women not leaving, 340
  *see also* dysphoric/borderline batterer; family-only batterer; generally violent/antisocial batterer; male batterers
  social learning theory and, 337–338
  types of, 332
  women as perpetrators of, 335
*DSM-IV. See Diagnostic and Statistical Manual of Mental Disorders*, Fourth Edition (*DSM-IV*)
Duluth Domestic Abuse Intervention Project, 345, 346
  criticisms of, 345
dynamic risk factors (criminogenic needs), 270
dysphoric/borderline batterer, 342

## E

École Polytechnique shootings, 381
Edmonton Police Service, 29
Edmonton Remand Centre, 221
epistemology, 19
ERPs. *See* event-related brain potentials (ERPs)
estimator variables, 120
*European Journal of Criminology*, 254
event-related brain potentials (ERPs), 97–98
  P300 type of, 98

evolutionary theories of sexual aggression, 364
ex-intimate stalker, 350
exhibitionists, 358
experimental forensic psychologists, 6
  research issues of, 6
  training for, 7
expert testimony, 16–18
  battered women's syndrome and, 198, 199
  challenges for, 18
  criteria for accepting, 20–22
  *Daubert* criteria for, 20, 21
  eyewitness testimony and, 139–140
  functions of, 18
  general acceptance test for, 20
  in Canada, 21
  in U.S., 20–21
  juries and, 196–197
  *Mohan* criteria for, 21
  psychopathy and, 293–294
externalizing problems, 314
  assessing, 315
extra-familial child molesters, 354, 358
extrajudicial measures, 311
*Eyewitness Evidence: A Guide for Law Enforcement*, 141
eyewitness testimony, psychology of, 9–10, 18
  absolute judgment, 131
  accuracy of confident, 135–136, 136*f*
  age variable in, 136–137
  culprit identification from, 127–128
  dependent variables in research into, 121
  expert testimony and, 139–140
  guidelines for, 141, 142
  independent variables in research into, 120–121
  race variable in, 137
  relative judgment, 131
  role of memory in, 118–119
  weapon focus effect, 138
Eysenck's biosocial theory of crime, 13

## F

fabricating, 148
factitious disorder, 108
false confessions, 67
  coerced-compliant, 68–69, 70
  coerced-internalized, 69–71
  compliance and, 72
  confabulation and, 72
  consequences of, 73–74
  frequency of, 67

internalization and, 72
research into, 71–73, 72t
types of, 68
voluntary, 68
false memory syndrome, 157
false negative outcome, 264
false positive outcome, 264
familicide, 375
Family Youth Clinic, 328, 329
family-only batterer, 342
family-supportive interventions (against youth violence), 324
FBI. *See* Federal Bureau of Investigation (FBI)
Federal Bureau of Investigation (FBI), 75, 76, 291
criminal profiling and, 77, 79, 80, 81
Federal Court of Appeal, 233
Federal Court of Canada, 232–233
female offenders, 279–281
femicide, 376
filicide, 372–373
maternal, 373
paternal, 375
fines, 238
FIT-R. *See* Fitness Interview Test-Revised (FIT-R)
Fitness Interview Test-Revised (FIT-R), 205
fitness to stand trial, 202
assessors of, 204
characteristics of, 205
criteria for, 202
numbers evaluated for, 203–204, 203t–204t
raising, 203
screening instruments for, 204–205, 207, 208
fixated child molesters, 359
fMRI. *See* functional magnetic resonance imaging (fMRI)
forensic anthropology, 6
forensic chemistry, 6
forensic entomology, 6
forensic linguistics, 6
forensic ondontology, 6
forensic pathology, 6
forensic psychiatry, 5
forensic psychology and, 5
forensic psychologists,
as clinicians, 4–5
as legal scholar, 7
clinical, 5
experimental, 6–7
roles of, 4

forensic psychology,
court cases in Canada and history of, 16
court cases in U.S. and history of, 14, 15
criminal justice system and, 12
definitions of, 2, 4
early European court cases and, 11
early research in, 9–10
forensic psychiatry and, 5
history of, 9–10, 10f, 11
legitimacy of, 15
media portrayal of, 1
North American advocates of, 12
free narrative. *See* open-ended recall (a.k.a. free narrative)
functional magnetic resonance imaging (fMRI), 98–99
fundamental principle of sentencing, 237

## G

GAM. *See* general aggression model (GAM)
general acceptance test (for expert testimony), 20
general aggression model (GAM), 383–383f
general deterrence, 236
General Social Survey (GSS), 335
stalking in, 348, 349, 350
generally violent/antisocial batterer, 342
*Geographic Profiling*, 86
geographic profiling, 84–85, 87f
cases, 85
heuristics and, 85
systems for, 85
Gottfredson and Hirschi's general theory of crime, 13
grudge stalker, 350
GSS. *See* General Social Survey (GSS)

## H

Hamilton Police Service, 33
Hare Psychopathy Checklist-Revised (PCL-R), 271, 276, 284, 289–290, 291, 295, 296, 304
Hare Psychopathy Checklist: Screening Version (PCL:SV), 296–297, 303
Hare Psychopathy Checklist: Youth Version (PCL:YV), 300, 302
Harvard University, 12
HCR-20 (risk assessment instrument), 278–279, 285, 318
females and, 281
*HCR-20* manual, 269

HCSA. *See* historic child sex abuse (HCSA)
Heart-Math Stress Management Program, 54
Her Majesty's Prison Service, 291
heuristics, 85
HIFVPP. *See* High Intensity Family Violence Prevention Program (HIFVPP)
High Intensity Family Violence Prevention Program (HIFVPP), 347
historic child sex abuse (HCSA), 159, 160
judge-only trials and, 160
jury trials and, 160
historical (static) risk factors, 270
homicide,
bimodal classification of, 372
evolutionary approach to, 383
general aggression model (GAM), 383–383f
juvenile, 375–376
offender treatments, 384–385
offenders, 369, 370
spousal, 376
theories, 380–383
types of, 370, 371–372

## I

IFI-R. *See* Interdisciplinary Fitness Interview-Revised (IFI-R)
IFI. *See* Interdisciplinary Fitness Interview (IFI)
illusory correlation, 266
impartiality (of juries), 178, 179
methods to keep, 180–182
threats to, 180
imprisonment, 238
in need of protection, 167
*In the Name of the Father* (motion picture), 69
Incredible Years Parenting Program, 325
infanticide, 373
mental illness and, 373–375
postpartum depression and, 374–375
postpartum psychosis and, 374, 375
Inmate Security Assessment (ISA): Young Offenders, 318
Innocence Project for Canadians, 141
insanity, 211
assessing, 215–216
defences, 213
numbers of, 215, 215t
review of legislation dealing with, 213
instigators, 338

instrumental (or predatory) aggression, 372
instrumental psychosis, 112
integrated model f sexual aggression, 363
Interdisciplinary Fitness Interview (IFI), 207–208
Interdisciplinary Fitness Interview-Revised (IFI-R), 207
internalizing problems, 314
International Dating Violence Study (2008), 335–337
interviewing eyewitnesses, 122
   cognitive interview, 125–127
   hypnosis to aid with, 124–125
intimate partner violence, 332
intoxication (as defence), 220
intra-familial child molesters (incest offenders), 358
Inuit peoples, 289
investigative psychology, 77–78
Investigative Support Unit (ISU) of FBI, 76
investigator bias during interrogation, 64–65
Inwald Personality Inventory (IPI), 35
IPI. *See* Inwald Personality Inventory (IPI)
ISA. *See* Inmate Security Assessment (ISA): Young Offenders
ISU. *See* Investigative Support Unit (ISU) of FBI

**J**

Jacobs, Brunton, Melville, Brittan, and McClemont's chromosomal theory (of crime), 13
John Hopkins University, 150
John Howard Society, 238, 251
*Journal of Abnormal Psychology*, 107
*Journal of Applied Psychology*, 132
JPO. *See* juvenile probation officer (JPO)
*Judging the Jury*, 198
juries,
   adjournment, 181
   attitude variables in predicting verdicts of, 193–194
   cases for, 176–177
   challenge for cause, 181–182
   change of venue, 180
   characteristics of, 178
   defendant characteristics influence on verdicts of, 194
   deliberating by, 186, 191
   demographic variables in predicting verdicts of, 192

expert testimony and, 196–197, 199
explanation models of decision making by, 190
field studies of, 185
functions of, 182
hung, 191
inadmissible evidence and, 187–189
judge's instructions to, 189
mathematical models of decision making by, 189
note-taking by, 186
nullification of, 182, 183
personality trait variables in predicting verdicts of, 192–193
post-trial interviews of, 184
questioning by, 187
selection of, 176, 177–178
simulation of, 185
verdicts of, 191
victim characteristics influence on verdicts of, 194–196
jury summons, 177
Juvenile Delinquents Act (JDA), 309, 309t
juvenile probation officer (JPO), 301

**K**

knowledge, 19
knowledge, skills, and abilities (KSAs), 30
known-groups design, 111
KSAs. *See* knowledge, skills, and abilities (KSAs)

**L**

*Larry King Live* (television series), 176
latitude, 19
*Law and Human Behavior* journal, 198
*Law and Order* (television series), 176
Law Reform Commission of Canada, 213
law, nature of, 19
leading questions, 122–123
leniency bias, 191
Level of Supervision Inventory-Revised (LSI-R), 279, 284
   females and, 281
Levenson Primary and Secondary Psychopathy Scale, 292
*Lie Detector* (television series), 104
*Lie to Me* (television series), 104
lineup, 121
   accuracy of identification, 129, 130t
   biased, 133, 134
   child witnesses and, 162

decision implications of identification, 130
distractors/foils, 129
elimination, 163
fair, 129
formats, 131
guidelines for, 141–142
identification, 128
multiple independent, 134–135
photo arrays *versus*, 130–131
   *see also* showup; walk-by
sequential, 131
simultaneous, 131
target-absent, 129
target-present, 129
Liquor Licensing Board, 232
long-term offender, 239
   criteria for, 239
love-obsessional stalker, 350
LSI-R. *See* Level of Supervision Inventory-Revised (LSI-R)

**M**

M-FAST. *See* Miller-Forensic Assessment of Symptoms Test (M-FAST)
MacArthur Competence Assessment Tool-Criminal Adjudication (MacCAT-CA), 208
MacArthur Violence Risk Assessment Study, 266
MacCAT-CA. *See* MacArthur Competence Assessment Tool-Criminal Adjudication (MacCAT-CA)
*Maclean's* magazine, 252
*Making Sense of Sentencing*, 254
male batterers,
   cognitive-behavioural therapy for, 345
   group therapy for, 345
   treatments for, 345, 346
male-emotional funnel system, 338
malingered psychosis, 111–112
   indicators of, 113–115, 114t
   interview-based methods to detect, 115–116
   self-report questionnaire to detect, 116
   testing for, 113
malingering, 108, 109
   explanatory models of, 109–110
   research, 110–111
mandatory charging policies, 343, 344–345
Manitoba Corrections, 318
Manitoba Court of Appeal, 16
mariticide, 376

Mark and Ervin's dyscontrol theory (of crime), 13
*Mask of Sanity, The*, 289, 291, 306
mass murderers, 380
Massachusetts Treatment Center *The Revised Rapist Typology* (MTC:R3), 299, 358, 359
maximization technique of interrogation, 60
MBP. *See* Munchausen syndrome by proxy (MBP)
McGill University, 42, 150
McGill-Montreal Children's Hospital Learning Centre, 150
McMaster University, 227, 382, 383
memory (concept of), 118–119
    hypnotically-refreshed, 125, 126
    recall, 119, 121
    recognition, 119, 128
    stages of, 120f
memory impairment hypothesis, 124
*mens rea* (criminal intent), 202
Mental Disorder Project, 213
mental disorders, 221
    as risk assessment factor, 273–274
    dealing with defendants with, 222
    infanticide and, 373–375
    offences committed by people with, 225
    police and offenders with, 223
    reasons for large numbers of offenders with, 222
    recidivism rates for those with, 226
    treatment for offenders with, 223–224, 226
    violence and offenders with, 224–225
Mental Health and the Law Advisory Committee of the Mental Health Commission of Canada, 42
mental health courts, 228
    effectiveness of, 228
Mental Health, Law and Policy Institute (MHLPI), 7
Merton's strain theory (of crime), 13
methodology, 19
MHLPI. *See* Mental Health, Law and Policy Institute (MHLPI)
Michigan Department of Corrections, 379
MIFVPP. *See* Moderate Intensity Family Violence Prevention Program (MIFVPP)
military courts, 232
Miller-Forensic Assessment of Symptoms Test (M-FAST), 116

minimization technique of interrogation, 60
Minnesota Multiphasic Personality Inventory (MMPI), 35, 116, 284
Minnesota Multiphasic Personality Inventory-version 2 (MMPI-2), 35
    malingered psychosis detection and, 116
*Miranda* rights (U.S.), 63
misinformation acceptance hypothesis, 124
misinformation effect, 123
    explanations for, 123–124
    research into, 123
MMPI-2. *See* Minnesota Multiphasic Personality Inventory-version 2 (MMPI-2)
MMPI. *See* Minnesota Multiphasic Personality Inventory (MMPI)
Moderate Intensity Family Violence Prevention Program (MIFVPP), 347
*Mohan* criteria (for expert testimony), 21
    problems with, 23
*Moment of Truth, The* (television series), 104
Monash University, Melbourne, Australia, 17
Mr. Big interrogation technique, 58
MTC:R3. *See* Massachusetts Treatment Center *The Revised Rapist Typology* (MTC:R3),
Multisystemic Therapy (MST), 327, 328
Munchausen syndrome by proxy (MBP), 108
    research, 110
Munchausen syndrome, 108
*Murderous Minds on Trial*, 295
*My Sister Sam* (television series), 351

# N

narrative elaboration, 155–156
National Advisory Commission on Criminal Justice Standards and Goals (U.S., 1973), 28
National Center for the Analysis of Violent Crime, 77
National Commission on Correctional Health Care, 291
National Crime Prevention Centre (NCPC), 322, 328
National Institute of Child Health and Human Development (NICHD), 156–157
National Parole Board (NPB), 232, 248, 249, 251–252
    factors in release decisions by, 250
    issues for assessments by, 248–249

pardons and, 252
    risk assessment and, 260, 262
    Sex Offender Registry and, 275
NCPC. *See* National Crime Prevention Centre (NCPC)
NCRMD. *See* not criminally responsible on account of mental disorder (NCRMD)
need principle, 246
neonaticide, 373
    maternal, 373
nested ecological model, 338
new technology,
    police recruitment and, 28
New York Police Department (NYPD), 45, 77
NICHD. *See* National Institute of Child Health and Human Development (NICHD)
Northwestern University, Chicago, 12, 198
not criminally responsible on account of mental disorder (NCRMD), 213, 214
    automatism and, 217, 219–220
    cases in Canada, 215, 215t
    offences committed by those, 225
    processes after a finding of, 216–217
NPB. *See* National Parole Board (NPB)
NRC. *See* United States National Research Council (NRC)
*Numb3rs* (television series), 76
NYPD. *See* New York Police Department (NYPD)

# O

observational learning, 337
Occupational Police Stress Questionnaire, 50
ODD. *See* oppositional defiant disorder (ODD)
offences, 176
    hybrid, 177
    indictable, 176–177
    summary, 176
*Offender Rehabilitation in Practice: Implementing and Evaluating Effective Programs*, 328
Offender Risk Assessment and Management System (ORAMS), 318
offenders with mental illness, 40
*On the Witness Stand*, 12
online dating services, 103
    accuracy of profiles on, 103

online dating services (*continued*)
  observed accuracy on, 103
  self-reported accuracy on, 103
Ontario Child Health Study (1987), 317
Ontario Court of Appeal, 16, 23, 65, 66,
  126, 140, 166, 183, 210
Ontario Mental Health Centre,
  Penetanguishene, 214, 227
Ontario Review Board, 210, 214, 269
Ontario Sex Offender Registry, 252, 275
Ontario Superior Court of Justice,
  166, 210
open-ended recall (a.k.a. free
  narrative), 121
oppositional defiant disorder (ODD),
  315, 316, 317
ORAMS. *See* Offender Risk Assessment
  and Management System
  (ORAMS)
Organizational Police Stress
  Questionnaire, 50
ORP. *See* SNAP Under 12 Outreach
  Project (ORP)
Osgoode Hall Law School, 141
own-race bias, 137

# P

pardons, 252
parent-focussed interventions (against
  youth violence), 324
parole, 248
  conditions, 251
  day, 250
  decision-making process, 248
  effectiveness of, 251–252
  full, 250–251
  myths, 249
  public attitudes towards, 253–254,
    255, 256
  revocation, 252, 253, 253f
  temporary absence, 250
pathway model of child sexual abuse, 363
patriarchy, 337
PCL-R. *See* Hare Psychopathy Checklist-
  Revised (PCL-R), 294
PCL:SV. *See* Hare Psychopathy
  Checklist: Screening Version
  (PCL:SV)
PCL:YV. *See* Hare Psychopathy
  Checklist: Young Version (PCL:YV)
PEACE model of interrogation, 66–67
pedophiles, 358
penile phallometry, 366
*Performance Monitoring Report*
  (2009), 251

photo arrays, 130–131
*Plenty of Fish* internet dating site, 103
polarization, 191
*Police Guidelines: Pretrial Eyewitness
  Identification Procedures*, 142
police interrogations, 57
  maximization technique of, 60
  minimization technique of, 60
  of psychopaths, 304–305
  PEACE model, 66–67
  *see also* Mr. Big interrogation technique;
    Reid model of interrogation
police officers, 26–27
  assessment centres for selection of, 36
  Canadian selection procedures for, 29
  cognitive ability tests for selection of, 34
  consequences of stress on, 51, 51t
  controlling discretion of, 45–46
  departmental policies for, 46–47
  discretion, 37
  divorce rates for, 52
  domestic violence and, 41–43
  informal action by, 39, 39f
  interviewing eyewitnesses, 122
  job analysis, 30
  job performance problems of, 52
  KSAs of, 30
  occupational stressors and, 49
  offenders with mental illness and,
    40, 223
  organizational stressors and, 49, 50–51
  personality tests for selection of, 35–36
  physical health and, 51–52
  psychological problems of, 52
  reasons for discretion of, 37
  routine decisions for, 37
  selection interview for, 32–34
  selection procedures for, 27, 28–29
  situational tests for selection of, 36
  stages in selection procedures for,
    29–30
  stress and, 48, 49, 49t
  stress maintenance for, 52–54
  suicide rates for, 52
  U.S. selection procedures for, 28–29, 29t
  use of force by, 44–45
  use-of-force situations and, 43–44
  validation of selection of, 30–31, 32
Police Public Contact Survey, 44
polygraph, 20, 90
  accuracy assessment of tests, 93–94
  accuracy of, 94–95
  admissibility of evidence, 97
  countermeasures to deceive, 96
  disclosure tests, 91

ground truth and, 94
*see also* Comparison Question Test
  (CQT) (polygraph type); Concealed
  Information Test (CIT) (polygraph
  type) (prev. Guilty Knowledge Test)
uses, 91
validity of, 96–97
post-event information effect, 123
post-traumatic stress disorder (PTSD), 357
power rapist, 359
PPI-R. *See* Psychopathic Personality
  Inventory-Revised (PPI-R)
PPI. *See* Psychopathic Personality
  Inventory (PPI)
PRA. *See* Primary Risk Assessment
  (PRA): Young Offenders
precondition model of child
  molestation, 363
*prima facie* case, 210
primary intervention strategies (against
  youth violence), 324
Primary Risk Assessment (PRA): Young
  Offenders, 318
principles, 19
Project Head Start, 325
protective factors, 282
provincial courts of appeal, 233
provincial/territorial "superior" courts,
  232–233
provincial/territorial courts, 232
*Psychological Science*, 107
psychology and the law, 7, 8
  differences between, 19
psychology in the law, 7, 8
*Psychology of Genocide, Massacres, and
  Extreme Atrocities, The*, 339
psychology of the law, 7, 8
Psychopathic Personality Inventory
  (PPI), 303
Psychopathic Personality Inventory-
  Revised (PPI-R), 290
psychopathy, 271–272, 288
  APD and, 293, 293f
  assessment of, 289–290
  descriptions, 289
  expert testimony and, 293–294
  family experiences and, 303–304
  genetics and, 302–303
  in animals, 296
  in community, 296–297
  in youth, 300, 302
  label of, 301
  law enforcement and, 304
  self-report measures to assess, 290
  sexual crimes and, 298–299

subclinical, 292
  theories on, 305–306
  treatments for, 299–300
  violence and, 294, 296
PTSD. *See* post-traumatic stress disorder
  (PTSD)
*Public Opinion, Crime, and Criminal
  Justice*, 254
Public Safety Canada, 322

# Q

quadripartite model of sexual
  aggression, 363
Queen's University, 42, 132, 269

# R

R-CRAS. *See* Rogers Criminal
  Responsibility Assessment Scales
  (R-CRAS)
racial bias, 192
Rape Empathy Scale, 365
rape trauma syndrome, 356–357
rapists, 358
  resistance and victim injury by, 360
  *see also* individual types of rapists
  subtypes of, 358
  typologies, 358
RCMP Police Aptitude Test
  (RPAT), 34
RCMP. *See* Royal Canadian Mounted
  Police (RCMP)
reactive (or effective) aggression, 372
recidivism, 246, 246t
  process, 280f
  rates, 344f
  risk factors to predict, 271
  sexual, 272, 369
*Red Dragon*, 298
regressed child molesters, 360
regulators, 338
Reid model of interrogation, 58, 59
  alternative to, 66–67
  deception detection and, 62
  goals of, 60
  investigator bias and, 64–65
  potential problems with, 61
  rights to legal counsel and, 63
  rights to silence and, 63–63t
  stages of, 59–60
  techniques of, 60
  usage of, 60–61t, 61t–62t
relapse prevention (RP) for sexual
  offenders, 367
Relevant/Irrelevant Test (polygraph
  type), 91

reparations, 237
representativeness (of juries), 178
  race and, 178, 179
*Research and Treatment for Aggression with
  Adolescent Girls*, 328
resilient youth, 323
resolution conference for young
  offenders, 39
response modulation deficit theory, 305
responsivity principle, 247
restitution, 238
restorative justice, 235, 236f
retroactive memory falsification, 11
review boards, 211, 213
  criteria taken into account by,
    217, 218f
  information taken into account by, 216
risk assessment, 259–260
  accuracy of various instruments, 279t
  adolescent, 316–317
  age of onset as factor in, 272
  base rates for, 265
  civil contexts for, 261
  criminal contexts for, 262
  demographics as factor in, 271
  evaluations for, 265–266
  females and instruments for, 281
  gender and, 279–281
  heuristics in, 266
  history of childhood maltreatment as
    factor in, 272
  history of, 263–264
  important risk factors in, 270
  instruments for adolescent,
    316–317, 318
  instruments, 276–279
  lack of social support as factor in,
    274–275
  limitations, 283–284
  mental disorder as factor in, 273–274
  methods of, 267, 268
  of youth under age 12, 314–316
  outcomes, 264
  past behaviour as factor in, 272
  personality as factor in, 271, 272
  practitioner usage of instruments,
    284–285
  prediction and management
    components of, 260
  probability and, 260
  protective factors and, 282
  risk factor predictors for, 270
  substance abuse as factor in, 273
  theories, 279
  weapon availability as factor in, 276

risk principle, 247
Rogers Criminal Responsibility
  Assessment Scales (R-CRAS),
  215–216
Royal Canadian Mounted Police
  (RCMP), 29, 291
  Sex Offender Registry and, 275
  taser use by, 46
  VICLAS and, 78
RP. *See* relapse prevention (RP) for
  sexual offenders
RPAT. *See* RCMP Police Aptitude Test
  (RPAT)

# S

sadistic rapist, 359
SARA. *See* Spousal Assault Risk
  Assessment (SARA)
Saskatchewan Court of Appeal, 180
Saskatchewan Justice Department, 179
SAVRY. *See* Structured Assessment of
  Violence Risk in Youth (SAVRY)
SCC. *See* Supreme Court of Canada
  (SCC)
*Scenes from the Class Struggle in Beverly
  Hills* (motion picture), 351
school-oriented strategies (against youth
  violence), 325
*Science* magazine, 113
secondary intervention strategies (against
  youth violence), 324, 327
selective serotonin-reuptake inhibitors
  (SSRIs), 367
Self-Report Psychopathy (SRP) Scale,
  290, 292
Sentencing Council of England and
  Wales, 254
sentencing disparity, 240
  research, 241–242, 243
  systematic, 240–241
  unsystematic, 240–241
  unwanted, 240
sentencing process, 236
  achieving goals of, 244, 245–246
  factors effecting, 239–240
  guidelines, 243
  options, 238, 239
  principles of, 237
  public attitudes towards, 253–254,
    255, 256
  purposes of, 236–237
  risk assessment as part of, 262
serial murderers, 376, 377
  characteristics of, 377
  comfort, 378, 379

serial murderers (*continued*)
  differences between male and female, 377*t*–378*t*
  female, 377
  hedonistic, 378
  lust, 378, 379
  mission-oriented, 378
  numbers of, 379
  power control, 378, 379
  thrill, 378, 379
  trauma-control model of, 380
  typologies for, 378–379
  visionary, 378
sex-force child molester, 360
sex-pressure child molester, 360
sexual assaults, 355
  definition of, 356
  effect on victims of, 356, 357
  offender categories, 358
  rape myths, 357
  rates, 355
  theories for, 363–364
sexual homicide, 298
sexual offenders,
  adolescent, 361
  aversion therapy for, 366
  cognitive distortions by, 364
  denial by, 364
  drugs for, 366
  effectiveness of treatments for, 368–369
  empathy and, 365–366
  female, 361–362
  masturbatory satiation for, 366
  penile phallometry and, 366
  rapists, 358
  social skills and, 366
  substance abuse and, 366
  treatments for, 364
  types of female, 362
sexual sadism, 299
SFU. *See* Simon Fraser University (SFU)
Sheldon's constitutional theory (of crime), 13
Shipley Institute of Living Scale (SILS), 35
showup, 132–133
*Silence of the Lambs, The* (motion picture), 1, 76, 298
SILS. *See* Shipley Institute of Living Scale (SILS)
Simon Fraser University (SFU), 7, 17, 76, 86, 269
simulation design, 110

SIRS. *See* Structured Interview of Reported Symptoms (SIRS)
situational risk factors, 270
SNAP Under 12 Outreach Project (ORP), 326
SNAP. *See* Stop Now And Plan (SNAP)
social learning theory, 320
  domestic violence and, 337–338
  homicide and, 381–382
Society for the Scientific Study of Psychopathy, 291
sociopathy, 293
  expert testimony and, 293–294
somatoform disorders, 108, 109
source misattribution hypothesis, 124
Sparwood Youth Assistance Program (SYAP), 39
specific deterrence, 236
SPJ. *See* structured professional judgment (SPJ)
Spousal Assault Risk Assessment (SARA), 277
spousal violence, 332
SRP Scale. *See* Self-Report Psychopathy (SRP) Scale
SSRIs. *See* selective serotonin-reuptake inhibitors (SSRIs)
St. Mary's University, 188
stalking. *See* criminal harassment (stalking)
Stanford-Binet Intelligence Test, 28
statement validity analysis (SVA), 152, 153
static risk factors, 270
Static-99 actuarial scale, 277–278, 284
Statistics Canada Violence Against Women Survey (1993), 334
statutory release, 251
stay proceedings, 211
step-wise interview, 154–155, 154*t*
Stop Now And Plan (SNAP), 326
Structured Assessment of Violence Risk in Youth (SAVRY), 318
Structured Interview of Reported Symptoms (SIRS), 115–116
structured professional judgment (SPJ), 268
Supreme Court of British Columbia, 179, 211
Supreme Court of Canada (SCC), 16, 65, 97, 126, 210, 213, 233
  abortions, 183
  automatism and, 217
  corporal punishment and, 166
  Gladue courts and, 235

jury characteristics, 178
*Mohan* criteria and, 21
NCRMD and, 213–214
overrepresentation of Aboriginal peoples in prisons, 234
public safety, 262
rape shield provisions, 196
Supreme Court of Iowa, 99
suspect, 128
Sutherland's differential association theory (of crime), 13
SVA. *See* statement validity analysis (SVA)
SYAP. *See* Sparwood Youth Assistance Program (SYAP)
system variables, 121

T
Tax Court of Canada, 233
TCO symptoms. *See* threat/control override (TCO) symptoms
Technical Working Group for Eyewitness Evidence (199), 141
tertiary intervention strategies (against youth violence), 324, 329
  music as, 329
Texas Court of Appeals, 374
Texas State University, 86
*Thin Blue Line, The* (documentary), 268
threat/control override (TCO) symptoms, 274
*To Catch a Predator* (television series), 172
trauma-control model of serial murder, 380
trial records, 184
true negative outcome, 264
true positive outcome, 264
truth-bias, 104

U
U.S. Bureau of Justice Statistics, 44
U.S. *See* United States (U.S.) of America
U.S. Supreme Court, 14, 20, 21, 135, 263–264
  *Daubert* criteria and, 21
UBC. *See* University of British Columbia (UBC)
*Understanding Public Attitudes to Criminal Justice*, 254
unfit to stand trial, 202
  characteristics of, 205
  competency restored, 209–211
  medication for, 209, 210
  staying proceedings for, 211

United Nations' Convention of the
Rights of the Child, 166
United States (U.S.) of America,
guidelines for eyewitness testimony in,
141, 142
HCSA in, 159
polygraph evidence in, 97
serial killers in, 379
use of force by police in, 44–45
youth crime in, 38
United States National Research
Council (NRC), 96
United States Supreme Court, 97
University of Alabama Law Enforcement
Academy, 35
University of Alberta, 132, 291
University of British Columbia (UBC),
7, 17, 107, 269, 289, 291, 339
University of Buffalo, 53
University of Calgary, 17
University of California, Berkeley, 71
University of California, Santa Cruz, 7
University of Guelph, 23
University of Nebraska, Lincoln, 17
University of Oxford, 254
University of Saskatchewan, 17
University of Toronto, 126, 227, 254,
269, 339, 382
University of Western Ontario, 198, 291,
328, 329, 374
unstructured clinical judgment, 267
distinctions between actuarial
prediction and, 267
use-of-force continuum, 45
uxoricide, 376
motives for, 376

## V

Vancouver Police Department (VPD),
27, 86
recruitment for, 28

VICLAS. *See* Violent Crime Linkage
Analysis System (VICLAS)
Violence Against Women in
Relationships Policy (B.C.), 41, 45
Violence Against Women Survey
(1996), 340
Violence Risk Appraisal Guide (VRAG),
276–278, 284
Violence Risk Scale (VRS), 277
Violent Crime Linkage Analysis System
(VICLAS), 78
Virginia Tech shootings, 380
voice identification, 134
factors in, 134
voyeurs, 358
VPD. *See* Vancouver Police Department
(VPD)
VRAG. *See* Violence Risk Appraisal
Guide (VRAG)
VRS. *See* Violence Risk Scale (VRS)

## W

*W-FIVE* (television series), 172
walk-by, 133
weapon focus effect, 138
unusualness as explanation for, 138–139
Wheaton College, Norton, Mass., 150
Wilfrid Laurier University, 157
Winnipeg Police Service, 143

## Y

Yale University, 80
YCJA. *See* Youth Criminal Justice
Act (YCJA)
Yerkes Regional Primate Centre,
Georgia, 296
YLS/CMI. *See* Youth Level of
Service/Case Management
Inventory (YLS/CMI)
YO-LSI. *See* Youthful Offenders-Level of
Service Inventory (YO-LSI)

YOA. *See* Young Offenders Act (YOA)
York University, 141, 198, 227
Yorkshire Ripper murders, 85
Young Offenders Act (YOA), 310,
310t, 328
*Young Offenders Act, The: A Revolution in
Canadian Young Justice*, 328
youth crime, 38–39
biological theories for, 319
cognitive theories for, 319
familial risk factors, 321
gangs and, 322, 322t
histories of those involved in,
317–319
individual risk factors, 320, 321
justice system and, 309–311
protective factors, 322–323
protective familial factors to, 323
rates of, 313, 313t–314t
resilience to, 322–323
resilient temperaments to, 323
*see also* Juvenile Delinquents Act
(JDA); Young Offenders Act
(YOA); Youth Criminal Justice
Act (YCJA)
social risk factors, 321–323
social theories for, 320
social/external protective factors
to, 324
Youth Criminal Justice Act (YCJA), 311,
313t–312t
interests of victims under, 313
releasing names under, 311
sentencing options under, 312
transferring to adult court under, 313
Youth Level of Service/Case
Management Inventory
(YLS/CMI), 318
Youth Psychiatric Inventory, 303
Youthful Offenders-Level of Service
Inventory (YO-LSI), 318